Frommer's®
Vancouver & Victoria

My Vancouver & Victoria

by Donald Olson

I FEEL A FRESH SENSE OF ADVENTURE EVERY TIME I RETURN TO BUSY, buzzing Vancouver. The backdrop of mountains, forests, and sea adds an unusual perspective to an urban landscape filled with soaring glass towers and an architectural sensibility more European than American. Vancouver—dubbed "Hollywood North" by some—is a new city, with an odd, appealing mixture of pioneer spirit and up-to-the-minute trendiness. Explore its neighborhoods and markets, and you'll pick up a distinct international vibe. But cultures don't clash here, they co-exist—each one contributing to the city's cosmopolitan flavor.

Victoria is another story—once so dowdy and dull that local cynics dubbed it a place for the newly wed and the nearly dead. But in the past few decades, the quaint capital of British Columbia has dusted itself off and rediscovered what has always made it so desirable: nature on a grand scale, and a city whose faded charms were ripe for a makeover. Today, Victoria is cozy and relaxing, a mini-maritime delight. Whether you come to watch whales, paddle a kayak, take tea at the venerable Empress Hotel, or stroll the century-old paths of Butchart Gardens (one of the greatest gardens in North America), you'll find Victoria to be an uncommonly pleasant place to visit. The photos in these pages show Vancouver and the surrounding region at its best.

© Floris Leeuwenberg/The Cover Story/Corbis

VANCOUVER AQUARIUM (left) An up-close and personal glimpse of a beluga whale in the icy-blue Arctic Canada exhibit at the Vancouver Aquarium Marine Science Center thrills landlubbers of all ages. For an extra fee, the aquarium also affords visitors the chance to help trainers feed the giant mammals throughout the day.

GASTOWN STEAM CLOCK (above) A quirky urban timepiece, the Steam Clock in Vancouver's historic Gastown gives a steamy rendition of the Westminster Chimes every 15 minutes, drawing its power from the underground steam-heat system. Vancouver's first neighborhood, established around "Gassy Jack's" saloon, Gastown is home to the city's oldest brick and cast-iron architecture and draws visitors to its art galleries, shops, pubs, clubs, and restaurants.

FIRST NATIONS TOTEM POLES (left):
Distinctive First Nations artwork is a living tradition throughout British Columbia. A stunning array of totem poles can be found in Vancouver—this one is in Stanley Park. Originally home to the Musqueam and Squamish nations, the park now boasts one of the city's largest collections of totem poles.

KITSILANO BEACH IN SUMMER (below) On warm, sunny days, Vancouver turns into a beach town, Northwest-style. There are many beaches to choose from, but Kitsilano is one of the grooviest. If you get tired of the beach, the adjacent Boho Kits neighborhood is a joy to explore.

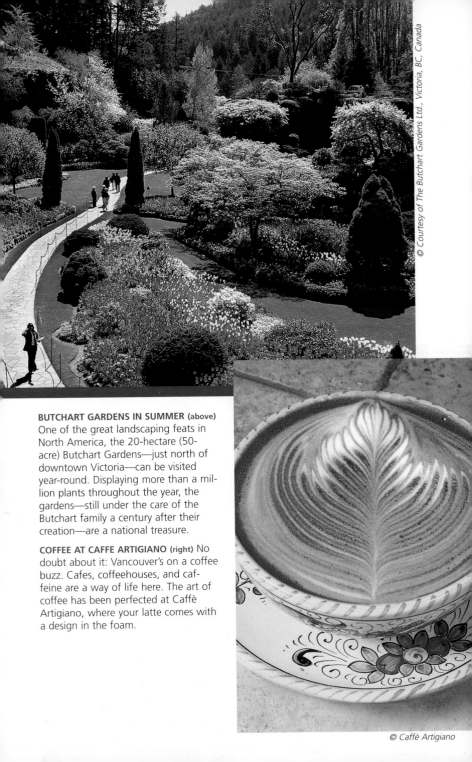

BUTCHART GARDENS IN SUMMER (above)
One of the great landscaping feats in North America, the 20-hectare (50-acre) Butchart Gardens—just north of downtown Victoria—can be visited year-round. Displaying more than a million plants throughout the year, the gardens—still under the care of the Butchart family a century after their creation—are a national treasure.

COFFEE AT CAFFE ARTIGIANO (right) No doubt about it: Vancouver's on a coffee buzz. Cafes, coffeehouses, and caffeine are a way of life here. The art of coffee has been perfected at Caffè Artigiano, where your latte comes with a design in the foam.

LIGHTHOUSE IN WEST VANCOUVER (above) On a rocky bluff overlooking the Strait of Georgia stands the Point Atkinson Lighthouse. Located in West Vancouver's Lighthouse Park, this iconic structure is just one of about 40 lighthouses that still survive along British Columbia's rugged and scenic coast.

GREAT BEAR RAINFOREST (right) Great Bear Rainforest on the western coast of Vancouver Island protects a magnificent swath of old-growth temperate rainforest, one of the last places in North America where several bear species—grizzly, black, and the rare Kermode, or spirit bear—thrive.

THE EMPRESS HOTEL Yes, it's touristy and expensive, but tea at the magnificent Empress is a must for visitors to Victoria. You'll be pleasantly pampered and shamelessly stuffed as an assortment of cakes, sandwiches, and scones with clotted cream appears— and disappears—at your table.

© Scott Markewitz/Getty Images

© Martin Bache/Alamy

WHISTLER (above) For what many consider the best skiing in North America, take the spectacular scenic Sea-to-Sky highway to Whistler Resort, just 2 hours north of Vancouver. Chosen as the site of the 2010 Winter Olympics, Whistler is a world unto itself. In the winter, you can ski from your hotel right to the slopes; in summer, the ski slopes are converted into a world-class mountain bike course.

VANCOUVER ISLAND (right) "Super-natural" is one way to describe British Columbia, which draws visitors to its spectacular landscapes of sea, forest, and mountains. In Pacific Rim National Park, on the rugged west coast of Vancouver Island, hikers discover the beauty and wonders of a coastal rainforest.

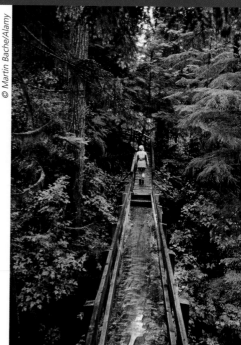

DR. SUN YAT-SEN CLASSICAL CHINESE GARDEN (right) One of Vancouver's hidden treasures, the Dr. Sun Yat-sen Classical Chinese Garden reflects the timeless tranquillity and painstaking artistry found in Taoist-inspired Chinese gardens.

SCIENCE WORLD (below) This big, blinking geodesic dome on the eastern end of False Creek is the home of Science World at Telus World of Science, Vancouver's child-oriented science museum. Hands-on adventures—plus a giant-screen Omnimax theater—give young visitors a fresh look at the world around them and how it works.

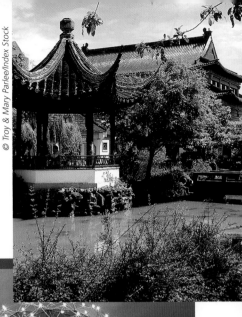

© Troy & Mary Parlee/Index Stock

© PCL/Alamy

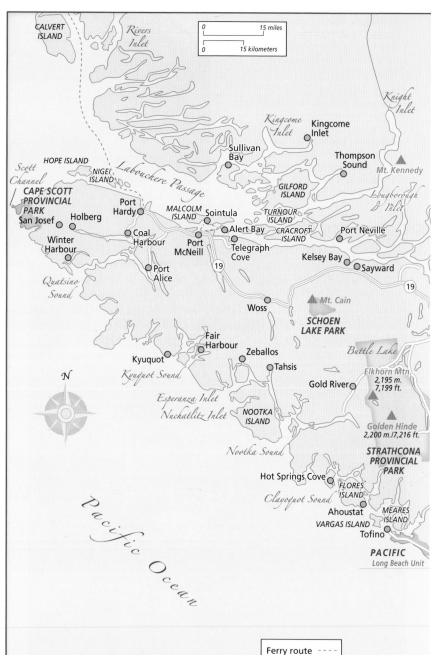

0   15 miles

0   15 kilometers

CALVERT ISLAND

Rivers Inlet

Knight Inlet

Kingcome Inlet

Kingcome Inlet

Sullivan Bay

Thompson Sound

Mt. Kennedy

Scott Channel

HOPE ISLAND

NIGEI ISLAND

Labouchere Passage

GILFORD ISLAND

Loughborough Inlet

CAPE SCOTT PROVINCIAL PARK

Port Hardy

MALCOLM ISLAND

Sointula

TURNOUR ISLAND

San Josef

Holberg

Coal Harbour

Port McNeill

Alert Bay

CRACROFT ISLAND

Port Neville

Winter Harbour

Telegraph Cove

Kelsey Bay

Sayward

Quatsino Sound

Port Alice

19

Woss

Mt. Cain

SCHOEN LAKE PARK

19

Fair Harbour

Zeballos

Buttle Lake

Kyuquot

Kyuquot Sound

Tahsis

Gold River

Elkhorn Mtn. 2,195 m. 7,199 ft.

N

Esperanza Inlet

Nuchatlitz Inlet

NOOTKA ISLAND

Golden Hinde 2,200 m.17,216 ft.

STRATHCONA PROVINCIAL PARK

Nootka Sound

Hot Springs Cove

FLORES ISLAND

Clayoquot Sound

Pacific Ocean

Ahoustat

MEARES ISLAND

VARGAS ISLAND

Tofino

PACIFIC Long Beach Unit

Ferry route - - - -

Ski area

Vancouver Island

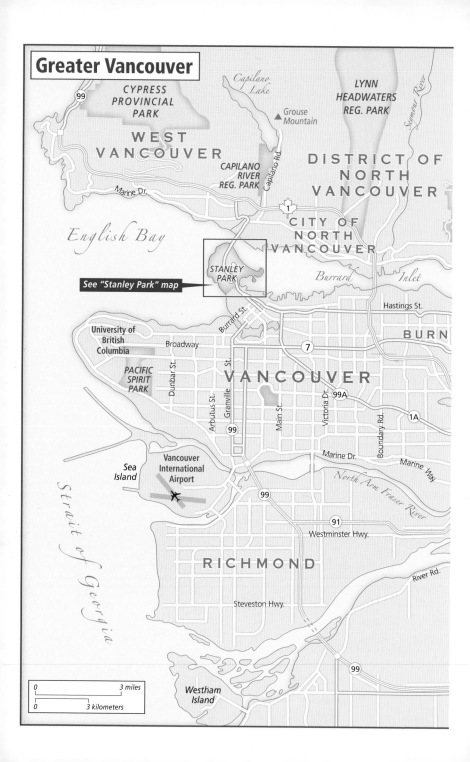

Greater Vancouver

99

CYPRESS PROVINCIAL PARK

Capilano Lake

LYNN HEADWATERS REG. PARK

▲ Grouse Mountain

Seymour River

WEST VANCOUVER

CAPILANO RIVER REG. PARK

Capilano Rd.

DISTRICT OF NORTH VANCOUVER

Marine Dr.

1

CITY OF NORTH VANCOUVER

English Bay

STANLEY PARK

See "Stanley Park" map

Burrard *Inlet*

Hastings St.

Burrard St.

University of British Columbia

Broadway

BURN

7

PACIFIC SPIRIT PARK

Dunbar St.

V A N C O U V E R

Arbutus St.

Granville St.

99

Main St.

Victoria Dr.

99A

Boundary Rd.

1A

Marine Dr.

Marine Way

Sea Island

Vancouver International Airport

North Arm Fraser River

99

91

Westminster Hwy.

Strait of Georgia

R I C H M O N D

River Rd.

Steveston Hwy.

99

Westham Island

0 ———— 3 miles
0 ———— 3 kilometers

Stanley Park

Ferguson Point **17**
Fish House Restaurant **20**
Girl in a Wet Suit statue **10**
Hollow Tree/Geographic Tree **15**
Horse-drawn Carriage Rides **4**
Hummingbird Trail/Malkin Bowl **3**
Japanese Monument **6**
Mallard Trail/Brockton Oval **8**
Nature Center **1**
Prospect Point **13**
Ravine Trail/Beaver Lake **12**
Second Beach **19**
Siwash Rock **14**
Teahouse Restaurant **18**
Third Beach **16**
Totem Poles **9**
Vancouver Aquarium & Marine
 Science Center **7**
Vancouver Children's Zoo/
 Variety Kids Farmyard **5**
Vancouver Rowing Club **2**
Variety Kids Water Park **11**

Downtown Victoria

Abkhazi Gardens **19**
Art Gallery of Greater Victoria **17**
British Columbia Aviation Museum **5**
Butchart Gardens **4**
Craigdarroch Castle **18**
Dominion Astrophysical Laboratory **5**
Emily Carr House **15**
The Fairmont Empress **11**
Fort Rodd Hill & Fisgard Lighthouse **3**
Hatley Park Castle and Museum **1**
Helmcken House **14**
Maritime Museum of British
   Columbia **7**
Market Square **6**
Miniature World **10**
Mount Douglas Park **5**
Pacific Undersea Gardens **9**
Parliament Buildings
   (Provincial Legislature) **12**
Point Ellice House **2**
Ross Bay Cemetery **20**
Royal British Columbia Museum **13**
Royal London Wax Museum **8**
Trans-Canada Highway Mile 0 **16**

Information ⓘ

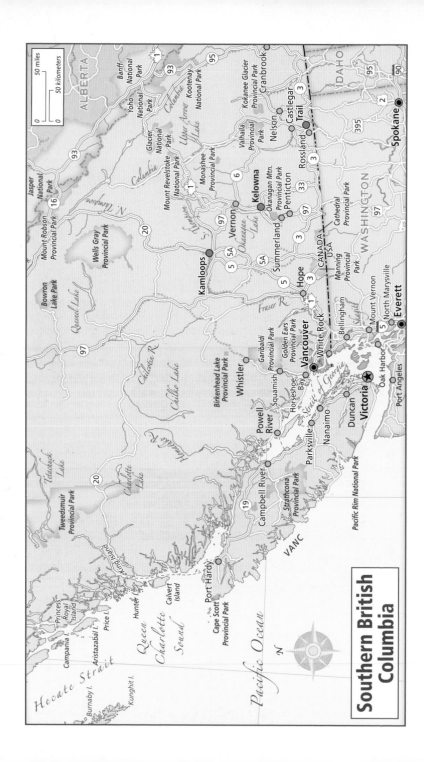

Southern British Columbia

Frommer's®

Vancouver & Victoria 2010

with Whistler

by Donald Olson

WILEY

Wiley Publishing, Inc.

Published by:

WILEY PUBLISHING, INC.

111 River St.
Hoboken, NJ 07030-5774

ISBN 978-0-470-50735-3

Editor: William Travis, with Melinda Quintero
Production Editor: Lindsay Conner
Cartographer: Andy Dolan
Photo Editor: Richard Fox
Production by Wiley Indianapolis Composition Services

Front cover photo: Science World at TELUS World of Science ©Masterfile.
Back cover photo: On the upper slopes of Whistler ©HP Canada/Alamy.

For information on our other products and services or to obtain technical support, please contact our Customer Care Department within the U.S. at 877/762-2974, outside the U.S. at 317/572-3993 or fax 317/572-4002.

Wiley also publishes its books in a variety of electronic formats. Some content that appears in print may not be available in electronic formats.

Manufactured in the United States of America

5 4 3 2 1

CONTENTS

VANCOUVER & VICTORIA

CONTENTS

8 EXPLORING VANCOUVER 112

9 VANCOUVER STROLLS 145

10 VANCOUVER SHOPPING 159

11 VANCOUVER AFTER DARK 171

12 WHISTLER BLACKCOMB 182

13 GETTING TO KNOW VICTORIA 203

14 WHERE TO STAY IN VICTORIA 209

LIST OF MAPS

ABOUT THE AUTHOR

Donald Olson is a novelist, playwright, and travel writer. His travel stories have appeared in *The New York Times, Travel + Leisure, Sunset, National Geographic,* and many other publications. His other guidebooks include *Best Day Trips from London, England For Dummies* (winner of the Lowell Thomas Travel Writing Award for best guidebook), *Germany For Dummies,* and *London For Dummies,* all published by Wiley. Under the pen name Swan Adamson, Donald Olson has published the novels *Memoirs Are Made of This* (also translated into Russian), *My Three Husbands* (published in France as *Vénus, quand tu nous tiens*), and *Confessions of a Pregnant Princess* (published in France as *Vénus à Rome*). His novel, *The Confessions of Aubrey Beardsley,* was published in the United Kingdom by Bantam Press, and his play, *Beardsley,* was produced in London. In 2010 his essay, "Confessions of a Faux Pa," will be featured in the new anthology *What I Would Tell Her: 28 Fathers on the Joys and Challenges of Raising their Daughters.*

HOW TO CONTACT US

In researching this book, we discovered many wonderful places—hotels, restaurants, shops, and more. We're sure you'll find others. Please tell us about them, so we can share the information with your fellow travelers in upcoming editions. If you were disappointed with a recommendation, we'd love to know that, too. Please write to:

Frommer's Vancouver & Victoria 2010
Wiley Publishing, Inc. • 111 River St. • Hoboken, NJ 07030-5774

AN ADDITIONAL NOTE

Please be advised that travel information is subject to change at any time—and this is especially true of prices. We therefore suggest that you write or call ahead for confirmation when making your travel plans. The authors, editors, and publisher cannot be held responsible for the experiences of readers while traveling. Your safety is important to us, however, so we encourage you to stay alert and be aware of your surroundings. Keep a close eye on cameras, purses, and wallets, all favorite targets of thieves and pickpockets.

FROMMER'S STAR RATINGS, ICONS & ABBREVIATIONS

Every hotel, restaurant, and attraction listing in this guide has been ranked for quality, value, service, amenities, and special features using a **star-rating system.** In country, state, and regional guides, we also rate towns and regions to help you narrow down your choices and budget your time accordingly. Hotels and restaurants are rated on a scale of zero (recommended) to three stars (exceptional). Attractions, shopping, nightlife, towns, and regions are rated according to the following scale: zero stars (recommended), one star (highly recommended), two stars (very highly recommended), and three stars (must-see).

In addition to the star-rating system, we also use **seven feature icons** that point you to the great deals, in-the-know advice, and unique experiences that separate travelers from tourists. Throughout the book, look for:

Finds	Special finds—those places only insiders know about
Fun Facts	Fun facts—details that make travelers more informed and their trips more fun
Kids	Best bets for kids and advice for the whole family
Moments	Special moments—those experiences that memories are made of
Overrated	Places or experiences not worth your time or money
Tips	Insider tips—great ways to save time and money
Value	Great values—where to get the best deals

The following **abbreviations** are used for credit cards:

AE	American Express	**DISC**	Discover	**V**	Visa
DC	Diners Club	**MC**	MasterCard		

TRAVEL RESOURCES AT FROMMERS.COM

Frommer's travel resources don't end with this guide. Frommer's website, **www.frommers. com**, has travel information on more than 4,000 destinations. We update features regularly, giving you access to the most current trip-planning information and the best airfare, lodging, and car-rental bargains. You can also listen to podcasts, connect with other Frommers.com members through our active-reader forums, share your travel photos, read blogs from guidebook editors and fellow travelers, and much more.

The Best of Vancouver & Victoria

The setting is majestic and the city is exciting so it's no wonder that **Vancouver** lures visitors from around the globe. The rest of the world has taken notice of the blessed life people in these parts lead, and surveys generally list Vancouver as one of the 10 best cities in the world to live in. It's also one of the 10 best to visit, according to *Condé Nast Traveler,* and won that magazine's Readers' Choice Award in 2005, 2006, and 2007 as "Best City in the Americas." In 2003, the International Olympic Committee named Vancouver the host of the 2010 Olympic and Paralympic Winter Games (see box on p. 32 for more information on the Winter Games). Heady stuff for a spot that less than 20 years ago was routinely derided as the world's biggest mill town. **Victoria,** British Columbia's capital city, exerts a siren call of its own. Located on the southeastern tip of Vancouver Island, a 90-minute ferry ride from Vancouver, Victoria is quieter and quainter than Vancouver, but it offers all the amenities you need for a wonderful holiday. Vancouver and Victoria are two very different cities, but their contrasting natures and easy accessibility offer visitors two wonderful opportunities to explore British Columbia's magnificent west coast.

1 THE MOST UNFORGETTABLE TRAVEL EXPERIENCES: VANCOUVER

- **Taking a Carriage Ride through Stanley Park:** One of the largest urban parks in the world, Stanley Park is nothing short of magnificent. Sample the highlights on a delightful 1-hour carriage ride that winds through the forest, along Burrard Inlet, past cricket fields, rose gardens, and the park's superlative collection of First Nations totem poles. See p. 116.

- **Wandering the West End:** Encompassing the über-shopping strip known as Robson Street, as well as cafe-lined Denman and a forest of high-rise apartments, the West End is the urban heart of Vancouver. Enjoy the lush trees lining the streets, the range of architecture, the diversity of cultures, the latest fashions and fashionistas, and neat little surprises on every side street. See "Walking Tour 1," p. 145.

- **Dining Out on Local Seafood:** Visitors are rightly amazed at the abundance of fresh-that-day seafood available in Vancouver's restaurants. This is a city where an appetizer of raw oysters often precedes a main course of wild salmon or halibut. See chapter 7.

- **Visiting the Vancouver Aquarium:** It's a Jacques Cousteau special, live and right there in front of you. Fittingly enough, the aquarium has an excellent display on the Pacific Northwest, plus sea otters (cuter than they have any right to be), beluga whales, sea lions, and a Pacific white-sided dolphin. See p. 119.

The Best Websites for Vancouver & Victoria

- **Entertainment Info** (www.ticketstonight.ca): This site is a great place for half-price night-of tickets and general entertainment information in the Vancouver area.
- **Pacific Rim Visitor Centre** (www.pacificrimvisitor.ca): This area-specific site is a great place to learn more about Vancouver Island's west coast.
- **Tourism B.C.** (www.hellobc.com): The official site of the provincial government tourism agency, this site provides good information on attractions, as well as higher-end accommodations.
- **Tourism Vancouver** (www.tourismvancouver.com): The official city tourism agency site provides a great overview of attractions, including an excellent calendar of events, plus a few last-minute deals on accommodations.
- **Tourism Victoria** (www.tourismvictoria.com): Victoria's official tourism site functions much the same as Vancouver's, with up-to-date, comprehensive information about what to do and see around the city.
- **Whistler Blackcomb Ski Resort** (www.whistlerblackcomb.com): This site offers a particularly helpful overview of activities and accommodations options available at North America's premier ski resort.

- **Exploring Chinatown:** Fishmongers call out their wares before a shop filled with crabs, eels, geoducks, and bullfrogs, while farther down the street elderly Chinese women haggle over produce as their husbands hunt for deer antler or dried sea horse at a traditional Chinese herbalist. When you're tired of looking and listening, head inside to any one of a dozen restaurants to sample succulent Cantonese cooking. See "Walking Tour 2," in chapter 9 (p.150) and "Gastown & Chinatown," in chapter 8 (p. 120).

- **Marveling at First Nations Artwork in the Museum of Anthropology:** The building—by native son Arthur Erickson—is worth a visit in itself, but this is also one of the best places in the world to see and learn about West Coast First Nations art and culture. See p. 123.

- **Browsing the Public Market on Granville Island:** Down on False Creek, this former industrial site was long ago converted into a truly eye-popping and sense-staggering indoor public market. Hop on the miniferry at the foot of Davie Street in Yaletown, and in 10 minutes you'll be there. At the market you'll find incredible food and goodies; put together a picnic and sit outside by the wharf to people- or boat-watch as you nosh. See p. 167.

- **Kayaking on Indian Arm:** Vancouver is one of the few cities on the edge of a great wilderness, and one of the best ways to appreciate its splendor is by kayaking on the gorgeous Indian Arm. Rent a kayak or go with an outfitter—they may even serve you a gourmet meal of barbecued salmon. See "Canoeing & Kayaking" on p. 137.

- **Discovering the Paintings of Emily Carr at the Vancouver Art Gallery:** It's always a thrill to discover a great artist, and Emily Carr's work hauntingly captures the primal appeal of B.C.'s rugged, rain- and wave-washed forests and shores. See p. 120.

- **Crossing the Capilano Suspension Bridge:** Stretched across a deep forested canyon, high above trees and a rushing river, this pedestrian-only suspension bridge has been daring visitors to look down for more than 100 years. Now you can explore the giant trees, too, on a series of artfully constructed tree-walks. See p. 125.

- **Watching the Sunset from a Water-side Patio:** Why else live in a city with such stunning views? Many places on False Creek, English Bay, and Coal Harbour have great waterside patios. See chapter 7.

2 THE MOST UNFORGETTABLE TRAVEL EXPERIENCES: VICTORIA

- **Strolling Victoria's Inner Harbour:** Watch the boats and aquatic wildlife come and go while walking along a paved pathway that winds past mani-cured flower gardens. The best stretch runs south from the Inner Harbour near the century-old Provincial Legisla-ture Buildings and the Fairmont Empress hotel. See "Walking Tour 1," p. 257.

- **Savoring Afternoon Tea:** Yes, it's expensive and incredibly touristy, but it's also a complicated and ritual-laden art form that goes on for at least an hour. Besides, it's good. See p. 232.

- **Marveling at Butchart Gardens:** This world-class garden, 20 minutes north of downtown Victoria, is a must-see attraction. Gorgeous during the day and subtly illuminated on summer eve-nings, it takes on a whole new personal-ity when the famous fireworks begin. Saturday nights in the summertime, you get both. See p. 240.

- **Touring the Royal B.C. Museum:** One of the best small museums in the world, the Royal B.C. does exactly what a good regional museum should do—explain the region and its people. See p. 243.

- **Whale-Watching:** Of all the species of orcas (killer whales), those on the Washington and B.C. coasts are the only ones that live in large and compli-cated extended families. This makes Victoria a particularly good spot to whale-watch because the orcas travel in large, easy-to-find pods. There's some-thing magical about being out on the water and seeing a pod of 15 animals surface just a few hundred feet away. See "Whale-Watching," in chapter 16.

- **Discovering the Paintings of Emily Carr at the Art Gallery of Greater Victoria:** If you didn't get to see the works by this great local artist at the Vancouver Art Gallery, you can view several canvases at the Art Gallery in Emily Carr's hometown. See p. 238.

- **Touring by Miniferry:** Catch a Victo-ria Harbour Ferry, and take a 45-min-ute tour around the harbor past the floating neighborhood of West Bay or up the gorge, where tidal waterfalls reverse direction with the changing tide. Moonlight tours depart every eve-ning at sunset. See "Getting Around," in chapter 13, and "Organized Tours," in chapter 16.

- **Biking the Dallas Road:** Where else can you find a bike path by an ocean with high mountain peaks for a back-drop? See p. 265.

3 THE MOST UNFORGETTABLE TRAVEL EXPERIENCES BEYOND VANCOUVER & VICTORIA

- **Skiing and Mountain Biking at Whistler Blackcomb Resort:** The two best resorts in North America merged in 1997 for a total of more than 200 runs on two adjoining mountains. In the summer, the same slopes become a world-class mountain biking network. See chapter 12.

- **Ziptrekking at Whistler:** Once you're strapped into your safety harness and hooked onto cables suspended hundreds of feet above a wild river, leap off, and away you go. Safe for everyone from 8 to 80, Ziptrek is an exhilarating adventure you'll never forget. See p. 199.

- **Looking for Bald Eagles in Squamish:** The bald eagle is the national symbol of the United States, but in winter, when the salmon are running, you can see more of these huge birds in Squamish than just about anywhere else in the world. See "Wildlife-Watching," in chapter 8.

- **Discovering Pacific Rim National Park:** The drive to this rugged maritime park on Vancouver Island's west coast is stunning, and once there, you're in a world of old-growth temperate rainforests and surf-pounded beaches. It's a place where you can experience the primal glories of nature amid the pampering luxuries of a first-class resort. See chapter 20.

4 THE BEST SPLURGE HOTELS: VANCOUVER

- **The Fairmont Hotel Vancouver** (900 W. Georgia St.; ℂ 866/540-4452 or 604/684-3131; www.fairmont.com): This grand hotel was built by the Canadian Pacific Railway and opened in 1939. The château-style exterior, the lobby, and even the rooms—now thoroughly restored—are built in a style and on a scale reminiscent of the great European railway hotels. See p. 72.

- **Opus Hotel** (322 Davie St.; ℂ 866/642-6787 or 604/642-6787; www.opushotel.com): A boutique hotel that's cool without the attitude, Opus has an offbeat location in hip Yaletown, an array of room types, and a luxurious but nontraditional aesthetic—plus good dining. See p. 74.

- **Pacific Palisades Hotel** (1277 Robson St.; ℂ 800/663-1815 or 604/688-0461; www.pacificpalisadeshotel.com): Large rooms decorated in apple greens and lemon yellows; a lobby of bold,

bright colors; a scene restaurant; and thoughtful freebies like the use of yoga gear make this West End high-rise one of the top choices for hip hotel aficionados. See p. 80.

- **Pan Pacific Vancouver Hotel** (300-999 Canada Place; ℂ 800/324-4856 or 604/662-8111; www.panpacific.com): Perched atop the Canada Place cruise-ship terminal and convention center, the Pan Pacific features rooms with stunning water, mountain, and city views; a great health club and spa; and first-class service. See p. 74.

- **Wedgewood Hotel** (845 Hornby St.; ℂ 800/663-0666 or 604/689-7777; www.wedgewoodhotel.com): The only boutique hotel in downtown, the Wedgewood is comfortably luxurious in that European style we love so much. Marble-clad bathrooms and a cozy bar/restaurant invite relaxing and romancing. See p. 75.

5 THE BEST MODERATELY PRICED HOTELS: VANCOUVER

- **Coast Plaza Hotel & Suites** (1763 Comox St.; ☎ **800/716-6199** or 604/688-7711; www.coasthotels.com): A former high-rise apartment building, the Coast houses large rooms with walk-out balconies and marvelous English Bay views, right in the heart of the West End. See p. 81.

- **West End Guest House** (1362 Haro St.; ☎ **888/546-3327** or 604/681-2889; www.westendguesthouse.com): Built in 1905 by two Vancouver photographers, this highly regarded B&B in the thick of the West End is filled with the artists' work as well as an impressive collection of Victorian antiques. See p. 82.

6 THE BEST SPLURGE HOTELS: VICTORIA

- **The Aerie** (600 Ebedora Lane, Malahat; ☎ **800/518-1933** or 250/743-7115; www.aerie.bc.ca): A red-tiled villa high atop Mount Malahat, this luxury accommodation features hand-carved king-size beds, massive wood-burning fireplaces, Jacuzzis, and a famed restaurant. Private terraces offer views across forested mountains to a long coastal fjord. See p. 221.

- **Brentwood Bay Lodge & Spa** (849 Verdier Ave.; ☎ **888/544-2079** or 250/544-2079; www.brentwoodbaylodge.com): Every detail in the rooms and bathrooms is perfect at this small luxury resort overlooking a pristine fjord 20 minutes north of Victoria (plus the food is great). You can get treatments for two at the fabulous Essence of Life spa. See p. 222.

- **Delta Victoria Ocean Pointe Resort and Spa** (45 Songhees Rd.; ☎ **800/667-4677** or 250/360-2999; www.deltavictoria.com): The glass-fronted hotel lobby and harbor-facing rooms provide the best vantage point in Victoria for watching the lights of the legislature switch on. This comfortable hotel

offers a host of services, including a calm, contemporary, Zen-like spa. See p. 211.

- **Hotel Grand Pacific** (463 Belleville St.; ☎ **800/663-7550** or 250/386-0450; www.hotelgrandpacific.com): The rooms in this high-rise luxury hotel beside the harbor come with a full array of amenities, and the fully equipped fitness center offers aerobics classes, a 25m (82-ft.) ozonated indoor pool, a separate kids' pool, a weight room, sauna, whirlpool, and massage therapist. See p. 212.

- **Inn at Laurel Point** (680 Montreal St.; ☎ **800/663-7667** or 250/386-8721; www.laurelpoint.com): With panoramic vistas of the harbor and an elegant, Japanese-influenced decor, this is the place for design junkies and aficionados. See p. 212.

- **Sooke Harbour House** (1528 Whiffen Spit Rd., Sooke; ☎ **800/889-9688** or 250/642-3421; www.sookeharbourhouse.com): In the little town of Sooke, just west of Victoria, this famed oceanside inn delivers quiet West Coast elegance and an exceptional restaurant. See p. 223.

7 THE BEST MODERATELY PRICED HOTELS: VICTORIA

- **Admiral Inn** (257 Belleville St.; ℂ **888/ 823-6472** or ℂ/fax 250/388-6267; www.admiral.bc.ca): Located on the edge of the Inner Harbour, the Admiral provides friendly service, free bikes, and the most reasonably priced harbor view around. See p. 215.
- **The Boathouse** (746 Sea Dr.; ℂ **866/ 654-9370** or 250/652-9370; www. accommodationsbc.com/boathouse. html): If you're seeking tranquillity, privacy, and a memorable location, check out this one-room cottage created from a converted boathouse. Built in a secluded cove on Brentwood Bay, within rowing distance of Butchart Gardens, it features its own private dock and dinghy. See p. 222.
- **The Magnolia Hotel & Spa** (623 Courtney St.; ℂ **877/624-6654** or 250/381-0999; www.magnoliahotel. com): With its central location, elegant lobby, well-designed rooms, and large

desks and dataports, the Magnolia is Victoria's best spot for business travelers and those who want understated luxury at a reasonable price. See p. 218.
- **Royal Scot Hotel & Suites** (425 Quebec St.; ℂ **800/663-7515** or 250/388-5463; www.royalscot.com): This family-friendly hotel occupies a converted apartment building and offers spacious suites that'll make you and yours feel comfortably at home. The suites come with fully equipped kitchens, and a video arcade and playroom are in the basement. See p. 215.
- **Swans Suite Hotel** (506 Pandora Ave.; ℂ **800/668-7926** or 250/361-3310; www.swanshotel.com): In the heart of the Old Town and just a block from the harbor, this newly refurbished boutique hotel is right above Swans Pub, one of the most pleasant restaurant/brewpubs in the city. See p. 218.

8 THE MOST UNFORGETTABLE DINING EXPERIENCES: VANCOUVER

- **C** (2-1600 Howe St.; ℂ **604/681-1164**): The creativity of the chef, the quality of the ingredients, and the freshness of the seafood all combine to make this contemporary restaurant overlooking False Creek the best place in Vancouver for innovative seafood. See p. 89.
- **Cin Cin** (1154 Robson St.; ℂ **604/ 688-7338**): For maximum buzz, dine at this Robson Street star on a Friday or Saturday night. It's a lively people-watching spot where the Italian menu is divided into Old World and New, and *tutto* tastes terrific. See p. 98.

- **Coast** (1054 Alberni St.; ℂ **604/685-5010**): "Catch it, cook it, eat it" is the motto of this superlative Yaletown restaurant. Fresh fish from around the world is cooked to elegant perfection in a beautiful space created with light wood and a dramatic center-island chef's kitchen. See p. 93.
- **Joe Fortes Seafood and Chop House** (777 Thurlow St.; ℂ **604/669-1940**): In the heart of the Robson shopping area, Joe Fortes has the best oyster bar in town and prepares its fresh fish the old-fashioned way, without a lot of culinary intervention. See p. 92.

- **Raincity Grill** (1193 Denman St.; ℂ 604/685-7337): Vancouver is loco for local fish, meat, produce, and wine. Raincity was one of the first and continues to be one of the best purveyors of fresh, locally sourced ingredients all assembled into dishes that show off the region's bounty, season by season. See p. 99.
- **Tojo's Restaurant** (1133 W. Broadway; ℂ 604/872-8050): The most sublime sushi in B.C., maybe in all of Canada.

Just remember to take out an extra mortgage and practice your so-what-if-you're-a-movie-star-I-don't-care look. See p. 102.

- **West** (2881 Granville St.; ℂ 604/738-8938): For dazzling fine dining that utilizes the freshest local seasonal ingredients, you can't go wrong with this stellar restaurant in Kitsilano. It's the culinary highlight of the entire region. See p. 103.

9 THE MOST UNFORGETTABLE DINING EXPERIENCES: VICTORIA

- **The Aerie** (600 Ebedora Lane, Malahat; ℂ 800/518-1933 or 250/743-7115): Even if you're not staying at the Aerie, you might want to consider eating there, because chef Christophe Letard's cooking is as unmistakably French as his accent, and *très fantastique*. See p. 236.
- **Camille's** (45 Bastion Sq.; ℂ 250/381-3433): Enjoy a glass of B.C. wine as you savor the fresh, comforting Pacific Northwest cuisine at this quiet, cozy, candlelit restaurant in downtown Victoria. See p. 231.
- **The Fairmont Empress** (721 Government St.; ℂ 250/384-8111): If you're doing the high tea thing only once, you may as well do it right, and there's no better place than Victoria's hotel crown

jewel, where the tea is delicious and the service impeccable. See p. 232.

- **SeaGrille** (Brentwood Bay Lodge, 849 Verdier Ave.; ℂ 888/544-2079 or 250/544-5100: The beautiful dining room of Brentwood Bay Lodge, about 20 minutes north of downtown, serves a regionally inspired menu that changes daily according to what is fresh and in season. The wine list is exemplary See p. 140.
- **Sooke Harbour House** (1528 Whiffen Spit Rd., Sooke; ℂ 800/889-9688 or 250/642-3421): Quality, inventiveness, and incredible attention to detail make this fabled inn the most memorable dining experience in (well, near) Victoria. It serves the best gifts from the sea and its own garden, and eating here is always a culinary adventure, well worth the money and the trip. See p. 237.

10 THE BEST THINGS TO DO FOR FREE (OR ALMOST): VANCOUVER

- **Walk the Stanley Park Seawall:** Or jog, blade, bike, skate, ride—whatever your favorite mode of transport is, use it, but by all means get out to enjoy this superlative and super-exhilarating path at the water's edge. See p. 140.
- **Watch the Fireworks Explode over English Bay:** Every August during the July/August HSBC Celebration of Light, three international fireworks companies compete by launching their best displays over English Bay. As many

as 500,000 spectators cram the beaches around English Bay, while those with boats sail out to watch from the water. See p. 29.

- **Stroll the Beach:** It doesn't matter which beach, there's one for every taste. Wreck Beach below the University of British Columbia is for nudists, Spanish Banks is for dog walkers, Jericho Beach is for volleyballers, Kitsilano Beach is for serious suntanning, and English Bay Beach is for serious people-watching. See p. 136.

- **Picnic at the Lighthouse:** One of the prettiest picnic spots is Lighthouse Park on the North Shore. Not only do you get to look back over at Vancouver, but also the walk down to the rocky water-line runs through a pristine, old-growth rainforest. See p. 129.

- **Hike the North Shore:** The forests of the North Shore are at the edge of a great wilderness and only 20 minutes from the city. Step into a world of muted light and soaring cathedral-like spaces beneath the tree canopy. See "Hiking," in chapter 8.

11 THE BEST THINGS TO DO FOR FREE (OR ALMOST): VICTORIA

- **Climb Mount Douglas:** Actually, you don't even have to climb. Just drive up and walk around. The whole of the Saanich Peninsula lies at your feet. See p. 244.

- **Beachcomb:** Just find a beach, prefera-bly a rocky one, and turn stuff over or poke through the tide pools. The best beaches are along Hwy. 14A, starting with East Sooke Regional Park, and moving out to French Beach, China Beach, Mystic Beach, and, the very best of all, Botanical Beach Provincial Park, some 60km (37 miles) away by Port Renfrew. Remember to put the rocks back once you've had a peek. See "Beaches," "Especially for Kids," and "Watersports," in chapter 16.

Vancouver & Victoria in Depth

Vancouver is imposing and intimate, sophisticated and laid-back, glossy and gritty, a bustling, prosperous city that almost miraculously combines a contemporary, urban-centered consciousness with the free-spirited magnificence of nature on a grand scale. In other words, it offers residents and visitors the best of both worlds: an exciting cityscape set within a landscape of rugged, eye-catching beauty.

Victoria, British Columbia's capital, is only a short ferry ride from Vancouver but the two cities are miles apart in their ambience and aesthetics. Where Vancouver trades on its image as a brash, glamorous, up-to-the-minute destination, Victoria, on the southeastern tip of Vancouver Island, leans more toward the quaint and the quiet (though you may not think so if you visit in the mobbed summer months).

This chapter delves into the past and dishes about the present. Just what is it that makes these two cities so unique and so popular? How did they get to be the way they are? Who are the people who left their mark in years gone by, and who are the people who live in Vancouver and Victoria today? What makes the landscapes they inhabit so unique and so memorable? If you're curious, read on. The answers may surprise you.

1 VANCOUVER & VICTORIA TODAY

BOOMTOWN VANCOUVER

With a population of 611,869 (2,249,725 in the metro area), Vancouver is the largest metropolitan area in Western Canada and the third-largest city in the country. It's an ethnically diverse place where 43% of the residents have a first language other than English. And it's a popular place, with a population expected to grow to over 3 million by 2021. Though you'd never think so, given the amount of greenery and water, Vancouver is one of the most densely populated cities in North America, coming in fourth after New York City, San Francisco, and Mexico City. If forecasts are correct, by 2021 Vancouver will be in second place for urban density.

Most people think of Vancouver as something of a glamour-puss, thanks to its booming film industry, and the overall impression is one of glossy affluence. But, in fact, the city's basic economic underpinnings are built on trade and industry. Its location on the Pacific Rim at the western terminus of Canada's transcontinental highway and rail routes has helped to make Vancouver one of the largest industrial centers in Canada. The Port of Vancouver, Canada's largest and most diversified, does more than C$43 billion in trade with over 90 countries annually. And it's no surprise, given that British Columbia's economy is based on what's euphemistically called "resource extraction," that Vancouver is also the headquarters of forest product and mining companies.

In recent years, however, the economy, like the population, has become more diverse, and right now, thanks in part to the upcoming 2010 Olympic Winter Games, it appears to be booming. Vancouver has become an increasingly important center for software development, biotechnology, and, of course, film development. Tourism is growing in importance, too. Over a million people annually pass through Vancouver, many of them en route to a cruise-ship vacation, usually to Alaska.

Vancouver is one of the "newest" cities you'll ever visit, and certainly it's one of the most cosmopolitan. A showy, energetic youthfulness pervades, along with a certain Pacific Northwest chic (and cheek). I can guarantee you that part of your trip will be spent trying to figure out what makes Canada's largest West Coast metropolis so appealing. Nature figures big in that equation, but so does enlightened city planning and the diversity of cultures. Vancouver is a city where people *want* to live.

AS DIVERSE AS IT GETS

Vancouver is the second-most popular destination for immigrants in Canada, after Toronto. People of English and Scottish origin formed the largest ethnic groups when the city was founded (the same was true in Victoria), and elements of British society and culture are still visible in the South Granville and Kerrisdale neighborhoods. But the largest visible

ethnic group in the city today is the Chinese. In the 1990s, an influx of immigrants from Hong Kong, mainland China, and Taiwan arrived to create one of the largest concentrations of ethnic Chinese residents in North America. Vancouver is home to the largest population of Chinese outside of Asia.

Not to suggest that Vancouver's population is either British or Chinese. Other significant Asian ethnic groups in Vancouver are South Asian (mostly Punjabi, usually referred to as Indo-Canadian), Vietnamese, Filipino, Indonesian, Korean, Cambodian, and Japanese. The city has a growing Latin-American population from Peru, Ecuador, and, more recently, Mexico. Vancouver and its surrounding metropolitan region are also home to the largest native (aboriginal) community in British Columbia and support a substantial gay community. British Columbia was the second Canadian jurisdiction to legalize same-sex marriage as a constitutional right, shortly after Ontario.

VICTORIA TODAY

For years Victoria marketed itself quite successfully as a little bit of England on the North American continent, a place that attracted "the newly wed and the nearly dead." Eventually the people of Victoria began to see the natural and very unique glories all around them instead of those reflected from a dying empire. When that

---

The Realities of Vancouver Real Estate

All the scenery, urban conveniences, and charm don't come cheap. Vancouver has the highest housing prices in Canada. Several 2006 studies ranked it as having the least affordable housing in Canada, with an average price of $757,853 for a two-story home, compared with $467,742 in Toronto and $322,853 in Calgary, the next most expensive major cities in Canada. The 11,000-square-foot house Oprah Winfrey bought in West Vancouver was on the market for a cool $18 million.

Impressions

Vancouver can dress up and act quite sophisticated when she wants to. But she'd rather put on her woollies and galoshes and go splash in a puddle.

—David Lansing, travel writer

happened, the city became a lot more interesting. Restaurants branched out into seafood, ethnic, and fusion cuisines. And as visitors showed more interest in exploring the natural world, Victoria added whale-watching and mountain-biking trips to its traditional London-style double-decker bus tours. The result? Victoria is the only city in the world where you can zoom out on a boat in the morning to see a pod of killer whales and make it back in time for an expansive afternoon tea. Still, life in Victoria remains much quieter and more laid-back than life in glam-seeking Vancouver. And that's part of Victoria's charm.

2 LOOKING BACK AT VANCOUVER & VICTORIA

Though **Vancouver** today has all the trappings of a sexy, showy, metrosexual metropolis, it began life as a hardscrabble pioneer town.

Victoria, on the other hand, has never shaken its colonial air and, in fact, embraces and celebrates it. The Victoria you see today retains much of its historic character and charm.

EUROPEAN CLAIMS

In 1791 José María Narváez of Spain became the first European to explore the coastline of present-day Vancouver (Point Grey). The following year, 1792, an English sea captain named George Vancouver explored the inner harbor of Burrard Inlet, giving various places British names. The explorer and fur trader Simon Fraser and his crew, working for the North West Company, were the first Europeans known to have set foot on the site of present-day Vancouver. In 1808, they descended the Fraser River perhaps as far as Point Grey, near where the University of British Columbia stands today. The entire region, including present-day Victoria, came under British rule in the mid–19th century, when the Strait of Juan de Fuca became one of the new dividing lines between the U.S. and Canada.

GOLD RUSH & BOOMTOWN

Though trappers and traders with the Hudson Bay Company had been active in the area since the 1820s (building forts in Victoria and Fort Langley near Vancouver), Vancouver really began its life as a boomtown during the Fraser Canyon Gold Rush of 1861, when 25,000 men, mostly from California, traveled to the mouth of the Fraser River and began prospecting for gold. The first European settlement was established in 1862, just east of the ancient village of Musqueam in what is now Marpole. Vancouver (and Victoria) boomed again during the 1898 Klondike Gold Rush, except this time the cities served as profitable trading posts where merchants sold equipment and provisions to gold-hungry prospectors on their way north.

Pulling Rank

Vancouver is consistently ranked one of the three "most livable cities" in the world. This "ranking" business always seems a bit silly to me, but of course it's also fascinating. Here are some other recent rankings for Vancouver:

- "3rd-highest quality of life in the world" (after Zurich and Geneva), tied with Vienna (Mercer Human Resource Consulting)
- "6th most overpriced real estate market in the world," second in North America after *really* overpriced Los Angeles (*Forbes*)
- "Canada's second most expensive city to live" after Toronto, and the "89th most expensive globally" (*Forbes*)
- "10th cleanest city in the world" (*Forbes*)

Vancouver's first sawmill was established on the north shore of Burrard Inlet in 1863 and was quickly followed by mills on the south shore. Hastings Mill, near the foot of Gore Street, formed the nucleus of nascent Vancouver, though the mill's central role in the city waned after the arrival of the Canadian Pacific Railway. The settlement of Gastown—the oldest section of Vancouver still standing today—grew up around a makeshift tavern established by "Gassy Jack" Deighton in 1867 on the edge of Hastings Mill. The British colonial government surveyed the settlement in 1870 and laid out a town site, renaming it "Granville," in honor of Granville Leveson-Gower, 2nd Earl Granville, the British Secretary of State for the Colonies.

EAST MEETS WEST: THE CANADIAN PACIFIC RAILWAY

Big changes were in store for the newly named settlement of Granville, for it was soon selected to be the terminus for the Canadian Pacific Railway (CPR), dashing the hopes of Victoria, which had also vied to be the railhead. The building of the railway was among the preconditions for British Columbia joining the Confederation in 1871. It was an enormous task, but finally, in 1886, the railway moved in and set up shop. A new era and a new name arrived with the railroad: The name Granville was scrapped, and the city was rechristened Vancouver. Just 4 years after the railway arrived, Vancouver's population grew from 400 to 13,000.

FROM 1886 TO 1986: ONE HELLUVA CENTURY

The year 1886 looms large in Vancouver's history. In that one year, the city incorporated, the first transcontinental Canadian Pacific train arrived, and a massive fire broke out and razed the entire city. Not surprisingly, 1886 was also the year the Vancouver Fire Department was established. The city quickly rebuilt and, thanks to the railroad and burgeoning port, grew even faster. Vancouver was now poised to become the key land and sea port for the natural bounty of British Columbia and the rest of Canada. Industry became the driving force behind Vancouver's phenomenal growth over the next century.

By 1901, the Steveston canneries were shipping out a record 16 million pounds of salmon. The opening of the Panama Canal in 1914 proved enormously beneficial to Vancouver by shortening ocean journeys between British Columbia and

A Short History of First Nations

When Captain Vancouver arrived in English Bay in 1792, he entered the traditional territories of the Skwxwú7mesh, Xwméthkwyiem, and Tsleil-Waututh peoples of the Coast Salish language group. Their villages dotted the land that we now recognize as Vancouver's Stanley Park, False Creek, the Burrard Inlet, West Vancouver, and Point Grey. Exactly where each tribe lived, when Captain Vancouver arrived, and how many members each had are matters of some controversy, but evidence suggests that the coastal areas around Vancouver and Victoria had about 10,000 native residents and had been settled for some 10,000 years. Pre-contact, First Nations society was divided into a nobility of chiefly families, commoners, and slaves, mostly war captives taken during raids. Living in the rainforest, all of these coastal peoples developed an extremely rich and complex culture, using cedar as their primary building material and, for food, harvesting marine resources such as herring, shellfish, and especially salmon. The richness of the local environment allowed these peoples ample surplus; their spare time was devoted to the creation of stories and art. Now undergoing a revival, coastal art, whether in wood, glass, or precious metals, usually depicts stylized figures from native mythology, including such universal figures as the Raven, or tribal totems such as the Bear, Frog, or Killer Whale.

The central ceremony of the coastal First Nations was and is the potlatch, a gathering of tribes held to mark a significant event such as the raising of a totem pole or the coming-of-age of a son or daughter. Invited tribes sing and dance traditional songs, while the host, both to thank his guests and to demonstrate his wealth, gives away presents.

In the years after contact, the coastal First Nations were decimated by disease. It's estimated that of some 10,000 people living along the coastal waterways all but 600 of them were killed by smallpox carried by white settlers. The loss of traditional fishing rights, the repression of traditional rituals such as the potlatch, and the forced assimilation into English-Canadian culture all had a major impact on First Nations life and culture. In the decades after World War II, an entire generation of native children was forced into residential schools, where speaking native languages and learning native stories were forbidden. (In 2008 the Canadian government issued a formal apology to all Canadian First Nations tribes and established a fund to pay for past abuses in the residential schools.) The 1970s saw the first steps toward a long and slow recovery. The term "First Nation" came into common usage in the '70s, replacing the word "Indian," which some regarded as derogatory. There is no legal definition of "First Nation," but the term "First Nations peoples" generally refers to all the indigenous peoples in Canada. Though still beset by problems, the First Nations communities are on their way back to becoming a powerful and important force on the B.C. coast.

Europe and spurring the port's continued growth in grain exports.

By 1923, Vancouver had become the third-largest city in Canada. Though the city struggled through the 1930s, World War II pulled Vancouver out of the Great Depression as shipyards began to build warships and minesweepers. But the war also fueled anti-Japanese sentiment and in 1942, following the Japanese bombing of Pearl Harbor, Japanese-Canadians were herded into holding areas at Hastings Park and removed to government camps in the Interior.

The turbulent 1960s was marked by anti-war protests, peace rallies, marches, and the appearance of hippies, who made Vancouver's West 4th Avenue (Kitsilano) their neighborhood. About the same time, the environmental activist group Greenpeace was formed in a Dunbar neighborhood living room.

The city's infrastructure was expanded in the 1970s with a new shipping-container facility and coal port that dramatically increased Canada's economic links to the Pacific Rim. At the same time, Granville Island was converted from an industrial island into the big public market and retail/restaurant sector that continues to be popular today.

Victoria's Secret

Founded in 1843, during Queen Victoria's reign, Victoria became the capital of British Columbia in 1866 when Vancouver Island united with the mainland—which is why a statue of the unamused monarch stands in front of the Provincial Legislature Buildings (still called "Parliament" by some). With colonyhood (and a big gold rush) came colonists, lots of them English and Scots, who imported British customs and brought a kind of domesticating old-world sensibility to their wild, new-world home. (They assumed they were bringing civilization, but that certainly wasn't how the First Nations tribes that had been in the area for at least 10,000 years saw it.) British patriotism and customs might have faded away altogether except that, in the 1920s, Victoria's population began to drop as business shifted over to Vancouver. Local merchants panicked. And it was then that San Francisco–born George Warren of the Victoria Publicity Bureau put forward his proposal: Sell the Olde England angle. Warren had never been to England and had no idea what it looked like, but to him, Victoria looked "English." Warren's scheme clicked big-time with the city's merchants and boosters, and for three-plus generations it served the city well. While Vancouver was leveling its "old" downtown in the name of urban renewal, Victoria nurtured and preserved its heritage buildings, adding gardens and city parks. Eventually it possessed that rarest of commodities for a North American city—a lively, walkable, historic city center. True, the "let's pretend we're in England" mindset meant ignoring certain details. Whales sometimes swam into the Inner Harbour; snowcapped mountain peaks loomed just across the water from Ross Bay; and trees in the surrounding forests towered far higher than Big Ben. So be it. It worked, and Victoria didn't turn into Disneyland in the process.

Impressions

To realize Victoria, you must take all that the eye admires most in Bournemouth, Tor-quay, the Isle of Wight, the Happy Valley at Hong Kong, the Doon, Sorrento and Camps Bay; add reminisces of the Thousand Islands, and arrange the whole round the Bay of Naples, with some Himalayas in the background.
　　　　　　　　　—Rudyard Kipling on Victoria (after visiting in 1908)

The whirlwind century ended with two milestones demonstrating just how far Vancouver had come from its humble frontier-town beginnings. Expo '86 (the last world's fair to be held in North America) coincided with Vancouver's 100th anniversary and drew more than 21 million visitors. By the end of the 1980s the Port of Vancouver was handling more imports/exports than any other port in North America.

3 VANCOUVER & VICTORIA ARCHITECTURE & ART

WOOD, BRICK & GLASS: THE FABRIC OF VANCOUVER

Old Vancouver was a city built of wood and brick, the complete antithesis of today's slender glass towers. The earliest wooden structures of pioneer Vancouver were destroyed in the Great Fire of 1886, after which brick became more common for commercial buildings. Walk through **Gastown** ("Walking Tour 2," p. 150) and you'll get a glimpse of what "downtown" Vancouver looked like in the late 19th century. If you stroll through the residential **West End** on the first walking tour in chapter 9, you'll encounter remnants of Old Vancouver in the form of big sturdy wooden houses with high front porches and sober, not-too-extravagant trim.

Though some "heritage buildings" still remain in Vancouver's Old Town and Chinatown, the face of the city you see today is undeniably new. Starting in the 1960s, misguided city planners and developers seemed intent on demolishing every last vestige of the city's pioneer past, replacing old brick and wood buildings with an array of undistinguished concrete high-rises and blocky eyesores. It was called "urban renewal." Citizen outcry finally got the bulldozers to stop their rampage. A few tiny pockets of original buildings are scattered among the downtown high-rises, most notably **Mole Hill** (See "Walking Tour 1: Downtown & the West End," in chapter 9).

What was lost? Vancouver as it used to be—a place where you could stand at any downtown street corner and have an unobstructed view of the sea in every direction. With a couple of notable exceptions, such as the **Sun Tower** (the tallest building in the British Empire when it was built at Beatty and Pender streets in 1911), the 25-story **Marine Tower** (which took over the title as tallest building in the British Empire when it was built in 1929 at Burrard and Hastings), and the **Fairmont Hotel Vancouver** (the big Canadian Pacific Railroad hotel built downtown in 1939), the city was more low-rise than high-rise. Luckily, all three of those landmarks remain, as does the **Vancouver Art Gallery,** a neoclassical gem built in 1907 to serve as the city's courthouse.

The same city planners responsible for bulldozing so much of the old city in the late 1950s and 1960s encouraged the development of high-rise residential towers in Vancouver's West End, a scheme that was intended to create a compact urban core amenable to public transit, cycling, and pedestrian traffic. According to the 2001 census, Vancouver's population density on the downtown peninsula is 121 people per hectare (or 49 people per acre). Vancouver is rare among North American cities for having this kind of dense (and desirable) downtown core where people live, work, and play.

A building boom for Expo '86 was spurred on by enormous amounts of cash pouring in (along with thousands of immigrants) from Hong Kong and Asia. The new quarter-block residential towers, made of glass and steel, are much lighter looking than those from times past, and have helped to generate Vancouver's hip, international image. It's this new construction, with the "view corridors" and sustainable urban planning that go with it, that have made Vancouver a model for livability.

A strong economy and the impending 2010 Winter Olympic Games have fueled Vancouver's latest building boom. The city continues to pursue progressive policies intended to increase density as an alternative to sprawl and to encourage environmental sustainability. The new buildings are characterized as mixed-use development, allowing street-level commerce and life to flourish. Though this booming city may now have its head in the clouds, it retains a street-level friendliness and accessibility. In fact, developing urban centers with mixed-use development has been referred to as "Vancouverism" because of the apparent success of such development in you-know-where.

VICTORIA'S ARCHITECTURAL CHARM

If you miss the old in Vancouver, you'll find plenty of it in Victoria. Victoria took the opposite approach from Vancouver and preserved nearly all its heritage buildings. As a result, British Columbia's capital, beautifully sited on its own Inner Harbour, is one of the most charming small cities you'll ever find (it has about 325,000 residents in the Greater Victoria area, compared to over two and a quarter million in Vancouver). The city's most famous architectural landmarks are the **Empress Hotel,** dating from 1908, and the **Legislature Building,** completed in 1898, both located on the Inner Harbour, the most visible spot in the city.

Most of the buildings in the downtown core are built of stone or brick and most of them are low-risers (newer hotels being the exception). But wood was the primary building material for houses, and a drive through any of Victoria's quiet residential neighborhoods will provide an architectural panorama of residential building styles from about the 1880s onward, including many English-style "cottages" that were popular in the 1920s. Victoria's neighborhoods are enhanced by lovely gardens, mature trees, and landscaping based on English gardening styles.

EMILY CARR: VISIONARY FROM VICTORIA

Victoria was the birthplace of one of British Columbia's most distinguished early residents, the painter and writer Emily Carr (1871–1945). Though trained in the classical European tradition, Carr developed her own style in response to the powerful landscapes of the Canadian west coast. Eschewing both marriage and stability, she spent her life traveling the coast, drawing inspiration from the land, seascapes, and native peoples for her vivid and striking works. In addition to visiting

Francis Rattenbury: Famous Architect & Murder Victim

Born in Leeds, England, Francis Mawson Rattenbury (1867–1935) moved to the new Canadian province of British Columbia in 1891 where he won, despite having no formal architectural training, a competition to build a new legislative building in Victoria. Built on a grand scale in the Romanesque style, the **Legislature (Parliament) Buildings** opened in 1898 and led to more commissions. In Victoria, as Western Division Architect for the Canadian Pacific Railway, Rattenbury designed the château-style **Empress Hotel,** which opened in 1914, and the CPR Steamship Terminal (1924; today the **Royal Waxworks Museum**). In Vancouver, he designed the Victorian **Roedde House** (1893) and the neoclassical Courthouse (1907) that serves today as the **Vancouver Art Gallery.** Then, as quickly as he'd become famous, Rattenbury and his architecture fell out of favor. Financial speculations led to conflicts with his business partners, and in 1923 he left his wife and two children for 27-year-old Alma Pakenham, an affair that led to public ostracism and contributed to his decision to leave Victoria and move to Bournemouth, England, in 1929. There, his relationship with Alma disintegrated as his financial problems worsened, and she began an affair with George Percy Stoner, her 18-year-old chauffeur. In 1935, aged 68, Rattenbury was murdered in his sitting room, suffering blows to the head with a carpenter's mallet from his killer. His wife and Stoner were charged and Stoner was convicted and sentenced to death, although the sentence was later commuted to a life imprisonment (he served 7 years). Alma committed suicide a few days after the charges against her were dropped. The event was made into the 1977 play *Cause Célèbre* by Terence Rattigan.

the great collection of Carr's paintings at the **Art Gallery of Greater Victoria** (p. 238), you can visit the **Emily Carr House** (p. 241), where she was born. The **Vancouver Art Gallery** (p. 120) also has a major collection of Carr's hauntingly evocative paintings.

BILL REID: FIRST AMONG FIRST NATION ARTISTS

William (Bill) Ronald Reid (1920–1998) is the best-known of Canada's aboriginal or First Nation artists and the man who helped to save and revitalize the traditions of Haida art and culture. Born in Victoria to a father of European descent and a mother from the Haida people, Reid first

learned about his aboriginal heritage from his maternal grandfather, a Haida artist of great renown. While working as a radio announcer in Toronto, Reid developed his interest in Haida art and studied jewelry making. In 1951 he returned to Vancouver to help salvage many intricately carved totem poles decaying in abandoned Haida village sites and to aid in the reconstruction of a Haida village in the University of British Columbia Museum of Anthropology. Working in traditional Haida forms, Reid made jewelry of gold, silver, and argillite before branching out into larger sculptures. Visitors to Vancouver can see two of Bill Reid's most magnificent works—the **Jade Canoe,** at **Vancouver**

Native Art of the Northwest: A Culture of Carving

The art of the first peoples of the Pacific Northwest is colorful, distinctive, and absolutely unique. It is, in its essence, sacred art meant to provide a bridge between the spirit and animal world (through a shaman) and the world of humans. Pacific Northwest First Nations art was almost always carved from rot-resistant cedar wood (or alder wood) and brightly painted with natural pigments; hairlike strands of cedar bark were sometimes attached. Totem poles, the most familiar pieces of native art, were originally erected in front of village longhouses to identify clans, memorialize ancestors, and denote status. But the great carving tradition of the First Nations artists also includes dramatic and sometimes frightening ceremonial and transformation masks; drums and rattles; boxes, feast dishes, and spoons; and canoes and paddles. The distinctive carvings and painted surfaces memorialize myths and mythological creatures, spirits both good and bad, and familiar animals of the sea, sky, and land.

By the 1950s, after a century of physical and cultural decimation, the great carving traditions were on the verge of being lost forever. Efforts by Bill Reid working with the University of British Columbia Museum of Anthropology (p. 123) in Vancouver and the Royal B.C. Museum (p. 243 in Victoria helped to save major First Nation artworks and revive the carving tradition.

Figures that recur over and over in Pacific Northwest First Nations art include the mythological Thunderbird and the more familiar animals that native tribes encountered, observed, and hunted: Raven, Bear, Salmon, Eagle, Killer Whale (Orca), Beaver, Hawk, Owl, Kingfisher, Wren, Grouse, Frog, and Bee. Stylized masks represent humans and elements of the natural world (Sun, Wind, Moon). Spirits whose images are carved into masks include (note that many variant spellings exist for these names):

Bakwas   Wild man of the woods, chief of the ghosts
Dzunukwa   Giant wild woman of the woods, bringer of gifts at the Potlatch
Huxwhukw   Cannibal bird
Kolus   One of the great thunderbirds, ancestor
Kumugwe   Lord of the Undersea
Noomis   Ancestor, born an old man at the beginning of time
Nulamal   Fool dancer
Pugmis   Sea equivalent of Bakwas, collector of souls
Pugwis   Messenger of the Lord of the Undersea
Pook-ubs   Figure who is a victim of the sea with white body and skeletal face
Sisiutl   Double-sided serpent with face in the middle

International Airport, is a large bronze sculpture of a canoe filled with human and animal figures; the **Legend of the Raven and the First Humans,** a Haida creation myth carved from Nootka cypress (yellow cedar), occupies pride of place at the **UBC Museum of Anthropology** (p. 123)—and also visit the **Bill Reid Gallery of Northwest Coast Art** (p. 116), which showcases a selection of his work. Reid's work is also featured on the **$20 note** in the Bank of Canada's *Canadian Journey* (2004) issue.

WAY BACK WHEN

Thousands of years ago, a giant glacier sliced along the foot of today's North Shore mountains, carving out a deep trench and piling up a gigantic moraine of rock and sand. When the ice retreated, water from the Pacific flowed in and the moraine became a peninsula, flanked on one side by a deep natural harbor (today's Port of Vancouver on Burrard Inlet) and on the other by a river of glacial meltwater (the Fraser River). Vast forests of fir and cedar covered the land and wildlife flourished. The First Nations tribes that settled in the area developed rich cultures based on cedar and salmon.

URBAN RECREATION

Although Vancouver is one of the most densely populated cities in North America, it also has over 1,298 hectares (3,200 acres) of parks and green space. At 404 hectares (1,000 acres), **Stanley Park** is the largest and most famous. Eighteen kilometers (11 miles) of **beaches** surround Vancouver, including one at English Bay (First Beach), and two in Stanley Park (Second Beach and Third Beach), all three easily reachable from anywhere in central Vancouver. Kitsilano Beach is the pride and joy of the west side Kitsilano neighborhood. The other city beaches—Jericho, Locarno, Spanish Bank East, Spanish Bank Extension, Spanish Bank West, and Sunset—are farther south, near the University of British Columbia.

Across **Burrard Inlet** and visible from just about anywhere in Vancouver, the nearby **North Shore Mountains** are home to three ski areas (Cypress Mountain, Grouse Mountain, and Mount Seymour), each within 20 to 30 minutes by car from downtown Vancouver. The **Capilano River, Lynn Creek,** and **Seymour River,** all less than half an hour from downtown, provide whitewater rafting during periods of rain and spring melt.

VICTORIA, WHERE ARE YOU?

Many visitors arrive thinking Victoria is on the British Columbia mainland. It's not. Victoria is on the southeastern tip of **Vancouver Island,** which lies southwest of Vancouver across the **Strait of Georgia** and **Haro Strait.** Victoria is 72km (45 miles) south of the 49th parallel, the border between most of Canada and the contiguous United States. British Columbia's island capital looks south across the **Strait of Juan de Fuca** to Port Angeles, Washington, and Washington state's snowcapped Olympic peninsula. Anacortes, Washington, is almost due east.

TIIIIIMBER!

The original vegetation of most of Vancouver and Victoria was dense temperate

---

Freeway-Free Vancouver

One of the first things you may notice in Vancouver is the conspicuous lack of freeways, with all the noise and congestion they bring. In the 1980s, as part of a long-term plan, city councils prohibited the construction of freeways. The only major freeway within city limits is Hwy. 1, which passes through the northeastern corner of the city. You'll see plenty of cars, of course, but car ownership has actually dropped in the past decade.

Ferry Tales

Instead of road rage, Victoria residents have "ferry stress." In order to get on or off their island, they have to take a ferry (or a floatplane), which takes time and involves some planning, especially on summer and holiday weekends. But gliding through the waters of the Pacific Northwest, with mountains gleaming and orcas (maybe) splashing, is really not the same as driving at breakneck speed along a freeway or sitting in bumper-to-bumper traffic. So the stress isn't really all that stressful.

rainforest, consisting of conifers—a mix of Douglas fir, Western red cedar, and Western hemlock—with scattered pockets of maple, alder, and, around Victoria, Garry oaks (indigenous to Vancouver Island). The forest you see today in Vancouver's Stanley Park is mostly second and third growth, and evidence of old-fashioned logging techniques such as springboard notches can still be seen there. British Columbia has been heavily logged, as you'll see if you venture out of Vancouver or Victoria, but it has also preserved the largest area of temperate rainforest left in the Northern Hemisphere (the **Great Bear Rainforest**, p. 289). Clear-cutting of old-growth forest has spurred major environmental action, especially in the area around Clayoquot Sound on the west coast of Vancouver Island (see chapter 20).

AS THE EAGLE FLIES

Keep your eyes open and you may spot a bald eagle or two in Vancouver and Victoria, though most of these magnificent raptors hang out in less populated and fishier areas. In fact, the largest concentration of American bald eagles in North America annually congregates at **Brackendale,** about an hour north of Vancouver. In 1994, 3,701 eagles were counted in one day along a 15km (6-mile) stretch of the Squamish Valley; in 2008, the number

dropped to 895, and in 2009 it fell to 755. The eagles congregate at the junction of Howe Sound at the mouths and tributaries of the Cheakamus, the Mamquam, and the Squamish rivers, to feed on spawning salmon. The mature trees, mixtures of fir, cedar, hemlock, and skeletal deciduous trees provide perfect roosting spots for these huge birds. The birds are also commonly sighted in and around Tofino and **Pacific Rim National Park** (p. 278). For more information on the annual Brackendale Eagle Count, see the Vancouver Calendar of Events for January, p. 26.

GREY WHALES & ORCAS

From mid- to late March, thousands of gray whales pass along the coast of British Columbia on their annual migration from Alaska down to their breeding grounds in Baja. The best places to view these giant mammals are **Tofino** and **Ucluelet** on the western coast of Vancouver Island, which celebrate the annual event with the Pacific Rim Whale Festival (see "Special Events," in chapter 20). But when companies in Victoria or Vancouver advertise "whale-watching" excursions, it is the orca, or killer whale, they are referring to. These animals are closer at hand and easier to spot—in fact, a pod of them lives year-round in the waters near Victoria on the southern tip of Vancouver Island.

5 VANCOUVER & VICTORIA IN POPULAR CULTURE: BOOKS, FILM, MUSIC

BOOKS

The following is a list of some titles that will give you a deeper insight into the multicultural richness of Vancouver and Victoria.

The Black Canoe: Bill Reid and the Spirit of the Haida Gwaii, Robert Bringhurst. A poet and storyteller pays tribute to the great Haida artist Bill Reid.

City of Glass: Douglas Coupland's Vancouver. Generation X author Coupland's homage to his hometown is both a personal memoir and an alternative history of Vancouver's cultural icons.

The Concubine's Children: Portrait of a Family Divided, Denise Chong. A moving narrative of a Chinese immigrant family at the dawn of the 20th century.

The Complete Writings of Emily Carr. Born in Victoria in the late 19th century, Emily Carr went on to become one of Canada's greatest and most original artists. In addition to painting, Carr also wrote, and this collection contains her remarkable autobiography, journals, and fiction. *Emily Carr,* part of the Extraordinary Canadians series, is a new biography of the artist by Lewis DeSoto. (For more on Emily Carr, see "Emily Carr: Visionary from Victoria," p. 16.)

Making Vancouver, by Robert A. J. McDonald is a scholarly history of Vancouver's development to 1913.

Obasan, Joy Kogawa. The author was 7 years old in 1942 when the outbreak of war with the Japanese prompted Canada to send its Japanese citizens to internment camps in the B.C. Interior. The book draws on her experiences during that period.

Shoeless Joe, W. P. Kinsella. This novel by Vancouver storyteller and raconteur Kinsella was adapted into the popular movie *Field of Dreams.*

Vancouver Cooks, edited by Jamie Maw. Fifty of the area's best-known chefs contributed to this celebration of the amazing food culture and restaurants of Vancouver, the Lower Fraser Valley, and southern Vancouver Island.

The Vancouver Stories: West Coast Fiction from Canada's Best Writers. With stories by the likes of Pauline Johnson, Emily Carr, Alice Munro, Malcolm Lowry, and many others, this wide array of short fiction reveals just how varied Vancouver really is.

Victoria: The Unknown City, Ross Crockford. Tales of hidden intrigue and historic curiosities in Canada's westernmost provincial capital, whose polite, "just-like-England" exterior conceals a surprisingly quirky and rough-edged heart.

MUSIC

A number of notable punk rock bands originated in Vancouver. D.O.A., the most famous, has been performing for 30 years and is often referred to as the founders of hardcore punk. Other early punk bands from Vancouver include the Subhumans; the Young Canadians; the Pointed Sticks; Active Dog; the Modernettes; UJ3RK5; I, Braineater; and Nomeansno (originally from Victoria). In the 1990s, when alternative rock hit the mainstream, several Vancouver groups rose to prominence, including 54-40, Odds, Moist, the Matthew Good Band, and Econoline Crush. More recent successes include Gob and Stabilo.

Today, Vancouver is home to a lively independent music scene, including bands such as the New Pornographers, Destroyer, Frog Eyes, the Organ, Veda Hille, and Black Mountain. Vancouver also produced

The City as Stand-In: Films Filmed in Vancouver

It's really a bit ironic: Though hundreds of films and television shows have been shot in and around Vancouver, the city and the surrounding region usually serve as stand-ins for some other metropolis, country, or region. The following is a very brief list of some of the better-known movies filmed in Vancouver.

The 6th Day (2000)   Arnold Schwarzenegger stars in this tale of a future when clones conspire to take over the world. The Vancouver Public Library serves as a stand-in for an evil corporation's headquarters.

The Accused (1988)   Jodie Foster won the Academy Award for Best Actress for her role as a rape victim who decides to strike back at her attackers. The Vancouver Art Museum stands in as a courthouse (which was its original function).

Best in Show (2000)   In Christopher Guest's hilarious "mockumentary" about celebrity canines and their owners, Vancouver's venerable old Coliseum building doubles as the venue for a dog show.

Bird on a Wire (1990)   Mel Gibson and Goldie Hawn star in this romantic comedy featuring a suite in the Metropolitan Hotel and various outdoor locales.

Christmas With the Kranks (2004)   The Pacific Centre Mall in downtown Vancouver is easy to spot in this comedy about a suburban family trying to skip the crass commercialism of Christmas.

The Chronicles of Riddick (2004)   This sci-fi epic was savaged by the critics, but who cares since it stars the always-watchable Judi Dench?

Dreamcatcher (2003)   The town of Steveston is meant to be a quaint Maine village in this Stephen King balderdash about aliens terrorizing a group of buddies vacationing in a cabin.

Elf (2003)   Vancouver does a stellar job of standing in for Manhattan in this Christmas flick starring Will Ferrell.

the influential metal band Strapping Young Lad and pioneering electro-industrial bands Skinny Puppy and Front Line Assembly. Popular musical artists from Vancouver include Bryan Adams, Sarah McLachlan, Michael Bublé, Nickelback, and Diana Krall. Notable hip hop artists from Vancouver include the Rascalz, Swollen Members, and Sweatshop Union.

6 EATING & DRINKING IN VANCOUVER & VICTORIA

In the past 2 decades Vancouver has become one of the top dining destinations in the world, bursting with an incredible variety of cuisines and making an international name for itself with its audacious and adventuresome Pacific Northwest cooking. The food mantra here is "buy locally, eat seasonally," a philosophy which lets chefs

The Exorcism of Emily Rose (2005)   The University of British Columbia campus gets screen time in this tale of a young girl killed by a priest during an exorcism.

The Five People You Meet in Heaven (2004)   A TV mini-series based on the book by Mitch Albom about a man who meets up with some important people in the afterlife.

Gods and Monsters (1998)   This fascinating film, starring Ian McKellen as James Whale, the director of the original Frankenstein, would be worth watching even if it weren't filmed in Vancouver.

A Guy Thing (2003)   Even though it's supposed to take place in Seattle, you'll see lots of obvious Vancouver landmarks in this so-so romantic comedy.

Herbie Fully Loaded (2005)   Lindsay Lohan starred in this family-friendly remake of a Disney movie about a cute little Volkswagen.

Night at the Museum (2006)   The Vancouver Art Gallery stars as the Museum of Natural History in New York.

Scary Movie (2000), **Scary Movie 4** (2006)   These idiotic horror-film spoofs filmed all over the Lower Mainland have raked in gazillions.

That Cold Day in the Park (1969)   I'm probably the only person alive who remembers this Robert Altman film about a neurotic spinster (Sandy Dennis) who kidnaps a young stud; it takes place in hippie-era Vancouver.

Timecop (1994)   Granville Island is featured in this time-warp thriller starring Jean-Claude Van Damme.

The X-Files (1998), **X-Men 2** (2003), **X-Men: The Last Stand** (2006)   These three movies (including the X-Files TV series) give nods to Robson Square in downtown Vancouver and that black-glass high-rise known as the Sheraton Wall Centre.

support local farmers and fishermen and take full advantage of bountiful local organic produce, game, and seafood.

REGIONAL RICHNESS

This part of the world has always been known for the bounty of its land, rivers, and sea. The First Nations tribes of the Pacific Northwest were among the richest in the world, thanks to the abundance and seasonal variety of their food, which included year-round fish, game, berries, and wild edible plants. During the tribal feast and gift-giving celebration known as potlatch, the natural wealth of the coastal rainforest and its rivers and coastlines was fully evident. You'll still find one of the most popular potlatch dishes—alderwood-smoked salmon—on menus in Vancouver and Victoria.

As you might expect, salmon and shellfish became dietary staples for the new immigrants arriving from England, Scotland, and Europe. An enormous salmon cannery (it's now a national historic landmark) in Steveston, on the Fraser River, packaged and exported millions of tons of sockeye—until the stocks dwindled and the industry collapsed in the 1970s.

100 Mile Menus

Some of the top dining spots in Vancouver now feature a "100 Mile Menu" in which every ingredient for every course is sourced from farms and fishermen within a 100-mile radius of the restaurant. It might feature fresh oysters, roasted beets or a soup made from stinging nettles, local Fraser Valley pork or halibut from the Queen Charlotte Islands, artisan cheeses from Salt Spring Island, or a dessert made from fresh seasonal berries or rhubarb.

The first European settlers were not known for inventive cooking. Victoria, in particular, took its culinary cues from England, and a large German population in Vancouver spawned so many delicatessens that Robson Street was known as Robsonstrasse. Up until the 1980s, restaurants in Vancouver and Victoria relied on the fried and true, serving fish, seafood, and area produce, but without the flair and imagination that rules the dining scene today.

What changed it all? A generation of young, creative, ambitious B.C. and Canadian chefs who trained in Europe and came back to experiment with the riches at home. That and a rising number of ethnic restaurants—at first mostly Chinese and Japanese, but today encompassing just about every cuisine you can think of. It wasn't long before chefs started crossing culinary lines and borrowing influences (and spices) from Asian and Indian cooking. Fusion is big. So are Italian (Vancouver has several excellent Italian restaurants), French, sushi, and dim sum.

The dining scene in Victoria isn't nearly as sophisticated or inventive as Vancouver's, but more and more attention is being paid to the glories of fresh, local, organic produce.

UNCORKING B.C. WINES

Be sure to try a British Columbian wine with your meal. B.C. wines are now winning international acclaim and rival vintages from California, Australia, France, and Germany. The big wine-producing areas are in the Okanagan Valley (in southern B.C.'s dry interior) and on southern Vancouver Island (the Cowichan Valley). Some of these wines are truly wonderful, but you won't find them outside of Canada (and sometimes not outside of Vancouver). They're not produced in large enough quantities to export, and the restaurants usually snap up what's available.

Planning Your Trip to Vancouver & Victoria

Whether visiting Vancouver and Victoria for fun and frivolity, business or shopping, dining or dancing, skiing or snowboarding, beachcombing or backwoods trekking, here are some tips to help you plan your trip.

Traveling to British Columbia is easy, but there is one important thing to remember: If you are not a Canadian citizen, you will need a passport or appropriate travel document to enter Canada (see "Entry Requirements," p. 34).

For additional help in planning your trip and for more on-the-ground resources in Vancouver and Victoria, please turn to "Fast Facts" on p. 292.

1 WHEN TO GO

WEATHER

A rainforest species like the western red cedar needs at least 76 cm (30 in.) of precipitation a year. Vancouver gets about 116 cm (46 in.) a year, a cause for celebration among the local cedar population. *Homo sapiens* simply learns to adjust.

Most of that precipitation (usually in the form of showers and drizzle, not downpours) arrives in the winter, when, with a 30-minute drive to the mountains, you can trade the rain for snow. Skiing and snowboarding are popular from mid-December until the mountain snowpack melts away in June. Except in Whistler, hotels in the winter are quiet and the restaurants less busy.

Both Vancouver and Victoria enjoy moderately warm, sunny summers and mild, rainy winters; their weather is the mildest in Canada. Victoria gets half as much rain as Vancouver (58 cm/23 in.),

thanks to the sheltering Olympic Peninsula to the south and its own southeasterly position on huge Vancouver Island. You can find **current weather conditions** for Vancouver at http://vancouver.weatherpage.ca.

Around mid-February, the winds begin to slacken, the sun shines a bit more, the buds on the cherry trees appear, and early daffodils blossom. By March, azaleas, rhododendrons, and most other flowers are in bloom, and the sun is more frequent.

June sees more sun per summer day than farther south (mid-June sees 16 hr. of daylight). Only 10% of the annual rainfall occurs during the summer months, and the sun stays out through summer until the rains close in again in mid-October. These spring/summer/early autumn months are prime visiting time and when most visitors arrive. The first cruise ships start appearing in April.

Daily Average High Temperatures & Total Precipitation for Vancouver, B.C.

	Jan	Feb	Mar	Apr	May	June	July	Aug	Sept	Oct	Nov	Dec
Temp (°F)	41	45	50	57	64	70	73	73	64	57	48	43
Temp (°C)	5	7	10	14	18	21	23	23	18	14	9	6
Precipitation (in.)	5.9	4.9	4.3	3	2.4	1.8	1.4	1.5	2.5	4.5	6.7	7

HOLIDAYS

The official British Columbia public holidays are as follows: New Year's Day (Jan 1); Good Friday, Easter, Easter Monday (Apr 2–5, 2010); Victoria Day (May 24, 2010); Canada Day (July 1); British Columbia Day (Aug 2, 2010); Labour Day (Sept 6, 2010); Thanksgiving (Oct 11, 2010); Remembrance Day (Nov 11); Christmas (Dec 25); and Boxing Day (Dec 26).

VANCOUVER & VICTORIA CALENDAR OF EVENTS

The BIG events in 2010 will be the Olympic and Paralympic Winter Games, both held in Vancouver and Whistler February 12–28 (Olympics) and March 12–21 (Paralympics). For those who are planning to attend these once-in-a-lifetime events, see "The 2010 Olympic & Paralympic Winter Games" box on p. 32.

Olympics aside, the various festivals and special events held in Vancouver and Victoria every year draw tens of thousands of visitors and reflect an extraordinary diversity of cultures. Things may seem a little quiet in the winter and early spring, but that's because most residents simply head for the ski slopes. Resorts in **Whistler Blackcomb** (📞 **800/944-7853;** www.whistler.com) have events happening nearly every weekend.

If no contact number or location is given for any of the events listed below, **Tourism Vancouver** (📞 **604/683-2000;** www.tourismvancouver.com) can provide further details.

For an exhaustive list of events beyond those listed here, check http://events.frommers.com, where you'll find a searchable, up-to-the-minute roster of what's happening in cities all over the world.

Vancouver Events

JANUARY

Polar Bear Swim, English Bay Beach. Thousands of hardy citizens show up in elaborate costumes to take a dip in the icy waters of English Bay. Call 📞 **604/665-3418** for more information, or visit http://vancouver.ca. January 1.

Dine Out Vancouver. For a limited time every January, Vancouver's hottest restaurants offer three-course dinners for C$18, C$28 and C$38 per person.

Annual Bald Eagle Count, Brackendale. The largest gathering of bald eagles in North America arrives every winter to feed on salmon near Brackendale. Call the **Visitor Centre** (📞 **604/692-9244**) or the **Brackendale Art Gallery** (📞 **604/898-3333**) for more information. First Sunday in January.

PuSh International Performing Arts Festival, venues throughout Vancouver. An international performing arts festival featuring over 100 performances involving 18 works in the main program, and seven satellite shows by 23 companies at 16 venues. For more information visit www.pushfestival.ca. January 20 to February 7, 2010.

FEBRUARY

Chinese New Year, Chinatowns in Vancouver and Richmond. This is when the Chinese traditionally pay their debts and forgive old grievances to start the new lunar year with a clean slate. These Chinese communities launch a 2-week celebration, ringing in the new year with firecrackers, dancing dragon parades, and other festivities. Call 📞 **604/415-6322** for information, or visit www.vancouverchinesegarden.com. Dates vary yearly.

International Bhangra Celebration, downtown Vancouver. Vancouver's East Indian population of 60,000-plus celebrates with Bhangra, a lively form of folk music and dance that originates in the Punjab. Events include live music and dance demonstrations, workshops, and competitions. Mid-February.

MARCH

CelticFest, downtown. For 5 days each year, the sounds of fiddles, bagpipes, bodhrans, dancing feet, and voices resound throughout downtown Vancouver in celebration of Celtic culture. Hundreds of local and international artists at more than 60 events are scheduled at dozens of popular venues and two outdoor stages along Granville Street. For information visit www.celtic festvancouver.com. Mid-March.

Vancouver Playhouse International Wine Festival. This is a major wine-tasting event featuring the latest international vintages. For more information, call ℂ **604/872-3313,** or visit www. playhousewinefest.com. Late March or early April.

APRIL

Baisakhi Day Parade. The Sikh Indian New Year is celebrated with a colorful parade around Ross Street near Marine Drive, and ends with a vegetarian feast at the temple. Contact **Khalsa Diwan Gurdwara Temple** (ℂ **604/324-2010;** www.kdsvancouver.com) for more information. Mid-April.

Vancouver Sun Run. This is Canada's biggest 10K race, featuring more than 40,000 runners, joggers, and walkers who race through 10 scenic kilometers (6.2 miles). The run finishes at B.C. Place Stadium. Call ℂ **604/689-9441** for information, or register online at www.sunrun.com.

MAY

Vancouver International Marathon. Runners from around the world compete

here. For information, call ℂ **604/872-2928,** or visit www.vanmarathon.com. First Sunday in May.

Cloverdale Rodeo, Cloverdale, Surrey. Professional cowboys from all over North America compete in roping, bull and bronco riding, barrel racing, and many other events. For information, call ℂ **604/576-9461,** or visit www. cloverdalerodeo.com. Mid-May.

International Children's Festival. Activities, plays, music, and crafts for children are featured at this annual event held in Vanier Park on False Creek. For information, call ℂ **604/ 708-5655,** or visit www.childrensfestival. ca. Mid-May.

JUNE

Festival d'Eté Francophone de Vancouver/Francophone Summer Festival. This 4-day festival celebrating French music uses various venues and includes a street festival. Call ℂ **604/ 736-9806** for information, or check www.lecentreculturel.com. Mid-June.

Alcan Dragon Boat Festival. Traditional dragon-boat racing is a part of the city's cultural scene. Watch the races from False Creek's north shore, where more than 150 local and international teams compete. Four stages of music, dance, and Chinese acrobatics are presented at the **Plaza of Nations,** 750 Pacific Blvd. For more info, call ℂ **604/ 561-6993,** or visit http://dragonboat bc.ca. Third weekend in June.

National Aboriginal Day Community Celebration. This event gives the public an opportunity to learn about Canada's First Nations cultures. Many events take place at the **Vancouver Aboriginal Friendship Centre,** 1607 E. Hastings St., at Commercial St., or visit www. vafcs.org. Call ℂ **604/251-4844** for information. June 21.

Vancouver International Jazz Festival. More than 800 international jazz and blues players perform at 25 venues ranging from the Orpheum Theatre to the Roundhouse. Many are free performances. Call the **Jazz Hot Line** (© 604/872-5200), or visit www. coastaljazz.ca for more information. Late June/early July.

Bard on the Beach Shakespeare Festival, Vanier Park. Four of Shakespeare's plays are performed in a tent overlooking English Bay. Call the box office (© 604/739-0559), or check www. bardonthebeach.org. Late May through late September, Tuesday through Sunday.

JULY

Canada Day. Canada Place Pier hosts an all-day celebration that begins with the induction of new Canadian citizens. Music and dance are performed outdoors throughout the day. A 21-gun salute at noon, precision acrobatics teams in the afternoon, and a nighttime fireworks display on the harbor lead the festivities. Granville Island, Grouse Mountain, and other locations also host Canada Day events. For more information, call © 604/683-2000 or check www.tourismvancouver.com. July 1.

Steveston Salmon Festival, Steveston. Steveston celebrates Canada Day with a big parade, marching bands, clowns, a carnival, a traditional salmon bake, and more. Call © 604/718-8080 for more info, or visit www.tourismrichmond. com. July 1.

BCMTA Kayak Marathon. Competitors race sea kayaks in Georgia Strait. The **Ecomarine Kayak Centre** (© 604/ 689-7575; www.ecomarine.com), at Jericho Beach, hosts the race and can provide details. Mid-July.

Harrison Festival of the Arts, Harrison Hot Springs, lower mainland. This arts festival in the Fraser River valley,

just east of Vancouver, attracts performing artists from around the world. Call © 604/796-3664 for more information, or visit www.harrisonfestival.com. Early to mid-July.

Dancing on the Edge. Canadian and international dance groups perform modern and classic works at the **Firehall Arts Centre** and other venues. For information, call © 604/689-0926, or visit www.dancingontheedge.org. Early to mid-July.

Vancouver Folk Music Festival. International folk music is performed outdoors at Jericho Beach Park. Contact the **Vancouver Folk Music Society** at © 604/602-9798 for more information, or visit www.thefestival.bc.ca. Second or third weekend in July.

Illuminares Lantern Festival, Trout Lake, John Hendry Park (Victoria Dr. and 15th Ave.). This evening lantern procession circling Trout Lake is a phantasmagoric experience, complete with drums, costumes, fire-breathing apparitions, and lots of elaborate handcrafted lanterns. Various performances start at dusk. For info, call © 604/879-8611, or visit www.publicdreams.org. Third or fourth Saturday in July.

Caribbean Days Festival, North Vancouver. The Trinidad and Tobago Cultural Society of B.C. hosts the city's premier Caribbean event at Waterfront Park in North Vancouver, featuring live music, authentic Caribbean food, arts, crafts, and a parade. For info, call © 604/ 515-2400, or visit www.ttcsbc.com. Third or fourth weekend in July.

Harmony Arts Festival, West Vancouver. This event highlights the talent of North Shore artists, offering free exhibitions, demonstrations, studio tours, theater, concerts, markets, and workshops. Call © 604/925-7268, or visit www.harmonyarts.net for more information. Late July and early August.

HSBC Celebration of Light. Three international fireworks companies compete for a coveted title by launching their best displays accompanied by music over English Bay Beach. Don't miss the big finale on the fourth evening. *Note:* Because of the crowds, some streets are closed to vehicles at night. Other prime viewing locations include Kitsilano Beach and Jericho Beach. Call ℂ **604/642-6835** for information, or check www.celebration-of-light.com. End of July to first week of August.

AUGUST

Summer Dancing in Robson Square. Every Friday night in August, Robson Square in downtown Vancouver hosts a free night of dancing under the stars. The evening starts with a free dance lesson given by a local instructor followed by showcase dancers and then a "general dance" where everyone (all ages and dance levels) is encouraged to join in. For more information visit www.dancesportbc.com.

Powell Street Festival. An annual fete of Japanese culture includes music, dance, food, and more. Contact the Powell Street Festival Society (ℂ **604/739-9388;** www.powellstreetfestival.com) for info. First weekend of August.

Gay Pride Parade, Vancouver. This huge and hugely popular gay- and lesbian-pride parade begins at noon and serves as the culmination of Pride Week. Celebrations at many local gay and lesbian nightclubs take place around town on the same long holiday weekend (B.C. Day weekend). For more info, contact the Pride Society (ℂ **604/687-0955;** www.vancouverpride.ca). First Sunday in August.

MusicFest Vancouver. National and international artists perform orchestral, choral, opera, world music, chamber music, and jazz concerts in venues throughout Vancouver. For information, call ℂ **604/688-1152,** or visit www.musicfestvancouver.ca. First 2 weeks in August.

Abbottsford International Air Show, Abbottsford. Barnstorming stuntmen and precision military pilots fly everything from Sopwith Camels to Stealth Bombers. This is one of the biggest air shows in the world. Call ℂ **604/852-8511,** or visit www.abbotsfordairshow.com for more info. Second weekend in August.

Pacific National Exhibition. The city's favorite fair includes one of North America's best all-wooden roller coasters. Special events include livestock demonstrations, logger competitions, fashion shows, and a midway. Call ℂ **604/253-2311,** or visit www.pne.bc.ca for more details. Mid-August to Labour Day.

Vancouver Wooden Boat Festival, Granville Island. Call ℂ **604/519-7400** for more info, or visit www.vancouverwoodenboat.com. Third weekend of August.

SEPTEMBER

Vancouver Fringe Festival. The Fringe Festival is centered on Granville Island, Commercial Drive, and Yaletown's Roundhouse, and features more than 500 innovative and original shows performed by more than 100 groups from Canada and around the world. Call ℂ **604/257-0350,** or see www.vancouverfringe.com for more info. First and second week of September.

CanWest Comedy Fest. Comedians from Canada and the U.S. perform around town. Contact **Ticketmaster** for tickets at ℂ **604/685-0881,** or check www.comedyfest.com for more information. Mid-September.

Mid-Autumn Moon Festival, Dr. Sun Yat-Sen Chinese Garden. This outdoor Chinese celebration includes a lantern festival, storytelling, music, and, of course, moon cakes. For info, call ✆ **604/662-3207,** or visit www. vancouverchinesegarden.com. Early to mid-September, according to the lunar cycle (15th day of the 8th month of the Chinese calendar).

Vancouver International Film Festival. This highly respected festival features 250 new works, revivals, and retrospectives, representing filmmakers from 40 countries (particularly Asia). Call ✆ **604/685-0260,** or visit www. viff.org for details. Late September and first 2 weeks of October.

OCTOBER

Vancouver International Writers and Readers Festival. Public readings by Canadian and international authors as well as writers' workshops take place on Granville Island and at other locations in the lower mainland. Call ✆ **604/ 681-6330,** or check www.writersfest. bc.ca for details. Mid-October.

Parade of the Lost Souls, Grandview Park. This bizarre and intriguing procession takes place around Commercial Drive to honor the dead and chase away bad luck. For more information, call ✆ **604/879-8611,** or visit www.public dreams.org. Last Saturday of October.

NOVEMBER

Remembrance Day. Celebrated throughout Canada, this day commemorates Canadian soldiers who gave their lives in war. Vintage military aircraft fly over Stanley Park and Canada Place, and at noon a 21-gun salute is fired from Deadman's Island. November 11.

Christmas Craft and Gift Market, VanDusen Botanical Garden. For info, call ✆ **604/878-9274,** or check www. vandusengarden.org. November and December.

DECEMBER

Carol Ship Parade of Lights Festival. Harbor cruise ships decorated with colorful Christmas lights sail around English Bay, while onboard guests sip cider and sing their way through the canon of Christmas carols. For more info, call ✆ **604/878-8999,** or check out www.carolships.org. First 3 weeks in December.

Festival of Lights. Throughout December, the VanDusen Botanical Garden is transformed into a magical holiday land with seasonal displays and more than 20,000 lights. Call ✆ **604/ 878-9274** for info, or visit www. vandusengarden.org.

Stanley Park Festival of Lights. Throughout December, the plaza in the middle of Stanley Park becomes a festive gathering point with more than a million twinkling lights transforming the surrounding forest and children's farmyard. The Stanley Park holiday train winds its way through the illuminated forest. For more information call ✆ **604/ 257-8400,** or visit http://vancouver.ca/ parks.

First Night. Vancouver closes its downtown streets for revelers in the city's New Year's Eve performing-arts festival and alcohol-free party. Events and venues change from year to year.

Victoria & Southern Vancouver Island Events

JANUARY

Annual Bald Eagle Count, Goldstream Provincial Park. Hundreds of bald eagles take up residence to feed on the salmon, which begin to run in October. The eagle count usually takes place in mid- to late January, when the numbers peak. Throughout December and January, the park offers educational programs, displays, and guest speakers. Call ✆ **250/478-9414,** or visit www. goldstreampark.com for exact dates.

Robert Burns's Birthday. Celebrating the birthday of the great Scottish poet, events around Victoria and Vancouver include Scottish dancing, piping, and feasts of haggis. Most events take place in pubs. January 25.

FEBRUARY

Chinese New Year, Chinatown. See "Vancouver Events," earlier in this chapter. Late January or early February.

Trumpeter Swan Festival, Comox Valley. A weeklong festival celebrates these magnificent white birds as they gather in the Comox Valley. Check dates with the Vancouver Island tourist office (✆ **250/754-3500**).

Flower Count. So many flowers bloom in Victoria and the surrounding area that the city holds an annual flower count. The third week in February is a great time to see the city as it comes alive with vibrant colors. Call ✆ **250/953-2033** for more info. Late February/early March.

MARCH

Pacific Rim Whale Festival, Tofino, Ucluelet, and Pacific Rim National Park. Every spring, more than 20,000 gray whales migrate past this coastline, attracting visitors to Vancouver Island's west coast beaches. The event features live crab races, storytelling, parades, art shows, guided whale-spotting hikes, and whale-watching boat excursions. Call ✆ **250/726-2688**, or visit www.pacificrimwhalefestival.org for more information. Mid-March to early April.

Annual Brant Wildlife Festival, Qualicum Beach. This 3-day celebration of the annual black brant migration to the area (20,000 birds) includes guided walks through old-growth forest and saltwater and freshwater marshes. For information, call ✆ **250/586-1311**, or visit www.brantfestival.bc.ca. March and April.

MAY

Swiftsure International Yacht Race. International sailing races make for spectacular scenery on the waters around Victoria. For information, call ✆ **250/953-2033,** or visit www.tourismvictoria.com. Third or fourth weekend in May.

JUNE

JazzFest International. Jazz, swing, bebop, fusion, and improv artists from across the globe perform at various venues around Victoria during this 10-day festival (✆ **250/388-4423;** www.jazzvictoria.ca). Late June/early July.

JULY

Canada Day. Victoria, the provincial capital, celebrates this national holiday with events centered on the Inner Harbour, including music, food, and fireworks. July 1.

Victoria Pride Celebration. Victoria's gay and lesbian community celebrates with a week of activities that culminates in a downtown parade and festival at Fisherman's Wharf Park. For more info visit www.victoriapridesociety.org. First week in July.

AUGUST

First Peoples Festival. This free event highlights the heritage of the Pacific Northwest First Nations with performances, carving demonstrations, and cultural displays at the Royal B.C. Museum (✆ **250/384-3211**). Second week in August.

Fringe Festival. Anything goes at this annual alternative-theater festival. The festival is a 12-day celebration of some of the most innovative theater offered anywhere in the country. For more information call ✆ **250/383-2663,** or visit www.intrepidtheatre.com. Late August/early September.

Classic Boat Festival. Boaters from around the world converge in Victoria's Inner Harbour for this annual Labour Day weekend celebration, which includes races, a parade of steam vessels, a cruise up the Gorge Waterway, and vessels open for tours. For more information call ✆ **250/383-8306.** Last weekend in August.

The 2010 Olympic & Paralympic Winter Games

The 2010 Olympic Winter Games will be staged in Vancouver and Whistler from February 12 to 28, 2010. These cities will also host the Paralympic Winter Games from March 12 to 21, 2010. If you hope to attend the 2010 Winter Games, pre-planning is essential.

For information on the Games, contact Vancouver 2010 Organizing Committee, #400–3585 Graveley St., Vancouver, B.C. V5K 5J5 (© **877/408-2010** or 604/966-2572; www.vancouver2010.com).

Olympic Torch Starts in Victoria   Vancouver and Whistler are grabbing all the attention, but Victoria was the symbolic starting point for the 2010 Winter Olympics. It was in Victoria, on October 30, 2009, that the torch relay began its journey across Canada; it will travel over 45,000 km (27,962 miles) before arriving back in Vancouver on February 10, 2010, signaling the start of the Vancouver 2010 Olympic Winter Games. For more information on the route the torch will follow, visit www.vancouver2010.com/torchrelay.

Events in Whistler   Alpine skiing (downhill, super G, giant slalom, slalom, combined); Nordic skiing (biathlon, cross-country skiing, ski jumping, Nordic combined); sliding (bobsleigh, luge, skeleton); Alpine skiing (Paralympic); biathlon (Paralympic); cross-Country skiing.

Events will take place in three major competition venues: Alpine skiing on Whistler Mountain's Creekside runs; bobsleigh, luge, and skeleton at the new Sliding Centre on Blackcomb Mountain; and Nordic, biathlon, and ski jumping at newly developed facilities (including two ski jumps, 14km/9 miles of competition trails, a day lodge, and two 12,000-seat stadiums) in Callahan Valley, about 10km (6 miles) southwest of Whistler.

The **Whistler Olympic and Paralympic Village** site is located within the Cheakamus Valley, near the so-called "Function Junction" at the western entrance to Whistler. A short shuttle ride will take athletes to the heart of Whistler Village and the nightly outdoor medal ceremonies at the Whistler Celebration Plaza. The Paralympic Closing Ceremony will also be presented at this site.

Events in Vancouver   Skiing (freestyle, snowboard); skating (speed, figure, pairs, ice dancing); curling (men/women's, wheelchair); ice hockey; ice sledge hockey.

Events will take place in six different venues: General Motors Place in downtown Vancouver (ice hockey); Hillcrest/Nat Bailey Park in central Vancouver near Queen Elizabeth Park (curling); Pacific Coliseum in Hastings Park, 15 minutes from downtown (figure skating); UBC Winter Sports Centre at the University of British Columbia on Vancouver's West Side (ice hockey, ice sledge hockey); Richmond Oval in Richmond, on the banks of the Fraser River, about 25 minutes from downtown (speed skating); and Cypress Mountain in West Vancouver (freestyle and snowboard skiing).

Tickets   The Vancouver 2010 Organizing Committee website at **www.vancouver 2010.com** is the best source of general information regarding tickets. If you are interested in attending the 2010 Winter Games, it is imperative to sign up at this website to receive ticket updates and announcements as they are made available. However, only Canadian citizens can buy tickets through the official website.

Non-Canadian residents must purchase tickets through the authorized sales agent for their respective National Olympic Committee. For example, U.S. citizens can purchase tickets to the 2010 Winter Games through **Jet Set Sports,** P.O. Box 366, Far Hills, NJ 07931 (✆ **908/766-1001;** fax 908/766-4646; www.jetsetsports. com), the authorized ticket sales agent of the U.S. Olympic Committee.

The ticket-buying process began in 2008 and has been staged in phases. In some cases, lotteries are held to distribute tickets fairly to events where demand for tickets exceeds supply. You want to see figure skating? How about settling for a ticket for curling? The starting price for event tickets is C$25, and half of all tickets are priced at C$100 or less.

Buyers should be aware that tickets bought from any unauthorized source may not be valid and may not be accepted for entry to 2010 Olympic Winter Games venues.

Accommodations Nearly all the hotels, condos, inns, and other lodging options in Whistler were asked to hold their rooms until all the groups that fall under the responsibility of the 2010 Organization Committee secured lodging. These included members of the International Olympic Committee, the National Olympic Committees of participating nations, International Sport Federations, international and domestic corporate sponsors, international and domestic news media, athletes' families, team coaches, support personnel, and security. At press time, it was impossible to know how many rooms in Whistler will remain for spectators after the bigwigs, officials, media, and family take their cut, but most of the hoteliers expect that few rooms will remain for the average tourist. Cruise ships may be docked at Squamish in Howe Sound (60km/37 miles from Whistler) to serve as hotels for stragglers. If you are hoping to stay in Whistler during the Olympics, you'll need to bird-dog the various hotel web-sites and monitor the official Olympics website at www.vancouver2010.com.

Once the unreserved rooms in Whistler are released, a huge surge of demand will drive up prices. Be very wary of using your credit card to purchase room reservations from unfamiliar sources—there is already a lot of fraud surrounding Internet ticket and reservation sales for Olympic events and services.

Transportation While the Games are on, nearly all transportation to, from, and within Whistler will be on public transport buses. Of course, the official line is that use of buses reduces impact on the environment, but the real reason has more to do with reducing traffic gridlock and enhancing security. If you have a ticket for an event in Whistler, be prepared to board a bus to take you there. Except for local residents, passenger cars will not be allowed on the Sea-to-Sky highway from Vancouver to Whistler.

Special Events in Vancouver If you can't visit Whistler during the Games, there will be special Olympics-related events in Vancouver to enjoy. "Live Sites" will be set up at Canada Place, at David Lam Park, and on Georgia Street. During the Olympic period, these alcohol-free sites will feature free main-stage enter-tainment, giant broadcast screens, local artists, and the opportunity to mingle with guests and athletes from around the world.

The Great Canadian Beer Festival. Featuring samples from the province's best microbreweries, this event is held at the Victoria Conference Centre, 720 Douglas St. For more information call ☎ **250/383-2332.** Early September.

OCTOBER

Royal Victoria Marathon. This annual race attracts runners from around the world (half-marathon course available, too). Call ☎ **250/658-4520,** or go to www.royalvictoriamarathon.com for more info. Early October (Canadian Thanksgiving weekend).

NOVEMBER

Remembrance Day. See "Vancouver Events," earlier in this chapter. November 11.

DECEMBER

Merrython Fun Run. This annual 8km (5-mile) race loops through Oak Bay and downtown Victoria. Call (☎ **250/953-2033**) for details. Early December.

First Night. See "Vancouver Events," earlier in this chapter. Call **Tourism Victoria** at ☎ **250/953-2033** for more details. December 31.

2 ENTRY REQUIREMENTS

ENTRY DOCUMENTS FOR U.S. CITIZENS

It is no longer possible to enter Canada and return to the U.S. by showing a government-issued photo ID (such as a driver's license) and proof of U.S. citizenship (such as a birth or naturalization certificate). The **Western Hemisphere Travel Initiative (WHTI),** which took full effect in 2009, requires all U.S. citizens returning to the U.S. from Canada to have a U.S. passport (this includes children under age 18).

In other words, if you are a U.S. citizen traveling to Canada by air, sea, or land, you must have a valid U.S. passport or a new passport card (see box below) in order to get back into the U.S.

You'll find current entry information on the website of the U.S. State Department at **www.travel.state.gov** and on the **Canada Border Services Agency** website, **www.cbsa-asfc.gc.ca.**

Permanent U.S. residents who are not U.S. citizens should carry their passport and Resident Alien Card (U.S. form I-151 or I-551). Foreign students and other non-citizen U.S. residents should carry their passport, a Temporary Resident Card (form

1688) or Employment Authorization Card (1688A or 1688B), a visitor's visa, an I-94 arrival-departure record, a current I-20 copy of IAP-66 indicating student status, proof of sufficient funds for a temporary stay, and evidence of return transportation.

Visitors arriving by ferry from the U.S. must fill out International Crossing forms, which are collected before boarding.

ENTRY DOCUMENTS FOR COMMONWEALTH CITIZENS

Citizens of Great Britain, Australia, and New Zealand don't need visas to enter Canada, but they do need to show **proof of Commonwealth citizenship** (such as a **passport**), as well as evidence of funds sufficient for a temporary stay (credit cards work well here). Naturalized citizens should carry their naturalization certificates. Permanent residents of Commonwealth nations should carry their passports and resident status cards.

Foreign students and other residents should carry their passport, a Temporary Resident Card or Employment Authorization Card, a visitor's visa, an arrival-departure

Passport Cards: The New Way to Enter Canada for U.S. Citizens

If you are traveling to and from Canada by land or sea in 2010, you can do so with the new **passport card** issued by the U.S. Department of State. The department adopted this idea in 2008 after vociferous complaints by border communities that requiring expensive passports for all visitors would harm local businesses dependent on easy cross-border access. Less expensive and more portable than the traditional passport book, the wallet-size passport card has the same validity period as a passport book: 10 years for an adult, 5 years for children 15 and younger. Adults who already have a passport book may apply for the card as a passport renewal and pay only $20. First-time applicants are charged $45 for adult cards and $35 for children.

The passport card contains a vicinity-read radio frequency identification (RFID) chip that links the card to a stored record in government databases. No personal information is written to the RFID chip itself. Note that **the passport card is valid for entry by land or sea only;** air travelers must have a valid U.S. passport. If you already have a passport, you may, of course, use that to enter Canada by land or sea. The passport card cannot be used for other international travel. First-time applicants can apply at any one of the 9,300 Passport Acceptance Facilities across the U.S. For more information on passport cards and to locate the application office nearest you, visit http://travel.state.gov.

record, a current copy of student status, proof of sufficient funds for a temporary stay, and evidence of return transportation. *Note:* With changing security regulations, it is advisable for all travelers to check with the Canadian consulate before departure to find out the latest in travel document requirements. You will also find current information on the **Canada Border Services Agency** website, **www.cbsa-asfc.gc.ca**; follow the links under "Help."

For Residents of Australia: You can pick up a passport application from your local post office or any branch of Passports Australia, but you must schedule an interview at the passport office to present your application materials. Call the **Australian Passport Information Service** at ✆ **131-232,** or visit the government website at **www.passports.gov.au**.

For Residents of Ireland: You can apply for a 10-year passport at the **Passport Office,** Setanta Centre, Molesworth Street, Dublin 2 (✆ **353/1671-1633** or 890/426-888; www.foreignaffairs.gov.ie). Those under age 18 and over 65 must apply for a 3-year passport. You can also apply at 1A South Mall, Cork (✆ **353/21494-4700** or 890/426-900) or at most main post offices.

For Residents of New Zealand: You can pick up a passport application at any New Zealand Passports Office or download it from their website. Contact the **Passports Office** at ✆ **0800/225-050** in New Zealand, or 04/474-8100, or log on to **www.passports.govt.nz**.

For Residents of the United Kingdom: To pick up an application for a standard 10-year passport (5-year passport for children under 16), visit your nearest passport office, major post office, or travel agency or contact the **United Kingdom Passport Service** at ✆ **0870/521-0410** or search its website at **www.ips.gov.uk**.

CUSTOMS

You'll pass through **Canadian Customs** (ⓒ **800/461-9999** in Canada, or 204/983-3500) upon arrival, and **U.S. Customs** (ⓒ **360/332-5771**), if you are traveling through the U.S., on your departure.

If you're **driving** from Seattle, you'll enter British Columbia, Canada, at the Peace Arch crossing (open 24 hr.; often there's a 30-min. or longer wait) in Blaine, Washington. You'll go through Customs when you cross the border into Canada and show your passport.

Arriving by air, you'll go through Customs at the airport once you clear passport control. (Even if you don't have anything to declare, Customs officials randomly select a few passengers and search their luggage.)

Visitors arriving by **train, ferry,** or **cruise ship** from the U.S. pass through U.S. Customs before boarding and Canadian Customs upon arrival.

What You Can Bring into Canada

Your personal baggage can include the following: boats, motors, snowmobiles, camping and sports equipment, appliances, TV sets, musical instruments, personal computers, cameras, and other items of a personal or household nature. If you are bringing excess luggage, be sure to carry a detailed inventory list that includes the acquisition date, serial number, and cost or replacement value of each item. It sounds tedious, but it can speed things up at the border. Customs will help you fill out the forms that allow you to temporarily bring in your effects. This list will also be used by U.S. Customs to check off what you bring out. You will be charged Customs duties for anything left in Canada.

A few other things to keep in mind:

• If you're over 18, you're allowed to bring in 40 ounces of liquor and wine or 24 12-ounce cans or bottles of beer and ale, and 50 cigars, 400 cigarettes, or

14 ounces of manufactured tobacco per person. Any excess is subject to duty.

• Gifts not exceeding C$60 and not containing tobacco products, alcoholic beverages, or advertising material can be brought in duty-free. Meats, plants, and vegetables are subject to inspection on entry. There are restrictions, so contact the Canadian Consulate for more details if you want to bring produce into the country, or check the Canada Border Services Agency website, www.cbsa-asfc.gc.ca.

• If you plan to bring your dog or cat, you must provide proof of rabies inoculation during the preceding 36-month period. Other types of animals need special clearance and health certification. (Many birds, for instance, require 8 weeks in quarantine.)

If you need more information concerning items you wish to bring in and out of the country, contact **Canada Border Services** (ⓒ **800/461-9999** in Canada, or 204/983-3500; www.cbsa-asfc.gc.ca).

What You Can Take Home from Canada

For information on what you're allowed to bring home, contact one of the following agencies:

U.S. Citizens: U.S. Customs & Border Protection (CBP), 1300 Pennsylvania Ave., NW, Washington, DC 20229 (ⓒ **877/227-5511;** www.cbp.gov).

U.K. Citizens: HM Customs & Excise at ⓒ **0845/010-9000** (from outside the U.K., 020/8929-0152), or consult their website at **www.hmrc.gov.uk**.

Australian Citizens: Australian Customs Service at ⓒ **1300/363-263,** or log on to **www.customs.gov.au**.

New Zealand Citizens: New Zealand Customs, The Customhouse, 17–21 Whitmore St., Box 2218, Wellington (ⓒ **04/473-6099** or 0800/428-786; **www.customs.govt.nz**).

3 GETTING THERE

This section outlines your options for getting to Vancouver and Victoria. You'll find specific information about getting around both cities by car, on foot, and by public transportation in the chapters "Getting to Know Vancouver" (chapter 5) and "Getting to Know Victoria" (chapter 13).

GETTING TO VANCOUVER
By Plane

Daily direct flights between major U.S. cities and Vancouver are offered by **Air Canada** (© 888/247-2262; www.aircanada. com), **Alaska Airlines** (© 800/252-7522; www.alaskaair.com), **American Airlines** (© 800/433-7300; www.aa.com), **Continental** (© 800/231-0856; www.continental. com), **Frontier Airlines** (© 800/432-1359; www.frontierairlines.com), **Northwest Airlines** (© 800/225-2525; www. nwa.com), and **United Airlines** (© 877/932-4259; www.united.com).

Domestic travelers within Canada have fewer options. **Air Canada** (© **888/247-2262**) operates flights to Vancouver and Victoria from all major Canadian cities, connecting with some of the regional airlines. Cheaper and reaching farther all the time is the no-frills airline **WestJet** (© **888/WEST-JET** [937-8358] or 800/538-5696; www.westjet.com), which operates regular flights from Vancouver and Victoria to Prince George, Kelowna, Edmonton, Calgary, Toronto, Montreal, Ottawa, Halifax, and farther afield.

Direct flights between London and Vancouver are offered by **Air Canada** (© **0871/220-1111;** www.aircanada.com). Other major carriers serving London (United, Continental, British Airways) make stops in the U.S. before continuing on to Vancouver.

Air Canada (© **0871/220-1111;** www. aircanada.com) also flies to Vancouver from Sydney, Australia, and Auckland, New Zealand.

By Ship & Ferry

Vancouver is the major embarkation point for cruises going up British Columbia's Inland Passage to Alaska. The ships carry more than one million passengers annually on their nearly 350 Vancouver-Alaska cruises. In the summer, up to four cruise ships a day berth at **Canada Place** cruise-ship terminal (p. 116; © **604/665-9000;** www.portmetrovancouver.com).

The following cruises dock at Canada Place or the nearby Ballantyne Pier: **Princess Cruises** (© 800/PRINCESS [774-6237]; www.princess.com), **Holland America Line** (© 800/724-5425; www. hollandamerica.com), **Royal Caribbean** (© 800/398-9819; www.royalcaribbean. com), **Crystal Cruises** (© 866/446-6625; www.crystalcruises.com), **Norwegian Cruise Line** (© 800/625-1166; www.ncl. com), **Radisson Seven Seas Cruises** (© 877/505-5370; www.rssc.com), and **Carnival** (© 888/CARNIVAL [227-6482]; www.carnivalcruise.com). Public transit buses and taxis greet new arrivals, but you can also easily walk to many major hotels (the **Pan Pacific Vancouver Hotel,** perched directly atop the cruise-ship terminal, is the most convenient; see p. 74).

If you're arriving from Vancouver Island or Victoria, **B.C. Ferries** (© **888/223-3779** or 250/386-3431; www.bcferries. com) has three daily routes. See "By Ship & Ferry," under "Getting to Victoria," below.

By Train

VIA Rail Canada, 1150 Station St., Vancouver (© **888/842-7245;** www.viarail. ca), connects with Amtrak at Winnipeg, Manitoba. From there you can transfer to the Canadian, the western transcontinental train that travels between Vancouver and Toronto, with stops in Kamloops, Jasper, Edmonton, Saskatoon, Winnipeg, and Sudbury Junction. For travel within

Canada only, the 12-day **Canrailpass** (C$576 off-peak; C$923 peak) is available through www.viarail.com.

Amtrak (© **800/872-7245;** www. amtrak.com) offers daily service from Seattle, though there's currently only one train in the morning (departing Seattle 7:10am, arriving Vancouver 11:35); otherwise, the Seattle-Vancouver route is covered by an Amtrak bus. Amtrak also has a route from San Diego to Vancouver. It stops at all major U.S. West Coast cities, and takes a little under 2 days to complete the entire journey.

By Car

You'll probably be driving into Vancouver along one of two routes. **U.S. I-5** from Seattle becomes **Hwy. 99** when you cross the border at the Peace Arch. The 210km (130-mile) drive from Seattle takes about 2½ hours. On the Canadian side of the border, you'll drive through the cities of White Rock, Delta, and Richmond, pass under the Fraser River through the George Massey Tunnel, and cross the Oak Street Bridge. The highway ends there and becomes Oak Street, a busy urban thoroughfare heading toward downtown. Turn left at the first convenient major arterial (70th, 57th, 49th, 41st, 33rd, 16th, and 12th aves. will all serve) and proceed until you hit the next major street, which will be Granville Street. Turn right on Granville Street. This street heads directly into downtown Vancouver via the Granville Street Bridge.

Trans-Canada Hwy. 1 is a limited-access freeway that runs to Vancouver's eastern boundary, where it crosses the Second Narrows Bridge to North Vancouver. When traveling on Hwy. 1 from the east, exit at Cassiar Street and turn left at the first light onto Hastings Street (Hwy. 7A), which is adjacent to Exhibition Park. Follow Hastings Street 6.4km (4 miles) into downtown. When coming to Vancouver from parts north, take exit 13 (the

sign says TAYLOR WAY, BRIDGE TO VANCOUVER) and cross the Lions Gate Bridge into Vancouver's West End.

Car insurance is compulsory in British Columbia (see chapter 21, "Fast Facts").

By Bus

Greyhound Bus Lines (© **800/231-2222** or 604/482-8747; www.greyhound. ca) offers daily bus service between Vancouver and all major Canadian cities, and between Vancouver and Seattle (at the border crossing, passengers disembark the bus and take their luggage through Customs). For information on Greyhound's cost-cutting **Canada Pass,** which allows for unlimited travel within Canada, and **Discovery Pass,** which allows for unlimited travel in the U.S. and Canada, consult their website. **Pacific Coach Lines** (© **604/ 662-7575;** www.pacificcoach.com) provides service between Vancouver and Victoria (see "Getting to Victoria," below).

GETTING TO VICTORIA
By Plane

The **Victoria International Airport** (© 250/953-7500; www.victoriaairport. com) is near the Sidney ferry terminal, 22km (14 miles) north of Victoria off the Patricia Bay Highway (Hwy. 17).

Air Canada (© **888/247-2262** or 800/661-3936; www.aircanada.com) and **Horizon Air** (© **800/547-9308;** www. alaskaair.com) offer direct connections from Seattle, Vancouver, Portland, Calgary, Edmonton, Saskatoon, Winnipeg, and Toronto. Canada's low-cost airline **WestJet** (© **888/WEST-JET** [937-8358]; www. westjet.com) offers flights to Victoria from Kelowna, Calgary, Edmonton, and other destinations; WestJet service now extends to a few U.S. cities as well.

Commuter airlines, including floatplanes that land in Victoria's Inner Harbour, provide service to Victoria from Vancouver and destinations within B.C. They include **Air B.C.** (reached through

Air Canada at ☏ **888/247-2262**), **Harbour Air Sea Planes** (☏ **604/274-1277** in Vancouver, or 250/384-2215 in Victoria; www.harbour-air.com), and **West Coast Air** (☏ **800/347-2222;** www.westcoastair. com).

Kenmore Air (☏ **800/543-9595;** www. kenmoreair.com) and **Helijet** (☏ **800/ 665-4354;** www.helijet.com) offer flights between Seattle, Port Angeles and Victoria.

By Ship & Ferry

Car-carrying **B.C. Ferries** (☏ **888/223-3779** or 250/386-3431; www.bcferries. com) has three routes from Vancouver to Vancouver Island and Victoria. In the summer, if you're driving, it's a good idea to reserve a space beforehand, especially on long weekends. Call B.C. Ferries reservations at ☏ **888/724-5223** (in B.C. only) or 604/444-2890.

The most direct B.C. Ferries route is the **Tsawwassen–Swartz Bay ferry,** which operates daily between 7am and 9pm (10pm on Sun). Ferries run every hour with extra sailings on holidays and in peak travel season. The crossing takes 95 minutes, but schedule an extra 2 hours for travel to and from both ferry terminals, including waiting time at the docks. Driving distance from Vancouver to Tsawwassen is about 20km (12 miles). Take Hwy. 99 south to Hwy. 17 and follow the signs to the ferry terminal.

Pacific Coach Lines (☏ **604/662-7575;** www.pacificcoach.com) provides regular bus service into Victoria for C$15 one-way, but you must book your seat on board the ferry and within the first 20 minutes of the ferry ride (a Pacific Coast Lines desk is on board the ferry). You can take Pacific Coach Lines all the way from Vancouver to Victoria for C$82 round-trip, which includes the ferry ride.

Exiting the Swartz Bay ferry terminal by **car,** you'll be on Hwy. 17 (there is no other option), which leads directly into downtown Victoria where it becomes Douglas Street.

The **Vancouver-Nanaimo ferry** operates between Tsawwassen and Duke Point, just south of Nanaimo, about 100km (62 miles) north of Victoria. The 2-hour crossing runs eight times daily between 5:15am and 10:45pm.

The **Horseshoe Bay–Nanaimo ferry** has nine daily sailings, leaving Horseshoe Bay near West Vancouver (to reach Horseshoe Bay from Vancouver, take the Trans-Canada Highway/Hwy. 99 and Hwy. 1 west across the Lions Gate Bridge) and arriving 95 minutes later in Nanaimo. From the Nanaimo ferry terminal on Vancouver Island, passengers bound for Victoria board the E&N Railiner (see "By Train," below) or drive south to Victoria via the Island Highway (Hwy. 1).

Three different **U.S. ferry** services offer daily, year-round connections between Port Angeles, Bellingham, or Seattle, Wash., and Victoria. All of these ferries dock at Victoria's Inner Harbour near the Empress Hotel and Parliament Buildings so you can walk right into town.

Black Ball Transport (☏ **250/386-2202** in Victoria, or 360/457-4491 in Port Angeles; www.cohoferry.com) operates between Port Angeles and Victoria. The crossing takes 1½ hours. There are four crossings per day in the summer (mid-June to Sept), and usually two sailings a day throughout the rest of the year (with a short 2-week closure in Jan).

Victoria Clipper (☏ **800/288-2535;** www.victoriaclipper.com) operates a high-speed catamaran between Seattle and Victoria, with some sailings stopping in the San Juan Islands. It's a passenger-only service; sailing time is approximately 3 hours with daily runs from downtown Seattle and Victoria.

From mid-June through September, the passenger-only MV *Victoria Star* operated by **Victoria San Juan Cruises** (☏ **800/ 443-4552** or 360/738-8099; www.whales. com) departs the Fairhaven Terminal in Bellingham, Wash., at 9am and arrives in

PLANNING YOUR TRIP TO VANCOUVER & VICTORIA

3

MONEY & COSTS

 Tips **Whale-Watching on the Way to Victoria**

If you're pressed for time, **Prince of Whales** (© 888/383-4884; www.princeof
whales.com) tours offers a great way to combine whale-watching with your trip
to Victoria. May to September, you can book a 5-hour whale-watching tour that
leaves from Vancouver's Burrard Inlet and docks right in front of the Fairmont
Empress in Victoria. The tour includes an excursion to world-famous Butchart
Gardens before heading back to Vancouver. Cost is C$300 for adults, C$280 for
youths 13–17, and C$260 for children 5–12.

Victoria at noon. It departs Victoria at
5pm, arriving in Bellingham at 8pm. This
service offers special on-board salmon
lunches and Victoria city tour add-ons and
overnights.

Note: If you're planning to ride the ferry
between the U.S. and Canada, remember
that you will need your **passport** or **passport card;** all passengers go through passport control and Customs on international
ferry trips.

By Train

Travelers on the **Horseshoe Bay–
Nanaimo ferry** (see "By Ship & Ferry,"
above) can board VIA Rail's **E&N Railiner**
train at Nanaimo and wind down Vancouver Island's Cowichan River valley through
Goldstream Provincial Park and to Victoria. The trip takes 2½ hours and ends at
E&N Station, 450 Pandora Ave. (© 800/
561-8630 in Canada), near the Johnson
Street Bridge. For more information, contact **VIA Rail Canada** (© 888/842-7245;
www.viarail.ca).

By Bus

Pacific Coach Lines (© 604/662-7575;
www.pacificcoach.com) provides service
between Vancouver and Victoria with
daily departures between 5:45am and
7:45pm. Pacific Coach Lines will pick up
passengers from the Vancouver cruise-ship
terminal and from most downtown hotels.
For more information, call or visit their
website.

4 MONEY & COSTS

The Value of the Canadian Dollar vs. Other Popular Currencies

Can$	US$	UK£	Euro (€)	Aus$	NZ$
1	.90	.55	.64	1.10	1.35

Frommer's lists exact prices in the local
currency. The currency conversions quoted
above were correct at press time. However,
rates fluctuate, so before departing consult
a currency exchange website such as **www.
oanda.com/convert/classic** to check up-
to-the-minute rates.

It's always advisable to bring money in
a variety of forms on a vacation: A mix of
cash and credit cards is most convenient
for most travelers today. You can exchange
currency or withdraw Canadian dollars
from an ATM upon arrival in Vancouver
or Victoria. ATMs offer the best exchange
rates and 24-hour access. Avoid exchanging money at commercial exchange
bureaus and hotels, which often have the
highest transaction fees.

What Things Cost in Vancouver & Victoria

The favorable exchange rate of the Canadian dollar against the U.S. dollar, the British pound, and the euro gives added value to whatever you buy. Prices in Vancouver are generally a bit higher than in Victoria. From mid-September to April, prices for hotel rooms in both cities generally drop by at least 20% and sometimes as much as 50%; the exception to this is Whistler, where winter is the high season and prices rise accordingly. The prices I've listed below are approximate.

Train to/from airport	C$4
Bus/train fare in city	C$2.50
Cup of coffee	C$1.75
Double latte	C$3.25
Glass of wine	C$7–C$10
Moderate hotel room	fall–spring C$175–C$200; summer C$225–C$250
Moderate 3-course dinner without wine	C$30–C$40
Expensive 3-course dinner without wine	C$60–C$755

CURRENCY

Canadian monetary units are dollars and cents, with dollar notes issued in different colors. The standard denominations are C$5, C$10, C$20, C$50, and C$100. The "loonie" (so named because of the loon on one side) is the C$1 coin that replaced the C$1 bill. A C$2 coin, called the "toonie" because it's worth two loonies, has replaced the C$2 bill. *Note:* If you're driving, it's a good idea to have a pocketful of toonies and loonies for parking meters. Avoid C$100 bills when exchanging money, as many stores refuse to accept these bills. Almost all stores and restaurants accept American currency, and most will exchange amounts in excess of your dinner check or purchase. However, these establishments are allowed to set their own exchange percentages and generally offer the worst rates of all.

TRAVELER'S CHECKS

Traveler's checks in Canadian funds are universally accepted by banks (which charge a fee to cash them), larger stores, and hotels. If your traveler's checks are in a non-Canadian currency, you can exchange them for Canadian currency at any major bank.

ATMS

The easiest and best way to get cash in Vancouver and Victoria is from an ATM. The **Cirrus** (© 800/424-7787; www.mastercard.com) and **PLUS** (© 800/843-7587; www.visa.com) networks span the globe; look at the back of your bank card to see which network you're on, then call or check online for ATM locations at your destination. Be sure you know your personal identification number (PIN) before you leave home, and be sure to find out your daily withdrawal limit before you depart. Many banks impose a fee every time a card is used at a different bank's ATM, and that fee can be higher for international transactions than for domestic ones. On top of this, the bank from which you withdraw cash may charge its own fee.

The 24-hour PLUS and Cirrus ATM systems are widely available throughout British Columbia. The systems convert Canadian withdrawals to your account's currency within 24 hours. Cirrus network cards work at ATMs at **BMO Bank** of Montreal (📞 800/555-3000), **CIBC** (📞 800/465-2422), **HSBC** (📞 888/310-4722), **RBC Royal Bank** (📞 800/769-2511), **TD Canada Trust** (📞 866/567-8888), and at all other ATMs that display the Cirrus logo.

CREDIT & DEBIT CARDS

Major U.S. credit cards are widely accepted in British Columbia, especially American Express, MasterCard, and Visa. British debit cards like Barclay's Visa are also accepted. Diners Club, Carte Blanche, Discover, JCB, and EnRoute are taken by

some establishments, but not as many. The amount spent in Canadian dollars will automatically be converted by your issuing company to your currency when you're billed—generally at rates that are better than you'd receive for cash at a currency exchange. However, the bank will probably add a 3% "adjustment fee" to the converted purchase price. You can also obtain a PIN on your credit card and use it in some ATMs. You usually pay interest from the date of withdrawal and often pay a higher service fee than when using a regular ATM card.

5 HEALTH

I list **hospitals** and **emergency numbers** in the "Fast Facts" section of the Vancouver (p. 65) and Victoria (p. 207) chapters.

If you become ill while traveling in Canada, you may have to pay all medical costs upfront and be reimbursed later. Medicare and Medicaid do not provide coverage for medical costs outside the U.S. Before leaving home, find out what medical services your health insurance covers. To protect yourself, consider buying medical travel insurance (see "Insurance," p. 292).

If you suffer from a chronic illness, consult your doctor before your departure. Pack **prescription medications** in your

carry-on luggage, and carry them in their original containers, with pharmacy labels—otherwise they won't make it through airport security. Carry the generic name of prescription medicines, in case a local Canadian pharmacist is unfamiliar with the brand name.

For conditions like epilepsy, diabetes, or heart problems, wear a **MedicAlert Identification Tag** (📞 **888/633-4298;** www.medicalert.org), which will immediately alert doctors to your condition and give them access to your records through MedicAlert's 24-hour hotline.

6 SAFETY

Overall, Vancouver is a safe city and Victoria is even safer. Violent-crime rates are quite low in both cities. However, property crimes and crimes of opportunity (such as items being stolen from unlocked cars) occur pretty frequently in Vancouver. Never leave valuable items on view in your parked car; put them in the trunk. Most hotels offer safe valet parking or parking in nearby lots.

Thanks to the mild climate and (controversially) lax laws, both Vancouver and Victoria have populations of transients living on the streets of certain neighborhoods. Vancouver's downtown East Side, between Gastown and Chinatown, is a troubled, drug-riddled neighborhood and should be avoided at night. In both Vancouver and Victoria, transients panhandle throughout downtown and tourist-heavy areas.

7 SPECIALIZED TRAVEL RESOURCES

In addition to the destination-specific resources listed below, please visit Frommers.com for additional specialized travel resources.

GAY & LESBIAN TRAVELERS

Since 2003, when the Province of British Columbia announced the legalization of same-sex marriage, Vancouver and Victoria have become favored sites for **gay and lesbian weddings.** (Same-sex marriage is now legal throughout Canada.) Information about the process is listed on the invaluable **www.gayvan.com** website. Vancouver's official tourism website, **www.tourismvancouver.com**, also has information for gay and lesbian travelers.

What San Francisco is to the United States, **Vancouver** is to Canada—a hip, laid-back town with a large, thriving gay community. In fact, the largest gay population in Western Canada lives here, primarily in the **West End** and **Commercial Drive.** You'll find hotels and restaurants in Vancouver to be very gay friendly. (The straight-friendly **West End Guest House,** described on p. 82, is owned and operated by a married gay couple).

The club, bar, and party scene is chronicled in the biweekly gay and lesbian tabloid, *Xtra! West,* available at cafes, bars, and businesses throughout the West End. For some gay nightlife options, also see section 5, "Gay & Lesbian Bars," in chapter 11.

The **Gay Lesbian Transgendered Bisexual Community Centre,** 2-1170 Bute St. (© **604/684-5307;** www.qmunity.ca), has all kinds of information on events and the current hot spots. Also check out the **Vancouver Pride Society** website (**www.vancouverpride.ca**) for upcoming special events, including the annual Vancouver Pride Parade in June, one of the largest gay-pride events in North America.

The **Vancouver Queer Film Festival** is held in mid-August; check **www.queerfilmfestival.ca** for more details. Also check out **Gay & Lesbian Ski Week** at Whistler, located 121km (75 miles) north of Vancouver; for information, go to **www.gaywhistler.com.**

The gay and lesbian scene in **Victoria** is small but active. Explore the gay and lesbian link under "Things to Do" at **www.tourismvictoria.com,** or go to the **www.gayvictoria.ca** website. At both sites you'll find information about special places to stay and dine, plus things to do. The **Victoria Pride Parade and Festival** is held every summer in early July. For nightlife options, see chapter 19.

The **International Gay and Lesbian Travel Association (IGLTA;** © **800/448-8550** or 954/776-2626; www.iglta.org) is the trade association for the gay and lesbian travel industry, and offers an online directory of gay- and lesbian-friendly travel businesses and tour operators.

Gay.com Travel (© **800/929-2268** or 415/644-8044; www.gay.com/travel) is an excellent online successor to the popular *Out & About* print magazine. It provides regularly updated information about gay-owned, gay-oriented, and gay-friendly lodging, dining, sightseeing, nightlife, and shopping establishments in every important destination worldwide. British travelers should click on the "Travel" link at **www.gay.co.uk** for advice and gay-friendly trip ideas.

SENIOR TRAVEL

Because B.C. has the mildest weather in all of Canada, Vancouver and Victoria have become havens for older and retired Canadians. Senior travelers often qualify for discounts at hotels and attractions throughout the area. Always ask; you'll be pleasantly surprised at the number of discounts available. **Discount transit passes** for persons over 65 (with proof of age) may be purchased at shops in Vancouver and Victoria that display a FAREDEALER sign (Safeway, 7-Eleven, and most newsstands). To locate a **FareDealer vendor,** contact B.C. Transit (© **604/521-0400;** www.transitbc. com).

If you're over 50, consider joining **AARP** (3200 E. Carson, Lakewood, CA 90712; © **800/424-3410;** www.aarp. org); their card offers additional restaurant and travel bargains throughout North America.

FAMILY TRAVEL

Vancouver and Victoria are two of the most child-friendly cosmopolitan cities in the world. Where else would you find a market especially for kids? In addition to the standard attractions and sights, you'll find a lot of free, adventurous, outdoor activities that both you and your kids will enjoy (see "Especially for Kids," in chapters 8 and 16).

To locate accommodations, restaurants, and attractions that are particularly kid friendly, refer to the "Kids" icon throughout this guide.

Recommended family travel websites include **Family Travel Forum** (www.family travelforum.com), a comprehensive site that offers customized trip planning; **Family Travel Network** (www.familytravelnetwork. com), an online magazine providing travel tips; and **Travelwithyourkids.com**, a comprehensive site written by parents, for parents, offering sound advice for long-distance and international travel with children.

TRAVELERS WITH DISABILITIES

Vancouver's former mayor, Sam Sullivan, is keenly aware of accessibility issues, having been a quadriplegic since breaking his neck in a skiing accident at age 19. He founded several nonprofit organizations

dedicated to improving the quality of life for disabled people throughout North America. However, even before Sam Sullivan, Vancouver was working to improve accessibility.

According to *We're Accessible,* a newsletter for travelers with disabilities, Vancouver is **"the most accessible city in the world."** There are more than 14,000 sidewalk wheelchair ramps, and motorized wheelchairs are a common sight in the downtown area. The stairs along Robson Square have built-in ramps, and most major attractions and venues have ramps or level walkways for easy access. Most Vancouver hotels have at least partial wheelchair accessibility; many have specially equipped rooms for travelers with disabilities. Most SkyTrain stations and the SeaBus are wheelchair accessible, and most bus routes are lift-equipped. For further information about accessible public transportation, contact **Translink** (© **604/953-3333;** www.translink.ca).

Many Vancouver hotels are also equipping rooms with visual smoke alarms and other facilities for hearing-impaired guests, while many crosswalks are now outfitted with beeping alerts to guide visually impaired pedestrians.

Victoria is similarly accessible. Nearly all Victoria hotels have rooms equipped to accommodate travelers with disabilities, and downtown sidewalks are equipped with ramps, though few intersections have beeping crosswalk signals for the visually impaired. The **Victoria Regional Transit System** (© **250/382-6161**) has a downloadable *Guide to Accessible Transit Services* on its website, **www.transitbc.com**, which includes information on which bus routes are equipped with lifts and/or low floors. The most notable spot in Victoria that isn't readily wheelchair accessible is the promenade along the water's edge in the Inner Harbour, which has only one rather challenging ramp near the Pacific Undersea Gardens.

The government of Canada hosts a comprehensive **Persons with Disabilities website** (www.accesstotravel.gc.ca) with resources for travelers with disabilities. In addition to information on public transit in cities across Canada, the site also lists accessible campsites, parks, coach lines, and a number of links to other services and associations of interest to travelers with disabilities. If you can't find what you need online, call ℂ **800/926-9105.**

Outside of Canada, organizations that offer a vast range of resources and assistance to disabled travelers include **MossRehab** (ℂ **800/CALL-MOSS** [225-5667]; www. mossresourcenet.org); the **American Foundation for the Blind (AFB;** ℂ **800/232-5463;** www.afb.org); and **SATH** (Society for Accessible Travel & Hospitality; ℂ **212/447-7284;** www.sath.org). **AirAmbulance Card.com** is now partnered with SATH and allows you to preselect top-notch hospitals in case of an emergency.

Access-Able Travel Source (ℂ **303/232-2979;** www.access-able.com) offers a comprehensive database on travel agents from around the world with experience in

accessible travel; destination-specific access information; and links to such resources as service animals, equipment rentals, and access guides.

Many travel agencies offer customized tours and itineraries for travelers with disabilities. Among them are **Flying Wheels Travel** (ℂ **507/451-5005;** www.flying wheelstravel.com); and **Accessible Journeys** (ℂ 800/846-4537 or 610/521-0339; www.disabilitytravel.com).

Flying with Disability (www.flying-with-disability.org) is a comprehensive information source on airplane travel. **Avis Rent a Car** (ℂ **888/879-4273**) has an "Avis Access" program that offers services for customers with special travel needs. These include specially outfitted vehicles with swivel seats, spinner knobs, and hand controls; mobility scooter rentals; and accessible bus service. Be sure to reserve well in advance.

Also check out the quarterly magazine *Emerging Horizons* (www.emerging horizons.com), available by subscription ($16.95 year in the U.S.; $21.95 outside the U.S.).

Getting Carded

Check out the **International Student Travel Confederation (ISTC;** www.istc. org) website for comprehensive travel services information and details on how to get an **International Student Identity Card (ISIC),** which qualifies students for substantial savings on rail passes, plane tickets, entrance fees, and more. It also provides students with basic health and life insurance and a 24-hour helpline. The card is valid for a maximum of 18 months. You can apply for the card online or in person at **STA Travel** (ℂ **800/781-4040** in North America; ℂ 132-782 in Australia; ℂ 087/1230-0040 in the U.K.; www.statravel.com), the biggest student travel agency in the world; check out the website to locate STA Travel offices worldwide. If you're no longer a student but are still under 26, you can get an **International Youth Travel Card (IYTC)** from the same people, which entitles you to some discounts. **Travel CUTS** (ℂ **800/592-2887;** www. travelcuts.com) offers similar services for both Canadians and U.S. residents. Irish students may prefer to turn to **USIT** (ℂ **01/602-1906;** www.usit.ie), an Ireland-based specialist in student, youth, and independent travel.

The "Accessible Travel" link at **Mobility-Advisor.com** (www.mobility-advisor.com) offers a variety of travel resources to disabled persons.

British travelers should contact **Holiday Care** (© 0845/124-9971 in the U.K.; www.tourismforall.org.uk) to access a wide range of travel information and resources for elderly people and individuals with disabilities.

STUDENT TRAVEL

The southwestern corner of B.C. is definitely student-oriented territory, and you'll find inexpensive youth hostels run by **Hostelling International** in Vancouver (chapter 6), Victoria (chapter 14), Whistler (chapter 12), and Tofino (chapter 20). These hostels make traveling in B.C. affordable and fun. For membership information check the **Hostelling International** websites at **www.hiusa.org** or **www.hihostels.ca**.

The University of British Columbia (UBC, with more than 30,000 students) in the Point Grey area, Burnaby's Simon Fraser University, and a number of smaller schools contribute to the enormous student population in **Vancouver.** Student travelers have a lot of free and inexpensive entertainment options, both day and night. Pick up a copy of *Georgia Straight* to find out what's happening. Many attractions and theaters offer discounts if you have your student ID with you. While many establishments will accept a school ID, the surest way to obtain student discounts is with an International Student Identity Card (ISIC; for information on obtaining one, see the box "Getting Carded").

In **Victoria,** the University of Victoria (referred to locally as "U. Vic.") has a sprawling campus just east of downtown. The student population accounts for most, if not all, of Victoria's nightlife. Student discounts abound. Pick up a copy of Victoria's weekly paper, *Monday Magazine* (which comes out on Thurs), for current nightclub listings.

8 SUSTAINABLE TOURISM

In 2006, after years of protests and negotiations by First Nations tribes and environmentalists, Canada declared British Columbia's Great Bear Rainforest off-limits to loggers. This landmark decision preserves the largest remaining temperate coastal rainforest in the world, some 6 million hectares (15 million acres) that are home to rare white bears and support the highest concentration of grizzly bears in North America (p. 289). It must also be noted that much of British Columbia's economy is based on "resource extraction" of one kind or another, logging being the most prevalent.

Vancouver and Victoria are meccas of ecotourism in all its many guises. From patronizing restaurants that use only locally harvested foods and nonendangered fish to enjoying natural, nonpolluting fun by paddling kayaks and hiking through beautiful rainforests, you can enjoy green holidays in both of these cities without sacrificing any fun or flavor. More and more hotels in both cities are revising their practices in order to be more sustainable. Restaurants throughout the region pride themselves on their fresh, organic produce. If you're ordering fish, look for the "OceanWise" logo on the menu–it indicates what fresh, nonendangered fish has been sustainably harvested for the restaurant.

Both Vancouver and Victoria are fit, outdoors-oriented cities. I list special low-impact walking tours and ecotours in and

General Resources for Green Travel

In addition to the resources for **Vancouver** and **Victoria** listed above, the following websites provide valuable wide-ranging information on sustainable travel. For a list of even more sustainable resources, as well as tips and explanations on how to travel greener, visit www.frommers.com/planning.

- **Responsible Travel** (www.responsibletravel.com) is a great source of sustainable travel ideas; the site is run by a spokesperson for ethical tourism in the travel industry. **Sustainable Travel International** (www.sustainable travelinternational.org) promotes ethical tourism practices, and manages an extensive directory of sustainable properties and tour operators around the world.

- In the U.K., **Tourism Concern** (www.tourismconcern.org.uk) works to reduce social and environmental problems connected to tourism. The **Association of Independent Tour Operators (AITO;** www.aito.co.uk) is a group of specialist operators leading the field in making holidays sustainable.

- In Canada, **www.greenlivingonline.com** offers extensive content on how to travel sustainably, including a travel and transport section and profiles of the best green shops and services in Toronto, Vancouver, and Calgary.

- In Australia, the national body that sets guidelines and standards for ecotourism is **Ecotourism Australia** (www.ecotourism.org.au). **The Green Directory** (www.thegreendirectory.com.au), **Green Pages** (www.thegreen pages.com.au), and **Eco Directory** (www.ecodirectory.com.au) offer sustainable travel tips and directories of green businesses.

- **Carbonfund** (www.carbonfund.org), **TerraPass** (www.terrapass.org), and **Carbon Neutral** (www.carbonneutral.org) provide info on "carbon offsetting," or offsetting the greenhouse gas emitted during flights.

- **Greenhotels** (www.greenhotels.com) recommends green-rated member hotels around the world that fulfill the company's stringent environmental requirements. **Environmentally Friendly Hotels** (www.environmentally friendlyhotels.com) offers more green accommodation ratings. The **Hotel Association of Canada** (www.greenkeyglobal.com) has a Green Key Eco-Rating Program, which audits the environmental performance of Canadian hotels, motels, and resorts.

- **Sustain Lane** (www.sustainlane.com) lists sustainable eating and drinking choices around the U.S.; also visit **www.eatwellguide.org** for tips on eating sustainably in the U.S. and Canada.

- For information on animal-friendly issues throughout the world, visit **Tread Lightly** (www.treadlightly.org). For information about the ethics of swimming with dolphins, visit the **Whale and Dolphin Conservation Society** (www.wdcs.org).

- **Volunteer International** (www.volunteerinternational.org) has a list of questions to help you determine the intentions and the nature of a volunteer program. For general info on volunteer travel, visit **www.volunteer abroad.org** and **www.idealist.org**.

around **Vancouver** in chapter 8 under "Organized Tours" (p. 133) and "Outdoor Activities" (p. 135). For **Victoria,** turn to "Organized Tours" (p. 249) and "Outdoor Activities" (p. 251) in chapter 16. Ecotours of various sorts are also available in **Whistler** (see section 4, "What to See &

Do Outdoors: Whistler's Raison d'Etre," in chapter 12), and they're especially popular in and around **Tofino** and the **Pacific Rim National Park** on the west coast of Vancouver Island (see "What to See & Do," in chapter 20).

9 SPECIAL INTEREST TRIPS, ESCORTED GENERAL INTEREST TOURS & PACKAGE TOURS

SPECIAL INTEREST TRIPS

Vancouver and Victoria are outdoors-oriented cities that offer a wealth of unique outdoor adventures. I list special low-impact walking tours and ecotours in and around **Vancouver** in chapter 8 under "Organized Tours" (p. 133) and "Outdoor Activities" (p. 135).

For **Victoria,** turn to "Organized Tours" (p. 249) and "Outdoor Activities" (p. 251) in chapter 16. Ecotours of various sorts are also available in **Whistler** (see section 4, "What to See & Do Outdoors: Whistler's Raison d'Etre," in chapter 12), and they're especially popular in and around **Tofino** and the **Pacific Rim National Park** on the west coast of Vancouver Island (see "What to See & Do," in chapter 20).

ESCORTED GENERAL-INTEREST TOURS

Escorted tours are structured group tours, with a group leader. The price usually includes everything from airfare to hotels, meals, tours, admission costs, and local transportation.

Uniglobe Specialty Travel (© 800/455-0007 or 604/688-8816; www.uniglobe specialtytravel.com) in Vancouver offers multiday escorted tours of Vancouver and Victoria highlighting the major attractions in both cities. **Globus Tours** (© 866/755-8581; www.globusjourneys.com), one of the largest tour companies in the U.S., provides escorted tours throughout Western

Canada, including Vancouver and Victoria as part of a larger West Coast itinerary.

PACKAGE TOURS

Package tours are simply a way to buy the airfare, accommodations, and other elements of your trip (such as car rentals, airport transfers, and sometimes even activities) at the same time and often at discounted prices.

One good source of package deals is the airlines themselves. **Air Canada Vacations** (© 888/247-2262; www.aircanada vacations.com) offers an array of package deals covering a whole series of travel bargains ranging from city packages to fly/drive tours, escorted tours, motor-home travel, and ski holidays. Other airlines with Canadian package holidays include **American Airlines** (© 800/321-2121; www.aavacations.com), Delta (© 800/221-6666; www.deltavacations.com), **Continental Airlines** (© 800/301-3800; www.covacations.com), and **United** (© 888/854-3899; www.unitedvacations.com).

Several big **online travel agencies**—Expedia, Travelocity, Orbitz, and Last minute.com—also do a brisk business in packages.

Travel packages are also listed in the travel section of your local Sunday newspaper. Or check ads in national travel magazines such as *Arthur Frommer's Budget Travel Magazine, Travel + Leisure, National Geographic Traveler,* and *Condé Nast Traveler.*

10 STAYING CONNECTED

TELEPHONES

Phones in British Columbia are identical to phones in the U.S. The country code is the same as the U.S. code (1). Local calls normally cost C25¢. Many hotels charge C$1 or more per local call and much more for long-distance calls, although more hotels are providing free local service. You can save considerably by using a calling card or your cellphone. You can buy **pre-paid phone cards** in various denominations at grocery and convenience stores.

To call Vancouver or Victoria:

1. If you're calling from outside North America, dial the international access code: 00 from the U.K., Ireland, or New Zealand; or 0011 from Australia. (Omit this step if you're calling from the U.S.)
2. Dial the country code 1.
3. For **Vancouver** or **Whistler**, dial the area code **604** and then the number. For **Victoria** or **Tofino/Ucluelet**, dial the area code **250** and then the number.

Calling within Vancouver and Whistler: If you are in Vancouver or Whistler and want to call another number in Vancouver or Whistler, you must use the area code **604,** followed by the number.

Calling within Victoria: If you are in Victoria and calling another Victoria number you do not need to add the area code. If you are calling from Victoria to anywhere else on Vancouver Island, however, you must use the area code **250** before the number.

To make international calls: To call the U.S. or elsewhere in Canada dial 1, followed by the area code and phone number. To call the U.K., Ireland, Australia, or New Zealand, first dial 00 and then the country code (U.K. 44, Ireland 353, Australia 61, New Zealand 64), followed by the area code and number.

For directory assistance: For automated toll-free directory assistance within Canada (and the U.S.), dial ℂ **1-800-555-1212.** You can also dial **411** if you're looking for a number inside Canada. Dial **0** for numbers to all other countries. (You will incur a charge if you use the 411 and 0 directory assistance numbers.)

For operator assistance: If you need operator assistance making a call, dial 0.

Toll-free numbers: Numbers within Canada beginning with 800, 866, 877, and 888 are toll-free from the U.S., but calling a 1-800 number in the States from Canada is not toll-free. In fact, it costs the same as an overseas call.

CELLPHONES

Canada is part of the **GSM** (Global System for Mobile Communications), a big, seamless network that makes for easy cross-border cellphone use. GSM phones function with a removable plastic SIM card, encoded with your phone number and account information. If your cellphone is on a GSM system, and you have a world-capable multiband phone such as many Sony Ericsson, Motorola, or Samsung models, you can make and receive calls across Canada. Just call your wireless operator and ask for "international roaming" to be activated on your account. (Many U.S. cellphones are already equipped with this capability and need no further modification to operate in Canada.)

You can **rent a cellphone** at a **Touristinfo Centre** at **Vancouver International Airport** (Touristinfo Centres are found in both the domestic and international terminals), or in the city at the **Vancouver Touristinfo Centre,** 200 Burrard St. (ℂ **604/683-2000**), for a minimum

Frommers.com: The Complete Travel Resource

Planning a trip or just returned? Head to **Frommers.com,** voted Best Travel Site by *PC Magazine.* We think you'll find our site indispensable before, during, and after your travels—with expert advice and tips; independent reviews of hotels, restaurants, attractions, and preferred shopping and nightlife venues; vacation giveaways; and an online booking tool. We publish the complete contents of over 135 travel guides in our **Destinations** section, covering over 4,000 places worldwide. Each weekday, we publish original articles that report on **Deals and News** via our free **Frommers.com Newsletters.** What's more, **Arthur Frommer** himself blogs 5 days a week, with cutting opinions about the state of travel in the modern world. We're betting you'll find our **Events** listings an invaluable resource; it's an up-to-the-minute roster of what's happening in cities everywhere—including concerts, festivals, lectures, and more. We've also added weekly **podcasts, interactive maps,** and hundreds of new images across the site. Finally, don't forget to visit our **Message Boards,** where you can join in conversations with thousands of fellow Frommer's travelers and post your trip report once you return.

charge (approx. C$50). For current rates and more information, contact the phone provider, **Cita Communications** © **604/ 671-4655;** www.cita.info).

INTERNET & E-MAIL
Without Your Own Computer

Almost all hotels in Vancouver and Victoria provide some kind of computer access to guests traveling without their own laptops. In some cases, it's a free public computer in the lobby; in other, more high-end hotels, there may be a charge to use computers in the hotel's business center. To find cybercafes in Vancouver and Victoria check **www.cybercaptive.com** and **www. cybercafe.com**.

With Your Own Computer

Almost all hotels, resorts, airports, cafes, and retailers have gone to **Wi-Fi** (wireless fidelity), offering free high-speed Wi-Fi access or charge a fee for 24-hour usage. In the service information for every hotel in this guide I note whether the hotel offers free Wi-Fi or high-speed Internet access; if not, I tell you what the hotel charges (it is always in the C$13–C$15 range for 24 hours). Almost invariably it is large upscale hotels and resorts (such as Westin and the Four Seasons) that charge guests for Internet or Wi-Fi use.

To locate public Wi-Fi "hotspots," go to **www.jiwire.com**; its Hotspot Finder holds the world's largest directory of public wireless hotspots.

4

Suggested Vancouver & Victoria Itineraries

Vancouver and Victoria are preeminently maritime cities, and the visitor is always aware of water and the closeness of the immense Pacific. Vibrant Vancouver is (mostly) on the British Columbia mainland, but charming Victoria occupies the southern tip of Vancouver Island, about 45km (30 miles) to the west. To get the most out of this glorious part of Canada, you'll need a car and you'll likely have to take a ferry to reach Victoria. In both Vancouver and Victoria, you can ditch your car and use public transportation or walk, but to enjoy the almost limitless sightseeing opportunities outside the cities, a car is essential.

In addition to the itineraries below, I provide walking tours of Vancouver in chapter 9 and Victoria in chapter 17.

1 THE BEST OF VANCOUVER IN 1 DAY

This tour is meant to show off the city as a whole, giving you an overview of what makes it so appealing. Some places you'll explore on foot, and for others you'll drive to reach the destination. Nature, art, culture, and coffee are all part of today's itinerary.

❶ Canada Place ★★
Start your day outside, on the upper (deck) level of the city's giant convention center and cruise-ship terminal, which juts out into Burrard Inlet across from the Touristinfo Centre. From here you'll get a good sense of Vancouver's natural and urban topography, with the North Coast Mountains rising up before you; low-rise, historic Gastown to the east; Stanley Park to the west; and a forest of glass residential towers in between. Canada Place is busiest in summer, when up to four giant cruise ships may dock in 1 day. For more on Canada Place, see "Walking Tour 2: Gastown & Chinatown," in chapter 9.

❷ Stanley Park ★★★
You can't really appreciate Stanley Park by driving through it in a car, so park your vehicle and head in on foot via Lagoon Drive. Surrounded by a famed pedestrian seawall, this giant park invites hours of exploration. A 1-hour carriage ride (p. 118) is the perfect way to see the highlights. See p. 116.

❸ Vancouver Aquarium Marine Science Centre ★★
One of the best aquariums in North America is located right in Stanley Park. Don't miss the Arctic Canada exhibit with its beluga whales, and the Marine Mammal Deck, where you can see Pacific white-sided dolphins, sea otters, and other denizens of Pacific Northwest waters. See p. 119.

> ☕ ENGLISH BAY BEACH ★★
> If the weather is warm, head to **English Bay Beach,** an all-seasons gathering spot on the south side of Stanley Park. You can pick up picnic eats or find takeout food on nearby Denman Street.

DAY ONE
1 Canada Place
2 Stanley Park
3 Vancouver Aquarium
4 English Bay Beach
5 Robson Square
6 Caffe Artigiano
7 Museum of Anthropology
8 Raincity Grill

DAY TWO
1 Gastown & Steam Clock
2 Salt
3 Chinatown
4 Granville Island
5 Kitsilano
6 Vancouver Art Gallery
7 West

Stanley Park

Lost Lagoon Dr.

Stanley Park Dr.

Lost Lagoon

Coal Harbour

Devonian Harbour Park

Lost Lagoon Dr.

Park Ln.

Chilco St.

Georgia St.

Gilford St.

Denman St.

Haro St.

Barclay St.

Robson St.

Alberni St.

Pender St.

Bidwell St.

Cardero St.

Nicola St.

Roedde House Museum

English Bay Beach Park

Beach Ave.

Pendrell St.

Comox St.

Bute St.

Davie St.

Jervis St.

Nelson St.

Inukshuk

Broughton St.

WEST END

Nelson Park

Thurlow St.

E n g l i s h

B a y

Burnaby St.

Sunset Beach Park

Harwood St.

Helmcken St.

Pacific St.

Burrard St.

Hornby St.

Howe St.

Vancouver Maritime Museum

Ogden Ave.

Vanier Park

Beach Ave.

Drake St.

Hadden Park

McNicoll Ave.

H.R. MacMillan Space Centre/ Vancouver Museum

Whyte Ave.

Chestnut St.

Granville St.

Kits Beach

Creelman Ave.

Granville Island Public Market

George Wainborn Park

Kitsilano Beach Park

Cornwall Ave.

Laburnum St.

Walnut St.

GRANVILLE ISLAND

York Ave.

Cypress St.

Johnston St.

Yew St.

Arbutus St.

W 2nd Ave.

Maple St.

W 3rd Ave.

Pine St.

Fir St.

Old Bridge St.

Cartwright St.

False

Sutcliffe Park

W 4th Ave.

KITSILANO

Burrard St.

Lamey's Mill Rd.

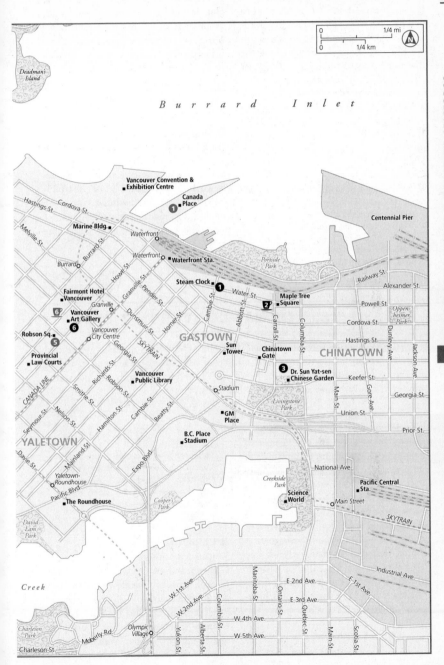

❺ Robson Street & the West End

How you explore the West End is up to you. You can walk from English Bay Beach down Denman Street, and then turn south on Robson, taking in as much of the throbbing shopping and cafe scene as you want. It's also fun to explore the West End as a living neighborhood—the most densely populated in North America. For extra suggestions on exploring the West End, see "Walking Tour 1: Downtown & the West End," in chapter 9.

> **☕ CAFFÈ ARTIGIANO ★★**
> For the best latte in town, as well as grilled Italian sandwiches and snacks, stop in at this busy cafe right across from the Vancouver Art Gallery. The patio in front is perfect for people-watching. 763 Hornby St. ℂ **604/694-7737.** See p. 109.

❼ Museum of Anthropology ★★★

Hop in your car or on the bus for the 20-minute drive to the outstanding Museum of Anthropology at the University of British Columbia. Here, in one of North America's preeminent collections of First Nations art, you'll encounter powerful totem poles, spirit masks, and totemic objects. See p. 123.

❽ Dinner

For a romantic dinner that will introduce you to the best of Vancouver's "eat local" food philosophy, reserve a table at **Raincity Grill,** 1193 Denman St. (ℂ **604/685-7337**), where the windows overlook English Bay, and the regional cuisine provides the perfect excuse to linger. See p. 99.

2 THE BEST OF VANCOUVER IN 2 DAYS

If you've already made your way through "The Best of Vancouver in 1 Day," you'll find that your second full-day tour takes in a roster of new sights and adventures. Today's itinerary will give you an entertaining handle on Vancouver's past, and introduce you to some of Vancouver's most appealing neighborhoods.

❶ Gastown & the Steam Clock

Gastown is the oldest part of Vancouver, a low-rise brick district from the late 19th century, now making a comeback after years of neglect. Stroll down Water Street, timing your visit so you'll be in front of the famous steam clock when it steams and chimes at noon. You might also want to shop for a piece of First Nations art at one of Gastown's specialty galleries (see "First Nations Art & Crafts," in chapter 10). For a complete tour of Gastown, see "Walking Tour 2: Gastown & Chinatown," in chapter 9.

> **☕ SALT ★**
> If it's lunchtime, head over to one of Gastown's smart new eateries. Salt (ℂ **604/633-1912**), in Blood Alley, is Vancouver's only charcuterie, serving cured meats, soup, and artisan cheeses. See p. 98.

❸ Chinatown

Vancouver's Chinatown lies just east of Gastown, and you can walk there or drive. Though parts of Chinatown are touristy, the street markets are lively and authentic. Don't miss the **Dr. Sun Yat-Sen Classical Chinese Garden ★★**. For a complete tour of Chinatown, see "Walking Tour 2: Gastown & Chinatown," in chapter 9.

④ Granville Island ★★★

You can easily drive to Granville Island via the Granville Bridge, but it's more fun to hop on a miniferry from Yaletown Landing and take the 10-minute trip across False Creek. The **public market** ★★★ is pure sensory overload, crammed with every kind of produce, seafood, and food product imaginable, while the area around it is a browser's heaven of shops, galleries, and outdoor-adventure outfitters. See p. 167. For a complete tour of Granville Island, see "Walking Tour 3," p. 154.

⑤ Kitsilano

You can drive, walk, or catch a bus to Kitsilano, the funky upbeat neighborhood west of Granville Island. Check out the buffed beach scene at Kitsilano Beach. One of the world's longest saltwater pools is here if you want a summertime swim.

For a complete walking tour of Kitsilano, see "Walking Tour 3," p. 154.

⑥ Vancouver Art Gallery ★★

You can drive or take a no. 4 or 7 bus on 4th Avenue for the 15-minute ride back to downtown Vancouver. Head for the Vancouver Art Gallery, and make your way specifically to the museum's collection of hauntingly atmospheric paintings by B.C. native Emily Carr. Her moodily expressive works sum up all that is grand and glorious in the Pacific Northwest landscape. See p. 120.

⑦ Dinner

Cap off your day with a memorable meal at **West** ★★★, 2881 Granville St. (✆ **604/738-8938**), a culinary high point of the city and winner of *Vancouver* magazine's Best Restaurant Award in 2008. See p. 103.

3 THE BEST OF VICTORIA IN 1 DAY

Victoria is less than a quarter of the size of Vancouver, and you can easily hit the highlights in 1 day if you arrive on an early ferry. The scenic ferry ride—from Vancouver, Seattle, Anacortes, or Port Angeles—is part of the fun. Although it's easy to experience Victoria by foot, bike, and public transportation, having a car will help to maximize your sightseeing.

① Inner Harbour

A stroll along the Inner Harbour takes you past the **Provincial Legislature Buildings** ★★, a massive stone edifice completed in 1898, and the famous Fairmont Empress hotel, which dates from 1908. Along the busy waterfront you'll also find information on whale-watching excursions, a popular Victoria pastime. For a complete walking tour of the Inner Harbour, see "Walking Tour 1," p. 257.

② Royal B.C. Museum ★★★

The highlight of this excellent museum is the First Peoples Gallery, an absorbing and thought-provoking showplace of First Nations art and culture. The other exhibits

pale by comparison, but do have a look at the life-size woolly mastodon. See p. 243.

> ⑶ THE FAIRMONT EMPRESS ★★
> Tea at the **Empress** is a traditional affair that has remained a real treat despite its fame. Make it your main meal of the day (seatings at 12:30, 2, 2:30, and 5pm), and be sure to reserve in advance. 721 Government St. ✆ **250/384-8111.** See "Taking Afternoon Tea," in chapter 15.

④ Butchart Gardens ★★★

This century-old garden is one of the gardening wonders of the world, meticulously planned and impeccably maintained.

① Inner Harbour
② Royal B.C. Museum
③ Fairmont Empress
④ Butchart Gardens
⑤ Il Terrazzo Ristorante

Though hordes of tourists can jam the paths in the summer months, time your visit for late afternoon, and you'll have more room, plus you can stay for the fabulous summer fireworks display. See p. 240.

⑤ **Dinner**

If there's time, have dinner at Victoria's best Italian restaurant, **Il Terrazzo Ristorante,** 555 Johnson St. (✆ **250/361-0028**). See p. 231.

4 THE BEST OF VANCOUVER, VICTORIA & WHISTLER IN 1 WEEK

Lucky the traveler who gets to spend a whole week or more exploring this ruggedly beautiful part of the Pacific Northwest. If you don't arrive with a car, you can rent one in either Vancouver or Victoria. Most visitors travel to Victoria by car ferry. The assumption here is that your week begins and ends in Vancouver, the major travel hub. For reference, see the map on the inside front cover of this book.

Days ① & ②: Vancouver ★★★

Start your week in Vancouver, following "The Best of Vancouver in 1 Day," and "The Best of Vancouver in 2 Days," above.

Day ③: North Vancouver

Use your third day to get out of the city. At **Capilano Suspension Bridge & Park** ★ (p. 125), you can test your

love-hate relationship with heights on the narrow, bouncy suspension footbridge that spans a scenic ravine, or you can hike under the canopies of the tallest trees on a series of tree bridges. Afterward, drive to the nearby **SkyRide gondola** and be transported to the summit of **Grouse Mountain** ★★★, where you'll enjoy panoramic views of the entire region

(p. 126). Capilano and Grouse Mountain have casual dining and picnic areas, or you can enjoy fine Pacific Northwest cuisine and a panoramic waterfront view at the **Beach House at Dundarave Pier** ★★ (p. 108; © **604/922-1414**), a restored 1912 teahouse located on the water's edge.

Day ❹: Vancouver to Whistler ★★★

Take Georgia Street from downtown Vancouver and head west through Stanley Park, across the scenic Three Lions Bridge, and hook up with the **Sea-to-Sky Highway,** which winds along the edge of Howe Sound and climbs into the mountains. It should take you about 2 hours to reach **Whistler Village.** Once you get to Whistler, ski (it is one of North America's greatest ski resorts, after all) . . . or mountain bike, or hike, or Ziptrek, or shop, or pamper yourself with a spa treatment. A casual and delicious lunch or dinner at **Ciao-Thyme Bistro** ★ (p. 194; © **604/932-7051**) will set you up for whatever activities are on your agenda. You'll find a complete rundown of Whistler possibilities in chapter 12.

Day ❺: Whistler to Vancouver

Spend the night in Whistler. Before leaving the area, drive to **Nairn Falls Provincial Park** ★★, where the Green River shoots through basaltic rock formations and forms a series of thundering waterfalls (p. 197). Once back in Vancouver, enjoy fresh oysters and fish at **Blue Water Cafe and Raw Bar** ★★★ (p. 93; © **604/688-8078**) or **Coast** ★★★ (p. 93; © **604/685-5010**).

Day ❻: Vancouver to Victoria ★★★

Spend day six of your weeklong adventure in Victoria, preferably taking an early-morning ferry through the Gulf Islands. For your day in Victoria, see "The Best of Victoria in 1 Day," above.

Day ❼: Victoria to Vancouver

If time allows, make a trip from Victoria to **Pacific Rim National Park** ★★★, a temperate rainforest with old-growth trees and a wildly magnificent coastline on the west coast of Vancouver Island (a 4½-hr. drive or 45-min. flight). For a complete summary of what's there, including famous lodges and dining choices, see chapter 20. Otherwise, this is the day you return to Vancouver by ferry. Back on the mainland, the Tsawassen ferry terminal is the closest to the Vancouver airport and hooks up with I-5 south to Seattle or north to Vancouver. Or you can travel back via Port Angeles, a gateway to Washington's Olympic National Park, or Anacortes.

Getting to Know Vancouver

Getting lost as you wander around a fascinating new neighborhood is part of the fun of traveling. And getting lost in Vancouver, or at least losing your directional bearings, is possible, mostly because the main grid of streets doesn't run strictly north-south, but rather northwest to southeast like a parallelogram. If you do become directionally challenged, just look for the mountains. They are to the north, across a body of water called Burrard Inlet. If you're facing the mountains, east is to your right, west is to your left, and the back of your head is pointing south. That one tip will generally keep you pointed in the right direction, no matter where you are. You'll also find that Vancouverites are incredibly friendly: If you're scratching your head over a map, almost inevitably someone will ask if he or she can help.

As the 2010 Olympic and Paralympic Winter Games approach, Vancouver and Whistler have entered the final stages of their 7-year boom-time frenzy. Tens of millions of dollars have been poured into new construction (including Olympic venues) and infrastructure. For complete information on the Games, including tickets, venues, and accommodations, see "The 2010 Olympic & Paralympic Winter Games," in chapter 3. For more information on Whistler, see chapter 12.

1 ORIENTATION

VANCOUVER AIRPORT

Vancouver International Airport (YVR; © **604/207-7077**; www.yvr.ca) is 13km (8 miles) south of downtown. The International Terminal features an extensive collection of First Nations sculptures and paintings set amid grand expanses of glass under soaring ceilings. Before you leave the International Terminal, catch a glimpse of Bill Reid's huge bronze sculpture, the *Jade Canoe.*

Tourist Information Centres (© **604/683-2000**), on Level 2 of the Main and International arrival terminals, are open daily from 8am to 11pm.

Getting into Town from the Airport & Vice Versa

The easiest, fastest and cheapest way to get into Vancouver from the airport is by the brand-new **Canada Line SkyTrain** operated by **Translink** (© **604/953-3333**; www. translink.ca). The train zips into Vancouver in 22 minutes, stopping at stations in Yaletown, City Centre (downtown), and Waterfront (the SeaBus Terminal, near the Canada Place cruise-ship terminal). The Canada Line had not yet opened as of press time, so I can't provide you with exact fares, but it will probably cost the same as Translink two-zone fares: C$3.75 for adults, C$2.50 after 6:30pm weekdays and all day on weekends.

The **YVR Airporter** (© **800/668-3141** or 604/946-8866; www.yvrairporter.com) provides **airport bus service** to downtown Vancouver's major hotels and cruise-ship terminal. It leaves from Level 2 of the Main Terminal every 15 minutes daily from 8:20am to 9:45pm. Fares for the 30-minute ride across the Granville Street Bridge into downtown Vancouver are C$13.75 for adults; C$10.75 for seniors; C$6.50 for children; and C$27.50 for families (two adults, two children). Buses leave from selected downtown hotels every half-hour between 7:30am and 9pm. Scheduled pickups serve the bus station, cruise-ship terminal, Four Seasons, Hotel Vancouver, Georgian Court, Sutton Place, Landmark, and others. Ask the driver on the way in or ask your hotel concierge for the nearest pickup stop and time.

Getting to and from the airport with **public bus** is much slower, requires at least one transfer, and will likely cost the same as the newly opened Canada Line SkyTrain. Public buses are operated by **Translink** (© **604/953-3333;** www.translink.ca). If you wish to travel into town this way, catch bus no. 424 at Ground Level of the Domestic Terminal; it will take you to Airport Station. From there, bus no. 98B (located in Bay 1) will take you into downtown Vancouver. B.C. Transit fares are by zone (airport to downtown costs C$3.75 during peak hours, and C$2.50 after 6:30pm and on weekends). You must have the **exact fare** because drivers do not make change. Transfers are free in any direction within a 90-minute period.

The average **taxi** fare from the airport to a downtown Vancouver hotel is approximately C$30 plus tip, but the fare can run up to C$40 if the cab gets stuck in traffic. **LimoJet** (© **604/273-1331;** www.limojetgold.com) offers flat-rate sedan or stretch-limousine service at C$39 per trip (not per person) to the airport from any downtown location, plus tax and tip, for up to three people (C$45 for up to six passengers). The drivers accept all major credit cards; no need to reserve in advance, just look for the Limojet Gold cars in front of the terminal.

Most major **car-rental firms** have airport counters and shuttles. Drivers heading into Vancouver from the airport should take the Arthur Laing Bridge, which leads directly to Granville Street, the most direct route to downtown.

THE TRAIN & BUS STATION

All trains and Greyhound buses arrive at **Pacific Central Station,** 1150 Station St. (at Main St. and Terminal Ave.; © **800/872-7245**), the main Vancouver railway station, located just south of Chinatown. You can reach downtown Vancouver from there by cab for about C$10. Plenty of taxis wait at the station entrance. One block from the station is the SkyTrain's Main Street Station (p. 63); within minutes, you'll be downtown. The Granville and Waterfront SkyTrain stations are two and four stops away, respectively.

VISITOR INFORMATION

The Vancouver Touristinfo Centre, 200 Burrard St., Plaza Level (© **604/683-2000;** www.tourismvancouver.com), is your single best travel information source about Vancouver and the North Shore. An incredibly helpful and well-trained staff provides information, maps, and brochures, and can help you with all your travel needs, including hotel, cruise-ship, ferry, bus, and train reservations. The center also has a **half-price ticket office** (Tickets Tonight) for same-day shows and events. The Touristinfo Centre is open daily from 8:30am to 6pm (closed Sunday in winter).

If you're driving, a **Tourist Info Centre,** 356 Hwy. 99, Surrey, is located just north of the **US-BC Peace Arch border crossing.** Visitors arriving by ship will find a Tourist Info Centre at the **Canada Place Cruise Ship Terminal,** 999 Canada Place. Both of these are walk-in offices (no phone).

The free weekly tabloid *Georgia Straight* (© 604/730-7000; www.straight.com), found in cafes, bookshops, and restaurants, provides up-to-date schedules of concerts, lectures, art exhibits, plays, recitals, and other happenings. Not free but equally good—and with more attitude—is the glossy city magazine *Vancouver* (© 604/877-7732; www.vanmag.com), available on newsstands. The free guide called *Where Vancouver* (© 604/736-5586; www.where.ca) is available in many hotels and lists attractions, entertainment, upscale shopping, and fine dining. It also has good maps.

Two free monthly tabloids, *B.C. Parent* (© 604/221-0366; www.bcparent.ca) and *West Coast Families* (© 604/689-1331), available at grocery stores and cafes around the city, are geared toward families with young children, listing many kid-friendly current events. Gay and lesbian travelers will want to pick up a copy of *Xtra! West* (© 604/684-9696), a free biweekly tabloid available in cafes, bars, shops, and restaurants throughout the West End.

CITY LAYOUT

For a map of Greater Vancouver, turn to the color insert at the beginning of this book.

With four different bodies of water lapping at its edges and miles of shoreline, Vancouver's geography can seem a bit complicated. **Downtown Vancouver** is on a peninsula: Think of it as an upraised thumb on the mitten-shaped Vancouver mainland. **Stanley Park,** the **West End, Yaletown,** and Vancouver's business and financial center (downtown) are located on this thumb of land bordered to the north by Burrard Inlet, the city's main deepwater harbor and port, to the west by English Bay, and to the south by False Creek. Farther west beyond English Bay is the Strait of Georgia, part of the Pacific Ocean. Just south across False Creek is **Granville Island,** famous for its public market, and the beach community of **Kitsilano.** This part of the city, called the **West Side,** covers the mainland, or the hand of the mitten. Its western shoreline looks out on the Strait of Georgia with the Pacific beyond, and the north arm of the Fraser River demarcates it to the south. Pacific Spirit Park and the University of British Columbia (UBC), a locus for visitors because of its outstanding Museum of Anthropology, take up most of the western tip of the West Side; the rest is mostly residential, with a sprinkling of businesses along main arterial streets. Both the mainland and peninsula are covered by a simple rectilinear street pattern. **North Vancouver** is the mountain-backed area across Burrard Inlet from downtown.

MAIN ARTERIES & STREETS On the downtown peninsula are four key **east-west streets** (to be more directionally exact, the streets run southeast to northwest). **Robson Street** starts at B.C. Place Stadium on Beatty Street, flows through the West End's more touristed shopping district, and ends at Stanley Park's Lost Lagoon on Lagoon Drive. **Georgia Street**—far more efficient for drivers than the pedestrian-oriented Robson—runs from the Georgia Viaduct on the eastern edge of downtown through Vancouver's commercial core, through Stanley Park, and over the Lions Gate Bridge to the North Shore. Three blocks north of Georgia is **Hastings Street,** which begins in the West End, runs east through downtown, and then skirts Gastown's southern border as it runs eastward to the Trans-Canada Highway. **Davie Street** starts at Pacific Boulevard near the Cambie Street Bridge, travels through Yaletown into the West End's more residential shopping district, and ends at English Bay Beach.

Three **north-south downtown streets** will get you everywhere you want to go in and out of downtown. Two blocks east of Stanley Park is **Denman Street,** which runs from West Georgia Street at Coal Harbour to Beach Avenue at English Bay Beach. This main

> ### ⓘ Tips   What's West
>
> The thing to keep in mind when figuring out what's where in Vancouver is that this is a city where property is king, and the word *west* has such positive connotations that folks have always gone to great lengths to associate it with their particular patch of real estate. Thus we have the **West End,** the **West Side,** and **West Vancouver,** which improbably enough is located immediately beside **North Vancouver.** It can be a bit confusing for newcomers, but fortunately each west has its own distinct character. The West End is a high-rise residential neighborhood on the downtown peninsula. The West Side is one-half of Vancouver, from Ontario Street west to the University of British Columbia. (The more working-class **East Side** covers the mainland portion of the city, from Ontario St. east to Boundary Rd.) Very tony West Vancouver is a city unto itself on the far side of Burrard Inlet. Together with its more middle-class neighbor, North Vancouver, it forms the **North Shore.**

West End thoroughfare is where locals dine out. It's also the shortest north-south route between the two ends of the Stanley Park Seawall.

Eight blocks east of Denman is **Burrard Street,** which starts near the Canada Place Pier and runs south through downtown, crosses the Burrard Street Bridge, and then forks. One branch, still **Burrard Street,** continues south and intersects West 4th Avenue and Broadway before ending at West 16th Avenue on the borders of the ritzy Shaughnessy neighborhood. The other branch becomes **Cornwall Avenue,** which heads west through Kitsilano, changing its name to **Point Grey Road** and then **Northwest Marine Drive** before entering the University of British Columbia campus.

Granville Street starts near the Waterfront Station on Burrard Inlet and runs the entire length of downtown, crosses the Granville Bridge to Vancouver's West Side, and carries on south across the breadth of the city before crossing the Arthur Laing Bridge to Vancouver International Airport.

On mainland Vancouver, the city's east-west roads are successively numbered from 1st Avenue at the downtown bridges to 77th Avenue by the banks of the Fraser River. The most important east-west route is **Broadway** (formerly 9th Ave.), which starts a few blocks from the University of British Columbia and extends across the length of the city to the border of neighboring Burnaby, where it becomes the **Lougheed Highway.** In Kitsilano, **W. 4th Avenue** is an important east-west shopping and commercial corridor. Intersecting with Broadway at various points are a number of important north-south commercial streets, each defining a particular neighborhood. The most significant of these streets are (from west to east) **Macdonald** in Kitsilano, **Granville, Cambie, Main,** and **Commercial Drive.**

FINDING AN ADDRESS   In many Vancouver addresses, the suite or room number precedes the building number. For instance, 100-1250 Robson St. is Suite 100 at 1250 Robson St.

In downtown Vancouver, Chinatown's **Carrall Street** is the east-west axis from which streets are numbered and designated. Westward, numbers increase progressively to Stanley Park; eastward, numbers increase approaching Commercial Drive. For example, 400 W. Pender would be 4 blocks from Carrall Street heading toward downtown; 400 E.

Pender would be 4 blocks on the opposite side of Carrall Street. Similarly, the low numbers on north-south streets start on the Canada Place Pier side and increase southward in increments of 100 per block (the 600 block of Thurlow St. is 2 blocks from the 800 block) toward False Creek and Granville Island.

Off the peninsula the system works the same, but **Ontario Street** is the east-west axis. Also, all east-west roads are avenues (for example, 4th Ave.), while streets (for example, Main St.) run exclusively north-south.

STREET MAPS   To get you off on the right foot, check out the detailed Vancouver map tucked inside the back cover of this guide. Tourist information centers (see "Visitor Information," above) and most hotels can also provide you with a detailed downtown map. *Where Vancouver* (📞 604/736-5586; www.where.ca), a free guide available at most hotels, has good maps. A good all-around metropolitan area map is the Rand McNally Vancouver city map. If you're an auto-club member, the Canadian Automobile Association (CAA) map is also good. It's not for sale, but is free to both AAA and CAA members, and is available at AAA offices across North America.

---

2 GETTING AROUND

BY PUBLIC TRANSPORTATION

Vancouver's public transportation system is the most extensive in Canada and includes service to all major tourist attractions, so it's not really necessary to have a car (especially if you're staying in the downtown area).

The **Translink** (otherwise known as B.C. Transit; 📞 604/521-0400; www.translink. ca) system includes electric buses, the SeaBus catamaran ferry, and the light-rail SkyTrain. It's an ecologically friendly, highly reliable, inexpensive system that allows you to get everywhere, including the beaches and ski slopes. Regular service runs from 5am to 2am.

Schedules and routes are available online, at tourist information centers, at many major hotels, and on buses. Pick up a copy of *Discover Vancouver on Transit* at one of the tourist information centers (see "Visitor Information," above). This publication gives transit routes for many city neighborhoods, landmarks, and attractions. The back cover of this book has a downtown Vancouver transit map.

FARES   Fares are based on the number of zones traveled, and are the same for buses, the SeaBus, and the SkyTrain. One ticket allows you to transfer from one mode of transport to another, in any direction, within 90 minutes. A one-way, one-zone fare (everything in central Vancouver) costs C$2.50. A two-zone fare—C$3.75—is required to travel to the airport or to nearby suburbs such as Richmond or North Vancouver, and a three-zone fare—C$5—is required for travel to the far-off city of Surrey. After 6:30pm on weekdays and all day on weekends and holidays, you can travel anywhere in all three zones for C$2.50. **DayPasses,** good on all public transit, cost C$9 for adults and C$7 for seniors, students, and children. They can be used for unlimited travel on weekdays or weekends and holidays.

Tip: Keep in mind that drivers do not make change, so you need the exact fare or a valid transit pass. Pay with cash or buy tickets and passes from ticket machines at stations, tourist information centers, both SeaBus terminals, and convenience stores, drugstores, and outlets displaying the FAREDEALER sign; most of these outlets also sell a transit map showing all routes.

Google Your Way There

Translink, British Columbia's transit authority, and Google Transit have produced a comprehensive tool to help you plan your trips by public transit. All you have to do is visit the Google Transit site, www.google.com/transit, plug in your starting point and destination, and you'll receive detailed instructions as well as a route plan on one of Google's maps. In many cases an address is not even necessary—just type in the name of hotel, restaurant, or the attraction that you want to visit.

BY BUS   Both diesel and electric-trolley buses service the city. Regular service on the busiest routes is every 12 minutes from 5am to 2am. Wheelchair-accessible buses and bus stops are identified by the international wheelchair symbol. Some key routes to keep in mind if you're touring the city by bus: **no. 5** (Robson St.), **no. 2** (Kitsilano Beach to downtown), **no. 50** (Granville Island), **no. 35** or **135** (to the Stanley Park bus loop), **no. 240** (North Vancouver), **no. 250** (West Vancouver–Horseshoe Bay), and buses **no. 4** or **10** (UBC–Exhibition Park via Granville St. downtown). From June until the end of September, the Vancouver Parks Board operates a **free bus through Stanley Park,** which stops at 14 points of interest. Call ✆ **604/953-3333** for general public transportation information.

BY SKYTRAIN   The SkyTrain is a fast, light-rail service between downtown Vancouver and the suburbs. The **Expo Line** trains operate from Waterfront to King George station, running along a scenic 27km (17-mile) route from downtown Vancouver east to Surrey through Burnaby and New Westminster in 39 minutes. There are 20 stations along this route; four downtown stations are underground and marked at street level. The **Millennium Line,** which opened in fall 2002, makes the same stops from Waterfront to Columbia, then branches to Sapperton, Braid, Lougheed town center, and beyond to Commercial Drive. All stations except Granville are wheelchair accessible; trains arrive every 2 to 5 minutes. **Canada Line,** the newest SkyTrain, began operating in October 2009, and links the Vancouver Airport to Yaletown, City Centre, and Waterfront Station (SeaBus terminal).

BY SEABUS   The SS *Beaver* and SS *Otter* catamaran ferries take passengers, cyclists, and wheelchair riders on a scenic 12-minute commute across Burrard Inlet between downtown's Waterfront Station and North Vancouver's Lonsdale Quay. On weekdays, a SeaBus leaves each stop every 15 minutes from 6:15am to 6:30pm, then every 30 minutes until 1am. SeaBuses depart on Saturdays every half-hour from 6:30am to 12:30pm, then every 15 minutes until 7:15pm, then every half-hour until 1am. On Sundays and holidays, runs depart every half-hour from 8:30am to 11pm. Note that the crossing is a two-zone fare on weekdays until 6:30pm.

BY TAXI

Cab fares start at C$2.85 and increase at a rate of C$1.66 per kilometer. In the downtown area, you can expect to travel for less than C$12 plus tip. The typical fare for the 13km (8-mile) drive from downtown to the airport is C$30.

Taxis are easy to find in front of major hotels, but flagging one down can be tricky. Most drivers are usually on radio calls. But thanks to built-in satellite positioning systems, if you call for a taxi, it usually arrives faster than if you go out and hail one. Call for a pickup from **Black Top** (✆ **604/731-1111**), **Yellow Cab** (✆ **604/681-1111**), or **MacLure's** (✆ **604/731-9211**).

BY CAR

Vancouver's road system and traffic are easier to handle than those in many other cities, in large part because the city has no freeways. Traffic thus tends to move more slowly. If you're just sightseeing around town, public transit and cabs will easily see you through. However, if you're planning to visit the North Shore mountains or pursue other out-of-town activities, then a car is necessary. Gas is sold by the liter, averaging at press time around C$1 per liter; a gallon of gas costs approximately C$3.75. Car insurance is compulsory in British Columbia (see chapter 21, "Fast Facts"). *Note:* In Canada, speeds and distances are posted in kilometers. The speed limit in Vancouver is 50kmph (31 mph); highway speed limits vary from 90 to 110kmph (56–68 mph).

RENTAL CARS   Rates vary widely depending on demand, style of car, and special offers. If you're over 25 and have a major credit card, you can rent a vehicle from **Avis,** 757 Hornby St. (© **800/879-2847** or 604/606-2868); **Budget,** 501 W. Georgia St. (© **800/472-3325** or 604/668-7000); **Enterprise,** 585 Smithe St. (© **800/736-8222** or 604/688-5500); **Hertz Canada,** 1128 Seymour St. (© **800/263-0600** or 604/606-4711); **National/Tilden,** 1130 W. Georgia St. (© **800/387-4747** or 604/685-6111); or **Thrifty,** 1015 Burrard St. or 1400 Robson St. (© **800/847-4389** or 604/606-1666). These firms all have counters and shuttle service at the airport as well. To rent a recreational vehicle, contact **Go West Campers,** 1577 Lloyd Ave., North Vancouver (© **800/661-8813** or 604/528-3900; www.go-west.com).

PARKING   All major downtown hotels have guest parking, either in-house or at nearby lots. Valet secure parking at most hotels costs about C$25 per day. Public parking is found at **Robson Square** (enter at Smithe and Howe sts.), the **Pacific Centre** (Howe and Dunsmuir sts.), and **the Bay** department store (Richards near Dunsmuir St.). You'll also find larger **parking lots** at the intersections of Thurlow and Georgia, Thurlow and Alberni, and Robson and Seymour streets.

   Street meters accept C$2 and C$1 coins. Rules are posted and strictly enforced; generally, downtown and in the West End, metered parking is in effect 7 days a week. (*Note:* Drivers are given about a 2-min. grace period before their cars are towed away when the 3pm no-parking rule goes into effect on many major thoroughfares.) Unmetered parking on side streets is often subject to neighborhood residency requirements: Check the signs. If you park in such an area without the appropriate sticker on your windshield, you'll get ticketed and towed. If your car is towed away or you need a towing service and aren't a CAA or an AAA member, call **Unitow** (© **604/251-1255**) or **Busters** (© **604/685-8181**). If you are parking on the street, remove all valuables from your car; break-ins are not uncommon.

SPECIAL DRIVING RULES   Though photo radar is no longer in use in B.C. (the new government got elected partially on its pledge to eliminate the hated system), photo-monitored intersections are alive and well. If you're caught racing through a red light, fines start at C$100. See also "Driving Rules," p. 292.

AUTO CLUB   Members of the American Automobile Association (AAA) can get assistance from the **Canadian Automobile Association (CAA)** (© **604/268-5600,** or for road service 604/293-2222; www.caa.ca).

BY BIKE

Vancouver is a biker's paradise. Along Robson and Denman streets near Stanley Park are plenty of places to rent bikes. (For specifics, see p. 137.) Paved paths crisscross through parks and along beaches. Helmets are mandatory and riding on sidewalks is illegal except on designated bike paths.

You can take your bike on the SeaBus anytime at no extra charge. Bikes are not allowed in the George Massey Tunnel, but a tunnel shuttle operates four times daily from mid-May to September to transport you across the Fraser River. From May 1 to Victoria Day (the third weekend of May), the service operates on weekends only. All of the West Vancouver blue buses (including the bus to the Horseshoe Bay ferry terminal) can carry two bikes, first-come, first-served, free of charge. In Vancouver, only a limited number of suburban bus routes allow bikes on board: no. 351 to White Rock, no. 601 to South Delta, no. 404 to the airport, and the no. 99 Express to UBC.

BY MINIFERRY

Crossing False Creek to Granville Island or beautiful Vanier Park on one of the zippy little miniferries is cheap and fun. These small, covered boats connect various points of interest; they are privately operated, so your public transit pass or ticket is not valid. It's well worth the extra money, though.

The **Aquabus** (© **604/689-5858;** www.theaquabus.com) docks at the south foot of Hornby Street, the Arts Club on Granville Island, Yaletown at Davie Street, Science World, and Stamp's Landing. Ferries operate daily from 6:40am to 10:30pm (9:30pm in winter) and run every 15 minutes to half-hour from 10am to 5pm (later in May and June). One-way fares are C$3 for adults and C$1.50 for seniors and children. A day pass is C$14 for adults and C$8 for seniors and children. You can take a 25-minute scenic boat ride (one complete circuit) for C$7 adults, C$4 seniors and children.

(Fast Facts) Vancouver

Business Hours Vancouver **banks** are open Monday through Thursday from 10am to 5pm and Friday from 10am to 6pm. Some banks, like Canadian Trust, are also open on Saturday. **Stores** are generally open Monday through Saturday from 10am to 6pm. Last call at **restaurant bars** and **cocktail lounges** is 2am.

Child Care If you need to rent cribs, car seats, playpens, or other baby accessories, **Cribs and Carriages** (© **604/988-2742;** www.cribsandcarriages.com) delivers them right to your hotel.

Dentists Most major hotels have a dentist on call. **Vancouver Centre Dental Clinic,** Vancouver Centre Mall, 11-650 W. Georgia St. (© **604/682-1601**), is another option. You must make an appointment. The clinic is open Monday to Friday 8:30am to 5pm (Wednesday until 6pm).

Doctors Hotels usually have a doctor on call. **Vancouver Medic Centre,** Bentall Centre, 1055 Dunsmuir St. (© **604/683-8138**), is a drop-in clinic open Monday through Friday 8am to 4pm. Another drop-in medical center, **Carepoint Clinic,** 1175 Denman St. (© **604/681-5338**), is open Monday through Thursday from 9am to 9pm, Friday through Sunday 9am to 8pm. See also "Hotlines," below.

Hospitals **St. Paul's Hospital,** 1081 Burrard St. (© **604/682-2344**), is the closest facility to downtown and the West End. West Side Vancouver hospitals include **Vancouver General Hospital Health and Sciences Centre,** 855 W. 12th Ave.

(© **604/875-4111**), and **BC Children's Hospital,** 4480 Oak St. (© **604/875-2345**). In North Vancouver, there's **Lions Gate Hospital,** 231 E. 15th St. (© **604/984-5785**).

Hotlines Emergency numbers include **Crisis Centre** (© 604/872-3311), **Rape Crisis Centre** (© 604/255-6228), **Rape Relief** (© 604/872-8212), **Poison Control Centre** (© 604/682-2344), **Crime Stoppers** (© 800/222-8477), and **SPCA** animal emergency (© 604/879-3571). Or dial **911** for any emergency police, fire, or ambulance service.

Internet Access Free Internet access is available at the Vancouver **Public Library** Central Branch, 350 W. Georgia St. (© **604/331-3600**). **Cyber Space Internet Café,** 1701 Robson St. (© **604/684-6004**), and **Internet Coffee,** 1104 Davie St. (© **604/682-6668**), are both open until at least midnight.

Laundry & Dry Cleaning **Davie Laundromat,** 1061 Davie St. (© **604/682-2717**), offers self-service, drop-off service, and dry cleaning. **Laundry & Suntanning,** 781 Denman St. (© **604/689-9598**), doesn't have dry-cleaning services, but you can work on your tan while you wait. Also, almost all hotels have laundry service.

Luggage Storage & Lockers Lockers are available at the main Vancouver railway station (which is also the main bus depot), **Pacific Central Station,** 1150 Station St., near Main Street and Terminal Avenue south of Chinatown (© **604/661-0328**).

Newspapers & Magazines The two local papers are the *Vancouver Sun* (www. vancouversun.com), published Monday through Saturday, and the *Province* (www.theprovince.com), published Sunday through Friday mornings. The free weekly entertainment paper, the *Georgia Straight* (www.straight.com), comes out on Thursday.

Pharmacies **Shopper's Drug Mart,** 1125 Davie St. (© **604/669-2424**), is open 24 hours. Several Safeway supermarket pharmacies are open late; the one on Robson and Denman is open until midnight.

Police For emergencies, dial © **911.** This is a free call. Otherwise, the **Vancouver City Police** can be reached at © **604/717-3535.**

Post Office The **main post office,** 349 W. Georgia St. at Homer Street (© **800/267-1177**), is open Monday through Friday from 8am to 5:30pm. You'll also find post office outlets in Shopper's Drug Mart and 7-Eleven stores with longer opening hours.

Weather Call © **604/664-9010** for weather updates. Each local ski resort has its own snow report line: **Cypress Ski area** © **604/419-7669; Whistler/Blackcomb** © **604/687-7507.**

Where to Stay in Vancouver

Everyone in Vancouver is excited about the 2010 Olympic and Paralympic Winter Games, and that includes the city's hotels, which have been upgrading, refurbing, and getting ready for the Olympic-size crowds.

If you are planning to be in Vancouver during the Olympics, start contacting hotels immediately. Some hotels have already been booked out for the entire period of the Games; others must reserve a certain number of their rooms for athletes and the thousands of others who are in some way officially involved with the Olympics. Keep in mind that if you do find a hotel room for the Olympic period (Feb 12–28, 2010), you'll be paying a hefty premium over the regular price of a room during the winter season. See "Reservations" below for additional information.

Most of Vancouver's hotels are in the downtown area or the West End. Central Vancouver is small and easily walkable, so in both of these neighborhoods you'll be close to major sights, services, and nightlife.

Downtown—the financial district, the area around Canada Place convention center and cruise-ship terminal, and the central shopping-business area around Robson Square—is buzzing during the day but pretty quiet at night. The **West End** is green, leafy, and residential, a neighborhood of high-rise apartment houses, beautifully landscaped streets, and close to Coal Harbour, Stanley Park, and the best beaches. While downtown gets quiet at night, the West End starts hopping; dozens of restaurants, cafes, and bars line Robson and Denman streets.

You'll also find a couple of hotels and some lovely B&Bs in great old houses on the **West Side**, the area south of False Creek on Granville Island, and in the **Kitsilano** neighborhood. Staying in "Kits" can be fun because it's a complete neighborhood unto itself and has its own hangout spots on 4th Avenue and around Kits Beach.

One thing to keep in mind when booking a room is that downtown hotels on south **Granville Street** (the Best Western Downtown Vancouver, Howard Johnson Hotel, and the Ramada Inn and Suites) offer a central location without the high price tag but the area they're in is not very attractive. Granville Street looks better now, however, than it has for years. It was given a makeover in 2009 and is becoming trendy because of its large concentration of bars and clubs (it's been dubbed the "Entertainment District"). It's not dangerous but be prepared for noisy revelry on warm summer Friday and Saturday nights.

(Tips) Fido-Friendly Hotels

Vancouver is one of the dog-friendliest cities in the world. Nearly all downtown and West End hotels allow you to check in your canine companion, usually for an added daily charge of C$25 to C$30.

Bed & Breakfast Registries

If you prefer to stay in a B&B, the following agencies specialize in matching guests with establishments that best suit their needs:

- **Vancouver Bed & Breakfast,** 4390 Frances St., Burnaby, B.C. V5C ZR3 (© **604/298-8815;** fax 604/298-5917; www.vancouverbandb.bc.ca)
- **Canada-West Accommodations,** P.O. Box 86607, North Vancouver, B.C. V7L 4L2 (© **800/561-3223** or 604/990-6730; www.b-b.com)

Quoted prices don't include the 10% **hotel room tax,** the 7% **provincial accommodations tax,** or the 6% **goods and services tax (GST).** I list the rack rates: the rates you would receive if you walked in off the street and requested a room. By checking the hotel's website, you'll almost always find lower rates, including special "romance packages" and weekend-getaway specials. The highest price I list is for high season (mid-June to Sept).

Bus and/or public transportation information is given only for those hotels listed below that are outside of the Vancouver city center.

Three noteworthy newcomers opened their doors in 2009. The 119-room **Shangri-La Hotel** (p. 74), the luxury Shangri-La brand's first North American property, opened in a convenient-to-everything downtown location and is home to one of the city's hottest new restaurants, **MARKET by Jean-Georges** (p. 94). The **Loden Vancouver** (p. 73), located in Coal Harbour at Melville and Bute streets, is a 130-room luxury boutique hotel with spa-like bathrooms and a stylish contemporary flair. The **St. Regis** (p. 76), one of the few Vancouver hotels to occupy a heritage building, opened after a complete makeover that transformed it into a cozy, business-friendly downtown charmer.

RESERVATIONS Reservations are highly recommended June to September and during holidays. They are essential if you are planning to be in Vancouver during the Winter Olympics (Feb 12–28, 2010). If you arrive without a reservation during that period, you may not be able to find a room. For additional information, call the **Super, Natural British Columbia,** at © **800/435-5622** or 800/663-6000. You can also book a room by going to **Tourism Vancouver,** 200 Burrard St. (across from Canada Place), or by visiting **www.tourismvancouver.com.** The official Vancouver 2010 Winter Games website, www.vancouver2010.com, is another place to find hotel information during the Winter Olympics period.

1 BEST VANCOUVER HOTEL BETS

For a quick overview of the city's best splurge and moderately priced hotels, see chapter 1, p. 4 and 5, respectively.

- **Best Historic Hotel: The Fairmont Hotel Vancouver,** 900 W. Georgia St. (© **866/540-4452** or 604/684-3131) harks back to a more gracious and traditional era. Even with all the modern amenities and services you could wish for, it wraps you up in old-fashioned charm and comfort. See p. 72.

- **Best for Business Travelers:** The **Shangri-La Hotel,** 1128 W. Georgia St. (© **604/ 689-1120**) provides comfortable desks with free Wi-Fi, easy access to faxes and printers, an efficient business center, and a location in the heart of downtown. See p. 74.

- **Best Boutique Hotel:** There are two. In trendy Yaletown, the stylish **Opus Hotel,** 322 Davie St. (© **866/642-6787** or 604/642-6787) houses an array of room types appointed in luscious colors and contemporary decor that sets it apart, plus an ultra-hip bar and a fine restaurant. See p. 74. The newer **Loden Vancouver,** 1177 Melville St. (© **877/225-6336** or 604/669-5060), a 14-story tower on the edge of Coal Harbour, envelops you in a sophisticated West Coast aesthetic that features spa-type bathrooms and a marvelous restaurant. See p. 73.

- **Best for a Romantic Getaway:** The **Wedgewood Hotel,** 845 Hornby St. (© **800/ 663-0666** or 604/689-7777), the only boutique hotel downtown, has a comfy, romantic, European elegance that brings out the romance in everyone. See p. 75.

- **Best for Families:** The **Rosedale on Robson Suite Hotel,** 838 Hamilton at Robson Street (© **800/661-8870** or 604/689-8033), offers two-bedroom suites and toys kids can enjoy in the pool. See p. 76.

- **Best Inexpensive Hotel:** With all the facilities of a convention center plus cheap, comfortable rooms, the **University of British Columbia Conference Centre,** 5961 Student Union Blvd. (© **888/822-1030** or 604/822-1000), is the best inexpensive choice in the city. See p. 84.

- **Best B&B:** Built in 1905 by two Vancouver photographers, the **West End Guest House,** 1362 Haro St. (© **888/546-3327** or 604/681-2889), is not only filled with the artists' work and a collection of Victorian antiques, but you also get fresh-baked brownies or cookies with your evening turndown service. See p. 82.

- **Best Location:** Everyone's definition of a great location is different, but the **Westin Bayshore Resort & Marina,** 1601 Bayshore Dr. (© **800/937-8461** or 604/682-3377), is right on the Seawall just steps from Stanley Park and Denman Street and only 10 blocks from downtown. See p. 80.

- **Best Views:** So many Vancouver hotels have outstanding views that it's difficult to choose just one—so how about three? There's something special about the upper floors at the **Pan Pacific Vancouver Hotel,** 300-999 Canada Place (© **877/324-4856** in the U.S., or 604/662-8111), where the harborside rooms have unimpeded views of Coal Harbour, Stanley Park, the Lions Gate Bridge, and the North Shore's mountains. See p. 74. Just as spectacular, and with windows that you can open to savor the freshness of the air along with the magnificence of the water/mountain/park views, is the **Westin Bayshore Resort & Marina,** 1601 Bayshore Dr. (© **800/937-8461** or 604/682-3377). See p. 80. Fashionistas may wince at the room decor in the **Empire Landmark,** 1400 Robson St. (© **800/830-6144** or 604/687-0511), but the panoramic views from most of the rooms in this 40-year-old tower are absolutely stunning. See p. 82.

2 DOWNTOWN & YALETOWN

All downtown hotels are within 5 to 10 minutes' walking distance of shops, restaurants, and attractions. Hotels in this area lean more toward the luxurious than the modest, a state of affairs reflected in their prices.

Barclay House Bed & Breakfast **7**
Best Western
  Downtown Vancouver **34**
Blue Horizon **10**
Buchan Hotel **2**
Chocolate Lily **40**
Coast Plaza Hotel & Suites **3**
Days Inn Downtown **21**
Delta Vancouver Suites **24**
Empire Landmark **5**
The Fairmont Hotel Vancouver **16**
The Fairmont Waterfront **22**
Four Seasons Hotel **18**
Georgian Court Hotel **26**
Granville Island Hotel **39**
Hostelling International Vancouver
  Downtown Hostel **38**
Hostelling International Vancouver
  Jericho Beach Hostel **42**
Howard Johnson Hotel **32**
Inn at False Creek–Quality
  Hotel Downtown **35**
Kenya Court Ocean Front
  Guest House **41**
The Kingston Hotel **29**
Le Soleil Hotel & Suites **20**
The Listel Hotel **8**
Loden Vancouver **12**
Metropolitan Hotel Vancouver **17**
Moda Hotel **30**
Opus Hotel **31**
Pacific Palisades Hotel **9**
Pan Pacific Vancouver **23**
Ramada Inn and Suites **33**
Rosedale on Robson Suite Hotel **27**

Stanley Park
Lost Lagoon Dr
Lost Lagoon
Coal Harbour
Lost Lagoon Dr
Devonian Harbour Park
Chilco St.
Georgia St.
Stanley Park Dr.
Pender St.
4
Gilford St.
2
Denman St.
Haro St.
Barclay St.
Robson St.
Alberni St.
Park Ln.
1
Beach Ave.
3
Bidwell St.
Cardero St.
Nicola St.
5
English Bay Beach Park
Pendrell St.
Roedde House Museum
6
8 **9**
7
10
Davie St.
Comox St.
Nelson St.
Bute St.
Broughton St.
Jervis St.
Inukshuk
Burnaby St.
Nelson Park
Thurlow St.
WEST END
English Bay
Sunset Beach Park
Harwood St.
37
38
36
Helmcken St.
Pacific St.
Burrard St.
Hornby St.
Hadden Park
Ogden Ave.
Vancouver Maritime Museum
Vanier Park
Beach Ave.
Howe St.
33 **32**
McNicoll Ave.
Chestnut St.
35
34
Drake St.
Whyte Ave.
H.R. MacMillan Space Centre/ Vancouver Museum
42
43
Kits Beach
Creelman Ave.
Laburnum St.
Walnut St.
Granville St.
40
Kitsilano Beach Park
Granville Island Public Market
George Wainborn Park
Cornwall Ave.
41
York Ave.
Cypress St.
GRANVILLE ISLAND
Johnston St.
Old Bridge St.
Cartwright St.
39
False
Yew St.
Arbutus St.
Maple St.
W. 2nd Ave.
Pine St.
W. 3rd Ave.
Fir St.
Sutcliffe Park
W. 4th Ave.
Lamey's Mill Rd.
KITSILANO

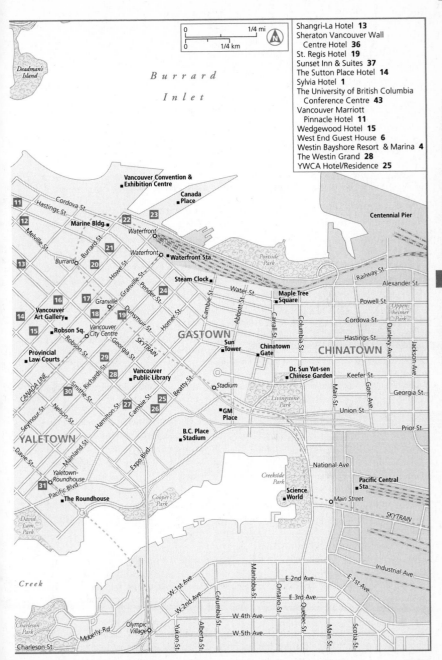

Shangri-La Hotel **13**
Sheraton Vancouver Wall
  Centre Hotel **36**
St. Regis Hotel **19**
Sunset Inn & Suites **37**
The Sutton Place Hotel **14**
Sylvia Hotel **1**
The University of British Columbia
  Conference Centre **43**
Vancouver Marriott
  Pinnacle Hotel **11**
Wedgewood Hotel **15**
West End Guest House **6**
Westin Bayshore Resort & Marina **4**
The Westin Grand **28**
YWCA Hotel/Residence **25**

Deadman's Island

Burrard

Inlet

Vancouver Convention & Exhibition Centre
Canada Place
Centennial Pier

Cordova St.
Hastings St.
Melville St.
Marine Bldg.
Waterfront
Waterfront
Waterfront Sta.
Portside Park
Railway St.
Alexander St.

Burrard St.
Howe St.
Granville St.
Pender St.
Steam Clock
Water St.
Maple Tree Square
Powell St.
Oppen-heimer Park
Cordova St.

Burrard
Hastings St.
Dunlevy Ave.
Jackson Ave.

Vancouver Art Gallery
Granville
Dunsmuir St.
Homer St.
Cambie St.
Abbott St.
Carrall St.
Columbia St.

GASTOWN
Sun Tower
Chinatown Gate
CHINATOWN

Robson Sq.
Vancouver City Centre
Robson St.
Georgia St.
SKYTRAIN
Dr. Sun Yat-sen Chinese Garden
Keefer St.
Gore Ave.
Georgia St.
Main St.

Provincial Law Courts
Smithe St.
Richards St.
Vancouver Public Library
Beatty St.
Stadium
Livingstone Park
Union St.
Prior St.

CANADA LINE
Seymour St.
Nelson St.
Hamilton St.
Cambie St.
GM Place
B.C. Place Stadium
Expo Blvd.
National Ave.

YALETOWN
Davie St.
Mainland St.
Pacific Blvd.
Yaletown-Roundhouse
The Roundhouse
Cooper's Park
Creekside Park
Science World
Main Street
Pacific Central Sta.
SKYTRAIN

David Lam Park

Creek

Charleson Park
Charleson St.
Moberly Rd.
Olympic Village
W. 1st Ave.
W. 2nd Ave.
Columbia St.
Manitoba St.
Ontario St.
Alberta St.
Yukon St.
W. 4th Ave.
W. 5th Ave.
E 2nd Ave.
E 3rd Ave.
Quebec St.
Main St.
E 1st Ave.
Industrial Ave.
Scotia St.

0 — 1/4 mi
0 — 1/4 km

11 12 13 14 15 16 17 18 19 20 21 22 23 24 25 26 27 28 29 30 31

Delta Vancouver Suites ★ (Kids) The Delta Vancouver Suites is a full-service, all-suites hotel with a special appeal to business travelers. It sits across the street from the Lookout observation tower (p. 120), just minutes from Canada Place, Gastown, China-town, and Robson Square. The look throughout is high-end, with an attractive lobby connecting to a state-of-the-art conference facility. Each suite has a desk and mini-office/living area. Corner 09 rooms are long and narrow with a full wall of floor-to-ceiling glass. A C$65 upgrade to the Signature Club gets you a room on the top three floors and access to the Signature Lounge, which puts out a good continental breakfast and afternoon hors d'oeuvres (both included in the upgrade). Kids are given a welcome pack on arrival.

550 W. Hastings St., Vancouver, B.C. V6B 1L6. (✆) **888/890-3222** or 604/689-8188. Fax 604/605-8881. www.deltahotels.com. 226 units. Oct 15–Apr C$349 double; May–Oct 14 C$409 double. Children 17 and under stay free in parent's room. AE, DC, DISC, MC, V. Valet parking C$26. **Amenities:** Restaurant; bar; babysitting; concierge; executive-level rooms; exercise room; indoor pool; room service; rooms for those w/limited mobility. *In room:* A/C, TV w/pay movies and games, hair dryer, high-speed Internet, minibar.

The Fairmont Hotel Vancouver ★★ (Kids) A landmark in the city since it first opened in 1939, the Fairmont Hotel has been brought up to 21st-century standards but retains its traditional, old-fashioned elegance. The rooms are spacious, quiet, and comfortable, if not particularly dynamic in layout or finish. The bathrooms (with tub/shower combinations) look a bit dated when compared with other downtown hotels in this price range, but that's part of the charm. Courtyard suites feature a luxuriously furnished living room, separated from the bedroom by French doors. Guests can use the state-of-the-art gym with heated indoor pool. The hotel is family friendly and even has two resident dogs (former Seeing Eye dogs) that can be taken out for walks.

900 W. Georgia St., Vancouver, B.C. V6C 2W6. (✆) **866/540-4452** or 604/684-3131. Fax 604/662-1929. www.fairmont.com. 556 units. C$299–C$439 double. Children 17 and under stay free in parent's room. AE, DC, DISC, MC, V. Parking C$33. **Amenities:** 2 restaurants; bar; babysitting; concierge; executive-level rooms; health club; Jacuzzi; indoor pool; room service; sauna; rooms for those w/limited mobility; rooms for hearing-impaired guests. *In room:* A/C, TV w/pay movies, hair dryer, high-speed Internet (C$15/day), minibar.

The Fairmont Waterfront ★★ (Kids) This large Fairmont hotel occupies a triangular high-rise tower right across the street from the Canada Place cruise-ship terminal. The Pan Pacific (p. 74) is the only other hotel in Vancouver as conveniently located for cruisers. The Fairmont features large, traditionally styled rooms with big windows and some great views; if you want to see the giant cruise ships right below you, ask for a harbor-view room on the ninth floor or above; for something really special and kid friendly, book one of the terrace rooms that have doors leading out to the hotel's rooftop garden and swimming pool. The more expensive Fairmont Gold rooms come with a dedicated concierge, breakfast, and evening hors d'oeuvres. At press time, the hotel was entirely booked out for February 2010.

900 Canada Place Way, Vancouver, B.C. V6C 3L5. (✆) **866/540-5409** or 604/691-1991. Fax 604/691-1999. www.fairmont.com. 457 units. C$299–C$439 double. Children 17 and under stay free in parent's room. AE, DC, DISC, MC, V. Parking C$30. SkyTrain: Waterfront Station. **Amenities:** Restaurant; bar; babysitting; concierge; executive-level rooms; health club; Jacuzzi; outdoor pool; room service; sauna; rooms for those w/limited mobility. *In room:* A/C, TV w/pay movies, hair dryer, high-speed Internet (C$14/day), minibar.

Four Seasons Hotel ★★★ (Kids) For over 30 years now, the Four Seasons has reigned as one of Vancouver's top hotels. From the outside, this huge high-rise hotel across from the Vancouver Art Gallery is rather unappealing. But the large, light-filled rooms are wonderfully comfortable with superb beds and interesting views of downtown with glimpses of the mountains. The marble bathrooms are on the small side but well designed. For a slightly larger room, reserve a deluxe corner room with wraparound floor-to-ceiling windows. One of the glories of this hotel is its health club with an enormous heated pool—half indoor, half outdoor—on a terrace. The Four Seasons kicked off the first stage of its top-to-bottom renovation in 2008 with the opening of its hip new bar/lounge/restaurant **Yew** (p. 94).

791 W. Georgia St., Vancouver, B.C. V6C 2T4. ☎ **800/819-5053** or 604/689-9333. Fax 604/684-4555. www.fourseasons.com/vancouver. 376 units. Nov–Apr C$250–C$330 double; May–Oct C$370–C$555 double. AE, DC, MC, V. Parking C$31. **Amenities:** 2 restaurants; bar; babysitting; concierge; exercise room; indoor and heated outdoor pool; room service; sauna; rooms for those w/limited mobility. *In room:* A/C, TV/VCR, hair dryer, minibar, Wi-Fi (C$17/day).

Le Soleil Hotel & Suites ★
A boutique hotel midway between Robson Square and the financial district, Le Soleil is a 1980s-era building decorated to look like a French manor, with crystal chandeliers, plush carpeting, and gilded ceilings. Except for 10 doubles, all the units are suites; for maximum space, corner suites are best. The problem with some of the units is that the sitting areas have no windows and consequently feel somewhat confined, despite the Biedermeier-style furniture and richly colored wallpapers and fabrics. Where Le Soleil shines is in its personal service, but if you're looking for a luxury boutique hotel, also check out the Wedgewood, the Loden, and the Opus (see below).

567 Hornby St., Vancouver, B.C. V6C 2E8. ☎ **877/632-3030** or 604/632-3000. Fax 604/632-3001. www.lesoleilhotel.com. 119 units. C$339–C$499 double. AE, DC, MC, V. Valet parking C$22. **Amenities:** Restaurant; concierge; access to YWCA fitness facilities next door; room service. *In room:* A/C, TV w/pay movies, hair dryer, minibar, free Wi-Fi.

Loden Vancouver ★★ (Finds)
Vancouver's newest downtown luxury boutique hotel opened in spring 2008 at the edge of Coal Harbour. The building is a narrow urban tower tucked in among other high-rise buildings just a couple of blocks from Burrard Inlet and the Seawall, and within easy walking distance to Robson Street and the West End. "Signature" (standard) rooms and one-bedroom suites are chic and comfortable at the same time, with a rich palette of fabrics, colors, and materials, and floor-to-ceiling windows that offer "view-corridor" views of the water and North Shore mountains. The bathrooms in every room have been designed to open up (if you want them to) into the bedroom area; it's like having your own private spa, with a soaker tub and a big glass-walled shower. **Voya** (p. 100), the Loden's restaurant, is a lovely spot to dine.

1177 Melville St. (at Bute St.), Vancouver, B.C. V6E 0A3. ☎ **877/225-6336** or 604/669-5060. www.lodenvancouver.com. 77 units. C$329–C$399 double "Signature" room, C$799 1-bedroom suite. Rates higher during Olympics. AE, DC, MC, V. Parking C$25. **Amenities:** Restaurant; bar; babysitting; concierge; exercise room; Jacuzzi; room service; sauna. *In room:* A/C, TV/DVD, hair dryer, minibar, free Wi-Fi.

Metropolitan Hotel Vancouver ★★
Centrally located between the financial district and downtown shopping areas, the Metropolitan is geared toward business and leisure travelers who want traditional luxury and full service. Guest rooms feature large, marble-tiled bathrooms with separate tub and shower, and wonderfully comfortable beds with Frette Italian linens. In 2008 the guest rooms were refurbished with new carpeting and furniture to add a splash of color to an otherwise muted scheme. Many units in the 18-story hotel have small balconies, but the views are not the hotel's selling point as the building is dwarfed by the Four Seasons across the street. Guests have use of a sauna and steam rooms. The hotel's restaurant, **Diva at the Met** (p. 92), is regarded as one of Vancouver's top eateries.

645 Howe St., Vancouver, B.C. V6C 2Y9. ☎ **800/667-2300** or 604/687-1122. Fax 604/602-7846. www. metropolitan.com. 197 units. C$249–C$399 double; C$249–C$699 suite. Children 17 and under stay free in parent's room. AE, DC, MC, V. Underground parking C$28. **Amenities:** Restaurant; bar; concierge; exercise room; Jacuzzi; indoor pool; room service; squash court. *In room:* A/C, TV w/pay movies, CD player, hair dryer, minibar, MP3 docking station, free Wi-Fi.

Opus Hotel ★★★   If you want to stay in a hip, happening, luxury hotel, try the Opus—in 2005, *Condé Nast Traveler* voted it one of the world's top 100 hotels. It's the only hotel in Yaletown, the trendiest area for shopping, nightlife, and dining. Each room is furnished according to one of five "personalities," with its own layout, color, and flavor—the luscious room colors are eye candy if you're tired of blah hotel interiors. Bathrooms are fitted with high-design sinks, soaker tubs, or roomy showers (or both). The cool Opus Bar serves an international tapas menu, and on weekends becomes one of Yaletown's see-and-be-seen scenes. (Be forewarned: This area of Yaletown is "club central", and can be noisy until the wee hours; book a Courtyard Room if you don't want to be disturbed.) Opus's top-notch restaurant, **Elixir** (p. 93), serves modern French bistro food.

322 Davie St., Vancouver, B.C. V6B 5Z6. ☎ **866/642-6787** or 604/642-6787. Fax 604/642-6780. www. opushotel.com. 96 units. May–Oct C$359–C$549 double, C$815 and up suite; Nov–Apr C$229–C$429 double, C$739 and up suite. Children 17 and under stay free in parent's room. AE, DC, MC, V. Valet parking C$29. **Amenities:** Restaurant; bar; bikes; concierge; small exercise room; room service. *In room:* A/C, TV w/pay movies, hair dryer, minibar, Wi-Fi (C$16/day).

Pan Pacific Vancouver ★★★   This 23-story luxury hotel atop Canada Place is a key landmark on the Vancouver waterfront. Despite its size, the hotel excels in comfort and service, and it provides spectacular views of the North Shore mountains, Burrard Inlet, and cruise ships arriving and departing from the terminal below. The rooms are spacious and comfortable, with contemporary furnishings and a soothing color palette. Bathrooms are large and luxurious. Guests have use of a heated outdoor pool and Jacuzzi overlooking the harbor. Spa Utopia offers a full array of pampering treatments. Café Pacifica puts on one of the best breakfast buffets in Vancouver.

300-999 Canada Place, Vancouver, B.C. V6C 3B5. ☎ **877/324-4856** in the U.S., or 604/662-8111. Fax 604/ 685-8690. www.panpacific.com. 504 units. May–Oct C$540–C$640 double, C$700–C$5,000 suite; Nov–Apr C$410–C$480 double, C$520 and up suite. AE, DC, DISC, MC, V. Valet parking C$30. **Amenities:** 2 restaurants; bar; babysitting; concierge; health club; Jacuzzi; outdoor heated pool; room service; sauna; spa. *In room:* A/C, TV w/pay movies, hair dryer, high-speed Internet (C$15/day), minibar.

Shangri-La Hotel ★★★   For all-around luxury and excellent, unobtrusive service, the new Shangri-La, opened in 2009, can't be beat; its only rival is the Four Seasons (reviewed above). This is the first North American property for Shangri-La, and it's an impressive one, with the hotel occupying the lower 15 floors of Vancouver's tallest residential tower. Attention to detail is what sets the Shangri-La apart; everything is geared to run smoothly. The rooms are large and furnished with a quiet good taste that combines contemporary furnishings with Asian accents; over half of them have balconies (the smaller balconies are more like a glass enclosure with an open window). Bathrooms, finished in white marble, are sumptuous. Chi, the hotel's spa, offers a unique menu of treatments utilizing Asian and Tibetan techniques. And to cap it all off, the hotel's restaurant, **MARKET by Jean-Georges** (as in Vongerichten), is one of Vancouver's hottest new haute spots.

1128 W. Georgia St., Vancouver, B.C. V6E 0A8. ☎ **604/689-1120**. Fax 604/689-1195. www.shangri-la.com. 119 units. C$275–C$850 double. AE, DC, DISC, MC, V. Valet parking C$30. **Amenities:** Restaurant; lounge; babysitting; concierge; health club; Jacuzzi; outdoor heated pool; room service; sauna; spa. *In room:* A/C, TV w/pay movies, hair dryer, minibar, free Wi-Fi.

Sheraton Vancouver Wall Centre Hotel ★ The tallest—and with 736 rooms the largest—hotel in the city, the Wall Centre is hard to miss. The hotel occupies a curved spire of black glass and a second, earlier tower with a fountain-filled urban garden in between. It may remind you of a futuristic office park, a feeling that's unfortunately reinforced in the rooms, which have floor-to-ceiling polarized glass windows that look out onto great views but can't be opened, so it feels like you're always wearing sunglasses. This is upscale Sheraton at its best (or worst, if you hate huge hotels), and because of its size it caters to tour groups. Rooms have a clean, contemporary look with blond-wood furnishings and nice bathrooms. Guests have the use of a huge health club with an indoor pool and an ayurvedic wellness spa.

1088 Burrard St., Vancouver, B.C. V6Z 2R9. (�C) **866/716-8101** or 604/331-1000. Fax 604/893-7200. www. sheratonvancouver.com. 733 units. C$399–C$539 double. AE, DC, MC, V. Valet parking C$26. **Amenities:** 2 restaurants; 2 bars; concierge; executive-level rooms; health club; Jacuzzi; indoor pool; room service; sauna; spa. *In room:* A/C, TV w/pay movies, hair dryer, high-speed Internet (C$11/day), minibar.

The Sutton Place Hotel ★★ Don't let the bland, corporate-looking exterior fool you: This hotel has won many awards, and is one of only two AAA five-diamond hotels in Canada. Once you enter the lobby, elegantly decorated with marble, fresh flowers, chandeliers, and French-leaning European furnishings, it's pure luxury, comparable to the Four Seasons (reviewed above). The rooms, decorated in a traditional European style, don't skimp on size or comfort. The European-style health club and spa has a big heated pool and sun deck.

845 Burrard St., Vancouver, B.C. V6Z 2K6. (℃) **866/378-8866** or 604/682-5511. Fax 604/682-5513. www. suttonplace.com. 397 units. C$375–C$450 double. AE, DC, DISC, MC, V. Underground, self-, or valet parking C$30. **Amenities:** Restaurant; lounge (w/bistro fare), bakery-cafe; bikes; concierge; health club & spa; Jacuzzi; indoor pool; room service; sauna. *In room:* A/C, TV w/pay movies, hair dryer, minibar, Wi-Fi (C$13/day).

Wedgewood Hotel ★★★ If you're searching for a romantic, sophisticated hotel with superb service, spacious rooms, fine detailing, a good restaurant, a full-service spa, and a central downtown location, you can't do any better than the Wedgewood. One feature that makes the award-winning Wedgewood so distinctive is that it's independently owned (by Greek-born Eleni Skalbania), and the owner's elegant personal touch is evident throughout. All 83 units are spacious and have balconies (the best views are those facing the Vancouver Art Gallery and Law Court). Furnishings and antiques are of the highest quality, and the marble-clad bathrooms with deep soaker tubs and separate walk-in Roman showers are simply the best. Bacchus, the cozy hotel restaurant, serves a fairly traditional menu of fish, pasta, and meat. In 2007, *Travel + Leisure* ranked the Wedgewood the best hotel in Vancouver. It has since become a member of the Relais & Châteaux group.

845 Hornby St., Vancouver, B.C. V6Z 1V1. (℃) **800/663-0666** or 604/689-7777. Fax 604/608-5349. www. wedgewoodhotel.com. 83 units. C$295–C$600 double; C$650 and up suite. AE, DC, MC, V. Valet parking C$20. **Amenities:** Restaurant; concierge; executive-level rooms; small exercise room; room service; spa; free Wi-Fi in common areas. *In room:* A/C, TV/VCR w/pay movies, CD player, hair dryer, minibar.

The Westin Grand ★★ (Kids) It's such a pleasure to find a luxury-level hotel that's elegant instead of garish, and understated rather than pompous. Located across from Library Square, the Westin Grand provides high-end all-suite accommodations within easy walking distance of Yaletown, GM Place, and Robson shopping. The spacious suites are brightened by natural light pouring in through the floor-to-ceiling windows; if you can, spring for one of the deluxe 09 or 03 units, which have balconies. Sitting rooms come with a concealed kitchenette and loads of business-friendly amenities. The furnishings throughout are clean-lined and contemporary; bathrooms are roomy, most with separate tub and shower. Kids get a special welcome kit, and the hotel's Aria restaurant has a kids' menu. Check the website for special deals; suites are often available for half the rack rate.

433 Robson St., Vancouver, B.C. V6B 6L9. ⓒ **888/680-9393** or 604/602-1999. Fax 604/647-2535. www.westingrandvancouver.com. 207 suites. Oct 12–Apr 13 C$429–C$639 suite; Apr 14–Oct 11 C$459–C$749 suite. Up to 2 children 16 and under stay free in parent's room. AE, DC, DISC, MC, V. Valet parking C$25. **Amenities:** Restaurant; babysitting; children's welcome bag; concierge; executive-level rooms; health club; Jacuzzi; outdoor pool; room service; sauna. *In room:* A/C, TV w/pay movies, hair dryer, kitchenette, minibar, Wi-Fi (C$15/day).

EXPENSIVE

Rosedale on Robson Suite Hotel ★ (Value) (Kids)

Across the street from Library Square, the Rosedale provides good value, particularly when it comes to amenities. All rooms are one- or two-bedroom suites, and feature separate living rooms with a pullout couch and full kitchenettes; the decor is contemporary but low-key rather than flashy. The designated two-bedroom family suites include two single beds in the kids' bedrooms. The lobby and the suites below the 15th floor have recently been refurbished. The small gym has an indoor pool with toys for the kids to enjoy. The hotel does a lot of business with tour groups, particularly Australians. Internet rates are considerably lower than the rack rates listed below.

838 Hamilton St. (at Robson St.), Vancouver, B.C. V6B 6A2. ⓒ **800/661-8870** or 604/689-8033. Fax 604/689-4426. www.rosedaleonrobson.com. 223 units. C$270–C$800 suite. Additional adult C$25. Rates include continental breakfast. AE, DC, MC, V. Parking C$11. **Amenities:** Restaurant; babysitting; concierge; executive-level rooms; exercise room; Jacuzzi; indoor lap pool; room service; sauna; steam room. *In room:* A/C, TV w/pay movies, fax, hair dryer, high-speed Internet (C$12/day), kitchenette.

St. Regis Hotel ★ (Finds)

Many hotels in downtown Vancouver occupy newer buildings, so it's a pleasure to find one—and especially one as nice as the St. Regis—in a so-called "heritage building" dating from 1913. The owners have transformed it into a unique boutique hotel that's handsome inside and out, filled with contemporary art, and wired for up-to-the-minute Wi-Fi. The redesigned rooms and suites are a bit small but have a savvy, comfy, contemporary look to them. Breakfast is included in the room rate, and there's a brewpub on the premises. You might think this part of downtown—close to Gastown is a little off—but it's convenient to everything in the commercial core of the city. The new Canada Line SkyTrain from the airport stops one block away at Granville and Dunsmuir. The only other heritage hotel in Vancouver to have this kind of updated flair is the Moda (p. 78).

602 Dunsmuir St., Vancouver, B.C. V6B 1Y6. ⓒ **800/770-7929** or 604/681-1135. Fax 604/683-1126. www.stregishotel.com. 65 units. C$214–C$310 double, C$275–C$509 suite. Breakfast included in room rate. AE, MC, V. **Amenities:** Restaurant; bar/pub; Starbucks; concierge; executive-level rooms; access to nearby health club. *In room:* A/C, TV w/pay movies, hair dryer, minibar (in suites), MP3 docking station, robes (in suites), free Wi-Fi.

MODERATE

Best Western Downtown Vancouver

The 12-story Best Western is just a 5-block walk from the theater area on Granville Street at the south end of downtown. All rooms are comfortable, and some have harbor views. The corner rooms are a bit smaller than the rest, but they receive more light. This hotel is not overflowing with amenities, but the rooms are well furnished and the location is convenient. Rooms with a full kitchen are available for an additional C$10 to C$15. Keep in mind, however, that while quite safe, the hotel is located in a nightlife-oriented downtown neighborhood. You shouldn't book here unless you have a reasonable tolerance for the realities of street life. You'll save by booking on the website.

718 Drake St. (at Granville St.), Vancouver, B.C. V6Z 2W6. (℃) **888/669-9888** or 604/669-9888. Fax 604/669-3440. www.bestwesterndowntown.com. 143 units, 32 with full kitchen. C$109–C$239 double. AE, DC, DISC, MC, V. Parking C$8. **Amenities:** Restaurant; babysitting; rooftop exercise room; Jacuzzi; sauna. *In room:* A/C, TV/VCR, hair dryer, free high-speed Internet.

Days Inn Downtown   Located in a heritage building dating from 1910, the well-maintained Days Inn Downtown is conveniently located in the heart of Vancouver's financial district and within easy walking distance of just about everything. For travelers who don't need all the amenities of a large hotel, these small, newly refurbished rooms are comfortable and convenient, but if you check out other hotel websites, you might find a much nicer place for not much more money. Ten of the rooms have showers only. Request a water view or consider a harbor-facing suite; rooms facing east stare directly at the concrete walls of the building next door.

921 W. Pender St., Vancouver, B.C. V6C 1M2. (℃) **877/681-4335** or 604/681-4335. Fax 604/681-7808. www.daysinnvancouver.com. 85 units, 10 with shower only. C$149–C$219 double. AE, DC, V. Valet parking C$20. **Amenities:** Restaurant; bar; concierge. *In room:* A/C, TV w/pay movies, fridge, hair dryer, high-speed Internet.

Georgian Court Hotel ★ (Value)   This modern, 14-story brick hotel is extremely well located, just a block or two from B.C. Place Stadium, GM Place Stadium, the Queen Elizabeth Theatre, the Playhouse, and the Vancouver Public Library. You can walk to Robson Square in about 10 minutes. The guest rooms are relatively large, nicely decorated, and have good-size bathrooms. And while the big-time celebs are usually whisked off to the glamorous top hotels, their entourages often stay at the Georgian Court, as it provides all the amenities and business-friendly extras such as two phones in every room, brightly lit desks, and complimentary high-speed Internet access—a service that other hotels almost always charge for.

773 Beatty St., Vancouver, B.C. V6B 2M4. (℃) **800/663-1155** or 604/682-5555. Fax 604/682-8830. www.georgiancourt.com. 180 units. May–Oct 15 C$199–C$279 double; Oct 16–Apr C$150–C$209 double. AE, DC, MC, V. Parking C$13. **Amenities:** Restaurant; bar; babysitting; concierge; exercise room; Jacuzzi; room service; sauna. *In room:* A/C, TV, fridge, hair dryer, free high-speed Internet.

The Inn at False Creek (Value) (Kids)   The Inn at False Creek went through a top-to-bottom refurbishment in 2007, making the rooms fresher and more contemporary. The upgraded decor, near-downtown (and Granville Island) location, and amenities make this a good choice for this price range, but street traffic is ever-present as the hotel sits next to the Granville Bridge on-ramp. Rooms are a good size, the tiled bathrooms have tubs and a shower, and the suites are great for families—some have full kitchens and narrow, glassed-in balconies. Rooms at the back are preferable but the traffic noise is minimized in the front by double-pane windows and blackout curtains. The Inn has a nice outdoor pool and patio (open summer only).

1335 Howe St. (at Drake St.), Vancouver, B.C. V6Z 1R7. (℃) **800/663-8474** or 604/682-0229. Fax 604/662-7566. www.innatfalsecreek.com. 157 units. C$149–C$249 double. AE, DC, DISC, MC, V. Parking C$12. **Amenities:** Restaurant; bar; babysitting; concierge; access to nearby health club; outdoor pool (summer only); room service. *In room:* A/C, TV, hair dryer, free Wi-Fi.

Moda Hotel ★ (Finds) Situated downtown, across from the Orpheum Theatre and close to the clubs on Granville Street, the Moda offers lots of style and excellent value. Rooms and suites in this 1908 heritage building feature a sleek, tailored, European look with dramatic colors, luxury beds and linens, flatscreen TVs, nice tiled bathrooms with a tub/shower, and double-glazed windows to dampen the traffic noise. The only thing the refurbers couldn't change was the slant in some of the old floors. For years, this hotel was called the Dufferin and catered to a mostly gay clientele; it's still gay friendly, but anyone with a bit of adventure and a taste for something out of the ordinary will enjoy a stay here. Suites offer an extra half-bathroom, corner locations with more light, and upgraded amenities.

900 Seymour St., Vancouver, B.C. V6B 3L9. (②) **877/683-5522** or 604/683-4251. Fax 604/683-0611. www.modahotel.ca. 57 units. C$119–C$229 double; C$219–C$289 suite. AE, DC, MC, V. **Amenities:** 2 restaurants; bar. In room: A/C, TV, high-speed Internet.

INEXPENSIVE

Hostelling International Vancouver Downtown Hostel Located in a converted nunnery, this modern, curfew-free hostel offers a convenient base of operations for exploring downtown. The beach is a few blocks south; downtown is a 10-minute walk north. Most beds are in quad dorms, with a limited number of doubles and triples available. Except for two rooms with a private bathroom, all bathroom facilities are shared. Rooms and facilities are accessible for travelers with disabilities. There are common cooking facilities, as well as a rooftop patio and game room. The hostel is extremely busy in the summertime, so book ahead. Many organized activities such as ski packages and tours can be booked at the hostel. The hostel also provides a free shuttle service to the bus/train station and Jericho Beach.

1114 Burnaby St. (at Thurlow St.), Vancouver, B.C. V6E 1P1. (②) **888/203-4302** or 604/684-4565. Fax 604/684-4540. www.hihostels.ca. 68 units, 44 4-person shared dorm rooms, 24 double or triple private rooms. C$26–C$30 dorm IYHA members, C$30–C$34 dorm nonmembers; C$68–C$80 double members, C$74–C$88 double nonmembers. Rates include full breakfast. Annual adult membership C$35. MC, V. Limited free parking. **Amenities:** Bikes; free Wi-Fi. In room: No phone.

Howard Johnson Hotel (Value) As yet another example of south Granville's ongoing gentrification, this formerly down-at-the-heels hotel was bought, gutted, renovated, and reopened with an eye to the budget-conscious traveler; the exterior was redone in 2009. The rooms are simply and adequately furnished; the suites have kitchenettes and sofa beds. To get any kind of view, request a unit facing Granville. The rooms are moderately larger and more comfortable than at the Ramada across the street. Keep in mind, however, that while quite safe, this is a downtown neighborhood full of clubs and bars and the street life can be loud and raucous on warm weekends.

1176 Granville St., Vancouver, B.C. V6Z 1L8. (②) **888/654-6336** or 604/688-8701. Fax 604/688-8335. www.hojovancouver.com. 110 units. June–Sept C$149–C$199 double, C$209–C$229 suite; Oct–May C$79–C$179 double, C$139–C$219 suite. Children 15 and under stay free in parent's room. AE, DC, MC, V. Parking C$18. **Amenities:** Restaurant; bar; concierge; access to nearby health club. In room: A/C, TV w/pay movies, hair dryer, free Wi-Fi.

The Kingston Hotel (Value) An affordable downtown hotel is a rarity for Vancouver, but if you can do without the frills, the Kingston offers a clean, safe, inexpensive place to sleep and a complimentary continental breakfast to start your day. You won't find a better deal anywhere, and the premises have far more character than you'll find in a cookie-cutter motel. The Kingston is a Vancouver version of the kind of small budget B&B hotels found all over Europe. Just 9 of the 55 rooms have private bathrooms and

TVs; the rest have hand basins and shared showers and toilets on each floor. The premises are well kept and the location is central so you can walk everywhere. The staff is friendly and helpful, and if you're just looking for a place to sleep and stow your bags, you'll be glad you found this place.

757 Richards St., Vancouver, B.C. V6B 3A6. ✆ **888/713-3304** or 604/684-9024. Fax 604/684-9917. www. kingstonhotelvancouver.com. 52 units, 13 with private bathroom. C$85–C$95 double with shared bathroom; C$125–C$170 double with private bathroom. Additional person C$10. Rates include continental breakfast. AE, MC, V. Parking C$20 across the street. **Amenities:** Restaurant; bar; sauna. *In room:* TV (in units w/private bathrooms), free Wi-Fi.

Ramada Inn and Suites   The Ramada, like the Howard Johnson across the street (reviewed above), was converted from a rooming house into a tourist hotel. The location is convenient for exploring downtown and Yaletown, as well as Granville Island or Kitsilano, but South Granville, though gentrifying, is not a scenic or shopping area. The motel-like rooms have dark-wood furniture and small desks; in 2008 all the beds were replaced and new bathrooms installed. For any kind of view, ask for a room facing Granville; otherwise, you may be looking out at a wall. Suites feature a sofa bed, kitchenette, and small dining area, making them useful for families. Guests have full access to a nearby sports club. The Ginger62 Ultra Lounge is a smart new addition. *Note:* Booking directly through the website below and using promotion code LNET will net you an additional 10% off the best rate of the day.

1221 Granville St., Vancouver, B.C. V6Z 1M6. ✆ **888/835-0078** or 604/685-1111. Fax 604/685-0707. www. ramadavancouver.com. 116 units. C$89–C$259 double. Children 16 and under stay free in parent's room. AE, DC, DISC, MC, V. Valet parking C$15. **Amenities:** Restaurant; bar/lounge; access to nearby health club; free Wi-Fi. *In room:* A/C, TV w/pay movies, hair dryer, kitchenette (in suites).

YWCA Hotel/Residence ★ (Value)   This attractive 12-story residence next door to the Georgian Court Hotel is an excellent choice for travelers on limited budgets. Bedrooms are simply furnished; some have TVs. Quite a few reasonably priced restaurants and a number of grocery stores are nearby. Three communal kitchens are available for guests' use, and all rooms have minifridges. The Y has three TV lounges and free access to the best gym in town, the nearby coed YWCA Fitness Centre.

733 Beatty St., Vancouver, B.C. V6B 2M4. ✆ **800/663-1424** or 604/895-5830. Fax 604/681-2550. www. ywcahotel.com. 155 units, 53 with private bathroom. C$66–C$94 double with shared bathroom; C$80–C$125 double with private bathroom. Weeklong discounts available. AE, MC, V. Parking C$14. **Amenities:** Access to YWCA facility. *In room:* A/C, TV, fridge, hair dryer, Wi-Fi (C$10/day).

3 THE WEST END

A 10-minute walk from downtown, the West End's hotels are nestled along Robson Street and amid the tree-lined, garden-filled residential streets bordering Stanley Park. Have no fear: You will not be out of the loop if you stay here, though the area's relaxed, beachy ambience is very different from downtown. While the area has fewer hotels than downtown, the choices are more diverse—and so are the people who live here.

EXPENSIVE
The Listel Hotel ★★ (Finds)   What makes the Listel unique is its artwork. Hallways and suites on the top two Gallery floors are decorated with original pieces from the Buschlen Mowatt Gallery or, on the Museum floor, with First Nations artifacts from the

UBC Anthropology Museum (see p. 123). Also unique is the fact that the Listel is the first Vancouver hotel to really go "green" with the use of solar power-generating panels. The hotel is luxurious without being flashy, and all the rooms and bathrooms feature top-quality bedding and handsome furnishings—though some bathrooms are larger than others, with separate soaker tub and shower. The roomy upper-floor suites facing Robson Street, with glimpses of the harbor and the mountains beyond, are the best bets. Rooms at the back are quieter but face the alley and nearby apartment buildings. In the evenings, you can hear live jazz at **O'Doul's** (p. 174), the hotel's restaurant and bar. Downtown or Stanley Park is a 10-minute walk away.

1300 Robson St., Vancouver, B.C. V6E 1C5. ℰ **800/663-5491** or 604/684-8461. Fax 604/684-7092. www. thelistelhotel.com. 129 units. C$229–C$269 standard to Gallery room double, C$400–C$600 suite. AE, DC, DISC, MC, V. Parking C$26. **Amenities:** Restaurant; bar; concierge; executive-level rooms; exercise room; Jacuzzi; room service; free Wi-Fi. *In room:* A/C, TV w/pay movies, hair dryer, minibar.

Pacific Palisades Hotel ★★★ Ⓚⓘⓓⓢ Ⓕⓘⓝⓓⓢ

It's hard not to like this place. Sherbet yellows and apple greens, pastel-colored fabrics, bright splashes of color, and whimsical touches make the hotel bright and welcoming (although the rock music playing in the lobby can be upbeat or annoying, depending on your mood), and the "green" policies are probably the most comprehensive in Vancouver. The rooms feature low-flow water valves, energy-efficient light bulbs, and the hotel as a whole uses eco-conscious cleaning products and has its own carbon-offset initiative. Guest rooms are spacious, airy, and equipped with kitchenettes (with minibar items priced at corner-store prices). The one-bedroom suites include large living/dining rooms and balconies. Other perks include the complimentary afternoon wine tasting in the attached art gallery, the large indoor pool and fitness rooms, and the fact that pets stay free. **Zin** (p. 101) is a cool spot for a drink and dinner. Internet is free if you sign up for Kimpton Hotels free InTouch service.

1277 Robson St., Vancouver, B.C. V6E 1C4. ℰ **800/663-1815** or 604/688-0461. Fax 604/688-4374. www. pacificpalisadeshotel.com. 233 units. C$150–C$425 double. AE, DC, DISC, MC, V. Valet parking C$25. **Amenities:** Restaurant; bar; babysitting; basketball court; concierge; health club; Jacuzzi; indoor pool; room service; spa services; yoga program. *In room:* A/C, TV, fridge, hair dryer, high-speed Internet (C$10/day), kitchenette, minibar, robes.

Vancouver Marriott Pinnacle Hotel

The high-rise Pinnacle gleams and glows between the West End and Coal Harbour. The rooms are designed to maximize the light and the views, though the views are often partially obstructed by surrounding high-rises (you can pay to upgrade to a better view). The rooms in general are fine, fitted up with all the things business travelers expect, but the decor is remarkably bland. Bathrooms are fairly large and well designed with a tub and separate shower. If you can, score one of the -19 rooms (2019, 2119, 2219, and so forth); aside from being the largest rooms, these oval-shaped units also max out on windows and views.

1128 W. Hastings St., Vancouver, B.C. V6E 4R5. ℰ **800/207-4150** or 604/684-1128. Fax 604/298-1128. www.vancouvermarriott.com. 434 units. Winter season C$199 double; summer season C$289 double. Children 18 and under stay free in parent's room. AE, DC, MC, V. Valet parking C$32. SkyTrain to Burrard Station. **Amenities:** Restaurant; bar; concierge; executive-level rooms; health club; Jacuzzi; indoor lap pool; room service; sauna. *In room:* A/C, TV w/pay movies, hair dryer, high-speed Internet (C$16/day), minibar.

Westin Bayshore Resort & Marina ★★★ Ⓚⓘⓓⓢ

This is Vancouver's only resort hotel with its own marina, and the views from all but a handful of its rooms are stunning. The Bayshore overlooks Coal Harbour and Stanley Park on one side, and Burrard Inlet and the city on the other. The hotel is in two buildings, the original low-rise from 1961 and a newer tower, with a giant pool, restaurant, and conference center between them. All the rooms received a makeover in 2009 with comfortable, contemporary West Coast decor and floor-to-ceiling windows that open wide. In the newer tower, the rooms are a bit larger and have narrow balconies. The bathrooms in both buildings are nicely finished but fairly small. A new spa opened in October 2009. Children receive their own welcome package and love the pools.

1601 Bayshore Dr., Vancouver, B.C. V6G 2V4. © **800/937-8461** or 604/682-3377. Fax 604/687-3102. www.westinbayshore.com. 510 units. C$460 double. Children 17 and under stay free in parent's room. AE, DC, MC, V. Self-parking C$23; valet parking C$28. **Amenities:** 2 restaurants; bar, Starbucks; babysitting; concierge; health club; Jacuzzi; 2 pools (indoor and outdoor); room service; sauna. *In room:* A/C, TV w/pay movies, hair dryer, minibar, Wi-Fi (C$15/day).

MODERATE

Barclay House Bed & Breakfast ★ (Finds)

The Barclay House is located on one of the West End's quiet maple-lined streets a block from historic Barclay Square. Built in 1904, this beautiful house is furnished in Victorian style; a number of the pieces are family heirlooms. The penthouse offers skylights, a fireplace, and a claw-foot tub; the south room contains a queen-size brass bed and an elegant sitting room. The parlors and dining rooms are perfect for lounging on a rainy afternoon or sipping a glass of complimentary sherry before dinner. On a summer day, the front porch, with its wooden Adirondack chairs, is a comfy spot to read and relax.

1351 Barclay St., Vancouver, B.C. V6E 1H6. © **800/971-1351** or 604/605-1351. Fax 604/605-1382. www. barclayhouse.com. 5 units. C$155–C$295 double. Rates include breakfast. AE, MC, V. Free parking. **Amenities:** Access to nearby fitness center. *In room:* TV/VCR w/pay movies, movie library, CD player, fridge, hair dryer, free Wi-Fi.

Blue Horizon (Value)

This 31-story high-rise built in the 1960s has a great location on Robson Street, just a block from the trendier Pacific Palisades and the tonier Listel Vancouver (see above for both). It's cheaper than those places and has views that are just as good if not better, but it lacks their charm and feels a bit like a high-rise motel. The rooms are fairly spacious, with a contemporary look, and every room is on a corner with wraparound windows and a small balcony; superior rooms on floors 15 to 30 offer the best views. The decor could use some updating, but overall these rooms are a good deal for this location. The hotel uses energy-efficient lighting, low-flow showerheads, and recycling bins, and the entire hotel is nonsmoking.

1225 Robson St., Vancouver, B.C. V6E 1C3. © **800/663-1333** or 604/688-1411. Fax 604/688-4461. www. bluehorizonhotel.com. 214 units. C$109–C$219 double; C$119–C$219 superior double; C$199–C$329 penthouse suite. Children 15 and under stay free in parent's room. AE, DC, MC, V. Self-parking C$16. **Amenities:** Restaurant; concierge; exercise room; Jacuzzi; indoor pool; sauna. *In room:* A/C, TV w/pay movies, fridge, hair dryer, free high-speed Internet, minibar.

Coast Plaza Hotel & Suites ★ (Finds)

Built originally as an apartment building, this 35-story hotel atop Denman Place Mall attracts a wide variety of guests, from business travelers and tour groups to film and TV actors. They come for the large rooms, the affordable one- and two-bedroom suites, and great views of English Bay. The two-bedroom corner suites are bigger than most West End apartments, and afford spectacular panoramas. The spacious one-bedroom suites and standard rooms feature floor-to-ceiling windows and balconies; about half the units have full kitchens, and all are nonsmoking. Furnishings are plain and comfortable. While the hotel has a good-size heated pool, it's in the not-particularly appealing basement.

1763 Comox St., Vancouver, B.C. V6G 1P6. ✆ **800/716-6199** or 604/688-7711. Fax 604/688-5934. www. coasthotels.com. 269 units. C$179–C$259 double; C$219–C$359 suite. AE, DC, DISC, MC, V. Valet parking C$8. **Amenities:** Restaurant; bar; babysitting; concierge; access to health club in mall below; Jacuzzi; indoor pool; room service; sauna. *In room:* A/C, TV, fridge; hair dryer, free high-speed Internet.

Empire Landmark   Originally a Sheraton, this 42-story tower-hotel is the tallest building in the West End. Here's the thing about the Empire Landmark: It's a big hotel that handles a lot of tour groups and conferences, so it feels pretty anonymous. The standardized rooms, though perfectly fine, are decorated in an old-fashioned style that seems to mask instead of emphasize the spectacular views, which you can savor from a small balcony. For the best panoramas, ask for a room on floor 28 or higher. The top floor features a revolving restaurant-lounge where you can have a drink with all of Vancouver spread out before you. Also in this hotel's favor is the location, right on Robson Street, close to English Bay and Stanley Park.

1400 Robson St. (btw. Broughton and Nicola sts.), Vancouver, B.C. V6G 1B9. ✆ **800/830-6144** or 604/687-0511. Fax 604/687-7267. www.empirelandmarkhotel.com. 357 units. C$190–C$330 double. AE, DC, DISC, MC, V. Self-service parking C$10/day. **Amenities:** Restaurant; bar; concierge. *In room:* A/C, TV, fridge, Wi-Fi (C$14/day).

Sunset Inn & Suites ★ (Value) (Kids)   Just a couple of blocks from English Bay on the edge of the residential West End, the Sunset Inn offers roomy studios or one-bedroom apartments with balconies and fully equipped kitchens. Like many other hotels in this part of town, the Sunset Inn started life as an apartment building, meaning the rooms are larger than at your average hotel. Request an upper floor since the views are better but the price remains the same. For those traveling with children, the one-bedroom suites have a separate bedroom and a pullout couch in the living room. All of the rooms were refurbished in 2008. The beds are comfy, the staff is helpful and friendly, and the location is great for this price.

1111 Burnaby St., Vancouver, B.C. V6E 1P4. ✆ **800/786-1997** or 604/688-2474. Fax 604/669-3340. www. sunsetinn.com. 50 units. Low season C$99–C$239 double; high season C$159–C$475 double. Additional person C$10. Rates include continental breakfast in lobby. Children 11 and under stay free in parent's room. Weekly rates available. AE, DC, MC, V. Free parking. **Amenities:** Small exercise room. *In room:* TV, kitchen, free Wi-Fi.

West End Guest House ★ (Finds)   A heritage home built in 1906, the West End Guest House is a handsome example of what the neighborhood looked like before concrete towers and condos replaced the original Edwardian homes in the early 1950s. Decorated with early-20th-century antiques and a serious collection of vintage photographs of Vancouver taken by the original owners, this gay-friendly B&B is a calm, charming respite from the hustle and bustle of the West End. The seven guest rooms feature feather mattresses and down duvets; the Grand Queen Suite, an attic-level bedroom with a brass bed, fireplace, sitting area, claw-foot bathtub, and skylights, is the best and most spacious room. Owner Evan Penner and his partner, Ron Cadurette, pamper their guests with a scrumptious breakfast and serve iced tea and sherry in the afternoon.

1362 Haro St., Vancouver, B.C. V6E 1G2. ✆ **888/546-3327** or 604/681-2889. Fax 604/688-8812. www. westendguesthouse.com. 9 units. Low season C$90–C$195 double; high season C$200–C$275 double. Rates include full breakfast. AE, DISC, MC, V. Free off-street parking. **Amenities:** Bikes. *In room:* TV/DVD, hair dryer, free Wi-Fi.

INEXPENSIVE

Buchan Hotel (Value)   Built in 1926, this three-story building is tucked away on a quiet residential street in the West End, 2 blocks from Stanley Park and Denman Street. Like the Kingston (see above) downtown, this is a small European-style budget hotel that doesn't bother with frills or charming decor; unlike the Kingston, it isn't a B&B, so don't expect the second B. The standard rooms are quite plain; be prepared for cramped quarters and tiny bathrooms, half of which are shared. The best rooms are the executive rooms: four nicely furnished front-corner rooms with private bathrooms. The hotel also has in-house bike and ski storage, and a reading lounge.

1906 Haro St., Vancouver, B.C. V6G 1H7. ℭ **800/668-6654** or 604/685-5354. Fax 604/685-5367. www. buchanhotel.com. 60 units, 30 with private bathroom. C$53–C$86 double with shared bathroom; C$80–C$135 double with private bathroom; C$110–C$138 executive room. Children 12 and under stay free in parent's room. Weekly rates available. AE, DC, MC, V. Limited street parking available. **Amenities:** Lounge. *In room:* TV, no phone.

Sylvia Hotel   Lots of folks love the Sylvia, mostly for its fabulous location, and many are eager to recommend it, but pretty as the old girl is from the outside, inside she's a very modest, plain Jane sort of place. This is a "heritage building" hotel (the original wing, anyway) that underplays style and doesn't believe in glamour. That's why you're not going to find waterfront accommodations anywhere else at Sylvia's prices. If you do stay, the best rooms are located on the higher floors facing English Bay. The suites have fully equipped kitchens and are large enough for families. The newer low-rise annex rooms offer less atmosphere.

1154 Gilford St., Vancouver, B.C. V6G 2P6. ℭ **604/681-9321.** Fax 604/682-3551. www.sylviahotel.com. 120 units. May–Sept C$160–C$255 double; Oct–Apr C$120–C$175 double. Children 17 and under stay free in parent's room. AE, DC, MC, V. Parking C$10. **Amenities:** Restaurant; bar; concierge; room service. *In room:* TV, hair dryer, free high-speed Internet.

4 THE WEST SIDE

Right across False Creek from downtown and the West End is Vancouver's West Side, where you'll find cozy B&Bs and hotels. It's the perfect location if your agenda includes a stop at Granville Island; exploration of the laid-back Kitsilano neighborhood and Kits Beach; visits to the Museum of Anthropology and famed gardens on the University of British Columbia campus; seeing the sunken garden at Queen Elizabeth Park; or being close to the airport without staying in an "airport hotel."

EXPENSIVE

Granville Island Hotel ★ (Finds   One of Vancouver's best-kept secrets, this hotel is tucked away on the edge of Granville Island in a unique waterfront setting, a short stroll from theaters, galleries, and the fabulous Granville Island Public Market (see p. 167). Rooms in the original wing are definitely fancier, so book these if you can, but the new wing is fine, too. Rooms are fairly spacious with traditional, unsurprising decor and large bathrooms with soaker tubs; some units have balconies and great views over False Creek. If you don't have a car, the only potential drawback to a stay here is the location. During the daytime when the False Creek ferries are running, it's a quick ferry ride to Yaletown or the West End. After 10pm, however, you're looking at a C$15 to C$20 cab ride or an hour walk. The Island after dark is reasonably happening, and the hotel's waterside restaurant and brewpub are good-weather hangout spots with outdoor seating.

1253 Johnston St., Vancouver, B.C. V6H 3R9. ℭ **800/663-1840** or 604/683-7373. Fax 604/683-3061. www. granvilleislandhotel.com. 85 units. Oct–Apr C$170 double, C$399 penthouse; May–Sept C$250 double, C$499 penthouse. AE, DC, DISC, MC, V. Parking C$12. **Amenities:** Restaurant; brewpub; babysitting; concierge; small fitness room w/Jacuzzi and sauna; room service; access to nearby tennis courts. *In room:* A/C, TV w/pay movies, hair dryer, minibar, free Wi-Fi.

MODERATE

Chocolate Lily ★ (**Finds**) (**Kids**) If you're looking for a self-catering place, this attractive, Craftsman-style house, just minutes from all the splash of Kits Beach and the dash of Kits shopping, is a real find. You don't need a car; public transportation can get you downtown in minutes. The two self-contained suites have private entrances and patios and are both small but carefully designed (a sofa in each makes into an extra bed) and furnished in a comfortable Northwest style. Both units have kitchenettes; the rear unit has only a shower. Breakfast is not served, but you're given a basket of fruit and baked goods upon arrival. In high season a 3-day minimum stay is required; special rates apply for longer stays.

1353 Maple St., Vancouver, B.C. V6J 3S1. (*C*) **866/903-9363** or 604/731-9363. www.chocolatelily.com. 2 self-catered suites. C$110–C$185. MC, V. Free parking. *In room:* TV, DVD player (in 1 unit), free high-speed Internet, kitchenette.

Kenya Court Ocean Front Guest House (**Finds**)   From the street this unusual B&B simply looks like the three-story 1926 apartment house that it is. But press button no. 5, and your hosts will welcome you into their pleasant establishment, where you'll find five furnished apartments rented on a B&B basis. Not only is the house in a fantastic location—directly across the street from Kits Beach—but every unit also has a view of English Bay, downtown Vancouver, and the Coast Mountains. The ground floor has a very nice little studio; the other units are larger, with a living room, bathroom, separate bedroom (or two), and full kitchen. Breakfast is served in a glass-walled solarium on the roof. In the summer, Kits Beach and Cornwall Avenue running past it are very busy—this can be either a plus or a minus, depending on your point of view.

2230 Cornwall Ave., Vancouver, B.C. V6K 1B5. (*C*) **604/738-7085**. h&dwilliams@telus.net. 5 units. C$150–C$175 double. Rates include breakfast. No credit cards. Free garage or street parking. **Amenities:** Outdoor pool and beach across the street; tennis court and jogging trails nearby. *In room:* TV, fridge, hair dryer, kitchenette.

INEXPENSIVE

Hostelling International Vancouver Jericho Beach Hostel   Located in a former military barracks, this hostel (open May–Sept only) is surrounded by an expansive lawn adjacent to Jericho Beach. Individuals, families with children over age 5, and groups are welcome. The 10 private rooms can accommodate up to six people. These particular accommodations go fast, so if you want one, call far in advance. The dormitory-style arrangements are well maintained and supervised. Linens are provided. Basic, inexpensive food is served in the cafe, or you can cook for yourself in the shared kitchen. The hostel's program director operates tours and activities.

1515 Discovery St., Vancouver, B.C. V6R 4K5. (*C*) **888/203-4303** or 604/224-3208. Fax 604/224-4852. www.hihostels.ca. 286 beds in 14 dorms; 10 private family units. No private bathrooms. C$20–C$24 dorm IYHA members, C$24–C$28 dorm nonmembers; C$60–C$72 private room members, C$68–C$80 private room nonmembers. MC, V. Parking C$5. Bus: 4. Children 4 and under not allowed. **Amenities:** Cafe; bikes. *In room:* No phone.

The University of British Columbia Conference Centre ★ (**Value**)   The University of British Columbia Conference Centre is in a pretty, forested setting on the tip of Point Grey, convenient to Kitsilano and the University itself. If you don't have a car, it's a half-hour bus ride from downtown. Although the on-campus accommodations are actually student dorms most of the year, rooms are usually available. The rooms are nice,

Staying on the North Shore (North Vancouver & West Vancouver)

The North Shore cities of North and West Vancouver are pleasant, lush, and much less hurried than Vancouver. Staying here also offers easy access to the North Shore mountains, including hiking trails, the Capilano Suspension Bridge & Park, and the ski slopes on Mount Seymour, Grouse Mountain, and Cypress Bowl. The disadvantage is that if you want to take your car into Vancouver, there are only two bridges, and during rush hour they're painfully slow. The passenger-only SeaBus, however, is quick and scenic.

The **Lonsdale Quay Hotel,** 123 Carrie Cates Court (© **800/836-6111** or 604/986-6111; www.lonsdalequayhotel.com), across the Burrard Inlet from the Canada Place Pier, sits at the water's edge above the Lonsdale Quay Market at the SeaBus terminal. Some rooms have unique harbor and city views. The hotel is completely nonsmoking. Doubles run C$139 to C$450.

but don't expect luxury. The 17-story Walter Gage Residence offers comfortable accommodations, many on the upper floors with sweeping views of the city and ocean. One-bedroom suites come equipped with private bathrooms, kitchenettes, TVs, and phones. Each studio has a twin bed; each one-bedroom features a queen-size bed; a six-bed Towers room—a particularly good deal for families—features one double bed and five twin beds. The West Coast Suites, renovated in 2007, are the most appealing, and have a very reasonable price.

5961 Student Union Blvd., Vancouver, B.C. V6T 2C9. © **888/822-1030** or 604/822-1000. Fax 604/822-1001. www.ubcconferences.com. About 1,500 units. Gage Towers units available May 10–Aug 26; Pacific Spirit Hostel units available May 15–Aug 15; West Coast Suites and Marine Drive Residence units (adjacent to the Gage Residence) available year-round. Gage Towers and Marine Drive Residences: C$39–C$53 single with shared bathroom; C$99–C$119 studio; C$119–C$139 1-bedroom suite. Pacific Spirit Hostel: C$33 single; C$66 double. West Coast Suites: C$159–C$199 suite. AE, MC, V. Parking C$7. Bus: 4, 17, 44 or 99. **Amenities** (on campus): Restaurant; cafeteria; pub; weight room; access to campus Olympic-size swimming pool; sauna (C$5 per person); tennis courts. *In room:* A/C, TV, hair dryer.

Where to Dine in Vancouver

For travelers who love to dine out and dine well, Vancouver is a delightful discovery. It's so good, in fact, that you could come here just to eat. And here's the capper: A fabulous meal at one of Vancouver's top restaurants costs about a third less than a similar meal would cost in New York, London, or San Francisco.

This is a city that likes to dine, and dine well, and you may be surprised at the sophistication of Vancouver's food scene. It's a place with an established food culture, celebrity chefs, and soap (soup?) operaish twists and turns that are grist for the gourmet gossip mills. That's part of the fun, of course, but it also means that the food scene is constantly changing and evolving and reinventing itself. But one thing is certain: You will not encounter any snotty waiters or wait staff in Vancouver. The friendly professionalism of everyone involved in the food industry in Vancouver adds to the pleasure of dining here.

Most of Vancouver's top restaurants offer tasting menus, and I recommend that you try them. In particular, the tasting menus at West, C, and Raincity Grill will give you a brilliant sampling of the best, freshest, and most creative cooking in Vancouver.

Sustainably harvested fish and seafood are available at most Vancouver restaurants; look for the OceanWise logo, which means the fish has been recommended by the Vancouver Aquarium as non-endangered.

Complement your dining experience with one of B.C.'s award-winning wines. Vineyards in the Okanagan Valley in eastern B.C., and the Cowichan Valley on Vancouver Island produce some remarkable reds and a couple of delicious sparkling whites. The province's viniculture has birthed a sophisticated wine culture in Vancouver, and every good restaurant has a sommelier or knowledgeable server who can steer you in the right direction.

Restaurant meals in British Columbia carry no provincial tax, but venues add the **6% goods and services tax (GST).** Restaurant hours vary. Lunch is typically served from noon to 1 or 2pm; Vancouverites begin dinner around 6:30pm, later in summer. Reservations are recommended at most restaurants and are essential at the city's top tables.

For more information see section 6, "Eating & Drinking in Vancouver & Victoria," in chapter 2.

1 BEST VANCOUVER DINING BETS

- **Best Spot for a Romantic Dinner:** Intimate, candlelit dining and tableside preparations make the long-established French restaurant **Le Gavroche,** 1616 Alberni St. (© **604/685-3924**), the most romantic dining spot in town. See p. 99.
- **Best Sustainable Dining:** There are two stand-outs in this category. **Raincity Grill,** 1193 Denman St. (© **604/685-7337**), was one of the first Vancouver eateries to source all its products locally and responsibly and features a memorable "100 Miles"

menu with food harvested, caught, or grown within 100 miles of Vancouver. See p. 99. Frank Pabst, the chef at **Blue Water Café and Raw Bar,** 1095 Hamilton St. (*C* **604/688-8078**), creates fabulously inventive dishes using only wild and sustainably harvested seafood.

- **Best Pacific Northwest Cuisine: West,** 2881 Granville St. (*C* **604/738-8938**), is the best—for an all-around, upscale, Pacific Northwest dining experience. But don't just take my word for it. This storied West Side eatery won *Vancouver* magazine's "Best Restaurant" award 4 years in a row. See p. 103.

- **Best View:** For a combination of top-notch food and a killer view of mountains, Burrard Inlet, and Stanley Park, try **Lift,** 333 Menchions Mews (*C* **604/689-5438**). See p. 99.

- **Best Chinese Cuisine:** The best Vancouver Chinese remains **Sun Sui Wah,** 3888 Main St. (*C* **604/872-8822**). It's definitely worth the trip. See p. 107.

- **Best Brunch:** Head across Burrard Inlet to West Vancouver and the **Beach House at Dundarave Pier,** 150 25th St. (*C* **604/922-1414**), the place where West Vanners go to enjoy the terrific view and the yummy weekend brunch.

- **Best Newcomer: MARKET by Jean-Georges,** 1115 Alberni St. (*C* **604/695-1115**), the famous chef's first foray into Vancouver, doesn't disappoint; the menu offers the greatest hits of the great Jean-Georges. See p. 94.

- **Best Sushi and Sashimi:** If you're looking for the best sushi and sashimi in Vancouver, **Tojo's Restaurant,** 1133 W. Broadway (*C* **604/872-8050**), is the place to go. It's expensive, but you'll be treated to the freshest fish and most exquisitely prepared seafood delicacies in B.C. See p. 102.

- **Best Outdoor Dining:** It's not fine dining, but for unsurpassed ocean views, reserve a table under the trees at **The Teahouse in Stanley Park,** Ferguson Point (close to Third Beach; *C* **604/669-3281**). This patio also doubles as the **best place to watch the sunset.** See p. 100.

- **Best Oysters: Joe Fortes Seafood and Chop House,** 777 Thurlow St. (*C* **604/669-1940**), has become a Vancouver institution, and if you try a few freshly shucked oysters before your grilled salmon or halibut, you'll go away happy. See p. 92.

- **Best Vegetarian: Annapurna,** 1812 W. 4th Ave. (*C* **604/736-5959**), has flavorful food, a cozy little room, and the most reasonable wines in town. Who says you have to sacrifice when you're a veggie eater? See p. 106.

2 RESTAURANTS BY CUISINE

American
Sophie's Cosmic Café (West Side, $, p. 107)
The Tomahawk Restaurant (North Shore, $, p. 109)

Barbecue
Memphis Blues Barbeque House ★ (West Side, $$, p. 103)

Belgian
Chambar Belgian Restaurant ★★ (Yaletown, $$$, p. 93)

Caribbean
The Reef (East Side, $$, p. 108)

Key to Abbreviations: $$$$ = Very Expensive $$$ = Expensive $$ = Moderate $ = Inexpensive

Casual
Bin 941 Tapas Parlour ★ (Downtown, $$, p. 95)
Café Zen (West Side, $$, p. 103)
The Locus Café (East Side, $$, p. 108)
The SandBar (Granville Island, $$, p. 103)

Charcuterie
Salt ★ (Gastown, $, p. 98)

Chinese/Dim Sum
Park Lock Seafood Restaurant (Chinatown, $$, p. 97)
Pink Pearl ★ (Chinatown, $$, p. 97)
Sha-Lin Noodle House (West Side, $, p. 107)
Sun Sui Wah ★★ (East Side, $$$, p. 107)

Coffee/Tea
Caffè Artigiano ★★ (Downtown, West End, $, p. 109)
Epicurean Delicatessen Caffè (Kitsilano, $, p. 110)
The Fish House in Stanley Park ★★ (West End, $$$, p. 99)
Mink, A Chocolate Cafe ★ (Gastown, $$$, p. 111)
Moonstruck Tea House (West End, $, p. 111)
Sciué ★ (Downtown, $, p. 96)
T (West Side, $, p. 111)

Desserts
La Casa Gelato ★ (East Side, $, p. 110)
Sciué ★ (Downtown, $, p. 96)

Family Style
Old Spaghetti Factory (Gastown, $, p. 98)
Romano's Macaroni Grill (West End, $$, p. 101)
Sophie's Cosmic Café (West Side, $, p. 107)
The Tomahawk Restaurant (North Shore, $, p. 109)

French
Elixir ★★ (Yaletown, $$$, p. 93)
Jules ★ (Gastown, $, p. 97)
Le Gavroche ★★ (West End, $$$, p. 99)
Nu (Yaletown, $$$, p. 94)
The Smoking Dog (Kitsilano, $$, p. 104)
West ★★★ (West Side, $$$$, p. 103)

Fusion
glowbal grill & satay bar ★★ (Yaletown, $$, p. 95)
MARKET by Jean-Georges ★★★ (Downtown, $$$, p. 94)
Yew ★★ (Downtown, $$$, p. 94)
Zin (West End, $$, p. 101)

Greek
Stephos (West End, $, p. 102)

Indian
Annapurna ★ (West Side, $, p. 106)
Rangoli (West Side, $, p. 106)
Vij ★★★ (West Side, $$, p. 105)

International
Coast ★★★ (Downtown, $$$, p. 93)
MARKET by jean-Georges ★★★ (Downtown, $$$, p. 94)
Sanafir ★★ (Downtown, $$, p. 96)

Italian
Amarcord ★ (Yaletown, $$$, p. 92)
Cin Cin ★★★ (West End, $$$, p. 98)
Gusto di Quattro ★ (North Shore, $$$, p. 108)
Il Giardino di Umberto Ristorante ★★ (Yaletown, $$$, p. 94)
Italian Kitchen ★★ (Downtown, $$, p. 95)
Old Spaghetti Factory (Gastown, $, p. 98)
Romano's Macaroni Grill (West End, $$, p. 101)
Sciué ★ (Downtown, $, p. 96)
Trattoria Italian Kitchen ★ (Kitsilano, $$, p. 105)

Japanese

Gyoza King (West End, $, p. 102)

Hapa Izakaya ★ (West End, $$, p. 100)

Ichiban-ya (West End, $$, p. 101)

Tanpopo (West End, $$, p. 101)

Tojo's Restaurant ★★★ (West Side, $$$$, p. 102)

Malaysian

Banana Leaf ★ (West End, $, p. 102)

Pacific Northwest

The Beach House at Dundarave Pier ★★ (North Shore, $$$, p. 108)

C ★★★ (Yaletown, $$$$, p. 89)

Diva at the Met ★ (Downtown, $$$$, p. 92)

The Fish House in Stanley Park ★★ (West End, $$$, p. 99)

Lift ★★ (West End, $$$, p. 99)

Raincity Grill ★★★ (West End, $$$, p. 99)

The Salmon House on the Hill ★ (North Shore, $$$, p. 109)

The Teahouse in Stanley Park (West End, $$$, p. 100)

Voya ★★ (West End, $$$, p. 100)

West ★★★ (West Side, $$$$, p. 103)

Yew ★★ (Downtown, $$$, p. 94)

Pizza

Incendio West ★ (Kitsilano, $, p. 106)

Seafood

Blue Water Cafe and Raw Bar ★★★ (Yaletown, $$$, p. 93)

C ★★★ (Yaletown, $$$$, p. 89)

The Cannery ★ (Gastown, $$$, p. 96)

Coast ★★★ (Downtown, $$$, p. 93)

The Fish House in Stanley Park ★★ (West End, $$$, p. 99)

Joe Fortes Seafood and Chop House ★ (Downtown, $$$$, p. 92)

The Salmon House on the Hill ★ (North Shore, $$$, p. 109)

Sun Sui Wah ★★ (East Side, $$$, p. 107)

Southwestern

The Locus Café (East Side, $$, p. 108)

Tapas

Bin 941 Tapas Parlour ★ (Downtown, $$, p. 95)

Zin (West End, $$, p. 101)

Thai

Simply Thai ★ (Yaletown, $$, p. 96)

Vegetarian

Annapurna ★ (West Side, $, p. 106)

The Naam Restaurant ★ (West Side, $, p. 106)

Vietnamese

Phnom Penh Restaurant ★ (Chinatown, $, p. 98)

---

3 DOWNTOWN & YALETOWN

VERY EXPENSIVE

C ★★★ SEAFOOD/PACIFIC NORTHWEST   Since opening in 1997, the popularity of this award-winning trendsetter hasn't flagged. The dining room is a cool white space with painted steel and lots of glass; the waterside location on False Creek is sublime (book an outside table if the weather is fine). Ingredients make all the difference here: The chef and his highly knowledgeable staff can tell you not only where every product comes from, but also the name of the boat or farm. Expect exquisite surprises and imaginative preparations: For appetizers, sample the fresh B.C. oysters with tongue-tingling sauces, candied salmon belly, or poached pear cannelloni. Mains are artfully

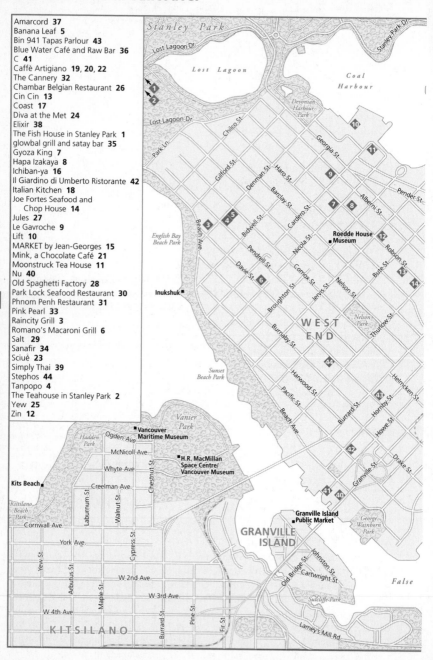

Amarcord **37**
Banana Leaf **5**
Bin 941 Tapas Parlour **43**
Blue Water Café and Raw Bar **36**
C **41**
Caffè Artigiano **19, 20, 22**
The Cannery **32**
Chambar Belgian Restaurant **26**
Cin Cin **13**
Coast **17**
Diva at the Met **24**
Elixir **38**
The Fish House in Stanley Park **1**
glowbal grill and satay bar **35**
Gyoza King **7**
Hapa Izakaya **8**
Ichiban-ya **16**
Il Giardino di Umberto Ristorante **42**
Italian Kitchen **18**
Joe Fortes Seafood and
    Chop House **14**
Jules **27**
Le Gavroche **9**
Lift **10**
MARKET by Jean-Georges **15**
Mink, a Chocolate Café **21**
Moonstruck Tea House **11**
Nu **40**
Old Spaghetti Factory **28**
Park Lock Seafood Restaurant **30**
Phnom Penh Restaurant **31**
Pink Pearl **33**
Raincity Grill **3**
Romano's Macaroni Grill **6**
Salt **29**
Sanafir **34**
Sciué **23**
Simply Thai **39**
Stephos **44**
Tanpopo **4**
The Teahouse in Stanley Park **2**
Yew **25**
Zin **12**

Deadman's Island

Burrard Inlet

0   1/4 mi
0   1/4 km

Vancouver Convention & Exhibition Centre

Canada Place

Centennial Pier

Hastings St.

Cordova St.

20 Marine Bldg.

Melville St.

Burrard St.

21 Waterfront

Waterfront Sta.

Portside Park

Railway St.

Alexander St.

15

Burrard

22

23

Granville St.

Pender St.

Steam Clock

Water St.

28

Maple Tree Square

Powell St.

Oppenheimer Park

16 17 18

Fairmont Hotel Vancouver

24 Howe St.

27

25

29

Cordova St.

Hastings St.

Jackson Ave.

19

Granville

Dunsmuir St.

Homer St.

Abbott St.

Carrall St.

Columbia St.

Dunlevy Ave.

Vancouver Art Gallery

Vancouver City Centre

Georgia St.

GASTOWN

Sun Tower

Chinatown Gate

CHINATOWN

Robson Sq.

SKYTRAIN

Robson St.

Richards St.

Dr. Sun Yat-sen Chinese Garden

30

Provincial Law Courts

26

Gore Ave.

Main St.

Keefer St.

Georgia St.

CANADA LINE

Smithe St.

Hamilton St.

Cambie St.

Beatty St.

Stadium

Vancouver Public Library

Livingstone Park

31

Union St.

Prior St.

24

Seymour St.

Nelson St.

GM Place

YALETOWN

B.C. Place Stadium

National Ave.

Pacific Central Sta.

36 35

Expo Blvd.

Creekside Park

Science World

Main Street

SKYTRAIN

37

Davie St.

38 39

Yaletown-Roundhouse

Mainland St.

Pacific Blvd.

The Roundhouse

Cooper's Park

David Lam Park

Creek

Charleson Park

Moberly Rd.

Charleson St.

Olympic Village

Yukon St.

W. 1st Ave.

W. 2nd Ave.

Columbia St.

Alberta St.

Manitoba St.

Ontario St.

E. 2nd Ave.

E. 3rd Ave.

W. 4th Ave.

W. 5th Ave.

Quebec St.

E. 1st Ave.

Industrial Ave.

Main St.

Scotia St.

created and might include twice-cooked sablefish with porcini fondue or crispy trout with black truffle puree. Give chef Robert Clark a chance to show off, and order a 6- or 10-course tasting menu as you watch the sun set over the marina. Excellent wine pairings, too.

1600 Howe St. 𝒞 **604/681-1164.** www.crestaurant.com. Reservations recommended. Main courses C$29–C$41; tasting menus C$98–C$130. AE, DC, MC, V. Dinner daily 5:30–11pm; lunch Mon–Fri 11:30am–2:30pm (May to Labour Day). Valet parking C$10. Bus: 1 or 2.

Diva at the Met ★ PACIFIC NORTHWEST   Diva's triple-tiered dining room with a giant wall of glass brick makes for an elegant dining experience at breakfast, lunch, or dinner. A few years ago this was the best hotel restaurant in Vancouver, and it still attracts diners who appreciate attentive service and good food (Yew, p. 94, at the Four Seasons has lured away some of the business). Diva's menu draws from the best of fresh seasonal ingredients and takes a light, international approach to spices and seasonings. Depending on the season, appetizers might include duck liver parfait, West Coast seafood chowder, or scallops with porcini risotto; mains include Queen Charlotte sablefish, roast duck breast with wild rice pilaf, and lamb sirloin. Diva's wine list is regularly rated one of the best in town.

In the Metropolitan Hotel (p. 73), 645 Howe St. 𝒞 **604/602-7788.** www.metropolitan.com/diva. Reservations recommended. Main courses lunch C$18–C$25, dinner C$22–C$34; breakfast C$9–C$18. AE, DC, DISC, MC, V. Daily 6:30am–1am. Bus: 4 or 7.

Joe Fortes Seafood and Chop House ★ SEAFOOD   Named after the burly Caribbean seaman who became English Bay's first lifeguard, Joe Fortes is great if you're hankering for fresh seafood served the "old-fashioned" way, without a lot of modern culinary intrusions. The downstairs dining room evokes a kind of turn-of-the-20th-century saloon elegance, but if the weather's fine, try for a table on the rooftop patio. Stick with the seafood because it's what they do best. The waiters will inform you what's just come in and where it's from. Although Joe's has added more fusion elements to boost the novelty, you can ask for your fish to be simply grilled or sautéed. My personal recommendation is the seasonal oysters (Joe Fortes has the best oyster bar in Vancouver) and grilled fresh fish or, a meal unto itself, the famous seafood tower, which comes with an iced assortment of marinated mussels, poached shrimp, grilled and chilled scallops, marinated calamari, tuna sashimi, Manila clams, Dungeness crab, and local beach oysters. They now offer a good, fixed-price, three-course dinner, too. Heavy on the white, the wine list is gargantuan and includes some wonderful pinots from the Okanagan Valley.

777 Thurlow St. (at Robson). 𝒞 **604/669-1940.** www.joefortes.ca. Reservations recommended. Main courses C$28–C$55; fixed-price dinner (from 4pm) C$28. AE, DC, DISC, MC, V. Daily 11am–10:30pm (brunch Sat–Sun 11am–4pm). Bus: 5.

EXPENSIVE

Amarcord ★ ITALIAN   The traditional Northern Italian cooking at Amarcord is based on recipes from Emilia-Romagna, considered one of the greatest food regions in Italy. This is not overly complicated or trendy cuisine. Come here for freshly made pasta or risotto teamed with lovingly prepared sauce. Think gnocchi with Italian sausage, fresh tomato, and basil; linguine with mussels, scallops, and tiger prawns; and veal scaloppine with lemon. Wines hail from Tuscany and California. The atmosphere is formal without being fussy.

104-1168 Hamilton St. 𝒞 **604/681-6500.** www.amarcord.ca. Reservations recommended. Main courses C$17–C$24. AE, DC, MC, V. Mon–Fri 11:30am–2:30pm; daily 5–10pm. Closed on holidays. Bus: 2.

Blue Water Cafe and Raw Bar ★★★ SEAFOOD If you had to describe this busy, buzzy place in one word, it would be *fresh,* as in only the best from sustainable and wild fisheries make it onto the menu. In fact, Blue Water won the top prize for "Best Seafood" at the 2008 and 2009 *Vancouver* magazine restaurant awards. If you love sushi and sashimi, the raw bar under the direction of Yoshihio Tabo offers up some of the city's best. On the other side of the room, Frank Pabst, the restaurant's executive chef, creates his dishes in a large open kitchen. For starters, try a medley of local oysters with various toppings; a sushi platter; or Dungeness crab salad with wakame seaweed and thinly sliced cucumber. Main courses depend on whatever is in season: It might be spring salmon, halibut, Arctic char, tuna, white sturgeon, or B.C. sablefish. The desserts are fabulous. A masterful wine list and an experienced sommelier assure fine wine pairings. Blue Water now offers a wonderful fixed-price menu between 5 and 6pm.

1095 Hamilton St. (at Helmcken). ℂ **604/688-8078.** www.bluewatercafe.net. Reservations recommended. Main courses C$29–C$45; fixed-price menu (5 to 6pm) C$45. AE, DC, MC, V. Daily 5–11pm. Valet parking C$10. Bus: 2.

Chambar Belgian Restaurant ★★ (Finds) BELGIAN One of Vancouver's favorite restaurants, Chambar occupies an intriguing space in a kind of no man's land on lower Beatty Street between Yaletown and Gastown. Michelin-trained chef Nico Scheuerman and his wife, Karri, have worked hard to make the place a success, and plenty of plaudits have come their way. The menu features small and large plates. Smaller choices typically include mussels cooked in white wine with bacon and cream (or with fresh tomatoes); beef carpaccio; or prosciutto and grilled pear. Main dishes feature tagine of braised lamb shank with honey, and roasted halibut with curried saffron risotto. For dessert, try the Belgian chocolate mousse or the mocha soufflé. Chambar specializes in Belgian beers, with some 25 varieties in bottles and on tap.

562 Beatty St. ℂ **604/879-7119.** www.chambar.com. Reservations recommended. Small plates C$15–C$21; main courses C$28–C$29; 3-course set menu C$60. AE, MC, V. Daily 6pm–midnight. Bus: 5 or 17.

Coast ★★★ (Finds) SEAFOOD/INTERNATIONAL This dashing restaurant moved from Yaletown to its new downtown location in 2009 and re-established itself as a culinary and people-watching spot of note. The concept at Coast is to offer an extensive variety of fresh and non-endangered seafood from coasts around the world. The dining room is a handsomely designed affair with a special "community table" that allows diners to watch the chef prepare culinary teasers such as the delicious lobster corn dog or the Dungeness crab-and-cucumber roll. The signature coastal platter with oysters, crab claws, clams, mussels, and more is a fabulous appetizer. Then, from the grill, you could order wild B.C. salmon, B.C. lingcod, or a seafood brochette. Other temptations include Creole lobster and prawn fettuccine, Arctic char over Alsatian sauerkraut, and (always) Liverpool-style fish and chips. Accompany your meal with a recommended wine from Coast's large cellar.

1054 Alberni St. ℂ **604/685-5010.** www.coastrestaurant.ca. Reservations recommended. Main courses C$17–C$34. AE, DC, MC, V. Daily 4:30–11pm. Bus: 1 or 22.

Elixir ★★ FRENCH Elixir, in the hip Opus Hotel, actually has three different dining areas: an enclosed space with dark-wood paneling and red velvet banquettes; the brighter garden room, more appropriate for an informal breakfast or brunch; and an adjacent bistro. The menu is the same in all three—modern brasserie food prepared with local ingredients and utilizing a medley of spices culled from former French colonies the world over. For appetizers, think mussels in cider, cream, and lemon thyme; for salads, warm *frissee* and bacon with a poached egg; and for main courses, pan-roasted halibut, or steak frites. A selection of local artisan cheeses is a perfect way to end your meal. Late in the evening, the restaurant becomes more like a Yaletown lounge and offers the same kind of small plates found in the Opus Bar.

In the Opus Hotel (p. 74), 350 Davie St. ⓒ **604/642-0557.** www.elixirvancouver.ca. Reservations recommended. Main courses C$14–C$26. AE, DC, MC, V. Mon–Sat 6:30am–2am; Sun 6:30am–midnight. Closed holidays. Bus: 1 or 22.

Il Giardino di Umberto Ristorante ★★ ITALIAN
Restaurant magnate Umberto Menghi started this small restaurant, tucked away in a yellow heritage house at the bottom of Hornby Street, about 3 decades ago. It still serves some of the best Italian fare, and has one of the prettiest garden patios in town. A larger restaurant now adjoins the original house, opening up into a bright, spacious dining room that re-creates the ambience of an Italian villa. The menu leans toward Tuscany, with dishes that emphasize pasta and game. Entrees usually include classics such as *osso buco* with saffron risotto, and that Roman favorite, spaghetti carbonara. A daily list of specials makes the most of seasonal fresh ingredients, often offering outstanding seafood dishes. The wine list is comprehensive and well chosen.

1382 Hornby St. (btw. Pacific and Drake). ⓒ **604/669-2422.** Fax 604/669-9723. www.umberto.com. Reservations recommended. Main courses C$15–C$35. AE, DC, MC, V. Mon–Fri noon–3pm and 6–11pm; Sat 6–11pm. Closed holidays. Bus: 1 or 22.

MARKET by Jean-Georges ★★★ FUSION/INTERNATIONAL
Jean-Georges Vongerichten is one of the world's most famous chefs, and his first restaurant in Vancouver is a paean to his long and highly successful career. You might call the menu here "The Greatest Hits of Jean-Georges" because what's on offer are the dishes he has perfected in his score of other restaurants. Try the sablefish in a nut-and-seed crust with sweet-and-sour broth, or soy-glazed short ribs with apple-jalapeno puree. The restaurant is calmly chic and not at all fussy; you can sit in the bar, in the cafe, or on the outdoor patio, and order from the same menu. The place is usually packed, and it should be, because the fixed-price lunch and dinner menus list a selection of wonderful dishes at a remarkably reasonable price.

1115 Alberni St. (Level 3 in the Shangri-La Hotel). ⓒ **604/695-1115.** Reservations recommended. Main courses C$15–C$35; fixed-price lunch C$30; fixed-price dinner C$65. AE, DC, MC, V. Restaurant Mon–Fri 11:30am–2:30pm; Mon–Sat 5:30–10:30pm. Cafe and bar Mon–Sat 11:30am–11:30pm.

Nu FRENCH
Nu means "naked" in French, but it's not clear how that applies to this stylish Yaletown hot spot. The same can be said for the 1970s airport-lounge decor. You're never quite sure if you're in a lounge or a dining room; Nu is both, obviously. But if the weather's nice, go out to the patio overlooking False Creek, because that's much more comfortable, and it's a great spot to enjoy a good lunch or a glass of wine and a snack, such as fried local oysters. More substantial fare includes flatiron steak, seafood salad, or caramelized lamb shanks. C (p. 89) is just steps away, and a better choice for a splurge dinner with a view; the same team runs both.

1661 Granville St. ⓒ **604/646-4668.** www.whatisnu.com. Reservations recommended. Main courses C$12–C$35. AE, DC, MC, V. Mon–Fri 11am–1am; Sat 10:30am–1am; Sun 10:30am–midnight. Bus: 1 or 2.

Yew ★★ PACIFIC NORTHWEST/FUSION
A multi-million-dollar makeover in 2008 transformed the old garden court dining room at the Four Seasons Hotel into a handsome new bar-lounge-restaurant that's drawing a whole new crowd of diners and

drinkers. A sandstone fireplace divides the lounge area from the restaurant with its raw bar and open kitchen, but you can order from the same menu wherever you sit. For a delicious shared appetizer, try the lobster and mango roll with a sweet chili dipping sauce. Then choose fresh fish or oysters from the raw bar, or dine on one of the fish, meat, or pasta dishes from the kitchen. Two noteworthy signature dishes are the grilled lamb striploin steak and the seafood paella for two. Wine lovers take note: With a two-glass minimum you can order wine by the glass from any of the 150 available vintages.

In the Four Seasons Hotel (p. 72), 791 W. Georgia St. ℭ **604/692-4939.** Reservations recommended. Main courses C$18–C$35. AE, DC, MC, V. Daily 6:30am–midnight. Bus: 240 or 242.

MODERATE

Bin 941 Tapas Parlour ★ TAPAS/CASUAL   Still booming after nearly a decade, Bin 941 remains the place for trendy tapas dining. True, the music's too loud and the room's too small, but the food that alights on the bar and eight tiny tables is delicious and fun, and the wine list is great. Look especially for local seafood such as scallops and tiger prawns tournedos. In this sliver of a bistro sharing is unavoidable, so come prepared for socializing. A second Bin, dubbed Bin 942, opened at 1521 W. Broadway (ℭ **604/ 734-9421**). The tables start to fill up at 6:30pm at both spots, and by 8pm, the hip and hungry have already formed a long and eager line.

941 Davie St. ℭ **604/683-1246.** www.bin941.com. Reservations not accepted. All plates are C$16. MC, V. Daily 5pm–1:30am. Bus: 4, 5, or 8.

glowbal grill & satay bar ★★ FUSION   Glowbal occupies a top spot in the trendy Yaletown dining scene. The dining room—divvied up into a long elevated bar, a rank of semi-secluded dining tables, a file of glowing dining cubes, and an open kitchen—maximizes the noise and drama. Have one of their famous martinis as you peruse the menu, and sample some of the delicious satays as an appetizer (glowbal started the Vancouver craze for these succulent skewers of grilled meat or fish served with a dipping sauce). Then, if you're in the mood for seafood, go with whatever is fresh: It may be wild salmon served with bok choy and lobster mashed potatoes, or spicy ahi tuna. Service is fun and friendly, the wine list exemplary. As the evening rolls on, the in-crowd rolls into Afterglow, the small lounge behind the dining room. If you want to try the food but avoid the scene, go for the reasonably priced lunch Monday to Friday.

1079 Mainland St. ℭ **604/602-0835.** www.glowbalgrill.com. Reservations recommended. Main courses lunch C$12–C$18, dinner C$16–C$29. AE, DC, MC, V. Daily 11:30am–midnight. Bus: 2.

Italian Kitchen ★★ ITALIAN   Italian Kitchen is a welcome addition to the downtown dining scene. At lunchtime it fills up with professionals who come for a reasonably priced lunch served in 45 minutes. At night it's dressier and more boisterous, with a noise level that mostly rules out intimate conversations. The menu spreads itself far and wide, incorporating classic tastes from all over Italy, but it ups the ante on some dishes, making them far richer than they'd ever be in their native settings. For an antipasto you can order beef tenderloin carpaccio with gorgonzola polenta, grilled calamari steak, or bruschetta with luscious toppings. From there, go on to an artisan pizza or one of the classic pastas. Chicken saltimbocca, veal scaloppine, and lamb shank are among the meat choices, and there are seasonal seafood entrees as well. Whatever you have, remember to share.

1037 Alberni St. ℭ **604/687-2858.** www.theitaliankitchen.ca. Reservations recommended. Main courses lunch C$11–C$19, dinner C$16–C$23. AE, DC, DISC, MC, V. Mon–Sat 11am–midnight, Sun 4–11pm. Bus: 240 or 242.

Sanafir ★★ (Finds) INTERNATIONAL   Influenced by the exotic dining and decor found along the Silk Road, Sanafir creates an opulent and fun dining experience that doesn't cost a fortune. The first-floor dining room is loud and buzzily exciting, but parties can also drink and dine upstairs while reclining on pillows beneath sexy harem-style draperies. The tapas-style plates come in three of five possible Silk Road variations: Asian, Mediterranean, Middle Eastern, Indian, or North African. And the trio of tastes costs only C$14. Order the chicken, for instance, and your three-dish tapas plate might contain Moroccan chicken tagine with saffron herb couscous, Indonesian chicken satays with lemon grass and peanut sauce, and Kashmir-style Tandoori chicken with mango chutney. Larger chef's specials are also available, such as the super-rich oxtail cappelletti with white truffle cream, Parmigiano-Reggiano, and shaved black truffle. There's no sign outside, so just look for the most glamorous place on gentrifying Granville Street, and you'll be there.

1026 Granville St. (at Nelson). ℂ **604/678-1049.** www.sanafir.ca. Reservations recommended. Tapas C$14; chef's specials C$17. AE, DC, MC, V. Daily 5pm–midnight. Bus: 4 or 7.

Simply Thai ★ THAI   At this small restaurant in trendy Yaletown, you can watch chef and owner Siriwan in the open kitchen as she cooks up a combination of northern and southern Thai dishes with some fusion sensations. The appetizers are perfect finger foods: *Gai satay* features succulent pieces of grilled chicken breast marinated in coconut milk and spices and covered in a peanut sauce, while the delicious *cho muang* consists of violet-colored dumplings stuffed with minced chicken. Main courses run the gamut of Thai cuisine: noodle dishes and coconut curries with beef, chicken, or pork, as well as a good number of vegetarian options. Don't miss the *tom kha gai*, a deceptively simple-looking coconut soup with chicken, mushrooms, and lemon grass. The set menu is a good way to sample a bit of everything.

1211 Hamilton St. ℂ **604/642-0123.** www.simplythairestaurant.com. Reservations recommended on weekends. Main courses C$13–C$18; set menu C$40. AE, DC, MC, V. Mon–Fri 11:30am–3pm and 5–10:30pm; Sat–Sun 5–10:30pm. Bus: 2.

INEXPENSIVE

Sciué ★ ITALIAN/DESSERTS/COFFEE   It's hard not to like a place that serves inexpensive Italian food and wonderful coffee in an airy, close-to-authentic Italian cafe setting. Sciué (pronounced *shoe*-eh) means "good and fast" in Italian regional slang, and that's how the food comes, but you can linger as long as you want and no one will bug you. Stop in for a double-shot espresso, a glass of Italian wine, or a dish of handmade gelato. For breakfast you can get a fresh Italian pastry or a light, healthy meal. Lunch options include *pane Romano* (thin Roman bread topped with a selection of sauces, vegetables, cheeses, meats, or seafood, and sold by weight), fresh pastas, salads, and soups.

110-800 E. Pender St. (at Howe St.). ℂ **604/602-7263.** www.sciue.ca. Main courses C$5–C$10. DC, MC, V. Mon–Fri 6:30am–8pm; Sat 9am–5pm. Bus: 2.

4 GASTOWN & CHINATOWN

EXPENSIVE

The Cannery ★ SEAFOOD   At least some of the pleasure of eating at The Cannery comes from the adventure of finding the place. (Drive or take a cab because it's impossible to get there on foot or by public transportation.) Hop the railroad tracks, thread your way past a harbor security checkpoint, pass container terminals and fish-packing plants, and there it is—a timber-framed rectangular building hanging out over the waters of Burrard Inlet. The interior, with its exposed beams and seafaring memorabilia, adds to the charm, but many come here for the view, one of the best in Vancouver. You'll find good, solid, traditional seafood, and ever-changing specials. Famous dishes include salmon Wellington (salmon, shrimp, and mushrooms baked in a puff pastry), smoked Alaskan black cod, and roasted mussels. Meat lovers can get a grilled New York steak or Alberta beef tenderloin. Chef Frederic Couton has been getting more inventive lately, but when an institution founded in 1971 is still going strong, no one's ever *too* keen to rock the boat. The wine list is stellar, and the desserts are wonderfully inventive.

2205 Commissioner St. (near Victoria Dr.). © 877/254-9606 or 604/254-9606. www.canneryseafood. com. Reservations recommended. Main courses C$24–C$41. AE, DC, DISC, MC, V. Tues–Fri 11:30am–2:30pm and 5:30–9pm; Sat 5–9:30pm; Sun 5–9pm. Closed Dec 24–26. From downtown, head east on Hastings St., turn left on Victoria Dr. (2 blocks past Commercial Dr.), then right on Commissioner St.

MODERATE

Park Lock Seafood Restaurant (Kids) CHINESE/DIM SUM   If you've never done dim sum, this large, second-floor dining room in the heart of Chinatown is a good place to give it a try, even though you'll have to listen to schlocky Western music while you dine. From 8am to 3pm daily, waitresses wheel little carts loaded with Chinese delicacies past the tables. When you see something you like, just point and ask for it. The final bill is based upon how many little plates are left on your table. Dishes include spring rolls, *hargow* (shrimp dumplings), *shumai* (steamed shrimp, beef, or pork dumplings), prawns wrapped in fresh white noodles, small steamed buns, sticky rice cooked in banana leaves, curried squid, and lots more. Parties of four or more are best—that way you get to try each other's food.

544 Main St. (at E. Pender St., on the 2nd floor). © 604/688-1581. Reservations recommended. Main courses C$10–C$25; dim sum C$3–C$7. AE, MC, V. Mon–Thurs 7:30am–4pm; Fri–Sun 7:30am–4pm and 5–9:30pm. Bus: 19 or 22.

Pink Pearl ★ (Kids) CHINESE/DIM SUM   Opened in 1981, the Pink Pearl remains Vancouver's best spot for dim sum. The sheer volume and bustle here are astonishing, and at peak times you may have to wait up to (or only, depending on your patience level) 15 minutes for a table. Dozens of waiters parade a cavalcade of trolleys stacked high with baskets, steamers, and bowls of dumplings, spring rolls, shrimp balls, chicken feet, and even more obscure and delightful offerings. At the tables, extended Chinese families banter, joke, and feast; towers of empty plates pile up in the middle, a tribute to the appetites of the brunchers, as well as the growing bill. Fortunately, dim sum is still a steal, perhaps the best and most fun way to sample Cantonese cooking.

1132 E. Hastings St. © 604/253-4316. www.pinkpearl.com. Main courses C$12–C$35; dim sum C$3–C$7. AE, DC, MC, V. Sun–Thurs 9am–10pm; Fri–Sat 9am–11pm (dim sum served daily 9am–2:30pm). Bus: 10.

INEXPENSIVE

Jules ★ (Finds) FRENCH   Jules is one of those places that is hard not to like. Like Salt (reviewed below), this casual French bistro is part of a mini-renaissance putting new life into Gastown. Jules can be really loud, but the staff is friendly and the food is honest, unpretentious, and reasonably priced. The menu's limited to just a few standard bistro items, all of them well prepared: steak frites (rib-eye or hanger steak with french fries), cassoulet, braised lamb shank, steamed mussels, or a vegetarian shepherd's pie. You can start with classics like French onion soup, escargots in garlic and herb butter, or country-style pâté. This is a good lunch spot, too.

216 Abbott St. 🕐 **604/669-0033.** Main courses C$11–C$24; 3-course fixed-price lunch C$24, fixed-price dinner C$26. AE, MC, V. Tues–Sat 11:30am–2:30pm and 5:30–10pm. Bus: 1 or 8.

Old Spaghetti Factory (Kids) (Value) FAMILY STYLE/ITALIAN The Old Spaghetti Factory has a convenient location in the Gastown heritage district and is a great place to take kids thanks to its selection of half-size, half-price pasta dishes, including spaghetti with meatballs. For the older and more adventurous are more complicated pastas with clam or Alfredo sauce, as well as veal and steak. All entrees come with a green salad or minestrone soup, sourdough bread, coffee or tea, and spumoni ice cream. A small list of wines is offered, plus beer and chocolate milk.

53 Water St. 🕐 **604/684-1288.** www.oldspaghettifactory.ca. Main courses C$9–C$15. AE, MC, V. Mon–Thurs 11am–10pm; Fri–Sat 11am–11pm; Sun 11am–9pm. Bus: 50.

Phnom Penh Restaurant ★ VIETNAMESE This family-run restaurant, serving Vietnamese and Cambodian cuisine, is a perennial contender for, and occasional recipient of, the *Vancouver* magazine award for the city's best Asian restaurant. Khmer dolls are suspended in glass cases, and the subdued lighting is a welcome departure from the harsh glare often found in inexpensive Chinatown restaurants. Try the hot-and-sour soup, loaded with prawns and lemon grass. The deep-fried garlic squid served with rice is a must-have. For dessert, the fruit-and-rice pudding is an exotic treat.

244 E. Georgia St., near Main St. 🕐 **604/682-5777.** Main courses C$6–C$11. AE, MC. Daily 10am–10pm. Bus: 8 or 19.

Salt ★ CHARCUTERIE The location of this new dining spot in Gastown's Blood Alley might put some visitors off, and that's really a shame because Salt is unique, and a wonderful place to get a good, inexpensive meal. The minimalistically modern room is set with communal spruce dining tables. Salt has no kitchen per se as it serves only cured meats and artisan cheeses plus a daily soup, a couple of salads, and grilled meat and cheese sandwiches. For the tasting plate you mix and match three of the meats and cheeses listed on the blackboard. To drink, choose from a selection of beers, and several good wines and whiskeys, or opt for a wine flight. As Blood Alley has no apparent street numbers, look for the salt shaker flag over the doorway. Try it for lunch if you're in Gastown.

45 Blood Alley, Gastown. 🕐 **604/633-1912.** www.salttastingroom.com. Tasting plates C$15; lunch specials C$12. AE, MC, V. Daily noon–midnight. Bus: 1 or 8.

5 THE WEST END

EXPENSIVE

Cin Cin ★★★ MODERN ITALIAN Vancouverites looking for great food and a romantic atmosphere frequent this award-winning, second-floor restaurant on Robson Street. The spacious dining room, done in a rustic Italian-villa style, surrounds an open kitchen built around a huge wood-fired oven and grill; the heated terrace is an equally pleasant dining and people-watching spot. The dishes, inspired by Italy but using locally sourced ingredients, change monthly, but your meal might begin with house-made Dungeness crab sausage with herb salad and lemon vinaigrette, followed by bison-filled gnocchi or biodynamic rice with scallops. Mouthwatering main courses include local fish and meat cooked in the wood-fired oven or on the wood grill, and a delicious pizza with sautéed wild mushrooms, peppercorn pecorino, and caramelized onions. The wine list is extensive, as is the selection of wines by the glass. The service is as exemplary as the food.

1154 Robson St. (*C*) **604/688-7338**. www.cincin.net. Reservations recommended. Main courses C$21–C$36; fixed-price menu (5–6pm) C$45. AE, DC, MC, V. Mon–Fri 11:30am–2:30pm and 5–11pm; Sat–Sun 5–11pm. Bus: 5 or 22.

The Fish House in Stanley Park ★★ SEAFOOD/PACIFIC NORTHWEST/TEA
Reminiscent of a more genteel era, this green clapboard clubhouse from 1929 is surrounded by lawns and old cedar trees, and looks out over English Bay (in the summer, try for a table on the veranda). Enjoy a traditional afternoon tea, Sunday brunch, or a memorable lunch or dinner of fresh B.C. oysters and shellfish, fresh seasonal fish, and signature dishes such as maple-glazed salmon, flaming prawns (done at your table with ouzo), and a seafood cornucopia. Chef Karen Barnaby often creates special theme menus and offers a reasonably priced three-course set dinner menu every month. The wine list is admirable; the desserts sumptuous.

8901 Stanley Park Dr. (*C*) **877/681-7275** or 604/681-7275. www.fishhousestanleypark.com. Reservations recommended. Main courses C$17–C$30; 3-course set menu (until 6:15pm) C$30; afternoon tea C$24. AE, DC, DISC, MC, V. Mon–Sat 11:30am–10pm; Sun 11am–10pm; afternoon tea daily 2–4pm. Closed Dec 24–26. Bus: 1, 35, or 135.

Le Gavroche ★★ FRENCH
This charmingly intimate French restaurant located in a century-old house celebrates its 30th anniversary in 2009. It's always been a place for special occasions and celebrations, and with food and wine of this caliber, there's a lot to celebrate. The food is classical French—but with inventive overtones and underpinnings. Try one of the tasting menus with wine pairings, and you won't regret a mouthful. Start with beef tartar or crab cakes with chili coulis, followed by a classic Caesar salad mixed at your table (Le Gavroche is known for its personal attention). Then, try slow-braised lamb shank, a venison chop with sour cherry jus, or mustard-crusted rack of lamb. Seafood and vegetarian choices are available as well. Finish your feast with a Grand Marnier soufflé or the incomparable "Lili" cake.

1616 Alberni St. (*C*) **604/685-3924**. www.legavroche.ca. Reservations recommended. Main courses C$25–C$45; set menus C$35–C$55. AE, DC, MC, V. Mon–Fri 11:30am–2:30pm and 5:30–10pm; Sat–Sun 5:30–10pm. Bus: 5.

Lift ★★ (Finds) PACIFIC NORTHWEST
Built on pilings right on Coal Harbour, Lift offers gorgeous mountain, water, and city views. Chef Dave Jorgenson's contemporary West Coast cuisine comes with a French twist and is equal to the sexy setting. The interior is luxe, with an illuminated onyx bar and different seating areas for drinking, eating, or both, as well as a rooftop patio. After 5pm, the restaurant serves "whet plates" (larger than an appetizer, but smaller than an entree), such as mussels with french fries, fried calamari with tsatsiki, or pan-seared chicken livers. Main courses include ahi tuna, bison ravioli, or veal Oscar. The Sunday brunch is hopping, too, and reasonably priced. The wine list here is good, but on the expensive side.

333 Menchions Mews (behind Westin Bayshore Resort). (*C*) **604/689-5438**. www.liftbarandgrill.com. Reservations recommended. Whet plates C$13–C$21; main courses C$29–C$49. AE, DC, MC, V. Mon–Fri 11:30am–midnight; Sat–Sun 11am–midnight; Sun brunch 11am–2:30pm. Bus: 240.

Raincity Grill ★★★ PACIFIC NORTHWEST
This top-starred restaurant on a busy, buzzy corner across from English Bay is a gem—painstaking in preparation, arty in presentation, and yet completely unfussy in atmosphere. Raincity Grill was one of the

very first restaurants in Vancouver to embrace the "buy locally, eat seasonally" concept and pioneered the OceanWise sustainable seafood organization. The menu focuses on seafood, game, poultry, and organic vegetables from British Columbia and the Pacific Northwest. The room is long, low, and intimate. To sample a bit of everything, I recommend the seasonal "100 miles" tasting menu, a bargain at C$70, or C$80 with wine pairings. One recent tasting menu included wild B.C. salmon with smoked turnip and potato roulade; roasted Berkshire pork belly with pear and parsnip puree; and spiced cider soup—all of it made with ingredients found within 161km (100 miles) of the restaurant. The wine list is huge and, in keeping with the restaurant's philosophy, sticks pretty close to home. From May through Labour Day, Raincity opens a takeout window on Denman Street, where you can get a gourmet sandwich, salad, and sweet to go for C$10.

1193 Denman St. ✆ **604/685-7337.** www.raincitygrill.com. Reservations recommended. Main courses C$17–C$33. AE, DC, MC, V. Mon–Fri 11:30am–2:30pm and 5–10:30pm; Sat–Sun 10:30am–3pm (brunch) and 5–10:30pm. Bus: 1 or 5.

The Teahouse in Stanley Park PACIFIC NORTHWEST   Perched on Ferguson Point overlooking English Bay, the Teahouse in Stanley Park is one of Vancouver's most venerable seaside landmarks. The menu sticks with safe tourist choices and a selection of what trendy Vancouverites are eating these days. Appetizers include wok-fried squid with Thai chiles and oyster sauce, and mushrooms stuffed with crab, shrimp, and cream cheese. Main courses are divided between seafood and meat, with pasta and risotto thrown in for good measure. The view is perhaps more memorable than the food, and after the sun fades, the lights cast a magical glow on the trees and garden. Try for a seat on the outdoor patio or at a window-side table in the conservatory.

Ferguson Point, Stanley Park. ✆ **604/669-3281.** www.vancouverdine.com. Reservations recommended. Small plates C$10–C$14; main courses C$18–C$36. AE, DC, MC, V. Mon–Fri 11:30am–9:45pm; Sat 11:30am–9:45pm (brunch 11:30am–2:30pm); Sun 10:30am–9:45pm (brunch 10:30am–2:30pm); small plates daily 2:30–5:30pm; dinner daily 5:30–9:45pm.

Voya ★★ PACIFIC NORTHWEST   The dining room of the new Loden Vancouver hotel (p. 73) is a lovely spot, with subdued Art Deco references and a chic, comfortable ambience. You can get breakfast and lunch here, but I'd suggest that you come for dinner so you can sample the globally inspired, regionally sourced cooking of Chef Marc-Andre Choquette, one of Vancouver's best chefs. There are plates for sharing, like blue-cheese risotto with pancetta, or veal cheek pappardella pasta. Delicious starters might include seared scallop with creamed leeks or tuna tartare. Main courses like braised lamb shank with butternut squash risotto and albacore tuna with cipollini onion puree and buttered sprouts are both artful and satisfying. Try one of the many B.C. wines with your meal.

1177 Melville St., in the Loden Vancouver. ✆ **604/638-8692.** www.voyarestaurant.com. Reservations recommended. Main courses dinner C$28–C$30. AE, MC, V. Daily 6:30am–10:30am, 11:30am–3pm, and 5:30–10:30pm.

MODERATE

Hapa Izakaya ★ JAPANESE   Dinner comes at almost disco decibels in Robson Street's hottest Japanese "eat-drink place" (the literal meaning of Izakaya), where chefs call out orders, servers shout acknowledgments, and the maitre d' and owner keep up a running volley to staff about the (often sizable) wait at the door. The menu features inventive nontraditional dishes such as bacon-wrapped asparagus, *negitori* (spicy tuna roll), and fresh tuna belly chopped with spring onions and served with bite-size bits of garlic bread. Inventive appetizers and meat dishes and a scrumptious Korean hot pot are also on the menu, for the non-raw fish eaters in your party. The crowd is about a third expat Japanese, a third Chinese (both local and expat), and a third Westerners. The service is fast and obliging, and the price per dish is reasonable. A second location is in Kitsilano at 1516 Yew St. (✆ **604/738-4272**).

1479 Robson St. ✆ **604/689-4272.** www.hapaizakaya.com. No reservations accepted 6–8pm. Main courses C$8–C$14. AE, MC, V. Sun–Thurs 5:30pm–midnight; Fri–Sat 5:30pm–1am. Bus: 5.

Ichiban-ya JAPANESE   In contrast to Hapa (see above), this small basement restaurant (with a rather dramatic red and black interior) has served old-fashioned, straight-up sushi for more than 2 decades. Options for non-sushiphiles include tempura, teriyaki, udon, and soba noodles.

770 Thurlow St. ✆ **604/682-6262.** www.ichiban-ya.com. Reservations accepted. Main courses C$7–C$19. AE, DC, MC, V. Daily 11:30am–10pm (until midnight in summer). Bus: 5.

Romano's Macaroni Grill (Kids) FAMILY STYLE/ITALIAN   It's almost worth eating here just to see the interior. Housed in a stone mansion built in 1900 by sugar baron B. T. Rogers, Romano's is a fun and casual chain restaurant with an Italian-influenced menu. This isn't high-concept Italian; the food is simple, understandable, and reliably good. The pastas are definitely favorites. The children's menu features lasagna, mac and cheese, spaghetti with meatball, and tasty pizzas. In the summer it's fun to dine outside on the beautiful garden patio, but the stunning interior, filled with handcrafted wood detailing and stained glass, is pretty amazing.

1523 Davie St. ✆ **604/689-4334.** www.macgrillbc.com. Reservations recommended. Main courses C$12–C$23; children's courses C$4.95. AE, DC, MC, V. Mon–Thurs noon–10pm; Fri–Sat noon–11pm. Bus: 5.

Tanpopo (Value) JAPANESE   Occupying the second floor of a corner building on Denman Street, Tanpopo has a partial view of English Bay, a large patio, and a huge menu of hot and cold Japanese dishes. But the line of people waiting 30 minutes or more every night for a table are here for the all-you-can-eat buffet. The unlimited fare includes the standards—makis, tuna and salmon sashimi, California and B.C. rolls—as well as cooked items such as tonkatsu, tempura, chicken kara-age, and broiled oysters. The quality is okay, a bit above average for an all-you-can-eat place. A couple of secrets to getting seated: You might try to call ahead, but they only take an arbitrary number of reservations for dinner each day. Otherwise, ask to sit at the sushi bar.

1122 Denman St. ✆ **604/681-7777.** Reservations recommended for groups. Main courses C$7–C$20; all-you-can-eat buffet C$22 for dinner, C$14 for lunch. AE, DC, MC, V. Daily 11:30am–10pm. Bus: 5.

Zin FUSION/TAPAS   Come to Zin for a restaurant meal (breakfast, lunch, or dinner) or tapas made with local ingredients and a global accent. The interior glows with candlelight and deep reddish hues offset by comfy sofas and chairs in the lounge and dining booths on the other side of the room. Small and shared plates are priced in the C$7-to-C$18 range and include standards such as burgers and steamed mussels, but you can also snack on truffled popcorn or an assortment of potato and yam fries. For your main course, try a rib-eye steak, seared B.C. sablefish, or a vegetarian pasta such as English pea ricotta agnolotti. Zin offers a large selection of martinis, wines by the glass, and the best selection of zinfandel in town. The restaurant is in the Pacific Palisades Hotel (p. 80) but managed separately.

In the Pacific Palisades Hotel, 1277 Robson St. ✆ **604/891-5195.** www.zin-restaurant.com. Main courses C$19–C$28. AE, DC, MC, V. Mon–Thurs 7am–midnight; Fri 7am–1am; Sat 8am–1am; Sun 8am–midnight.

Banana Leaf ★ MALAYSIAN   One of the city's best spots for Malaysian food, Banana Leaf is just a hop and a skip from English Bay. The menu includes inventive specials such as mango and okra salad, delicious South Asian mainstays such as *gado gado* (a salad with hot peanut sauce), *mee goreng* (fried noodles with vegetables topped by a fried egg), and occasional variations such as an assam curry (seafood in hot-and-sour curry sauce), with okra and tomato. Must-tries are sambal green beans and a signature chili crab. For dessert, don't pass up *pisang goreng*—fried banana with ice cream. The seven-course tasting menu (C$30) lets you sample a bit of everything. The small room is tastefully decorated in dark tropical woods; service is very friendly. Other locations at 820 W. Broadway (© **604/731-6333**) and in Kitsilano at 3005 W. Broadway (© **604/734-3005**); same prices and hours apply.

1096 Denman St. © **604/683-3333.** www.bananaleaf-vancouver.com. Main courses C$11–C$20. AE, MC, V. Sun–Thurs 11:30am–10pm; Fri–Sat 11:30am–11pm. Bus: 5.

Gyoza King JAPANESE   Gyoza King features an entire menu of *gyoza*—succulent Japanese dumplings filled with prawns, pork, vegetables, and other combinations—as well as Japanese noodles and staples like *katsu-don* (pork cutlet over rice) and *udon* (a rich, hearty soup). This is the gathering spot for hordes of young Japanese students and visitors looking for reasonably priced eats that approximate home cooking. The staff is very courteous and happy to explain the dishes.

1508 Robson St. © **604/669-8278.** Main courses C$5–C$10. AE, MC, V. Mon–Fri 11:30am–3pm and 5:30pm–2am; Sat 11:30am–2am; Sun 11:30am–midnight. Bus: 5.

Stephos Value GREEK   A long-time fixture on the Davie Street dining scene, Stephos offers Greek food at its simplest and cheapest. Customers line up outside for a seat amid Greek travel posters, potted ivy, and whitewashed walls (the average wait is about 10–15 min., but it could be as long as 30 min., as once you're inside, the staff will never rush you out the door). Order some pita and dip (hummus, spicy eggplant, or garlic spread) while you peruse the menu. An interesting appetizer is the *avgolemono* soup, a delicately flavored chicken broth with egg and lemon, accompanied by a plate of piping hot pita bread. When choosing a main course, keep in mind that portions are huge. The roasted lamb, lamb chops, fried calamari, and a variety of souvlakia are served with rice, roast potatoes, and Greek salad. The beef, lamb, or chicken pita come in slightly smaller portions served with fries and *tsatsiki* (a sauce made from yogurt, cucumber, and garlic).

1124 Davie St. © **604/683-2555.** Reservations accepted for parties of 5 or more. Main courses C$6–C$11. AE, MC, V. Daily 11am–11:30pm. Bus: 5.

6 THE WEST SIDE

VERY EXPENSIVE

Tojo's Restaurant ★★★ JAPANESE   Tojo's is considered Vancouver's top Japanese restaurant, the place where celebs and food cognoscenti come to dine on the best sushi in town. It's expensive, but the food is absolutely fresh, inventive, and boy is it good. The dining room's main area wraps around Chef Tojo and his sushi chefs with a giant curved maple sake bar and an adjoining sushi bar. Tojo's ever-changing menu offers such specialties as sea urchin on the half shell, herring roe, lobster claws, tuna, crab, and barbecue eel. Go for the Chef's Arrangement—tell them how much you're willing to spend (per **103** person), and let the good times roll.

1133 W. Broadway. © **604/872-8050.** www.tojos.com. Reservations required. Main courses C$16–C$30; sushi/sashimi C$8–C$28; Chef's Arrangement C$50–C$100. AE, DC, MC, V. Mon–Sat 5–10pm. Closed Christmas week. Bus: 9.

West ★★★ FRENCH/PACIFIC NORTHWEST   Every meal I've had at this award-winning restaurant—it was voted "Best Restaurant in Vancouver" by *Vancouver* magazine 4 years in a row—has been memorable. The credo at West is deceptively simple: "True to our region, true to the seasons." That means fresh, organic, locally harvested seafood, game, and produce are transformed into extraordinary creations. The menu changes three to four times a week, but first courses might include lightly poached B.C. spot prawns in a rhubarb and watermelon essence or quail tortellini with roasted sweet corn puree. For a main course you might find fillet of smoked sablefish, seared Qualicum Bay scallops with smoked veal tongue, or crisp sliced porchetta with black garlic and toasted gnocchi. For the ultimate dining experience, try one of the seasonal tasting menus—a multicourse progression through the best the restaurant has to offer. A carefully chosen wine list includes a selection of affordable wines by the glass and half-bottle. If you're really into cooking, reserve one of the two "chef tables" adjacent to Chef Warren Geraghty's bustling kitchen.

2881 Granville St. © **604/738-8938.** www.westrestaurant.com. Reservations recommended. Main courses C$22–C$32 lunch, C$37–C$44 dinner; tasting menus C$85–C$98. AE, DC, MC, V. Mon–Fri 11:30am–2:30pm and 5:30–11pm; Sat–Sun 5:30–11pm. Bus: 8.

MODERATE

Café Zen CASUAL   A huge brunch menu, fast and efficient service, reasonable prices, and great eggs Benedict (plus the best French toast in Vancouver) turn this little cafe into a packed dining room by 10am on weekends, when guests spill out the doorway and up the long, steep sidewalk. Sandal-clad traffic from Kits Beach (next door) heads here for breakfast and lunch during the week.

1631 Yew St. (at York). © **604/731-4018.** Main courses C$6–C$12. MC, V. Daily 7am–4pm. Bus: 2, 4, 7, or 22.

Memphis Blues Barbeque House ★ (Finds) BARBECUE   At the busy intersection of Granville and Broadway, this hole-in-the-wall barbecue pit has made a name for itself with corn-pone, Southern-boy barbecue smoked for hours over a low-heat, hardwood fire. Ribs come out tender enough to pull apart with your fingers (which is how food is eaten here; the cutlery is mostly for show), yet still sweet and firm. The beef brisket is cooked long enough that the fat is all rendered out, while the lean flesh remains juicy and tender. The pork butt is slow cooked until you can pull it apart with a fork. Those three meats (plus catfish and Cornish game hen) are essentially what's offered here. Put that meat on greens, and you've got a Southern salad. Put it on bread, and it becomes a sandwich. Serve it on a plate with beans and a potato, and it becomes a meal. Wines are sold by the glass and bottle, but what you want is the ice-cold, home-brewed beer. A second location has opened at 1342 Commercial Dr. (© **604/215-2599**); same hours apply.

1465 W. Broadway. © **604/738-6806.** www.memphisbluesbbq.com. Main courses C$7–C$15; complete meals C$15–C$40. AE, DC, MC, V. Mon–Thurs 11am–10pm; Fri 11am–midnight; Sat noon–midnight; Sun noon–10pm. Bus: 4, 7, or 10.

The SandBar CASUAL   On Fridays and Saturdays, the bar and patio here fill up with 20-something singles and an assortment of baby boomers; a DJ spins at 9pm. Those who aren't ready to tear into the pickup scene can sink their teeth into a number of fairly

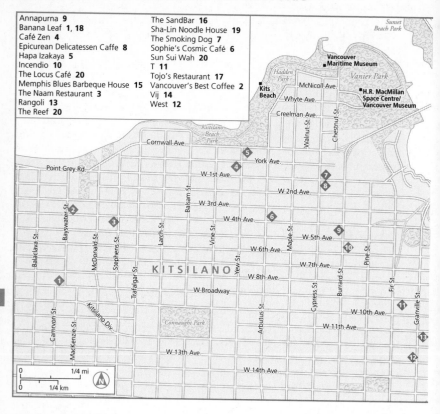

Annapurna **9**	The SandBar **16**
Banana Leaf **1, 18**	Sha-Lin Noodle House **19**
Café Zen **4**	The Smoking Dog **7**
Epicurean Delicatessen Caffe **8**	Sophie's Cosmic Café **6**
Hapa Izakaya **5**	Sun Sui Wah **20**
Incendio **10**	T **11**
The Locus Café **20**	Tojo's Restaurant **17**
Memphis Blues Barbeque House **15**	Vancouver's Best Coffee **2**
The Naam Restaurant **3**	Vij **14**
Rangoli **13**	West **12**
The Reef **20**	

decent tapas and entrees. Shrimp and pork dumplings, lettuce wraps, pad thai, and wok dishes provide the Asian component of a menu that spans the globe. Main courses range from cedar-planked grilled salmon to daily pasta and pizza specials. In summer, the third-floor patio is great for lazing about in the sunshine.

1535 Johnston St., Granville Island. ✆ **604/669-9030.** www.vancouverdine.com. Reservations not accepted for patio. Main courses C$11–C$29; tapas C$6–C$13. AE, MC, V. Sun–Thurs 11:30am–10pm; Fri–Sat 11:30am–11pm. Bus: 50 to Granville Island.

The Smoking Dog FRENCH   To date, the little Kitsilano neighborhood of Yorkville Mews has remained a local secret, perhaps because the few tourists who do venture into this delightful 1-block stretch are immediately confronted with a confusing variety of choices. This bistro with international French-fusion overtones is generally a safe bet for a good meal. The menu features striploin steak with bordelaise sauce, pan-roasted salmon, steamed mussels and fries, sandwiches, and good pastas. If weather permits, take a seat on the heated patio and enjoy the bustling street life. Enjoy live jazz Wednesday and Friday nights.

1889 W. 1st Ave. ✆ **604/732-8811.** www.thesmokingdog.com. Main courses C$15–C$30. AE, DC, MC, V. Mon–Fri 11:30am–10:30pm; Sat 5:30–9:30pm. Bus: 2 or 22.

Trattoria Italian Kitchen ★ ITALIAN The group behind glowbal, Coast, Sanafir, and Italian Kitchen have scored again, this time in Kitsilano. Trattoria is Kits-friendly, meaning it's more casual than their other restaurants, but the standards remain just as high and the prices just as reasonable. You can't make a reservation here, so plan accordingly. The line begins to form at 5:30pm and by 7 you may have to wait an hour or more for a table (you can order a drink while you're waiting). The menu is much the same as Italian Kitchen: excellent pizzas with delicious toppings (lamb sausage with wild mushrooms or mascarpone and fingerling potatoes); pastas like strozzapreti with smoked chicken, linguine carbonara, or the sharable platter of spaghetti and meatballs (the meatballs are made of Kobe beef). Main courses are seasonal and might include seared wild spring salmon or roasted whole trout. The wine list includes all the major Italian vintages.

1850 W. 4th Ave. © **604/732-1441.** www.trattoriakitchen.ca. Reservations not accepted. Main courses C$12–C$16. AE, MC, V. Mon–Fri 11:30am–midnight; Sat–Sun 10:30am–midnight. Bus: 2 or 22.

Vij ★★★ INDIAN Vij doesn't take reservations, as is apparent by the line outside every night, but patrons huddled under the neon sign don't seem to mind since they're treated to tea and *papadums* (a thin bread made from lentils). Inside, the decor is as warm and subtle as the seasonings, which are all roasted, hand-ground, and used with studied delicacy. The menu changes monthly, though some of the more popular entrees remain constant. Recent offerings included beef short ribs in a cinnamon and red-wine curry; eggplant and papaya curry with chickpeas and roasted almonds; and chicken breast in clove, garlic, and yogurt curry. Vegetarian selections abound, including curried vegetable rice pilaf with cilantro cream sauce, and Indian lentils with naan and *raita* (yogurt-mint sauce). The wine and beer list is short but carefully selected. And for teetotalers, Vij has developed a souped-up version of the traditional Indian chai, the chaiuccino. Vij recently opened Rangoli (see below), right next door, for lunch and takeout.

1480 W. 11th Ave. ✆ **604/736-6664.** www.vijs.ca. Reservations not accepted. Main courses C$23–C$26. AE, DC, MC, V. Daily 5:30–10pm. Closed Dec 24–Jan 8. Bus: 8 or 10.

INEXPENSIVE

Annapurna ★ (**Value**) INDIAN/VEGETARIAN   A Kitsilano favorite, Annapurna's small dining room is hung with dozens of white, red, yellow, and orange rice-paper lamps that emanate a soft, warm glow. The menu is all vegetarian, but with the amazing combinations of Indian spices, herbs, and local vegetables, the dishes are rich and satisfying. Appetizers include samosas, *pakoras,* and lentil dumplings soaked in tangy yogurt with chutney. A variety of breads, such as *paratha,* naan, and *chapatis,* are served piping hot. Entrees such as *aloo-ghobi* (potato curry with cauliflower, onions, and cilantro) or *navrattan korma* (seasonal vegetables simmered in poppy-seed paste, flavored with saffron, aniseed, and sliced almonds) can be prepared from mild to screaming hot. The wine list is small but very reasonably priced.

1812 W. 4th Ave. ✆ **604/736-5959.** Main courses C$11–C$13. AE, MC, V. Daily 11:30am–10pm. Bus: 4 or 7.

Incendio West ★ (**Finds**) PIZZA   If you're looking for something casual and local that won't be full of other tourists, this Kitsilano pizzeria is just the spot. The 22 pizza combinations are served on fresh, crispy crusts baked in a wood-fired oven; pastas are homemade. The wine list is decent; the beer list is inspired.

2118 Burrard St. ✆ **604/736-2220.** Main courses C$14–C$24. AE, MC, V. Mon–Thurs 11:30am–3pm and 5–10pm; Fri 11:30am–3pm and 5–11pm; Sat 5–11pm; Sun 4:30–10pm. Closed Dec 23–Jan 3. Bus: 1 or 8.

The Naam Restaurant ★ (**Kids**) VEGETARIAN   Back in the '60s, when Kitsilano was Canada's hippie haven, the Naam was tie-dye central. Things have changed since then, but Vancouver's oldest vegetarian and natural-food restaurant still retains a pleasant granola feel, and it's open 24/7. The decor is simple, earnest, and welcoming, and includes well-worn wooden tables and chairs, plants, an assortment of local art, a nice garden patio, and live music every night. The brazenly healthy fare ranges from all-vegetarian burgers, enchiladas, and burritos to tofu teriyaki, Thai noodles, and a variety of pita pizzas. The sesame spice fries are a Vancouver institution. And though the Naam is not quite vegan, they do offer specialties like the macrobiotic Dragon Bowl of brown rice, tofu, sprouts, and steamed vegetables.

2724 W. 4th Ave. ✆ **604/738-7151.** www.thenaam.com. Reservations accepted on weekdays only. Main courses C$7–C$12. AE, MC, V. Daily 24 hr. Live music every night 7–10pm. Bus: 4 or 22.

Rangoli INDIAN   Vij, reviewed above, takes Indian cuisine to inventive new heights and tastes. But Vij is only open for dinner, so right next door you can get lunch and takeout versions of Vij's curries and other specialties. Try lamb stewed in Vij's masala, spicy pulled pork, or beef in garlic and green-onion curry. A sweet and savory snacks menu is offered from 4 to 8pm: Rice and *paneer* cakes with fresh mango salsa, vegetable samosas, and warm mango custard are some of the offerings. Rangoli has a hip, simple-looking interior with just a few tables and a lot of stainless steel.

1488 W. 11th Ave. ✆ **604/736-5711.** www.vijsrangoli.ca. Reservations not accepted. Main courses C$8.50–C$15. AE, DC, MC, V. Daily 11am–10pm. Bus: 8 or 10.

Sha-Lin Noodle House (Value) CHINESE/DIM SUM   Ever wonder how fresh your noodles really are? At Sha-Lin, you can watch the noodle chef make them right before your eyes. Unique for Vancouver, Sha-Lin is one of the few places where each order of noodles is made from scratch. The chefs mix, knead, toss, stretch, and compress the dough until it almost magically gives way to thin strands. Two or three dishes make a satisfying meal for two; choose from a wide variety of meat and vegetable dishes. For a little entertainment, order the special tea, and watch the server pour it from a meter-long (3-ft.) pot originally designed to allow male servants to maintain a polite distance from an 18th-century Chinese empress. Bare-bones decor but worthwhile food.

548 W. Broadway. ✆ **604/873-1816.** Main courses C$5–C$11. No credit cards. Lunch Wed–Mon 11:30am–3pm; dinner daily 5:30–9:30pm. Bus: 9.

Sophie's Cosmic Café (Kids) FAMILY STYLE/AMERICAN   For a fabulous home-cooked, diner-style breakfast in a laid-back but buzzy atmosphere, come to this Kitsilano landmark. On Sunday morning get here early, or you may have to wait a half-hour or more to get in. You can also have a good, filling lunch or dinner here. Every available space in Sophie's is crammed with toys and knickknacks from the 1950s and 1960s so, understandably, children are inordinately fond of the place. Crayons and coloring paper are always on hand. The menu is simple and includes pastas, burgers and fries, great milkshakes, and a few classic Mexican and "international" dishes, but it's the breakfast menu that draws the crowds.

2095 W. 4th Ave. ✆ **604/732-6810.** www.sophiescosmiccafe.com. Main courses C$5–C$17. MC, V. Daily 8am–9:30pm. Bus: 4 or 7.

7 THE EAST SIDE

These "east side" restaurants are on Main Street, which is on the borderlands between upscale west and working-class east. Main thus has some funky urban authenticity to go with its ever-increasing trendiness.

EXPENSIVE

Sun Sui Wah ★★ CHINESE/DIM SUM/SEAFOOD   One of the most visited and sophisticated Chinese restaurants in town, the award-winning Sun Sui Wah is well known for its seafood. Fresh and varied, the catch of the day can include fresh crab, geoduck, scallops, oyster, prawns, and more. Pick your meal from the tank, or order from the menu if you'd rather not meet your food eye-to-eye before it's cooked. Dim sum is a treat, with the emphasis on seafood. Choices abound for meat lovers and vegetarians, though they will miss out on one of the best seafood feasts in town. The decor is in need of a shake-up, but don't let that stand in your way.

3888 Main St. ✆ **604/872-8822.** www.sunsuiwah.com. Main courses C$12–C$50. AE, DC, MC, V. Daily dim sum 10am–3pm; dinner 5–10:30pm. Bus: 3.

The Locus Café CASUAL/SOUTHWESTERN Even if you arrive by your lonesome, you'll soon have plenty of friends because the Locus is a cheek-by-jowl kind of place, filled with a friendly, funky crowd of artsy Mount Pleasant types. The big bar is overhung with "swamp-gothic" lacquer trees and surrounded by a tier of stools with booths and tiny tables. The cuisine originated in the American Southwest and picked up an edge along the way, as demonstrated in the roasted half-chicken with a cumin-coriander crust and sambuca citrus demi-glace. Keep an eye out for fish specials, such as grilled tomba tuna with a grapefruit and mango glaze. The pan-seared calamari makes a perfect appetizer. Bowen Island Brewing Company provides the beer, so quality's high. Your only real problem is catching the eye of the busy bartender.

4121 Main St. (C) **604/708-4121.** www.locusonmain.com. Reservations recommended. Main courses C$10–C$16. MC, V. Mon–Sat 11am–1:30am; Sun 11am–midnight. Bus: 3.

The Reef (Value) CARIBBEAN The "JERK" in the phone number refers to a spicy marinade of bay leaves, Scotch bonnet peppers, allspice, garlic, soya, green onions, vinegar, and cloves. The Reef serves a number of jerk dishes, including their signature quarter jerk chicken breast. Other dishes are equally tasty, including a tropical salad of fresh mango, red onions, and tomatoes; shrimp with coconut milk and lime juice; grilled blue marlin; and Trenton spiced ribs. With a glass of wine from the thoughtfully selected list you have good dining at a bargain price. Afternoons, the tiny patio is drenched in sunlight, while in the evenings a DJ spins the sounds of the Islands.

4172 Main St. (C) **604/874-JERK** [5375]. www.thereefrestaurant.com. Main courses C$9–C$17. AE, DC, MC, V. Sun–Wed 11am–midnight; Thurs–Sat 11am–1am. Bus: 3.

8 THE NORTH SHORE

EXPENSIVE

The Beach House at Dundarave Pier ★★ PACIFIC NORTHWEST The Beach House offers a panoramic view of English Bay from its waterfront location. Diners on the heated patio get more sunshine, but they miss out on the rich interior of this restored 1912 teahouse. The food is consistently good—innovative, but not so experimental that it leaves the staid West Van burghers gasping for breath. Appetizers include fresh oysters with shaved horseradish; spicy calamari with citrus yogurt; and a salad of crab, shrimp, avocado, and tomato. Entrees usually include linguine with wild prawns, scallops, tomatoes, and chilies; seared tuna in black truffle and red-wine sauce; and braised beef short ribs. The wine list is award winning. The Beach House is a favorite West Van spot for Saturday and Sunday brunch.

150 25th St., West Vancouver. (C) **604/922-1414.** www.thebeachhouserestaurant.ca. Reservations recommended. Main courses C$22–C$35. AE, DC, MC, V. Daily 11am–10pm. Bus: 255 to Ambleside Pier.

Gusto di Quattro ★ ITALIAN West Vancouverites have always had numerous fine-dining options, but for folks in more working-class North Vancouver (to the east of Lions Gate Bridge), times were always tougher. That is until the father-and-son Corsi team opened Gusto di Quattro just steps from the Lonsdale Quay SeaBus Terminal. The menu focuses on central Italy, and the food just seems to get better as the years go by. To start, try the fresh mozzarella wrapped in prosciutto and radicchio and drizzled with cherry vinaigrette, or the grilled calamari in a tomato coulis. Signature main courses include pistachio-crusted black cod; roasted loin pork chop with braised escarole, smoked bacon and rosemary parmesan; and spaghetti quattro, a spicy concoction of minced chicken, black beans, garlic, and chile. The wine list leans heavily toward Italy, offering a good selection of chianti and other table wines.

1 Lonsdale Ave., North Vancouver. © **604/924-4444.** www.quattrorestaurants.com. Reservations recommended. Main courses C$17–C$35. AE, DC, MC, V. Mon–Fri 11:30am–2pm and 5–10pm; Sat–Sun 5–10pm. SeaBus to Lonsdale Quay.

The Salmon House on the Hill ★ PACIFIC NORTHWEST/SEAFOOD High above West Vancouver, the Salmon House offers a spectacular view of the city and Burrard Inlet. An alder-wood-fired grill dominates the kitchen, lending a delicious flavor to many of the dishes. Try the "Uniquely B.C." menu, a three-course meal prepared with ingredients from British Columbia's different regions (C$49). You might start with bison tartare or sablefish eschabeche, go on to alder-grilled salmon with sticky rice, and finish with homemade Frangelico tiramisu.

2229 Folkstone Way, West Vancouver. © **604/926-3212.** www.salmonhouse.com. Reservations recommended for dinner. Main courses C$14–C$32. AE, DC, MC, V. Mon–Sat 11:30am–2pm and 5–10pm; Sun 11am–2pm (brunch) and 5–10pm. Bus: 251 to Queens St.

INEXPENSIVE

The Tomahawk Restaurant (Finds) (Kids) FAMILY STYLE/AMERICAN This is a typical American-style diner with one critical difference that makes it worth a visit: The Tomahawk is packed with native knickknacks and some truly first-class First Nations art. It all started back in 1926 when proprietor Chick Chamberlain began accepting carvings from Burrard Band First Nations in lieu of payment. Over the years, the collection just kept growing. So how's the food? Great, in a burgers-and-fries kind of way. Portions are large, burgers are tasty (many made with organic beef), and milkshakes come so thick the spoon stands up straight as a totem pole. For an "only in B.C." treat, try the oysters on toast.

1550 Philip Ave., North Vancouver. © **604/988-2612.** www.tomahawkrestaurant.com. Reservations not accepted. Main courses C$5–C$17. AE, DC, MC, V. Sun–Thurs 8am–9pm; Fri–Sat 8am–10pm. Bus: 239 to Philip Ave.

9 COFFEE, TEA, SWEETS & ICE CREAM

Caffè Artigiano ★★ (Finds) Absolutely the best lattes in town. The trick is to start with the perfect beans, brew the coffee to an exact temperature, give the steamed milk the respect it deserves, and pour it out ever so slowly, forming a leaf- or heart-shaped pattern in your cup. This is latte-making as an art form. Pop in for a light lunch or pastry, too. The original location at 1101 W. Pender (at Thurlow) in the financial district is less intimate than the digs on Hornby, right across from the Vancouver Art Gallery; the Hornby location has a little outdoor patio perfect for people-watching. A new location is at 740 W. Hastings.

763 Hornby St. © **604/694-7737.** www.caffeartigiano.com. Sweets and sandwiches C$3–C$10. AE, MC, V. Mon–Sat 6:30am–9:30pm; Sun 6:30am–7pm (other locations closed evenings, West Pender closed Sun). Bus: 22.

Epicurean Caffè Bistro (Finds)   The Epicurean brews a mean espresso, a real Italian *caffè* in Kitsilano. Locals and visitors flock to this tiny neighborhood deli, packing the sidewalk spots on nice days or the cozy small tables inside when the weather turns gray. Italian sweets, biscotti, and sorbet go well with any of the coffees, but for a savory treat, have a peek at the glass display case in the back. Freshly made antipasti, cold cuts, salads, panini sandwiches, and risotto are just some of the delectables available for lunch or takeout. Eat-in guests can sip a glass of wine with the fab food. The menu changes regularly, as the owners try out new recipes.

1898 W. 1st Ave. (📞 **604/731-5370.** Everything under C$10. MC, V. Daily 8am–9pm. Bus: 22 to Cornwall and Cypress.

La Casa Gelato ★ (Finds)   No self-respecting ice-cream fiend could possibly pass up a visit to La Casa Gelato, where ice-cream lovers gather for a taste of one or more of the 198 flavors in store. Of course you don't get that many flavors by simply serving up chocolate, vanilla, and strawberry. How about garlic, lavender, durian, basil, or hot chile ice cream, or pear with Gorgonzola sorbet? You're entitled to at least several samples before committing to one or two flavors, so go ahead and be adventurous. The downside: It's quite a trek out to this obscure industrial area near Commercial Drive, and sometimes the novelty tastes don't work as well as they should.

1033 Venables St. (📞 **604/251-3211.** www.lacasagelato.com. Everything under C$7. MC, V. Daily 10am–11pm. Bus: 10 to Commercial and Venables.

Caffeine Nation

"I've never seen so much coffee in all my life. The whole town is on a caffeine jag," said Bette Midler, when she performed in Vancouver.

Though the population had been softened up to the idea by a generation of Italian immigrants, the fine-coffee explosion started first in Seattle, Vancouver's sister city to the south. Vancouver now has more than 60 of the Seattle-based **Starbucks,** as well as **Blenz, Roastmasters,** and other chain cafes. The Starbucks franchises facing each other on Robson and Thurlow are famed for the movie stars who drop in and the regular crowd of bikers who sit sipping lattes on their hogs. Some claim that the city's best java joint—fittingly enough—is **Vancouver's Best Coffee,** 2959 W. 4th Ave. (📞 **604/739-2136**), on a slightly funky section of West 4th Avenue at Bayswater.

Nearly as good and far more politically correct is **Joe's Cafe,** 1150 Commercial Dr. (📞 **604/255-1046;** www.joescafebar.com), in the heart of the immigrant- and activist-laden Commercial Drive area, where lesbian activists, Marxist intellectuals, Guatemalan immigrants, and little old Portuguese men all sit and sip their cappuccinos together peacefully.

For the best lattes, see the review above for Caffè Artigiano. Latte competition has become more intense with the opening of Sciué (p. 96).

Tea for You?

Everyone knows Vancouver runs on coffee, but tea has become the latest craze. The quality of tea depends on its growing region, soil, weather, harvesting season, and ways of processing. You can see (and taste) the difference at **T,** a tasting boutique located on the West Side at 1568 W. Broadway (btw. Granville and Fir; **604/730-8390;** www.tealeaves.com), where over 100 varieties and blends of tea from the four corners of the world are available. Visitors can sample whole leaf, premium leaf iced, and whole leaf pyramid teabags. The boutique also sells spa kits, including the popular Jetlag AM and PM packs. **Moonstruck Tea House,** 1590 Coal Harbour Quay (**604/602-6669;** www.moonstruckteahouse.com), located across from the Westin Bayshore Resort right on the water, has a vast selection of teas, edible flowers, and herbs direct from China's best tea farms. Moonstruck also offers Chinese tea ceremonies for two to four people.

Mink, A Chocolate Cafe ★ (Finds) Baristas can make a fabulous cup of coffee, but chocolate—both hot and cold—is what Mink is all about. This unique chocolate cafe serves exceptionally fine chocolate beverages made with special spices and ingredients (like chipotle). Their little handcrafted (made in Vancouver) chocolate bars are heavenly, and the bonbons . . . well, try one and you'll know what I mean.

863 W. Hastings St. (at Hornby, on west side of Terminal City Club). **866/283-5181** or 604/633-2451. www.minkchocolates.com. Coffee and chocolate drinks C$3.75–C$5.95; chocolates C$1.50–C$5.25. MC, V. Mon–Fri 8am–6pm; Sat–Sun 10am–6pm. Bus: 10, 16, or 20.

Exploring Vancouver

A city perched on the edge of a great wilderness, Vancouver offers unrivaled opportunities for exploring the outdoors. But within the city limits, Vancouver is intensely urban, with buzzy sidewalk cafes and busy shopping streets. The forest of high-rises ringing the central part of the city reminds some visitors of New York or Shanghai, and Chinatown inevitably invites comparisons to San Francisco. But similarities with other places begin to pall as you come to realize that Vancouver is entirely its own creation: a young, self-confident, sparklingly beautiful city like no other place on earth.

1 NEIGHBORHOODS TO EXPLORE

DOWNTOWN Most of Vancouver's commercial and office space is found in a square patch starting at Nelson Street and heading north to the harbor, with Homer and Burrard streets forming the east and west boundaries, respectively. **Canada Place,** on the waterfront facing Burrard Inlet, is the city's huge convention center and cruise-ship terminal. The most interesting avenues for visitors are Georgia, Robson, and Granville streets. **Georgia Street**—in addition to being the prime address for class-A commercial property—is where you'll find the **Vancouver Art Gallery** (p. 120), the Coliseum-shaped **Vancouver Public Library** (p. 154), and the Pacific Centre regional shopping mall. **Robson Street** is "trend central," crammed with designer boutiques, restaurants, and cafes. Rapidly gentrifying **Granville Street** is the home of bars, clubs, theaters, pubs, and restaurants (along with one or two remaining porn shops to add that key touch of seedy authenticity).

THE WEST END This was Vancouver's first upscale neighborhood, settled in the 1890s by the city's budding class of merchant princes. By the 1930s, most of the grand Edwardian homes had become rooming houses, and in the late 1950s some of the Edwardians came down and high-rise apartments went up. The resulting neighborhood owes more to the verticality of Manhattan than to the sprawling cities of the west, though the lush landscaping, gardens, and gorgeous beaches along English Bay and Stanley Park are pure Northwest. All the necessities of life are contained within the West End's border, especially on **Denman** and **Robson streets:** great cafes, good nightclubs, many and varied bookshops, and some of the city's best restaurants. That's part of what makes it such a sought-after address, but it's also the little things, like the street trees, the mix of high-rise condos and sturdy old Edwardians, and the way that, in the middle of such an urban setting, you now and again stumble on a view of the ocean or the mountains.

GASTOWN The oldest section of Vancouver, Gastown has a charm that shines through the souvenir shops and panhandlers. It can be seedy—druggies and winos hang out around its fringes—but it's recently become home to some great new restaurants and stores. It's worth visiting, though, because it's the only section of the city that has the feel of an old Victorian town—the buildings stand shoulder to shoulder, and cobblestones

Legend:

Bill Reid Gallery of Northwest Art **4**

Canada Place **5**

Dr. Sun Yat-sen Classical Chinese Garden **10**

H.R. MacMillan Space Centre **2**

Science World at TELUS World of Science **11**

Steam Clock **6**

Vancouver Art Gallery **3**

Vancouver Centennial Police Museum **9**

Vancouver Lookout **7**

Vancouver Maritime Museum **1**

Vancouver Museum **2**

Vancouver Public Library **8**

**Map labels:**

Burrard Inlet

CHINATOWN

GASTOWN

YALETOWN

WEST END

False Creek

English Bay

Burrard Inlet

Portside Park

Creekside Park

Livingstone Park

Cooper's Park

Crab Park

David Lam Park

George Wainborn Park

Nelson Park

Sunset Beach Park

Vanier Park

Main St.

Powell St.

Hastings St.

National Ave.

Main Street

Columbia St.

Carrall St.

Maple Tree Square

Chinatown Gate

Water St.

Abbott St.

Sun Tower

GM Place

Cambie St.

B.C. Place Stadium

Stadium

Beatty St.

Expo Blvd

Pender St.

Granville St.

Dunsmuir St.

Homer St.

Georgia St.

Robson St.

SKYTRAIN

Cambie St.

Hamilton St.

Mainland St.

Yaletown-Roundhouse

The Roundhouse

Pacific Blvd

Vancouver Convention & Exhibition Centre

Waterfront Sta.

Waterfront

Marine Bldg.

Howe St.

Burrard St.

Cordova St.

Hastings St.

Pender St.

Melville St.

Granville

Vancouver City Centre

CANADA LINE

Richards St.

Smithe St.

Nelson St.

Seymour St.

Helmcken St.

Fairmont Hotel Vancouver

Robson Sq.

Provincial Law Courts

Drake St.

Alberni St.

Robson St.

Haro St.

Barclay St.

Comox St.

Pendrell St.

Davie St.

Harwood St.

Pacific St.

Beach Ave.

Burrard St.

Hornby St.

Howe St.

Granville St.

Bute St.

Thurlow St.

Jervis St.

Nicola St.

Cardero St.

Bidwell St.

Roedde House Museum

Nelson Park

Burnaby St.

Broughton St.

Chestnut St.

Granville Island Public Market

Inukshuk

1/4 mi

1/4 km

line the streets. The current Gastown was built from scratch just a few months after an 1886 fire wiped out the entire city. (Photographs of the time show proper-looking men in black coats selling real estate out of tents erected on the still-smoking ashes.) Also, rents in Gastown have stayed low, so it's still the place to look for a new and experimental art gallery, a young fashion designer setting up shop, or a piece of beautiful, hand-carved First Nations art in one of the galleries along **Water** and **Hastings streets.** It's also the setting for the famous Steam Clock on Water Street (see "Walking Tour 2: Gastown & Chinatown," in chapter 9).

Alcohol has always been a big part of Gastown's history. The neighborhood is named for a saloonkeeper—Gassy Jack Deighton—who, according to local legend, talked the local mill hands into building a saloon as Vancouver's first structure in return for all the whiskey they could drink. Nowadays, Gastown is still liberally endowed with pubs and clubs—it's one of two or three areas where Vancouverites congregate when the sun goes down.

CHINATOWN   Even though much of Vancouver's huge Asian population has moved out to Richmond, Chinatown remains a kick because it hasn't become overtly touristy. For the tens of thousands of Cantonese-speaking Canadians who live in the surrounding neighborhoods, Chinatown is simply the place they go to shop. And for many others who have moved to more outlying neighborhoods, it's still one of the best places to come and eat. One of North America's more populous Chinatowns, the area was settled about the same time as the rest of Vancouver, by migrant laborers brought in to build the Canadian Pacific Railway. Many white settlers resented the Chinese labor, and race riots periodically broke out. At one point, Vancouver's Chinatown was surrounded with Belfast-like security walls. By the 1940s and 1950s, however, the area was mostly threatened with neglect. The 1970s saw a serious plan to tear the whole neighborhood down and put in a freeway, but a huge protest stopped that, and now the area's future seems secure. For visitors, the fun is to simply wander, look, and taste.

YALETOWN & FALSE CREEK NORTH   Vancouver's former meatpacking and warehouse district, Yaletown has been converted to an area of apartment lofts, nightclubs, restaurants, and a fledgling multimedia biz. It's a relatively tiny area, and the main streets of interest are **Mainland, Hamilton,** and **Davie.** For visitors, it features some interesting cafes, high-end shops, and a kind of gritty urban feel. This old-time authenticity provides an essential anchor to the brand-new bevy of towers that have risen in the past 10 years on **Pacific Boulevard** along the north edge of False Creek. Officially (and unimaginatively) called False Creek North, the area is more often referred to as "the Concorde lands" after the developer, or "the Expo lands" after the world's fair held in 1986 on the land where the towers now stand. Where the shiny newness of Concorde can prove a little disconcerting, gritty Yaletown provides the antidote. And vice versa. The two neighborhoods are slowly melding into one wonderful whole.

GRANVILLE ISLAND   Part crafts fair, part farmers market, part artist's workshop, part mall, and part industrial site, Granville Island seems to have it all. Some 25 years ago, the federal government decided to try its hand at a bit of urban renewal, so they took this piece of industrial waterfront and redeveloped it into . . . well, it's hard to describe. But everything you could name is here: theaters, pubs, restaurants, artists' studios, bookstores, crafts shops, an art school, a hotel, a cement plant, and lots and lots of people. One of the most enjoyable ways to experience the Granville Island atmosphere is to head down to the **Granville Island Public Market** (p. 167), grab a latte (and perhaps a piece of cake or pie to boot), then wander outside to enjoy the view of the boats, the buskers, and the children endlessly chasing flocks of squawking seagulls.

KITSILANO   Hard to believe, but in the 1960s Kitsilano was a neighborhood that had fallen on hard times. Nobody respectable wanted to live there—the 1920s homes had all been converted to cheap rooming houses—so hippies moved in. The neighborhood became Canada's Haight-Ashbury, with coffeehouses, head shops, and lots of incense and long hair. Once the boomer generation stopped raging against the machine, they realized that Kitsilano—right next to the beach, but not quite downtown—was a very groovy place to live indeed, and a fine place to own property. Real estate began an upward trend that has never stopped, and "Kits" became thoroughly yuppified. Nowadays, it's a fun place to wander. You will discover great bookstores and trendy furniture and housewares shops, lots of consignment clothing stores, snowboard shops, coffee everywhere, and lots of places to eat (every third storefront is a restaurant). The best parts of Kitsilano are the stretch of **West 4th Avenue** between Burrard and Balsam streets, and **West Broadway** between Macdonald and Alma streets. Oh, and **Kits Beach** (p. 136), of course, with that fabulous heated saltwater swimming pool.

COMMERCIAL DRIVE   Known as "The Drive," Commercial Drive is the 12-block section from Venables Street to East 6th Avenue. The Drive has a less glitzy, more down-to-earth, fading counterculture feel to it. It's an old immigrant neighborhood that, like everyplace else in Vancouver, has been rediscovered. The first wave of Italians left old-fashioned, delightfully tacky cafes such as **Calabria,** 1745 Commercial Dr. (✆ **604/253-7017**), and **Caffe Amici,** 1344 Commercial Dr. (✆ **604/255-7879**). More recent waves of Portuguese, Hondurans, and Guatemalans have also left their mark. And lately, lesbians, vegans, and artists have moved in—the shops and restaurants reflect the mix. Think Italian cafe next to the Marxist bookstore across from the vegan deli. After the relentless see-and-be-seen scene in the West End, it's nice to come out to the Drive for a bit of unpretentious fun.

SHAUGHNESSY   Distances within the Shaughnessy neighborhood aren't conducive for a comfortable stroll, but Shaughnessy is a great place to drive or bike, especially in the spring when trees and gardens are blossoming. Designed in the 1920s as an enclave for Vancouver's budding elite, this is Vancouver's Westmount or Nob Hill. Thanks to the stranglehold Shaughnessy exerts on local politics—every second mayor hails from this neighborhood—traffic flow is carefully diverted away from the area, and it takes a little bit of driving around to find your way in. It's an effort worth making, however, if only to see the stately homes and monstrous mansions, many of which are now featured in film shoots or rented by Hollywood movie stars while they're in town filming. This is also home to many old Vancouver families with a pioneer past. To find the neighborhood, look on the map for the area of curvy and convoluted streets between Cypress and Oak streets and 12th and 32nd avenues. The center of opulence is the Crescent, an elliptical street to the southwest of Granville and 16th Avenue.

RICHMOND   Twenty years ago, Richmond was mostly farmland with a bit of sleepy suburb. Now it's Asia West, an agglomeration of shopping malls geared to the new—read: rich, educated, and successful—Chinese immigrant. The residential areas of the city are not worth visiting (unless tract homes are your thing), but malls like the **Aberdeen Mall** or the **Yaohan Centre** are something else. It's like getting into your car in Vancouver and getting out in Hong Kong. For information on the famous Richmond Night Market, see "A Special Vancouver Experience: Asian Night Markets," p. 162.

PUNJABI MARKET   India imported. Most of the businesses on this 4-block stretch of Main Street, from 48th up to 52nd Avenue, are run by and cater to Indo-Canadians, primarily Punjabis. The area is best seen during business hours, when the fragrant scent of spices wafts out from food stalls, and the sound of Hindi pop songs blares from hidden speakers. Young brides hunt through sari shops or seek out suitable material in discount textile outlets. **Frontier Cloth House,** 6695 Main St. (© **604/325-4424**), specializes in richly colored silk saris, shawls, fabrics, and costume jewelry.

2 THE TOP ATTRACTIONS

DOWNTOWN & THE WEST END

Bill Reid Gallery of Northwest Coast Art ★★   Newly opened in 2008, this downtown museum-gallery showcases the work of the great Northwest coast aboriginal artist Bill Reid, who died in 1994 (see "Bill Reid: First Among First Nation Artists," in chapter 2). Permanent installations include the Raven's Trove: Gold Masterworks by Bill Reid; the monumental bronze sculpture Mythic Messengers, Reid's masterful composition of 11 intertwined figures recounting traditional Haida myths; a monumental cedar tribute pole carved by Haida Chief 7idansuu (Jim Hart) honoring Reid. Two exhibition spaces feature rotating exhibitions of Northwest Coast art, cultural performances, and lectures. The gift shop offers a good selection of Northwest Coast Native art, books, jewelry, and museum-quality collectibles.

639 Hornby St. © 604/682-3455. www.billreidgallery.ca. Admission C$10 adults, C$7 seniors and students, C$5 children 6–17, C$25 families. Summer Tues–Fri 10am–5pm, Sat–Sun 11am–5pm; winter Weds–Sun 11am–5pm.

Canada Place ★★   If you've never been to Vancouver, this is a good place to orient yourself and see some of what makes B.C.'s largest city so special. (Or you may arrive here on a cruise ship, in which case this will be your first introduction to Vancouver.) With its five tall Teflon sails and bowsprit jutting out into Burrard Inlet, Canada Place is meant to resemble a giant sailing ship. Inside it's a convention center on one level and a giant cruise-ship terminal below, with the Pan Pacific Hotel (p. 74) perched on top. Around the perimeter is a promenade, offering wonderful views across Burrard Inlet to the North Shore peaks and toward nearby Stanley Park, with plaques explaining the sights and providing historical tidbits. Continue around the promenade, and you'll get great city views and be able to see the older, low-rise buildings of Gastown, where Vancouver began. Bus sightseeing tours begin here, there's an **IMAX Theatre** (© **604/682-IMAX** [4629]), and the Tourism Vancouver Touristinfo Centre (see "Visitor Information," chapter 5) is right across the street. In 2009 the new addition to the Canada Place Convention Centre opened. With its amazing "green" roof, marvelous light-filled interior spaces, and wonderful plazas and walkways, it has transformed the area adjacent to the "old" Canada Place.

Canada Place at the end of Burrard St. Promenade daily 24 hr. Bus: 1 or 5.

Stanley Park ★★★ **(Kids)**   The green jewel of Vancouver, Stanley Park is a 400-hectare (1,000-acre) rainforest jutting out into the ocean from the edge of the busy West End. Exploring the second-largest urban forest in Canada is one of Vancouver's quintessential experiences.

The park, created in 1888, is filled with towering western red cedar and Douglas fir, manicured lawns, flower gardens, placid lagoons, and countless shaded walking trails that meander through it all. The famed **seawall** ★★★ runs along the waterside edge of the

Horse-drawn Carriage Rides **2**
Lost Lagoon Nature House **1**
Stanley Park's Children's Farm **5**
Stanley Park's Miniature Railway **6**
Totem Poles **3**
Vancouver Aquarium
Marine Science Centre **4**

Burrard   Inlet

Brockton Pt.

Girl in a Wet Suit

Brockton
Oval

*Deadman's
Island*

Brockton Oval Tr.

Anson W.

Brockton Point Tr.

Stanley Park Dr.

*Coal
Harbour*

Malkin
Bowl

Vancouver
Rowing Club

Japanese Monument

Garden of
Remembrance

Stanley Park Dr.

Tunnel Tr.

Pipeline Rd

Lions Gate Bridge

Prospect Pt.

*Beaver
Lake*

Beaver Lake Tr.

Hanson Tr.

Lake Tr.

Stanley Park Causeway

North Creek Tr.

Bridle Path

Raccoon Tr.

Thompson Tr.

Tatlow Walk

Lovers Walk

Lee's Tr.

Rawlings Tr.

Lagoon Dr. N

Lost Lagoon

Georgia St.

Alberni St.

Chilco St.

Fish House
Restaurant

Stanley Park Dr.

Seawall Walk

Siwash Rock

Fergson Pt.

Third   Beach

Second
Beach

*English
Bay*

EXPLORING VANCOUVER

8

THE TOP ATTRACTIONS

1/4 mi

1/4 km

N

Stanley (Fun) Park

Stanley Park is the scene of several yearly events that have become part of the collective consciousness of Vancouverites. From the last weekend in November to early January, the Miniature Railway becomes the **Bright Nights Christmas Train** and runs through a forest illuminated with thousands of festive lights. For three weeks in October, the train is transformed into the **Stanley Park Halloween Ghost Train,** with actors portraying vampires and ghouls scaring delighted passengers as the train puffs through the forest. From June to August, **Dance at Dusk** takes place Monday through Wednesday (on good-weather evenings) from 7 to 9:30pm, near Ceperley Playground's red fire engine. No partner is required, all ages are welcome, instruction is provided, and it's free. Summer is also the time to enjoy **Theatre Under the Stars,** a Stanley Park tradition at the Malkin Bowl since 1934. In mid-July thousands of Vancouverites participate in the **Walk With the Dragon** festival, following a giant Chinese dragon along the entire length of the seawall. See the Stanley Park website (http://vancouver.ca/parks) for dates and details.

park, allowing cyclists and pedestrians to experience the magical interface of forest, sea, and sky. One of the most popular free attractions in the park is the **collection of totem poles** ★★★ at Brockton Point, most of them carved in the 1980s to replace the original ones that were placed in the park in the 1920s and 1930s. The area around the totem poles features open-air displays on the Coast Salish First Nations and a small gift shop/ visitor information center.

The park is home to lots of wildlife, including beavers, coyotes, bald eagles, blue herons, cormorants, trumpeter swans, brant geese, ducks, raccoons, skunks, and gray squirrels imported from New York's Central Park decades ago and now quite at home in the Pacific Northwest. (No, there are no bears.) For directions and maps, brochures, and exhibits on the nature and ecology of Stanley Park, visit the **Lost Lagoon Nature House** (© 604/257-8544; open 10am–7pm July 1 to Labour Day, weekends only outside this period; free admission). On Sundays at 1pm, rain or shine, they offer Discovery Walks of the park (pre-registration recommended). Equally nature-focused but with way more wow is the **Vancouver Aquarium** ★★ (see below). The **Stanley Park's Children's Farm** (© 604/257-8531) is a petting zoo with peacocks, rabbits, calves, donkeys, and Shetland ponies. Next to the petting zoo is **Stanley Park's Miniature Railway** ★ (© 604/257-8531), a diminutive steam locomotive that pulls passenger cars on a circuit through the woods.

Swimmers head to **Third Beach** and **Second Beach** (p. 136), the latter with an outdoor pool beside English Bay. For kids there's a free **Spray Park** near Lumberman's Arch, where they can run and splash through various water-spewing fountains. Perhaps the best way to explore the park is to rent a bike (p. 137) or in-line skates, and set off along the seawall. If you decide to walk, remember the free shuttle bus that circles the park every 15 minutes, allowing passengers to alight and descend at most of the park's many attractions. The wonderful **horse-drawn carriage ride** ★★★ operated by **AAA Horse &**

Carriage Ltd. (© 604/681-5115; www.stanleypark.com) is one of the most enjoyable **119** ways to tour the park. Carriage tours depart every 20 minutes mid-March through October from the lower aquarium parking lot on Park Drive near the Georgia Street park entrance. The ride lasts an hour and covers portions of the park that many locals have never seen. Rates are C$27 for adults, C$25 for seniors and students, and C$15 for children 3 to 12.

Of the three restaurants located in the park, the best is the **Fish House in Stanley Park** (p. 99), where you can have lunch, afternoon tea, or dinner.

Stanley Park. © **604/257-8400.** http://vancouver.ca/parks. Free admission; charge for individual attractions. Park does not close. Bus: 23, 35, or 135; free "Around the Park" shuttle bus circles the park at 15-min. intervals mid-June to late Sept (visitors can get off and on at 14 points of interest). Parking entire day C$7 summer, C$4 winter.

Vancouver Aquarium Marine Science Centre ★★ (Kids) One of North America's largest and best, the Vancouver Aquarium houses more than 8,000 marine species. From platforms above or through underwater viewing windows you can watch the white beluga whales flashing through their pools. (One of the belugas gave birth in June 2008, and as of press time another one is expecting.) There are also sea otters, Steller sea lions, and a Pacific white-sided dolphin. During regularly scheduled shows, the aquarium staff explains marine-mammal behavior while working with these impressive creatures. The Wild Coast area features a fascinating assortment of fish and sea creatures found in local waters, and an exhibit called "Frogs Forever" is dedicated to our friends, the amphibious frogs.

For a substantial extra fee (C$150 per person, C$210 adult and one child age 8–12), you can have a behind-the-scenes Beluga Encounter, helping to feed these giant white cetaceans, then head up to the Marine Mammal deck to take part in the belugas' regular training session. Beluga encounters are available daily from 9 to 10:30am, with extra encounters on weekends between 2 and 4pm. Other Animal Encounter tours take visitors behind the scenes to interact with dolphins (C$195 adult, C$270 adult and child), or help feed the Steller sea lions (C$35 adult, C$15 child), sea turtles (C$35 adult, C$15 child), and sea otters (C$25 adult, C$15 child). Animal Encounter tours are available daily but times vary. Call © **800/931-1186** to reserve all of these programs ahead of time. Children must be 8 or older to participate.

Stanley Park. © **604/659-FISH** [3474]. www.vanaqua.org. Admission C$20 adults; C$15 seniors, students, and youths 13–18; C$12 children 4–12; free for children 3 and under. Summer daily 9am–7pm; winter daily 9:30am–5pm. Bus: 135; "Around the Park" shuttle bus June–Sept only. Parking C$7 summer, C$4 winter.

A Mighty Wind

In the early morning hours of December 15, 2006, a major windstorm struck Stanley Park and left, after 2 short hours of gale-force winds, a level of devastation that had not been seen since Hurricane Frieda in 1962. The gusting winds blew down an estimated 5,000 to 10,000 trees, mostly on the west side, leveling more than 41 hectares (100 acres) of the park's 243 hectares (600 acres) of forest. Large waves and falling trees also damaged sections of the seawall. The structural damage has now been repaired, but it will be decades before Stanley Park's forest regenerates to anything like what it was.

Vancouver Art Gallery ★★   Designed as a courthouse by B.C.'s leading early-20th-century architect Francis Rattenbury (the architect of Victoria's Empress Hotel and the Parliament buildings), and renovated into an art gallery by B.C.'s leading late-20th-century architect Arthur Erickson, the Gallery is an excellent stop to see what sets Canadian and West Coast art apart from the rest of the world. Along with an impressive collection of paintings by B.C. native **Emily Carr** ★★★ are examples of a unique Canadian art style created during the 1920s by members of the "Group of Seven," which included Vancouver painter Fred Varley. The Gallery also hosts rotating exhibits of contemporary sculpture, graphics, photography, and video art from around the world. Geared to younger audiences, the Annex Gallery offers rotating presentations of visually exciting educational exhibits.

750 Hornby St. 📞 **604/662-4719.** www.vanartgallery.bc.ca. Admission C$18 adults, C$13 seniors, C$12 students, C$7 children 5–12, C$47 families, Tues 5–9pm by donation. Wed and Fri–Mon 10am–5:30pm; Tues and Thurs 10am–9pm. SkyTrain: Granville. Bus: 3.

GASTOWN & CHINATOWN

Dr. Sun Yat-Sen Classical Chinese Garden ★★   This small reproduction of a Classical Chinese scholar's garden truly is a remarkable place, but to get the full effect, it's best to take the free guided tour. Untrained eyes will only see a pretty pond surrounded by bamboo and oddly shaped rocks. The engaging guides, however, can explain this unique urban garden's Taoist yin-yang design principle, in which harmony is achieved through dynamic opposition. To foster opposition (and thus harmony) in the garden, Chinese designers place contrasting elements in juxtaposition: Soft-moving water flows across solid stone; smooth, swaying bamboo grows around gnarled immovable rocks; dark pebbles are placed next to light pebbles in the paving. Moving with the guide, you discover the symbolism of intricate carvings and marvel at the subtle, ever-changing views from covered serpentine corridors. This is one of two Classical Chinese gardens in North America (the other is in Portland, OR) created by master artisans from Suzhou, the garden city of China.

578 Carrall St. www.vancouverchinesegarden.com. C$8.75 adults, C$7 seniors and students, free for children 5 and under, C$20 family pass. Free guided tour included. May–June 14 and Sept daily 10am–6pm; June 15–Aug daily 9:30am–7pm; Oct–Apr Tues–Sun 10am–4:30pm. Bus: 19 or 22.

Vancouver Centennial Police Museum   If you have a real fascination with crime, this museum will occupy an hour of your time; if not, I wouldn't recommend a visit. It's a well-meaning, old-fashioned place housed in the old Vancouver Coroner's Court

---

360 Degrees of Vancouver

The most popular (and most touristed) spot from which to view Vancouver's skyline and surrounding topography is high atop the space needle observation deck at the **Vancouver Lookout** ★, 555 W. Hastings St. (📞 **604/689-0421;** www.vancouver lookout.com). It's a great place for first-time visitors who want a panorama of the city. The 360-degree view is remarkable (yes, that is Mt. Baker looming above the southeastern horizon), but the signage could be a lot better. Skylift admission is C$13 for adults, C$11 for seniors, C$9 for students and youths 11 to 17, C$6 children 4 to 10, and free for children 3 and under. It's open daily in summer from 8:30am to 10:30pm and in winter from 9am to 9pm. Tickets are valid for the entire day.

In a Summer Garden

Every Friday evening at 7:30pm from mid-July through the first weekend in September, the Dr. Sun Yat-Sen Classical Chinese Garden is the scene of musical performances and dances. The eclectic repertoire includes classical, Asian, world, Gypsy jazz, Slavic soul, and fusion music. Shows cost C$18 and often sell out. The website provides a full listing of concerts; call ℭ **604/662-3207** to reserve tickets.

(where actor Errol Flynn was autopsied in 1959 after dropping dead in the arms of a 17-year-old girl) and dedicated to memorializing some of the best cops and worst crimes in the city's short but colorful history. The confiscated illegal-weapons display is hair-raising; you can also see the old morgue, a simulated autopsy room (with pieces of damaged body parts in specimen bottles), and a forensics lab (sleuths of all ages can partake in the Forensic Science program on Sun noon–4pm). More fun and a lot more fascinating is the 2-hour **Sins of the City Walking Tour** ★, which departs from the museum Wednesdays at 2pm and Fridays and Saturdays at 4pm (early May to late Sept) and covers (or uncovers) the history of vice in a 10-block area around the museum. Tour cost (which includes museum entrance) is C$15 for adults, C$12 seniors and students; it's essential to make reservations 1 day ahead.

240 E. Cordova St. ℭ **604/665-3346.** www.vancouverpolicemuseum.ca. Admission C$7 adults; C$5 seniors, students, and youths 7–13; C$20 families. Mon–Sat 9am–5pm. Bus: 4 or 7.

THE WEST SIDE

Granville Island ★★★ (**Kids**)   Almost a city within a city, Granville Island is a good place to browse away a morning, an afternoon, or a whole day. You can wander through a busy public market jammed with food stalls, shop for crafts, pick up some fresh seafood, enjoy a great dinner, watch the latest theater performance, rent a yacht, stroll along the waterfront, or simply run through the sprinkler on a hot summer day; it's all there and more. If you only have a short period of time, make sure you spend at least part of it in the **Granville Island Public Market** ★★★, one of the best all-around markets in North America.

Once a declining industrial site, Granville Island started transforming in the late 1970s when the government encouraged new, people-friendly developments. Maintaining its original industrial look, the former warehouses and factories now house galleries, artist studios, restaurants, and theaters; the cement plant on the waterfront is the only industrial tenant left. Access to Granville Island is by Aquabus from the West End, Yale-town, or Kitsilano (see "By Miniferry," in chapter 5; the Aquabus drops you at the public market) or by foot, bike, or car across the bridge at Anderson Street (access from W. 2nd Ave.). Avoid driving over on weekends and holidays—you'll spend more time trying to find a parking place than in the galleries. Check the website for upcoming events or stop by the information center, behind the Kids Market. Also see "Walking Tour 3," p. 154.

If you can't bear to leave the island, consider staying at the **Granville Island Hotel** (p. 83). Even if you don't stay, it's worth stopping by the hotel's brewpub restaurant, the Dockside Brewery Company, for a brew with a view.

Granville's Greatest Hits

Even though the bustling **Public Market** ★★★ makes a fine destination in itself, Granville Island offers much more. To really get a feel for this neighborhood, stroll along the side streets and explore the alleys and lanes away from the main entrance. Check out the recommended attractions below.

- Railspur Alley's 12 artist studios are perfect for browsing; stop in at **Al'Arte Silk** in the Alley Gallery (1369 Railspur Alley; *©* **604/357-1300**) to see some of the beautifully hand-painted wearable silk art; check out the wares at **Artisan Sake** (1339 Railspur Alley; *©* **604/685-7253**), Canada's first boutique premium sake winery; or pause at the **Agro Café** (1363 Railspur Alley; *©* **604/669-0724**) for a latte and pastry.

- Art exhibits in the North Building at the **Emily Carr Institute of Art + Design,** 1399 Johnston St., (*©* **604/844-3800;** www.ecuad.ca), showcase the works of the institute's grads and students. You may be looking at the next Andy Warhol. Media and Concourse Galleries are free and open daily 10am to 5pm; the Charles H. Scott Gallery, showing exhibits of international work, is open Monday to Friday noon to 5pm, Saturday and Sunday 10am to 5pm.

- In summer, check the **Performance Works** (*©* **604/687-3020;** www.gi culturalsociety.org) schedule for free outdoor Shakespearean plays, or see what's playing at the **Arts Club Theatre** (*©* **604/687-1644;** www.artsclub. com) or **Waterfront Theatre** (*©* **604/685-1731**).

- Paddle off into the sunset by renting a kayak from one of the marinas on the west side of the island. Beginners can take lessons or head out on a guided tour. **Ecomarine Ocean Kayak Centre** (*©* **604/689-7575;** www. ecomarine.com) has everything to get you started. A 3-hour kayak lesson for C$72 teaches you the basic strokes. Or explore the waters of False Creek and English Bay on a 2¹⁄₂-hour tour with a guide for C$59. Experienced paddlers can rent single or double kayaks (C$69 single kayak, C$99 double kayak for full day).

- Granville Island is one big playground. On a rainy day, duck into the **Kids Only Market** (daily 10am–6pm) to check out toys, kites, clothes, art supplies, and an indoor play area. On warm days, the free **waterpark** is the place to be. Open daily (weather permitting) from 10am to 6pm, late May until Labour Day.

Located on the south shore of False Creek, under the Granville St. Bridge. For studio and gallery hours and other information about Granville Island, contact the information center at *©* **604/666-5784.** www. granvilleisland.com. Public market daily 9am–7pm. For information on getting to Granville Island, see "By Miniferry," in chapter 5. Bus: 50.

H. R. MacMillan Space Centre ★ **Kids** In the same building as the Vancouver Museum (see below), the space center and observatory has hands-on displays and exhibits that will delight budding astronomy buffs and their parents (or older space buffs and their children). Displays are highly interactive: In the Cosmic Courtyard, you can try

Arts Club Theatre **6**
Emily Carr Institute **1**
Kids Market **5**
Museums **7**
Net Loft **8**
Public Market **9**
Railspur Alley **2**
Waterfront Theatre **4**
Waterpark **3**

designing a spacecraft or maneuvering a lunar robot. Or, punch a button and get a video explanation of the *Apollo 17* manned-satellite engine that stands before you. The exciting **Virtual Voyages Simulator** ★★ takes you on a voyage to Mars—it's a thrilling experience for kids and adults. In the GroundStation Canada Theatre, video presentations explore Canada's contributions to the space program and space in general. The Star Theatre shows movies—many of them for children—on an overhead dome. The Planetarium Star Theatre features exciting laser shows in the evening.

1100 Chestnut St., in Vanier Park. © **604/738-7827.** www.hrmacmillanspacecentre.ca. Admission C$15 adults; C$11 seniors, students, and children 5–10; C$7 children 4 and under; C$45 families (up to 5, maximum 2 adults). Evening laser shows C$11 each. Tues–Sun 10am–5pm; evening laser shows Fri–Sat 8, 9:15, and 10:20pm. Closed Dec 25. Bus: 22.

Museum of Anthropology ★★★ (Kids) This isn't just any old museum. In 1976, B.C. architect Arthur Erickson created a classic native post-and-beam-style structure out of poured concrete and glass to house one of the world's finest collections of Northwest Coast Native art. A major renovation in 2009 more than doubled the gallery space and added new luster to this remarkable showplace.

Enter through doors that resemble a huge, carved, bent-cedar box. Artifacts from different coastal communities flank the ramp leading to the Great Hall's **collection of totem poles.** Haida artist Bill Reid's cedar bear and sea wolf sculptures sit at the Cross Roads; Reid's masterpiece, ***The Raven and the First Men,*** is worth the price of admission all by itself. The huge carving in glowing yellow cedar depicts a Haida creation myth, in which Raven—the trickster—coaxes humanity out into the world from its birthplace in a clamshell. Some of Reid's fabulous jewelry creations in gold and silver are also on display.

The **Masterpiece Gallery**'s argillite sculptures, beaded jewelry, and hand-carved ceremonial masks lead the way to the Visible Storage Galleries, where more than 15,000 artifacts are arranged by culture. You can open the glass-topped drawers to view small treasures and stroll past larger pieces housed in tall glass cases.

Also at the museum is the somewhat incongruous Koerner Ceramics Gallery, a collection of European ceramics.

Behind the museum, overlooking Point Grey, are two **longhouses** built according to the Haida tribal style, resting on the traditional north-south axis. Ten hand-carved totem poles stand in attendance along with contemporary carvings on the longhouse facades. *Note:* You might want to visit the nearby UBC Botanical Garden and Nitobe Japanese Garden (see below). A number of trails also lead down to a few of Vancouver's most pristine beaches (p. 136).

6393 NW Marine Dr. (at Gate 4). 🄒 **604/822-3825.** www.moa.ubc.ca. Admission C$9 adults; C$7 seniors, students, and children 6–18; free for children 5 and under; free Tues 5–9pm. Summer Wed–Mon 10am–5pm, Tues 10am–9pm; winter Wed–Sun 11am–5pm, Tues 11am–9pm. Closed Dec 25–26. Bus: 4 or 99 (10-min. walk from UBC bus loop).

Science World at TELUS World of Science ★ 🄺ids   Science World is impossible to miss: It's the big blinking geodesic dome (built for Expo '86 and now partnered with TELUS, a telephone company, hence the branded name) on the eastern end of False Creek. Inside, it's a hands-on scientific discovery center where you and your kids can light up a plasma ball, walk through a 160-sq.-m (1,722-sq.-ft.) maze, wander through the interior of a camera, create a cyclone, watch a zucchini explode as it's charged with 80,000 volts, stand inside a beaver lodge, play in wrist-deep magnetic liquids, create music with a giant synthesizer, and watch mind-bending three-dimensional slide and laser shows as well as other optical effects. Science World is loaded with first-rate adventures for kids from toddler age to early teens; you'll want to spend at least a couple of hours here. Throughout the day, special shows, many with nature themes, are presented in the OMNIMAX Theatre—a huge projecting screen equipped with surround sound.

1455 Quebec St. 🄒 **604/443-7443.** www.scienceworld.ca. Admission C$18 adults, C$15 seniors and students, C$12 children 4–17, free for children 3 and under, C$62 family pass for 6 related people. Combination tickets additional C$5 for OMNIMAX film. Sept–June Mon–Fri 10am–5pm, Sat–Sun 10am–6pm; July–Aug daily 10am–6pm; holidays 10am–6pm. SkyTrain: Main St.–Science World.

Steam Clock 🄺ids   The Steam Clock in Gastown is a favorite photo op for tourists, but you're not missing much if you miss it. Built by horologist Raymond Saunders in 1977 (based on an 1875 design), it's the only steam clock in the world, powered by steam from an underground system of pipes that supply heat to many downtown buildings. The clock is supposed to sound its whistles (playing "The Westminster Chimes") every quarter-hour as the steam shoots out from vents at the top. Sometimes, however, it simply steams with no musical accompaniment. It's a stop on my "Gastown & Chinatown" walking tour in chapter 9.

Gastown, at the intersection of Water and Cambie sts. Free.

UBC Botanical Garden & Nitobe Japanese Garden ★   Serious plant lovers will love the University of British Columbia. The prime attraction on campus, besides the must-see Museum of Anthropology (see above), is the 28-hectare (69-acre) **UBC Botanical Garden,** home to more than 10,000 species of trees, shrubs, and flowers grouped into a B.C. native garden, a physic (or medicinal) garden, a food garden, and several others. You can also peruse the excellent plant and seed store. (*Note:* You can't bring plants in soil across the U.S. border, or back into most countries, including the U.K.) Give yourself at least an hour if you want to explore this garden; an audio guide is available for C$2. Nearby is the **Nitobe Memorial Garden,** a beautiful traditional Japanese garden considered among the top five Japanese gardens in North America and one of the most authentic Tea and Stroll Gardens outside of Japan. Cherry blossoms peak in April and May, the irises bloom in June, and autumn brings colorful leaf displays. Both gardens are free from mid-October to mid-March.

Botanical Garden: 6804 SW Marine Dr., Gate 8. ✆ **604/822-9666.** www.ubcbotanicalgarden.org. Admission C$8 adults; C$6 seniors, students, and youths; free for children 5 and under. Nitobe Japanese Garden: 6565 NW Marine Dr., Gate 4. ✆ **604/822-6038.** www.nitobe.org. Admission C$6 adults, C$5 seniors, free for children 11 and under. Dual pass for both gardens C$12. Mid-Mar to mid-Oct daily 10am–6pm; mid-Oct to mid-Mar daily 10am–5pm. Both gardens closed late Dec to early Jan.

Vancouver Maritime Museum (Kids)   This is a well-meaning but dull museum unless you're a real nautical nut. The museum's main attraction is the 1920s RCMP Arctic patrol vessel *St. Roch,* the first ship to find the Northwest Passage, preserved with most of its original stores and equipment onboard. Tours of the *St. Roch* are popular with kids—they get to clamber around the boat poking and prodding stuff.

The other half of the museum displays model ships, maps, prints, and a number of permanent exhibits. If the weather is pleasant, walk across the front lawn at the edge of False Creek to Heritage Harbour, where the museum keeps a collection of vintage boats. You can also catch the miniferry there to Granville Island or the West End.

1905 Ogden Ave., in Vanier Park. ✆ **604/257-8300.** www.vancouvermaritimemuseum.com. Admission C$10 adults, C$7.50 seniors and youths 6–19, free for children 5 and under, C$25 families. June–Aug daily 10am–5pm; Sept–May Tues–Sat 10am–5pm, Sun noon–5pm. Bus: 22, then walk 4 blocks north on Cypress St. Boat: False Creek ferries dock at Heritage Harbour.

Vancouver Museum   Located in the same building as the H. R. MacMillan Space Centre (see above), the Vancouver Museum is dedicated to the city's history, from its days as a native settlement and European outpost to its 20th-century maturation into a modern urban center. The exhibits have been remounted and revitalized to make them more interesting to the casual visitor. Of most importance here is the wonderful collection of First Nations art and artifacts. Hilarious, campy fun abounds in the 1950s Room, where a period film chronicles "Dorothy's All-Electric Home." Next to this is another fun, and socially intriguing, room devoted to Vancouver's years as a hippie capital, with film clips, commentary, and a replica hippie apartment.

1100 Chestnut St. ✆ **604/736-4431.** www.museumofvancouver.ca. Admission C$11 adults, C$9 seniors, C$7 youths 4–19. Fri–Wed 10am–5pm; Thurs 10am–9pm. Closed Mon Sept–Apr. Bus: 22, then walk 3 blocks south on Cornwall Ave. Boat: Granville Island Ferry to Heritage Harbour.

NORTH VANCOUVER & WEST VANCOUVER

Capilano Suspension Bridge & Park ★   Vancouver's first and oldest tourist trap (built in 1889), this attraction still works—mostly because there's still something inherently thrilling about walking across a narrow, shaky walkway 69m (226 ft.) above a

Doin' the Grouse Grind

The "Grouse Grind," a popular 2.9km (1.8-mile) trail commonly referred to by locals as "Mother Nature's Stairmaster," generally opens late spring or early summer. Over 110,000 hikers per year take on the challenge of the rugged terrain and steep climb. By the time you reach the plateau, your ascent will have gained 853m (2,799 ft.). Average completion time is usually 1¹/₂ hours, with the fastest completion time just over 26 minutes. Once you reach the top, you can take the tram back down for just C$5. For a look at the terrain, visit www.vancouvertrails.com/trails/grouse-grind.

canyon floor, held up by nothing but a pair of tiny cables. Set in a beautiful 8-hectare (20-acre) park about 15 minutes from downtown, the suspension bridge itself is a 135m-long (443-ft.) cedar-plank and steel-cable footbridge, which sways and bounces gently above the Capilano River. Visitors nervously cross above kayakers and salmon shooting the rapids far below. A new attraction called **"Treetops Adventure"** features more bridges and walkways, only these are attached to giant tree trunks 24m (79 ft.) above the rainforest floor.

In addition to the bridge, the park has a **carving center** where native carvers demonstrate their skill; an exhibit describing the region's natural history; guides in period costume who recount Vancouver's frontier days; and a pair of overpriced and poorly serviced restaurants. Though overall it's quite well done, it's hard to justify the exorbitant entrance fee, and the summer crowds can be off-putting. If the admission price is a roadblock, you can have a similar experience at the nearby Lynn Canyon Suspension Bridge, which is almost as high, set in a far larger forest, almost untouristed, and absolutely free (see "The *Other* Suspension Bridge," p. 129).

3735 Capilano Rd., North Vancouver. ✆ **604/985-7474.** www.capbridge.com. Admission winter/summer C$28 adults, C$26 seniors, C$22 students, C$17 youths 13–16, C$8.75 children 7–12, free for children 6 and under. Hours change monthly; generally, May–Sept daily 8:30am–dusk; Oct–Apr daily 9am–5pm. Closed Dec 25. Bus: 246 from downtown Vancouver, 236 from Lonsdale Quay SeaBus terminal. Car: Hwy. 99 north across Lions Gate Bridge to exit 14 on Capilano Rd.

Grouse Mountain ★★ (Kids) Once a local ski hill, Grouse Mountain has developed into a year-round mountain recreation park that claims to be the number-one attraction in Vancouver. It's fun if you're sports minded or like the outdoors; if not, you might find it disappointing. Located only a 15-minute drive from downtown, the **SkyRide gondola** ★★ transports you to the mountain's 1,110m (3,642-ft.) summit. (Hikers can take a near vertical trail called the Grouse Grind. See "Doin' the Grouse Grind" below.) On a clear day, the **view** ★★★ from the top is the best around: You can see the city and the entire lower mainland, from far up the Fraser Valley east across the Strait of Georgia to Vancouver Island. In the lodge, **Theater in the Sky** ★ shows wildlife movies. Outside, in the winter, you can ski and snowboard (26 runs, 13 runs for night skiing/snowboarding; drop-in ski lessons available), go snowshoeing, skate on the highest outdoor rink in Canada, take a brief "sleigh ride" (behind a huge snow-cat), and the kids can play in a special snow park. In warmer weather, you can wander forest trails, take a scenic chair ride, enjoy a lumberjack show or Birds in Motion demonstrations, visit the Refuge for Endangered Wildlife, or ride on the mountain-bike trails. Most of these activities are

a lift ticket and equipment rentals. Casual and fine-dining options, and a Starbucks, are
in the lodge.

6400 Nancy Greene Way, North Vancouver. ℂ **604/984-0661.** www.grousemountain.com. SkyRide C\$35
adults, C\$33 seniors, C\$21 youths 13–18, C\$13 children 5–12, free children 4 and under. Full day ski-lift
tickets C\$50 adults, C\$40 seniors and youths, C\$22 children, C\$150 families (2 adults, 2 children 17 and
under). SkyRide free with advance Observatory Restaurant reservation. Daily 9am–10pm. Bus: 232, then
transfer to bus 236. SeaBus: Lonsdale Quay, then transfer to bus 236. Car: Hwy. 99 north across Lions Gate
Bridge, take North Vancouver exit to Marine Dr., then up Capilano Rd. for 5km (3 miles). Parking C\$3 for
2 hr. in lots below SkyRide.

---

3 VANCOUVER'S PLAZAS & PARKS

PLAZAS

Unlike many cities, Vancouver's great urban gathering places stand not at the center but
on the periphery, on two opposite sides of the **seawall** that runs around Stanley Park:
English Bay, on the south side of Denman Street, and **Coal Harbour,** on the northern,
Burrard Inlet side, are where Vancouverites go to stroll and be seen. On warm sunny
days, these two areas are packed. Another waterside gathering spot is **Canada Place**
(p. 116), built for Expo '86 and just enlarged to add more convention space. Built in the
shape of a cruise ship and serving as the city's cruise-ship terminal, it has wide walkways
all around it that are super for strolling and offers fabulous views of the mountains.

Designed by architect Arthur Erickson to be Vancouver's central plaza, **Robson
Square**—downtown, between Hornby and Howe streets from Robson to Smithe
streets—has never really worked. The square, which anchors the north end of the Provincial Law Courts complex designed by Erickson in 1972, suffers from a basic design
flaw: It's sunk one story below street level, making it difficult to see and to access. The
Law Courts complex, which sits on a higher level, raised above the street, is beautifully
executed with shrubbery, cherry trees, sculptures, and a triple-tiered waterfall, but Robson Square below is about as appealing as a drained swimming pool. Just opposite Robson Square, however, the steps of the **Vancouver Art Gallery** (p. 120) are a great people
place, filled with loungers, political agitators, and old men playing chess. It just goes to
show that grandiose urban theory and urban design, especially back in the 1970s, doesn't
always take the human element into account.

Library Square—a few blocks east from Robson Square at the corner of Robson
and Homer streets—is an example of a new urban space that does work. It's been popular with locals since it opened in 1995. People sit on the steps, bask in the sunshine,
read, harangue passersby with half-baked political ideas, and generally seem to enjoy
themselves.

PARKS & GARDENS

Park and garden lovers are in heaven in Vancouver. The wet, mild climate is ideal for
gardening, and come spring the city blazes with blossoming cherry trees, rhododendrons,
camellias, azaleas, and spring bulbs—and roses in summer. Gardens are everywhere.
For general information about Vancouver's parks, call ℂ **604/257-8400,** or try http://
vancouver.ca/parks. For information on **Stanley Park** ★★★, the queen of them all, see
p. 116.

On the West Side you'll find the magnificent **UBC Botanical Garden,** one of the largest living botany collections on the West Coast, and the sublime **Nitobe Japanese Garden** ★; for descriptions of both, see p. 125.

In Chinatown, the **Dr. Sun Yat-Sen Classical Chinese Garden** ★★ (p. 120) is a small, tranquil oasis in the heart of the city, built by artisans from Suzhou, China; right next to it, accessed via the Chinese Cultural Centre on Pender Street, is the pretty (and free) **Dr. Sun Yat-Sen Park,** with a pond, walkways, and plantings.

On the West Side, **Queen Elizabeth Park**—at Cambie Street and West 33rd Avenue—sits atop a 150m-high (492-ft.) extinct volcano and is the highest urban vantage point south of downtown, offering panoramic views in all directions. Along with the rose garden in Stanley Park, it's Vancouver's most popular location for wedding-photo sessions, with well-manicured gardens and a profusion of colorful flora. There are areas for lawn bowling, tennis, pitch-and-putt golf, and picnicking. The **Bloedel Conservatory** (© 604/257-8584) stands next to the park's huge sunken garden, an amazing reclamation of an abandoned rock quarry. A 42m-high (138-ft.) domed structure, the conservatory (open daily 10am–5pm) houses a tropical rainforest with more than 100 plant species as well as free-flying tropical birds. Admission to the conservatory is C$5 for adults, with discounts for seniors, children, and families. Take bus no. 15 to reach the park.

Vancouver's 22-hectare (54-acre) **VanDusen Botanical Gardens,** 5251 Oak St., at West 37th Avenue (© 604/878-9274; www.vandusengarden.org), located just a few blocks from Queen Elizabeth Park and the Bloedel Conservatory, concentrates on whole ecosystems. From towering trees to little lichens on the smallest of damp stones, the gardeners at VanDusen attempt to re-create the plant life of a number of different environments. Depending on which trail you take, you may find yourself wandering through the Southern Hemisphere section, the Sino-Himalayan garden, or the Northern California sequoia garden. Should all this tree gazing finally pall, head for the farthest corner of the garden to the devilishly difficult Elizabethan garden maze. Admission April through September: C$9 adults, C$6.50 seniors and youths 13 to 18, C$5 children 6 to 12, C$20 families, and free for children 5 and under. Admission is about C$2 less from October through March. Open daily 10am to dusk. Take bus no. 17. *Note:* The garden lost hundreds of trees in the December 2006 windstorm that also devastated Stanley Park.

Adjoining the University of British Columbia (UBC) on the city's west side at Point Grey, **Pacific Spirit Regional Park,** called the **Endowment Lands** by longtime Vancouver residents, is the largest green space in Vancouver. Comprising 754 hectares (1,863 acres) of temperate rainforest, marshes, and beaches, the park includes nearly 35km (22 miles) of trails ideal for hiking, riding, mountain biking, and beachcombing.

Across the Lions Gate Bridge, six provincial parks delight outdoor enthusiasts year-round. Good in winter or for those averse to strenuous climbing is the publicly maintained **Capilano River Regional Park,** 4500 Capilano Park Rd. (© 604/666-1790), surrounding the **Capilano Suspension Bridge & Park** (p. 125). Hikers can follow a gentle trail by the river for 7km (4.4 miles) down the well-maintained **Capilano trails** to the Burrard Inlet and the Lions Gate Bridge, or about a mile upstream to **Cleveland Dam,** a launching point for white-water kayakers and canoeists.

The **Capilano Salmon Hatchery,** on Capilano Park Road (© 604/666-1790), is on the river's east bank about .5km (⅓ mile) below the Cleveland Dam. Approximately two million coho and chinook salmon are hatched annually in glass-fronted tanks connected to the river by a series of channels. You can observe the hatching fry (baby fish) before

(Finds) **The *Other* Suspension Bridge**

Lynn Canyon Park, in North Vancouver between Grouse Mountain and Mount Seymour Provincial Park on Lynn Valley Road, offers a free alternative to the Capilano Suspension Bridge. True, the **Lynn Canyon Suspension Bridge** ★ is both shorter and a little lower than Capilano (p. 125), but the waterfall and swirling whirlpools in the canyon below add both beauty and a certain fear-inducing fascination. Plus, it's free.

The park is located in a gorgeous 247-hectare (610-acre) rainforest of cedar and Douglas fir and is also home to an **Ecology Centre** (3663 Park Rd.; ⓒ **604/990-3755**), which presents natural-history films, tours, and displays that explain the local ecology. Staff members lead frequent walking tours. The center is open daily from 10am to 5pm (Sat–Sun Oct–May noon–4pm). The park itself is open from 7am to 7pm in spring and fall, 7am to 9pm in summer, and 7am to dusk in winter; it's closed December 25 and 26 and January 1. To get there, take the SeaBus to Lonsdale Quay, then transfer to bus no. 229; by car, take the Trans-Canada Highway (Hwy. 1) to the Lynn Valley Road exit (about a 20-min. drive from downtown), and follow Lynn Valley Road to Peters Road, where you turn right. The park's cafe serves sit-down and takeout meals.

Six kilometers (3¾ miles) up Lynn Valley Road from the highway is **Lynn Headwaters Regional Park** (ⓒ **604/985-1690** for trail conditions), one of the best places close to the city to experience the breathtaking nature of the Northwest. Until the mid-1980s, this was inaccessible wilderness and bear habitat. The park and the bears are now managed by the Greater Vancouver Regional Parks Department. Some of the 12 marked trails of various levels of difficulty meander by the riverbank, while others climb steeply up to various North Shore peaks, and one trail leads to a series of cascading waterfalls.

they depart for open waters, as well as the mature salmon that return to the Capilano River to spawn (Sept–Dec is best viewing time). Admission is free, and the hatchery is open daily from 8am to 7pm (until 4pm in the winter). Drive across Lions Gate Bridge and follow the signs to North Vancouver and the Capilano Suspension Bridge. Or take the SeaBus to Lonsdale Quay and transfer to bus no. 236; the trip takes less than 45 minutes.

Eight kilometers (5 miles) west of Lions Gate Bridge on Marine Drive West, West Vancouver, is **Lighthouse Park** ★. This 74-hectare (183-acre) rugged-terrain forest has 13km (8 miles) of groomed trails and—because it has never been clear-cut—some of the largest and oldest trees in the Vancouver area. One of the paths leads to the 18m (59-ft.) **Point Atkinson Lighthouse,** on a rocky bluff overlooking the Strait of Georgia and a fabulous view of Vancouver. It's an easy trip on bus no. 250. For information about other West Vancouver parks, call ⓒ **604/925-7200** on weekdays.

Driving up-up-up the mountain from **Lighthouse Park** will eventually get you to the top of **Cypress Provincial Park.** Stop halfway at the scenic viewpoint for a sweeping vista of the Vancouver skyline, the harbor, the Gulf Islands, and Washington State's Mount

Steveston: Small-Town Charm in Suburban Vancouver

Steveston, located at the southwest corner of Richmond by the mouth of the Fraser River, once existed for nothing but salmon. Fishermen set out from its port to catch the migrating sockeye, and returned to have the catch cleaned and canned. Huge processing plants covered its waterfront, where thousands of workers gutted millions of fish. Industrial-scale fishing ended long ago, and Steveston's waterfront and boardwalk have been restored and put to new uses. With public fish sales, charter trips up the river or out to the Fraser delta, first-rate restaurants, fish and chips, and, above all, a laid-back, small-town atmosphere, Steveston is a wonderful escape from downtown Vancouver.

Much of Steveston's fishy history is on display in the **Gulf of Georgia Cannery National Historic Site,** near the wharf at Bayview Street and 4th Avenue (© **604/664-9009**). A picturesque boardwalk passes the Cannery and leads into **Garry Point Park,** fronting the Strait of Georgia. Dunes, reeds, and wild flowers fill the park year-round, while the spring and summer attract kite fly-ers—July is host to the Steveston International Kite Flying Competition.

Steveston offers visitors a wealth of good restaurants, most of them concentrated along the wharf. For alfresco dining, and arguably the best fish and chips in all of Metro Vancouver, pull up a bench at **Pajo's** (© **604/272-1588;** www.pajos.com), either on the wharf or at the entrance to Garry Point Park. The menu covers the basics of chippy fare but also includes a yellowfin tuna burger and poutine. Plus, the chips are hand cut and everything is locally sourced.

For something a bit different, visit the not-for-profit **London Heritage Farm** (6511 Dyke Rd.; © **604/271-5220**), a restored 1880s farmhouse. The farm has a traditional tea service for a fraction of the cost and formality in Victoria (p. 232). Tea and clotted cream is accompanied by scones, cakes, and cookies made on the farm and topped with homemade jams from local fruit. The service is done by volunteers or the farm's proprietor. The whole affair will cost you C$6. During July and August, the farm is open daily, 10am to 4pm; otherwise, it's only open Saturday and Sunday, noon to 4pm. Take a taxi from the Steveston waterfront.

Several buses run from downtown Vancouver Burrard Station to Steveston (Mon–Fri morning and evening rush hours): Bus no. 491 runs in the mornings and afternoons, bus nos. 490 and 496 run in the afternoons only. Otherwise, take the no. 98 B-line bus from Burrard Station to Richmond Centre, then transfer to no. 401, 402, 407, or 410. The whole trip takes about an hour, ending at the Steveston wharf and boardwalk.

Stop in at the **Tourism Richmond Visitor Centre** (www.tourismrichmond.com), in front of the Gulf of Georgia Cannery, for more information. The office is only open seasonally, May to September, though only on the weekends during May, July, and September.

Baker, which peers above the eastern horizon. The park is 12km (7½ miles) north of Cypress Bowl Road and the Hwy. 99 junction in West Vancouver. Cypress Provincial Park has trails for hiking during the summer and autumn and for downhill and cross-country skiing during the winter.

Rising 1,430m (4,692 ft.) above Indian Arm, **Mount Seymour Provincial Park,** 1700 Mt. Seymour Rd., North Vancouver (© **604/986-2261**), offers another view of the area's Coast Mountains range. Higher than Grouse Mountain, Mount Seymour provides a spectacular view of Washington State's Mount Baker on clear days. It has challenging hiking trails that go straight to the summit, where you can see Indian Arm, Vancouver's bustling commercial port, the city skyline, the Strait of Georgia, and Vancouver Island. The trails are open all summer for hiking; during the winter, the paths are maintained for skiing, snowboarding, and snowshoeing. Mount Seymour is open daily from 7am to 10pm.

HISTORIC LANDMARKS & ATTRACTIONS

The **Burnaby Village Museum,** 6501 Deer Lake Ave., Burnaby (© **604/293-6501;** www.burnabyvillagemuseum.ca), is a 3.5-hectare (8¾-acre) re-creation of the town as it might have appeared in the 1920s. You can walk along boardwalk streets among costumed townspeople, shop in a general store, ride a vintage carousel, peek into an authentic one-room schoolhouse, and visit a vintage ice-cream parlor that's been in the same location since the turn of the 20th century. At Christmastime, the whole village is aglow in lights and Victorian decorations. Admission is C$12 for adults; C$9 for seniors, students, and youths 13 to 18; C$6 for children 6 to 12; and free for children 5 and under. It's open daily early May through early September from 11am to 4:30pm; October 28–31 ("Haunted Village") from 6 to 9 p.m.; November 24 through December 9 noon to 5pm; December 10 through December 23 ("Holiday Village") from noon to 8pm; closed December 24 and 25. From the Metrotown Skystation take bus no. 110 to Deer Lake.

The **Fort Langley National Historic Site,** 23433 Mavis Ave., Fort Langley (© **604/ 513-4777;** www.pc.gc.ca/fortlangley), is the birthplace of British Columbia. In 1827, the Hudson's Bay Company established this settlement to supply its provincial posts. Costumed craftspeople demonstrate blacksmithing, coopering, and woodworking, bringing this landmark back to life. It's open year-round, daily from 9am to 8pm in July and August; 10am to 5pm the rest of the year. Admission is C$7.80 for adults, C$6.55 for seniors, C$3.90 for children 6 to 16, and free for children 5 and under; a family pass is C$20. To get there, take the SkyTrain to Surrey Central Station and transfer to bus no. 501. *Note:* The main street of Fort Langley Village, Glover Road, is packed with antiques shops, a bookstore, and cafes, and it's only a 2-minute stroll away.

---

4 ESPECIALLY FOR KIDS

Pick up copies of the free monthly newspapers *B.C. Parent* (© **604/221-0366;** www. bcparent.ca); and *West Coast Families* (© **604/249-2866;** www.westcoastfamilies. com). *West Coast Families'* centerfold, "Fun in the City," and event calendar list all current events, including **CN IMAX** shows at Canada Place Pier, **OMNIMAX** (© **604/443-7443**) shows at Science World at TELUS World of Science (p. 124), and free children's programs. Both publications, and Tourism Vancouver's **Kids' Guide,** are available at Granville Island's Kids Market and at neighborhood community centers throughout the city.

To give kids an overview of the city, take the fun trolley tour offered by **Vancouver Trolley Company** (© **888/451-5581** or 604/801-5515; www.vancouvertrolley.com). Gas-powered trolleys run through Downtown, Chinatown, the West End, and Stanley Park (for more info, see "Organized Tours," below).

Stanley Park ★★★ (p. 116) offers a number of attractions for children, including a fabulous and free **Spray Park** near Lumberman's Arch. **Stanley Park's Children's Farm** (© **604/257-8531**) has peacocks, rabbits, calves, donkeys, and Shetland ponies. Next to the petting zoo is Stanley Park's **Miniature Railway** ★ (© **604/257-8531**), a diminutive steam locomotive with passenger cars that runs on a circuit through the woods. The zoo and railway are open from 11am to 4pm daily June through early September, plus Christmas week, spring break, and on weekends October through March depending on weather. Admission for the petting zoo or the miniature railroad is C$6 for adults, C$4.25 for seniors, C$4 for youths 13 to 18, and C$3 for kids 2 to 12. **Second Beach** on the park's western rim has a playground, a snack bar, and an immense heated oceanside **pool** ★ (© **604/257-8371**), open from May through September. Admission is C$5.15 for adults, C$3.60 for seniors and youths 13 to 18, and C$2.60 for children 6 to 12. Kids will also be impressed with the collection of giant **totem poles** ★★★ in Stanley Park, and the entire family will enjoy the **horse-drawn carriage rides** ★★★ that begin near Lost Lagoon (p. 118).

Also in Stanley Park, the **Vancouver Aquarium Marine Science Centre** ★★ (p. 119) has sea otters, sea lions, whales, and numerous other marine creatures, as well as many exhibits and special programs geared to children.

Right in town, **Science World at TELUS World of Science** (p. 124) is a terrific interactive kids' museum where budding scientists can get their hands into everything.

A trip to **Granville Island** ★★★ will delight kids, and there are a couple of specific places they will really enjoy. Granville Island's **Kids Market,** 1496 Cartwright St. (© **604/689-8447**), is open daily from 10am to 6pm. Playrooms and shops filled with toys, books, records, clothes, and food are all child-oriented. At **Granville Island's Water Park and Adventure Playground,** 1496 Cartwright St., kids can really let loose with movable water guns and sprinklers. They can also have fun on the water slides or in the wading pool. The facilities are open during the summer daily (weather permitting) from 10am to 6pm. Admission is free; changing facilities are nearby at the False Creek Community Centre (© **604/257-8195**).

Across Burrard Inlet, **Maplewood Farm,** 405 Seymour River Place, North Vancouver (© **604/929-5610;** www.maplewoodfarm.bc.ca), has more than 200 barnyard animals (from cows to chickens) living on its 2-hectare (5-acre) farm. A few working farms once operated in the area but were put out of business by competition from the huge agricultural concerns in Fraser River valley. The parks department rescued this one and converted it into an attraction. The ticket booth (a former breeding kennel) sells birdseed for feeding the ducks and other fowl. The farm also offers pony rides. Special events include the summertime Sheep Fair, the mid-September Farm Fair, 101 Pumpkins Day in late October, and the Country Christmas weekend. The farm is open daily April through mid-September (closed Mon the rest of the year) from 10am to 4pm. Admission is C$5.25 for adults, C$3 for seniors and children. Take bus no. 210 and transfer to the no. 211 or 212.

Greater Vancouver Zoo, 5048 264th St., Aldergrove (© **604/856-6825;** www.gvzoo. com), located 48km (30 miles) east of downtown Vancouver (about a 45-min. drive), is a lush 48-hectare (119-acre) reserve filled with lions, tigers, ostriches, buffalo, elk, antelope, zebras, giraffes, a rhino, and camels; 124 species in all. The zoo also has food service and a playground. It's open daily 9am to 4pm from October through March; 9am to 7pm from April through September. Admission is C$18 for adults, C$14 for seniors and children 3 to 15, free for children 2 and under, and C$60 for families. Take the Trans-Canada Highway to Aldergrove, exit 73; parking is C$4 per day.

Walk high above the rushing waters at the **Capilano Suspension Bridge & Park** (p. 125) and the **Lynn Canyon Suspension Bridge** (p. 129). In winter, **Mount Seymour Provincial Park** (p. 141) and **Grouse Mountain Resort** (p. 126) offer ski programs for kids and adults; in summer, both are great for hikes.

A 45-minute drive north of Vancouver, the **B.C. Museum of Mining,** Hwy. 99, Britannia Beach (© **800/896-4044;** www.bcmuseumofmining.org), is impossible to miss. Located at the head of Howe Sound, it's marked by a 235-ton truck parked in front. During the summer it offers guided tours of the old copper mine, demonstrations of mining techniques, and even a gold-panning area where anyone can try straining gravel for the precious metal. It's open daily from mid-March to mid-October from 9am to 4:30pm; the rest of the year it's closed on weekends. Call ahead for the tour schedule; allow about 1½ to 2 hours. Admission is C$19 for adults, C$14 for seniors and students, C$12 youths, C$55 for families, and free for children under 5.

A whale-watching excursion is one of the most exciting adventures you can give a kid. See "Wildlife-Watching" later in this chapter for information.

5 ORGANIZED TOURS

Please note that the 6% General Services Tax (GST) may be applied to the tour prices listed below.

AIR TOURS

West Coast Air ★★★, 1177 W. Hastings St. (© **800/347-2222** or 604/606-6800; www.westcoastair.com), operates daily floatplane flights from its downtown Vancouver terminal next to Canada Place cruise-ship terminal. Floatplanes are single-prop, six-seater planes that take off and land on water. The 20-minute "Vancouver Scenic" tour (C$99 per person) flies over Stanley Park and all around the metro region, giving you an unparalleled bird's-eye view of the magnificent terrain; the 5-hour "Whistler Plane and Train" tour (C$288 adults, C$238 children 2–11) includes a 4-hour stopover in Whistler Village and return via Whistler Mountaineer scenic train. Other tours will take you to Victoria, glacial lakes, and prime fly-fishing and whale-watching spots. The 6-hour "Victoria and Butchart Gardens" tour (C$289 adults, C$139 children 2–11) flies you across the Strait of Georgia to Vancouver Island, where you have a 3-hour tour that includes the world-famous Butchart Gardens.

Harbour Air (© **800/665-0212** or 604/274-1277; www.harbour-air.com) is on Coal Harbour just west of the Canada Place Pier. Thirty-minute seaplane flights over downtown, Stanley Park, and the North Shore cost C$99 per person. Longer tours to alpine lakes, glaciers, and nearby islands, as well as regularly scheduled flights to Victoria, Nanaimo, and Prince Rupert, are also available.

From April through September, **Helijet Charters** (☎ **800/987-4354** or 604/270-1484; www.helijet.com) offers a variety of daily tours that depart from their terminal next to Canada Place and their helipad on top of Grouse Mountain. The "Coastal Scenic Tour" is a 20-minute tour of the city, Stanley Park, and North Shore mountains for C$169 per person.

BOAT TOURS

Harbour Cruises, no. 1, north foot of Denman Street (☎ **604/688-7246;** www.boatcruises.com), will take you on a 2½-hour Sunset Dinner Cruise, including a buffet meal and onboard entertainment. Cost is C$75 for adults, seniors, and students; C$65 for children 2 to 11. The cruise leaves at 7pm May through October. The 4-hour Indian Arm Luncheon Cruise (May–Sept) includes a salmon or chicken lunch, with departure at 11am. Cost is C$65 per person.

Harbour Cruises also conducts a 75-minute narrated Harbour Tour aboard the MPV *Constitution,* a 19th-century sternwheeler with a smokestack. Tours depart at 11am, 12:15pm, 1:30pm, and 2:45pm daily from early May to late September and twice a day at 1:30 and 2:45pm mid-April through early May and late September through October (dates vary yearly). Fares are C$30 for adults, C$25 for seniors and youths 12 to 17, C$10 for children 5 to 11, and free for children 4 and under. This tour allows you to see harbor facilities and gets you out onto Burrard Inlet, but the narration, read from a script, is rather dull and unengaging.

Accent Cruises, 1676 Duranleau St. (☎ **800/993-6257** or 604/688-6625; www.champagnecruises.com), runs a 2½-hour Sunset Cruise departing Granville Island daily at 5:45pm. Cost for adults is C$60 with dinner, C$25 for the cruise only.

Paddlewheeler River Adventures, New Westminster Quay, New Westminster (☎ **604/525-4465;** www.vancouverpaddlewheeler.com), operates Fraser River tours from New Westminster aboard the 19th-century vessel SS *Native.* The company offers a 4-hour Dine and Dance cruise Saturday evenings at 7pm. Ticket prices are C$65 for adults, C$60 seniors. More interesting but not regularly scheduled are day trips to historic Fort Langley; call or visit the website for dates.

BUS TOURS

Big Bus, 317 Water St. (☎ **877/299-0701** or 604/299-0700; www.bigbus.ca) runs a fleet of double-decker buses on a 90-minute "hop-on, hop-off" sightseeing loop around the city for C$35 adults, C$30 students and seniors, C$17 children, and C$75 families. Buses depart from Canada Place daily between 9am and 6pm, running every 20 minutes during peak summer hours; tickets are valid for 2 days.

Vancouver Tours (☎ **888/321-3635;** www.vancouvertours.com), offers a wide array of tour options, including a 3½-hour excursion through Vancouver in a 15-person van. Offered year-round at 9am and 2pm, the tour costs C$69 for adults, C$45 for children. The van picks you up from downtown hotels. You can also take a tour up to Grouse Mountain and the Capilano Suspension Bridge. Departing at 11am (and 2pm from mid-May to mid-Oct), it costs C$125 for adults, C$89 for children 3 to 12. Other options are tours of wineries, Victoria, and Whistler.

Vancouver Trolley Company, 875 Terminal Ave. (☎ **888/451-5581** or 604/801-5515; www.vancouvertrolley.com), operates gas-powered trolleys on a route through downtown, Chinatown, the West End, and Stanley Park. Between 9am and 6pm in summer (4:30pm in winter), passengers can get on and off at any of the 23 stops, explore, and catch another scheduled trolley. Onboard, drivers provide detailed commentary.

Purchase tickets from the driver (or at the Gastown ticket booth at 157 Water St.) for C$35 for adults, C$32 for seniors, and C$18 for children 4 to 12.

FIRST NATIONS TOURS

The Tsleil-Waututh Nation of North Vancouver leads a number of cultural and ecotours that provide an introduction to both First Nations culture and the stunning Indian Arm fjord. Their company, **Takaya Tours,** Cates Park Paddling Centre, Cates Park, North Vancouver (© **604/985-2925;** www.takayatours.com), conducts a roster of outdoor tours such as excursions in traditional northwest canoes, plant nature walks, full-moon paddles, and salmon feasts at prices running from C$55 to C$140.

SPECIALTY TOURS

Playing off Vancouver's growing reputation as a culinary tourism destination, **Chef and Chauffeur,** 103-4900 Cartier St. (© **604/267-1000;** www.chefandchauffeur.com), has launched several tours of the Fraser Valley, located an hour east of the city, and the more distant Okanogan Valley, famed for its fruit, produce, meats, cheeses, and wines. Participants start the day with coffee, fresh orange juice, and cinnamon buns while their guide maps out the day's adventures. The tours, in a luxury SUV, visit a variety of wineries, farms, bakeries, and cheese makers. Optional dinner and overnight add-ons are available. Tours range from C$395 to C$2,995.

Early Motion Tours, 1-1380 Thurlow St. (© **604/687-5088**), gives private sightseeing tours around Vancouver aboard a restored 1930 Model A Ford Phaeton convertible that holds up to four passengers plus the driver. Reservations are required. Limousine rates apply: C$100 per hour for up to four people with a 1-hour minimum. The office is open daily from 7:30am to 8pm.

WALKING TOURS

Walkabout Historic Vancouver (© **604/720-0006;** www.walkabouthistoricvancouver. com) offers 2-hour walking tours through Vancouver and Granville Island historic sites, complete with guides dressed as 19th-century schoolmarms. Tours depart daily at 10am and 2pm February through November, and by request during other months. Tours are wheelchair accessible. The cost is C$25 per person.

During the summer months (June–Aug), the **Architectural Institute of B.C.** (© **604/683-8588,** ext. 306; www.aibc.ca) offers a number of **architectural walking tours** ★★★ of downtown Vancouver neighborhoods, including Chinatown and Granville Island, for only C$5 per person. The 2-hour tours run Tuesday through Saturday and depart at 1pm from the AIBC Architecture Centre, 440 Cambie St. Call or visit the website for details and to book.

The **Vancouver Centennial Police Museum** offers an entertaining "Sins of the City" walking tour; see the museum description (p. 120) for details.

Or, devise your own walking tour with brochures from the Tourism Vancouver **Touristinfo Centre** at 200 Burrard St. (p. 59). Otherwise, turn to chapter 9.

---

6 OUTDOOR ACTIVITIES

If you don't find your favorite sport listed here, take a look at chapter 12; also check out "Parks & Gardens" earlier in this chapter.

An excellent resource for outdoor enthusiasts is **Mountain Equipment Co-op,** 130 W. Broadway (© **604/872-7858;** www.mec.ca).

Only 10% of Vancouver's annual rainfall occurs during June, July, and August; 60 days of summer sunshine is not uncommon, although the Pacific never really warms up enough for a comfortable swim. Still, **English Bay Beach** ★★, at the end of Davie Street off Denman Street and Beach Avenue, is a great place to see sunsets. The bathhouse dates to the turn of the 20th century, and a huge playground slide is mounted on a raft just off the beach every summer.

On **Stanley Park**'s western rim, **Second Beach** ★ is a short stroll north from English Bay Beach. A playground, a snack bar, and an immense heated oceanside **pool** ★ (© 604/257-8370), open from May through September, make this a convenient and fun spot for families. Admission to the pool is C$5.15 for adults, C$3.60 for seniors and youths 13 to 18, and C$2.60 for children 6 to 12. Farther along the seawall, due north of Stanley Park Drive, lies secluded **Third Beach.** Locals tote along grills and coolers to this spot, a popular place for summer-evening barbecues and sunset-watching.

South of English Bay Beach, near the Burrard Street Bridge, is **Sunset Beach** ★. Running along False Creek, it's actually a picturesque strip of sandy beaches filled with enormous driftwood logs that serve as windbreaks and provide a little privacy for sunbathers and picnickers. A snack bar, a soccer field, and a long, gently sloping grassy hill are available for people who prefer lawn to sand.

On the West Side, **Kitsilano Beach** ★★★, along Arbutus Drive near Ogden Street, is affectionately called Kits Beach. It's an easy walk from the Maritime Museum and the False Creek ferry dock. If you want to do a saltwater swim but can't handle the cold, head to the huge (135m/443-ft.) heated (25°C/77°F) **Kitsilano Pool** ★★. Admission is the same as for Second Beach Pool, above.

Farther west on the other side of Pioneer Park is **Jericho Beach** (Alma St. off Point Grey Rd.), another local after-work and weekend social spot. **Locarno Beach,** off Discovery Street and Marine Drive, and **Spanish Banks,** NW Marine Drive, wrap around the northern point of the UBC campus and University Hill. (Be forewarned that beachside restrooms and concessions on the promontory end abruptly at Locarno Beach.) Below UBC's Museum of Anthropology is **Point Grey Beach,** a restored harbor-defense site. The next beach is **Wreck Beach** ★★★—Canada's largest nude beach. You get down to Wreck Beach by taking the very steep Trail 6 on the UBC campus near Gate 6 down to the water's edge. Extremely popular with locals, and maintained by its own preservation society, Wreck Beach is also the city's most pristine and least-developed sandy stretch, bordered on three sides by towering trees.

At the northern foot of the Lions Gate Bridge, **Ambleside Park** is a popular North Shore spot. The quarter-mile beach faces the Burrard Inlet.

For information on any of Vancouver's many beaches, call © 604/738-8535 (summer only).

BOATING

With thousands of miles of protected shoreline along B.C.'s West Coast, boaters enjoy some of the finest cruising grounds in the world. You can rent powerboats for a few hours or up to several weeks at **Bonnie Lee Boat Rentals,** 1676 Duranleau St., Granville Island (© 866/933-7447 or 604/290-7447; www.bonnielee.com), a company that has been renting boats and offering chartered fishing expeditions since 1980. Rates for a 5.8m (19-ft.) sport boat with 115-horsepower motor begin at C$60 per hour (plus C$9 insurance fee and fuel), or C$375 for an 8-hour package. **Jerry's Boat Rentals,** Granville

Island (© **604/696-5500**), is steps away and offers similar deals. **Delta Charters,** 3500
Cessna Dr., Richmond (© **800/661-7762** or 604/273-4211; www.deltacharters.com),
has weekly and monthly rates for skippered boats that sleep four.

CANOEING & KAYAKING

Both placid, urban False Creek and the incredibly beautiful 30km (19-mile) North Vancouver fjord known as Indian Arm have launching points that can be reached by car or
bus. Prices range from about C$40 per 2-hour minimum rental to C$70 per 5-hour day
for single kayaks and about C$60 for canoe rentals. Customized tours range from C$75
to C$150 per person.

    Ecomarine Ocean Kayak Centre, 1668 Duranleau St., Granville Island (© **888/
425-2925** or 604/689-7575; www.ecomarine.com), has 2-hour, daily, and weekly kayak
rentals, as well as courses and organized tours. The company also has an office at the
Jericho Sailing Centre, 1300 Discovery St., at Jericho Beach (© **604/224-4177;** www.
jsca.bc.ca). In North Vancouver, **Deep Cove Canoe and Kayak Rentals,** 2156 Banbury
Rd. (at the foot of Gallant St.) (© **604/929-2268;** www.deepcovekayak.com), is an easy
starting point for anyone planning an Indian Arm run. It offers hourly and daily rentals
of canoes and kayaks, as well as lessons and customized tours.

    Lotus Land Tours, 2005-1251 Cardero St. (© **800/528-3531** or 604/684-4921;
www.lotuslandtours.com), runs guided kayak tours on Indian Arm that come with hotel
pickup, a barbecue salmon lunch, and incredible scenery. The wide, stable kayaks are
perfect for first-time paddlers. One-day tours cost C$165 for adults, C$119 for children
4 to 12.

    See also **Takaya Tours,** an excellent First Nations eco-outfitter (p. 135).

CYCLING & MOUNTAIN BIKING

Cycling in Vancouver is fun, amazingly scenic, and very popular. Cycling maps are available at most bicycle retailers and rental outlets. Some West End hotels offer guests bike
storage and rentals. Hourly rentals run around C$7 for a one-speed "Cruiser" to C$17
for a top-of-the-line mountain bike or tandem; C$30 to C$80 for a day, helmets and
locks included. Popular shops that rent city and mountain bikes, child trailers, child
seats, and in-line skates (protective gear included) include **Spokes Bicycle Rentals &
Espresso Bar,** 1798 W. Georgia St. (© **604/688-5141;** www.spokesbicyclerentals.com),
at the corner of Denman Street at the entrance to Stanley Park; **Alley Cat Rentals,** 1779
Robson St., in the alley (© **604/684-5117**); and **Bayshore Bicycle and Rollerblade
Rentals,** 745 Denman St. (© **604/688-2453;** www.bayshorebikerentals.ca). *Note:* Be
advised that wearing a helmet is mandatory, and one will be included in your bike rental.

    The most popular cycling path in the city runs along the **seawall** ★★★ around the
perimeter of Stanley Park. Offering magnificent views of the city, the Burrard Inlet, the
mountains, and English Bay, this flat, 10km (6¼-mile) pathway attracts year-round
bicyclists, in-line skaters, and pedestrians. (*Note:* Runners and cyclists have separate lanes
on developed park and beach paths.) Another popular route is the **seaside bicycle route,**
a 15km (9⅓-mile) ride that begins at English Bay and continues around False Creek to
the University of British Columbia. Some of this route follows city streets that are well
marked with cycle-path signs; the sights include the Plaza of Nations, Science World,
Granville Island, the Pacific Space Centre, the Kitsilano Pool, the Jericho Sailing Centre,
and the University of British Columbia, home to the UBC Botanical Garden and Nitobe
Japanese Garden (p. 125), and the lush Pacific Spirit Park (p. 128).

8

Serious mountain bikers also have a wealth of world-class options within a short drive from downtown Vancouver. The trails on **Grouse Mountain** (p. 126) are some of the lower mainland's best. The very steep **Good Samaritan Trail** on **Mount Seymour** connects to the Baden-Powell Trail and the Bridle Path near Mount Seymour Road. Local mountain bikers love the cross-country ski trails on **Hollyburn Mountain** in **Cypress Provincial Park,** just northeast of Vancouver on the road to Whistler on Hwy. 99. Closer to downtown, both **Pacific Spirit Park** and **Burnaby Mountain** offer excellent beginner and intermediate off-road trails.

ECOTOURS

Lotus Land Tours runs guided kayak tours on Indian Arm (see "Canoeing & Kayaking," above). From late November to the end of January, this small local company also offers unique float trips on the Squamish River to see the large concentration of bald eagles up close. **Rockwood Adventures** (© 888/236-6606 or 604/741-0802; www.rockwood adventures.com) has 4-hour **guided walks of the North Shore rainforest ★,** complete with a trained naturalist, stops in Capilano Canyon and at the Lynn Canyon Suspension Bridge (p. 129), and lunch. Cost is C$85 for adults, C$78 for seniors and students, and C$60 for children 6 to 11.

FISHING

Five species of salmon, rainbow and Dolly Varden trout, steelhead, and sturgeon abound in the local waters around Vancouver. To fish, anglers over the age of 16 need a **nonresident saltwater or freshwater license.** Licenses are available province-wide from more than 500 vendors, including tackle shops, sporting-goods stores, resorts, service stations, marinas, charter-boat operators, and department stores. Saltwater (tidal waters) fishing licenses for nonresidents cost C$7.50 for 1 day, C$20 for 3 days, and C$33 for 5 days. Fly-fishing in national and provincial parks requires special permits, which you can get at any park site for a nominal fee. Permits are valid at all Canadian parks.

The B.C. *Tidal Waters Sport Fishing Guide* and *B.C. Sport Fishing Regulations Synopsis for Non-Tidal Waters,* and the *B.C. Fishing Directory and Atlas,* available at many tackle shops, are good sources of information. Another good source of general information is the **Fisheries and Oceans Canada** website (www.pac.dfo-mpo.gc.ca).

Hanson's Fishing Outfitters, 102-580 Hornby St. (© 604/684-8988), and **Bonnie Lee Fishing Charters Ltd.,** 1676 Duranleau St., Granville Island © 866/933-7447 or 604/290-7447; www.bonnielee.com), are outstanding outfitters that also sell fishing licenses.

GOLF

With five public 18-hole courses, half a dozen pitch-and-putt courses in the city, and dozens more nearby, golfers are never far from their love. For discounts and short-notice tee times at more than 30 Vancouver-area courses, contact the **A-1 Last Minute Golf Hot Line** (© 800/684-6344 or 604/878-1833; www.lastminutegolfbc.com).

A number of excellent public golf courses, maintained by the **Vancouver Board of Parks and Recreation** (© 604/280-1818 to book tee times; http://vancouver.ca/parks), can be found throughout the city. **Langara Golf Course,** 6706 Alberta St., around 49th Avenue and Cambie Street (© 604/713-1816), built in 1926 and recently renovated and redesigned, is one of the most popular golf courses in the province. Depending on the course, summer greens fees range from C$24 to C$49 for an adult, with discounts for seniors, youths, and off-season tee times.

The public **University Golf Club,** 5185 University Blvd. (© **604/224-1818;** www. universitygolf.com), is a great 6,560-yard, par-71 course with a clubhouse, pro shop, locker rooms, bar and grill, and sports lounge.

Leading private clubs are situated on the North Shore and in Vancouver. Check with your club at home to see if you have reciprocal visiting memberships with one of the following: **Capilano Golf and Country Club,** 420 Southborough Dr., West Vancouver (© **604/922-9331;** www.capilanogolf.com); **Marine Drive Golf Club,** West 57th Avenue and SW Marine Drive (© **604/261-8111;** www.marine-drive.com); **Seymour Golf and Country Club,** 3723 Mt. Seymour Pkwy., North Vancouver (© **604/929-2611;** www.seymourgolf.com); **Point Grey Golf and Country Club,** 3350 SW Marine Dr. (© **604/261-3108;** www.pointgreygolf.com); and **Shaughnessy Golf and Country Club,** 4300 SW Marine Dr. (© **604/266-4141;** www.shaughnessy.org). Greens fees range from C$42 to C$75.

HIKING

Great trails for hikers of all levels run through Vancouver's dramatic environs. You can pick up a local trail guide at any bookstore. Good trail maps are also available from **International Travel Maps and Books,** 12300 Bridgeport Rd., Richmond (© **604/ 273-1400;** www.itmb.com), which also stocks guidebooks and topographical maps. The retail store is open daily from 9:30am to 5pm or you can order maps online.

If you're looking for a challenge without a longtime commitment, hike the aptly named **Grouse Grind** from the bottom of **Grouse Mountain** (p. 126) to the top; then buy a one-way ticket down on the Grouse Mountain SkyRide gondola.

For a bit more scenery with a bit less effort, take the Grouse Mountain SkyRide up to the **Grouse chalet** and start your hike at an altitude of 1,100m (3,609 ft.). The trail north of **Goat Mountain** is well marked and takes approximately 6 hours round-trip, though you may want to build in some extra time to linger on the top of Goat and take in the spectacular 360-degree views of Vancouver, Vancouver Island, and the snowcapped peaks of the Coast Mountains.

Lynn Canyon Park, Lynn Headwaters Regional Park, Capilano River Regional Park, Mount Seymour Provincial Park, Pacific Spirit Park, and **Cypress Provincial Park** (see "The Top Attractions" and "Parks & Gardens," earlier in this chapter) have good, easy-to-challenging trails that wind up through stands of Douglas fir and cedar and contain a few serious switchbacks. Pay attention to the trail warnings posted at the parks (some have bear habitats), and always remember to sign in with the park service at the start of your chosen trail.

A little farther outside the city, the 6- to 10-hour hike to **Black Tusk** is one of the finest day hikes in North America. The trail head is located in **Garibaldi Provincial Park** (© **604/898-3678**), located 13km (8 miles) north of Squamish, which is 97km (60 miles) north of Vancouver along Hwy. 99 on the road to Whistler. The park has five access points; Black Tusk/Garibaldi Lake is the second marked turnoff (it takes about an hour to get there). The trail switchbacks up 1,000m (3,281 ft.) in about 6km (3¾ miles), then levels onto a rolling alpine plateau with fabulous views. The best time to make this climb is from July to October.

ICE-SKATING

The highest ice-skating rink in Canada is located on **Grouse Mountain;** see the Grouse Mountain description under "The Top Attractions," earlier in this chapter. In the city, the **West End Community Centre,** 870 Denman St. (© **604/257-8333**), rents skates at its enclosed rink, open January through March, as is the **Kitsilano Ice Rink,** 2690 Larch St. (© **604/257-6983;** http://vancouver.ca/parks). The enormous **Burnaby 8 Rinks Ice Sports Centre,** 6501 Sprott St., Burnaby (© **604/291-0626**), is the Vancouver Canucks' official practice facility. It has eight rinks, is open year-round, and offers lessons and rentals. Call ahead to check hours for public skating at all these rinks.

IN-LINE SKATING

All over Vancouver you'll find lots of locals rolling along beach paths, streets, park paths, and promenades. If you didn't bring a pair of blades, try **Bayshore Bicycle and Roller-blade Rentals,** 745 Denman St. (© **604/688-2453;** www.bayshorebikerentals.com). Rentals run C$5 per hour or C$20 for 8 hours. For information on in-line skating lessons and group events, visit www.inlineskatevancouver.com.

JOGGING

Local runners traverse the **Stanley Park seawall** ★★★ and the park paths around **Lost Lagoon** and **Beaver Lake.** If you're a dawn or dusk runner, take note that this is one of the world's safer city parks. However, if you're alone, don't tempt fate—stick to open and lighted areas. Other prime jogging areas are **Kitsilano Beach, Jericho Beach,** and **Spanish Banks** (see "Beaches," earlier in this chapter); all of them offer flat running paths along the ocean. You can also take the seawall path from English Bay Beach south along **False Creek.** If you feel like doing a little racing, competitions take place throughout the year; ask for information at any runners' outfitters such as **Forerunners,** 3504 W. 4th Ave. (© **604/732-4535**), or **Running Room,** 679 Denman St. (corner of Georgia; © **604/684-9771**). Check www.runningroom.com for information on clinics and events around Vancouver and British Columbia.

The **Sun Run** in April and the **Vancouver International Marathon** in May attract runners from around the world. Contact the **Vancouver International Marathon Society,** 1601 Bayshore Dr., in the Westin Bayshore Hotel (© **604/872-2928;** www.bmovanmarathon.ca), or the **Vancouver Sun Run,** 655 Burrard St. (© **604/689-9441;** www.sunrun.com), for information.

PARAGLIDING

In Surrey, **Deimos Paragliding Flight School** (© **877/359-7413** or 604/418-7328; www.deimospg.com) offers tandem flights from Burnaby Mountain and other locations for C$160. No experience is necessary for this unforgettable adventure; the actual flight, controlled by an experienced instructor, takes approximately 20 minutes.

SKIING & SNOWBOARDING

World-class skiing lies outside the city at the **Whistler Blackcomb Ski Resort,** 110km (68 miles) north of Vancouver; see chapter 12. However, you don't have to leave the city to get in a few runs. It seldom snows in the city's downtown and central areas, but Vancouverites can ski before work and after dinner at the three ski resorts in the North Shore mountains. These local mountains will play host to the freestyle and snowboard events in the 2010 Winter Games.

Grouse Mountain Resort, 6400 Nancy Greene Way, North Vancouver (© **604/984-0661,** snow report 604/986-6262; www.grousemountain.com), is about 3km (1¾ miles) from the Lions Gate Bridge and overlooks the Burrard Inlet and Vancouver skyline (p. 126). Four chairs, two beginner tows, and two T-bars take you to 24 alpine runs. The resort has night skiing, special events, instruction, and a spectacular view, as well as a 90m

(295-ft.) half-pipe for snowboarders. All skill levels are covered, with two beginner trails, three blue trails, and five black-diamond runs, including Coffin and Inferno, which follow the east slopes down from 1,230 to 750m (4,035–2,461 ft.). Rental packages and a full range of facilities are available. Lift tickets good for all-day skiing are C$50 for adults, C$42 for seniors and youths, C$22 for children 5 to 12, and free for children 4 and under. Lift prices do not include your gondola ride to the summit.

Mount Seymour Provincial Park, 1700 Mt. Seymour Rd., North Vancouver (© **604/ 986-2261**; www.mountseymour.com), has the area's highest base elevation; it's accessible via four chairs and a tow. Lift tickets are C$42 all day for adults, C$30 for seniors, C$35 for youths 12 to 19, and C$21 for children 6 to 11. Nighttime skiing from 4 to 10pm costs less. In addition to day and night skiing, the facility offers snowboarding, snowshoeing, and tobogganing along its 22 runs, as well as 26km (16 miles) of cross-country trails. The resort specializes in teaching first-timers. Camps for children and teenagers, and adult clinics, are available throughout the winter. Mount Seymour has one of Western Canada's largest equipment rental shops, which will keep your measurements on file for return visits. Shuttle service is available during ski season from various locations on the North Shore, including the Lonsdale Quay SeaBus. For more information, call © **604/953-3333.**

Cypress Bowl, 1610 Mt. Seymour Rd. (© **604/926-5612,** snow report 604/419-7669; www.cypressmountain.com), has the area's longest vertical drop (525m/1,722 ft.), challenging ski and snowboard runs, and 16km (10 miles) of track-set cross-country ski trails (including 5km/3 miles set aside for night skiing). Full-day lift tickets are C$56 to C$60 for adults, with reduced rates for youths, seniors, and children. Cross-country full-day passes are C$17 for adults, with reduced rates for youths, seniors, and children. Snowshoe tours and excellent introductory ski packages are available. *Note:* Cypress will be home to the 2010 Winter Olympics freestyle skiing (moguls and aerials), snowboarding (half-pipe and parallel giant slalom), and brand-new skicross events. In winter 2008 Cypress opened nine new runs for intermediate and expert skiers and snowboarders, accessed by a new quad chairlift. A new day lodge opened for the winter 2008/2009 season.

SWIMMING

The **Vancouver Aquatic Centre,** 1050 Beach Ave., at the foot of Thurlow Street (© **604/ 665-3424**), has a heated, 50m (164-ft.) Olympic pool, saunas, whirlpools, weight rooms, diving tanks, locker rooms, showers, child care, and a tot pool. Admission is C$5.65 for adults, C$2.80 for children 2 to 12. The new, coed **YWCA Fitness Centre,** 535 Hornby St. (© **604/895-5800;** www.ywcavan.org), in the heart of downtown, has a 6-lane, 25m (82-ft.), ozonated (much milder than chlorinated) pool, steam room, whirlpool, conditioning gym, and aerobic studios. A day pass is C$18 for adults. UBC's **Aquatic Centre,** 6121 University Blvd. (© **604/822-4522;** www.aquatics.ubc.ca), located next door to the Student Union Building and the bus loop, sets aside time for public use. Admission is C$5 for adults, C$4 for youths and students, and C$3 for seniors and children 3 to 12.

See also "Beaches," p. 136.

TENNIS

The city maintains 180 outdoor hard courts that have a 1-hour limit and accommodate patrons on a first-come, first-served basis from 8am until dusk. Local courtesy dictates that if people are waiting, you surrender the court on the hour. (Heavy usage times are evenings and weekends.) With the exception of the Beach Avenue courts, which charge a nominal fee in summer, all city courts are free.

Stanley Park has four courts near Lost Lagoon and 17 courts near the Beach Avenue entrance, next to the Fish House Restaurant. During the summer season (May–Sept), six courts are taken over for pay tennis and can be pre-booked by calling ✆ 604/605-8224. Queen Elizabeth Park's 18 courts service the central Vancouver area, and Kitsilano Beach Park's ★ 10 courts service the beach area between Vanier Park and the UBC campus.

Play at night on the Langara Campus of Vancouver Community College, on West 49th Avenue between Main and Cambie streets. The UBC Coast Club, 6160 Thunderbird Blvd. (✆ 604/822-2505; www.tennis.ubc.ca), has 10 outdoor and four indoor courts. Indoor courts are C$12 to C$22 per hour, depending on the time; outdoor courts are C$5 per person.

WHITE-WATER RAFTING

A 2½-hour drive from Vancouver, on the wild Nahatlatch River, Reo Rafting, 845 Spence Way, Anmore (✆ 800/736-7238 or 604/461-7238; www.reorafting.com), offers some of the best guided white-water trips in the province, at a very reasonable price. One-day packages—including lunch, all your gear, and 4 to 5 hours on the river—start at C$105 for adults. Multiday trips and group packages are available, and they can provide transportation from Vancouver.

Only a 1½-hour drive from the city is Chilliwack River Rafting (✆ 800/410-7238; www.chilliwackriverrafting.com), which offers half-day trips on the Chilliwack River and in the even hairier Chilliwack Canyon. The cost is C$89 for adults and C$69 for children.

WILDLIFE-WATCHING

Orcas, or killer whales, are the largest mammals to be seen in Vancouver's waters. Three pods (families), numbering about 80 whales, return to this area every year to feed on the salmon that spawn in the Fraser River starting in May and continuing into October. The eldest female leads the group; the head of one pod is thought to have been born in 1911. From April through October, daily excursions offered by Vancouver Whale Watch, 12240 2nd Ave., Richmond (✆ 604/274-9565; www.vancouverwhalewatch.com), focus on the majestic whales plus Dall's porpoises, sea lions, seals, eagles, herons, and other wildlife. The cost is C$125 per person (slightly lower rates for a semi-covered boat). Steveston Seabreeze Adventures, 12551 No. 1 Rd., Richmond (✆ 604/272-7200) also offers whale-watching tours for about the same price. Both companies offer a shuttle service from downtown Vancouver.

Thousands of migratory birds following the Pacific flyway rest and feed in the Fraser River delta south of Vancouver, especially at the 340-hectare (840-acre) George C. Reifel Bird Sanctuary, 5191 Robertson Rd., Westham Island (✆ 604/946-6980; www.reifel birdsanctuary.com), which was created by a former bootlegger and wetland-bird lover. Many other waterfowl species have made this a permanent habitat. More than 263 species have been spotted, including a Temminck's stint, a spotted redshank, bald eagles, Siberian (trumpeter) swans, peregrine falcons, blue herons, owls, and coots. The Snow Goose Festival, celebrating the annual arrival of the huge, snowy white flocks, is held here during the first weekend of November. The snow geese stay in the area until mid-December. (High tide, when the birds are less concealed by the marsh grasses, is the best time to visit.) An observation tower, 3km (2 miles) of paths, free birdseed, and picnic tables make this wetland reserve an ideal outing spot from October to April, when the birds are wintering in abundance. The sanctuary is wheelchair accessible and open daily from 9am to 4pm. Admission is C$4 for adults and C$2 for seniors and children.

The **Richmond Nature Park,** 11851 Westminster Hwy. (© **604/718-6188**), was established to preserve the Lulu Island wetlands bog. It features a Nature House with educational displays and a boardwalk-encircled duck pond. On Sunday afternoons, knowledgeable guides give free tours. Admission is by donation.

To hook up with local Vancouver birders, try the **Vancouver Natural History Society** (© **604/737-3074;** www.naturevancouver.ca). This all-volunteer organization runs birding field trips most weekends; many are free.

During the winter, thousands of bald eagles—in fact, the largest number in North America—line the banks of the **Squamish, Cheakamus,** and **Mamquam** rivers to feed on spawning salmon. To get there by car, take the scenic **Sea-to-Sky Highway** (Hwy. 99) from downtown Vancouver to Squamish and Brackendale; the trip takes about an hour. The route winds along the craggy tree-lined coast of Howe Sound through the town of Britannia Beach and past two beautiful natural monuments: Shannon Falls and the continent's tallest monolithic rock face, the Stawamus Chief. Alternatively, you can take a **Greyhound** bus from Vancouver's Pacific Central Station, 1150 Station St. (© **604/482-8747;** www.greyhound.ca); trip time is 1¼ hours. Contact **Squamish & Howe Sound Visitor Info Centre** (© **604/815-4994;** www.squamishchamber.com) for more information.

The annual summer salmon runs attract more than bald eagles. Tourists also flock to coastal streams and rivers to watch the waters turn red with leaping coho and sockeye. The salmon are plentiful at the **Capilano Salmon Hatchery** (p. 128), **Goldstream Provincial Park** out on Vancouver Island, and numerous other fresh waters.

Stanley Park (p. 116) and **Pacific Spirit Park** (p. 128) are both home to heron rookeries. You can see these large birds nesting just outside the Vancouver Aquarium. Ravens; dozens of species of waterfowl, raccoons, skunks, beavers, gray squirrels (imported from New York's Central Park decades ago), and even coyotes are also full-time residents. The **Stanley Park Ecology Society** (© **604/257-8544**) runs regular nature walks in the park. Call or check their website (www.stanleyparkecology.ca) for more information, or drop by the **Lost Lagoon Nature House** in Stanley Park (p. 118).

WINDSURFING

Windsurfing is not allowed at the mouth of False Creek near Granville Island, but you can bring a board to **Jericho** (p. 136) and **English Bay beaches** (p. 136) ★★ or rent one there. Equipment sales, rentals (including wet suits), and instruction can be found at **Windsure Windsurfing School,** 1300 Discovery St., at Jericho Beach (© **604/224-0615;** www.windsure.com). Rentals start at about C$19 per hour, wet suit and life jacket included.

7 SPECTATOR SPORTS

You can get schedules for all major events at Tourism Vancouver's **Touristinfo Centre,** 200 Burrard St. (© **604/683-2000;** www.tourismvancouver.com). Purchase tickets from Ticketmaster at the **Vancouver Ticket Centre,** 1304 Hornby St. (© **604/280-4444;** www.ticketmaster.ca), or from 40 outlets in the Greater Vancouver area. Popular events such as Canucks games sell out weeks or months in advance, so be sure to book ahead.

The Canadian Football League's B.C. Lions (✆ 604/589-7627; www.bclions.com) play their home and Grey Cup championship games (in good seasons) in the 60,000-seat B.C. Place Stadium, 777 Pacific Blvd. S. (at Beatty and Robson sts.). Canadian football differs from its American cousin: It's a three-down offense game on a field that's 10 yards longer and wider. Some of the plays you see will have American fans leaping out of their seats in surprise. Tickets for individual games are available from Ticketmaster (✆ 604/ 280-4639; www.ticketmaster.ca); prices run from C$30 to C$80

HOCKEY

The National Hockey League's **Vancouver Canucks** play at **General Motors Place** (otherwise known as GM Place, or the Garage), 800 Griffiths Way (✆ **604/899-4600;** event hotline 604/899-7444; www.canucks.com). Tickets are C$55 to C$100 and while difficult to obtain because the season tends to sell out in advance, some individual seats are made available for every home game.

HORSE RACING

Thoroughbreds run at **Hastings Park Racecourse,** Exhibition Park, 188 N. Renfrew St. (✆ **604/254-1631;** www.hastingspark.com), from mid-April to October. Call ahead or check the website for the latest schedule. The racecourse has a decent restaurant, so you can make a full afternoon or evening of dining and racing.

RUNNING

The **Vancouver Sun Run** in April and the **Vancouver International Marathon** (Canada's largest) in May attract thousands of runners from around the world and even more spectators. Contact the **Vancouver International Marathon Society** (✆ **604/872-2928;** www.bmovanmarathon.ca), or the **Vancouver Sun Run,** 655 Burrard St. (✆ **604/ 689-9441;** www.sunrun.com), for information.

SOCCER

The American Professional Soccer League's **Vancouver Whitecaps** (✆ **604/899-9283**) play at Swangard Stadium (✆ **604/435-7121;** www.whitecapsfc.com) in Burnaby. Admission is typically C$21 to C$42.

Vancouver Strolls

Down below's Stanley Park. On the side of the trees there's a beach. You can't see it [points over to left]. Steveston's over there. [points to left] Coast Guard station. There's the Yacht Club, and beyond it, the docks. Then over on the other side of the inlet, there's Grouse Mountain. It's about 4,000 feet high. There's a restaurant on top of it. Nice restaurant.

—from the screenplay for Playback, by Raymond Chandler

Chandler's detective Philip Marlow was one of Hollywood's most popular creations, but studio executives so hated his set-in-Vancouver screenplay that it never made it onto celluloid. That was back in the days before Vancouver came to be called "Hollywood North" because of all the films that are shot here. Chandler's geography in the above excerpt was a bit off, but that's quite understandable, since it can be a little difficult to orient yourself in this city surrounded by water. If you have directional problems, just remember that the grid of streets basically runs northwest to southeast rather than straight north-south, and that the mountains (which you can almost always see) are north. The best way to get acquainted with this unique city is to explore its various neighborhoods on foot. The tours below provide a good overall introduction.

WALKING TOUR 1	DOWNTOWN & THE WEST END

START:	The Fairmont Hotel Vancouver.
FINISH:	Cathedral Place.
TIME:	2 to 3 hours, not including museum, shopping, and eating stops.
BEST TIME:	Daytime, particularly during the week when the Law Courts building is open.
WORST TIME:	Late in the evening when the shops and offices have closed.

Vancouver's West End is said to be the densest residential district west of Manhattan. I don't know if that's true or not, but what I do know is that urban density has never been more beautifully planned or landscaped than in Vancouver. Every Edwardian house and every high-rise residential tower in the West End is surrounded by lush, beautiful plantings of trees, shrubs, and flowers. This appealingly green idea of the urban working *with* nature instead of against it carries over into Vancouver's commercial downtown, where the placement and orientation of buildings has been carefully controlled to preserve view corridors to the mountains and bodies of water. Remember to look up as you wander downtown—more often than not, you'll be rewarded with a peekaboo view of a North Shore peak.

❶ The Fairmont Hotel Vancouver
At 900 W. Georgia St. and dating from 1939, this hotel is owned by the Canadian Pacific Railway (CPR), just as the city itself was for many, many years. In return for agreeing in 1885 to make Vancouver its western terminus, the CPR was given 2,400 hectares (5,931 acres) of prime real

estate—nearly the whole of today's downtown. The Hotel Vancouver is built in the CPR's signature château style, with a verdigris-green copper roof. It's worth stepping inside to see the grand, old-fashioned ambience of the lobby.

Leaving by the Burrard Street exit, turn left. When you reach the corner, turn right, cross Burrard Street, and you're on:

❷ Robson Street

The shops on this corner get more foot traffic than any others in Canada. Things were different back in the 1950s, when so many German delis and restaurants opened up that for a time the street was nicknamed "Robsonstrasse." Beginning in the 1980s, the older businesses were replaced with high-end clothiers and new restaurants and gift shops with signs in Japanese. Whether you're into shopping or not, Robson Street is a great place to walk and people-watch. The street has an international cosmopolitan feel to it, and chances are you'll hear Cantonese, Croatian, Japanese, and other tongues as you stroll.

Two blocks farther down Robson at Bute Street, turn left and walk 1 block through a minipark to Barclay Street, and you've entered:

❸ The West End

Beginning in about 1959, this down-at-its-heels neighborhood of once-grand Edwardian houses was transformed by the advent of the concrete high-rise. By 1970, most of the Edwardian houses had been replaced by apartment towers, and the West End was on its way to becoming one of the densest—and simultaneously one of the most livable—inner cities on the continent. The minipark at Bute and Barclay is one of the things that makes the neighborhood so successful: traffic is kept to a minimum on the tree-lined West End streets, so that residents—though they live in the city center—can enjoy a neighborhood almost as quiet as a small town.

Beautiful landscaping, and plenty of it, adds to the area's appealing allure.

Turn right and walk 3 blocks down Barclay Street to Nicola Street. Along the way you'll see some of the elements that make the West End such a sought-after enclave: the gardens, street trees, and the range and variety of buildings—including a few surviving Edwardians, like the Arts and Crafts house at 1351 Barclay, and the pair of houses at the corner of Barclay and Nicola streets, otherwise known as:

❹ Barclay Square

This beautifully preserved bit of 19th-century Vancouver consists of Barclay Manor, built in the Queen Anne style in 1890, and **Roedde House,** a rare domestic design by British Columbia's leading 19th-century institutional architect, Francis Rattenbury. Roedde House is now a museum, open for guided tours Tuesday through Friday 2 to 4pm; admission C$5. On Sundays, tea and cookies are served and the admission price is C$1 more.

Turn left and walk south down Nicola Street for 1 block—past Fire Station No. 6—then turn right and go 1 block on Nelson, then left again onto Cardero Street, passing by the tiny Cardero Grocery at 1078 Cardero St. All the grocery needs of the West End were once supplied by little corner stores like this one. Turn right and walk 2 blocks on Comox Street to reach Denman Street, the perfect place to:

TAKE A BREAK
If Robson Street is the place Vancouverites go for hyperactive shopping sprees, Denman is where they go to sit back, sip a latte, and watch their fellow citizens stroll past. **Urban Rush,** 1040 Denman St. (✆ **604/685-2996**), is a fine spot for coffee and baked goods, particularly if you can nab a table on their outdoor terrace. One block down on the opposite side of the street, **Delaney's on Denman,** 1105 Denman St. (✆ **604/662-3344**), is a favorite coffee hangout for members of the West End's sizable gay community. Everyone's welcome, of course, and the pies and cakes at this little cafe are great.

1 Fairmont Hotel Vancouver
2 Robson Street
3 The West End
4 Barclay Square
5 English Bay Beach
6 Alexandra Park
7 The Gabriola
8 Pendrell Street
9 Mole Hill
10 B.C. Hydro Building
11 Provincial Law Courts
12 Robson Square
13 Vancouver Art Gallery
14 Christ Church Cathedral
15 Cathedral Place

VANCOUVER STROLLS

9

DOWNTOWN & THE WEST END

When you're ready to continue the walking tour, go 2 blocks farther down Denman Street and you're at:

5 English Bay Beach

This is the place to be when the sun is setting, or on one of those crystal-clear days when the mountains of Vancouver Island can be seen looming in the distance—or any day at all, really, so long as the sun is shining. Every January 1, shivering Vancouverites in fancy costumes surround the bathhouse here at the very foot of Denman Street (entrance at beach level) to take part in the annual Polar Bear Swim.

Walk southeastward (left, as you're facing the water) on Beach Avenue, and you come to a tiny green space with a band shell known as:

6 Alexandra Park

Back around the turn of the 20th century, a big Bahamian immigrant named Joe Fortes used to make his home in a cottage near this spot—that is, when he wasn't down on the beach teaching local kids to swim. In recognition of his many years of free service, the city finally appointed Fortes its first lifeguard. Later, a marble water fountain was erected in his memory by the Beach Avenue entrance to the park.

When you're finished looking around the park, head up Bidwell Street 2 blocks to Davie Street, cross the street, turn right, walk 2 blocks farther on Davie Street, and on your left at no. 1531 you'll see:

❼ The Gabriola

This was the finest mansion in the West End when it was built in 1900 for sugar magnate B. T. Rogers. Its name comes from the rough sandstone cladding, quarried on Gabriola Island in the Strait of Georgia. Unfortunately for Rogers, the Shaughnessy neighborhood soon opened up across False Creek, and the West End just wasn't a place a millionaire could afford to be seen anymore. By 1925, the mansion had been sold off and subdivided into apartments. Since 1975, it's been a restaurant of one sort or another—currently Romano's Macaroni Grill (reviewed in chapter 7). The wrought-iron tables in the garden are nice spots to sit on a summer day.

Cut through the garden and walk up through the Nicola Street minipark, turning right on:

❽ Pendrell Street

A few interesting bits of architecture reside on this street. One block farther, at the corner of Broughton Street, is the **Thomas Fee house,** 1119 Broughton St., where one of the city's leading turn-of-the-20th-century developer-architects made his home. Farther along, at the southeast corner of Pendrell and Jervis streets, is **St. Paul's Episcopal Church,** a 1905 Gothic Revival church built entirely of wood. A block away at 1254 Pendrell is the **Pendrellis**—a piece of architecture so unbelievably awful, one gets a perverse delight just looking at it. Built as a seniors' home at the height of the 1970s craze for concrete, the multistory tower is one great concrete block, with nary a window in sight.

At Bute Street, turn left and walk 1 block to Comox Street, and you're at:

❾ Mole Hill

These 11 preserved Edwardian homes provide a rare view of what the West End looked like in, say, 1925. That they exist at all is more or less a fluke. The city bought

the buildings in the 1970s but continued renting them out, thinking one day to tear them down for a park. By the 1990s, however, heritage had become important. The residents of the houses waged a sophisticated political campaign, renaming the area Mole Hill and bringing in nationally known architectural experts to plead the case for preservation. The city soon gave in.

Cut across the park to Nelson Street and continue down Nelson Street past Thurlow Street to 970 Burrard St., where stands:

❿ The B.C. Hydro Building

Built in 1958 by architect Ned Pratt, it was one of the first modernist structures erected in Canada, and has since become a beloved Vancouver landmark, thanks in no small part to its elegant shape and attention to detail. Note how the windows, the doors, and even the tiles in the lobby and forecourt echo the six-sided lozenge shape of the original structure. In the mid-'90s, the building was converted to condominiums and rechristened the Electra.

From here, continue on Nelson Street, crossing Burrard Street and Hornby Street to:

⓫ The Provincial Law Courts

Internationally recognized architect Arthur Erickson has had an undeniable impact on his native city of Vancouver. His 1973 Law Courts complex covers 3 full city blocks, including the Erickson-renovated Vancouver Art Gallery at its north end. Linking the two is Robson Square, which Erickson—and everyone else—envisioned as the city's main civic plaza. As with so many Erickson designs, this one has elements of brilliance—the boldness of the vision itself, the tiered fountains (behind them are the offices of the Crown attorney—the Canadian equivalent of a district attorney—the cathedral-like space of the courthouse atrium—but, raised above street level, the entire ensemble is removed from all the life around it.

To reach the courthouse, take the concrete stairway up and follow the elevated pedestrian concourse. The courthouse, with its giant glass-covered atrium, is worth a visit.

When you've seen the Law Courts, backtrack along the concourse, and you'll end up at:

⑫ Robson Square

As a civic plaza, Robson Square should be grand, but in fact it's pretty underwhelming. Its basic problem is that it has been sunk 6m (20 ft.) below street level, so it's never exactly appealing or inviting to passersby. Although there's a pleasant cafe in the square and a UBC bookstore, Robson Square lacks the throngs of people that add the essential ingredient—life—to a civic plaza. But just look across the street, and you'll see all the life that Robson Square lacks.

Directly across from Robson Square at 750 Hornby St. is the:

⑬ Vancouver Art Gallery

On sunny days, people bask like seals on the steps of the old courthouse-turned-art-gallery, a great gathering place and the perfect spot to see jugglers and buskers, pick up a game of outdoor speed chess, or listen to an activist haranguing the world at large about the topic du jour.

Designed as a courthouse by Francis Rattenbury (architect of Roedde House, described above, and the Legislature Buildings and Fairmont Empress hotel in Victoria) and renovated into an art gallery by Arthur Erickson, the Vancouver Art Gallery (p. 120) is home to a tremendous collection of works by iconic West Coast painter Emily Carr, as well as rotating exhibits ranging from native masks to video installations. Film buffs may remember the entrance steps and inside lobby from the movie *The Accused.*

To continue the tour, go around the gallery and proceed down Hornby Street. Note the fountain on the Art Gallery's front lawn. It was installed by a very unpopular provincial government as a way—according to some—of forever blocking protesters from gathering on what was then the courthouse lawn. In 2007, the 2010 Olympic Winter Games countdown clock was placed here.

Cross Georgia Street and have a glance inside the **Hong Kong Bank building,** 885 W. Georgia St., where a massive pendulum designed by artist Alan Storey slowly swings back and forth.

Cross Hornby and continue west on Georgia Street to 690 Burrard, where stands:

⑭ Christ Church Cathedral

A Gothic Revival sandstone church with a steep gabled roof, buttresses, and arched stained-glass windows, the Anglican Christ Church Cathedral was completed in 1895. It was nearly demolished in the 1930s, when developers offered a lot of money to the church for the land. A local reporter uncovered the clergy's plot to raze the landmark in exchange for a big profit, and publicized it while negotiations were in the final stages. The public outcry marked the first shift in local sentiment toward the preservation of heritage sites.

Backtrack east to Hornby, turn left, walk half a block, and climb the few steps into:

⑮ Cathedral Place

Often overlooked by Vancouverites, peaceful Cathedral Place is a charming example of an urban park. The building behind it, at 639 Hornby, is a postmodern structure with small Art Deco parts melded onto a basically Gothic edifice. Some of the panels on its front were salvaged from the Georgia Medical-Dental building, a much-loved skyscraper that used to stand on this site. As for the Cathedral Place courtyard itself, it has the formality and calm of a French garden, the perfect spot to sit and enjoy a bit of peace.

START:	Canada Place.
FINISH:	Maple Tree Square.
TIME:	2 to 4 hours, not including shopping, eating, and sightseeing stops.
BEST TIME:	Any day during business hours, but Chinatown is particularly active in the mornings. If you arrive between noon and 2pm, you can enjoy dim sum at many of the restaurants.
WORST TIME:	Chinatown's dead after 6pm, except on weekends in the summer, when they close a few streets to traffic and hold a traditional Asian night market from 6:30 to 11pm.

Chinatown and Gastown are two of Vancouver's most fascinating neighborhoods. Gastown has history and the kind of old-fashioned architecture that no longer exists downtown or in the West End. Chinatown has brightly colored facades, street markets, and the buzz of modern-day Cantonese commerce. One small travel advisory, however: The two neighborhoods border on Vancouver's Downtown Eastside, a skid-row area troubled by alcoholism and drug use. While there's actually little danger for outsiders, there is a good chance you'll cross paths with a down-and-outer here and there, particularly around Pigeon Park at the corner of Carrall and Hastings streets. The tour route has been designed to avoid these areas.

Begin the tour at:

❶ Canada Place

With its five tall Teflon sails and bowsprit jutting out into Burrard Inlet, Canada Place is meant to resemble a giant sailing ship. Inside it's a convention center and giant cruise-ship terminal, with the Pan Pacific Hotel (p. 74) perched on top. Around the perimeter is a promenade with plaques at regular intervals explaining the sights or providing historical tidbits. During the summer months, this area is jammed with tourists and passengers arriving and departing from Alaskan cruises; the rest of the year you'll have it pretty much to yourself. A huge expansion to add more convention space and additional docking facilities should be completed in 2009.

To follow the promenade, start by the fountain flying the flags of Canada's provinces and territories, and head north along the walkway. On the roof at the far end of the pier, a pair of leaping bronze lions point up and out toward a pair of peaks on the North Shore called the Lions, so named for their supposed resemblance to

the bronze lions in Trafalgar Square, but really because the local morality squad wanted to eliminate forever the name given to the peaks by the rough-minded early settlers—Sheila's Paps. Continue around the promenade, and you'll turn and look back toward the city: The line of low-rise older buildings just beyond the railway tracks is Gastown.

To continue the tour, walk back toward the shore along the promenade, go down the steps, turn left, and curve along the sidewalk until you pass the Aqua Riva restaurant. Then turn left and go up the steps to an elevated plaza. You're now at:

❷ Granville Square

Had some ill-advised politicians and developers had their way, all of Gastown and Chinatown would have been replaced by towers like the one you see here at 200 Granville. In 1970, the plans were drawn up and the bulldozers were set to move when a coalition of hippies, heritage lovers, and Chinatown merchants took to the barricades in revolt. This undistinguished building was the only one ever built, and the plan was abandoned soon afterward.

1 Canada Place
2 Granville Square
3 Waterfront Station
4 Steam Clock
5 Maple Tree Square
6 Sun Tower
7 T&T Supermarket
8 Sam Kee Building
9 Chinese Cultural Centre/
    Dr. Sun Yat-sen Park and
    Chinese Classical Garden
10 Kuomintang Building
11 St. James Anglican Church
12 Vancouver Centennial Police
    Museum
13 Crab Park Overpass

At the east end of the plaza a doorway leads into:

❸ Waterfront Station

Though this Beaux Arts edifice at 601 W. Cordova St. was converted into the SeaBus terminal in the 1970s (SkyTrain was added in 1986), the building was originally the CPR's Vancouver passenger-rail terminal. Look up high on the walls, and you'll see oil paintings depicting scenes you might encounter if you took the train across Canada (much easier then than now). On the main floor is a Starbucks and some tourist shops. This is also where you can catch the SeaBus over to Lonsdale Quay in North Vancouver.

Leave by the front doors, turn left, and proceed to cobblestoned Water Street, Gastown's main thoroughfare. The Landing, at 375 Water St., is home to some high-end retail stores and offices. Like most of Gastown's buildings, The Landing was built in the boom years between the Great Fire of 1886 and World War I. Klondike gold fueled much of the construction. As you walk along, note the Magasin Building at 322 Water St. Each of the column capitals bears the bronze head of a Gastown notable, among them Ray Saunders, the man who designed the:

❹ Steam Clock

A quirky urban timepiece, the Steam Clock at Water and Cambie streets gives a steamy rendition of the Westminster Chimes every 15 minutes, drawing its

power from the city's underground steam-heat system. A plaque on the base of the clock explains the mechanics of it all. (*Note:* The chimes can be erratic.)

Continue down Water Street, past Hill's Native Art (165 Water St.), where Bill Clinton picked up a little bear statuette as a gift for you-know-who. At Abbot Street, cross over to the south side and continue on Water Street until you come to the Gaoler's Mews building (12 Water St.). Duck in through the passageway and cross Carrall Street to reach:

TAKE A BREAK

The **Irish Heather,** 210 Carrall St. (☎ **604/688-9779**), an old Vancouver favorite in a new (since 2009) location, serves excellent beer and good pub food. Once you leave the pub, continue down Carrall to:

❺ Maple Tree Square

A historic spot, Maple Tree Square is where Vancouver first began. The statue by the maple tree (not the original tree, but a replacement planted in the same spot) is of Gassy Jack Deighton, a riverboat captain and innkeeper who erected Vancouver's first significant structure—a saloon—in 1867. Deighton got the nickname Gassy because of his propensity to jaw on at length (gassing, as it was known) about whatever topic happened to spring to mind. In 1870, when the town was officially incorporated as Granville, it was home to exactly six businesses: a hotel, two stores, and three saloons. Most folks called it Gastown, after Jack. More recent history: On August 7, 1971, some 1,500 hippies gathered in the square for the Grasstown Smoke-in & Street Jamboree. There were riots, arrests, and lots of stoned people.

Continue south on Carrall Street to West Cordova, turn right, and walk 1 block to Abbot Street. Turn left and walk 2 blocks down Abbot, crossing West Hastings Street and stopping at West Pender Street, where you get a great view of the:

❻ Sun Tower

At 500 Beatty St., it was the tallest building in the British Empire when it was built in 1911 to house the publishing empire of Louis D. Taylor, publisher of *Vancouver World.* Not only was the building tall, but it was also slightly scandalous, thanks to the nine half-nude caryatids that gracefully support the cornice halfway up the building. Three years after the building opened, Louis D. was forced to sell it.

Cross West Pender Street and continue on Abbot Street until you come to the entrance at 179 Keefer Place of:

❼ T&T Supermarket

Think you know supermarkets? Unless your hometown is Hong Kong or Singapore, you haven't seen one like this. Just have a gander at the seafood display inside the doors: king crab, scallops, three different kinds of oysters, lobster, and geoducks. Farther in is a host of other wondrous products, including strange Asian fruits like rambutan, lychee, and the pungent durian. Browse, maybe pick up something you don't recognize, and have an impromptu picnic in nearby Andy Livingstone Park.

Outside, walk 1 block east on Keefer Street to Taylor Street. Andy Livingstone Park is farther ahead to your right, but to continue the tour, turn left on Taylor Street and walk 1 block north to Pender Street. Turn right on Pender, and walk 1 block. Now you're in one of North America's most populous Chinatowns. Our first Chinatown stop, at 8 W. Pender St., is the:

❽ Sam Kee Building

The world's thinnest office building—just shy of 1.5m deep (4 ft. 11 in. to be exact)—was Sam Kee's way of thumbing his nose at both the city and his greedy next-door neighbor. In 1912, the city expropriated most of Kee's land in order to widen Pender Street, but refused to compensate him for the tiny leftover strip. Kee's neighbor, meanwhile, hoped to pick up the leftover sliver dirt-cheap. The building was Kee's response. Huge bay windows helped maximize the available space, as did the extension of the basement

well out underneath the sidewalk (note the glass blocks in the pavement).

Just behind the Sam Kee Building is the forlorn-looking **Shanghai Alley,** which just 40 years ago was jampacked with stores, restaurants, a pawnshop, a theater, rooming houses, and a public bath. (**Canton Alley,** on your right between E. Pender and E. Hastings sts., still gives an idea of what these teeming alleyways looked like a few decades ago, but it's now an unsavory hangout for drug users.) More interesting is the **Chinese Freemason's building,** just across the street at 1 W. Pender. The building could be a metaphor for the Chinese experience in Canada. On predominantly Anglo Carrall Street, the building is the picture of Victorian conformity. On the Pender Street side, on the other hand, the structure is exuberantly Chinese.

Walk 1 block farther (east) on Pender Street and you'll come to the:

❾ Chinese Cultural Centre/Dr. Sun Yat-Sen Park & Chinese Classical Garden

A modern building with an impressive traditional gate, the cultural center provides services and programs for the neighborhood's thousands of Chinese-speaking residents. Straight ahead as you enter the courtyard, a door set within a wall leads into the **Dr. Sun Yat-Sen Park,** a small urban park with a pond, walkways, and a nice gift shop selling scaled-down replicas of the ancient terra-cotta warriors unearthed in the tomb of Chinese Emperor Qon Shi Huang. Admission to the park is free.

Adjoining the park, and accessible through another small doorway to the right of it, is the **Dr. Sun Yat-Sen Classical Chinese Garden** (p. 120). Modeled after a Ming period (1368–1644) scholar's retreat in the Chinese city of Suzhou, this garden is definitely worth a visit. Dr. Sun Yat-Sen (1866–1925), for whom the park

and garden are named, is known as the **153** father of modern China.

Exit the Chinese Classical Garden by the gate on the east side, turn left on Columbia Street, and you'll find the **Chinese Cultural Centre Museum and Archives** at 555 Columbia St.

From here, continue on Columbia Street up to Pender, turn right and continue east, peeking in here and there to explore Chinese herbalist shops like Vitality Enterprises at 126 E. Pender. At Main Street, turn right and walk south 1 block to Keefer Street and:

TAKE A BREAK
Though it's Canada's largest Chinese restaurant, **Floata Seafood Restaurant,** 180 Keefer St. (𝒸 **604/ 602-0368**), isn't easy to find. In classic Hong Kong restaurant style, it's on the third floor of a bright red shopping plaza/ parking garage. Time your arrival for mid-morning dim sum (a kind of moving Chinese smorgasbord) if you can. Alternatively, you might want to check out the recommended Chinatown restaurants in chapter 7.

To continue the tour, stroll east on Keefer Street, lined with sidewalk markets selling fresh fish, fruit, and vegetables. Turn left on Gore Avenue, and walk 1 block north to Pender Street. On your left, at 296 E. Pender St., is the:

❿ Kuomintang Building

Though often a mystery to outsiders, politics was and remains an important part of life in Chinatown. Vancouver was long a stronghold of the Chinese Nationalist Party, or Kuomintang (KMT), whose founder, Dr. Sun Yat-Sen, stayed in Vancouver for a time raising funds. In 1920, the party erected this building to serve as its western Canadian headquarters. When the rival Chinese Communist party emerged victorious from the Chinese civil war in 1949, KMT leader Chiang Kaishek retreated to Taiwan. Note the Taiwanese flags on the roof.

Return to Gore Avenue, and turn left (north) for 2 blocks. At the corner of Gore Avenue and Cordova Street (303 E. Cordova St.) stands:

⑪ St. James Anglican Church

Just before getting this commission, architect Adrian Gilbert Scott had designed a cathedral in Cairo—and it shows.

One block west on Cordova brings you to the:

⑫ Vancouver Centennial Police Museum

Located in the former Coroner's Court at 240 E. Cordova, the **Vancouver Centennial Police Museum** (p. 120) is worth a visit if you're in a macabre mood. Among other displays, the museum has the autopsy report of Errol Flynn, who died in Vancouver in 1959 in the arms of his 17-year-old girlfriend.

Back on Gore Avenue walk north 2 blocks to Alexander Street. Turn left, and walk 1 block west on Alexander to the:

⑬ Crab Park Overpass

City Hall calls it Portside Park, and that's how it appears on the map, but to everyone else it's Crab Park. It was created after long and vigorous lobbying by eastside activists, who reasoned that poor downtown residents had as much right to beach access as anyone else. The park is pleasant enough, though not worth the trouble of walking all the way up and over the overpass. What is worthwhile, however, is walking halfway up to where two stone Chinese lions stand guard. From here, you can look back at Canada Place—where the tour started—or at the container port and fish plant to your right.

To bring the tour to an end, return to Alexander Street and walk 2 blocks west back to Maple Tree Square (stop 5).

WALKING TOUR 3	YALETOWN, GRANVILLE ISLAND & KITSILANO

START:	The Vancouver Public Library Central Branch at Homer and Georgia streets.
FINISH:	The Capers Building, 285 W. 4th Ave. (at Vine), in Kitsilano.
TIME:	2 to 4 hours, not including shopping, eating, and sightseeing stops.
BEST TIME:	Any time during business hours.
WORST TIME:	After 6pm, when Granville Island's shops have closed.

This tour takes you through three of Vancouver's most interesting neighborhoods: the trendy warehouse-turned-retail/restaurant district of Yaletown, the industrial-area-turned-public-market called Granville Island, and the laid-back enclave of Kitsilano. The tour includes a brief ferry ride and a stroll along the waterfront and beach.

We begin at:

① Vancouver Public Library

Designed by architect Moshe Safdie, the library, at 350 W. Georgia St., was enormously controversial when it opened in 1995. Though Safdie denied that the ancient Roman coliseum served as inspiration, the coliseum is exactly what comes to mind when you first see the exterior of this postmodern building. Architectural critics pooh-poohed it as derivative and ignorant

of West Coast architectural traditions, but for the public it was love at first sight. The steps out front have become a popular public gathering place, the lofty atrium inside a favored hangout spot and "study-date" locale. Go inside the atrium and then into the high-tech library itself: It's light, airy, and wonderfully accessible.

From the library, walk south down Homer Street and turn left on Nelson Street. At Hamilton Street you're in:

1 Vancouver Public Library
2 Yaletown
3 The Roundhouse
4 Yaletown Landing
5 Granville Island Aquabus
   Ferry Dock
6 Granville Island Public Market
7 Government Fish Dock
8 Burrard Bridge
9 Heritage Harbour
10 Maritime Museum
11 Totem Pole
12 Kitsilano Beach
13 The Capers Building

Vancouver's former meatpacking warehouse district, Yaletown was where roughneck miners from Yale (up the Fraser Valley) used to come to drink and brawl. The city considered leveling the area in the 1970s until someone noticed that the raised loading docks would make great outdoor terraces and the low brick buildings themselves could be renovated into commercial space. Though it's taken years for the neighborhood to really catch on, the result is a funky upscale district of furniture shops, restaurants, multimedia companies, "New York–style" lofts, and lots and lots of clubs. Hamilton Street and Mainland Street are the trendiest arteries in Yaletown. Note the metal canopies over the loading docks on many buildings—they used to keep shipping goods dry; now they do the same for tourists and latte-sipping computer programmers.

Walk down Mainland and turn left at Davie. Continue southeast down Davie Street, turn right on Pacific Boulevard, and across the street you'll see:

❸ The Roundhouse

The Roundhouse is so named because that's exactly what this brick-and-timber frame building was, back when this land was the CPR's switching yard. The structure has since been converted into a community center. It's worth ducking inside to have a look at the locomotive that pulled the first passenger train into Vancouver, way back in 1887; you can also see the locomotive from the street, through a giant glass window.

Follow Davie Street south to the False Creek waterfront and the:

❹ Yaletown Landing (at the Foot of Davie St.)

The forest of high-rises ringing the north shore of False Creek, where you're now standing, is the creation of one company—Concorde Pacific, owned by Hong Kong billionaire Li Ka Shing. Formerly a railway switching yard, the area was transformed for the Expo '86 World's Fair. When the fair came to an end, the provincial government sold the land to Li Ka Shing for a song on the understanding he would build condominiums. And did he ever.

At the landing site, note the large art piece, *Street Light,* designed by Bernie Miller and Alan Tregebov and installed in 1997. The large panels, each of which depicts a seminal event in False Creek's history, have been arranged so that on the anniversary of that event, the sun will shine directly through the panel, casting a shadowed image on the street.

From here, at the end of the dock, catch the **Aquabus miniferry** (✆ **604/689-5858**) for Granville Island, right across False Creek. The little boats leave about every 15 minutes through the day; the fare is C$2.50 for adults.

The Aquabus will scoot you across False Creek harbor in about 5 minutes and let you off at:

❺ Granville Island Ferry Dock

To be topographically honest, Granville Island (p. 114) is not really an island; it's more of a protuberance. But it contains a fascinating collection of shops, restaurants, theaters, artists' workshops, housing, a hotel, and still-functioning heavy industry—one of the few successful examples of 1970s urban renewal. The **Granville Island Information Centre,** 1592 Johnston St. (✆ **604/666-5784**), near the Public Market, has excellent free maps, but they're not really necessary—the place is so compact, the best thing to do is simply wander and explore.

Right at the top of the Aquabus dock is an entrance into the:

❻ Granville Island Public Market

This is an amazing place that sells just about anything and everything that's edible. The market is a wonderful place to stop and:

TAKE A BREAK
If it's edible, the **Granville Island Public Market** probably has it, from chocolate and fresh salmon to fresh bread and strawberries picked that morning out in the Fraser Valley. Those with an immediate hunger gravitate to the far side of the market, where **A La Mode** (© 604/685-8335) sells lattes and fabulous rhubarb-strawberry pie. The most fun way to feed yourself, however, is to roam the market stalls for sandwiches, sausages, or picnic supplies—artichoke hearts, artisan cheese, cold smoked salmon, Indian candy, pepper pâté, freshly baked bread—then head outside for an alfresco feast at one of the tables on the dock overlooking False Creek. The views are great, the fresh air invigorating, and, if you've brought small children along, it's the perfect place to play that endlessly fascinating (to kids) game of Catch the Seagull.

From Triangle Square, the small plaza in front of the public market, head south (left) on Duranleau Street, where you'll pass enticing shops and marine charter services. At Anderson Street turn right and right again on waterside Island Park Walk, following it north to the:

⑦ Government Fish Dock

Want to buy fresh from the boat? This is the place to do it. Find fresh salmon in season (summer and early fall), prawns, scallops, and other shellfish much of the rest of the year. Sales take place every day in high season and on weekend mornings the rest of the year. Hours and availability, of course, depend on the catch.

Continue on the seaside walkway, and eventually you pass beneath the:

⑧ Burrard Bridge

In 1927, the city fathers commissioned noted urban planner Harland Bartholomew to provide some guidance on how to expand their rather raw seaport city. One of Bartholomew's first injunctions: Build beautiful bridges. The Burrard Bridge is the result, an elegant steel span with two castles guarding the approaches at either end.

Walk beneath the bridge and continue along the waterside pedestrian path in Vanier Park to:

⑨ Heritage Harbour

Many older wooden boats find shelter here, including the seiner BCP45 shown on the back of the old Canadian $5 bill. Those interested in a shortcut can pick up a ferry (**False Creek Ferries;** © 604/684-7781) at this point and ride back to Granville Island (stop 5) or over to the West End. On weekdays and in the off season, the ferries run less frequently. Hours and fares are posted on the sign at the end of the dock.

If you're continuing the walk, proceed west along the shoreline. To your left stands artist Chung Hung's massive iron sculpture *Gate to the Northwest Passage.* Just beyond that, the conical building is the **Vancouver Museum** (p. 125) and **H. R. MacMillan Space Centre** (p. 122). The low building next to that is the **Vancouver Archives,** 1150 Chestnut St. (© 604/736-8561), home to some truly fascinating panoramic photographs of Vancouver back in the early days.

Continue on the waterside path until you come to the:

⑩ Vancouver Maritime Museum

For centuries, the quest of every European explorer was to find the Northwest Passage, the seagoing shortcut to the riches of the East. The little ship housed inside the **Vancouver Maritime Museum** (p. 125) is the one that finally did it. Tours of the RCMP vessel, the *St. Roch,* are available at regular intervals throughout the day. Out back of the museum, the junk on the lawn by the north side all comes from various ships wrecked on the B.C. coast.

In front of the museum, you'll see the:

⑪ Totem Pole

Carved by the exceptional Kwakiutl carver Mungo Martin (who also did many of the poles displayed in the Museum of Anthropology and in Stanley Park), the 10 figures on this 30m-tall (98-ft.) pole each represent an ancestor of the 10 Kwakiutl clans.

An identical pole was presented to Queen Elizabeth in 1958 to mark B.C.'s centenary. It now stands in Windsor Great Park in England.

Continue on the waterside pathway to:

⑫ Kitsilano Beach

Vancouver is blessed with beaches. From here, they stretch almost unbroken to the University of British Columbia, 10km (6¼ miles) west on the tip of the Point Grey peninsula. Each beach has its own distinct personality. Below UBC, Wreck Beach is a semiwild strand for nudists and nature lovers. Beaches in between cater to dogs, picnicking families, and hikers. Kitsilano Beach (Kits Beach for short) is home to a spandex-and-testosterone set that loves a fast and furious game on the volleyball courts. But relaxers love Kits, too. The logs lined up on the beach make it a fine place to lay out a blanket and laze the day away. Small children love to play on the nearby swings, while older kids favor the life-guarded swimming area or the world's largest outdoor saltwater swimming pool. On a clear day, the views of the mountains are tremendous.

About midway down Kits Beach, a sidewalk veers left and takes you up to Yew Street. Follow Yew uphill to 4th Avenue and turn right. At 2285 W. 4th Ave. you'll find:

⑬ The Capers Building

Back in the 1960s, Kitsilano was Canada's Hippie Central, a Haight-Ashbury–like enclave of head shops, communes, and coffeehouses. In the early 1970s, Vancouver's supersquare mayor, Tom Campbell, went so far as to propose rounding up all the tie-dyed long-hairs and shipping them off to a detention center. As the years passed, the hippies' waistlines and wallets got thicker, run-down communes and boardinghouses were renovated or replaced with new apartments and condos, and the shops came to reflect Kitsilano's new affluence, though still with a touch of counterculture.

The retail/office/apartment building at 2285 W. 4th Ave. was built according to an innovative energy-efficient design, and now serves as home to an excellent bookstore called **Duthie's,** and to **Capers,** an organic supermarket.

The walk ends here. You may want to explore the shopping opportunities along 4th Avenue. Or you can catch a no. 4 or 7 bus to take you back to downtown Vancouver.

Vancouver Shopping

Vancouver's a fun place to shop because it's international and cosmopolitan but hasn't lost its funky, fun-loving edge. There are stores galore, and most of them are not in malls. Blessed with a climate that seems semitropical in comparison to the rest of Canada, Vancouverites never really developed a taste for indoor malls (though there is one, the Pacific Centre, right downtown). Below are a few thoughts on where to start your shopping expeditions.

---

1 THE SHOPPING SCENE

Outside of malls, stores in Vancouver are generally open Monday through Saturday from 9am to 6pm. A few exceptions: Stores on Robson Street stay open later (usually until 9pm), while stores in Kitsilano open later (around 10am). On Sunday most stores are open 11am to 6pm, but a few remain closed all day. Malls such as the Pacific Centre are open from 10am to 7pm Monday and Tuesday, 10am to 9pm Wednesday through Friday, 10am to 7pm on Saturday, and 10am to 6pm on Sunday. During Christmas shopping season, stores extend their hours.

ROBSON STREET It's been said that the corner of Robson and Burrard gets more foot traffic than any other corner in Canada. It's a busy, colorful parade of humanity, with many students, visitors, and residents from Asia (hence the sushi bars and shops with Japanese signs), most with money. Over the past few years, rents have risen so much that Robson Street now mostly offers upscale chain shops and international designer boutiques, though here and there a few local stores survive. Look for high-end clothing and accessories, with a focus on young designer fashions.

SOUTH GRANVILLE The 10-block stretch of Granville Street, from 6th Avenue up to 16th Avenue, is where Vancouver's old-money enclave of Shaughnessy comes to shop. Classic and expensive clothiers, and housewares and furniture boutiques predominate. This is also the heart of the gallery district.

WATER STREET & GASTOWN Though a little too heavy on the souvenir shops, Water Street and Gastown are by no means just a tacky tourist enclave. Look for antiques and cutting-edge furniture, galleries of First Nations art, funky basement retro shops, and up-to-the-minute fashions by local designers.

MAIN STREET Antiques, and lots of 'em. From about 19th up to 27th, Main Street is chockablock with antiques shops. Rather than outbid each other, the stores have evolved so that each covers a particular niche, from Art Deco to country kitchen to fine Second Empire. It's fun to browse, and if your eyes start to glaze over at the thought of yet another divan, the area also has cafes, bookshops, and clothing stores.

GRANVILLE ISLAND A rehabilitated industrial site beneath the Granville Street Bridge, the Public Market is one of the best places to pick up salmon and other seafood. It's also a great place to browse for crafts and gifts. You can also observe potters, silversmiths, and glass blowers as they work their magic. Particularly interesting is Kids Market, a kind of minimall for children, featuring play areas and services for the not-yet-10 demographic. See the Granville Island listing (p. 114).

ASIA WEST   If you've never been to Hong Kong, or are just itching to get back, this new commercial area on Richmond's No. 3 Road between Capstan and Alderbridge roads is the place to shop. Stores in four new malls—the Yaohan Centre, President Plaza, Aberdeen Centre, and Parker Place—cater to Vancouver's Asian community by bringing in goods directly from the Far East. If the prices seem a bit high, a simple inquiry is often enough to bring them plummeting by as much as 80%. The **Aberdeen Centre,** 4151 Hazelbridge Way (corner of Hazelbridge Way and Cambie St.; ℃ **604/270-1234**), and the adjacent **Yaohan Centre,** 3700 No. 3 Rd. (between Cambie and Capstan Way; ℃ **604/231-0601**) are the best. Both malls have large food courts and specialty shops selling everything from cellphones to candied ginseng.

PUNJABI MARKET   Just like an imported India, the 4 blocks of Main Street on either side of 49th Avenue contain the whole of the subcontinent, shrunk down to a manageable parcel. Look for fragrant spice stalls, sari shops, and textile outlets selling luxurious fabrics—at bargain-basement prices.

---

2 SHOPPING A TO Z

ANTIQUES

Bakers Dozen Antiques   This charming shop specializes in antique toys, model ships and boats, folk art, and unusual 19th- and early-20th-century furniture. 3520 Main St. ℃ **604/879-3348.** www.dodaantiques.com.

DoDa Antiques (Finds)   A colorful and eclectic collection of mid-20th-century pieces—costume and estate jewelry, art glass from Canada, Scandinavia, and Italy, pottery, paintings, and curios—fills this shop. 434 Richards St. ℃ **604/602-0559.**

Mihrab (Finds)   Part museum and part subcontinental yard sale, Mihrab specializes in one-of-a-kind Indian antiques for the house and garden. Think intricately carved teak archways or tiny jewel-like door pulls, all selected by partners Lou Johnson and Kerry Lane on frequent trips to the subcontinent. 4578 Main St. ℃ **778/737-5959.**

Uno Langmann Limited   Catering to upscale shoppers, Uno Langmann specializes in European and North American paintings, furniture, silver, and objets d'art from the 18th through early 20th centuries. 2117 Granville St. ℃ **604/736-8825.** www.langmann.com.

Vancouver Antique Centre   Housed in a heritage commercial building, this maze contains about a dozen separate shops on two levels, specializing in everything from china, glass, and jewelry to military objects, sports, toys, retro '50s and '60s collectibles, home furnishings, and watches. Neighboring buildings house even more shops. 422 Richards St. ℃ **604/684-9822.**

BOOKS

Blackberry Books   Although this small Granville Island store tends toward general interest, they have a healthy selection of books about art, architecture, and cuisine. They're right across from the public market. 1663 Duranleau St. ℃ **866/685-6188** or 604/685-6188. www.bbooks.ca.

Chapters   Chapters chain bookstores are pleasant and well planned, with little nooks, comfy benches, and a huge stock of titles. 788 Robson St. ℂ 604/682-4066. A 2nd location is at 2505 Granville St. ℂ 604/731-7822. www.chapters.indigo.ca.

Duthie Books Fourth Avenue   This well-known local bookstore on Granville Island has been in business since 1957. It's a good place to find local authors and stocks an excellent inventory of Canadian and international titles. 2239 W. 4th Ave. ℂ 604/732-5344. www.duthiebooks.com.

International Travel Maps and Books (Finds)   This store has the best selection of travel books, maps, charts, and globes in town, plus an impressive selection of special-interest British Columbia guides. This is the hiker's best source for detailed topographic charts of the entire province. The only problem is that they've closed their handy downtown store and moved out to Richmond. 12300 Bridgeport Rd., Richmond. ℂ 604/273-1400.

Kidsbooks (Kids)   The largest and most interesting selection of children's literature in the city also has an amazing collection of puppets and holds regular readings. 3083 W. Broadway. ℂ 604/738-5335. A 2nd location is at 3040 Edgemont Blvd., North Vancouver. ℂ 604/986-6190. www.kidsbooks.ca.

Macleod's Books   The kind of dusty, old-fashioned, used bookstore true booklovers and bibliophiles love to explore, stacked high with reasonably priced books covering every conceivable subject. 455 Pender St. ℂ 604/681-7654.

CAMERAS

Dunne & Rundle foto source   Dunne & Rundle, located downtown in the Bentall Shopping Centre, can handle repairs for most major brands, and sells parts, accessories, and film. 595 Burrard St. (at Pender St.). ℂ 604/681-9254. www.dunneandrundle.com.

Lens & Shutter   Located in Kitsilano, Lens & Shutter provides film and camera advice, sells and repairs cameras, and develops photos. 2912 W. Broadway. ℂ 604/736-3461. www.lensandshutter.com.

CERAMICS, CHINA, SILVER & CRYSTAL

Gallery of B.C. Ceramics   This Granville Island gallery is owned and operated by the Potters Guild of British Columbia and features a collection of sculptural and functional ceramic works from 100 B.C. potters. Gallery hours change seasonally, so phone ahead to confirm hours of operation. Closed on Mondays in January and February. 1359 Cartwright St. ℂ 604/669-3606. www.bcpotters.com.

Martha Sturdy Originals (Finds)   Local designer Martha Sturdy—once best known for her collectible, usable, handblown glassware trimmed in gold leaf—is now creating a critically acclaimed line of cast-resin housewares, as well as limited-edition couches and chairs. Expensive, but, if you've got the dough, the furniture is well worth it. 3039 Granville St. ℂ 604/737-0037. www.marthasturdy.com.

CHINESE GOODS

Silk Road Art Trading Co. (Finds)   This store, with an entrance on Columbia Street and another within Dr. Sun Yat-Sen Park in the Chinese Cultural Centre, sells reproductions of Chinese art objects, including the ancient terra-cotta warriors unearthed in a Chinese emperor's tomb. 561 Columbia St. ℂ 604/683-8707.

A Special Vancouver Experience: Asian Night Markets

Whether you're hoping to sample steamed dumplings, pick up a tin of oolong tea, or just poke around a fascinating scene, visiting one of Vancouver's Asian night markets is great fun. Throughout the summer, both Pender and Keefer streets in historic Chinatown are closed to make room for the **Chinatown Night Market** (www.vcma.shawbiz.ca). Styled after Asian marketplaces where shopping is personal and haggling is the name of the game, stalls and tables are loaded with bargain-price merchandise, including CDs, garments, novelties, watches, food, and accessories. Enjoy horse-drawn carriage rides on Fridays, entertainment shows on Saturdays, and family fun and games on Sundays. The market runs every Friday, Saturday, and Sunday, May 18 to September 9, from 6:30 to 11pm.

In Richmond, about 30 minutes from downtown Vancouver, the **Richmond Night Market** (www.summernightmarket.com) is an all-out event that feels like a summer festival with up to 15,000 visitors in 1 night. Over 300 booths sell merchandise from all over the world, and over 50 food vendors cook up a storm. Entertainment is also a big part of the market with various performers during the evening. The market runs from May 18 through October 8 every Friday, Saturday, and Sunday.

T&T Supermarket (Finds)   This store has racks and racks of goods you won't find at home (unless your home is China), but the real entertainment is the seafood and produce, where strange and ungainly comestibles lurk: fire-dragon fruit, lily root, and enoki mushrooms. 179 Keefer Place. ✆ 604/899-8836. www.tnt-supermarket.com.

Ten Ren Tea & Ginseng Co.   Whether you prefer the pungent aroma of Chinese black tea or the exotic fragrance of chrysanthemum, jasmine, or ginger flower, you must try the numerous varieties of drinking and medicinal teas in this Chinatown shop. It also carries Korean, American, and Siberian ginseng for a lot less than you might pay elsewhere. 550 Main St. ✆ 604/684-1566. www.tenren.com.

Tung Fong Hung Foods Co. (Finds)   If you've never been to a Chinese herbalist, this is the one to try: jars, bins, and boxes full of such things as dried sea horse, thinly sliced deer antler, and bird's nest. It's fun to explore and potentially good for what ails you. Chinese remedies can have side effects, however, so before ingesting anything unfamiliar, consult the on-site herbalist. 536 Main St. ✆ 604/688-0883.

CIGARS & TOBACCO

Americans, remember: If they're Cuban, you can't bring them into the U.S.

La Casa del Habano   Directly across from Planet Hollywood on Robson Street, Casa del Habano has Vancouver's largest walk-in humidor. Cigars range in price from a few dollars to more than a hundred. 402 Hornby St. ✆ 604/609-0511.

Vancouver Cigar Company   The selection here is reputed to be the city's most extensive, featuring brands such as Cohiba, Monte Cristo, Macanudo, Hoyo de Monterrey, Romeo y Julieta, Partagas, Ashton, and A. Fuente. The shop also carries a complete line of accessories. 250-780 Beatty St. ✆ 604/685-0445. www.vancouvercigar.com.

DEPARTMENT STORES

The Bay (Hudson's Bay Company) From the establishment of its early trading posts during the 1670s to its modern coast-to-coast department-store chain, The Bay has built its reputation on quality goods. You can still buy a Hudson's Bay woolen "point" blanket (the colorful stripes originally represented how many beaver pelts each blanket was worth in trade), but you'll also find Tommy Hilfiger, Polo, DKNY, and more. 674 Granville St. ℰ **604/681-6211.** www.hbc.com.

Hills of Kerrisdale ⟨**Value**⟩ This neighborhood department store in central Vancouver is a city landmark. Carrying full lines of quality men's, women's, and children's clothes, as well as furnishings and sporting goods, it's a destination for locals because the prices are often lower than those in the downtown core. 2125 W. 41st Ave. ℰ **604/266-9177.** www. hillsofkerrisdale.com.

DISCOUNT SHOPPING

The strip of West 4th Avenue between Cypress and Yew streets has recently emerged as consignment-clothing central. New shops open regularly.

In-Again Clothing ⟨**Value**⟩ This shop has a good variety of seasonal consignment clothing, and the selection keeps up with fashion trends. Don't miss the collection of purses, scarves, and belts. 1962 W. 4th Ave. ℰ **604/738-2782.**

Second Suit for Men & Women ⟨**Value**⟩ This resale- and sample-clothing store has the best in men's and women's fashions, including Hugo Boss, Armani, Donna Karan, Nautica, Calvin Klein, and Alfred Sung. The inventory changes rapidly. 2036 W. 4th Ave. ℰ **604/732-0338.** www.secondsuit.com.

FASHION
For Children

Isola Bella ⟨**Kids**⟩ This store imports an exclusive collection of rather expensive, high-fashion newborn and children's clothing from designers like Babar, Milou, Petit Bateau, and Paul Smith. 5692 Yew St. ℰ **604/266-8808.** www.isolabella.ca.

Please Mum ⟨**Kids**⟩ This Kitsilano store sells attractive Canadian-made toddler's and children's cotton clothing. 2951 W. Broadway. ℰ **604/732-4574.** www.pleasemum.com.

For Men & Women

Vancouver has the Pacific Northwest's best collection of clothes from Paris, London, Milan, and Rome, in addition to a great assortment of locally made, cutting-edge fashions. It seems that almost every week a new designer boutique opens in Yaletown, Kitsilano,

---

⟨**Finds**⟩ **Facials to Go**

For a great facial, head to **skoah,** 1011 Hamilton St. (ℰ **888/697-5624** or 604/642-0200; www.skoah.com). This Yaletown spa is open 7 days a week, specializes in facials for men and women, and sells its own line of organic, locally made skin-care products. The 75-minute "Facialiscious" treatment (C$100) includes deep cleansing, exfoliating, delicate extractions, detoxifying, stimulating masks, and a soothing foot and hand massage.

or Kerrisdale. International designer outlets include **Chanel Boutique,** 900 W. Hastings St. (© 604/682-0522); **Salvatore Ferragamo,** 918 Robson St. (© 604/669-4495); **Gianni Versace Boutique,** 757 W. Hastings St. (© 604/683-1131); **Polo/Ralph Lauren,** the Landing, 375 Water St. (© 604/682-7656); and **Plaza Escada,** Sinclair Centre, 757 W. Hastings St. (© 604/688-8558).

Dorothy Grant (Finds) Designed to look like a Pacific Northwest longhouse, this shop is where First Nations designer Dorothy Grant exhibits her unique designs as well as her husband's (acclaimed artist Robert Davidson) collection of exquisitely detailed Haida motifs, which she appliqués on coats, leather vests, jackets, caps, and accessories. The clothes are gorgeous and collectible. She also carries contemporary Haida art and jewelry. 138 W. 6th Ave., Unit 1B. © 604/681-0201. www.dorothygrant.com.

Dream 311 Big-name designs can be found anywhere, but this little shop is one of the few places to show early collections—clothing and jewelry—of local designers. 311 W. Cordova St.. © 604/683-7326.

Leone Shop where the stars shop. Versace, Donna Karan, Byblos, Armani, and fabulous Italian and French accessories are sold in this very elegant building; valet parking provided, and private after-hours shopping by appointment for VIPs. Sinclair Centre, 757 W. Hastings St. © 604/683-1133. www.leone.ca.

Obakki Visit this great new fashion boutique in Gastown for original garments created by talented new Canadian designers; high-quality fabrics and attention to design are the hallmarks. 44 Water St. © 604/669-9727. www.obakki.com.

Roots Canada Proudly Canadian, this chain features sturdy casual clothing, including leather jackets and bags, footwear, outerwear, and athletic wear for the whole family. 1001 Robson St. (corner of Burrard St.). © 604/683-4305. www.roots.com.

Swimco Located near Kitsilano Beach, this store sells a large variety of bikinis and other bathing suits in the latest styles for men, women, and children. 2166 W. 4th Ave. © 604/732-7946. www.swimco.com.

Venus & Mars (Finds) Add some drama to your life. This Gastown boutique features Vancouver designer Sanné Lambert's work, specializing in one-of-a-kind handmade gowns and velvet robes. Some plus sizes also available. 315 Cambie St. © 604/687-1908. www.venusandmars.biz.

Zonda Nellis Design Ltd. (Finds) Rich colors and intricate patterns highlight this Vancouver designer's imaginative hand-woven separates, pleated silks, sweaters, vests, and soft knits. Nellis has also introduced a new line of hand-painted silks and sumptuous, sheer, hand-painted evening wear. 2203 Granville St. © 604/736-5668. www.zondanellis.com.

Vintage Clothing

Deluxe Junk Co. The name fits—there's tons of junk here. However, some real bargains have been known to pop up among the polyester jackets and worn-out dress shirts. 310 W. Cordova St. © 604/685-4871. www.deluxejunk.com.

Legends Retro-Fashion Specializing in unique retro clothing, Legends is well known among vintage purists for its cache of one-of-a-kind pieces. Most of the clothes, such as evening dresses, shoes, kid gloves, and other accessories, are in immaculate condition. Closed Monday and Tuesday. 4366 Main St. © 604/875-0621.

True Value Vintage Clothing   This underground shop has a collection of funky
fashions from the 1930s through the 1990s, including tons of fake furs, leather jackets,
denim, soccer jerseys, vintage bathing suits, formal wear, smoking jackets, sweaters, and
accessories. 710 Robson St. ✆ 604/685-5403.

FIRST NATIONS ART & CRAFTS

You don't have to purchase a pricey antique to acquire original Coast Salish or Haida
work. As the experts at the **Museum of Anthropology** explain, if an item is crafted by
any of the indigenous Pacific Northwest artisans, it's a real First Nations piece of art.
Galleries will tell you about the artist, and explain how to identify and care for these
beautifully carved, worked, and woven pieces. Bold, traditional, and innovative geomet-
ric designs, intricate carvings, strong primary colors, and rich wood tones are just a few
of the elements you'll find in First Nations crafts.

Even if you're not in the market, go gallery-hopping to see works by Haida artists **Bill
Reid** (the province's best-known native artist) and **Richard Davidson,** and by
Kwakwaka'wakw artist and photographer **David Neel.**

Coastal Peoples Fine Arts Gallery   This Yaletown boutique showcases an extensive collection of fine First Nations jewelry. The motifs—Bear, Salmon, Whale, Raven,
and others—are drawn from local myths and translated into 14-karat or 18-karat gold
and sterling silver creations. Inuit sculptures and items made of glass or wood are also
worth a look. Custom orders can be filled quickly and shipped worldwide. 1024 Mainland
St. ✆ 604/685-9298. www.coastalpeoples.com.

Hill's Native Art ★   In a re-creation of a trading post interior, this shop, established
in 1946 and claiming to be North America's largest Northwest Coast native art gallery,
sells ceremonial masks, Cowichan sweaters, moccasins, wood sculptures, totem poles,
silk-screen prints, soapstone sculptures, and gold, silver, and argillite jewelry. 165 Water
St. ✆ 604/685-4249. www.hillsnativeart.com.

Images for a Canadian Heritage ★ **(Finds)**   This store and the Inuit Gallery of
Vancouver (see below) are government-licensed First Nations art galleries, featuring traditional and contemporary works such as native designs on glass totems and copper-
plates. With a museum-worthy collection, this shop deserves a visit whether you're
buying or not. 164 Water St. (at Cambie St.). ✆ 604/685-7046. www.imagesforcanada.com.

Inuit Gallery of Vancouver   This store is home to one of Canada's foremost collections of Inuit and First Nations art. Prices are for serious buyers, but it's worth a visit.
206 Cambie St. ✆ 604/688-7323. www.inuit.com.

Khot-La-Cha Salish Handicrafts **(Finds)**   Hand-tanned moose-hide crafts, wood-
carvings, Cowichan sweaters, porcupine-quill jewelry, and bone, silver, gold, and tur-
quoise accessories are just a few of the selections at this Coast Salish crafts shop. 270
Whonoak St., North Vancouver. ✆ 604/987-3339. Turn south on Capilano Rd. (off Marine Dr.) and
make the first left (Whonoak is parallel to Capilano Rd.). www.khot-la-cha.com.

Lattimer Gallery **(Finds)**   This beautiful gallery showcases museum-quality Pacific
Northwest First Nations art, including ceremonial masks, totem poles, limited-edition
silk-screen prints, argillite sculptures, and expensive gold and silver jewelry. 1590 2nd Ave.
✆ 604/732-4556. www.lattimergallery.com.

Marion Scott Gallery   For more than 30 years, this gallery has been well regarded for its Inuit and First Nations art collections. 308 Water St. ℂ **604/685-1934.** www.marion scottgallery.com.

Museum of Anthropology   Works by contemporary First Nations artisans as well as books about the culture and publications on identifying and caring for Pacific Northwest crafts. University of British Columbia, 6393 NW Marine Dr. ℂ **604/822-5087.** www.moa. ubc.ca.

FOOD

You'll find **salmon** everywhere in Vancouver. Many shops package whole, fresh salmon with ice packs for visitors to take home. Shops also carry delectable smoked salmon in travel-safe, vacuum-packed containers. Some offer decorative cedar gift boxes; most offer overnight air transport. Try other salmon treats such as salmon jerky and Indian candy (chunks of marinated smoked salmon), which are available at public markets such as **Granville Island Public Market** and **Lonsdale Quay Market.**

Chocolate Arts ⒻFinds   The works at this chocolatier are made with exquisite craftsmanship. Seasonal treats include pumpkin truffles around Halloween or eggnog truffles for Christmas. They even make chocolate toolboxes filled with tiny chocolate tools. Look for the all-chocolate diorama in the window—it changes every month or so. 2037 W. 4th Ave. ℂ **604/739-0475.** www.chocolatearts.com.

The Lobsterman   Live lobsters, Dungeness crabs, oysters, mussels, clams, geoducks, and scallops are just a few of the varieties of seafood swimming in the saltwater tanks at this Granville Island fish store. The staff steams the food fresh on the spot, free. Salmon and other seafood can also be packed for air travel. 1807 Mast Tower Rd. ℂ **604/687-4531.** www.lobsterman.com.

Murchie's Tea & Coffee   This Vancouver institution has been the city's main tea and coffee purveyor for more than a century. You'll find everything from Jamaican Blue Mountain and Kona coffees to Lapsang Souchong and Kemun teas. The knowledgeable staff will help you decide which flavors and blends fit your taste. A fine selection of bone china and crystal serving ware as well as coffeemakers and teapots are also on sale. 970 Robson St. ℂ **604/669-0783.** www.murchies.com.

Salmon Village   If you want some salmon to take home, Salmon Village has a good selection to choose from. Smoked salmon or jerky are vacuum sealed for travel, and fresh salmon can be packed in an ice box or (for a price) shipped to you anywhere on the planet. 779 Thurlow St. ℂ **604/685-3378.** www.salmonvillage.com.

South China Seas Trading Company   The South Seas have always been a source of intrigue. This shop re-creates a bit of that wonder, with a remarkable collection of rare spices and hard-to-find sauces. Look for fresh Kaffir lime leaves, Thai basil, young ginger, sweet Thai chile sauce, and occasional exotic produce like mangosteens and rambutans. Pick up recipes and ideas from the knowledgeable staff. Granville Island Public Market. ℂ **604/681-5402.** www.southchinaseas.ca.

GALLERIES

On the first Thursday of every month, many galleries host free openings from 5 to 8pm. Check the *Georgia Straight* or *Vancouver* magazine for listings, or visit **www.art-bc.com** for more details on Vancouver's art scene.

Buschlen Mowatt This is the city's leading "establishment" gallery. Look for paintings, sculptures, and prints from well-known Canadian and international artists. 111-
1445 W. Georgia St. ✆ **604/682-1234.** www.buschlenmowatt.com.

Diane Farris Gallery Come here to see contemporary painting and sculpture from
up-and-coming and established artists. 1590 W. 7th Ave. ✆ **604/737-2629.** www.dianefarris
gallery.com.

Monte Clark Gallery ⟨**Value**⟩ This cutting-edge gallery—in the otherwise slightly
staid confines of south Granville's gallery row—is one of the best spots to look for that
rising superstar without the rising prices. 2339 Granville St. ✆ **604/730-5000.** www.monte
clarkgallery.com.

HOME FURNISHINGS & ACCESSORIES

Farfalla ⟨**Finds**⟩ Relocated in 2007 to the Koret Lofts in Gastown, Farfalla features a
choice array of products rarely found outside their country of origin, including Artel glass
from Prague, Santa Maria Novella toiletries from Florence, Lomonosov tea ware from St.
Petersburg, and various lines from the Weavers Guild of Europe. They do custom mono-
gramming and even have a tearoom where they serve Hediard tea from Paris. 57 E. Cordova St. (near Carrall St.). ✆ **604/215-8707.** www.shopfarfalla.ca.

Inform Interiors ⟨**Finds**⟩ Chances are you won't be lugging a sofa back home, but this
classy interior-design store in Gastown has contemporary lighting, home accessories, and
design books in addition to furniture. Their new bed and bath store is right across the
street at 50 Water St. 97 Water St. ✆ **604/682-3868.** www.informinteriors.com.

JEWELRY

Costen Catbalue ⟨**Finds**⟩ One-of-a-kind pieces in platinum and gold are made on the
premises here by a team of four goldsmiths and artists Mary Ann Buis and Andrew
Costen. The two artists' styles complement each other; Buis favors contemporary and
clean lines, and Costen's designs tend toward a more ornate Renaissance style. 1832 W. 1st
Ave. ✆ **604/734-3259.** www.costencatbalue.com.

Forge & Form Master Granville Island metal designers Dietje Hagedoorn and Jürgen
Schönheit specialize in customized gold and silver jewelry. Renowned for their gold and
silver bow ties, they also create unique "tension set" rings, which hold a stone in place
without a setting. Their studio (open by appointment) is located just past the False Creek
Community Centre. 1334 Cartwright St. ✆ **604/684-6298.**

Karl Stittgen and Goldsmiths ⟨**Finds**⟩ Karl Stittgen's gold pins, pendants, rings,
and other accessories demonstrate his eye for crisp design and fine craftsmanship. Each
work is a miniature architectural wonder. 2203 Granville St. ✆ **604/737-0029.**

The Raven and the Bear If you've never seen West Coast native jewelry, it's worth
making a trip here. Deeply inscribed with stylized creatures from Northwest mythology,
these rings, bangles, and earrings are unforgettable. (See also "First Nations Art &
Crafts," above.) 1528 Duranleau St. ✆ **604/669-3990.**

MARKETS

Granville Island Public Market ★★★ This 4,645-sq.-m (49,998-sq.-ft.) public
market features produce, meats, fish, wines, cheeses, arts and crafts, and lots of unique
fast-food counters offering a little of everything. The market is open daily 9am to 6pm.

From mid-June to September, the Farmers' Truck Market operates here Thursday from 10am to 7pm. 1669 Johnston St. ℂ **604/666-6477.** www.granvilleisland.com.

Lonsdale Quay Market (Kids)   Located at the SeaBus terminal, this public market is filled with produce, meats, fish, specialty fashions, gift and book shops, food counters, coffee bars, a hotel, and Kids' Alley (a section dedicated to children's shops and a play area). 123 Carrie Cates Court, North Vancouver. ℂ **604/985-6261.** www.lonsdalequay.com.

New Westminster Quay Public Market   A smaller version of the Granville Island Public Market, this market is located 25 minutes away by SkyTrain from downtown Vancouver. Here you'll find a variety of gift shops, specialty stores, a food court, a delicatessen, and produce stands. Once you're finished browsing, make sure to have a gander at the neighboring Fraser River. A walkway extends along the river and allows great views of the waterfront, the busy boat traffic, and the occasional seal or sea lion. 810 Quayside Dr., New Westminster. ℂ **604/520-3881.** www.rivermarket.ca.

Vancouver Flea Market (Value)   Near the train/bus terminal, Vancouver's largest flea market is filled with more than 350 stalls. Go early, or the savvy shoppers will have already cleaned out the gems. Open weekends and holidays 9am to 5pm. 703 Terminal Ave. ℂ **604/685-0666.** www.vancouverfleamarket.com.

MUSIC
Zulu Records (Finds)   Zulu Records specializes in alternative music, local and import, new and used. You'll also find a good selection of vinyl and magazines. The staff is happy to make recommendations and bring you up to speed on what's hot in the local music scene. 1972 W. 4th Ave. ℂ **604/738-3232.** www.zulurecords.com.

SHOES
David Gordon   Vancouver's oldest Western boot, hat, and accessories store is far from stodgy. Boots include an extensive selection of Tony Lama, Boulet, Durango, HH Brown, and Dan Post. You'll also find Vans, Doc Martens, and a lineup of other funky footwear that attracts skateboarders and club kids. 822 Granville St. ℂ **604/685-3784.**

John Fluevog Boots & Shoes Ltd.   This native Vancouverite has a growing international cult following of designers and models clamoring for his under-C$200 urban and funky creations. You'll find outrageous platforms and clogs, Angelic Sole work boots, and a few bizarre experiments for the daring footwear fetishist. You may even meet the designer, who often spends his time at this flagship store on Granville. A new store has now opened in Gastown at 65 Water St. 837 Granville St. ℂ **604/688-2828.** www.fluevog.com.

SPECIALTY
Buddha Supply Centre (Finds)   Want money to burn? At Chinese funerals, people burn *joss*—paper replicas of earthly belongings—to help make the afterlife for the deceased more comfortable. This shop has more than 500 combustible products to choose from, including $1-million notes (drawn on the bank of hell), luxury penthouse condos, and that all-important cellphone. 4158 Main St. ℂ **604/873-8169.**

Cookworks   This attractive downtown store stocks a finely tuned selection of high-quality, well-designed kitchenware and accessories for the table. 377 Howe St. ℂ **604/662-4918.** www.cookworks.ca.

Escents   Beautifully displayed, the large collection of soaps, bath oils, shampoos, and other body products here come in a variety of scents, such as the fresh ginger-citrus twist or the relaxing lavender sea. Locally produced and made with minimal packaging, the all-natural, environmentally friendly products come in convenient sizes and prices and can be individually blended to fit your mood. An additional store is at 1744 Commercial Dr. 2579 W. Broadway ℂ **604/687-4700.** www.escentsaromatherapy.com.

Lush   Lush has the look of an old-fashioned deli with big wheels of cheese, slabs of sweets, and vats of dips and sauces, but all those displays are really soaps (custom cut from a block), shampoos, skin treatments, massage oils, and bath bombs made from all-natural ingredients. 1025 Robson St. ℂ **604/687-5874.** www.lush.ca.

The Market Kitchen Store   This store has everything you'd like to have (or could even imagine) on your kitchen counters or in your drawers—gourmet kitchen accessories, baking utensils, gadgets, and the like. 2-1666 Johnston St. (Net Loft, Granville Island). ℂ **604/681-7399.**

The Ocean Floor   If you want to bring home a few gifts from the sea, then select from this Granville Island shop's collection of seashells, ship models, lamps, chimes, coral, shell jewelry, stained glass, and marine brass. 1522 Duranleau St. ℂ **604/681-5014.**

Three Dog Bakery   Beagle Bagels, Scottie Biscotti, or Gracie's Rollovers. Canines will have a hard time deciding on a favorite treat from this gone-to-the-dogs bakery. The store also has leashes, collars, greeting cards, and other dog paraphernalia. 2186 W. 4th Ave. ℂ **604/737-3647.** www.threedog.com.

The Umbrella Shop ★ ⟨**Finds**⟩   A family business since 1935, this shop carries an amazing assortment of quality umbrellas in every size, shape, and color. 526 W. Pender St. ℂ **604/669-1707.** Factory store: 1106 W. Broadway. ℂ **604/669-9444.** www.theumbrellashop.com.

SPORTING GOODS

A 2-block area near the Mountain Equipment Co-op (see below) has become "outdoor central," with at least a half-dozen stores such as **Altus Mountain Gear,** 137 W. Broadway (ℂ **604/876-2525**); **Great Outdoors Equipment,** 222 W. Broadway (ℂ **604/872-8872**); and **AJ Brooks,** 147 W. Broadway (ℂ **604/874-1117;** www.ajbrooks.com). Just down the street, you'll find **Taiga,** 301 W. Broadway (ℂ **604/875-8388;** www.taiga works.ca), which carries inexpensive fleece and other quality outdoor gear.

In the past few years, the corner of 4th Avenue and Burrard Street has become the spot for high-quality snow/skate/surfboard gear as well as the place to see top-level boarders and their groupies hanging out. Shops here include **Pacific Boarder,** 1793 W. 4th Ave. (ℂ **604/734-7245;** www.pacificboarder.com), and the particularly noteworthy **Westbeach,** 1766 W. 4th Ave. (ℂ **604/731-6449;** www.westbeach.com), which sometimes hosts pro-skate demos on the half-pipe at the back of the store. **Thriller,** 3467 Main St. (ℂ **604/736-5651;** www.thrillershop.com), is another well-known shop carrying independent labels and accessories for surfers and boarders real and wannabe.

Comor Sports   "Go play outside" is Comor's motto, and they certainly have the goods to get you out there. Pick up some skateboard garb, swimwear, hiking shoes, in-line skates, skis, boards, and snow toys. 1090 W. Georgia St. ℂ **604/736-7547.** www.comor sports.com.

Mountain Equipment Co-op   A true West Coast institution and an outdoor-lover's dream come true, this block-long store houses the best selection of top-quality outdoor equipment: rain gear, clothing, hiking shoes, climbing gear, backpacks, sleeping bags, tents, and more. Memorize the MEC label; you're sure to see it later—at the beach, the bar, or the concert hall. 130 W. Broadway (between Manitoba and Columbia). ✆ 604/872-7858. www.mec.ca.

TOYS

The Games People ⟨**Kids**⟩   The Games People carries a huge selection of board games, strategy games, role-playing games, puzzles, models, toys, hobby materials, and other amusements. It's difficult to walk past this store—whether you're an adult or a kid. 157 Water St. ✆ 604/685-5825.

Kids Market ⟨**Kids**⟩   Probably the only mall in North America dedicated to kids, the Kids Market on Granville Island features a Lilliputian entryway; toy, craft, and book stores; play areas; and services for the younger set, including a "fun hairdresser." 1496 Cartwright St. (on Granville Island). ✆ 604/689-8447. www.kidsmarket.ca.

Kites on Clouds ⟨**Kids**⟩   This little Gastown shop has every type of kite. Prices range from C$10 to C$20 for nylon or Mylar dragon kites to around C$200 for more elaborate ghost clippers and nylon hang-glider kites. The Courtyard, 131 Water St. ✆ 604/669-5677.

WINE

Ten years of restructuring, reblending, and careful tending by French and German master vintners have won the province's vineyards world recognition. When buying B.C. wine, look for the VQA (Vintner Quality Alliance) seal on the label; it's a guarantee that all grapes used are grown in British Columbia and meet European standards for growing and processing.

Summerhill, Cedar Creek, Mission Hill, and **Okanagan Vineyards** are just a few of the more than 50 local estates producing hearty cabernet sauvignons, honey-rich ice wines, and oaky merlots. These wines can be found at any government-owned **BC** liquor store, such as the one at 1716 Robson St. (✆ **604/660-9031**) and at some privately owned wine stores.

Marquis Wine Cellars   If you're looking for a particular B.C. vintage, try this place first. The owner and staff of this West End wine shop are dedicated to educating their patrons about wines. They conduct evening wine tastings, featuring selections from their special purchases. They also publish monthly newsletters. In addition to carrying a full range of British Columbian wines, the shop also has a large international selection. 1034 Davie St. ✆ 604/684-0445. www.marquis-wines.com.

The Okanagan Estate Wine Cellar   This department store annex, located in the Pacific Centre Shopping Mall, sells a great selection of British Columbian wines by the bottle and the case. The Bay, 674 Granville St. ✆ 604/681-6211.

Vancouver After Dark

Vancouver's evening social calendar is filled with a variety of events, from productions by cutting-edge theater companies and a top-notch opera to symphony, folk, and jazz festivals that draw people from all over the world. And then there are the bars, lounges, pubs, clubs, and cafes—lots of them—for every taste, budget, and fetish. Dining out at a fine restaurant is also considered an evening out; at a restaurant like C or West (both reviewed in chapter 7), the presentation is theater on a plate; in a restaurant-lounge like Sanafir, the theatricality of the decor will wow you.

For the best overview of Vancouver's nightlife, pick up a copy of the weekly *Georgia Straight* (www.georgiastraight. com). The Thursday edition of the *Vancouver Sun* contains the weekly entertainment section *Queue.* The monthly *Vancouver* magazine (www.vanmag.com) is filled with listings and strong views about what's really hot in the city. Or, get a copy of *Xtra! West*

(www.xtra.ca), the free gay and lesbian biweekly tabloid, available in shops and restaurants throughout the West End.

The **Alliance for Arts and Culture,** 100-938 Howe St. (© **604/681-3535;** www.allianceforarts.com), is a great information source for all performing arts, literary events, and art films. The office is open Monday through Friday from 9am to 5pm.

Ticketmaster (Vancouver Ticket Centre), 1304 Hornby St. (© **604/280-4444;** www.ticketmaster.ca), has 40 outlets in the Vancouver area.

Half-price tickets for same-day shows and events are available at the **Tickets Tonight** (www.ticketstonight.ca) kiosk (open Tues–Sat 11am–6pm) in the **Vancouver Touristinfo Centre,** 200 Burrard St. (© **604/684-2787** for recorded events info). The Touristinfo Centre is open from May to Labour Day daily from 8am to 6pm; the rest of the year, it's open Monday through Saturday from 8:30am to 5pm.

1 THE PERFORMING ARTS

Three major theaters in Vancouver regularly host touring performances. The **Orpheum Theatre,** 801 Granville St. (© **604/665-3050;** www.vancouver.ca/theatres), is a 1927 theater that originally hosted the Chicago-based Orpheum vaudeville circuit. The theater now hosts the Vancouver Symphony and pop, rock, and variety shows. The Queen Elizabeth Theatre and the Vancouver Playhouse comprise the **Queen Elizabeth Complex,** 600 Hamilton St., between Georgia and Dunsmuir streets (© **604/665-3050;** www.vancouver.ca/theatres), home to the Vancouver Opera and Ballet British Columbia. The 670-seat Vancouver Playhouse presents chamber-music performances and recitals. Located in a converted turn-of-the-20th-century church, the **Vancouver East Cultural Centre** (the "Cultch" to locals), 1895 Venables St. (© **604/251-1363;** www.thecultch. com), coordinates an impressive program that includes avant-garde theater productions, performances by international musical groups, and children's programs.

On the UBC campus, the **Chan Centre for the Performing Arts,** 6265 Crescent Rd. (© **604/822-2697;** www.chancentre.com), showcases the work of the UBC music and

> **(Finds) Art on the Edge**
>
> For more original performance fare, don't miss **Vancouver's International Fringe Festival** (© 604/257-0350; www.vancouverfringe.com). Centered on Granville Island, the Fringe Festival features more than 500 innovative and original shows each September, all costing under C$20.

acting students and hosts a winter concert series. Designed by local architectural luminary, Bing Thom, the Chan Centre's crystal-clear acoustics are the best in town.

THEATER

An annual summertime Shakespeare series, **Bard on the Beach,** is presented in Vanier Park (© **604/737-0625;** www.bardonthebeach.org). You can also bring a picnic dinner to Stanley Park and watch **Theatre Under the Stars** (see below), which features popular musicals and light comedies.

Arts Club Theatre Company The 425-seat **Granville Island Stage** presents dramas, comedies, and musicals, with post-performance entertainment in the Backstage Lounge. The Arts Club **Revue Stage** is an intimate, cabaret-style showcase for small productions, improvisation nights, and musical revues. The Art Deco **Stanley Industrial Alliance Theatre** plays host to longer-running plays and musicals. The box office is open 9am to 7pm. Granville Island Stage, 1585 Johnston St. Stanley Industrial Alliance Theatre, 2750 Granville St. © **604/687-1644.** www.artsclub.com. Tickets C$25–C$45.

Frederic Wood Theatre (Value) Some students at UBC are actors in training, and their productions are extremely high caliber. For the price, they're a steal. Presentations range from classic dramatic works to new plays by Canadian playwrights. All shows start at 7:30pm. The theater goes dark during the summer. 6354 Crescent Rd., Gate 4, University of British Columbia. © **604/822-2678.** www.theatre.ubc.ca. Tickets C$20 adults, C$14 seniors, C$12 children.

Theatre Under the Stars From mid-July to mid-August, favorite musicals like *Annie, West Side Story,* and *Thoroughly Modern Millie* are performed outdoors by a mixed cast of amateur and professional actors. Bring a blanket (it gets chilly once the sun sets) and a picnic for a relaxing evening. Malkin Bowl, Stanley Park. © **604/734-1917** or 604/687-0174. www.tuts.ca. Tickets C$30 adults, C$25 seniors and youths, C$20 children 6–10, C$85 families (2 adults and 2 children).

Vancouver Playhouse The company at the Vancouver Playhouse presents a program of six plays each season, usually a mix of the internationally known, nationally recognized, and locally promising. 600 Hamilton St. (between Georgia and Dunsmuir sts. in the Queen Elizabeth complex). © **604/665-3050.** www.vancouverplayhouse.com. Tickets C$25–C$55.

CLASSICAL MUSIC & OPERA

Vancouver Bach Choir ★★ Vancouver's international, award-winning amateur choir, a 150-voice ensemble, presents five major concerts a year at the Orpheum Theatre. Specializing in symphonic choral music, the choir's singalong performance of Handel's *Messiah* during the Christmas season is a favorite. 805-235 Keith Rd., West Vancouver. © **604/921-8012.** www.vancouverbachchoir.com. Tickets C$20–C$35.

Vancouver Cantata Singers ★ This semiprofessional, 40-person choir specializes works by Bach, Brahms, Monteverdi, Stravinsky, and Handel, as well as Eastern European choral music. The season normally includes three programs: in October, December, and March, all at various locations. 1254 W. 7th Ave. © **604/730-8856.** www.vancouvercantata singers.com. Tickets C$10–C$30.

Vancouver Chamber Choir ★★★ Western Canada's only professional choral ensemble presents an annual concert series at the Orpheum Theatre, the Chan Centre, and Ryerson United Church. Under conductor John Washburn, the choir has gained an international reputation. 1254 W. 7th Ave. © **604/738-6822.** www.vancouverchamberchoir. com. Tickets C$15–C$35 adults, C$13–C$25 seniors and students.

Vancouver Opera ★★★ I've always been impressed with the quality of the stagings and performances at the Vancouver Opera. The company produces both concert versions and fully staged operas, often sung by international stars. The season runs October through May, with most performances in the Queen Elizabeth Theatre. 835 Cambie St. © **604/683-0222.** www.vancouveropera.ca. Tickets C$24–C$140.

Vancouver Symphony ★★★ At its home in the Orpheum Theatre during the fall, winter, and spring, Vancouver's excellent orchestra, under the baton of maestro Branwell Tovey, presents a variety of year-round concerts. The box office is open from 6pm until showtime. 601 Smithe St. © **604/876-3434.** www.vancouversymphony.ca. Tickets C$20–C$75; discounts available for seniors and students.

DANCE

The new **Scotiabank Dance Centre,** 677 Davie St., provides a focal point for the Vancouver dance community. Renovated by Arthur Erickson, the former bank building now offers studio and rehearsal space to more than 30 dance companies, and is open to the general public for events, workshops, and classes. For more information, call © **604/606-6400,** or check www.thedancecentre.ca.

For fans of modern dance, the time to be here is early July, when the **Dancing on the Edge Festival** (© **604/689-0926;** www.dancingontheedge.org) presents 60 to 80 original pieces over a 10-day period. For more information about other festivals and dance companies around the city, contact the **Dance Centre** at © **604/606-6400** or www. thedancecentre.ca.

Ballet British Columbia ★ This established company strives to present innovative works, such as those by choreographers John Cranko and William Forsythe, along with more traditional productions by visiting companies, such as the American Ballet Theatre and the Moscow Classical Ballet. Performances are usually at the Queen Elizabeth Theatre, at 600 Hamilton St. 1101 W. Broadway. © **604/732-5003.** www.balletbc.com. Tickets C$25–C$60.

2 LAUGHTER & MUSIC

COMEDY CLUB/IMPROV SHOW

Vancouver TheatreSports League ★★ Part comedy, part theater, and partly a take-no-prisoners test of an actor's ability to think extemporaneously, TheatreSports involves actors taking suggestions from the audience and spinning them into short skits or full plays, often with hilarious results. Since moving to the Arts Club Stage, Vancouver's TheatreSports leaguers have had to rein in their normally raunchy instincts for the more family-friendly audience—except, that is, for Friday and Saturday at 11:45pm, when the Red-Hot Improv show takes the audience into the R-rated realm. Shows are Wednesday and Thursday at 7:30pm and Friday and Saturday at 8, 10, and 11:45pm. New Revue Stage, 1601 Johnston St. (✆ 604/738-7013. www.vtsl.com. Tickets C$11–C$20.

STRICTLY LIVE

The **Vancouver International Jazz Festival** (✆ 604/872-5200; www.coastaljazz.ca) takes over many venues and outdoor stages around town every June. The festival includes a number of free concerts.

The **Vancouver Folk Music Festival** (✆ 604/602-9798; www.thefestival.bc.ca) is one of the big ones on the West Coast. It takes place outdoors in July on the beach at Jericho Park.

The Commodore Ballroom ★   Every town should have one, but sadly very few do: a huge old-time dance hall, complete with a suspended hardwood dance floor. And though the room and floor date back to the Jazz Age, the lineup nowadays includes many of the best modern bands coming through town (and also groups like the Harlem Gospel Choir). In fact, the Commodore is one of the best places to catch a midsize band. 868 Granville St. (✆ 604/739-4550. Tickets C$5–C$50.

O'Doul's Restaurant & Bar ★★   Every night, the restaurant for the Listel Hotel (p. 79) becomes the venue for Vancouver's top jazz performers. You can dine on West Coast cuisine by candlelight or enjoy a drink while listening to the mellow sounds. During the Vancouver International Jazz Festival in late June, O'Doul's becomes the scene of late-night jam sessions with world-renowned musicians. 1300 Robson St. (at Jervis St.). (✆ 604/661-1400. www.odoulsrestaurant.com.

The Roxy   Live bands play every day of the week in this no-holds-barred club, which also features bartenders with Tom Cruise *Cocktail*-style moves. Theme parties (often with vacation giveaways)—Extreme Karaoke, '80s only, Sunday Country Night (with two-step)—and other events add to the entertainment and the uninhibited and sometimes pretty raucous scene. On weekends, the lines are long, the patrons often soused. Dress code: No bags, no backpacks, no track suits, no ripped jeans; everything else is okay. 932 Granville St. (✆ 604/331-7999. www.roxyvan.com. Cover C$5–C$15.

The WISE Club (Finds)   In the far-off reaches of East Vancouver (okay, Commercial Dr. area), The WISE Club was unplugged long before MTV ever thought of reaching for the power cord. Bands are local and international, and the room's a lot of fun—like a church basement or community center with alcohol. 1882 Adanac St. (✆ 604/254-5858. www.wisehall.ca. Cover depends on show; C$15 for most bands.

Yale Hotel   This century-old tavern on the far south end of Granville is Vancouver's one-and-only home of the blues. Visiting heavyweights have included Stevie Ray Vaughan and Jeff Healey. When outside talent's not available, the Yale features the home-grown, including Long John Baldry and local bluesman Jim Byrne. Shows are Monday through Saturday at 9:30pm. On Saturday and Sunday is an open-stage blues jam from 3 to 7pm. 1300 Granville St. (✆ 604/681-9253. www.theyale.ca. Cover Thurs–Sat C$15–C$28.

3 BARS, PUBS & OTHER WATERING HOLES

11

Vancouver has loosened up a great deal in the past few years. Until recently, patrons in a restaurant could drink only if they were eating or *had the intention of eating.* Nowadays, Vancouver drinkers can stand tall and order that beer with no fear of being forced to purchase a token cookie or french fry. Even better, bars can now regularly stay open until 2am, and as late as 4am in peak summer months.

That said, officialdom in the city still doesn't love the late-night crowd. They seem to look on drinkers and revelers as an unfortunate byproduct of urbanism, and bars as a necessary evil. City policy has been to concentrate the city's pubs and clubs into two ghettos—er, *entertainment zones*—one along **Granville Street** and the other along **Water and Pender streets** in Gastown. **Yaletown** has recently become a third, more upscale, bar/lounge/club zone. Pubs and clubs can be found in other places, and many are listed below, but if you just want to wander out for a serendipitous pub-crawl, the Granville or Water Street strips are best. Granville Street tends more to Top 40 discos and upscale lounges, while down in Gastown, it's dark cellars spinning hip-hop and house. Yaletown is the newest late-night entertainment/drinking area, a place where martinis reign and some of the restaurants turn into cocktail lounges at 11pm.

BARS MASQUERADING AS RESTAURANTS

One holdover from the bad old days of the liquor license drought is the relatively large number of restaurants that look suspiciously like pubs. You can order food in these places. Indeed, it used to be a condition of drinking (wink, wink), but most patrons stick to a liquid diet.

The Alibi Room　This high-end, trendy restaurant/bar has new owners and a new chef creating modern-British-pub-style cuisine, but there's still a DJ and a dance floor. Located on the eastern edge of Gastown. 157 Alexander St. (at Main St.). © **604/623-3383.** www.alibi.ca.

The Atlantic Trap and Gill　Regulars in this sea shanty of a pub know the words to every song sung by the Irish and East Coast bands that appear onstage Thursday and Saturday night. 612 Davie St. (at Seymour St.). © **604/806-6393.** www.trapandgill.com.

The Jupiter Cafe (Finds　Located just off busy Davie Street in the West End, the Jupiter Cafe combines a postapocalyptic industrial look with lounge chic. Black ceilings, exposed pipes, and roof struts mix surprisingly well with chandeliers, velvet curtains, and plush chairs. More important, the Jupiter is open late (until 4am some nights). True, it can be a challenge to flag down your waiter, but that gives you more time to scope out the crowd: gay and straight, funky and preppy, casual and dressed to kill. A huge outdoor patio provides a pleasant refuge from the street, but on colder nights, it's the exclusive domain of die-hard smokers. The menu—burgers, pastas, and pizzas—is largely decorative. 1216 Bute St. (at Davie St.). © **604/609-6665.** www.jupitercafe.com.

Monsoon Restaurant　What this slim little bistro in the otherwise sleepy (but starting-to-wake-up) section of Main and Broadway does really well is beer and fusion-induced tapas, accompanied by a buzzing atmosphere generated by interesting and sometimes beautiful people. The kitchen is open noon until 11pm on weekdays, later on weekends. 2526 Main St. (at Broadway). © **604/879-4001.**

Urban Well   The taut and tanned from nearby Kits Beach drop into the Well as the sun goes down, and often don't emerge until the next day. Monday and Tuesday features stand-up comedy, while a DJ keeps things groovy the rest of the week. 1516 Yew St. ✆ **604/737-7770.** www.urbanwell.com.

ACTUAL BARS

The Irish Heather   A bright, pleasant Irish pub in the dark heart of Gastown, the Heather boasts numerous nooks and crannies, some of the best beer in town, and a menu that does a lot with the traditional Emerald Isle spud. The clientele is from all over the map, from artsy types to urban pioneers. 210 Carrall St. ✆ **604/688-9779.** www.irishheather. com.

The Lennox Pub   Part of the renewal of Granville Street, this new pub fills a big void in the neighborhood; it's a comfortable spot for a drink without having to deal with lines or ordering food. The beer list is extensive, featuring such hard-to-find favorites as Belgian Kriek, Hoegaarden, and Leffe, along with a great selection of single-malt Scotches, too. The menu covers all the pub-food basics. 800 Granville St. ✆ **604/408-0881.**

A SPORTS BAR

The Shark Club Bar and Grill   The city's premier sports bar, the Shark Club—in the Sandman Inn—features lots of wood and brass, TVs everywhere, and on weekend evenings, lots of young women who don't look terribly interested in sports. 180 W. Georgia St. (at Beatty St.). ✆ **604/687-4275.** www.sharkclubs.com. Cover Fri–Sat C$6–C$8.

BARS WITH VIEWS

You're in Vancouver. Odds are you're aware that this is a city renowned for its views. The entire population could make more money living in a dull flat place like Toronto, but they stay here because of the seductive scenery. As long as that's your raison d'être, you may as well drink in style at one of the places below. Also check out the view at the new restaurant, **Lift** (p. 99).

Cardero's Marine Pub   On the water at the foot of Cardero Street, this Coal Harbour pub and restaurant offers a great view of Stanley Park, the harbor, and the North Shore. Overhead heaters take away the chill when the sun goes down. 1583 Coal Harbour Quay. ✆ **604/669-7666.**

Cloud Nine   As this sleek hotel-top lounge rotates 6 degrees a minute, your vantage point circles from volcanic Mount Baker, the Fraser estuary, and English Bay to Stanley Park, the towers of downtown, the harbor, and East Vancouver. Live entertainment Friday and Saturday nights. 1400 Robson St. (42nd floor of the Empire Landmark Hotel). ✆ **604/662-8328.** Cover Fri–Sat after 8:30pm C$5.

The Dockside Brewing Company   The Dockside is located in the Granville Island Hotel (reviewed in chapter 6) and looks out across False Creek to Yaletown and Burnaby Mountain far in the distance. The grub's not much to write about, but the beer is among the best in town—brewed-on-the-premises lagers, ales, and porters. Even with the overhead gas heaters on chillier evenings, it's a good idea not to arrive too late: An hour or two after the sun goes down, the mostly 30-something patrons remember that they have homes to go to. 1253 Johnson St. ✆ **604/685-7070.** www.docksidebrewing.com.

The Flying Beaver Bar (Finds)   Located beneath the flyway of Vancouver International, the Beaver offers nonflyers great views of incoming jets, along with mountains, bush planes, river craft, and truly fine beer. 4760 Inglis Dr., Richmond. © 604/273-0278.

LOUNGES

Afterglow   Intimate couches and a soft soundtrack (which gets cranked up to deafening decibels as the evening wears on) make for candlelit foreplay to a meal at glowbal grill (p. 95); you can also stay in the low-slung love seats for a long evening's cuddle. 350 Davie St. © 604/602-0835.

The Arts Club Backstage Lounge   The Arts Club Lounge has a fabulous location under the Granville Bridge by the water on the edge of False Creek. The crowd is a mix of tourists and art school students from neighboring Emily Carr College. A live band plays on Friday and Saturday evenings. Most other times, if the sun's out, the waterfront patio is packed. 1585 Johnston St. © 604/687-1354. www.thebackstagelounge.com.

Bacchus Lounge ★   This luxuriously comfy hot spot in the tony Wedgewood Hotel (p. 75) stages a powerhouse cocktail hour for mostly well-to-do professionals, then becomes an irony-free piano bar. In the Wedgewood Hotel, 845 Hornby St. © 604/608-5319. www.wedgewoodhotel.com.

George Ultra Lounge ★   Small, loud, crowded, and hedonistic. Look for local glitterati and primo cocktails from the mixologist who started Vancouver's high-end cocktail trend. 1137 Hamilton St. © 604/628-5555. www.georgelounge.com.

Ginger Sixty-Two   A mix of lounge, restaurant, and club, Ginger is the darling of the fashion-industry trendsetters who love to be spotted here. The room is funky warehouse-chic-meets-adult-rec-room, decorated in red, orange, and gold. Comfy crash pads are strategically placed throughout the room, and plenty of pillows help prop up those less-than-young in the joints. 1219 Granville St. © 604/688-5494. www.ginger62.com.

Gotham Cocktail Bar   A clear case of the law of unintended consequences: The lounge adjoining this new steakhouse was designed for a male clientele—thick leather benches and a mural of sensuous women in Jazz Age fashions. Men do show up—well-off suits in their 30s and 40s particularly—but they're often a minority amid the great gaggles of women, all seemingly 30-somethings with romantic aspirations. 615 Seymour St. (between Dunsmuir and Georgia sts.). © 604/605-8282. www.gothamsteakhouse.com.

MARKET by Jean-Georges ★   Jean-Georges Vongerichten opened this new restaurant on Level 3 in the new Shangri-La Hotel in 2009. Besides the restaurant, there's a cafe, an outdoor patio, and a bar. And because it's new and a be-seen scene, it's usually crowded. In the Shangri-La Hotel, 1128 Georgia St. © 604/695-1115. www.shangri-la.com.

Opus Bar ★   Supertrendy decor, great drinks, and a succulent small-plates menu have helped the Opus Bar in the cool Opus Hotel (p. 74) become a Yaletown hot spot for a pre-dinner martini or an extended evening schmooze. In the Opus Hotel, 50 Davie St. © 604/642-0577. www.elixir-opusbar.com.

BREWPUBS

Don't forget the **Dockside Brewing Company,** 1253 Johnson St. (© 604/685-7070), in the Granville Island Hotel, listed under "Bars with Views," above.

Steamworks Pub & Brewery   Winding your way from room to room in this Gastown brewery is almost as much fun as drinking. Upstairs, by the doors, it's a London city pub where stockbrokers ogle every new female entrant. Farther in by the staircase, it's a refined old-world club, with wood paneling, leather chairs, and great glass windows overlooking the harbor. Down in the basement, it's a Bavarian drinking hall with long lines of benches, set up parallel to the enormous copper vats. Fortunately, the beer's good. Choose from a dozen in-house beers. 375 Water St. ℂ 604/689-2739. www.steamworks.com.

Yaletown Brewing Company   Every Sunday, all pints of brewed-on-the-premises beer are C$3.75 and pizzas are half-price. The excellent beer is complemented by an extremely cozy room, a great summertime patio, and a good appetizer menu. 1111 Mainland St. (at Helmcken St.). ℂ 604/681-2739. www.markjamesgroup.com.

4 DANCE CLUBS

Generally clubs are open until 2am every day but Sunday, when they close at midnight. In the summer months (mid-June through Labour Day), opening hours are extended to 4am. The city's clubs and discos are concentrated around two "entertainment zones," downtown around Granville Street, and along Water and Pender streets in Gastown.

Au Bar   An address is unnecessary for Au Bar; the long Seymour Street line of those not-quite-beautiful-enough for expedited entry immediately gives it away. Inside, this downtown bar is packed with beautiful people milling from bar to dance floor to bar (there are two) and back again. Observing them is like watching a nature documentary on the Discovery Channel: Doelike women prance and jiggle while predatory men roam in packs, flexing pecs and biceps. 674 Seymour St. ℂ 604/648-2227. www.aubarnightclub. com. Cover C$5–C$8.

Caprice   Upstairs, it's the Lounge, with dark wood, a fireplace, a big-screen TV showing old Audrey Hepburn movies, and a Granville Street patio. Downstairs, it's the Nightclub, a large room with a funky semicircular glowing blue bar, big comfy wall banquettes, a secluded circular passion pit in one corner, and a medium-size dance floor. Earlier in the week the DJ spins house, but on weekends, when the older, richer 25-and-overs come out to play, the cover goes up and the DJ retreats to the safety of Top 40. 965 Granville St. ℂ 604/685-3288. www.capricenightclub.com. Cover Tues–Thurs C$6, Fri–Sat C$10.

The Cellar   The Cellar inhabits that netherworld between dance club, bar, meat market, and personals ads. Dance-club characteristics include a cover charge, small dance floor, and a DJ who mostly spins Top 40. But Cellar patrons are far less interested in groovin' than they are in meeting other Cellar dwellers, a process facilitated by a wall-length message board upon which pickup lines are posted. 1006 Granville St. ℂ 604/605-4350. www.cellarvan.com. Cover C$5–C$8.

Fabric Nightclub   Located in the heart of Gastown, one of Vancouver's biggest and most legendary rooms (it was formerly Sonar) has been revitalized and reborn as Fabric Nightclub. With a 500-plus capacity, couches, a VIP balcony section that overlooks the giant dance floor, plus some of the biggest name DJs in the world, the club doesn't disappoint. 66 Water St. ℂ 604/683-6695. www.fabricvancouver.com. Cover C$10–C$20.

Maxine's Hideaway In a funky Spanish Revival building with a seedy past as a bordello, Maxine's serves loungey martinis, wine, and tapas until the wee hours (2am), plus houses two small dance floors, each with its own DJ, and hosts floor shows on Friday and Saturday nights. 1215 Bidwell St. (at Davie St.). ✆ **604/689-8822**. www.maxineshideaway. com. Cover Fri–Sat C$15–C$20.

The Red Room This basement warren has two bars, numerous intimate cubby holes, and a DJ that does progressive house and hip-hop, plus a live band sometimes on the weekend. And if that weren't enough, there's also a pool. 398 Richards St. ✆ **604/687-5007**. www.redroomonrichards.com. Cover C$7–C$15.

Richard's on Richards For years, this club was a notorious pickup spot. Things have mellowed since then, but as the line of limos out front on busy nights attests, Dick's is still hot. Inside are two floors, four bars, a laser light system, and lots of DJ'ed dance tunes and concerts. 1036 Richards St. ✆ **604/687-6794**. www.richardsonrichards.com. Cover Fri–Sat C$8 for the club, C$10–C$30 for concerts.

Shine This downstairs cellar in Gastown plays house and hip-hop, with occasional forays into other genres such as reggae. 364 Water St. ✆ **604/408-4321**. www.shinenightclub. com. Cover C$5–C$10.

The Stone Temple Here, frat boys from America are tickled pink that the drinking age in B.C. is only 19. And dude, the beer's so cheap! Opens at 9pm. 1082 Granville St. ✆ **604/488-1333**. www.stonetemplenightclub.com. Cover weeknights C$5, weekends C$10.

Tonic Squeeze past the well-endowed door bunnies, and you're in a narrow room with a soaring ceiling, oversize paintings of hard-liquor bottles, and an impressive-looking disco ball. The crowd is post-university but as yet unmated. Music is Latin, Brazilian, and Top 40 mix on weekends. 919 Granville St. ✆ **604/669-0469**. www.thetonicclub.com. Cover C$6–C$10.

5 GAY & LESBIAN BARS

B.C.'s enlightened attitude—remember, same-sex couples can wed in Canada—has had a curious effect on Vancouver's queer dance-club scene: It's so laid-back and attitude-free that it's often hard to tell straight from gay, male go-go dancers and naked men in showers notwithstanding. The "Gay Village" is in the West End, particularly on Davie and Denman streets. Many clubs feature theme nights and dance parties, drag shows are ever popular, and every year in early August, as Gay Pride nears, the scene goes into overdrive. The **Gay Lesbian Transgendered Bisexual Community Centre,** 2-1170 Bute St. (✆ **604/684-5307;** www.qmunity.ca), has information on the current hot spots, but it's easier just to pick up a free copy of *Xtra West!,* available in most downtown cafes.

The Fountain Head Pub Reflecting the graying and—gasp!—mellowing of Vancouver's boomer-age gay crowd, the hottest hangout for gays is the Fountain Head, a pub located in the heart of the city's gay ghetto on Davie Street. The Head offers excellent microbrewed draft, good pub munchies, and a pleasant humming atmosphere until the morning's wee hours. 1025 Davie St. ✆ **604/687-2222**. www.thefountainheadpub.com.

Lotus Hotel Once among the most disreputable of Gastown gay bars, this aging hotel was given a face-lift and is now home to three bars and lounges, all with a largely but not exclusively gay clientele. Downstairs, the Lotus Lounge is one of the hottest house music venues in town, particularly on Straight Up Fridays with an all-female DJ team on the turntables. Lick, on the main floor, is a lesbian bar. The third venue, also on the main floor, is Honey, a comfortable lounge where a mixed crowd gathers for cocktails or beers. On most nights, the DJs keep the music on a mellow, conversational level. However, on Saturdays, decibels go up significantly when the Queen Bee review, a New York–style cabaret drag show, fills the house. 455 Abbott St. ✆ **604/685-7777.** Cover Milk and Lotus C$5–C$12 (some nights); Honey C$7 (only on Sat).

Numbers A multilevel dance club with five floors and three bars, Numbers hasn't changed much over the years. Extroverts hog the dance floor while admirers look on from the bar above. On the second floor, carpets, wood paneling, pool tables, darts, and a lower volume of music give it a neighborhood pub feel. 1042 Davie St. ✆ **604/685-4077.** www.numbers.ca. Cover Fri–Sat C$3.

The Odyssey Odyssey is the hottest and hippest gay/mixed dance bar in town (alley entrance is for men; women go in by the front door). The medium-size dance space is packed. Shows vary depending on the night. Saturday it's Fallen Angel go-go dancers, and Sunday it's the Feather Boa drag show. And on Thursday, it's "Shower Power"—yes, that is a naked man in the shower above the dance floor. 1251 Howe St. ✆ **604/689-5256.** www.theodysseynightclub.com. Cover Thurs–Tues C$3–C$5.

6 CINEMA

Thanks to the number of resident moviemakers (both studio and independent), Vancouver is quite a film town. First-run theaters show the same Hollywood junk seen everywhere in the world, but for those with something more adventurous in mind, plenty of options can be found.

Attendance at the **Vancouver International Film Festival** (✆ **604/685-0260;** www.viff.org) reaches more than 100,000, not including the celebs who drop in. At this highly respected October event, more than 250 new films are shown, representing filmmakers from 40 countries. Asian films are particularly well represented.

SPECIALTY THEATERS

Since 1972, the **Pacific Cinematheque,** 1131 Howe St. (✆ **604/688-FILM** [3456]; www.cinematheque.bc.ca), has featured classic and contemporary films from around the world. Screenings are organized into themes, such as "Jean-Luc Godard's Early Efforts," film noir, or the "Hong Kong Action Flick: A Retrospective." Schedules are available in hipper cafes, record shops, and video stores around town, and on the website. Admission is C$9.50 for adults, C$8 for seniors and students; double features cost C$2 extra. Annual membership, required to purchase tickets, is C$3.

At the **CN IMAX,** Canada Place (✆ **604/682-IMAX** [4629]), a gargantuan screen features large-format flicks about denizens of the animal kingdom (sharks, wolves, elephants, extreme athletes). A similar large screen at the **Alcan OMNIMAX,** Science World (✆ **604/443-7443**), features flicks about empty, wide-open spaces, colorful coral reefs, and the like. See the Canada Place and Science World at TELUS World of Science listings under "The Top Attractions," in chapter 8.

Way off in the strip-mall lands of farthest Kingsway stands the **Raja,** 3215 Kingsway (℗ **604/436-1545;** www.rajacinema.com), a modest single-screen movie house dedicated to bringing in the best Bollywood flicks from Bombay, the world's moviemaking capital. Expect unbelievable plots mixed with big-production musical numbers. Some have English subtitles, though strictly speaking they're not necessary. If Kingsway is too far off, another Raja is at 639 Commercial Dr. (℗ **604/253-0402**).

Whistler Blackcomb

One of the world's greatest ski resorts, **Whistler Blackcomb** will be hosting the 2010 Olympic and Paralympic Winter Games (p. 32). This favored spot, less than 2 hours by car from Vancouver, has more vertical runs, lifts, and varied ski terrain than any other ski resort in North America. Winter sports rule from December through April: Downhill, backcountry, cross-country and heli-skiing, snowboarding, sledding, and sleigh riding are just the tip of the glacier.

In the summer, Whistler is a mecca for mountain bikers, with a world-class mountain bike park to match its world-class winter skiing. If you're not a fan of biking, you can spend your summer days in Whistler rafting, hiking, golfing, and horseback riding. Or, for some wonderful low-tech, eco-friendly fun, try zipping across Fitzsimmons Creek on Ziptrek (p. 199) and exploring the sublime coastal rainforest hidden between Whistler and Blackcomb mountains.

The focus for all the action is **Whistler Village.** This resort community is sophisticated and international, but so new that at first glance it might strike you as a bit like Disneyland, or a huge mall with hotels (what the retail industry calls a "lifestyle center"). Back in the 1970s, a few visionary planners made the decision to build a resort town and set about creating a carefully planned infrastructure and aesthetic. The results are impressive—a compact resort, at the base of two mountains, arranged around a stroll-able, ski-able, and completely carless village street lined with upscale shopping, great restaurants, lots of pubs and cafes with outdoor patios, and plenty of plazas. What was sacrificed in this drive to become the perfectly planned community was space for the odd, the funky, the quaint, and the nonconforming. It's just too new and too affluent (at least in the winter; in the summer mountain-biking season it becomes more family oriented). When word went out that the 2010 Olympic Winter Games would be held here, real estate prices skyrocketed and more luxury hotels went up.

1 ESSENTIALS

128km (80 miles) N of Vancouver

Prices for hotels jump considerably during the high season from December through April, and that's also—not surprisingly—when Whistler is at its most seductive, blanketed with snow and twinkling with lights. July, August, and September are the best months for summer recreation on the mountains. During the shoulder seasons, May and June and October and November, you can expect rain—the area is, after all, a coastal rainforest. For information on accommodations during the 2010 Winter Olympics, see the box "The 2010 Olympic & Paralympic Winter Games" on p. 32.

GETTING THERE

Note: During the 2010 Winter Olympics period (Feb 12–28, 2010), special regulations involving transportation to and from Whistler will be in effect. In general, passenger cars will not be allowed on the Sea-to-Sky Highway going up to Whistler, and ticket holders

ACCOMODATIONS

Alpine Chalet Whistler **4**
Cedar Springs Bed & Breakfast Lodge **1**
Chalet Beau Sejour **3**
Durlacher Hof Pension Inn **2**
Hostelling International Whistler **5**

CAMPGROUNDS ●

Alice Lake Provincial Park **A**
Birkenhead Lake Provincial Park **C**
Nairn Falls **B**

Skiing
Golfing
Hiking
Parking **P**

0   1 mi
0   1 km

Green Lake

Fitzsimmons Creek

Chateau
Whistler
Golf Club

LOST LAKE
PARK

Lost
Lake

Blackcomb
Benchlands

Alpine
Meadows

Alpine Way

Alta Lake Rd.

Nicklaus North
Golf Course

River of Golden Dreams

99

99

White
Gold Estates

3

Wizard Express

Magic Chair

Excalibur

Gondola

BLACKCOMB
MOUNTAIN

Village
North

2

Upper
Village

P

Northlands Blvd

Blackcomb Way

P

P

Whistler
Cay

Fairway Dr.

Whistler
Golf Club

Fitzsimmons Express

Whistler Village Gondola

see "Whistler Village" map

Alta Vista

Brio

Alta Lake

Scotia Creek

Nita
Lake

Nordic Estates

WHISTLER MOUNTAIN

Creekside
Gondola

Whistler
Creek

Alpha Lake

Bayshores

Alta Lake Rd.

99

Function Junction

Cheakamus River

0   100 miles

BRITISH
COLUMBIA

Gold Bridge

D'Arcy

Lytton

Fraser R.

99

Garibaldi
Provincial Park

Golden Ears
Provincial Park

5

Whistler

A

B

Squamish

Vancouver

99

Strait of Georgia

Bellingham

WA

5

Victoria

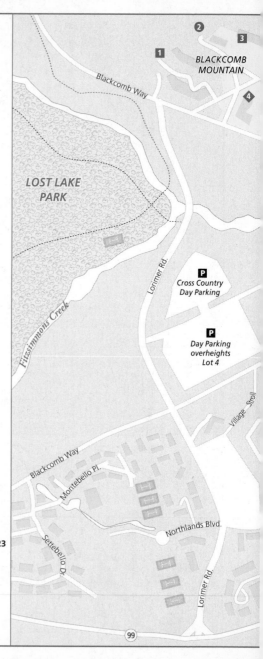

WHISTLER BLACKCOMB

12

ESSENTIALS

ACCOMMODATIONS ■
Adara Whistler Hotel **16**
Delta Whistler Village Suites **21**
The Fairmont Chateau Whistler **3**
Four Seasons Resort Whistler **1**
Pan Pacific Whistler Mountainside **5**
Pan Pacific Whistler Village Centre **13**
Summit Lodge & Spa **24**
The Westin Resort & Spa Whistler **8**

DINING ◆
Araxi **14**
Bearfoot Bistro **19**
Caramba! Restaurant **11**
Ciao-Thyme Bistro and the Fitz Pub **4**
Citta Bistro **18**
Dubh Linn Gate Irish Lounge/Pub **5**
Hy's Steakhouse **22**
Ingrid's Village Café **15**
Quattro **25**
Rimrock Cafe and Oyster Bar **26**
Whistler BrewHouse **9**

NIGHTLIFE ▼
Boot Pub **26**
Buffalo Bills **17**
Dubh Linn Gate Irish Lounge/Pub **5**
Garfinkel's **12**
Maxx Fish **15**
Savage Beagle **14**
Tommy Africa's **14**
Whistler BrewHouse **9**

OTHER ATTRACTIONS ●
Blackcomb Gondola **6**
Maurice Young Millennium Place **10**
Squamish Lil'Wat Cultural Centre **2**
Tourism Whistler Activity and
  Information Center **20**
Whistler Museum & Archives Society **23**
Whistler Village Gondola **7**

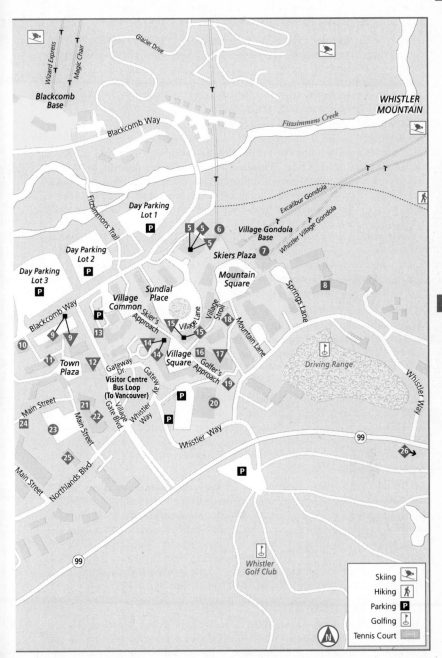

to Olympic events will have to board special buses at Horseshoe Bay for the 2-hour trip to Whistler. Visit the website **www.vancouver2010.com** for more information. The information below is for the pre- and post-Winter Olympics period.

BY BUS The **Whistler Express,** 8695 Barnard St. (© **888/717-6606** or 604/717-6600; www.perimeterbus.com), operates bus service from Vancouver International Airport to the Whistler Bus Loop, as well as drop-off service at many of the hotels. In summer, there are seven daily departures; in winter, there are nine. The trip takes about 2½ to 3 hours; roundtrip fares are C$103 adults, C$53 for children 5 to 11 and free for children under 5. Reservations are required year-round.

SnowBus (© **866/685-7669;** www.snowbus.ca) is a luxury coach featuring hosts, movies, snacks, drinks, and a hot breakfast option for early-morning departures from Vancouver during the winter ski season. They can also arrange lift tickets and rentals. Roundtrip adult fare is C$43. **Whistler Direct Shuttle** (© **888/405-2410;** www. whistlerdirectshuttle.com) operates a deluxe highway coach service between Vancouver and Whistler. The service is by reservation only and is licensed to pick up from the airport and all downtown Vancouver hotels. Adult one-way fare from a Vancouver hotel is C$49; the fare from the airport is C$65.

Greyhound, Pacific Central Station, 1150 Station St. (© **800/661-8747** or 604/683-8133; www.greyhound.ca), operates daily bus service (six trips a day 5:30am–5:30pm) from the Vancouver airport or downtown bus depot to the Whistler Creekside bus stop. The trip takes about 2½ hours; round-trip fares are C$48 for adults, C$21 for children 5 to 12, and free for children 4 and under.

BY CAR Whistler is about a 2-hour drive from Vancouver along **Hwy. 99,** also called the **Sea-to-Sky Highway.** The drive is spectacular, winding first along the edge of Howe Sound before climbing through the mountains. In preparation for the 2010 Winter Games, the highway was completely overhauled. Parking is free for day skiers and visitors in Whistler. Most hotels in Whistler Village and Upper Village charge a minimum of C$20 for underground parking.

BY PLANE **Howe Sound Seaplanes** (© **866/882-3252;** www.howesoundseaplanes. com) offers two daily flights from Victoria to the Whistler area. Passengers fly from Victoria's Inner Harbour via the Vancouver Airport to Squamish, located 30 minutes south of Whistler, where a courtesy shuttle transfers them to Whistler. The flight from Victoria to Vancouver is 35 minutes and from Vancouver to Squamish 30 minutes. Fares begin at C$149.

BY TRAIN Between May 1 and October 16, **Rocky Mountaineer Vacations** (© **877/460-3200** or 604/606-7245; www.rockymountaineer.com) offers daily service between North Vancouver and Whistler on the **Whistler Mountaineer** ★★★, a refurbished train with a vintage observation car. Trains depart North Vancouver at 8:30am (transportation to the train station is provided by most Vancouver hotels) and arrive at 11:30am; departure time from Whistler is 3pm, arriving back in North Vancouver at 6pm. Breakfast is served on the way up, and a light meal on the return. Standard round-trip "Coach Classic" fares are C$199 for adults and C$109 for children ages 2 to 11.

VISITOR INFORMATION

The **Whistler Visitor Info Centre,** 4230 Gateway Dr., off Village Gate Boulevard from Hwy. 99 (© **877/991-9988** or 604/935-3357; www.whistlerchamber.com), is open daily from 8am to midnight during the winter ski season (otherwise daily 8am to 10pm),

ism Whistler Activity Centre (© 877/991-9988 or 604/938-2769; www.whistler.
com), located in front of the TELUS Conference Centre near the Whistler gondola, is
open daily 10am to 6pm, and can assist you with ski-lift and other activity tickets and
information, plus last-minute accommodations bookings. For **hotel reservations,** call
© **800/WHISTLER** [944-7853].

Another good website for general information is **www.whistlerblackcomb.com**.

GETTING AROUND

Compact and pedestrian-oriented, Whistler Village has signed trails and pathways linking hotels, shops, and restaurants with the gondolas up to Whistler and Blackcomb
mountains. If you're staying in the Village, you can park and leave your car for the duration of your stay.

The resort is divided into **Whistler Village** (where you get the gondola for Whistler
Mountain) and the **Upper Village** (where you get the gondola for Blackcomb Mountain); it takes about 5 minutes to walk between them, and 11 minutes if you take the new
Peak to Peak gondola (p. 195). At some of the hotels, you can ski from the front entrance
directly to the gondolas.

BY BUS   **Whistler and Valley Express (WAVE;** © **604/932-4020;** www.busonline.
ca), a year-round public transit service, runs from the Gondola Transit Exchange to the
neighboring districts of Nester's Village, Alpine Meadows, and Emerald Estates. Service
from the Village to Village North and Upper Village accommodations is free; other
routes, one-way fares are C$1.50 for adults, C$1.25 for seniors and students, and free for
children 4 and under.

BY CAB   **Sea-to-Sky Taxi** (© **800/203-5322** or 604/932-3333) operates 24 hours.

BY CAR   Rental cars are available from **Avis,** 4315 Northlands Blvd. (© **800/879-**
2847 or 604/932-1236), and **Budget,** 4005 Whistler Way (© **800/299-3199** or 604/
493-4122).

SPECIAL EVENTS

For information on events taking place during the **2010 Olympic and Paralympic**
Winter Games, see p. 32.

Non-Olympic downhill **ski competitions** are held December through May. Contact
Tourism Whistler (see "Visitor Information," above) for event listings.

Cornucopia (© **800/766-0449;** www.whistlercornucopia.com) is Whistler's premier
wine-and-food festival. Held in November, the opening gala showcases 50 top wineries
from the Pacific region. Other events include a celebrity chef competition, food and wine
seminars, and wine tastings.

For other month-by-month event listings, visit www.whistler.com.

2 WHERE TO STAY

The first and biggest decision to make is whether to stay in or outside of Whistler Village.
If you stay in the Village, you can forget about your car for the duration of your visit and
walk along paved pathways from hotel to ski lift to restaurant to pub. Staying outside the
Village, you'll have a short drive to the parking lots on the perimeter of Whistler Village

(many hotels outside the Village offer shuttle service). Accommodations within the Village are top quality, while outside the Village affords a bit more variety, including some fine European-style inns.

To get the best rates on the hotels listed below, check the hotel's website to see if special packages are available or promotions are going on. In some cases, you can nab incredible ski/hotel packages.

Note: If you are planning to visit Whistler during the 2010 Olympic and Paralympic Winter Games, it's important that you read the information about accommodations in "The 2010 Olympic & Paralympic Winter Games," p. 32. The rates for any available accommodation during the Olympic period will be considerably higher than the highest rack rate listed below.

Whistler Central Reservations (✆ **800/944-7853;** www.whistler.com) can book a wide range of accommodations in the Whistler area, and provide a customized package with lift tickets and transportation from and to Vancouver.

IN THE VILLAGE
Very Expensive

Adara Whistler Hotel ★★   Adara, right in the center of the village, offers guests a stylish alternative to Whistler's lodge-style hotels by using all the traditional Whistler "ingredients" (stone and wood) in a more playful manner. The guest rooms come in four configurations (including a loft studio) with contemporary furnishings that give a comfortable, carefree look. The bathrooms are functional rather than luxurious, with showers only. The outside pool overlooks the village.

4122 Village Green, Whistler, B.C. V0N 1B4. ✆ **866/502-3272** or 604/905-4009. www.adarahotel.com. 41 units. Low season C$129–C$279 double; high season C$299–C$809 double. AE, MC, V. Underground valet parking C$20. **Amenities:** Restaurant; bikes; executive-level rooms; heated outdoor pool (seasonal); sauna; ski rental; spa. *In room:* A/C, TV/DVD w/pay movies, hair dryer, kitchenette (in some), minibar, free Wi-Fi.

The Fairmont Chateau Whistler ★★   The Fairmont Chateau Whistler in the Upper Village at the foot of Blackcomb Mountain is absolutely enormous, and built in the style of the great old Canadian Pacific lodge hotels. The rooms and suites are quite large (the Mountain Suites, in fact, are huge), very quiet, and have good-size bathrooms with a separate soaker tub and shower. The heated outdoor pool and Jacuzzis look out over the base of the ski hill. Massive wooden beams, double-sided stone fireplaces, and an on-site spa help create an elegant if old-fashioned ambience.

4599 Chateau Blvd., Whistler, B.C. V0N 1B4. ✆ **800/606-8244** or 604/938-8000. Fax 604/938-2291. www. fairmont.com. 550 units. Spring–fall C$259–C$499 double, C$319–C$699 suite; winter C$359–C$799 double, C$489–C$1,949 suite. AE, MC, V. Underground valet parking C$28. **Amenities:** 4 restaurants, bar; babysitting; children's programs; concierge; concierge-level rooms; health club; Jacuzzi; 2 heated outdoor pools; room service; spa; 3 tennis courts; rooms for those w/limited mobility. *In room:* A/C, TV w/pay movies, hair dryer, high-speed Internet, minibar.

Four Seasons Resort Whistler ★★★   If you want the best, this is it. In the Upper Village, the Four Seasons has set a new standard for luxury and service in Whistler. The guest rooms, suites, and town houses are the largest in Whistler. All feature beautifully detailed wood-trimmed interiors, gas fireplaces, and views of the mountains, forest, valley, pool, or courtyard from step-out balconies. The decor is an updated version of a 1920s grand mountain lodge. The beds are fitted with Frette sheets. You won't find larger or more luxurious bathrooms anywhere in Whistler; each one has a deep soaker tub, a separate glass-enclosed shower, and two sinks. Every amenity you can think of is available here, including valet ski service. **189**

4591 Blackcomb Way, Whistler, B.C. V0N 1B4. (C) **888/935-2460** or 604/935-3400. Fax 604/935-3455. www.fourseasons.com. 273 units. Summer–fall C$265–C$505 double, C$395 and up suite; winter C$305–C$1,325 double, C$615 and up suite. AE, DC, MC, V. Underground valet parking C$33. **Amenities:** Restaurant, bar; babysitting; concierge; executive-level rooms; health club; Jacuzzi; heated outdoor pool; room service; sauna; spa; rooms for those w/limited mobility. *In room:* A/C, TV w/pay movies, DVD/CD player, fireplace, hair dryer, minibar, free Wi-Fi.

Expensive

Delta Whistler Village Suites ★ (Kids)

Just minutes from all the major attractions in Whistler, the Delta offers a variety of comfortable, unpretentious, one- and two-bedroom suites with gas fireplaces, balconies, living rooms, fully equipped kitchens, and washer-dryers. They have standard double rooms as well. The beds are firm and comfortable, and the bathrooms are plain but adequate. You won't find the fine finishes and furnishings of a luxury hotel, but you will get great service and the use of a large heated pool with three Jacuzzis. **Hy's Steakhouse** (p. 193) is in the same building. The hotel welcomes children and has special kids' programs.

4308 Main St., Whistler, B.C. V0N 1B4. (C) **888/299-3987** or 604/905-3987. Fax 604/938-6335. www.delta hotels.com. 207 units. May–Dec 15 C$109–C$209 double, C$129–C$399 suite; Dec 16–Apr C$189–C$499 double, C$299–C$999 suite. AE, MC, V. Underground valet parking C$24. **Amenities:** Restaurant; babysitting; children's programs; concierge; executive-level rooms; health club; indoor and outdoor Jacuzzis; heated outdoor pool; room service; sauna; ski rental; spa; rooms for those w/limited mobility. *In room:* A/C, TV w/pay movies, hair dryer, fireplace (in suites), high-speed Internet (C$14/day), kitchen, minibar.

Pan Pacific Whistler Mountainside ★★

The Pan Pacific's location, overlooking the Whistler gondola and ski slopes, puts this hotel right in the center of the action. You can literally ski out the door straight to the gondola. The look here is contemporary lodge-style, sophisticated, and very comfortable, with lots of warm wood in the rooms. Every suite has a fully equipped kitchenette and balcony. The studio suites with fold-down Murphy beds are the smallest units available; the one- and two-bedroom suites are quite roomy. One of the best features is the huge heated outdoor pool and Jacuzzi deck overlooking the snowy slopes. The hotel's **Dubh Linn Gate Irish Lounge/Pub** is a popular après-ski rendezvous point.

The **Pan Pacific Whistler Village Centre,** 4299 Blackcomb Way ((C) **888/966-5575** or 604/966-5500; www.panpacificwhistler.com), run by the same company, is an all-suite, boutique hotel with fine amenities and a village location. Spring-fall rates for a one-bedroom suite are C$179 to C$429; winter rates for a one-bedroom suite are C$249 to C$999.

4320 Sundial Crescent, Whistler, B.C. V0N 1B4. (C) **888/905-9995** or 604/905-2999. Fax 604/905-2995. www.panpacificwhistler.com. 121 units. Spring–fall C$139–C$329 studio, C$179–C$629 suite; winter C$219–C$869 studio, C$319–C$1,619 suite. AE, MC, V. Underground valet parking C$25. **Amenities:** Restaurant, pub; concierge; fitness center; Jacuzzi; heated outdoor pool; room service; rooms for those w/limited mobility. *In room:* A/C, TV, fridge, hair dryer, free high-speed Internet, kitchen, minibar.

Summit Lodge & Spa ★★

Peace and harmony reign at this classy boutique hotel located just a short stroll from the slopes and featuring a unique, full-service spa. All of the guest rooms are suites with kitchenettes, fireplaces, and balconies. All the units showcase granite countertops, custom-designed cherrywood furnishings, original artwork, and oversize beds with down-filled duvets and pillows. The bathrooms feature soaker tubs. Among the complimentary services are a yoga program and hot chocolate every evening;

you can also borrow portable Zen waterfalls and tranquillity rock/sand gardens. The hotel's new dining spot, Elements Urban Tapas Lounge, offers upscale tapas, fresh seafood, infused martinis, and rare wines. The hotel's on-site Taman Sari Royal Heritage Spa features traditional Javanese spa treatments.

4359 Main St., Whistler, B.C. V0N 1B4. (© **888/913-8811** or 604/932-2778. Fax 604/932-2716. www.summit lodge.com. 81 units. C$119–C$425 suite. AE, MC, V. Underground valet parking C$19. **Amenities:** Restaurant; concierge; Jacuzzi; heated outdoor pool; ski shuttle; full-service spa; rooms for those w/limited mobility. *In room:* A/C, TV, fridge, hair dryer, free high-speed Internet, kitchenette.

The Westin Resort & Spa Whistler ★★★
Located just a few hundred yards from the Whistler gondola, this two-tower hotel provides outstanding service and luxury-level amenities. All 419 generously sized suites include upscale kitchens, gas fireplaces, and most have balconies—and all were refurbished in 2009. The bathrooms are roomy, with separate bathtubs and showers in most units. Some rooms in the back have lovely mountain views, but you can hear distant traffic noise from Hwy. 99, so ask about this when booking. Little luxuries include ski valet, boot-warming services, and the full-service spa, Avello, one of the best in Canada, offering more than 75 treatments. There's also an award-winning restaurant, Aubergine Grille, for fine dining.

4090 Whistler Way, Whistler, B.C. V0N 1B4. (© **888/634-5577** or 604/905-5000. Fax 604/905-5640. www. westinwhistler.com. 419 units. C$189–C$949 junior suite; C$239 and up 1-bedroom suite. Children 17 and under stay free in parent's room. AE, MC, V. Underground valet parking C$28. **Amenities:** 2 restaurants; bar; babysitting; concierge; health club; indoor and outdoor Jacuzzi; outdoor pool; room service; sauna; spa. *In room:* TV w/pay movies, hair dryer, kitchen, Wi-Fi (C$15/day).

OUTSIDE THE VILLAGE
Expensive
Alpine Chalet Whistler ★
This elegant chalet was built to the exact specifications of a Czech couple who took up a second career as innkeepers. The common room is a dream, with comfy chairs and a big fireplace. The adjoining dining area is flooded with natural light from the overhead skylights. Rooms are named after trees and come in essentially two configurations: Standard rooms are comfortable but not huge, with two twins or a king-size bed, bathrooms with heated floors, and a functional tub/shower combo; signature rooms are larger, with vaulted ceilings, the same bed combinations but with Italian linen, as well as a gas fireplace and comfy leather armchairs. Several of these rooms also have pocket balconies, though with views of nothing much. Breakfasts are a top-quality feast prepared by a Swiss chef.

3012 Alpine Crescent, Whistler, B.C. V0N 1B3. (© **800/736-9967** or 604/935-3003. Fax 604/935-3008. www. alpinechaletwhistler.com. 8 units. C$139–C$399 double. Rates include full breakfast. MC, V. Free parking. Take Hwy. 99 about 2km (1¼ miles) past Whistler Creekside (before Whistler Village), turn left onto Alta Vista and Hillcrest Dr., then a quick right onto Alpine Crescent; the chalet is on the left side about a block away. No pets. **Amenities:** Hot tub; ski and bike storage; small steam room. *In room:* TV, free Wi-Fi.

Durlacher Hof Pension Inn ★ (Finds)
This lovely inn has an Austrian feel and a wonderfully sociable atmosphere. Both are the result of the exceptional care and service shown by owners Peter and Erika Durlacher. The guest rooms in this two-story chalet-style property vary in size from comfortable to spacious, and come with goose-down duvets and Ralph Lauren linens on extralong twin- or queen-size beds, and private bathrooms (some with jetted tubs) with deluxe toiletries. The private balconies give way to incredible mountain views. Better still is the downstairs lounge, with a welcoming fireplace and complementary après-ski appetizers baked by innkeeper Erika, who also provides a substantial gourmet breakfast.

7055 Nesters Rd., Whistler, B.C. V0N 1B7. ✆ **877/932-1924** or 604/932-1924. Fax 604/938-1980. www. durlacherhof.com. 8 units. C$129–C$299 double. Extra person C$35. Rates include full breakfast and afternoon tea. MC, V. Free parking. Take Hwy. 99 about .8km (1/2 mile) north of Whistler Village to Nesters Rd.; turn left and the inn is immediately on the right. **Amenities:** Jacuzzi; sauna; ski and bike storage; 1 room for those w/limited mobility. *In room:* Hair dryer, no phone.

Moderate

Cedar Springs Bed & Breakfast Lodge (Kids) This is one of Whistler's few B&Bs
that welcomes children. Guests at this charming lodge have a choice of king-, queen-, or twin-size beds in comfortably modern surroundings. The largest room (no. 4) features a fireplace and balcony, though the bathroom is shower only. Room no. 8 has a queen-size bed, two single futons, and a big soaker tub, while room no. 7 has two queen-size and a shower only. The guest sitting room has a fireplace, TV, VCR, and video library; a sauna and hot tub on the sun deck (overlooking the gardens) fill out the list of amenities. An excellent breakfast is served by the fireplace in the dining room, and guests are welcome to enjoy afternoon tea. A complimentary shuttle service takes you to and from the ski lifts.

8106 Cedar Springs Rd., Whistler, B.C. V0N 1B8. ✆ **800/727-7547** or 604/938-8007. Fax 604/938-8023. www.whistlerbb.com. 8 units, 6 with private bathroom (5 with shower only). Winter C$85–C$255 double; summer C$85–C$229 double. Rates include full breakfast. AE, MC, V. Free parking. Take Hwy. 99 north toward Pemberton 4km (2 1/2 miles) past Whistler Village; turn left onto Alpine Way, go a block to Rainbow Dr., and turn left; go a block to Camino St. and turn left; the lodge is a block down at the corner of Camino St. and Cedar Springs Rd. **Amenities:** Bikes; Jacuzzi; sauna. *In room:* Hair dryer, no phone.

Chalet Beau Sejour (Value) The standout feature of the Beau Sejour is a large common room with a fireplace and a fine view of Whistler Mountain and the valley. The medium-size rooms are comfortable and clean, with two single beds that can be joined together to make a king-size. Of the four units, one is a self-contained suite with a queen-size bed and its own fireplace and full kitchen, although all units provide the best value you're likely to find in a Whistler B&B. The back patio has a large hot tub for guests' use. The B&B is on a public bus route, and located only about a 15-minute walk from the Village via pedestrian paths. Guests are provided with lockers at the base of Whistler for the duration of their stay, plus a shuttle to/from the Chalet on their first/last day (so you can drop off/pick up your ski gear).

7414 Ambassador Crescent, Whistler, B.C. V0N 1B7. ✆ **604/938-4966.** Fax 604/938-6296. www.beau sejourwhistler.com. 4 units, shower only. Summer C$99–C$120 double; winter C$120–C$165 double. Rates include full breakfast. AE, MC, V. Free parking. Take Hwy. 99 north toward Pemberton about 2km (1 1/4 miles) past Whistler Village; turn right onto Nancy Green Dr., go over the creek and 3 blocks to Ambassador Crescent, and turn right. No children 11 or under. **Amenities:** Jacuzzi. *In room:* No phone.

Inexpensive

Hostelling International Whistler (Value) One of the few inexpensive spots in
Whistler, this hostel also happens to have a great location on the south edge of Alta Lake, with a dining room, deck, and lawn overlooking the lake to Whistler Mountain. Inside this pleasant hostel is a lounge with a wood-burning stove, a common kitchen, a piano, Ping-Pong tables, and a sauna, as well as a drying room for ski gear and storage for bikes, boards, and skis. In the summer, guests have use of a barbecue, canoe, and rowboat. As with all hostels, most rooms and facilities are shared, but some private rooms are available. Book by September at the latest for the winter ski season.

5678 Alta Lake Rd., Whistler, B.C. V0N 1B5. ✆ **604/932-5492.** Fax 604/932-4687. www.hihostels.ca. 32 beds in 4- to 8-bed dorms. C$20–C$60 IYHA members, C$24–C$68 nonmembers; annual adult membership C$35. MC, V. Free parking. The turnoff for Alta Lake Rd. is before the main village, to the left of Hwy. 99. **Amenities:** Bikes; sauna; watersports equipment.

You can reserve spots for the campgrounds listed here through **Discover Camping** (© **800/689-9025;** www.discovercamping.ca). Reservation fees are uniformly C$6.30 per night with a maximum of C$19 for 3 nights. South of Whistler on the Sea-to-Sky corridor is the very popular **Alice Lake Provincial Park.** Free hot showers, flush toilets, and a sani-station are among the available facilities. Hiking trails, picnic areas, sandy beaches, swimming areas, and fishing spots are also on the grounds. Twenty-seven kilometers (17 miles) north of Whistler, the well-maintained campground at **Nairn Falls** on Hwy. 99 is more adult oriented, with pit toilets, pumped well water, fire pits and firewood, but no showers. Its proximity to the roaring Green River and the town of Pemberton makes it appealing to many hikers, and the sound of the river is sweeter than any lullaby. The 85 campsites at **Birkenhead Lake Provincial Park,** off Portage Road, Birken, fill up quickly in summer. Boat launches, great fishing, and well-maintained tent and RV sites make the park an angler's paradise and one of the province's top 10 camping destinations. Facilities include fire pits, firewood, pumped well water, and pit toilets. Please note that many provincial parks now charge a day-use parking fee of C$3 to C$5 per vehicle; you may also encounter a C$2 charge for using the sani-station.

3 WHERE TO DINE

Whistler overflows with dining choices, and a stroll through the Village will take you past 25 or 30 restaurants. Some serve overpriced resort food, but a number of them stand out for either atmosphere or the quality of their meals. For those willing to spend a bit more, Whistler has some outstanding fine-dining options.

On the Village Square, **Ingrid's Village Cafe** (© **604/932-7000;** www.ingridswhistler. com), open daily 7am to 6pm, is a local favorite for quality and price; it's been around for over 20 years, making it one of Whistler's oldest businesses. A large bowl of Ingrid's daily soup costs C$4.50; a veggie burger, C$7. Right across from Ingrid's, **Citta Bistro** (© **604/932-4177;** www.cittabistro.com) is a favorite dining and night spot, open daily 10am (9am Fri–Sat) to 1am. It serves thin-crust pizzas, gourmet burgers, and various appetizers. Besides having good food and good prices (main courses are C$10–C$17), it has terrace seating perfect for people-watching.

For good beer and stick-to-your-ribs grub, try the family-friendly **Whistler Brew-House,** 4355 Blackcomb Way (© **604/905-2739;** www.drinkfreshbeer.com), located just over the creek in Upper Village. It's open daily 11:30am to midnight (Fri and Sat to 1am). Shared plates run from C$6 to C$13; dinner entree prices are C$14 to C$38. Equally fun indoor dining can be had at the **Dubh Linn Gate Irish Lounge/Pub** (© **604/905-4047**) in the Pan Pacific hotel (p. 189). The Gate offers solid pub grub and the atmosphere of the Emerald Isle. Open Monday through Saturday 7am to 1am, Sundays 7am to midnight; main courses cost C$11 to C$20.

VERY EXPENSIVE

Bearfoot Bistro ★★★ FRENCH   What began as a fairly simple bistro has become Whistler's most elegant French restaurant. The kitchen procures the finest wild and cultivated products, and almost everything is prepared "a la minute" with an emphasis on the quality of the ingredients without over-complication. Diners create their own tasting menus from selections that change daily. For an appetizer, you might choose a raw plate with hamachi, wild salmon, and yellowfin tuna or wild Arctic caribou with a lentil-bacon

ragout. Your main course might be buffalo short ribs or fresh fish. The wine list at Bearfoot
Bistro is outstanding, and the expert sommelier can help you with wine pairings. For the proper experience, allot at least 2 hours to dine here and be prepared for wonderful service.

4121 Village Green. (C) **604/932-3433.** www.bearfootbistro.com. Reservations essential. Tasting menus C$39–C$79. AE, MC, V. Daily 5–10pm.

EXPENSIVE

Araxi ★★★ PACIFIC NORTHWEST   If you're looking for sublime food and an atmosphere of relaxed but sophisticated elegance, Araxi is as good as it gets. The haute spot of Whistler cuisine, this Village restaurant was voted "Best Restaurant in Whistler" by *Vancouver* magazine for 10 consecutive years. The menu is nominally Italian but with a Pacific Northwest bent that emphasizes fresh regional products. The seafood is extraordinary, with appetizers such as fresh oysters and a Dungeness crab roll. Main courses might include herb- and arugula-crusted Queen Charlotte halibut, prawn risotto, or prime beef tenderloin. When in doubt, try one of the tasting menus. Araxi's wine list is an awe-inspiring 27 pages long and offers a great selection of wines by the glass. Dinner is served in a warm, woody, beautifully designed space that looks out on the main village street; they also have an outdoor patio. Araxi now serves small tasting plates and a C$39 fixed-price meal.

4222 Village Sq. (C) **604/932-4540.** www.araxi.com. Reservations recommended. Main courses C$27–C$34; tasting menus C$79–C$89; small plates C$13–C$18. AE, MC, V. Daily 11am–3pm and 5pm–midnight.

Hy's Steakhouse ★ NORTH AMERICAN   This is the place to go if you're hungering for a big slab of roast beef with garlic mashed potatoes or a juicy steak (Hy's is famous for the quality of its beef). The menu also has seafood and even a vegetarian dish.

In the Delta Whistler Village Suites (p. 189), 4308 Main St. (C) 604/905-5550. www.hyssteakhouse.com. Main courses C$29–C$50. AE, DC, MC, V. Oct and May–June daily 8am–3pm; July–Sept and Nov–Apr daily 8am–3pm and 5–10pm.

Quattro ★★ ITALIAN   Quattro is in the Village, but it's a little off the beaten path. The room is warm and slightly quirky, while the food is fairly simple (fresh ingredients in uncomplicated seasonings), but satisfyingly well done. Though menus change regularly, typical appetizers include fresh minestrone with pesto, while main courses include a variety of great pastas (if you can't decide, order the *pazza a pezzi* and sample all five), as well as daily specials such as saltimbocca (veal scaloppine with sage and prosciutto in a butter sauce). The wine list is extraordinary, with a few token vintages from B.C. and California, but a heart and soul residing in Italy.

4319 Main St. (C) **604/905-4844.** www.quattrorestaurants.com. Reservations recommended. Main courses C$21–C$39. AE, MC, V. Daily 5:30–11pm. Closed Mon–Tues mid-Apr to June.

Rimrock Cafe and Oyster Bar ★★ SEAFOOD   Rimrock is like a Viking hall of old, with a long, narrow room, high ceiling, and a great stone fireplace. It's not the atmosphere, however, that draws folks in, it's the superlative food. The first order of business should be a plate of oysters. The chef serves them up in half a dozen ways, from raw with champagne to "cooked in hell" (broiled with fresh chilies). Entrees are seafood oriented but also include steak and fresh game (caribou, anyone?). Look for wild salmon grilled with fresh herbs, and pan-fried sablefish in an almond-ginger crust. The accompanying wine list has a number of fine vintages from B.C., California, New Zealand, and Australia.

2117 Whistler Rd. (C) **877/932-5589** or 604/932-5565. www.rimrockwhistler.com. Reservations recommended. Main courses C$24–C$42. AE, MC, V. Daily 6–11:30pm, but call ahead in the low season (May–June and Sept–Nov) as hours may change.

Side text (vertical): WHISTLER BLACKCOMB

12

WHAT TO SEE & DO OUTDOORS: WHISTLER'S RAISON D'ETRE

Caramba! Restaurante (Kids) MEDITERRANEAN   The food here won't win any awards, but Caramba! remains a good spot for casual dining; parents can bring their kids and not feel like they're "eating down." The nominally Mediterranean menu is something of an anomaly when it comes to culinary influences. Try the pasta, free-range chicken, or roasted pork loin. If you're into sharing, order a pizza or two and a plate of sliced prosciutto and bullfighter's toast (toasted Spanish bread with herbs).

12-4314 Main St., Town Plaza. ✆ **604/938-1879.** Main courses C$13–C$39. AE, MC, V. Daily 11:30am–10:30pm.

Ciao-Thyme Bistro and Fitz Pub ★ (Finds) (Kids) CASUAL/PACIFIC NORTHWEST   This popular spot in the Upper Village is a favorite with locals and a dream come true for visitors who want to eat well on a limited budget. The space is small, and the lines can be long (reserve if you're coming for dinner), but the fresh, delicious food is worth the wait. The bistro is a great spot for breakfast (until 3pm), lunch, or dinner (the only meal they serve in the winter), with a simple menu that reaches from free-range egg omelets to delicious sandwiches (try the pulled pork) and wraps. The special kids' menu features standards like grilled cheese sandwiches and pasta. The menu is the same in both the bistro and the nonsmoking pub next door.

4573 Chateau Blvd., Upper Village. ✆ **604/932-7051.** www.ciaothymebistro.com. Main courses C$13–C$25. AE, DC, MC, V. Spring–fall daily 8am–4pm and 6–10pm (closed Mon–Tues in May); winter daily dinner only 6–10pm.

4 WHAT TO SEE & DO OUTDOORS: WHISTLER'S RAISON D'ETRE

Whistler and Blackcomb Mountains ★★★ (Kids)   Both mountain resorts are operated by Intrawest, so your pass gives you access to both ski areas. Whistler is generally considered better for beginners and middle-range skiers, while steeper Blackcomb is geared to the experienced. A new gondola—the longest in the world—now links the two mountains (see "A Peak to Peak Experience: The New Intermountain Ski Lift," below). **Whistler Mountain** has 1,502m (4,928 ft.) of vertical (and more than 100 marked runs) serviced by a high-speed gondola and eight high-speed chairlifts, plus four other lifts and tows. Helicopter service from the top of the mountain provides access to another 100-plus runs on nearby glaciers. The peak has cafeterias, gift shops, and a restaurant. **Blackcomb Mountain** has 1,584m (5,197 ft.) of vertical (and more than 100 marked) runs serviced by nine high-speed chairlifts, plus three other lifts and tows. The cafeteria, restaurant, and gift shop aren't far from the peak. Both mountains also have bowls and glade skiing, with Blackcomb Mountain offering glacier skiing well into August. A family-friendly Tube Park, located at Base II on Blackcomb, offers a 385m (1,263-ft.) run with six lanes, accessed by a carpet-style lift. *Note:* You can save about 20% on your lift tickets by booking online.

4545 Blackcomb Way, Whistler, B.C. V0N 1B4. ✆ **800/766-0449** in North America, or 0800/587-1743 in the U.K.; snow report 604/687-7507 in Vancouver, 604/932-4211 in Whistler. www.whistlerblackcomb.com. Winter lift tickets C$55 adults, C$47 seniors and youths 13–18, C$27 children 7–12, free for children 6 and under. A variety of multiday passes are available. Tube park per hour C$16 adults, C$13 children. Lifts daily 8:30am–3:30pm (until 4:30pm mid-Mar until the end of season, depending on weather and conditions).

A Peak to Peak Experience: The New Intermountain Ski Lift

A new gondola linking the peaks of Whistler (elev. 2,182m/7,159 ft.) and Blackcomb (elev. 2,284m/7,493 ft.) mountains opened in December 2008. The longest free-span lift in the world, at 3km (2 miles), and with a total length of 4.4km (2³/₄ miles), the **Peak to Peak Gondola** is also the highest detachable lift in the world, at 415m (1,362 ft.) above the valley floor. The gondola has 28 cars, each carrying up to 28 passengers, and leaves about once every minute. The lift takes 11 minutes to travel from peak to peak. The new gondola offers skiers greater flexibility for skiing the highest runs of both mountains, and provides summer visitors with one of the most thrilling gondola rides in the world. The price for a gondola ride is C$40 for adults, C$33 for seniors and youths, and C$17 for children. To reach the Peak to Peak gondola, you must first take either the Whistler or Blackcomb gondola up to the new gondola boarding area.

DIFFERENT SLOPES FOR DIFFERENT FOLKS: THE LOWDOWN ON SKIING IN WHISTLER

Whistler Blackcomb offers **ski** and **snowboarding lessons** and **ski guides** for all levels and interests. Phone **Guest Relations** at © 604/932-3434 for details.

You can **rent ski and snowboard gear** at the base of both Whistler and Blackcomb Villages just prior to purchasing your lift pass. No appointment is necessary (or accepted), and the system is first-come, first-served. Arrive at 8am, and you'll be on the gondola by 8:15. Arrive at 8:30am, and you won't be up until 9:15 at the earliest.

Summit Ski (© 866/608-6225 or 604/932-6225; www.summitsport.com), at various locations including the Delta Whistler Resort and Market Pavilion, rents high-performance and regular skis, snowboards, telemark and cross-country skis, and snowshoes.

BACKCOUNTRY SKIING   The **Spearhead Traverse,** which starts at Whistler and finishes at Blackcomb, is a well-marked backcountry route that has become extremely popular in the past few years.

Garibaldi Provincial Park (© 604/898-3678) maintains marked backcountry trails at **Diamond Head, Singing Pass,** and **Cheakamus Lake.** These are ungroomed and unpatrolled rugged trails, and you have to be at least an intermediate skier and bring (and know how to use) appropriate clothing and avalanche gear. Several access points to the trails are along Hwy. 99 between Squamish and Whistler. If you're not sure of yourself off-*piste*, hire a guide through **Whistler Alpine Guides Bureau** (© 604/938-9242; www.whistlerguides.com) or **Whistler Cross Country Ski and Hike** (© 888/771-2382; www.whistlerski-hike.com).

CROSS-COUNTRY SKIING   Well-marked, fully groomed cross-country trails run throughout the area. The 30km (19 miles) of easy-to-very-difficult marked trails at **Lost Lake** start a block away from the Blackcomb Mountain parking lot. These trails are groomed for track skiing and ski-skating, are patrolled by Whistler employees, and are at their best from mid-December to mid-March. Passes are C$17 per day; a 1-hour cross-country lesson including pass and equipment rental runs about C$79, and can be booked at the same station where you buy your trail pass. For more information, contact **Lost Lake Cross Country Connection** (© 604/905-0071; www.crosscountryconnection.ca).

The **Valley Trail System** in the village becomes a well-marked cross-country ski trail during winter.

HELI-SKIING   For intermediate and advanced skiers who can't get enough fresh powder or vertical on the regular slopes, there's always heli-skiing. **Whistler Heli-Skiing** (© **888/435-4754** or 604/905-3337; www.whistlerheliskiing.com) offers a three-run day, with 2,400 to 3,000m (7,874–9,843 ft.) of vertical helicopter lift, for C$795 per person. A four-run day for expert skiers and riders only, with 3,000 to 3,600m (9,843–11,811 ft.) of vertical helicopter lift, is also available.

OTHER WINTER PURSUITS

SLEIGHING & DOG SLEDDING   For a horse-drawn sleigh ride, contact **Blackcomb Horsedrawn Sleigh Rides,** 103-4338 Main St. (© **604/932-7631;** www.blackcomb sleighrides.com). In winter, tours go out every evening and cost C$55 for adults and C$35 for children under 12. Other options include daylight and dinner sleigh rides.

From mid-December through March, **Whistler Blackcomb** (© **866/218-9690;** www. whistlerblackcomb.com) offers dog-sled rides. A backcountry dog-sled tour costs C$400 for one or two people.

SNOWMOBILING & ATVS   Year-round combination ATV and snowmobile tours of the Whistler Mountain trails are offered by **Canadian Snowmobile Adventures Ltd.,** Carleton Lodge, 4290 Mountain Sq. (© **604/938-1616;** www.canadiansnowmobile. com). All tours are weather and snow conditions permitting. A 2-hour tour costs C$125 for a driver and C$99 for a passenger. Drivers on both the snowmobile and the ATV must have a valid driver's license. A 3-hour Mountain Safari on Blackcomb Mountain costs C$159 for a driver and C$125 for a passenger.

Blackcomb Snowmobile (© **604/932-8484;** www.blackcombsnowmobile.com) offers a variety of guided snowmobile tours, including family tours on Blackcomb Mountain. A 2-hour tour costs C$129 for one adult, C$99 each for two adults, and half-price for children.

SNOWSHOEING   Snowshoeing is the world's easiest and most environmentally friendly form of snow-comotion; it requires none of the training and motor skills of skiing or boarding, and it's quiet, so it lets you appreciate nature in a different way. You can wear your own shoes or boots, provided they're warm and waterproof, strap on your snowshoes, and off you go. Rentals are available at the ski-and-board rental companies listed above. One of the best rental and trail companies is **Lost Lake Cross Country Connection** (© **604/905-0071;** www.crosscountryconnection.ca), which rents snowshoes for C$18.

SUMMER PURSUITS

CANOEING & KAYAKING   The 3-hour River of Golden Dreams Kayak & Canoe Tour is a great way for novices, intermediates, and experts to get acquainted with the beautiful stretch of slow-moving glacial water running between Green Lake and Alta Lake behind the village of Whistler. Contact the **Whistler Activity and Information Centre** (© **877/991-9988**) for information. Packages begin at C$30 per person, unguided, and include all gear and return transportation to the village center. The Whistler Activity and Information Centre also offers lessons and clinics, as well as sailboat and windsurfing rentals.

FISHING   Everything from rainbow trout to coho salmon attracts anglers from around the world to the area's many glacier-fed lakes and rivers and to **Birkenhead Lake Provincial Park,** 67km (42 miles) north of Pemberton.

Whistler River Adventures (📞 888/932-3532 or 604/932-3532; www.whistlerriver. com), offers half- and full-day catch-and-release fishing trips in the surrounding glacial rivers. Rates are C$240 per person for a half day, based on two people, which includes all fishing gear, round-trip transport to/from the Whistler Village Bus Loop, and a snack or lunch. A 1-day fishing license is an additional C$20.

GOLFING   Robert Trent Jones, Jr.'s, **Fairmont Chateau Golf Club,** at the base of Blackcomb Mountain (📞 877/938-2092, or pro shop 604/938-2097; www.golfwhistler. com), is an 18-hole, par-72 course. With an elevation gain of more than 120m (394 ft.), this course traverses mountain ledges and crosses cascading creeks. A panoramic view of the Coast Mountains unfolds midcourse. Greens fees range from C$125 to C$195, including power-cart rental.

Nicklaus North at Whistler (📞 800/386-9898 or 604/938-9898; www.golfwhistler. com) is a 5-minute drive north of the Village on the shores of Green Lake. The par-71 course's mountain views are spectacular. It's only the second Canadian course designed by Nicklaus, and, of all the courses he's designed worldwide, the only one to bear his name. Greens fees are C$37 to C$185.

Whistler Golf Club (📞 800/376-1777 or 604/932-3280; www.golfwhistler.com), designed by Arnold Palmer, features nine lakes, two creeks, and magnificent vistas. This 18-hole, par-72 course offers a driving range, putting green, sand bunker, and pitching area. Greens fees are C$59 to C$159.

A-1 Last Minute Golf Hotline (📞 800/684-6344 or 604/878-1833) can arrange a next-day, last-minute tee time at Whistler golf courses and elsewhere in B.C. at more than 30 courses. Savings can be as much as 40%. No membership is necessary. Call between 3 and 9pm for the next day or before noon for the same day. The hotline also arranges group and advanced bookings (as much as a year ahead).

HIKING   Numerous easy hiking trails can be found in and around Whistler. Besides taking a lift up to Whistler and Blackcomb mountains' high mountain trails (you can somewhat easily hike to the foot of a glacier) during summer, you have a number of other choices.

Lost Lake Trail starts at the northern end of the Day Skier Parking Lot at Blackcomb Mountain. The lake is less than a mile from the entry. The 30km (19 miles) of marked trails that wind around creeks, beaver dams, blueberry patches, and lush cedar groves are ideal for biking, cross-country skiing, or just strolling and picnicking. The **Valley Trail System** is a well-marked paved trail that connects parts of Whistler. The trail starts on the west side of Hwy. 99 adjacent to the Whistler Golf Course and winds through quiet residential areas as well as golf courses and parks.

Garibaldi Provincial Park's **Singing Pass Trail** is a 4-hour hike of moderate difficulty. The fun way is to take the Whistler Mountain gondola to the top and walk down the well-marked path that ends on an access road in the Village. Winding down from above the tree line, the trail takes you through stunted alpine forest into Fitzsimmons Valley. Along Hwy. 99 between Squamish and Whistler are several access points into the park.

Nairn Falls Provincial Park ★★, about 33km (21 miles) north of Whistler on Hwy. 99, features a mile-long trail that leads you to a stupendous view of the glacial Green River as it plunges 59m (194 ft.) over a rocky cliff into a narrow gorge on its way downstream. You will also spy an incredible view of Mount Currie peeking over the treetops.

On Hwy. 99 north of Mount Currie, **Joffre Lakes Provincial Park** has an intermediate-level hike that leads past several brilliant blue glacial lakes up to the very foot of a glacier. The **Ancient Cedars** area of Cougar Mountain is an awe-inspiring grove of towering cedars and Douglas firs. (Some of the trees are more than 1,000 years old and measure 3m/9¾ ft. in diameter.)

Guided nature hikes provide an excellent opportunity to learn more about the ecology of the region. Contact the **Whistler Activity and Information Centre** (© 877/991-9988 or 604/938-2769; www.tourismwhistler.com) for guided hikes and interpretive tours. Two- to 3-hour nature walks start at C$35.

HORSEBACK RIDING **Adventure Ranch,** 1641 Airport Way, Pemberton (© 604/894-5200; www.adventureranch.net), offers 2-hour trail rides along the Green River, through the forest, and across the Pemberton Valley from its 4-hectare (10-acre) riverside facility, a 35-minute drive north of Whistler. The 2-hour ride costs C$69; longer rides can be arranged.

JET BOATING **Whistler River Adventures,** Whistler Mountain Village Gondola Base (© 888/932-3532 or 604/932-3532; www.whistlerriver.com), takes guests up the Green River just below Nairn Falls, where moose, deer, and bear sightings are common in the canyon (although the noise of the jet boat might scare them away). Later in the season, tours go up the Lillooet River past ancient petroglyphs, fishing sites, and the tiny native village of Skookumchuck. Tours range from C$109 to C$155.

MOUNTAIN BIKING A rumor is afloat that within 5 years, mountain biking at Whistler will be bigger than skiing. **Whistler Mountain Bike Park** ★★★ (© 866/218-9688; www.whistlerblackcomb.com/bike) offers some of the best mountain-biking trails, skill centers, and jump parks in the world. When the snow melts the slope is reconfigured for biking—with 48km (30 miles) of marked trails, open daily mid-May to mid-October from 10am to 5pm (until 8pm Sat; additional late openings June–July). The variety of trails can accommodate almost all ages and experience levels. Single-day ticket prices with gondola are C$40 for adults, C$36 for seniors and youths 13 to 18, and C$21 for children 10 to 12. *Note:* Children 12 and under are not permitted in the bike park unless accompanied by a parent.

You can rent the best mountain bikes (about C$70 for 4 hr.) and body armor (C$20) right next to the bike park. **Lost Lake Cross Country Connection** (© 604/905-0071; www.crosscountryconnection.ca) offers bike rentals and guided tours for levels from beginner to expert.

RAFTING **Whistler River Adventures** (© 888/932-3532 or 604/932-3532; www.whistlerriver.com) offers 2-hour, 4-hour, and full-day round-trip rafting runs down the Green, Birkenhead, Elaho, and Squamish rivers. They include equipment and ground transportation for C$75 to C$89 for a 2- to 4-hour tour, or C$159 for a full day on the Elaho and Squamish rivers. Children are welcome as long as they can hold on by themselves and weigh a minimum of 41kg (90 lb.). Novices are taken to the Green River on a half-day trip, where small rapids and snowcapped mountain views are the highlights. Experts are transported to the Elaho River or Squamish River for full-day, Class 4 excitement. May through August, trips depart daily. The full-day trip includes a salmon barbecue lunch.

For first-timers, **Wedge Rafting,** Carleton Lodge, Whistler Village (© 604/932-7171; www.wedgerafting.com), offers Green River, Birkenhead River, and Cheakamus River tours. For the Green River trip, about 2½ hours, the shuttle picks up rafters in Whistler and takes them to the wilderness launch area for briefing and equipping. It's an exciting hour or more on the icy rapids. After the run, rafters can relax at the outfitter's log lodge with a snack and soda before being shuttled back into town. Tours cost C$59,

Zipping with Ziptrek ★★★

One of Whistler's most exciting year-round adventures is offered by **Ziptrek Ecotours** (📞 **866/935-0001** or 604/935-0001; www.ziptrek.com). On guided 2¹/₂-hour tours, you're taken through Whistler's ancient temperate rainforest on a network of five zipline rides joined by canopy bridges, boardwalks, and trails. Along the way, you're harnessed into a safety contraption that lets you whiz out on cables suspended hundreds of feet above glacier-fed Fitzsimmons Creek. It sounds hair-raising, but it's completely safe for all ages and abilities, and you'll never forget the experience. Individual Ziptrekkers must be 7 or older and weigh between 29kg and 125kg (64–276 lb.); children can ride tandem with one of the guides. Choose from two five-line tours, or you can do a 10-line zip all the way back to Whistler for C$149. The five-line tour costs C$98 for adults, C$78 for seniors 65 and older and children 14 and under. If you don't want to zip, consider the **Treetrek,** which explores the rare and ancient temperate rainforest along a network of suspension bridges, boardwalks, and treetop viewing platforms. The sales desk is located in the Carleton Lodge right across from the Whistler Village Gondolas.

with up to three daily departures. The Birkenhead River tour takes about 4 hours and costs C$89. Discounts are available for youths 10 to 16; however, they must weigh at least 41kg (90 lb.).

Located in the gorgeous Squamish valley, **Sun Wolf Outdoor Centre** (📞 **877/806-8046;** www.sunwolf.net) has summer rafting trips on the Elaho River and winter eagle-viewing trips on the Cheakamus and Squamish rivers. Full-day summer rafting trips cost C$149 per person, and the winter eagle trips cost C$99 per person.

ROCK CLIMBING   **The Great Wall,** 4340 Sundial Crescent (📞 **604/905-7625**), has a year-round indoor climbing center and summer outdoor climbing wall, as well as guided climbs and instruction. The indoor center is on the lower level of the Westbrook Hotel at the base of Whistler. The outdoor center is in the Blackcomb Upper Village near the Wizard Chair. An adult day pass is C$18.

TENNIS   The **Whistler Racquet & Golf Resort,** 4500 Northlands Blvd. (📞 **604/932-1991;** www.whistlertennis.com), has three covered courts, seven outdoor courts, and a practice cage. Indoor courts are C$32 per hour, outdoor courts C$16 per hour. Adult and junior tennis camps are offered in summer. Camp prices run C$300 to C$370 for a 3-day adult camp. Kids' camps cost about C$50 per day drop-in, or C$198 for a week.

The **Mountain Spa & Tennis Club,** Delta Whistler Resort, Whistler Village (📞 **604/938-2044**), and the **Chateau Whistler Resort,** Fairmont Chateau Whistler Hotel, Upper Village (📞 **604/938-8000**), also offer courts to drop-in players. Prices run about C$20 per hour per court; racquet rentals are available for C$5 per hour.

Free public courts (📞 **604/935-7529**) are located at Myrtle Public School, Alpha Lake Park, Meadow Park, Millar's Pond, Brio, Blackcomb Benchlands, White Gold, and Emerald Park.

WHISTLER BLACKCOMB

12

WHAT TO SEE & DO OUTDOORS: WHISTLER'S RAISON D'ETRE

A New First Nations Cultural Center

The new **Squamish Lil'wat Cultural Centre** (© 866/441-7522; www.slcc.ca) is an architecturally stunning showcase of soaring glass and stone, designed to celebrate the joint history and living cultures of the Squamish and Lil'wat Nations. Anchored by a monumental Great Hall with traditional artifacts and 67m (220-ft.) glass walls revealing spectacular mountain and forest views, the center also features a gallery of Squamish and Lil'wat sacred cultural treasures and icons, plus a shop for First Nations art. Outdoors you'll find a longhouse, which was the traditional dwelling of the Squamish people, and a replica Lil'wat "ístken" or "Pit House," the traditional dwelling of the Lil'wat people. The cultural center is located at the entrance to the Upper Village, along Lorimer Road, on a wedge of land between the Four Seasons Resort and the Fairmont Chateau Whistler. The Centre is open daily year-round from 9:30am to 5pm. Admission is C$18 for adults, C$14 for seniors, C$11 for youths 13–18, and C$8 for children.

INDOOR PURSUITS

For **performing arts,** from classical and choral to folk and blues, check out the **Maurice Young Millennium Place** (© 604/935-8410; www.myplacewhistler.org).

A MUSEUM To learn more about Whistler, visit the **Whistler Museum & Archives,** 4333 Main St., off Northlands Boulevard (© 604/932-2019; www.whistlermuseum. com). The museum exhibits reveal the life and culture of the First Nations tribes that have lived in the lush Whistler and Pemberton valleys for thousands of years. There are also re-creations of the village's early settlement by British immigrants during the late 1800s and early 1900s. The museum is open daily from 10am to 4pm in July and August, and Thursday through Sunday 10am to 4pm September through June (Thurs until 8pm year-round). Admission is C$5 for adults, C$4 for seniors and students, C$3 for children 7 to 18, and free for children 6 and under.

SHOPPING The **Whistler Marketplace** (in the center of Whistler Village) and the area surrounding the **Blackcomb Mountain lift** brim with clothing, jewelry, crafts, specialty, and equipment shops that are generally open daily from 10am to 6pm. **Horstman Trading Company** (© 604/938-7725), next to the Fairmont Chateau Whistler, carries casual wear, from swimwear and footwear to polar-fleece vests and nylon jacket shells. **Escape Route** (© 604/938-3228), at Whistler Marketplace and Crystal Lodge, has a great line of outdoor clothing and equipment.

For some of the finer things in life, visit the **Whistler Village Art Gallery** (© 604/938-3001; www.whistlerart.com) and **Adele Campbell Gallery** (© 604/938-0887; www.adelecampbell.com). Their collections include fine art, sculpture, and glass. **Keir Fine Jewelry,** Village Gate House (© 604/932-2944; www.keirfinejewellery.com), sells Italian gold, Swiss watches, and handmade Canadian jewelry. For a list and map of all the galleries in town, as well as information on events, contact the **Whistler Community Arts Council** (© 604/935-8232; www.whistlerartscouncil.com).

SPAS The **Taman Sari Royal Heritage Spa** (© 888/913-8811; www.tamansarispa. com) offers an unusual array of Javanese and European spa treatments. The Westin's **Avello** (© 877/935-7111; www.whistlerspa.com) has a variety of signature treatments, including hot rock, Chinese, and Satago massage. The **Spa at Chateau Whistler Resort** (© **604/938-2086**) provides massage therapy, skin care, and body wraps.

If something didn't quite go right on the slopes or on the trails, **Whistler Physiotherapy** specializes in sports therapy. There are two locations: 339-4370 Lorimer Rd., at Marketplace (© **604/932-4001;** www.whistlerphysio.com), and 202-2011 Innsbruck Dr., next to Boston Pizza in Creekside (© **604/938-9001**).

ESPECIALLY FOR KIDS

Whistler Village and the Upper Village sponsor daily activities for kids of all ages near the base of the mountains. Mountain-bike races; an in-line skating park; trapeze, trampoline, and wall-climbing lessons; summer skiing; snowboarding; snowshoeing; bungee jumping; and a first-run multiplex movie theater are just a few of the options.

Based at Blackcomb Mountain, the **Dave Murray Summer Ski and Snowboard Camp** (© **604/932-3238;** www.skiandsnowboard.com) is North America's longest-running summer ski camp. Junior programs cost C$2,195 for 8 days, or C$1,195 for a 5-day package; both are available from mid-June to mid-July. Packages include food, lodging (day-camp packages without the hotel are also available), lift passes, and tennis, trapeze, and mountain biking options. Days are spent skiing, boarding, or free-riding on the excellent terrain parks and half-pipes. This camp accommodates a range of abilities from beginners to champion-level skiers and riders; the age group is 10 to 18 years. The comprehensive instruction and adult supervision at this activity-oriented camp are excellent.

---

5 WHISTLER AFTER DARK

For a town of just 10,000, Whistler has a pretty good nightlife scene. Of course, it *is* considered the preeminent ski resort in North America, and attracts millions of year-round visitors. Bands touring through Vancouver regularly make the trip up the Sea-to-Sky Highway; some even make Whistler their Canadian debut. Concert listings can be found in *Pique*, a free local paper available at cafes and food stores.

Tommy Africa's (© **604/932-6090;** www.tommyafricas.com), beneath the Pharma-save at the entrance to the Main Village, and the dark and cavernous **Maxx Fish** (© **604/932-1904;** www.maxxfish.moonfruit.com), in the Village Square below the Amsterdam Cafe, cater to the 18- to-22-year-old crowd: lots of beat and not much light. The crowd at **Garfinkel's** (© **604/932-2323;** www.garfswhistler.com), at the entrance to Village

---

ⓜ **Moments** Après-Ski

"Après-ski" refers to that delicious hour after a hard day on the slopes, when you sit back with a cold or hot drink and nurse the sore spots in your muscles. On the Whistler side, the many loud and kicky beer bars will be in your face the moment your skis cease to schuss. On the Blackcomb side, **Merlin's Bar** (© **604/938-7735**) is almost as obvious and equally young and lubricated. However, **The Mallard Lounge and Terrace** ★ (© **604/938-8000**), inside the Fairmont Chateau Whistler (p. 188), is one of the most civilized après-ski bars on earth.

North, is similar, though the cutoff age can reach as high as 27. **Buffalo Bills** (© 604/932-6613; www.buffalobills.ca), across from the Whistler Gondola, and the **Savage Beagle** (© 604/938-3337), in the Village Square, cater to the 30-something crowd. Bills is bigger, with a pool table, video ski machine, a small dance floor, and music straight from the 1980s. The Beagle has a fabulous selection of beer and bar drinks, with a pub upstairs and a house-oriented dance floor below.

If all you want to do is savor a beer and swap ski stories, try the **Whistler BrewHouse** (© 604/905-2739) in the Upper Village, or the fun and very Irish **Dubh Linn Gate Irish Lounge/Pub** (© 604/905-4047) in the Pan Pacific Whistler Mountainside hotel (p. 189).

13

Getting to Know Victoria

The new keeps intruding upon the old in Victoria. And that's part of its charm. If you want to experience "colonial" Victoria, head over to the Bengal Lounge in the Fairmont Empress, sink into a leather armchair, and order a drink. Overhead, breezes gently waft down from the old ceiling fans, while the light from the roaring fire sparkles off the glass eyeballs of the poor Bengal tiger mounted above the mantelpiece. In this time-warped atmosphere, you might think you're in some outpost of the empire on the edge of an unknown island . . . Except that your drink might be a fluorescent blue martini, the music from the sound system is mellow jazz, and the coats piled up on a nearby armchair are made of Gore-Tex and fleece instead of wool or oilskin.

Once a little patch of the British Empire, Victoria is now wading into the shoals of a highly internationalized 21st century, and doing it with an appealing vitality that tweaks nostalgia for the past with a thoroughly modern sensibility.

As in Vancouver, you'll be amazed at how nice the people of Victoria are. Of course, you'd be nice, too, if you lived in such a pleasant place surrounded by such generous doses of natural beauty. Victoria, after all, with a population of about 325,000, occupies just a tiny corner of an island one-fifth the size of England but far more wild—so wild, in fact, that parts of it still have no roads and the only way to get around is by boat or on foot.

The city is one thing, its location something else. Only in the past decade or so has Victoria finally begun to capitalize on its stunning physical surroundings. Whale-watching is now a major industry; kayak tours are becoming ever more popular; mountain bikes have taken to competing for road space with the bright-red double-decker tour buses; ecotourism is big; and "outdoor adventures" are available in just about every form you can think of. Your trip will be even more memorable if you move a bit beyond "Tourist Central" (the Inner Harbour area) and put yourself in touch with Mother Nature.

Afterward, you can sip a lovely cream tea or a bright blue martini.

1 ORIENTATION

Victoria is on the southeastern tip of Vancouver Island, which lies southwest of the city of Vancouver across the Strait of Georgia and Haro Strait. B.C.'s island capital looks south across the Strait of Juan de Fuca to Port Angeles, WA, and Washington's snow-capped Olympic peninsula. Many people arrive in Victoria by ferry (see "Getting to Victoria," in chapter 3): The ferry from Port Angeles is the only one that arrives in the Inner Harbour downtown; the ferries from Vancouver and Anacortes arrive in Swartz Bay or Sidney, about 20 minutes north of Victoria.

Several **car-rental** firms have desks at the airport, including **Avis** (© **800/879-2847** or 250/656-6033; www.avis.ca), **Budget** (© **800/668-9833** or 250/953-5300; www.budget victoria.com), **Hertz** (© **800/654-3131** or 250/656-2312; www.hertz.com), and **National** (© **800/222-9058** or 250/656-2541; www.nationalcar.com). If you're driving from the airport, take Hwy. 17 south to Victoria; it becomes Douglas Street as you enter downtown.

The **Akal Airporter shuttle bus** (© **250/386-2525;** www.victoriaairportshuttle.com) has a ticket counter at the airport, and makes the trip downtown in about a half-hour. Buses leave every 30 minutes daily from 4:30am to midnight; the fare is C$16 one-way; C$10 per person for groups of four or more. Drop-offs are made at most hotels and bed-and-breakfasts, and pickups can be arranged as well. A limited number of hotel courtesy buses also serve the airport. A cab ride into downtown Victoria costs about C$45 plus tip. **Empress Cabs** and **Blue Bird Cabs** (p. 207) make airport runs.

VISITOR INFORMATION

Tourism Victoria Visitor Centre, 812 Wharf St. (© **800/663-3883** or 250/953-2033; www.tourismvictoria.com), is located on the Inner Harbour, across from the Fairmont Empress hotel. The center is open daily September through June 5 from 9am to 5pm, and June 6 through August from 9am to 8:30pm.

If you want to explore the rest of the 459-km-long (285-mile) Vancouver Island (it's roughly the size of Holland), this office will help put you on the right track; you'll find a list of all the **regional tourism offices** on Vancouver Island at **www.vancouverisland.travel**.

For details on the after-dark scene, pick up a copy of *Monday Magazine,* available free in cafes around the city; it's an excellent guide to Victoria's nightlife and has also driven at least one mayor from office with its award-winning muckraking journalism. The online version (www.mondaymag.com) has detailed entertainment listings.

CITY LAYOUT

Victoria was born at the edge of the Inner Harbour in the 1840s and spread outward from there. The areas of most interest to visitors, including **downtown** and **Old Town,** lie along the eastern edge of the **Inner Harbour.** (North of the Johnson St. Bridge is the **Upper Harbour,** which is largely industrial but taking on new life as old buildings are redeveloped.) A little farther east, the **Ross Bay** and **Oak Bay** residential areas around Dallas Road and Beach Drive reach the beaches along the open waters of the Strait of Juan de Fuca.

Victoria's central landmark is the **Fairmont Empress** hotel on Government Street, right across from the Inner Harbour. If you turn your back to the hotel, downtown and Old Town are on your right, while the **Provincial Legislature Buildings** and the **Royal B.C. Museum** are on your immediate left. Next to them is the dock for the **Seattle–Port Angeles ferries,** and beyond that the residential community of **James Bay,** the first neighborhood in the city to be developed.

MAIN ARTERIES & STREETS   Three main **north-south arteries** intersect just about every destination you may want to reach in Victoria.

Government Street goes through Victoria's main downtown shopping-and-dining district. Wharf Street, edging the harbor, merges with Government Street at the Fairmont Empress. **Douglas Street,** running parallel to Government Street, is the main business thoroughfare as well as the road to Nanaimo and the rest of the island. It's also Trans-Canada Hwy. 1. The "Mile 0" marker sits at the corner of Douglas and Dallas Road. Also running parallel to Government and Douglas streets is **Blanshard Street** (Hwy. 17), the

route to the Saanich Peninsula—including the Sidney-Vancouver ferry terminal—and
Butchart Gardens.

Important **east-west streets** include the following: **Johnson Street** lies at the northern end of downtown and the Old Town, where the small E&N Station sits opposite Swans Hotel at the corner of Wharf Street. The Johnson Street Bridge is the demarcation line between the Upper Harbour and the Inner Harbour. **Belleville Street** is the Inner Harbour's southern edge. The Legislative Buildings and the ferry terminal are here. Belleville Street loops around westward toward Victoria Harbour before heading south, becoming **Dallas Road.** Dallas Road follows the water's edge past residential areas and beaches before it winds northward up to Oak Bay.

FINDING AN ADDRESS   Victoria addresses are written like those in Vancouver: The suite or room number precedes the building number. For instance, 100-1250 Government St. refers to suite 100 at 1250 Government St.

Victoria's streets are numbered from the city's southwest corner and increase in increments of 100 per block as you go north and east. (1000 Douglas St., for example, is 2 blocks north of 800 Douglas St.) Addresses for all the east-west streets (Fort, Yates, Johnson, and so on) downtown start at 500 at Wharf Street; thus, all buildings between Wharf and Government streets fall between 500 and 599, while all buildings between Government and Douglas streets fall between 600 and 699, and so on.

STREET MAPS   Street maps are available free at the **Tourism Victoria Visitor Centre** (see "Visitor Information," above). The best map of the surrounding area is the **B.C. Provincial Parks** map of Vancouver Island, also available at the Info Centre.

Neighborhoods in Brief

DOWNTOWN & OLD TOWN   These areas have been the city's social and commercial focal points since the mid-1800s, when settlers first arrived by ship. This is also the area of the city most popular with visitors, filled with shops, museums, heritage buildings, and lots of restaurants. The area's fascinating Barbary Coast history—which includes rum smuggling, opium manufacturing, gold prospecting, whaling, fur trading, and shipping—is reflected in the hundreds of heritage buildings, once home to chandleries, warehouses, factories, whorehouses, and gambling dens.

The two neighborhoods are usually listed together because it's difficult to say where one leaves off and the other begins. The Old Town consists of the pre-1900 commercial sections of the city that grew up around the original Fort Victoria at View and Government streets. Roughly speaking, it extends from Fort Street north to Pandora and from Wharf Street east to Douglas. Downtown is everything outside of that, from the Inner Harbour to Quadra Street in the east and from Belleville Street in the south up to Herald Street at the northern edge of downtown.

CHINATOWN   Victoria's Chinatown is tiny—only 2 square blocks—but venerable. In fact, it's the oldest Chinese community in North America. At one time, legal opium manufacturing took place in the hidden courtyard buildings flanking the 1.2m-wide (4-ft.) Fan Tan Alley, Canada's narrowest commercial street.

JAMES BAY, ROSS BAY & OAK BAY   When Victoria was a busy port and trading post, the local aristocracy would retire to homes in these neighborhoods to escape the hustle and bustle in the city center. Today, they remain beautiful residential communities. Houses are perched on hills overlooking the straits or nestled amid lushly landscaped gardens. Golf courses, marinas, and a few cozy inns edge the waters, where you can stroll the beaches or go for a dip if you don't mind a chill.

2 GETTING AROUND

BY PUBLIC TRANSPORTATION

BY BUS The **Victoria Regional Transit System** (**B.C. Transit**; ✆ **250/382-6161;** www.bctransit.com) operates 40 bus routes through greater Victoria as well as the nearby towns of Sooke and Sidney. Buses run to both the Butchart Gardens and the Vancouver Ferry Terminal at Sidney. Regular service on the main routes runs daily from 6am to just past midnight.

Schedules and route maps are available at the Tourism Victoria Visitor Centre (see "Visitor Information," above), where you can pick up a copy of the *Victoria Rider's Guide* or *Discover Vancouver on Transit: Including Victoria.* Popular Victoria bus routes include **no. 2** (Oak Bay), **no. 5** (downtown, James Bay, Beacon Hill Park), **no. 14** (Victoria Art Gallery, Craigdarroch Castle, University of Victoria), **no. 61** (Sooke), **no. 70** (Sidney, Swartz Bay), and **no. 75** (Butchart Gardens).

Fares are good throughout the Greater Victoria area. One-way fares are C$2.25 for adults and students and C$1.40 for seniors and children 5 to 13. Transfers are good for travel in one direction only, with no stopovers. A **DayPass,** C$7 for adults and students, and C$5 for seniors and children 5 to 13, covers unlimited travel throughout the day. You can buy passes at the Tourism Victoria Visitor Centre (see "Visitor Information," above), convenience stores, and ticket outlets throughout Victoria displaying the FARE-DEALER sign.

BY FERRY Crossing the Inner, Upper, and Victoria harbors by one of the blue 12-passenger **Victoria Harbour Ferries** (✆ **250/708-0201;** www.victoriaharbourferry.com) is cheap and fun. May through September, the ferries to the Fairmont Empress, Coast Harbourside Hotel, and Ocean Pointe Resort hotel run about every 15 minutes daily from 9am to 9pm. In March, April, and October, ferry service runs daily 11am to 5pm. November through February, the ferries run only on sunny weekends 11am to 5pm. The cost per hop is C$4 for adults and C$2 for children.

Instead of just taking the ferry for a short hop across, try the 45-minute **Harbour tour** ★ or the 55-minute **Gorge tour** ★; both cost C$20 adults, C$18 seniors, and C$10 children 12 and under.

BY CAR

You can easily explore the downtown area of Victoria on foot. If you're planning out-of-town activities, you can rent a car in town or bring your own on one of the car-passenger ferries from Vancouver, Port Angeles, or Anacortes. Traffic is light in Victoria, largely because the downtown core is so walkable.

(Moments) The Ferry Ballet

Starting at 9:45am every Sunday during summer, the ferries gather in front of the Fairmont Empress to perform a **ferry "ballet"**—it looks a bit like the hippo dance in Disney's *Fantasia.*

RENTALS   Car-rental agencies in Victoria include the following: **Avis,** 1001 Douglas St. (© **800/879-2847** or 250/386-8468; www.avis.ca; bus no. 5 to Broughton St.); **Budget,** 757 Douglas St. (© **800/668-9833** or 250/953-5300; www.budgetvictoria. com); **Hertz,** 655 Douglas St., in the Queen Victoria Inn (© **800/654-3131** or 250/ 952-3765; www.hertz.com); and **National,** 767 Douglas St. (© **800/227-7368** or 250/ 386-1213; www.nationalvictoria.com). These latter three can be reached on the no. 5 bus to the Convention Centre.

PARKING   Metered **street parking** is available downtown, but be sure to feed the meter because rules are strictly enforced. Unmetered parking on side streets is rare. All major downtown hotels have guest parking. Parking lots can be found at **View Street** between Douglas and Blanshard streets, **Johnson Street** off Blanshard Street, **Yates Street** north of Bastion Square, and **The Bay** on Fisgard at Blanshard Street.

DRIVING RULES   Some of the best places on Vancouver Island can be reached only via gravel logging roads, on which logging trucks have absolute right of way. If you're on a logging road and see a logging truck coming from either direction, pull over to the side of the road and stop to let it pass. See also "Driving Rules," p. 292.

BY BIKE

Biking is the easiest way to get around the downtown and beach areas. The city has numerous bike lanes and paved paths in parks and along beaches. Helmets are mandatory, and riding on sidewalks is illegal, except where bike paths are indicated. You can rent bikes starting at C$7 per hour and C$24 per day (lock and helmet included) from **Cycle B.C.,** 707 Douglas St. (© **866/380-2453** or 250/380-2453; www.cyclebc.ca).

BY TAXI

Within the downtown area, you can expect to travel for less than C$10, plus tip. It's best to call for a cab; you won't have much luck if you try to flag one down on the street. Drivers don't always stop, especially when it's raining. Call for a pickup from **Empress Cabs** (© **250/381-2222**) or **Blue Bird Cabs** (© **250/382-2222**).

BY PEDDLE-CAB

You get to sit while an avid bicyclist with thighs of steel peddles you anywhere you want to go for C$1 per minute (C$2 per min. if there are four of you). You'll see these two- and four-seater bike cabs along the Inner Harbour at the base of Bastion Square, or you can call **Kabuki Kabs** (© **250/385-4243;** www.kabukikabs.com) for 24-hour service.

(Fast Facts   **Victoria**

Business Hours Victoria **banks** are open Monday through Thursday 10am to 3pm and Friday 10am to 6pm. **Stores** are generally open Monday through Saturday 10am to 6pm. Some establishments are open later, as well as on Sundays, in summer. Last call at the city's **bars** and **cocktail lounges** is 2am.

Currency Exchange The best exchange rates in town can be found at banks and by using ATMs. **Royal Bank,** 1079 Douglas St. at Fort Street, is in the heart of downtown. Take bus no. 5 to Fort Street.

FAST FACTS: VICTORIA / **GETTING TO KNOW VICTORIA** / 13

Dentist Most major hotels have a dentist on call. **Cresta Dental Centre,** 3170 Tillicum Rd., at Burnside Street in the Tillicum Mall (© **250/384-7711;** bus no. 10), is open Monday through Friday 8am to 9pm, Saturday 9am to 5:30pm, and Sunday 11am to 5pm.

Doctor Hotels usually have doctors on call. The **Tillicum Mall Medical Clinic,** 3170 Tillicum Rd., at Burnside Street (© **250/381-8112;** bus no. 10 to Tillicum Mall), accepts walk-in patients daily 9am to 9pm.

Hospitals Local hospitals include the **Royal Jubilee Hospital,** 1952 Bay St. (© **250/370-8000,** emergency 250/370-8212), and the **Victoria General Hospital,** 1 Hospital Way (© **250/727-4212,** emergency 250/727-4181). You can get to both hospitals on bus no. 14.

Internet Access In the heart of Old Town, **Stain Internet Café,** 609 Yates St. (© **250/382-3352**), is open daily 10am to 2am (C$2.50 per half-hour). Closer to the Legislature, try **James Bay Coffee and Books,** 143 Menzies St. (© **250/386-4700**), open daily 7:30am to 10pm (C$1 per 10 min.). Most hotels have Internet access, as does the Victoria Public Library; see below.

Library The **Greater Victoria Public Library** (© **250/382-7241;** bus no. 5 to Broughton St.) is at 735 Broughton St., near the corner of Fort and Douglas streets.

Luggage Storage & Lockers Coin lockers are available outside the bus station (behind the Fairmont Empress). Take bus no. 5 to the Convention Centre.

Pharmacies **Shopper's Drug Mart,** 1222 Douglas St. (© **250/381-4321;** bus no. 5 to View St.), is open Monday through Friday 7am to 8pm, Saturday 9am to 7pm, and Sunday 9am to 6pm.

Police Dial © **911.** This is a free call. The **Victoria City Police** can also be reached by calling © **250/995-7654.**

Post Office The **main post office** is at 714 Yates St. (© **250/953-1352;** bus no. 5 to Yates St.). There are also postal outlets in **Shopper's Drug Mart** (see "Pharmacies," above) and in other stores displaying the CANADA POST postal outlet sign. Supermarkets and many souvenir and gift shops also sell stamps.

14

Where to Stay in Victoria

Victoria has been welcoming visi-tors and adventurers for more than a century, so it knows how to do so with style. As in Vancouver, you'll find a disarming friendliness when you check into a Victoria hotel. The city has a wide choice of fine accommodations in all price ranges, most in the Old Town, in downtown, or around the Inner Harbour and within easy walking distance of the city's main attractions (except for Butchart Gardens). But you don't have to limit yourself to Victoria proper. A 20-minute or half-hour drive north, east, or west takes you to all manner of marvelous resorts and inns, some on the ocean, some next to quiet bays and harbors, and some perched on mountaintops. You'll find information on the hotel choices in Brentwood Bay, Sooke, Sidney, Bear Mountain, and Malahat in "Outside the Central Area," later in this chapter.

Spas are now an almost essential part of big hotels in Victoria—so much so that the Inner Harbour has been dubbed Spa Harbour, with major spas at the Fairmont Empress, the Delta Ocean Pointe, the Hotel Grand Pacific, and The Magnolia.

You can get fine spa treatments at all four and also at Brentwood Bay Lodge, Westin Bear Mountain Golf Resort & Spa, and the new Sidney Pier Hotel & Spa.

Be sure to check the hotel websites for special packages, and promotional or seasonal rates cheaper than the rack rates listed here.

You'll save big-time if you schedule your holiday from October to May. When the high summer season starts in June, rates tend to skyrocket, especially at the finer resort hotels.

Reservations are essential in Victoria June through September. If you arrive without a reservation and have trouble finding a room, **Tourism Victoria** (© **800/663-3883** or 250/953-2033; www.tourismvictoria.com) can make reservations for you at hotels, inns, and B&Bs. It deals only with establishments that pay a fee to list with them; fortunately, most do.

Prices quoted here don't include the 10% **hotel room tax,** the 7% **provincial accommodations tax,** or the 6% **goods and services tax (GST).**

1 BEST VICTORIA HOTEL BETS

- **Best Historic Hotel:** She's a grande dame, no doubt about it, and she sits on Victoria's Inner Harbour like an Empress on her throne. For sheer showoffy splendor the **Fairmont Empress,** 721 Government St. (© **866/540-4429** or 250/384-8111), has no peers. See p. 211.
- **Best for Business Travelers: The Magnolia,** 623 Courtney St. (© **877/624-6654** or 250/381-0999), sits in a convenient location right downtown and features business-friendly amenities. The views are nothing to write home about, but the rooms are comfortable and the bathrooms surprisingly luxe. See p. 218.

- **Best Place to Pretend You Died & Went to Hollywood:** Perched above a fjord, the **Aerie,** 600 Ebedora Lane, Malahat (© **800/518-1933** or 250/743-7115), is famed for its over-the-top splendor. Some find it a bit too pretentious, but others love it for just that reason. The restaurant is one of Vancouver Island's best, and the possibilities for pampering are endless. See p. 221.

- **Best Hotel Lobby:** The two-story, plate-glass windows in the lobby of the **Delta Victoria Ocean Pointe Resort and Spa,** 45 Songhees Rd. (© **800/667-4677** or 250/360-2999), provide the best vantage in Victoria for watching the lights on the Legislature switch on. The comfy chairs and fireplaces also make this a great place to warm up. See p. 211.

- **Best for Families:** Honest, thrifty, and down-to-earth, the **Royal Scot Hotel & Suites,** 425 Quebec St. (© **800/663-7515** or 250/388-5463), is great if you have kids in tow thanks to the in-suite kitchens and communal pool, game room, and arcade. See p. 215.

- **Best B&B:** With rooms double the size of those in other B&Bs and every possible need taken care of, the friendly innkeepers at the **Haterleigh Heritage Inn,** 243 Kingston St. (© **866/234-2244** or 250/384-9995), do themselves proud. See p. 212.

- **Best Inexpensive Hotel:** While the rooms in the main hotel are just okay, the next-door suites and cottage operated by the **James Bay Inn,** 270 Government St. (© **800/836-2649** or 250/384-7151), are a veritable steal. See p. 217.

- **Most Romantic Hotel: Brentwood Bay Lodge & Spa,** 849 Verdier Ave. (© **888/544-2079** or 250/544-2079), is a small luxury resort overlooking a pristine fjord. Every detail in the rooms and bathrooms is perfect, from fabrics to fireplace, and couples can have side-by-side treatments in the lovely spa. See p. 222.

- **Most Environmentally Conscious Hotel: Sooke Harbour House,** 1528 Whiffen Spit Rd., Sooke (© **800/889-9688** or 250/642-3421), wins hands down in the go-green department: It has its own bioreactor to reprocess wastewater, which is then used to water its gardens, and it has a green parking lot. Incidentally, this hotel also has the **best hotel restaurant** and the **best oceanside location.** See p. 223.

- **Best Alternative Accommodations: The Boathouse,** 746 Sea Dr. (© **866/654-9370** or 250/652-9370), is a real (converted) boathouse, with a private dock and a rowing dinghy. Built in a secluded cove, the tiny cottage is a perfect spot for those seeking privacy and a glorious outlook right on the water. See p. 222.

- **Best Location:** The **Fairmont Empress,** 721 Government St. (© **866/540-4429** or 250/384-8111), sits right on the Inner Harbour and is minutes away from all the sightseeing and shopping in and around downtown Victoria. See p. 211.

- **Best Spa:** One spa in the city and two about a 20-minute drive from downtown qualify in this category. Considered one of the best spas in Canada, the luxurious Willow Stream spa at the **Fairmont Empress,** 721 Government St. (© **866/540-4429** or 250/384-8111), offers about 20 different types of spa treatments (p. 211). The Essence of Life spa at **Brentwood Bay Lodge & Spa,** 849 Verdier Ave. (© **888/544-2079** or 250/544-2079), has the most impressive hydrobath in British Columbia, and provides massage treatments for couples (p. 222). Nonsurgical skin treatments (such as Botox and microdermabrasion) are available at the Santé Spa at Bear Mountain in the **Westin Bear Mountain Victoria Golf Resort & Spa,** 1999 Country Club Way (© **888/533-2327** or 250/391-7160); see p. 224. All three spas offer complete skin and body treatments, aesthetics, and aromatherapy treatments to pamper the body and spirit.

- **Best View:** Score a newly redesigned and redecorated suite in the South Wing of the **Inn at Laurel Point,** 680 Montreal St. (© **800/663-7667** or 250/386-8721), facing the harbor and you may never want to leave (p. 212). Outside of town, the **Aerie,** 600 Ebedora Lane, Malahat (© **800/518-1933** or 250/743-7115), offers private terraces with views across tree-clad mountains to a long blue coastal fjord (p. 221). For the best view on Vancouver Island, **The Wickaninnish Inn** in Tofino (© **800/333-4604** or 250/725-3100) has no peers (p. 284).

2 THE INNER HARBOUR & NEARBY

VERY EXPENSIVE

Delta Victoria Ocean Pointe Resort and Spa ★★ (Kids)
The "OPR," located across the Johnson Street Bridge on the Inner Harbour's north shore, is a big, bright, modern hotel with commanding views of downtown, the Legislature, the Fairmont Empress, and the busy harbor itself. The rooms here are nice and big, and so are the bathrooms. The decor, like the hotel itself, is a blend of contemporary and traditional. A few extra dollars buys a few extra perks, like breakfast and evening hors d'oeuvres in the third-floor Signature Lounge. All guests have use of the big indoor pool, a really good whirlpool, and a fully equipped gym with racquetball and tennis courts. Lots of guests come for the new spa, one of the best in Victoria. Kids receive a free welcome kit, and they'll love the pool.

45 Songhees Rd., Victoria, B.C. V9A 6T3. © **800/667-4677** or 250/360-2999. Fax 250/360-1041. www.deltavictoria.com. 239 units. C$119–C$499 double; C$449–C$999 suite. Children 16 and under stay free in parent's room. AE, DC, MC, V. Underground valet parking C$15. Bus: 24 to Colville. **Amenities:** Restaurant/lounge; babysitting; concierge; executive-level rooms; health club; Jacuzzi; indoor pool; room service; sauna; spa; outdoor tennis courts; rooms for those w/limited mobility. *In room:* A/C, TV/VCR w/pay movies, hair dryer, free high-speed Internet, minibar.

The Fairmont Empress ★★★ (Kids)
The world-renowned Empress is the most famous celebrity on the Victoria waterfront, and staying at this full-service landmark hotel makes for a memorable experience. But to get the most out of your stay, it's a good idea to book a room at the Gold level, which comes with larger rooms, a dedicated concierge, breakfast, and evening hors d'oeuvres; it's like a smaller hotel within the hotel. The hotel's 256 standard rooms are smallish and offer little in the way of view. The Deluxe rooms are bigger, with high ceilings, and most of them have a view of the harbor. The Signature rooms are large corner rooms. The hotel's fabulous location and first-class amenities—including a kid-friendly indoor pool and luxurious Willow Stream spa—add to the pleasure of staying here. The enormous Empress is firmly traditional (old-fashioned) in terms of decor. If you don't stay here, you may want to come for the famous afternoon tea (see "Taking Afternoon Tea," in chapter 15), a relaxing session at the spa, or a cocktail in the wood-paneled Bengal Lounge (which also serves a lunchtime curry buffet).

721 Government St., Victoria, B.C. V8W 1W5. © **866/540-4429** or 250/384-8111. Fax 250/381-4334. www.fairmont.com/empress. 477 units. C$169–C$569 double; C$269–C$769 Gold level double. AE, DC, DISC, MC, V. Underground valet parking C$28. Bus: 5. **Amenities:** 2 restaurants; bar/lounge; tearoom; babysitting; concierge; executive-level rooms; high-quality health club; Jacuzzi; indoor lap pool; room service; sauna; spa; rooms for those w/limited mobility. *In room:* TV w/pay movies, hair dryer, high-speed Internet (C$15/day).

The Haterleigh Heritage Inn ★ Haterleigh innkeeper Paul Kelly is a fount of information, on Victoria in general and on this lovingly restored 1901 home in particular. With his wife, Elizabeth, he runs this exceptional B&B that captures the essence of Victoria's romance with a combination of antique furniture, original stained-glass windows, and attentive personal service. The rooms feature high arched ceilings, large windows, sitting areas, and large bathrooms, some with hand-painted tiles and Jacuzzi tubs. On the top floor, the cozy Angel's Reach room features a big four-poster bed. The second-floor Secret Garden room has a small balcony with views of the Olympic mountain range. A full gourmet breakfast with organic produce is served family-style at 8:30am, and complimentary sherry is available in the drawing room each evening.

243 Kingston St., Victoria, B.C. V8V 1V5. (C) **866/234-2244** or 250/384-9995. Fax 250/384-1935. www. haterleigh.com. 7 units. C$165–C$299 double. Rates include full breakfast. MC, V. Free parking. Bus: 30 to Superior and Montreal sts. **Amenities:** Jacuzzi; free Wi-Fi. *In room:* Hair dryer.

Hotel Grand Pacific ★★ On Victoria's bustling Inner Harbour, directly across the street from the Port Angeles–Victoria ferry dock, the Grand Pacific is more luxurious than the Delta Ocean Pointe, and has rooms that are generally more spacious than standard rooms at the Fairmont Empress. Like those other two hotels on the Inner Harbour, the Grand Pacific has its own spa; its health club is better than the others, and features a huge ozonated indoor pool. All rooms have balconies and are attractively and comfortably furnished. Suites provide the best views, overlooking the harbor and the Empress. Bathrooms throughout are fairly small. Fine dining options include the informal Pacific Restaurant and the **Mark** (p. 228).

463 Belleville St., Victoria, B.C. V8V 1X3. (C) **800/663-7550** or 250/386-0450. Fax 250/380-4475. www. hotelgrandpacific.com. 304 units. C$159–C$289 double; C$219–C$399 suite. Additional person C$30. AE, DC, DISC, MC, V. Self-parking C$12; valet parking C$24. Bus: 30 to Superior and Oswego sts. **Amenities:** 2 restaurants; cafe, bar; concierge; superior health club; Jacuzzi; indoor pool; room service; spa; squash courts. *In room:* A/C, TV w/pay movies, hair dryer, free high-speed Internet, minibar.

Inn at Laurel Point ★★★ The three stars are for the Erickson Wing suites featuring stylish, contemporary furnishings, Asian artwork, balconies overlooking a Japanese garden, shoji-style sliding doors, and luxurious marble bathrooms with deep soaker tubs and glassed-in showers. This art-filled, resort-style hotel occupies a prettily landscaped promontory jutting out into the Inner Harbour, and consists of the original north wing and the newer south wing designed by noted Vancouver architect Arthur Erickson in 1989. The overall design reflects the elegant simplicity of Japanese artistic principles and is a refreshing change from the chintz and florals found in so many Victoria hotels. Rooms in the older north wing come with pocket balconies (every room in the hotel has

The Best Bed & Breakfast Registry

If you prefer to stay at a B&B other than those listed in this chapter, **Canada-West Accommodations Bed & Breakfast Registry,** P.O. Box 86607, North Vancouver, B.C. V7L 4L2 ((C) **800/561-3223** or 604/990-6730; www.b-b.com), specializes in matching guests to the B&Bs that best suit their needs.

Abbeymoore Manor Inn **32**
Abigail's Hotel **28**
Admiral Inn **13**
Andersen House Bed & Breakfast **18**
The Beaconsfield Inn **29**
The Bedford Regency Hotel **10**
Best Western Carlton Plaza **8**
Chateau Victoria Hotel & Suites **25**
Coast Victoria Harbourside Hotel & Marina **11**
Dashwood Manor **31**
Days Inn on the Harbour **21**
Delta Victoria Ocean Pointe Resort and Spa **2**
Executive House Hotel **26**
The Fairmont Empress **23**
The Gatsby Mansion Boutique Hotel and Restaurant **14**
Harbour Towers Hotel & Suites **16**
The Haterleigh Heritage Inn **17**
Hostelling International Victoria **4**
Hotel Grand Pacific **22**
Huntingdon Hotel and Suites **15**
Inn at Laurel Point **12**
Isabella's Guest Suites **5**
The James Bay Inn **30**
The Magnolia **24**
Ocean Island Backpackers Inn **9**
The Oswego Hotel **19**
Paul's Motor Inn **7**
Royal Scot Suite Hotel **20**
Spinnakers Guest House **1**
Swans Suite Hotel **6**
Victoria Marriott Inner Harbour **27**
The Victoria Regent Hotel **3**

a water view) and nice bathrooms—but the Erickson Wing is where you want to be. The hotel's Aura restaurant is a new dining hot spot.

680 Montreal St., Victoria, B.C. V8V 1Z8. *©* **800/663-7667** or 250/386-8721. Fax 250/386-9547. www. laurelpoint.com. 200 units. C$149–C$269 double; C$249–C$369 suite. Additional adult C$25. Children 17 and under stay free in parent's room. AE, DC, DISC, MC, V. Secure parking C$12. Bus: 30 to Montreal and Superior sts. **Amenities:** Restaurant; bar; babysitting; concierge; free access to YMCA facilities; indoor pool; room service; rooms for those w/limited mobility. *In room:* A/C, TV, hair dryer, free high-speed Internet.

MODERATE

Andersen House Bed & Breakfast ★

The art and furnishings in Andersen House are drawn from the whole of the old British Empire and a good section of the modern world beyond. The 1891 house has the high ceilings, stained-glass windows, and ornate fireplaces typical of the Queen Anne style, but the art and decorations are far more eclectic. Each room has a unique style: the sun-drenched Casablanca room on the top floor, for example, boasts Persian rugs, a four-poster queen-size bed, and a boxed window seat. All rooms have private entrances and come with two-person Jacuzzis, books, CD players and CDs, and complimentary Wi-Fi.

301 Kingston St., Victoria, B.C. V8V 1V5. *©* **877/264-9988** or 250/388-4565. Fax 250/388-4508. www. andersenhouse.com. 4 units. C$125–C$285 double. Rates include breakfast. AE, MC, V. Free off-street parking. Bus: 30 to Superior and Oswego sts. Children 11 and under not accepted. *In room:* TV/VCR, hair dryer, Jacuzzi, free Wi-Fi.

The Gatsby Mansion Boutique Hotel and Restaurant

Built in 1897, this white clapboard Victorian across from the Seattle–Port Angeles ferry terminal has been fully restored and now serves as a B&B-style inn. With its hand-painted ceramic-tiled fireplace, rich wood paneling, stained-glass windows, frescoed ceilings, and crystal chandeliers, it evokes a turn-of-the-20th-century elegance. The spacious rooms feature down duvets, fine linens, and lots of Victorian antiques. Some rooms have views of the Inner Harbour, while others have private parlors. It's a pretty property, with an on-site spa, but because it's part of the larger Huntingdon hotel complex (see listing below), it lacks that owner-operated B&B feel.

309 Belleville St., Victoria, B.C. V8V 1X2. *©* **800/563-9656** or 250/388-9191. www.gatsbymansion.com. 20 units. C$139–C$319 double. Rates include breakfast. AE, DC, MC, V. Free parking. Bus: 30 or 31 to Belleville and Government sts. **Amenities:** Restaurant; bikes; Jacuzzi; room service; sauna; spa. *In room:* TV w/pay movies, hair dryer, free Wi-Fi.

The Oswego Hotel ★★

The stylish and eco-friendly Oswego, a boutique hotel in the quiet James Bay neighborhood, 2 blocks from the Inner Harbour, opened in 2009. All the studios, one-bedroom, and two-bedroom suites have fully equipped kitchens and floor-to-ceiling windows; most have balconies, too. The styling throughout is crisp and contemporary, which is a refreshing change in Victoria. For the absolute best here, book one of the penthouse suites with enormous balconies and fabulous views. The O Bistro is one of Victoria's best new restaurants. Check the website for special rates that are lower than the rack rates listed below.

500 Oswego St., Victoria, B.C. V8V 5C1. *©* **877/767-9346** or 250/294-7500. Fax 250/294-7509. www. oswegovictoria.com. 80 units. C$159–C$289 double; C$199–C$499 suite; C$569–C$699 penthouse. AE, DC, MC, V. Free parking. Bus: 31 to Oswego and Michigan sts. **Amenities:** Restaurant; lounge; small exercise room; room service. *In room:* TV w/pay movies, fridge, hair dryer, kitchen, free Wi-Fi.

Royal Scot Hotel & Suites (Value) (Kids)   A block from the Inner Harbour, the Royal **215**
Scot provides friendly service and good value, particularly if you opt for a studio or one-
bedroom suite. It was constructed as an apartment building, so the rooms are larger than
average. Each studio suite has a divider separating the bedroom from the living room.
One-bedroom suites have separate bedrooms with king-size, queen-size, or twin beds. All
suites have lots of closet space, fully equipped kitchens, complimentary refreshments, and
sofa beds in the living rooms. The decor is comfortable but uninspired, and bathrooms
tend to be on the small side. In summer, the Royal Scot fills up with families. Kids make
heavy use of the pool and game room.

425 Quebec St., Victoria, B.C. V8V 1W7. (C) **800/663-7515** or 250/388-5463. Fax 250/388-5452. www.
royalscot.com. 176 units. C$155–C$249 double; C$185–C$435 suite. AE, DC, MC, V. Parking C$6. Bus: 5 to
Belleville and Government sts. **Amenities:** Restaurant; exercise room; Jacuzzi; indoor pool; room service;
sauna. *In room:* TV, hair dryer, free high-speed Internet, kitchen.

Spinnakers Guest House ★ (Value)   This bed-and-breakfast-style guesthouse offers
good accommodations at a moderate price. The two separate buildings are owned and
operated by the same local entrepreneur who runs Spinnakers Brewpub. The 1884 heritage building on Catherine Street is the more luxurious. Rooms feature queen-size beds,
lovely furnishings, in-room Jacuzzis, fireplaces, high ceilings, and lots of natural light.
The four Garden Suites units on Mary Street are really self-contained apartments, with
separate bedrooms and full kitchens, perfect for longer stays or for families. Guests at
both buildings get an in-room breakfast. The waterfront location is a 10- to 20-minute
walk from downtown; the harbor ferry stops nearby.

308 Catherine St., Victoria, B.C. V9A 3S8. (C) **877/838-2739** or 250/384-2739. Fax 250/384-3246. www.
spinnakers.com. 10 units. C$129–C$279 double. Rates include breakfast. AE, MC, V. Free parking. Bus: 24
to Catherine St. *In room:* Fireplace (some units), Jacuzzi, kitchen (some units), free Wi-Fi.

INEXPENSIVE

Admiral Inn (Value) (Kids)   The family-operated Admiral is in a three-story building on
the Inner Harbour, near the Port Angeles–bound ferry terminal and close to restaurants and
shopping. The combination of clean comfortable rooms and reasonable rates attracts young
couples, families, seniors, and other travelers in search of a harbor view at a moderate price.
The rooms are pleasant and comfortably furnished, a bit motel-like, with small bathrooms
and balconies or terraces. The more expensive rooms come with a kitchenette with a small
fridge and stove. The suites come with full kitchens. Some units can sleep up to six (on two
double beds and a double sofa bed). The owners provide sightseeing advice as well as extras
like free bicycles, free local calls, and an Internet terminal in the lobby.

257 Belleville St., Victoria, B.C. V8V 1X1. (C) **888/823-6472** or (C)/fax 250/388-6267. www.admiral.bc.ca.
29 units. C$99–C$199 double; C$139–C$229 suite. Additional person C$10. Children 11 and under stay
free in parent's room. Rates include continental breakfast. AE, DC, MC, V. Free parking. Bus: 5 to Belleville
and Government sts. **Amenities:** Complimentary bikes; free Wi-Fi in lobby. *In room:* A/C, TV, fridge, hair
dryer, kitchen/kitchenette (in some units).

Coast Victoria Harbourside Hotel & Marina ★ (Value)   With its harborside location, fine-dining restaurant, and amenities, this hotel is a really good value, giving it a
special edge over all others in this price range. Spring for a Premium room on the 10th
floor and you'll be looking out over the Inner Harbour from a balcony. The rooms in this
hotel are not fancy but they are comfortable and nicely appointed with contemporary
decor; they all have balconies or sliding windows that open wide. The least expensive

rooms have a city rather than water view. The **Blue Crab Bar & Grill** (p. 228) is one of Victoria's best seafood restaurants. The path in front of the hotel winds around the entire harbor; downtown is a 10-minute walk. In the summer or on weekends year-round, you can take one of the little harbor ferries to the hotel's dock.

146 Kingston St., Victoria, B.C. V8V 1V4. (✆) **800/716-6199** or 250/360-1211. Fax 250/360-1418. www. coasthotels.com. 132 units. C$109–C$199 double. AE, DC, MC, V. Free parking. Harbor ferry. **Amenities:** Restaurant; small exercise room; Jacuzzi; indoor-outdoor pool; room service. *In room:* TV w/pay movies, fridge, hair dryer, free Wi-Fi.

Days Inn on the Harbour

This hotel across from the MV *Coho* ferry terminal on the Inner Harbour has small, motel-like rooms that aren't very distinguished but at least put you in a great location. Half the rooms face the Inner Harbour; the other half have views of the nearby residential area. View rooms cost a little more. The rooms come with queen-size, king-size, or two double beds, and are outfitted with standard furnishings and step-up bathtubs. Eighteen rooms are equipped with kitchenettes. A small outdoor pool is in back and a patio overlooking the harbor is in front.

427 Belleville St., Victoria, B.C. V8V 1X3. (✆) **800/665-3024** or 250/386-3451. Fax 250/386-6999. www. daysinnvictoria.com. 71 units. C$99–C$203 double. Additional person C$10. Children 11 and under stay free in parent's room. AE, DC, MC, V. Free parking. Bus: 5 to Belleville and Government sts. **Amenities:** Restaurant; bar; Jacuzzi; seasonal heated outdoor pool. *In room:* TV, hair dryer, free high-speed Internet, kitchenettes (in some units).

Harbour Towers Hotel & Suites ★ (Kids)

Though this 12-story tower by the Inner Harbour has a few standard rooms, the one- and two-bedroom suites with fully equipped kitchens are a better value. In recent years, the hotel has added some great features, such as an impressively upscale lobby, a day spa, and an improved fitness center with indoor pool. The rooms also received a complete overhaul, but the traditional-looking decor, though comfy, is fairly uninspired, and plastic plants look decidedly weird in verdant Victoria. Most units feature floor-to-ceiling windows opening onto private balconies, some with spectacular harbor views. The larger suites are great for families, and the gym has a glass-walled kids' play area.

345 Quebec St., Victoria, B.C. V8V 1W4. (✆) **800/663-5896** or 250/385-2405. Fax 250/480-6593. www. harbourtowers.com. 196 units. C$94–C$169 standard double or suite; C$499 penthouse suite. Additional person C$19. Children 16 and under stay free in parent's room. AE, DC, MC, V. Underground parking C$12. Bus: 31 to Superior and Oswego sts. **Amenities:** Restaurant; bar; babysitting; fitness center; indoor pool; room service; sauna; spa. *In room:* TV w/pay movies, hair dryer, free high-speed Internet.

Huntingdon Hotel and Suites (Value) (Kids)

Set within a stone's throw of the Inner Harbour, the Huntingdon Hotel and the adjacent Gatsby Mansion Inn (owned by the same company) are set on a landscaped block with a courtyard, cafes, and shops. Built in 1981, the three-story Huntingdon is a pleasant low-key hotel that's particularly good if you're traveling with children. The standard rooms are fairly large, and all rooms come equipped with fridges. The prime rooms are the split-level gallery rooms or lofts on the third floor, which have a sitting room with TV, a pullout double bed on the ground floor, and a master bedroom (and second TV) upstairs; all sleep four comfortably; some accommodate six. Some units have fully equipped kitchens, but you have to pay an additional C$10 charge to use them.

330 Quebec St., Victoria, B.C. V8V 1W3. (✆) **800/663-7557** or 250/381-3456. Fax 250/382-7666. www. bellevillepark.com. 116 units. C$79–C$189 double; C$109–C$249 suite. AE, DC, MC, V. Parking C$5. Bus: 5, 28, or 30. **Amenities:** Restaurant; bar; Jacuzzi; room service; sauna. *In room:* A/C (3rd-floor gallery suites only), TV, fridge, hair dryer, kitchen (in some units), free Wi-Fi.

The James Bay Inn (Value)   The Inner Harbour/James Bay area isn't especially blessed
with cheap digs, but this Edwardian manor on the edge of Beacon Hill Park is one of the
few. Built in 1907, it still offers one of the best accommodations deals downtown. The
standard rooms in the main building of this four-story walk-up are small and simply
furnished. The real bargains: the adjacent cottage and four suites located next door in a
renovated heritage property. The two studios are on the small side but come with a full-
size kitchen; the larger one-bedroom suites also feature a full kitchen, a bedroom with
queen-size bed, and a separate living room area. The cottage is a fully furnished, two-
bedroom house cater-cornered to the James Bay Inn. With space for eight people and a
peak-season price of C$240, it's a steal.

270 Government St., Victoria, B.C. V8V 2L2. © **800/836-2649** or 250/384-7151. Fax 250/385-2311. www.
jamesbayinn.bc.ca. 45 units. C$79–C$172 double; C$105–C$230 suite; C$145–C$240 cottage. AE, MC, V.
Free limited parking. Bus: 5 or 30 to Niagara St. **Amenities:** Restaurant; bar. *In room:* TV, hair dryer, free
Wi-Fi.

---

3 DOWNTOWN, OLD TOWN & NEARBY

EXPENSIVE

Abigail's Hotel ★★   Located in a residential neighborhood just east of downtown,
Abigail's began life in the 1920s as a luxury apartment house before being converted to
a boutique hotel. If you like small, personalized bed-and-breakfast hotels, you'll enjoy
this impeccably maintained property. Everything is done well here, and the quality is
high throughout. In the original building, some of the 16 rooms are bright and sunny
and beautifully furnished, with pedestal sinks and goose-down duvets. Others feature
soaker tubs and double-sided fireplaces, so you can relax in the tub by the light of the
fire. The six Celebration Suites in the Coach House are even more luxurious. Recent
renovations added Italian-marble bathrooms, new furniture, and a new spa. Abigail's chef
prepares a multicourse gourmet breakfast served in the sunny breakfast room, on the
patio, or in your room.

906 McClure St., Victoria, B.C. V8V 3E7. © **800/561-6565** or 250/388-5363. Fax 250/388-7787. www.
abigailshotel.com. 23 units. C$139–C$450 double. Rates include full breakfast. AE, MC, V. Free parking.
Bus: 1 to Cook and McClure sts. **Amenities:** Concierge. *In room:* A/C, TV, fireplace (in some rooms), hair
dryer, Jacuzzi (in some rooms), free Wi-Fi.

The Beaconsfield Inn ★   Built in 1905, this elegantly restored Edwardian mansion
is located just a few blocks from Beacon Hill Park and the Inner Harbour. The inn features fir paneling, mahogany floors, antique furnishings, and stained-glass windows. The
nine guest rooms are prettily decorated and filled with fresh flowers from the garden.
Some suites have skylights and French doors that open onto the garden. For couples who
want to get away from it all, book the cozy Beaconsfield Suite. Located on the third floor,
this room has a four-poster canopy bed, a sitting area in front of a wood-burning fireplace, a jetted tub, and a window seat. A full hot breakfast is served in the sunroom or
the dining room, and afternoon tea is served in the library. Children 12 and under, pets,
and smoking are not permitted.

998 Humboldt St., Victoria, B.C. V8V 2Z8. © **888/884-4044** or 250/384-4044. Fax 250/384-4052. www.
beaconsfieldinn.com. 9 units. C$109–C$299 double. Full breakfast, afternoon tea, and sherry hour
included. AE, MC, V. Free parking. Bus: 1 or 2 to Humboldt and Quadra sts. Children 12 and under permitted. **Amenities:** Access to nearby health club; Jacuzzi. *In room:* TV, fireplace, free Wi-Fi.

Two suites located above Willy's bakery provide affordable, fun, and surprisingly stylish accommodations in the heart of the city. The front suite is a large studio with a bed/sitting room that opens into a dining room and full kitchen. Bright colors and cheerful accents, upscale rustic furniture, high ceilings, large windows, and plenty of space make this a great home base for exploring Victoria. The second unit, a one-bedroom suite, overlooks the alley and patio of Il Terrazzo restaurant (reviewed in chapter 15). The living room is painted in bright red, which goes surprisingly well with the wood floors and funky furniture. Both units have king-size beds and are nonsmoking. Breakfast is included and served at the bakery. Parking is free, and you have your own entrance.

537 Johnson St., Victoria, B.C. V8W 1M2. ☎ **250/812-9216.** Fax 250/381-8415. www.isabellasbb.com. 2 units. C$150–C$195 double. Rates include continental breakfast. MC, V. Free parking. Bus: 5. *In room:* A/C, TV, hair dryer, kitchen.

The Magnolia ★★

A boutique hotel in the center of Victoria, the Magnolia was completed in 1999 and offers a taste of luxury at a reasonable price. Room decor manages to be traditional without feeling frumpy, with high-quality linens, down duvets, and quality furnishings. The large marble bathrooms feature walk-in showers and deep soaker tubs. The windows extend floor to ceiling, letting in lots of light, but the hotel really does not have any great views. For business travelers there are large, well-lit work desks with high-speed Internet access. Local calls are complimentary. The Diamond Suites on the sixth and seventh floors feature a sitting room with fireplace. In 2009 the hotel opened a new steakhouse, **Prime** (p. 232), and a full-service Aveda spa.

623 Courtney St., Victoria, B.C. V8W 1B8. ☎ **877/624-6654** or 250/381-0999. Fax 250/381-0988. www.magnoliahotel.com. 63 units. C$149–C$339 double. Rates include continental breakfast. AE, DC, MC, V. Valet parking C$15. Bus: 5. **Amenities:** Restaurant; bar; concierge; executive-level rooms access to nearby health club; room service; spa. *In room:* A/C, TV w/pay movies, fridge, hair dryer, minibar, free Wi-Fi.

Swans Suite Hotel ★★ (Kids)

In 1988, this heritage building was turned into a hotel, restaurant, brewpub, and nightclub. Located near the Johnson Street Bridge, it's just minutes from Bastion Square, Chinatown, and downtown. Like any good boutique hotel, Swans is small, friendly, and charming. The suites are large and many are split-level, featuring open lofts and huge exposed beams. All come with fully equipped kitchens, dining areas, living rooms, queen-size beds, and original artwork. The two-bedroom suites are like little town houses; they're great for families, accommodating up to six comfortably. Swan's Brewpub is one of the most popular in the city and features nightly live entertainment. The one potential drawback to this otherwise fine hotel is that a homeless shelter is located across the street.

506 Pandora St., Victoria, B.C. V8W 1N6. ☎ **800/668-7926** or 250/361-3310. Fax 250/361-3491. www.swanshotel.com. 30 units. C$179–C$199 studio; C$219–C$359 suite. Children 12 and under stay free in parent's room. AE, DC, DISC, MC, V. Parking C$9. Bus: 23 or 24 to Pandora Ave. **Amenities:** Restaurant; brewpub; room service. *In room:* TV, hair dryer, kitchen, free Wi-Fi.

The Victoria Regent Hotel (Kids)

An outside upgrade freshened the exterior of this hotel, which sits right on the Inner Harbour, closer to the water than any other hotel in Victoria. Rooms are fairly large and comfortable, though the decor is not very inspired. The 10 large one-bedroom suites feature king-size beds, small balconies (with big views), and standard serviceable bathrooms. The 36 two-bedroom suites have larger bathrooms and great views of the harbor (you're right on it). All the suites have full kitchens, so the hotel is popular with families.

1234 Wharf St., Victoria, B.C. V8W 3H9. ✆ **800/663-7472** or 250/386-2211. Fax 250/386-2622. www.
victoriaregent.com. 48 units. C$209 double; C$269–C$709 suite. Rates include continental breakfast.
Additional person C$20. Children 15 and under stay free in parent's room. AE, DC, DISC, MC, V. Free
underground parking. Bus: 6, 24, or 25 to Wharf St. **Amenities:** Restaurant; babysitting; concierge; access
to nearby health club; rooms for those w/limited mobility. *In room:* TV/VCR, CD player, hair dryer, minibar,
free Wi-Fi.

MODERATE

Abbeymoore Manor Inn ★★ (**Finds**)   This impressive 1912 mansion is in Rockland, an area of "Old Victoria" where grand homes were built by Victoria's elite. It's one
of the best B&Bs you'll find, with large, attractive rooms, lots of period antiques and
finishes, and an overall charm that's hard to beat. All the rooms are individually decorated
and have private bathrooms and beds fitted with fine linens. Two ground-floor garden
suites have separate entrances and fully equipped kitchens; the penthouse suite has views
of the ocean. A delicious gourmet breakfast is served, and complimentary beverages are
available throughout the day.

1470 Rockland Ave., Victoria, B.C. V8S 1W2. ✆ **888/801-1811** or 250/370-1470. Fax 250/370-1470. www.
abbeymoore.com. 7 units. C$109–C$159 double; C$149–C$179 suite. Additional person C$40. Rates
include full breakfast. MC, V. Free street parking. Bus: 11 or 14. No children 12 and under. *In room:* TV (in
suites), CD player, free Wi-Fi.

Best Western Carlton Plaza (**Kids**)   In the heart of Victoria's shopping and entertainment district, the Best Western Carlton is ideally located for those who like to step right
into the hustle and bustle of downtown. Rooms are comfortably furnished. Almost half
the units come with a fully equipped kitchen, and even the standard rooms are pretty
large. Perfect for families, the junior suites have two double beds, a sitting area with a
pullout couch, a dining room table, and full kitchen. The Best Western prides itself on
being a child-friendly hotel, and pets are also welcome.

642 Johnson St., Victoria, B.C. V8W 1M6. ✆ **800/663-7241** or 250/388-5513. Fax 250/388-5343. www.
bestwesterncarlton.com. 103 units. C$94–C$190 double; C$114–C$239 suite. Additional person C$20.
Children 17 and under stay free in parent's room. AE, MC, V. Free parking winter; $9 May–Oct. Bus: 5 to
Douglas and Johnson sts. **Amenities:** Restaurant; concierge; exercise room; room service; rooms for
those w/limited mobility. *In room:* A/C, TV w/pay movies, hair dryer, free Wi-Fi.

Chateau Victoria Hotel (**Value**)   This 18-story hotel was built in 1975 as a high-rise
apartment building, so the hotel's rooms and one-bedroom suites are unusually spacious;
many suites have kitchenettes, and all have balconies. The one-bedroom suites were
renovated in 2006 and there have been some decor changes throughout, making this a
good value for your money (including free local phone calls and free high-speed Internet
access). Prices are higher for the 5th through 15th floors, where the views are better; if
you can, get one of the corner 09 rooms with windows on two sides. The Vista 18 Rooftop Lounge offers one of the best views of downtown Victoria.

740 Burdett Ave., Victoria, B.C. V8W 1B2. ✆ **800/663-5891** or 250/382-4221. Fax 250/380-1950. www.
chateauvictoria.com. 177 units. C$105–C$165 double; C$129–C$229 suite. Children 16 and under stay
free in parent's room. AE, DC, DISC, MC, V. Free parking. Bus: 2 to Burdett Ave. **Amenities:** Rooftop restaurant; bar; babysitting; concierge; small exercise room; Jacuzzi; indoor pool; room service. *In room:* A/C, TV
w/pay movies, fridge, hair dryer, free high-speed Internet.

Dashwood Manor ★   This lovely old Elizabethan-style, half-timbered manor sits in
a great location on the edge of Beacon Hill Park, just across Dallas Road from the beach
and the Strait of Juan de Fuca. The landmark heritage property has recently been

upgraded into a comfortable and rather distinctive all-suites hotel. The rooms are large and bright, with carefully chosen furniture and wood-paneled walls. Bathrooms have been updated with new tile and fixtures, including deep-jetted tubs, and several of the rooms have large Jacuzzis. All of the rooms offer excellent ocean views; some have balconies. Complimentary sherry, port, and wine are laid out in the lobby in the evenings; a gourmet breakfast is served in the morning.

1 Cook St., Victoria, B.C. V8V 3W6. (C) **800/667-5517** or 250/385-5517. Fax 250/383-1760. www.dashwood manor.com. 11 units. C$129–C$279 suite. Additional person C$45. Rate includes breakfast. AE, DC, MC, V. Free parking. Bus: 5 to Dallas Rd. and Cook St. *In room:* TV, fridge, hair dryer, kitchen, free Wi-Fi.

Executive House Hotel (Kids)   You can't miss the Executive House, a concrete high-rise looming above the Fairmont Empress on Old Town's east side. Inside, the rooms are bigger than average in size, and—as in the adjacent and very similar Chateau Victoria (see above)—some intelligent thought has gone into their layout. A recent renovation freshened up the decor and furnishings. Bathrooms are small and functional. Each penthouse-level suite has a Jacuzzi in its own little atrium, a fireplace, a garden terrace with a panoramic view, a dining table, and a fully equipped kitchen.

777 Douglas St., Victoria, B.C. V8W 2B5. (C) **800/663-7001** or 250/388-5111. Fax 250/385-1323. www. executivehouse.com. 181 units. C$195–C$210 double; C$219–C$325 suite; C$395–C$895 penthouse rooms and suites. Additional person C$15. Children 15 and under stay free in parent's room. AE, DC, DISC, MC, V. Parking C$4 per night. Bus: 2 to the Convention Center. **Amenities:** 2 restaurants; 3 bars; babysitting; concierge; executive-level rooms; exercise room; room service; spa. *In room:* TV w/pay movies, fridge, hair dryer, free Wi-Fi.

Victoria Marriott Inner Harbour   The Marriott is a high-rise hotel with lots of marble in the lobby, and all the usual Marriott amenities, including an added-price concierge level that offers a pleasant lounge with breakfast and evening hors d'oeuvres. What you won't find is a whole lot of personality. The rooms are nice enough, especially the concierge-level suites on the 16th floor, but they're decorated in an indefinable style that's meant to look traditional but doesn't convey much beyond a cookie-cutter corporate aesthetic. The hotel has a good workout room and a nice big indoor pool and the service here is friendly and efficient. If you're a fan of Marriott, you'll find it all to your liking.

728 Humboldt St., Victoria, B.C. V8W 3Z5. (C) **866/306-5451** or 250/480-3800. Fax 250/480-3838. www. marriottvictoria.com. 236 units. C$149–C$259 double. AE, DC, MC, V. Valet or self-parking C$12 per day. Bus: 2 to the Convention Center. **Amenities:** Restaurant; lounge; babysitting; executive-level and concierge-level rooms; health club; Jacuzzi; indoor pool; room service. *In room:* A/C, TV, hair dryer, free high-speed Internet, minibar.

INEXPENSIVE

The Bedford Regency Hotel (Value)   If you're looking for a budget hotel right smack-dab in the middle of downtown, this heritage property is it. The Bedford Regency occupies the oldest building in Victoria (dating from 1869); it's not glamorous, but it's well maintained and has some surprising features, such as wood-burning fireplaces, harbor views, and spa-type bathrooms in the Superior rooms. The furnishings here are decidedly old-fashioned, but not without a certain charm. A new Café Artigiano (my favorite coffee bar in Vancouver and Victoria) opened in 2009 next to the lobby, and the hotel also houses Garrick's Head, the oldest pub in Victoria, where pub food and microbrews are served.

1140 Government St., Victoria, B.C. V8W 1Y2. (C) **800/665-6500** or 250/384-6835. Fax 250/386-8930. www.bedfordregency.com. 49 units. C$89–C$199 double. AE, DC, MC, V. **Amenities:** Coffee bar, pub. *In room:* A/C, TV, fridge, free Wi-Fi.

Hostelling International Victoria   The location is perfect—right in the heart of Old Town. In addition, this hostel has all the usual accouterments, including two kitchens (stocked with utensils), a dining room, a TV lounge, a game room, a common room, a library, laundry facilities, an indoor bicycle lockup, 24-hour security, and hot showers. The dorms are on the large side (16 people to a room), showers are shared and segregated by gender, and a couple of family rooms are available (one of which has a private toilet). There's an extensive ride board, and the collection of outfitter and tour information rivals that of the tourism office. The front door is locked at 2:30am, but you can make arrangements to get in later. *Note:* At press time there was talk of a complete renovation at the end of 2009, and a price increase of about C$5.

516 Yates St., Victoria, B.C. V8W 1K8. © **888/883-0099** or 250/385-4511. Fax 250/385-3232. www.hihostels. ca. 104 beds. C$20–C$25 dorm bed IYHA members, C$24–C$29 dorm bed nonmembers; C$45–C$61 private room IYHA members, C$49–C$65 private room nonmembers. Wheelchair-accessible unit available. MC, V. Parking on street. Bus: 70 from Swartz Bay ferry terminal. **Amenities:** Lounge; kitchens; free Wi-Fi.

Ocean Island Backpackers Inn ★ (Value)   All sorts of travelers make their way to this inexpensive, centrally located hostel (an alternative to the Hostelling International network), from families with children to on-the-go seniors and young adults with global wanderlust. The big, comfy lounge/common area always has all kinds of stuff going on, including live music and open-mic evenings. You can buy cheap meals and snacks, use the kitchen, or kick back with a beer or glass of wine. In addition to the dorm rooms there are 60 private rooms, in various configurations, including some with their own bathrooms. The staff here goes out of its way to help guests make the most of their time in Victoria and on Vancouver Island, including arranging day trips to out-of-the-ordinary places.

791 Pandora Ave., Victoria, B.C. V8W 1N9. © **888/888-4180** or 250/385-1788. Fax 250/385-1780. www. oceanisland.com. 50 units. C$21–C$27 dorm bed; C$27–C$75 private room (some with private bathroom). MC, V. Parking C$5. Bus: 70 to Pandora Ave. and Douglas St. **Amenities:** Restaurant; lounge. *In room:* TV (in some rooms), Wi-Fi (C$3/hr).

Paul's Motor Inn (Value)   Sometimes nothing but an inexpensive motor inn or motel will do, and that's where Paul's comes in. It's been around for ages, it's very well maintained, and it's within walking distance to downtown. The rooms are pleasant for what they are, and much nicer than those in many motel chains. The staff here is friendly and helpful and there's an above-average restaurant. Clean and cheerful all around.

1900 Douglas St., Victoria, B.C. V8T 4K8. © **866/333-7285** or 250/382-9231. Fax 250/384-1435. www. paulsmotorinn.com. 78 units. C$69–C$124 double. AE, DC, DISC, MC, V. Free parking. Bus: 30 to Douglas and Chatham sts. **Amenities:** Restaurant. *In room:* TV, fridge, free Wi-Fi.

4 OUTSIDE THE CENTRAL AREA

EXPENSIVE

The Aerie ★★   On a forested mountain slope high above a fjord about half an hour from town, this Mediterranean-inspired villa enjoys a spectacular view and is one of the most luxurious retreats you'll find on Vancouver Island, though some may find the European-inspired decor and design a bit over-the-top. Accommodations are in three separate buildings. All rooms include big comfortable beds with top-quality linen, and all but the lowest-priced Deluxe rooms include a soaker tub for two; master and residence suites have private decks and fireplaces. An on-site full-service spa offers a variety of aesthetic treatments. Dining is an integral part of the experience, and the **Aerie restaurant** (p. 236) is among the best restaurants on the island. A full breakfast is included in the room rate.

600 Ebedora Lane (P.O. Box 108), Malahat, B.C. V0R 2L0. (☎) **800/518-1933** or 250/743-7115. Fax 250/743-4766. www.aerie.ca. 29 units. C$195–C$295 double; C$300–C$565 suite. Rates include breakfast. AE, DC, MC, V. Free parking. Take Hwy. 1 north, turn left at the Spectacle Lake turnoff, take the first right, and follow the winding driveway. **Amenities:** Restaurant; bar; concierge; small weight room; indoor and outdoor Jacuzzis; small indoor pool; room service; spa; tennis courts. *In room:* A/C, TV, hair dryer, minibar, free Wi-Fi.

The Boathouse ★★★ (Finds)

Vancouver Island has nothing else like it, and I can almost guarantee you'll fall in love with this tiny, secluded cottage—a former boathouse—set on pilings over Saanich Inlet on Brentwood Bay. The only passersby you're likely to encounter are seals, bald eagles, otters, herons, and raccoons, plus the occasional floatplane flying in. The converted boathouse is at the end of a very long flight of stairs (if you have mobility issues, this is not the place for you). Outside there's a waterside porch you may never want to leave; inside are a queen-size bed, a dining table, a kitchen area with a small refrigerator and toaster oven, an electric heater, and a reading alcove. Toilet and shower facilities are in a separate bathhouse, 17 steps back uphill. A small dinghy is reserved exclusively for guests' use. It's wonderful.

746 Sea Dr., Brentwood Bay, Victoria, B.C. V8M 1B1. (☎) **866/654-9370** or 250/652-9370. www.accommodations bc.com/boathouse.html. 1 unit. C$215 double with continental breakfast; C$195 double without breakfast. 2-night minimum. AE, MC, V. Free parking. Closed Oct–Feb. Bus: 75 to Wallace Dr. and Benvenuto Ave. No children 17 and under. *In room:* Fridge, hair dryer.

Brentwood Bay Lodge & Spa ★★★ (Finds)

Located on a pristine inlet about 20 minutes north of downtown Victoria, this contemporary timber-and-glass lodge offers the best of everything, including a fabulous spa, boat shuttle to Butchart Gardens, and all manner of eco-adventures, including kayaking, scuba diving, fishing, and boat trips through the surrounding waters. The rooms are beautifully outfitted with handcrafted furnishings, gas fireplaces, luxurious bathrooms with soaker tubs and body massage showers, balconies, and king-size beds fitted with the highest quality Italian linens. The **SeaGrille** dining room and pub (p. 236) offers fine seasonal menus and great pub food. The hotel has its own marina and is a licensed PADI (Professional Association of Diving Instructors) dive center—the fjord on which it sits is considered one of the best diving spots in the world.

849 Verdier Ave. on Brentwood Bay, Victoria, B.C. V8M 1C5. (☎) **888/544-2079** or 250/544-2079. Fax 250/544-2069. www.brentwoodbaylodge.com. 33 units. C$179–C$419 double; C$369–C$699 suite. Rates include continental breakfast. AE, DC, MC, V. Free parking. Take Pat Bay Hwy. north to Keating Crossroads, turn left (west) to Saanich Rd., turn right (south) to Verdier Ave. **Amenities:** Restaurant; pub; concierge; Jacuzzi; heated outdoor pool; room service; spa. *In room:* A/C, TV/DVD, fireplace, hair dryer, Jacuzzi (in suites), minibar, free Wi-Fi.

Miraloma on the Cove ★ (Finds)

If you're looking for a small, quiet, luxury boutique hotel off the beaten tourist track, consider the Miraloma in Sidney. The building, with a three-story central atrium lobby area, offers well-decorated rooms with sumptuous beds, large bathrooms, gas fireplaces, and a high-end kitchen or kitchenette; all but two have balconies. Surrounded by a pretty garden, the hotel is next door to a historic home that once served as the lieutenant governor's getaway residence, and a 5-minute walk to Van Isle marina. The Swartz Bay–Vancouver ferry terminals are 10 minutes to the north,

Victoria is 20 minutes to the south, or you can bike into the seaside town of Sidney on one of the hotel's complimentary bikes.

2326 Harbour Rd., Sidney, B.C. V8L 2P8. ✆ **877/956-6622** or 250/656-6622. Fax 250/656-1212. www. miraloma.ca. 22 units. C$159–C$449 double. Rates include buffet continental breakfast. AE, MC, V. Free parking. Bus: 70 to Resthaven Dr. **Amenities:** Bikes; small fitness center; outdoor Jacuzzi. *In room:* TV/ DVD, CD player, fridge, hair dryer, free high-speed Internet, kitchen, washer-dryer (in suites).

Poets Cove Resort & Spa ★

To reach Pender Island, one of the Gulf Islands between the mainland and Vancouver Island, you have to take a ferry or water taxi from Sidney, north of Victoria; you can also skipper your own boat and dock it at the 110-slip marina (with a Customs clearance checkpoint). Overlooking Bedwell Harbour and its own marina, Poets Cove opened in 2004 as a 22-room lodge with a cluster of seaside cottages, all built with a contemporary Craftsman-style Pacific Northwest look and ambience. All the accommodations feature ocean or forest-and-water views, fireplaces, big bathtubs for soaking, and all the amenities of an upscale resort. You can dine on fresh Pacific Northwest cuisine at the Aurora Restaurant in the lodge, or enjoy snacks and comfort food in the lounge. Susurrus Spa offers a full complement of relaxation and aesthetic treatments, including spa treatments for couples.

9801 Spalding Rd., Pender Island, B.C. V0N 2M3. ✆ **888/512-7638** or 250/629-2100. www.poetscove. com. 22 lodge units, 15 cottages, 9 villas. C$169–C$279 double in lodge; C$299–C$489 villa; C$319–C$659 cottage. AE, DC, MC, V. Free parking. Ferry from Sidney to Pender Island (www.bcferries.com); take Island Hwy. from ferry terminal. **Amenities:** Restaurant; lounge; concierge; fitness center; 2 heated outdoor pools and hot tubs (seasonal); spa. *In room:* TV/DVD/CD, fireplace, hair dryer, outdoor Jacuzzi (some units), kitchen (in cottages and villas).

Sidney Pier Hotel & Spa ★★ (Finds) (Kids)

This seaside boutique hotel has brought a splash of stylish (but low-key) glamour to Sidney's waterfront (the Vancouver and Anacortes ferry terminals are less than 5 min. away and the new Sidney Aquarium is right next door). The guest rooms are well designed and comfortable, with calm, minimalist interiors and a refreshing lack of froufrou. Most of the rooms have ocean views; the suites have balconies, fireplaces, and connect with adjoining rooms, making them very family-friendly. Bathrooms are equally well designed, some with showers only, others with soaker tubs and walk-in showers. Haro's, the hotel's restaurant; it serves fresh area specialties, including salads, fish, and lamb. At Haven Spa, all manner of rejuvenating and refreshing treatments are available.

9805 Seaport Place, Sidney, B.C. V8L 4X3. ✆ **866/659-9445** or 250/655-9445. Fax 250/655-0715. www. sidneypier.com. 55 units. C$129–C$259 double; C$289–C$529 suite. AE, MC, V. Underground parking: C$5. From Victoria, drive north on Patricia Bay Hwy. (Hwy. 17) to Sidney, turn right (east) on Beacon Ave. and continue toward waterfront, turn left (north) on Seaport Place. **Amenities:** Restaurant; bar; small fitness center; spa. *In room:* TV/DVD, fireplace (in suites), hair dryer, free high-speed Internet, kitchen (in suites).

Sooke Harbour House ★★★

This quirkily distinctive inn, located right on the ocean at the end of a sand spit about 30km (19 miles) west of Victoria, has earned an international reputation for its sumptuous rooms, each furnished and decorated according to a particular Northwest theme, and its outstanding restaurant (p. 237), which makes use of fragrant herbs and edible flowers from the inn's magnificent seaside gardens. Thanks to some clever architecture, all the rooms are awash in natural light and have fabulous ocean views. All have wood-burning fireplaces and sitting areas, most have sun decks and Jacuzzis or soaker tubs. Breakfast (served in your room) is included in the room rate.

1528 Whiffen Spit Rd., Sooke, B.C. V9Z 0T4. ℂ **800/889-9688** or 250/642-3421. Fax 250/642-6988. www. sookeharbourhouse.com. 28 units. C$305–C$650 double. Rates include full breakfast. MC, V. Free parking. Take the Island Hwy. (Hwy. 1) to the Sooke/Colwood turnoff (junction Hwy. 14); follow Hwy. 14 to Sooke; about 1.6km (1 mile) past the town's only traffic light, turn left onto Whiffen Spit Rd. **Amenities:** Restaurant; babysitting; nearby golf course; access to nearby health club; room service; sauna; spa. *In room:* CD player, fireplace, fridge, hair dryer, minibar, free Wi-Fi.

Westin Bear Mountain Victoria Golf Resort & Spa ★★★   This resort hotel overlooks an 18-hole mountaintop golf course designed by Jack Nicklaus and his son. Part of a high-end resort-community development covering some 486 hectares (1,201 acres), the hotel is big and handsomely crafted, with fine natural finishes of wood and stone and the overall ambience of a giant West Coast mountain lodge. Rooms (in two separate buildings) are spacious, well designed, and furnished in a way that's both luxurious and comfortable; each has a balcony. The extra-large bathrooms feature soaker tubs and separate showers. The gym is the best on Vancouver Island, and the spa offers medically supervised dermatology services. Dining options include the Copper River Grille, open for breakfast, lunch, and dinner, and the more exclusive Panache, serving both traditional and fusion-inspired fare.

1999 Country Club Way, Victoria, B.C. V9B 6R3. ℂ **888/533-2327** or 250/391-7160. Fax 250/391-3792. www.bearmountain.ca. 156 units. C$179–C$349 double; C$249–C$419 1-bedroom suite. AE, MC, V. Valet parking C$15. Take the Island Hwy. (Hwy. 1) to exit 14, then follow Millstream Rd. to Bear Mountain Pkwy. and follow the signs. **Amenities:** Restaurant; sports bar; babysitting; world-class golf course w/driving range; health club w/outdoor pool; room service; spa. *In room:* TV w/pay movies, fireplace, fridge, hair dryer, kitchen, Wi-Fi (C$15/day).

MODERATE

Birds of a Feather Oceanfront Bed & Breakfast   Located on an oceanfront lagoon 20 minutes west of Victoria, this quiet, ecofriendly B&B run by Annette Moen and Dieter Gerhard is super for bird-watchers and nature lovers. The lagoon is on the Pacific Flyway and attracts thousands of migratory birds and other wildlife. The three guest rooms, in their own separate wing, are furnished with Arts and Crafts–inspired beds and comfy leather chairs; they all have a good-size bathroom, kitchen, gas fireplace, and patio area with views of the water. The Honeymoon Suite is flooded with light on two sides; the family room has two levels with a spiral staircase.

206 Portsmouth Dr., Victoria, B.C. V9C 1R9. ℂ **800/730-4790** or 250/391-8889. www.victorialodging. com. 3 units. C$165–C$215 double. Rates include full breakfast. AE, MC, V. From Victoria take Hwy. 1 to exit 10 (Colwood/View Royal), turn left on Ocean Blvd., right on Lagoon Rd., right on Heatherbell, right on Portsmouth Dr. **Amenities:** Complimentary bikes, canoes, and kayaks. *In room:* TV/DVD, fireplace, fridge, hair dryer, kitchen, free Wi-Fi.

INEXPENSIVE

Point-No-Point Resort ★ ⓕ**Finds**   Away from it all in your own snug cabin, you'll have 16 hectares (40 acres) of wilderness around you and a wide rugged beach in front of you, with nothing to do but laze away the day in your hot tub. Or stroll along the beach. Or roam in the forest. Or look at an eagle. This oceanfront resort has been welcoming guests since 1950. Cabins vary depending on when they were built. All have fireplaces, full kitchens, and bathrooms; newer ones have hot tubs on their private decks. Lunch and afternoon tea are available daily in the small, sunny central dining room. Dinner is served Wednesday through Sunday. The dining room tables are conveniently equipped with binoculars, so you won't miss a bald eagle as you dine.

10829 West Coast Rd., Shirley, B.C. V9Z 1G9. ✆ **250/646-2020.** Fax 250/646-2294. www.pointnopoint resort.com. 25 units. C$140–C$270. AE, MC, V. Free parking. No public transit. Take Hwy. 14 to exit 10 (Sooke); resort is 20 min. past Sooke. **Amenities:** Jacuzzi. *In room:* Kitchen, no phone.

University of Victoria Housing, Food, and Conference Services (Value) One

of the best deals going is found at the University of Victoria, when classes aren't in session and summer visitors are welcomed. All rooms have single or twin beds and basic furnishings; bathrooms, pay phones, and TV lounges are on every floor. Linens, towels, and soap are provided. The suites are an extremely good value—each has four bedrooms, a kitchen, a living room, and 1½ bathrooms. For C$5 extra per day, you can make use of the many on-campus athletic facilities. Each of the 28 buildings has a coin laundry. The disadvantage is that the U. Vic. campus is a painfully long way from everywhere—the city center is about a 20-minute drive away.

P.O. Box 1700, Sinclair at Finerty Rd., Victoria, B.C. V8W 2Y2. ✆ **250/721-8395.** Fax 250/721-8930. www. hfcs.uvic.ca. 898 units. May–Aug C$45 single; C$55 double; C$150 suite (sleeps 4 people). Rates for single and double rooms include continental breakfast and taxes. MC, V. Parking C$6. Closed Sept–Apr. Bus: 4 or 14 to University of Victoria. **Amenities:** Access to athletic facilities; indoor pool. *In-room*: Free Wi-Fi.

Where to Dine in Victoria

Victoria has jumped on the foodie bandwagon and offers a cornucopia of culinary styles from around the world. It's not as savvy and sophisticated as Vancouver, and never will be, but with more than 700 restaurants in the area, something is available for every taste and wallet.

The touristy restaurants along Wharf Street serve mediocre food for folks they know they'll never have to see again, so avoid them. The canny visitor knows to head inland (even a block is enough), where the proportion of tourists to locals drops sharply and the quality jumps by leaps and bounds.

The one time-honored aspect of English cuisine Victoria is still known for is the custom of afternoon tea. American visitors in particular should give it a try.

For the best places, see "Taking Afternoon Tea," later in this chapter.

Victoria is not the kind of late-night, show-off, see-and-be-seen dining city that Vancouver is. Most restaurants in Victoria close at 10pm. Reservations are strongly recommended for prime sunset seating during summer, especially on Friday and Saturday. No provincial tax is added to restaurant meals in British Columbia, just the **6% goods and services tax (GST).**

Note: Because Victoria is so compact, most of the restaurants listed in this chapter are in downtown or Old Town and no more than a 10-minute walk from most hotels. Thus, in this chapter, I've listed public transit information only for those spots that are a bit farther out.

1 BEST VICTORIA DINING BETS

- **Best Spot for a Romantic Dinner: Camille's,** 45 Bastion Sq. (© **250/381-3433**), offers a quiet, intimate, candlelit room and a wine list with a bottle or glass for every occasion. See p. 231.
- **Best Pacific Northwest:** Much of the menu at **Sooke Harbour House,** 1528 Whiffen Spit Rd., Sooke (© **800/889-9688** or 250/642-3421), is picked fresh from the adjacent garden, a treasure-trove of edible beauty. You'll find unique seasonal flavors, inventive cooking, and a superlative wine cellar. See p. 237.
- **Best Local Crowd: Café Brio,** 944 Fort St. (© **250/383-0009**), one of Victoria's top dining spots, celebrated its 10th anniversary in 2007 and remains a local fave. See p. 231.
- **Best for Kids: rebar,** 50 Bastion Sq. (© **250/361-9223**), offers large portions, terrific quality, and a funky laid-back atmosphere. See p. 235.
- **Best Burgers & Beer: Six Mile Pub,** 494 Island Hwy. (© **250/478-3121**), offers 10 house brews, juicy burgers (even veggie burgers), and loads of British pub-style atmosphere. See p. 237.

- **Best Afternoon or High Tea:** How can you brag about your trip to Victoria if you don't include tea at the **Fairmont Empress,** 721 Government St. (© **250/384-8111**)? It's more than a tradition—it's a legendary experience, and the closest you'll come to reliving a bygone era. See p. 232.
- **Best Newcomer: Prime Steakhouse & Lounge,** 621 Courtney St. (© **250/386-2010**), in the Magnolia Hotel, serves up the best steaks and prime rib in the city.
- **Best Small Plates: Stage,** 1307 Gladstone Ave. (© **250/388-4222**), a new bistro in the Fernwood neighborhood, has a full menu of small plates that are big on taste.
- **Best Eco-Eats:** At the busy take-out stand at **Red Fish/Blue Fish,** 1006 Wharf St. (© **250/298-6877**), the seafood is delicious and comes only from sustainable sources, and every plate and container is biodegradable and/or recyclable.
- **Best Hang-Out for Under 30s:** With its busy Bastion Square location, views of the Inner Harbour, great beers and cocktails, and casual menu, **The Local Kitchen,** 1205 Wharf St. (© **250/385-1999**), draws a big crowd, especially on warm days when you can sit outside at a sidewalk table.

---

2 RESTAURANTS BY CUISINE

Bakery
Ottavio ★ (Oak Bay, $, p. 234)
Q V Bakery & Café (Downtown, $, p. 235)
Willie's (Old Town, $, p. 234)

Bistro
Stage ★ (Fernwood, $, p. 236)

Chinese
J&J Wonton Noodle House ★ (Downtown, $, p. 234)

Deli
Sam's Deli (Downtown, $, p. 235)

Eastern European
Paprika Bistro ★★ (East of Downtown, $$$, p. 235)

Fish & Chips
Barb's Place (Inner Harbour, $, p. 230)
Fairfield Fish and Chips (East of Downtown, $, p. 236)
Red Fish/Blue Fish (Inner Harbour, $, p. 230)

French
The Aerie ★★★ (Greater Victoria, $$$$, p. 236)
Brasserie L'Ecole ★★ (Old Town, $$$, p. 230)

Italian
Café Brio ★★★ (Downtown, $$$, p. 231)
Il Terrazzo Ristorante ★★ (Downtown, $$$, p. 231)
Pagliacci's (Downtown, $$, p. 232)
Zambri's ★ (Downtown, $$, p. 233)

Pacific Northwest
Café Brio ★★★ (Downtown, $$$, p. 231)
Camille's ★★★ (Downtown, $$$, p. 231)
Canoe ★ (Inner Harbour, $$, p. 229)
The Local Kitchen (Inner Harbour, $, p. 230)
The Mark ★★ (Inner Harbour, $$$, p. 228)
SeaGrille ★★★ (Greater Victoria, $$$$, p. 236)

Key to Abbreviations: $$$$ = Very Expensive $$$ = Expensive $$ = Moderate $ = Inexpensive

Sooke Harbour House ★★★ (Greater Victoria, $$$$, p. 237)

Spinnakers Brewpub (Inner Harbour, $$, p. 230)

Stage ★ (Fernwood, $, p. 236)

Pub Grub

Canoe ★ (Inner Harbour, $$, p. 229)

Six Mile Pub (Greater Victoria, $, p. 237)

Spinnakers Brewpub (Inner Harbour, $$, p. 230)

Seafood

The Blue Crab Bar and Grill ★★★ (Inner Harbour, $$$, p. 228)

Red Fish/Blue Fish ★ (Inner Harbour, $, p. 230)

Steak

Prime Steakhouse & Lounge ★★ (Downtown, $$$, p. 232)

Tapas

The Tapa Bar (Old Town, $$, p. 233)

Tea

Abkhazi Garden (Greater Victoria, $, p. 233)

Butchart Gardens Dining Room Restaurant ★★★ (Greater Victoria, $$$, p. 233)

The Fairmont Empress ★★★ (Downtown, $$$$, p. 232)

Point Ellice House (Greater Victoria, $$, p. 232)

White Heather Tea Room ★★ (Greater Victoria, $, p. 233)

Thai

Siam Thai Restaurant (Downtown, $, p. 235)

Vegetarian

Green Cuisine (Downtown, $, p. 234)

rebar (Downtown, $, p. 235)

---

3 THE INNER HARBOUR

EXPENSIVE

The Blue Crab Bar and Grill ★★★ SEAFOOD   One of Victoria's best bets for seafood, the Blue Crab combines excellent fresh ingredients and a fairly uncomplicated preparation. It sits right on the Inner Harbour and has a wonderful view across the water. Like other top-end restaurants in town, the Crab sources most of its ingredients locally, and it's a member of OceanWise, a group dedicated to sustainable fishing practices. For lunch you can tuck in to Pacific seafood chowder or a grilled arctic char sandwich; at dinner, try the fresh oysters, a Cortes Island clam and mussel pot, fresh halibut with pasta, or the signature hot pot of local seafood prepared with ginger and lemon grass broth. The award-winning wine list (*Wine Spectator* Award of Excellence from 2003–07) features midrange and top-end vintages, drawn mostly from B.C., Washington, and California. The service is deft and obliging.

In the Coast Hotel, 146 Kingston St. ⓒ **250/480-1999.** www.bluecrab.ca. Reservations recommended. Main courses lunch C$12–C$21, dinner C$15–C$35. AE, DC, MC, V. Daily 6:30am–10pm (dinner from 5pm).

The Mark ★★ PACIFIC NORTHWEST   The fine dining room at the Hotel Grand Pacific is a small, candlelit haven. Here you can enjoy highly personalized service, delicious food prepared with locally grown ingredients, and fine wines chosen by an astute sommelier. To sample the best of everything, try the seasonal tasting menu, priced at C$70, or C$112 with wine pairings. The menu might start with a Buttercup squash confit with fresh ricotta, then on to roasted Alberta lamb and lamb chorizo, with a finish of a cardamom and Delicata squash custard. The a la carte menu features meat dishes

Barb's Place **26**
The Blue Crab Bar and Grill **25**
Brasserie L'Ecole **3**
Café Brio **8**
Caffe Artigiano **17**
Camille's **16**
Canoe **2**
Fairfield Fish and Chips **6**
The Fairmont Empress **23**
Green Cuisine **10**
Il Terrazzo Ristorante **11**
J&J Wonton Noodle House **7**
The Local Kitchen **13**

The Mark **24**
Pagliacci's **20**
Prime Steakhouse & Lounge **21**
Q V Bakery & Café **4**
rebar **14**
Red Fish/Blue Fish **19**
Sam's Deli **22**
Siam Thai Restaurant **18**
Spinnakers Brewpub **1**
Stage **5**
The Tapa Bar **15**
Willy's **12**
Zambri's **9**

such as matsuke-glazed venison loin or center-cut beef tenderloin. The hotel's casual **Pacific Restaurant** is also a good choice for lunch or dinner, with nicely done dishes such as West Coast seafood linguine, vegetarian pizzas, and high-quality steak and lamb. The Pacific has a great outdoor patio overlooking the harbor.

In the Hotel Grand Pacific (p. 212), 463 Belleville St. ☏ **250/380-4487.** www.themark.ca. Reservations required for the Mark, recommended for Pacific Restaurant. The Mark main courses C$30–C$34; Pacific Restaurant main courses C$16–C$30. AE, DC, MC, V. The Mark daily 5–9:30pm; Pacific Restaurant daily 6:30am–10pm.

MODERATE

Canoe ★ PUB GRUB/PACIFIC NORTHWEST   What was once a Victorian power station is now one of Victoria's loveliest and liveliest brewpub restaurants, with an outdoor patio overlooking the harbor toward the Johnson Street Bridge and an industrial-inspired interior with massive masonry walls and heavy timber crossbeams. Canoe is popular because it has something tasty for every palate, all made with local ingredients whenever possible. The kitchen offers intriguing variations on standard pub fare and bar snacks, including thin-crust pizzas (but with grilled lamb or chili prawns), classic burgers, and their signature pot pie. Head upstairs for finer fare such as premium top sirloin steak, seafood curry, or the day's fresh fish. The beer is excellent, the award-winning wine list is small but select. This is a good spot for lunch, too.

450 Swift St. © **250/361-1940.** www.canoebrewpub.com. Reservations recommended for weekend dinner and Sun brunch. Main courses C$13–C$23; pub fare and bar snacks C$9–C$17; lunch special C$12. AE, MC, V. Sun–Wed 11:30am–11pm; Thurs 11:30am–midnight; Fri–Sat 11:30am–1am.

Spinnakers Brewpub PUB GRUB/PACIFIC NORTHWEST Spinnakers beer has always been extraordinary—rich ales, stouts, and lagers are all craft-brewed on the premises. The cuisine has changed over the years and evolved into above-average gastro-pub fare with some adventurous fresh West Coast seafood, all served in a fun, bustling pub atmosphere with great Inner Harbour views. It's hard to go wrong with the burgers, steamed mussels, or fish and chips.

308 Catherine St. © **250/384-2739.** www.spinnakers.com. Main courses C$7–C$20. AE, MC, V. Daily 11am–11pm.

INEXPENSIVE

Barb's Place (Kids) FISH & CHIPS The best "chippie" in town, Barb's is a no-frills harborside stand that serves lightly breaded halibut (and other locally caught fish) and hand-hewn chips, plus a good seafood chowder, seafood specialties, and burgers. Picnic tables are nearby at Fisherman's Wharf.

Fisherman's Wharf, Erie St. © **250/384-6515.** www.barbsplace.ca. Menu items C$2–C$7; meals C$9–C$19. MC, V. Daily 11am–sunset.

The Local Kitchen PACIFIC NORTHWEST Located right at the base of Bastion Square, with outdoor sidewalk seating in good weather, The Local Kitchen is a great place to hang out for a couple of hours with a beer, a cocktail, a shared mix of small plates, or a more substantial meal. For main courses, try the Bengal halibut curry or the West Coast linguine with seafood. Smaller plates include seafood chowder and Dungeness crab cakes. This is a fave spot for thirtysomethings and the generation that came after. Summer Sunday brunch is very popular.

1205 Wharf St. (at Bastion Sq.) © **250/385-1999.** www.thelocalkitchen.ca. Small plates C$4–C$15; main courses C$23–C$30. MC, V. Mon–Sat 11:30am–11pm; Sun 9:30am–6pm.

Red Fish/Blue Fish ★ (Finds) FISH & CHIPS/SEAFOOD Locals and tourists alike flock to this waterside stand for fresh, fast, sustainably harvested seafood delights. Wild Pacific fish and chips, oyster or wild salmon tacos, and fresh fish sandwiches are generally on the menu, as well as fish chowder and an organic vegetarian salad. Every paper plate and container used here is recycled. If the weather's nice, you can sit at an outdoor table. This popular place is located on the pier next to the floatplane terminal right on the Inner Harbour.

1006 Wharf St. © **250/298-6877.** www.redfish-bluefish.com. Menu items C$5–C$16. AE, MC, V. Daily 11:30am–6pm (later in summer).

4 DOWNTOWN & OLD TOWN

EXPENSIVE

Brasserie L'Ecole ★★ FRENCH In the overheated world of food fashion, it's so refreshing to find simple French bistro fare deftly prepared and served at amazingly reasonable prices. Honesty is what's on offer at this warm, comfortable restaurant, the **231** brainchild of longtime Victoria chef Sean Brenner. L'Ecole's menu changes daily, depending entirely on what comes in fresh from Victoria's hinterland farms. Preparation is simple, no big reductions or complicated *jus,* just shellfish, local fish, meats with red-wine sauces, and fresh vegetables with vinaigrettes. The wine list is small, with no hugely expensive vintages, but has good straightforward wine to match the excellent food. Very satisfying in every way.

1715 Government St. © **250/475-6260.** www.lecole.ca. Reservations recommended. Main courses C$22–C$24. AE, MC, V. Tues–Sat 5:30–11pm.

Café Brio ★★★ PACIFIC NORTHWEST/ITALIAN   Café Brio is one of Victoria's best and buzziest spots for casual but top-flight dining. The Tuscan-influenced cuisine strongly reflects the seasons, fresh local meats and produce, and Pacific seafood. The menu changes daily, but appetizers always include locally harvested oysters, a wonderful house-made paprika sausage, and a delicious charcuterie plate (the chef makes all his charcuterie on the premises). For entrees, choose from handmade pasta (such as fresh herb-ricotta agnolotti) or roasted or poached wild fish. The wine list is excellent, with an impressive selection of B.C. and international reds and whites. The service is deft, friendly, and knowledgeable, and the kitchen stays open as long as guests keep ordering. An all-around winner.

944 Fort St. © **250/383-0009.** www.cafe-brio.com. Reservations recommended. Main courses C$14–C$49. AE, MC, V. Daily 5:30–9:30pm.

Camille's ★★★ PACIFIC NORTHWEST   The most romantic of Victoria's restaurants, Camille's is also one of the very best. Tucked away in two rooms beneath the old Law Chambers, its decor contrasts white linen with century-old exposed brick, stained-glass lamps, and candlelight. Chef and owner David Mincey was one of the founders of a Vancouver Island farm cooperative that brings local farmers together with local restaurants, so you're usually dining on foods found within a 100-mile radius of the restaurant. The ever-changing menu displays Mincey's love for cheeky invention and the seasonal bounty of Vancouver Island. To sample a bit of everything try the five-course tasting menu, a fantastic bargain at C$50, or C$75 with wine pairings. The reasonable and extensive wine list comes with liner notes that are amusing and informative. A meal here is a quiet, memorable occasion abetted by the professionalism of the staff.

45 Bastion Sq. © **250/381-3433.** Reservations recommended. Main courses C$22–C$37. AE, MC, V. Tues–Sun 5:30–10pm.

Il Terrazzo Ristorante ★★ ITALIAN   This charming spot in a converted heritage building off Waddington Alley is always a top contender for Victoria's best Italian restaurant. You can be assured of a good meal here. The northern Italian cooking includes wood-oven-roasted meats, fish, and pizzas, as well as homemade pastas. An emphasis on fresh produce and local seafood sets the tone for the menu, with appetizers such as artichokes stuffed with salmon and crabmeat drizzled with a light lemon-cream sauce, and entrees like salmon crusted with almond and black pepper and baked in the wood-burning oven, or a fabulous rack of lamb. The mood is bustling and upbeat, complete with an atmospheric courtyard furnished with flowers, marble tables, wrought-iron chairs, and heaters. The wine list is enormous, with some 1,200 vintages. Service is friendly and helpful.

555 Johnson St. (off Waddington Alley). © **250/361-0028.** www.ilterrazzo.com. Reservations recommended. Main courses C$15–C$37. AE, MC, V. Mon–Sat 11:30am–3pm and 5–10pm, Sun 5–10pm.

ⓂMoments Taking Afternoon Tea

Far from a simple cup of hot water with a Lipton tea bag beside it, a proper afternoon tea is both a meal and a ritual.

Any number of places in Victoria serve afternoon tea; some refer to it as high tea. Both come with sandwiches, berries, and tarts, but high tea usually includes some more substantial savory fare such as a meat-and-vegetable-filled turnover. Though the caloric intake can be hefty, it's really more about the ritual than the potential weight gain. For that reason, you don't want to go to any old teahouse. Note that in summer it's a good idea to book *at least* a week ahead.

If you want, and can afford, the best experience, head to the **Fairmont Empress** ★★★, 721 Government St. (ⓒ **250/384-8111;** p. 211), where tea is served in the Tea Lobby, a busy and beautifully ornate room at the front of the hotel. Price depends on the time and season, and runs from C$49 to C$60. For that, you'll be pampered with fresh berries and cream or a fruit compote; sandwiches of smoked salmon, cucumber, and curried chicken; scones with strawberry preserves and thick Jersey cream; and an assortment of tarts and chocolates. Seatings are every 15 minutes four times a day starting at noon, until 3:45pm; reservations are essential and a "smart casual" dress code is in effect (no torn jeans, short shorts, or flip-flops).

More affordable, less crowded, and just as historic is tea on the lawn of **Point Ellice House,** 2616 Pleasant St. (ⓒ **250/380-6506;** www.pointellicehouse.ca), where the cream of Victoria society used to gather in the early 1900s. On the Gorge waterway, Point Ellice is just a 5-minute trip by ferry from the Inner

15

Prime Steakhouse & Lounge ★★ STEAK   Prime opened in 2009 and quickly established itself as Victoria's best steakhouse. They dry age their New York steak to preserve its full flavor and succulence. Thick, juicy prime rib, another house specialty, is served with a great Yorkshire pudding and fresh horseradish. For lunch you can get a spiced lamb burger, a fresh fish, or pasta. If you like oysters, start your meal with those. They have a good and reasonably priced wine list that features B.C. and international vintages.

In The Magnolia Hotel, 621 Courtney St. ⓒ **250/386-2010.** www.primesteak.ca. Reservations recommended. Main courses lunch C$13–C$16, dinner C$25–C$50. AE, MC, V. Daily 11:30am–11pm.

MODERATE

Pagliacci's Ⓚ Kids ITALIAN   Victoria's night owls used to come here when Pagliacci's was one of the few places to offer late-night dining. Though the city's evening scene has improved since expatriate New Yorker Howie Siegal opened the restaurant in 1979, Pagliacci's can still boast an un-Victoria kind of big-city buzz and energy. Tables jostle against one another as guests ogle each other's food and eavesdrop on conversations. The menu is southern Italian—veal parmigiana, tortellini, and 19 or 20 other a la carte pastas, all fresh and made by hand, many quite inventive. Live jazz, swing, blues, or Celtic music

Harbour, or take bus no. 14 to Pleasant Street. Afternoon tea costs C$23 and includes a half-hour tour of the mansion and gardens, plus the opportunity to play a game of croquet. Open daily 11am to 5pm (tea served noon–4pm) May through the first Monday of September (weather permitting); phone ahead for reservations and Christmas hours.

If you want your tea in a historic garden setting, head over to **Abkhazi Garden,** 1964 Fairfield Rd. (© 250/598-8096; by car or bus no. 1 from downtown), where tea is served daily in the small, modernist house built by Russian Prince and Princess Abkhazi; see p. 238 for a description of the garden.

Set in impeccably maintained gardens, "Afternoon Tea at the Gardens" at the **Butchart Gardens Dining Room Restaurant ★★★**, 800 Benvenuto Ave. (© 250/652-8222; www.butchartgardens.com; bus no. 75), is a memorable experience. Sitting inside the Butchart mansion and looking out over the flowers, you can savor this fine tradition for C$27 per person. Tea is served daily year-round noon to 3pm; reservations recommended. Call ahead for winter hours.

What the **White Heather Tea Room ★★**, 1885 Oak Bay Rd. (© 250/595-8020), lacks in old-time atmosphere it makes up for with the sheer quality and value of the tea, and the charm of proprietress and tea mistress Agnes. Of all the numerous options on offer, all of them are less expensive than a similar experience at the Empress. For those feeling not so peckish, try the Wee Tea at C$14; for those a little hungrier, the Not So Wee Tea at C$18. If you feel like going the whole hog, try the Big Muckle Great Tea for Two at C$42. Open Tuesday through Saturday 10am to 5pm, tea served from 11:30am. Call for reservations.

starts at 8:30pm, Sunday through Wednesday. Howie hosts a very good brunch, also on Sunday. Children are welcome and enjoy this fun, laid-back environment.

1011 Broad St. © 250/386-1662. Reservations not accepted. Main courses C$12–C$26; Sun brunch C$10–C$15. AE, MC, V. Mon–Thurs 11:30am–10pm; Fri–Sat 11:30am–11pm; Sun 10am–10pm.

The Tapa Bar (Finds TAPAS The perfect meal for the commitment-shy, tapas are small and flavorful plates that you combine together to make a meal. Tapas to be sampled in this warm and welcoming spot include fried calamari, hearts of palm, and grilled portobello mushrooms. However, don't pass up on the *gambas al ajillo*—shrimp in a rich broth of garlic. The martini list is likely longer than the list of wines, but between the two there's plenty to keep the room buzzing until the witching hour.

620 Trounce Alley. © 250/383-0013. www.tapabar.ca. Tapas plates C$7–C$15. AE, MC, V. Mon–Thurs 11:30am–11pm; Fri–Sat 11:30am–midnight; Sun noon–10pm.

Zambri's ★ (Finds ITALIAN This little deli-restaurant in a strip mall off Yates Street has earned numerous accolades for its honest and fresh Italian cuisine served in an unpretentious, no-nonsense style. The lunch menu, served cafeteria-style, includes daily pasta specials and a handful of entrees such as fresh rockfish or salmon. In the evenings, the atmosphere is slightly more formal with table service and a regularly changing a la carte

Finding High-Octane Coffee

Good coffee is one of the great joys of life. Fortunately, Victoria's tea-party Englishness hasn't stopped it from buzzing into the same coffee-cuckooness that's engulfed Vancouver and the rest of the Pacific Northwest. Some to savor:

- On a sunny day, head for **Willie's,** 537 Johnson St. (ⓒ **250/381-8414**). Order your brew from the counter, and take a seat on the patio. This bakery serves up excellent sweets and great hot breakfasts. It's open Monday to Friday 7am to 5pm, Saturday 8am to 5pm, and Sunday 8:30am to 4:30pm.
- Out in Oak Bay, **Ottavio** ★, 2272 Oak Bay Ave. (ⓒ **250/592-4080;** www. ottaviovictoria.com), is a charming cafe, bakery, and deli with great Italian pastries, snacks, and coffee. It's open Tuesday to Saturday from 8am to 6pm, and Sunday from 10am to 6pm. Take bus no. 2 Oak Bay to Oak Bay Avenue and Monterey Street.
- The best coffee in Victoria, for my money, is served at the new **Caffè Artigiano,** 1140 Government St. (ⓒ **250/388-4147**). For years Caffè Artigiano steamed up its artful lattes only in Vancouver; this new outpost opened beside the lobby of the Bedford Regency Hotel in Victoria's oldest (1867) building. It's open Monday through Friday from 6am to 6pm, Saturday and Sunday from 7am to 6pm.

menu. Menu items veer from penne with sausage and tomato to pasta with chicken liver pâté or peas and Gorgonzola. Many diners come for the three-course dinner (C$40–C$45), though this is not served every night (call ahead).

110-911 Yates St. ⓒ **250/360-1171**. www.zambris.com. Reservations not accepted. Lunch C$8–C$14; dinner main courses C$22–C$25. MC, V. Tues–Sat 11:30am–2:30pm and 5–9pm.

INEXPENSIVE

Green Cuisine (Value) VEGETARIAN In addition to being undeniably healthy, Victoria's only fully vegan eatery offers remarkably tasty choices, with a self-serve salad bar, hot buffet, dessert bar, and full bakery. Available dishes range from pasta primavera salad to pumpkin tofu cheesecake, not to mention a wide selection of freshly baked breads (made with natural sweeteners and fresh-ground organic flour). Green Cuisine also has a large selection of freshly squeezed organic juices, smoothies, and shakes, as well as organic coffees and teas.

560 Johnson St. (in Market Sq.). ⓒ **250/385-1809**. www.greencuisine.com. Main courses C$4–C$10. AE, MC, V. Daily 10am–8pm (Sun 10am–5pm in winter).

J&J Wonton Noodle House ★ (Finds) CHINESE This place doesn't go overboard on the atmosphere, but it's perfectly pleasant and, more importantly, you won't find better noodles anywhere in Victoria. The kitchen is glassed in so you can watch the chefs spinning out noodles. Lunch specials—which feature different fresh seafood every day—are good and cheap, so expect a line of locals at the door. If you miss the specials, noodle soups, wontons, and other dishes are also quick, delicious, and inexpensive. Dinner is pricier.

Q V Bakery & Café BAKERY   The main attraction of this diner on the edge of downtown isn't so much its quality—though the coffee, muffins, cookies, and light meals like lasagnas and salads are all good—as its availability. On weekends, Q V is open 24 hours, which in Victoria is enough to make it very special indeed.

1701 Government St. ☏ **250/384-8831.** Main courses C$4–C$10. MC, V. Sun–Thurs 6am–3am; Fri–Sat 24 hr.

rebar (Kids) VEGETARIAN   Even if you're not hungry, it's worth dropping in here for a juice blend—say grapefruit, banana, melon, and pear with bee pollen or blue-green algae for added oomph. If you're hungry, rejoice: rebar is the city's premier purveyor of vegetarian comfort food. Disturbingly wholesome as that may sound, rebar is not only tasty, but fun, and a great spot to take the kids for brunch or breakfast. The room—in the basement of an 1890s heritage building—is bright and funky; the service is friendly and casual; and the food tends toward the simple and wholesome. The menu features quesadillas, omelets, and crisp salads. Juices are still the crown jewels, with more than 80 blends on the menu.

50 Bastion Sq. ☏ **250/361-9223.** www.rebarmodernfood.com. Main courses C$10–C$18. AE, MC, V. Mon–Thurs 8:30am–9pm; Fri–Sat 8:30am–10pm; Sun 8:30am–3:30pm. Reduced hours in the winter.

Sam's Deli DELI   If you don't like lines, avoid the lunch hour, for Sam's is *the* lunchtime soup-and-sandwich spot in Victoria. Sandwiches come in all tastes and sizes (mostly large), but the shrimp and avocado is the one to get. The homemade soups are excellent, as is the chili. And Sam's is right across the street from the harbor, making it unbeatably convenient.

805 Government St. ☏ **250/382-8424.** www.samsdeli.com. Main courses C$5–C$10. MC, V. Summer Mon–Fri 7:30am–10pm, Sat–Sun 8am–10pm; winter Mon–Fri 7:30am–5pm.

Siam Thai Restaurant (Value) THAI   Tucked away just half a block or so from the waterfront, this little local favorite offers good-quality Thai cooking. Menu items are starred from mild to spicy (one to four peppers), so there's no risk of having your tongue scorched, and include many signature Thai dishes such as pad thai noodles and a variety of curries (red, yellow, and green). The lunch specials are a great deal.

512 Fort St. ☏ **250/383-9911.** www.siamthai.ca. Main courses C$5–C$10. MC, V. Tues–Sun 11:30am–2pm and 5–9:30pm, Mon 5–9:30pm

---

5 EAST OF DOWNTOWN

EXPENSIVE

Paprika Bistro ★★ EASTERN EUROPEAN   Veteran chef George Szasz does the cooking and his wife Linda does the welcoming. It's a winning combo, and it's dedicated to the concept of "slow food." Paprika, a short walk from Willows Beach in Estevan Village, is housed in an attractive old building updated with a warm contemporary interior. The menu is classic bistro with Hungarian underpinnings. Start with some house-made sausage, then try the chicken curry with homemade chutney, the crispy, slow-braised pork belly, or potato strudel with duck confit and a sauce made from sour cherries and ginger. All the produce is local and organic. Paprika is a place to go for a memorable meal just a bit off the beaten track.

2524 Estevan Ave. ☏ **250/592-7424.** www.paprika-bistro.com. Reservations recommended. Main courses C$26–C$30. AE, MC, V. Mon–Sat 5–10pm. Bus: 11.

Fairfield Fish and Chips (Value) FISH & CHIPS   A colorful storefront sit-down restaurant on Fairfield Road welcomes budget-minded diners to this great neighborhood "chipper." The menu is limited to fish (halibut, haddock, cod, rockfish) burgers, and hand-cut chips, all excellent. The halibut burger is a scrumptious treat; so is the oyster burger. You can order your fish lightly or richly battered.

1277 Fairfield Rd. (C) **250/380-6880.** http://members.shaw.ca/fairfieldfishandchips. Main courses C$4–C$9. AE, MC, V. Tues–Sat 11:30am–8pm (Sun 10am–5pm in winter). Bus: 7.

Stage ★ BISTRO/PACIFIC NORTHWEST   Just a few minutes from downtown, in the funky Fernwood neighborhood, this smart, bustling new bistro and wine bar takes its name from the nearby Belfry Theatre (p. 273). Stage serves excellent and reasonably priced small plates that you can share. Choose from charcuterie, cheese, fish, meat, and vegetarian selections, all of them fresh and flavorful. There's a great selection of wines by the glass, as well.

1307 Gladstone Ave. (at Fernwood Rd.). (C) **250/388-4222.** Small plates C$3.50–C$12. AE, MC, V. Daily 5–10pm. Bus: 22.

6 OUTSIDE THE CENTRAL AREA

VERY EXPENSIVE

The Aerie ★★★ FRENCH   The dining room of this hotel enjoys a breathtaking view over Finlayson Inlet, the Strait of Juan de Fuca, and, on a clear day, the Olympic Mountains. The room itself is decorated with a 14-carat gold-leaf ceiling, crystal chandeliers, and a large open-hearth fireplace. As for the food—well, eating at this award-winning restaurant is definitely a culinary event. Chef Castro Boateng combines West Coast freshness with a "slow food" philosophy. A recent tasting menu included lobster and Dungeness crab salad, wild garlic soup, pan-seared sablefish, truffle and herb-crusted veal tenderloin, and a chocolate trio dessert. Excellent wine pairings, featuring local vintages, and impeccable service help to make meals even more memorable.

In the Aerie hotel (p. 221), 600 Ebedora Lane, Malahat. (C) **800/518-1933** or 250/743-7115. www.aerie. ca. Reservations required. Main courses C$38–C$43; tasting menu C$85. AE, DC, MC, V. Daily noon–3pm and 5:30–8:30pm (Sun brunch noon–2pm). Take Hwy. 1 to the Spectacle Lake turnoff; take the first right, and follow the winding driveway.

SeaGrille ★★★ PACIFIC NORTHWEST   The dining room of beautiful Brentwood Bay Lodge (p. 222), about a 20-minute drive north of Victoria, is all warm wood with giant windows overlooking Saanich Inlet. The food prepared here emphasizes fresh, seasonal, sustainable seafood such as B.C. salmon, arctic char, halibut, and sablefish. You can also choose from sushi, steaks, chops, and chicken breast, plus a vegetarian special, or order from the more casual pub menu, which includes thin-crust pizzas and staples such as fish and chips and a great halibut burger. To sample the best of what's on offer, go for the reasonably priced Chef's Menu. SeaGrille is a lovely place to dress up and dine well, but you won't feel out of place if you're in casual garb.

In Brentwood Bay Lodge and Spa, 849 Verdier Ave., Brentwood Bay. (C) **888/544-2079** or 250/544-5100. www.brentwoodbaylodge.com. Reservations recommended. Main courses C$22–C$42; Chef's Menu C$55. AE, DC, MC, V. Daily 11:30am–10:30pm (Fri–Sat until midnight). From Victoria, take Pat Bay Hwy. north to Keating Crossroads, turn left (west) to Saanich Rd., turn right (south) to Verdier Ave.

Sooke Harbour House ★★★ PACIFIC NORTHWEST   The dining room of this celebrated restaurant/inn offers spectacular views of Sooke Harbour, a relaxed atmosphere, and some of Canada's best and most inventive food. Dishes on the daily changing, seasonally adjusted menu are prepared with care, imagination, and flair. Ingredients are resolutely local: Many come from the inn's own organic garden or from the ocean at the Harbour House's doorstep. Depending on the season, dishes might include yellow split-pea-crusted ling cod or grilled pork tenderloin with a red wine meat-stock reduction and dried cherry and thyme compote. The wine cellar is one of the best in Canada. A four-course set menu or a seven-course Gastronomical Menu is offered nightly.

In the Sooke Harbour House Hotel (p. 223), 1528 Whiffen Spit Rd., Sooke. ✆ **800/889-9688** or 250/642-3421. www.sookeharbourhouse.com. Reservations required. Set menus C$75–C$125. MC, V. Daily 5:30–9pm. Take the Island Hwy. to the Sooke/Colwood turnoff (Junction Hwy. 14); continue on Hwy. 14 to Sooke; about 2km (1¼ miles) past the town's only traffic light, turn left onto Whiffen Spit Rd.

INEXPENSIVE

Six Mile Pub PUB GRUB   This pub dates from 1855 and has a rich history. Originally named the Parson's Bridge Hotel, it was filled with sailors when the Esquimalt Naval Base opened nearby in 1864. When Victoria elected to continue Prohibition until 1952, the Six Mile Pub became the hub for provincial bootleggers. Loyal locals still come for the atmosphere and the dinner specials. You can enjoy the warm ambience of the fireside room, or sit on the outdoor patio. Start with one of the 10 house brews on tap, then enjoy a hearty Cornish pasty (pronounced *pass*-tee, filled with mystery meat, peas, potatoes, and carrots in a pastry envelope), steak-and-mushroom pie, or juicy prime rib. If meat isn't part of your diet, try a veggie burger. They've recently gone "international," too, and serve various tapas, pot stickers, and more adventuresome seafood dishes. Just don't bring the kids—you must be at least 19 years old to enter.

494 Island Hwy. ✆ **250/478-3121.** www.sixmilepub.com. Main courses C$7–C$15. MC, V. Mon–Thurs 11am–11pm; Fri–Sat 11am–1am; Sun 10am–11pm.

WHERE TO DINE IN VICTORIA

OUTSIDE THE CENTRAL AREA

16

Exploring Victoria

Victoria's top draws are its waterfront—the beautiful view created by the Fairmont Empress and the Provincial Legislature Buildings on the edge of the Inner Harbour—and its historic Old Town. Two must-see attractions are the Butchart Gardens, about a 20-minute drive from downtown, and the Royal B.C. Museum on the Inner Harbour.

So attractive is this small capital city, though, that folks sometimes forget what a beautiful and wild part of the world it's set in. If you have time, step out of town and see some nature: sail out to see killer whales, beachcomb for crabs, kayak along the ocean shorelines, or hike into the hills for fabulous views and scenery. Pacific Rim National Park, a wild and wonderful wonderland on the west coast of Vancouver Island, is covered in Chapter 20.

1 SEEING THE SIGHTS

THE TOP ATTRACTIONS

Abkhazi Garden ★ (Finds)   It's a bit out of the way, about 5 minutes east of downtown by car, but if you're a nature lover, you'll love discovering this .4-hectare (1-acre) jewel box of a garden and the romantic story behind its creation. The wealthy Marjorie (Peggy) Pemberton-Carter met Russian Prince Nicholas Abkhazi in Paris in the 1920s, but they didn't meet again until 1946, by which time both had endured incarceration in prisoner-of-war camps (she in Shanghai as a British national, he in Germany). They wed, moved to Victoria, and set about creating a landscape garden that takes full advantage of a dramatic site that contains quiet woodland, rocky slopes, and lovely vistas. The Abkhazi's modernist summerhouse has been lovingly restored, as has the small, charming house where they eventually lived. The house is used as a tearoom and gift shop. Allow 1 hour.

1964 Fairfield Rd. (© **250/598-8096.** www.abkhazi.com. Admission Mar–Sept C$10 adults, C$7.50 seniors and students, free for children 12 and under; Oct–Feb by donation. Daily Mar–Sept 11am–5pm, Oct–Feb 11am–3pm, closed Dec 24–Jan; tearoom Mar–Sept daily 11:30am–4pm, otherwise 11am–3pm. Bus: 1 to Fairfield Rd. and Foul Bay.

Art Gallery of Greater Victoria ★★   Housed in a combination of contemporary exhibition space and a historic 19th-century mansion called Gyppeswick, the Art Gallery of Greater Victoria features a permanent collection of more than 15,000 objets d'art, drawn from Asia, Europe, and North America, though the gallery's primary emphasis is on Canada and Japan. The permanent **Emily Carr and Her Contemporaries** exhibit ★★ integrates Carr's works—from her earliest British-style watercolors to her compelling B.C. coast paintings to her final landscapes—with the works of her contemporaries in B.C. and Canada. (For more on Emily Carr, see "Emily Carr: Visionary from Victoria," p. 16.) There is also a gallery devoted to contemporary Canadian art. This museum is beautifully integrated into the neighborhood around it, and small enough so that you can see everything in about an hour.

Abkhazi Garden **13**
Art Gallery of Greater Victoria **11**
Craigdarroch Castle **12**
Emily Carr House **10**
The Fairmont Empress **4**
Helmcken House **5**
Maritime Museum of
  British Columbia **1**
Miniature World **3**
Pacific Undersea Gardens **8**
Provincial Legislature
  (Parliament Buildings) **7**
Royal B.C. Museum **6**
Royal London Wax Museum **9**
Victoria Bug Zoo **2**

1040 Moss St. © **250/384-4101.** www.aggv.bc.ca. Admission C$12 adults, C$10 seniors and students, C$2 children 6–17. Tues–Sat 10am–5pm (Thurs until 9pm); Sun noon–5pm. Bus: 11, 14, or 22.

British Columbia Aviation Museum ★   Located adjacent to Victoria International Airport, this small hangar is crammed with a score of original, rebuilt, and replica airplanes. The collection ranges from the first Canadian-designed craft ever to fly (a bizarre kitelike contraption) to slightly more modern water bombers and helicopters. Thursdays you can watch the all-volunteer crew in the restoration hangar working to bring these old aircraft back to life.

1910 Norseman Rd., Sidney. © **250/655-3300.** www.bcam.net. Admission C$7 adults, C$5 seniors, free for children 12 and under. Summer daily 10am–4pm; winter daily 11am–3pm. Closed Dec 25, Jan 1. Bus: Airport.

Butchart Gardens ★★★   These internationally acclaimed gardens were created after Robert Butchart exhausted the limestone quarry near his Tod Inlet home, about 22km (14 miles) from Victoria. His wife, Jenny, gradually landscaped the deserted eyesore into the resplendent Sunken Garden, opening it for public display in 1904. Over the years, a Rose Garden, Italian Garden, and Japanese Garden were added. The gardens—still in the family—now display more than a million plants throughout the year. On one stroll, passing through all of them, you'll be amazed at the gardeners' painstaking care and the beauty of the plantings.

On summer evenings, the gardens are illuminated with a variety of softly colored lights. June through September, musical entertainment is provided free Monday through Saturday evenings. You can even watch **fireworks displays** ★★★ on Saturdays in July and August. A very good lunch, dinner, and afternoon tea are offered in the Dining Room Restaurant (p. 233) in the historic residence; afternoon and high teas are also served in the Italian Garden (reservations recommended). Allow 2 to 3 hours; in peak summer months you'll encounter less congestion in the garden if you come very early or after 3pm. Admission prices vary according to season.

800 Benvenuto Ave., Brentwood Bay. © **866/652-4422** or 250/652-4422; dining reservations 250/652-8222. www.butchartgardens.com. Admission C$15–C$28 adults, C$7.75–C$14 youths 13–17, C$2–C$3 children 5–12, free for children 4 and under. Daily 9am–sundown (call or visit website for seasonal closing times); visitors can remain in gardens for 1 hr. after gate closes. Bus: 75; C$4.50 round-trip. Take Blanshard St. (Hwy. 17) north toward the ferry terminal in Saanich, then turn left on Keating Crossroads, which leads directly to the gardens—about 20 min. from downtown Victoria; it's impossible to miss if you follow the trail of billboards.

Craigdarroch Castle ★   What do you do when you've clawed, scraped, and bullied your way up from indentured servant to coal baron and richest man in British Columbia? You build a castle, of course, to show the other buggers what you're worth. Located in the highlands above Oak Bay, Robert Dunsmuir's home, built to cement his status and please his socially ambitious wife in the 1880s, is a stunner. The four-story, 39-room Highland-style castle is topped with stone turrets and chimneys, and filled with opulent Victorian splendor: detailed woodwork, Persian carpets, stained-glass windows, paintings, and sculptures. The nonprofit society that runs Craigdarroch does an excellent job showcasing the castle. You're provided with a self-tour booklet; several volunteer docents are happy to provide further information. The castle also hosts many events throughout the year, including theater performances, concerts, and dinner tours. Allow 30 minutes to 1 hour for castle tour. After visiting Craigdarroch, you might want to visit Hatley Park, the castle built by Dunsmuir's son in 1910 (see description below).

1050 Joan Crescent (off Fort St.). *©* **250/592-5323.** www.craigdarrochcastle.com. Admission C$12
adults, C$11 seniors, C$3.75 children 5–12, free for children 4 and under. June 15 to Labour Day daily
9am–7pm; day after Labour Day to June 14 daily 10am–4:30pm. Closed Dec 25–26 and Jan 1. Bus: 11 to
Joan Crescent. Take Fort St. out of downtown, just past Cook, and turn right on Joan Crescent.

Emily Carr House ★
The house where the great artist and writer Emily Carr was
born (see "Emily Carr: Visionary from Victoria," p. 16) has been restored to the condition it would have been in when Carr lived there. Many of the rooms have also been
hung with reproductions of her art or quotations from her writings, providing a good
introduction to this true B.C. original. On selected days throughout the year, Molly
Raher Newman, a local actress, portrays Emily Carr and regales visitors with Carr family
stories; call ahead to see if she is performing.

207 Government St. *©* **250/383-5843.** www.emilycarr.com. Admission C$6 adults, C$5 seniors and
students, C$4 youths 6–18, C$15 families. May–Sept Tues–Sat 11am–4pm.

Fort Rodd Hill & Fisgard Lighthouse
Perched on an outcrop of volcanic rock, the
Fisgard Lighthouse has guided ships toward Victoria's sheltered harbor since 1873. The
light no longer has a keeper (the beacon has long been automated), but the site itself has
been restored to its 1873 appearance. Two floors of exhibits in the light keeper's house
recount stories of the lighthouse, its keepers, and the terrible shipwrecks that gave this
coastline its ominous moniker "the graveyard of the Pacific."

Adjoining the lighthouse, **Fort Rodd Hill** is a preserved 1890s coastal artillery fort
sporting camouflaged searchlights, underground magazines, and its original guns. Audio-
visual exhibits bring the fort to life with the voices and faces of the men who served at
the outpost. Displays of artifacts, room re-creations, and historic film footage add to the
experience. Allow 1 to 2 hours.

603 Fort Rodd Hill Rd. *©* **250/478-5849.** www. fortroddhill.com. Admission C$4 adults, C$3.50 seniors,
C$2 children 6–16, free for children 5 and under, C$10 families. Feb 15–Oct daily 10am–5:30pm; Nov–Feb
14 daily 9am–4:30pm. Head north on Douglas St. until it turns into Hwy. 1. Stay on Hwy. 1 for 5km (3
miles), then take the Colwood exit (exit 10). Follow Hwy. 1A for 2km (1¹/₄ miles), then turn left at the 3rd
traffic light onto Ocean Blvd.; follow the signs to the site.

Hatley Park National Historic Site ★
Craigdarroch Castle (see above) was built
during the 1880s to serve as Scottish coal-mining magnate Robert Dunsmuir's home. In
1908, Dunsmuir's son, James, after a bitter inheritance battle with his mother, built his
own palatial manse, Hatley Castle, on a 226-hectare (559-acre) waterfront estate about
25 minutes from Victoria. The younger Dunsmuir reportedly commissioned architect
Samuel Maclure with the words, "Money doesn't matter, just build what I want." The bill
came to more than C$1 million (equivalent to about US$40 million today). The impressive castle, built of local stone in a hybrid Norman-Tudor fantasy style, is open to visitors
on guided tours on the weekend or on weekdays by appointment; the admission price is
way too high, but Hatley does make for an interesting excursion. As you're shown around
the castle, you have to use your imagination, since all the furniture was sold in 1937
(much of it is now in Craigdarroch Castle) and the rooms are either empty or filled with
office modules and equipment. The paneling and wood floors are truly remarkable,
though. The surrounding estate features several heritage gardens, including the tranquil
Japanese Garden, designed almost a century ago by the Japanese architect Isaburo
Kishida, who also designed the Japanese Gardens at Butchart Gardens. Allow 1 to 2 hours.

Royal Roads University, 200 Sooke Rd., Colwood. *©* **866/241-0674** or 250/391-2666. www.hatleypark.
ca. 1-hr. castle tour and garden access C$18 adults, C$12 youths 13–17, C$9.50 children 6–12, C$50
families (2 adults, 3 children). Gardens only C$4.75 adults, C$4.25 seniors, C$3.25 youths 13–17, children

12 and under free. Castle tours weekends year-round 10am–4pm, weekdays by appt; gardens and museum daily 10am–4pm. From Victoria, take Government St. north for about 2km (1¼ miles), turn left onto Gorge Rd. (Hwy. 1A) and follow about 20km (12 miles); turn left onto Sooke Rd. (Hwy. 14A) and look for signs to Royal Roads University or Hatley Park National Historic Site.

Maritime Museum of British Columbia

Housed in the former provincial courthouse, this museum is dedicated to recalling B.C.'s rich maritime heritage. The displays do a good job of illustrating maritime history, from the early explorers to the grand ocean liners. An impressive collection of ship models and paraphernalia—uniforms, weapons, gear—is complemented by photographs and journals. The museum also shows films in its Vice Admiralty Theatre. Allow 1 hour.

28 Bastion Sq. (© **250/385-4222.** www.mmbc.bc.ca. Admission C$10 adults, C$8 seniors and students, C$5 children 6–11, free for children 5 and under, C$25 families. Sept 16–June 14 daily 9:30am–4:30pm; June 15–Sept 15 daily 9:30am–5pm. Closed Dec 25. Bus: 5 to View St.

Miniature World (Kids)

It sounds cheesy—hundreds of dolls, miniatures, and scenes from old fairy tales, but Miniature World, inside the Fairmont Empress (the entrance is around the corner), is actually kinda cool, and kids love it. You walk in, and you're plunged into darkness, except for a moon, some planets, and a tiny spaceship flying up to rendezvous with an orbiting mother ship. This is the most up-to-date display. Farther in are re-creations of battle scenes, a miniature Canadian Pacific Railway running all the way across a miniature Canada, Victorian dollhouses, and a three-ring circus and midway. Better yet, most of these displays do something: The train moves at the punch of a button, and the circus rides whirl around and light up as simulated darkness falls. Allow about 30 minutes to see it all.

649 Humboldt St. (© **250/385-9731.** www.miniatureworld.com. Admission C$12 adults, C$9 youths, C$7 children 4–12, free for children 3 and under. Summer daily 8:30am–9pm; fall/winter daily 9am–5pm; spring daily 9am–7pm. Bus: 5, 27, 28, or 30.

Pacific Undersea Gardens

Savvy locals aren't very keen on the sight of this conspicuous white structure floating in the Inner Harbour, and those with some knowledge of Vancouver Island's marine environment will tell you that many of the creatures on display here are not indigenous to these waters. But your kids might enjoy a visit—or they might not, since the place is dark and kind of scary for little ones. A gently sloping walkway leads down to a glass-enclosed viewing area. One of the star attractions is a remarkably photogenic octopus (reputedly the largest in captivity). Injured seals and orphaned seal pups are cared for in holding pens alongside the observatory as part of a provincial marine-mammal rescue program. Allow 1 hour.

490 Belleville St. (© **250/382-5717.** www.pacificunderseagardens.com. Admission C$9.75 adults, C$8.75 seniors, C$7.75 youths 12–17, C$5.75 children 5–11, free for children 4 and under. Sept–Mar daily 10am–5pm; Apr–May daily 10am–6pm; June–Aug daily 9am–8pm. Bus: 5, 27, 28, or 30.

Provincial Legislature Buildings (Parliament Buildings) ★★

Designed by a 25-year-old Francis Rattenbury (see "Francis Rattenbury: Famous Architect and Murder Victim," in chapter 2) and built between 1893 and 1898 at a cost of nearly C$1 million, the Provincial Legislature Buildings (which some diehard Anglophiles insist on calling "the Parliament buildings") is one of the most noteworthy landmarks on Victoria's Inner Harbour. The 40-minute tour comes across at times like an eighth-grade civics lesson, but it's worth it to see the fine mosaics, marble, woodwork, and stained glass.

501 Belleville St. (© **250/387-3046.** www.leg.bc.ca. Free admission. Victoria Day (late May)–Labour Day Mon–Thurs 9am–5pm, Fri–Sun 9am–7pm; Sept–late May Mon–Fri 9am–5pm. Tours offered every 20–30 min. in summer; in winter call ahead for the public tour schedules as times vary due to school-group bookings. Bus: 5, 27, 28, or 30.

Something Fishy in Sidney

The **Ocean Discovery Centre** (© 250/665-7511; www.newmarinecentre.ca) in Sidney, 25 minutes north of Victoria, is Vancouver Island's newest way to learn about ocean ecology and explore British Columbia's unique sea life. Opened in June 2009, the center features 17 giant aquarium habitats that house hundreds of fish, invertebrates, and plant life—including octopus, wolf eels, rock fish, and colorful anemones. With floor-to-ceiling viewing panels highlighting the breath-taking array of local marine life, visitors are transported to the ocean depths and coastal environments. The center promotes environmental awareness and con-servation of the ocean environment and has a multimedia classroom designed to engage and inspire students from pre-school to high school about human con-nectivity to the ocean. The Ocean Discovery Centre is located in the Sidney Pier Building at the end of Beacon Street. Hours are 9am to 5pm daily. Admission is C$12 for adults, C$6 for children 6 to 17, and free for children 5 and under.

Royal B.C. Museum ★★★ (Kids)   One of North America's best regional museums, the Royal B.C. has a mandate to present the land and the people of coastal British Columbia. The second-floor **Natural History Gallery** showcases the coastal flora, fauna, and geography from the Ice Age to the present; it includes dioramas of a temperate rain-forest, a seacoast, and (particularly appealing to kids) a life-size woolly mastodon. The third-floor **Modern History Gallery** presents the recent past, including historically faith-ful re-creations of Victoria's downtown and Chinatown. On the same floor, the **First Peoples Gallery** ★★★ is an incredible showpiece of First Nations art and culture with rare artifacts used in day-to-day native life, a full-size re-creation of a longhouse, and a hauntingly wonderful gallery with totem poles, masks, and artifacts. The museum also has an **IMAX theater** showing an ever-changing variety of large-screen movies. On the way out (or in), be sure to stop by **Thunderbird Park,** beside the museum, where a cedar longhouse (Mungo Martin House, named after a famous Kwakiutl artist) houses a work-shop where native carvers work on new totem poles. To see and experience everything takes at least 2 hours.

675 Belleville St. © **888/447-7977** or 250/356-7226. www.royalbcmuseum.bc.ca. Admission C$15 adults; C$9.50 seniors, students, and youths; free for children 5 and under; C$38 families. IMAX C$11 adults, C$9.50 students, C$8.75 seniors and children 6–18, C$5 children 5 and under. Museum daily 9am–5pm (June–Sept Fri–Sat 9am–10pm); IMAX daily 9am–8pm. Closed Dec 25 and Jan 1. Bus: 5, 28, or 30.

Royal London Wax Museum (Overrated)   I've never understood why one of Victoria's most beautiful classical buildings, designed by Francis Rattenbury as a steamship ticket office and prominently perched right on the waterfront, had to be turned into a wax museum. And a pretty cheesy one at that. Inside, you can see the same dusty royal fam-ily and other figures ranging from Buddha to Goldie Hawn (the most recent addition, probably because she has a house in B.C.). It's doubtful even your kids will much enjoy it, except, of course, for the gory Chamber of Horrors (which might put off some kids). An hour is more than enough.

470 Belleville St. © **877/929-3228** or 250/388-4461. www.waxmuseum.bc.ca. Admission C$12 adults, C$11 seniors, C$9 students 13 and older, C$6 children 6–12, free for children 5 and under. Daily 9:30am–5pm. Bus: 5, 27, 28, or 30.

On the Lookout: Victoria's Best Views

In town, the best view of the Fairmont Empress and the Legislature comes from walking along the pedestrian path in front of the **Delta Ocean Pointe Resort,** off the Johnson Street Bridge. In summer, sit and enjoy a coffee or glass of wine with the view from the patio.

When the fishing fleets come in early in the morning, head over to **Fisherman's Wharf,** at St. Lawrence and Erie streets, to watch as the fishermen unload their catches. Later on, you can enjoy the sunset from the wharf along the eastern edge of the Inner Harbour or from the 18th floor of the **Vista 18 Restaurant,** 740 Burdett Ave. (© **250/382-9258**). Just south of downtown, you can see across the Strait of Juan de Fuca and the San Juan Islands to the mountains of the Olympic Peninsula from the **Ogden Point** breakwater, the top of the hill in **Beacon Hill Park,** or the walking path above the beach along **Dallas Road.** Farther afield, **Fort Rodd Hill** and **Fisgard Lighthouse** offer equally good views of the mountains, as well as a view of the ships in Esquimalt Harbour.

Mount Douglas ★, a 15-minute drive north of the city on Shelbourne Street, affords a panoramic view of the entire Saanich Peninsula, with a parking lot just a 2-minute walk from the summit. To the east, **Mount Work** offers an equally good view, but the walk up takes about 45 minutes. At the top of Little Saanich Mountain (about 16km/10 miles north of Victoria) stands the **Dominion Astrophysical Observatory,** 5071 W. Saanich Rd. (© **250/363-8262**), and its new **Centre of the Universe** interpretive center, which offers guided tours of the observatory from May to mid-June Monday through Friday from 1 to 4:30pm; cost is C$9 adults, C$8 seniors and students, C$5 youths 6 to 18, and C$23 families. Mid-June through August, hours are Tuesday through Saturday from 3 to 11pm; prices are C$12 adults, C$10 seniors and students, and C$7 youths 6 to 18. The observatory is closed to the public from September to May. There is no public transportation to the observatory, so you'll have to take a cab or drive.

Victoria Butterfly Gardens ★ (Kids)   This is a great spot for kids, nature buffs, or anyone who just likes butterflies. An ID chart allows you to identify the hundreds of exotic, colorful butterflies fluttering freely through this lush tropical greenhouse. Species range from the tiny Central American Julia (a brilliant orange butterfly about 3 in. across) to the Southeast Asian Giant Atlas Moth (mottled brown and red, with a wingspan approaching a foot). Naturalists are on hand to explain butterfly biology, and a display allows you to see the beautiful creatures emerge from their cocoons. You'll also see tropical birds, fish, and exotic plants, including an orchid collection. Allow 1 hour.

1461 Benvenuto Ave. (P.O. Box 190), Brentwood Bay. © **877/722-0272** or 250/652-3822. www.butterfly gardens.com. Admission C$12 adults, seniors, and students; C$6.50 children 3–12; free for children 2 and under. Daily Feb 10am–4pm; Mar–Apr and Nov–Dec 9:30am–4:30pm; May–Oct 9am–5pm. Closed Jan. Bus: 75.

First a trading post, and then a gold-rush town, a naval base, and a sleepy provincial capital, Victoria bears architectural witness to all these eras. What Vancouver mostly demolished, Victoria saved, so you really do have a feast of heritage buildings to enjoy. The best of Victoria's buildings date from the pre–World War I years, when gold poured in from the Fraser and Klondike rivers, fueling a building boom responsible for most of downtown.

Perhaps the most intriguing downtown edifice isn't a building but a work of art. The walls of **Fort Victoria,** which once spanned much of downtown, have been demarcated in the sidewalk with bricks bearing the names of original settlers and traders. Look on the sidewalk on the corner of Government and Fort streets.

Most of the retail establishments in Victoria's Old Town area are housed in 19th-century shipping warehouses that have been carefully restored as part of a heritage-reclamation program. You can take a **self-guided tour** of the buildings, most of which were erected between the 1870s and 1890s; their history is recounted on easy-to-read outdoor plaques. The majority of the restored buildings are between Douglas and Government streets from Wharf Street to Johnson Street. The most impressive structure once housed a number of shipping offices and warehouses, and is now the home of a 45-shop complex known as **Market Square,** 560 Johnson St./255 Market Sq. (© **250/386-2441**).

Some of the British immigrants who settled Vancouver Island during the 19th century built magnificent estates and mansions. In addition to architect Francis Rattenbury's crowning turn-of-the-20th-century achievements—the **Provincial Legislature Buildings,** 501 Belleville St. (completed in 1898), and the opulent **Fairmont Empress,** 721 Government St. (completed in 1908)—you'll find a number of other magnificent historic architectural sites.

Helmcken House, 610 Elliott St. Sq. (© **250/356-7226**), is the oldest house in B.C. still standing on its original site. Dr. John Sebastian Helmcken, a surgeon with the Hudson's Bay Company, set up house here in 1852 when he married the daughter of Governor Sir James Douglas. Originally a three-room log cabin, the house was built by Helmcken and expanded as both the prosperity and size of the family grew. It still contains its original furnishings, imported from England. Helmcken went on to become a statesman and helped negotiate the entry of British Columbia as a province into Canada. Helmcken House is open daily May through September from 10am to 5pm. Admission is C$5 for adults, C$4 for seniors and students, and C$3 for children.

CEMETERIES

Ross Bay Cemetery, 1495 Fairfield Rd., has to be one of the finest locations in all creation to spend eternity. Luminaries interred here include the first governor of the island, James Douglas; frontier judge Matthew Begbie; and West Coast painter Emily Carr. *An Historic Guide to Ross Bay Cemetery,* available in Munro's Books (p. 268) as well as other bookstores, gives details on people buried here and directions to grave sites.

Pioneer Square, on the corner of Meares and Quadra streets beside Christ Church, is one of British Columbia's oldest cemeteries. Hudson's Bay Company fur traders, ship captains, sailors, fishermen, and crew members from British Royal Navy vessels lie beneath the worn sandstone markers.

Contact the **Old Cemeteries Society** (© **250/598-8870;** www.oldcem.bc.ca) for more information on tours of both of these graveyards.

A Provincial Park, a Native Village & a Few Wineries

A short drive north from Victoria along the Island Highway takes you to three spots discussed below. The drive—along the ocean, up over the Malahat mountains, and then through the beautiful Cowichan Valley—is short enough to complete in one fairly leisurely day.

Goldstream Provincial Park   This quiet little valley overflowed with prospectors during the 1860s gold-rush days. Trails take you past abandoned mine shafts and tunnels as well as 600-year-old stands of towering Douglas fir, lodgepole pine, red cedar, indigenous yew, and arbutus trees. The **Gold Mine Trail** leads to Niagara Creek and the abandoned mine that was operated by Lt. Peter Leech, a royal engineer who discovered gold in the creek in 1858. **The Goldstream Trail** leads to the salmon spawning areas. (You might also catch sight of mink and river otters racing along this path.)

For general information on Goldstream Provincial Park and all other provincial parks on the South Island, contact **B.C. Parks** at ℂ **250/391-2300,** or check www.bcparks.ca. Throughout the year, Goldstream Park's **Freeman King Visitor Centre** (ℂ **250/478-9414**) offers guided walks, talks, displays, and programs geared toward kids but interesting for adults, too. Open daily 9am to 4pm. Take Hwy. 1 about 30 minutes north of Victoria. Note that B.C. government cutbacks have significantly reduced the number of events and services in most provincial parks. There is now a C$3 day-use parking fee at Goldstream.

Three species of salmon (chum, chinook, and steelhead) make **annual salmon runs** up the Goldstream River during October, November, December, and February. You can easily observe this natural wonder along the riverbanks. Contact the park's visitor center for details.

Quw'utsun' Cultural & Conference Centre ★   The main reason for visiting the town of Duncan is to see the Quw'utsun' Cultural and Conference Centre, 200 Cowichan Way (ℂ **877/746-8119** or 250/746-8119; www.quwutsun.ca). Created by the Cowichan People, the center brings First Nations culture to visitors in a way that's commercially successful yet still respectful of native traditions.

Longhouses along the crystal-clear Cowichan River give you an idea of the lodgings and ceremonial structures built by the aboriginal tribes who have lived in the area for thousands of years. Totem poles placed throughout the grounds represent traditional stories and legends. Though you can visit and take a self-guided tour year-round, it's best to tour the 2.4-hectare (6-acre) site with one of the native guides in July or August when there are ceremonial midday dances beside the river and a salmon barbecue (Tues–Sat at 1pm). Master and apprentice carvers create poles, masks, and feasting bowls in workshops open to the public; the traditional Cowichan art of knitting sweaters is also demonstrated. Original tools, clothing, and pictures are on display and a film presents an oral history of the Cowichan culture. A large gift shop in the complex sells native-made carvings, crafts, jewelry, clothing, silk-screen prints, and other items. The center and gift shops are open daily 9am to 5pm (until 4pm on weekends); closed weekends October through March. Summer admission is C$15 for adults, C$12 for seniors and youths 12 to 18, and C$8 for children 6 to 11; prices reduced October through March. (Salmon barbecue and dance performance costs C$35 for adults, C$33 for seniors and students, and C$24 for children.) You can enjoy authentic native foods (salmon, oysters, venison) at the **River Walk Café,** open June through September for lunch Monday through Saturday 11am to 4pm. All in all, a unique experience.

The **Duncan-Cowichan Visitor Info Centre** is at 381A Trans-Canada Hwy. (in the Overwaitea Mall), Duncan, B.C. V9L 3R5 (© **888/303-3337**). During July and August, it's open daily from 9am to 6pm; September through June, hours are Monday through Saturday 9am to 3pm.

The Cowichan Valley Wineries The vintners of gorgeous agricultural Cowichan Valley have gained a solid reputation for producing fine wines. Several of the wineries offer 1-hour tours—a great introduction for novices. They usually include a tasting of the vintner's art as well as a chance to purchase bottles or cases of your favorites. (Great gift idea because you will not find any of these wines outside British Columbia.)

Cherry Point Vineyards, 840 Cherry Point Rd., Cowichan (© **250/743-1272;** www.cherrypointvineyards.com), looks like a slice of California's Napa Valley. The wine-tasting room and gift shop are open daily April through September from 10am to 5pm (Oct–Mar Tues–Sat until 4pm). From May through September you can have lunch at the on-site bistro (main courses about C$15). **Blue Grouse Vineyards,** 4365 Blue Grouse Rd., Duncan (© **250/743-3834;** www.bluegrousevineyards.com), is a smaller winery that began as a hobby. April through September, it's open for tastings and on-site purchases Wednesday through Sunday 11am to 5pm (Oct–Dec Wed–Sat, Jan–Mar Sat only). **Merridale Cidery,** located just south of Cowichan Bay at 1230 Merridale Rd. (© **800/998-9908** in B.C. only, or 250/743-4293; www.merridalecider.com), is worth a stop to taste their artisan ciders, or for lunch at their bistro. Open daily 10:30am to 4:30pm (phone ahead to confirm open hours).

Cowichan Bay (off Hwy. 1, south of Duncan) is a pleasant half-hour drive from the wine country. Just southeast of Duncan, Cowichan Bay is a pretty little seaside town with a view of the ocean and a few attractions. The **Cowichan Bay Maritime Centre,** 1761 Cowichan Bay Rd., Cowichan Bay (© **250/746-4955;** www.classicboats.org), is a unique museum where boats are displayed in special pods seen from atop an old, picturesque pier that stretches out into the bay. It's open daily 9am to dusk; admission is by donation.

From the time the Hudson's Bay Company settled here in the mid-1800s, the historic **Old Town** was the center of the city's bustling business in shipping, fur trading, and legal opium manufacturing. Market Square and the surrounding warehouses once brimmed with exports like tinned salmon, furs, and timber bound for England and the United States. Now part of the downtown core, this is still a terrific place to find British, Scottish, and Irish imports (a surprising number of these shops date back to the early 1900s), souvenirs of all sorts, and even outdoor equipment for modern-day adventurers. Just a block north on Fisgard Street is **Chinatown.** Founded in 1858, it's the oldest Chinatown in Canada.

The **James Bay** area on the southern shores of the Inner Harbour is a quiet, middle-class, residential community. As you walk along its tree-lined streets, you'll find many older private homes that have maintained their original Victorian flavor.

Beautiful residential communities such as **Ross Bay** and **Oak Bay** have a more modern West Coast appearance, with houses and apartments perched on hills overlooking the beaches amid lush, landscaped gardens. Private marinas in these areas are filled with perfectly maintained sailing craft.

PARKS & GARDENS

With the mildest climate in Canada, Victoria's gardens are in bloom year-round. In addition to the world-renowned **Butchart Gardens** ★★★ (p. 240) the **Abkhazi Garden** ★ (p. 238), and the gardens at **Hatley Park National Historic Site** ★ (p. 241), several city parks attract strollers and picnickers. The 61-hectare (151-acre), 128-year old **Beacon Hill Park** ★ stretches from Southgate Street to Dallas Road between Douglas and Cook streets. In 1882, the Hudson's Bay Company gave this property to the city. Stands of indigenous Garry oaks (found only on Vancouver, Hornby, and Salt Spring islands) and manicured lawns are interspersed with floral gardens and ponds. Hike up Beacon Hill to get a clear view of the Strait of Georgia, Haro Strait, and Washington's Olympic Mountains. The children's farm (see "Especially for Kids," below), aviary, tennis courts, lawn-bowling green, putting green, cricket pitch, wading pool, and playground make this a wonderful place to spend a few hours with the family. The **Trans-Canada Highway's "Mile 0" marker** stands at the edge of the park on Dallas Road.

Just outside downtown, **Mount Douglas Park** has great views of the area, several hiking trails, and—down at the waterline—a picnic/play area with a trail leading to a good walking beach.

About 45 minutes southwest of town, **East Sooke Park** ★ is a 1,400-hectare (3,460-acre) microcosm of the West Coast wilderness: jagged seacoast, native petroglyphs, and hiking trails up to a 270m (886-ft.) hilltop. Access is via the Old Island Highway and East Sooke Road.

(**Finds**) **Strolling the Governor's Gardens**

Government House, the official residence of the lieutenant governor, is at 1401 Rockland Ave., in the Fairfield residential district. Around back, the hillside of Garry oaks is one of the last places to see what the area's natural fauna looked like before European settlers arrived. The rose garden at the front is quite sumptuous.

2 ESPECIALLY FOR KIDS

Victoria offers unique opportunities for kids to view creatures from whales and butter-flies to sea anemones and hermit crabs. The oldest of petting zoos is the **Beacon Hill Children's Farm,** Circle Drive, Beacon Hill Park (℃ **250/381-2532;** www.beaconhill park.ca), where kids can ride ponies; pet goats, rabbits, and other barnyard animals; and cool off in the wading pool. May to Labour Day, the farm is open daily 10am to 5pm (11am–4pm in the fall; 10am–4pm in the spring). Admission is by donation.

To see and touch (or be touched by) even smaller creatures, visit the **Victoria But-terfly Gardens** (p. 244). Closer to town is the **Victoria Bug Zoo,** 631 Courtney St. (℃ **250/384-BUGS** [2847]; www.bugzoo.bc.ca), home to praying mantises, stick insects, and African cockroaches. Admission is C$8 for adults, C$7 for seniors, C$6 for youths 13–19, C$5 for children 3 to 12, and free for children 2 and under; open Monday to Friday 11am to 4:30pm, Saturday 10am to 5pm, and Sundays 11am to 5pm.

The **Pacific Undersea Gardens** (p. 242) is a face-to-face introduction to some of the sea creatures of the Pacific coast. Better still, take the kids out to explore any of the tide pools on the coast. **Botanical Beach Provincial Park** ★★★, near Port Renfrew, is excel-lent, though the 60km (37-mile) drive west along Hwy. 14A may make it a bit far for some. Closer to town, try **French Beach** ★ or **China Beach** ★ (also along Hwy. 14A), or even the beach in **Mount Douglas Park.** Find a good spot, bend down over a tide pool, and look—or else pick up a rock to see crabs scuttle away. Remember to put the rocks back where you found them.

In **Goldstream Provincial Park** (p. 246), the Visitor Centre (℃ **250/478-9414**) has nature programs and activities geared especially for children. The **Swan Lake Christmas Hill Nature Sanctuary,** 3873 Swan Lake Rd. (℃ **250/479-0211;** www.swanlake.bc.ca), offers a number of nature-themed drop-in programs over the summer, including Insect-mania and Reptile Day.

Back in the city, the **Royal B.C. Museum** ★★★ (p. 243) has many displays geared toward kids, including a rather dramatic and amazing life-size reconstruction of a woolly mastodon.

Miniature World (p. 242), with its huge collection of dolls and dollhouses, model trains, and diminutive circus displays, is a favorite with kids of all ages.

Located in Elk and Beaver Lake Regional Park (p. 252), **Beaver Lake** is a great fresh-water spot where kids can enjoy a day of watersports and swimming in safe, lifeguard-attended waters.

3 ORGANIZED TOURS

BUS TOURS

Gray Line of Victoria, 4196 Glanford Ave. (℃ **800/663-8390** or 250/388-6539; www. grayline.com), conducts a number of tours of Victoria and Butchart Gardens. The 1½-hour "Grand City Tour" costs C$28 for adults and C$18 for children ages 5 to 11. There are daily departures throughout the year, usually at noon and 2pm. For other tours, check the website.

Victoria Harbour Ferries, 1234 Wharf St. (© **250/708-0201;** www.victoriaharbour ferry.com), offers a terrific 45-minute **harbor tour** ★ for C$20 adults, C$18 seniors, and C$10 for children under 12. Harbor tours depart from seven stops around the Inner Harbour every 15 or 20 minutes daily 10am to 4pm (longer hours May–Sept). If you wish to stop for food or a stroll, you can get a token good for reboarding at any time during the same day. A 50-minute **Gorge Tour** ★ takes you to the gorge opposite the Johnson Street Bridge, where tidal falls reverse with each change of the tide. The price is the same as for the harbor tour; June through September, gorge tours depart from the dock in front of the Fairmont Empress every half-hour 9am to 8:15pm; at other times the tours operate less frequently, depending on the weather. The ferries are 12-person, fully enclosed boats, and every seat is a window seat.

Heritage Tours and Daimler Limousine Service, 713 Bexhill Rd. (© **250/474-4332**), guides you through the city, Butchart Gardens, and Craigdarroch Castle in a six-passenger British Daimler limousine. Rates start at C$75 for the Daimler per hour per vehicle (not per person).

The bicycle-rickshaws operated by **Kabuki Kabs,** 613 Herald St. (© **250/385-4243;** www.kabukikabs.com), can usually be found on the causeway in front of the Fairmont Empress or hailed in the downtown area. Prices for a tour are C$1 per minute for a two-person cab.

Tallyho Horse-Drawn Tours, 2044 Milton St. (© **250/383-5067;** www.tallyho tours.com), has conducted tours of Victoria in horse-drawn carriages and trolleys since 1903. Horse-drawn trolley and carriage excursions start at the corner of Belleville and Menzies streets. Fares for the trolley are C$15 for adults, C$12 for seniors, C$9 for students, and C$7 for children 17 and under. Trolley tours operate daily every 30 minutes 9am to 3pm during summer. An assortment of private carriage tours (maximum six people) are available throughout the year and in the summer from 10am to 10pm; cost runs from C$50 for 15 minutes, to C$240 for 2 hours.

To get a bird's-eye view of Victoria, take a 30-minute tour with **Harbour Air Sea-planes,** 1234 Wharf St. (© **800/665-0212** or 250/384-2215; www.harbour-air.com). Rates are C$99 per person. For a romantic evening, try the "Fly and Dine" to Butchart Gardens deal; C$229 per person includes the flight to the gardens, admission, dinner, and a limousine ride back to Victoria.

Fresh Air Tours Ltd. (© **877/868-7790**) offers year-round scenic sightseeing mini-coach and cycling tours to Victoria's highlights, wineries, Butchart Gardens, the town of Sidney, Salt Spring Island, and seasonal tours such as the Halloween pumpkin patch and Christmas lights. The company provides complimentary hotel pickup and drop-off; on cycling tours, bicycles, helmets, and support van are provided.

WALKING TOURS

Chapter 17 has two self-guided walking tours around Victoria. If you'd prefer to have a guide, **Victoria Bobby Walking Tours** (© 250/995-0233; www.walkvictoria.com) offers a leisurely story-filled walk around Old Town. Tours depart at 11am daily, May through September 15, from the Visitor Centre on the Inner Harbour; cost is C$15 per person.

Discover the Past (© 250/384-6698; www.discoverthepast.com) organizes interesting walks year-round. In the summer, **Ghostly Walks** explores Victoria's haunted Old Town, Chinatown, and historic waterfront; tours depart from the front of the Visitor Info Centre nightly at 7:30pm from May through October, Saturdays at 7:30pm from

> **Finds**   **Victoria's Cemetery Tours**
>
> The **Old Cemetery Society of Victoria** (📞 **250/598-8870;** www.oldcem.bc.ca)
> runs regular cemetery tours throughout the year. Particularly popular are the
> **Lantern Tours of the Old Burying Ground** ★, which begin at the Cherry Bank
> Hotel, 845 Burdett Ave., at 9pm nightly in July and August. The tour lasts about 1
> hour. On Sundays throughout the year, the Society offers historically focused
> tours of **Ross Bay Cemetery.** Tours depart at 2pm from Starbucks in the Fairfield
> Plaza, 1594 Fairfield Rd., across from the cemetery gate. Both tours are C$5 per
> person. Call first to make certain the tour is on.

November through February, and Fridays and Saturdays at 7:30pm in March and April.
The cost is C$12 adults, C$10 seniors and students, C$8 children 6 to 10, and C$30 for
families. Check the website for other walks.

The name says it all for **Walkabout Historical Tours** (📞 **250/592-9255;** www.
walkabouts.ca). Charming guides lead tours of the Fairmont Empress, Victoria's Chinatown, Antique Row, and Old Town Victoria, or will help you with your own itinerary.
The Empress Tour costs C$10 and begins at 10am daily in the Empress Tea Lobby. Other
tours have different prices and starting points.

The **Victoria Heritage Foundation,** No. 1 Centennial Sq. (📞 **250/383-4546**), offers
the excellent free pamphlet *James Bay Heritage Walking Tour.* The well-researched pamphlet (also available at the Visitor Info Centre) describes a self-guided walking tour
through the historic James Bay neighborhood.

ECOTOURS

The 2-hour **wilderness cruise** ★★★ departing from the marina at **Brentwood Bay
Lodge & Spa** (p. 222; 📞 **888/544-2079** or 250/544-2079), provides an extremely informative and enjoyable exploration of Finlayson Inlet, a deep fjord with a fascinating history.
On the cruise it's not uncommon to spot eagles, seals, and sometimes whales. Cost is C$69
per person; cruises are available from mid-May through mid-October; call to reserve.

4 OUTDOOR ACTIVITIES

Sports Rent, 1950 Government St. (📞 **250/385-7368;** www.sportsrentbc.com), is a
great general equipment and watersports rental outlet.

BEACHES

The most popular beach is Oak Bay's **Willows Beach,** at Beach and Dalhousie roads
along the esplanade. The park, playground, and snack bar make it a great place to spend
the day building a sand castle. **Gyro Beach Park,** Beach Road on Cadboro Bay, is
another good spot for winding down. At the **Ross Bay Beaches,** below Beacon Hill Park,
you can stroll or bike along the promenade at the water's edge.

For a taste of the wild and rocky west coast, hike the oceanside trails in beautiful **East
Sooke Regional Park** ★. Take Hwy. 14A west, turn south on Gillespie Road, and then
take East Sooke Road.

Two inland lakes give you the option of swimming in fresh water. **Elk and Beaver Lake Regional Park,** on Patricia Bay Road, is 11km (6¾ miles) north of downtown Victoria; to the west is **Thetis Lake,** about 10km (6¼ miles; Hwy. 1 to exit 10 or 1A onto Old Island Hwy. 14, turn right at Six Mile Pub and follow the signs), where locals shed all their clothes but none of their civility.

BIKING

Biking is one of the best ways to get around Victoria. The 13km (8-mile) **Scenic Marine Drive bike path** ★★ begins at Dallas Road and Douglas Street, at the base of Beacon Hill Park. The paved path follows the walkway along the beaches before winding up through the residential district on Beach Drive. It eventually turns left and heads south toward downtown Victoria on Oak Bay Avenue. The **Inner Harbour pedestrian path** has a bike lane for cyclists who want to take a leisurely ride around the entire city seawall. The new **Galloping Goose Trail** (part of the Trans-Canada Trail) runs from Victoria west through Colwood and Sooke all the way up to Leechtown. If you don't want to bike the whole thing, you can park at numerous places along the way, as well as several places where the trail intersects with public transit. Contact **B.C. Transit** (✆ **250/382-6161;** www.bctransit.com) to find out which bus routes take bikes. Bikes and child trailers are available at **Cycle B.C. Rentals,** 707 Douglas St. (May–Oct; ✆ **250/380-2453;** www.cyclebc.ca). Rentals run C$7 per hour and C$24 per day; helmets and locks included.

BIRDING

The **Victoria Natural History Society** (www.vicnhs.bc.ca) runs regular weekend birding excursions. Their **event line** (✆ **250/479-2054**) lists upcoming outings and gives contact numbers. **Goldstream Provincial Park** (p. 246) and the village of **Malahat**—both off Hwy. 1 about 40 minutes north of Victoria—are filled with dozens of varieties of migratory and local birds, including eagles. **Elk and Beaver Lake Regional Park,** off Hwy. 17, has some rare species such as the rose-breasted grosbeak and Hutton's vireo. Ospreys also nest there. **Cowichan Bay,** off Hwy. 1, is the perfect place to observe ospreys, bald eagles, great egrets, and purple martins.

BOATING, CANOEING & KAYAKING

Ocean River Sports, 1824 Store St. (✆ **800/909-4233** or 250/381-4233; www.oceanriver.com), can equip you with everything from a single or double kayak or a canoe to life jackets, tents, and dry-storage camping gear. Rental costs for a single kayak range from C$25 for 2 hours to C$40 per day. Multiday and weekly rates are also available. The company also offers numerous **guided tours** ★ of the Gulf Islands and the coast. For beginners, try the guided 5½-hour Explorer Tour of the coast around Victoria or Sooke for C$115. They also offer a guided 3-day/2-night trip to the nearby Gulf Islands for C$635.

Rowboats, kayaks, and canoes are available for hourly or daily rental from **Great Pacific Adventures,** 811 Wharf St. (✆ **877/733-6722** or 250/386-2277; www.greatpacificadventures.com).

Blackfish Wilderness Expeditions (✆ **250/216-2389;** www.blackfishwilderness.com) offers a number of interesting kayak-based tours such as the kayak/boat/hike combo, where you boat to the protected waters of the Discovery Islands, hike one of the islands, and kayak to see the pods of resident killer whales that roam the waters around Victoria. Day tours start at C$70 per person.

DIVING

The coastline of **Pacific Rim National Park** (see chapter 20) is known as "the graveyard of the Pacific." Submerged in the water are dozens of 19th- and 20th-century shipwrecks and the marine life that has taken up residence in them. Underwater interpretive trails help identify what you see in the artificial reefs. If you want to take a look for yourself, contact the **Ogden Point Dive Centre,** 199 Dallas Rd. (© **888/701-1177** or 250/380-9119; www.divevictoria.com), which offers a two-day Race Rocks and Shipwreck Tour package that starts at C$299 per person, including all equipment and transportation. The **Saanich Inlet,** about a 20-minute drive north of Victoria, is a pristine fjord considered one of the top cold-water diving areas in the world (glass sponges are a rarity found only here). Classes and underwater scuba adventures can be arranged through **Brentwood Bay Lodge & Spa** (p. 222), Canada's only luxury PADI (Professional Association of Diving Instructors) dive resort.

FISHING

Saltwater fishing's the thing out here, but unless you know the area, it's best to take a guide. **Adam's Fishing Charters** (© **250/370-2326;** www.adamsfishingcharters.com) is located on the Inner Harbour down below the Visitor Info Centre. Chartering a boat and guide starts at C$95 per hour per boat, with a minimum of 5 hours.

To fish, you need a saltwater fishing license. Licenses (including the salmon surcharge) for nonresidents cost C$7.50 for 1 day, C$20 for 3 days, and C$33 for 5 days. Tackle shops sell licenses, have details on current restrictions, and often carry copies of the *B.C. Tidal Waters Sport Fishing Guide* and *B.C. Sport Fishing Regulations Synopsis for Non-Tidal Waters.* Independent anglers should also pick up the *B.C. Fishing Directory and Atlas.* **Robinson's Sporting Goods Ltd.,** 1307 Broad St. (© **250/385-3429**), is a reliable source for information, recommendations, lures, licenses, and gear. For the latest fishing hot spots and recommendations on tackle and lures, check out **www.sportfishingbc.com**. You'll find official fishing information at the Fisheries and Oceans Canada website, **www.pac.dfo-mpo.gc.ca**.

GOLFING

Victoria's Scottish heritage doesn't stop at the tartan shops. The greens here are as beautiful as those at St. Andrews. The **Cedar Hill Municipal Golf Course,** 1400 Derby Rd. (© **250/475-7151;** www.golfcedarhill.com), the busiest course in Canada, is an 18-hole, par-67 public course 3km (1¾ miles) from downtown Victoria. It's open on a first-come, first-served basis; daytime weekday greens fees are C$40 to C$45 and twilight fees (after 3pm) are C$25 to C$30. Golf clubs can be rented for C$15. The **Cordova Bay Golf Course,** 5333 Cordova Bay Rd. (© **250/658-4444;** www.cordovabaygolf.com), is northeast of the downtown area. Designed by Bill Robinson, the par-71, 18-hole course features 66 sand traps and some tight fairways. Greens fees are C$46 to C$60 depending on day and season; twilight fees range from C$39 to C$59.

The newest star of Vancouver Island golf courses, and the most expensive to play, is the 18-hole, 7,212-yard, par-72 course designed by Jack Nicklaus and his son for **Westin Bear Mountain Golf Resort & Spa,** 1999 Country Club Way (© **888/533-2327** or 250/391-7160 tee time bookings). Golf carts (included with fee) and collared shirts (blue jeans not permitted) are mandatory on this upscale, mountaintop course that features breathtaking views and a spectacular 19th hole for recreational betting. Nonmember greens fees, depending on when you reserve and the time you play, range from C$65 to C$145.

253

EXPLORING VICTORIA

16

OUTDOOR ACTIVITIES

You can call **A-1 Last Minute Golf Hot Line** at $\textcircled{c}$ **800/684-6344** for substantial discounts and short-notice tee times.

HIKING

Goldstream Provincial Park (30 min. west of downtown along Hwy. 1; p. 246) is a tranquil site for a short hike through towering cedars and past clear, rushing waters.

The hour-long hike up **Mount Work** provides excellent views of the Saanich Peninsula and a good view of Finlayson Arm. The trail head is a 30- to 45-minute drive. Take Hwy. 17 north to Saanich, then take Hwy. 17A (W. Saanich Rd.) to Wallace Drive, turn right on Willis Point Drive, and right again on Ross-Durrance Road, looking for the parking lot on the right. Signs are posted along the way. Equally good, though more of a scramble, is the hour-plus climb up **Mount Finlayson** in Gowland-Tod Provincial Park (take Hwy. 1 west, get off at the Millstream Rd. exit, and follow Millstream Rd. north to the very end).

The very popular **Sooke Potholes** trail wanders up beside a river to an abandoned mountain lodge. Take Hwy. 1A west to Colwood, then Hwy. 14A (Sooke Rd.). At Sooke, turn north on Sooke River Road, and follow it to the park.

For a taste of the wild and rocky west coast, hike the oceanside trails in beautiful **East Sooke Regional Park** ★★. Take Hwy. 14A west, turn south on Gillespie Road, and then take East Sooke Road.

For serious backpacking, go 104km (65 miles) west of Victoria on Hwy. 14A to Port Renfrew and the challenging **West Coast Trail** ★★★, extending 77km (48 miles) from Port Renfrew to Bamfield in a portion of **Pacific Rim National Park** ★★★ (p. 278). The trail was originally a lifesaving trail for shipwrecked sailors. Plan a 7-day trek for the entire route; reservations are required, so call $\textcircled{c}$ **604/663-6000.** The trail is rugged and often wet, but the scenery changes from old-growth forest to magnificent secluded sand beaches, making it worth every step. You may even spot a few whales along the way. **Robinson's Outdoor Store,** 1307 Broad St. ($\textcircled{c}$ **250/385-3429;** www.robinsonsoutdoors. com), is a good place to gear up before you go. At Robinson's, ask about the newer, less challenging 48km-long (30-mile) **Juan de Fuca Marine Trail** ★★ connecting Port Renfrew and the Jordan River.

Island Adventure Tours ($\textcircled{c}$ **866/812-7103** or 250/812-7103; www.islandadventure tours.com) has a number of options for folks wanting to explore the outdoors. The 6-hour guided **rainforest walks** cost C$95 or a full-day hike including transportation and lunch. For the deluxe Juan de Fuca experience, sign up for a 3-day, fully catered backpacking trip along the rugged West Coast Trail for C$499.

For something less strenuous but still scenic, try the **Swan Lake Christmas Hill Nature Sanctuary,** 3873 Swan Lake Rd. ($\textcircled{c}$ **250/479-0211;** www.swanlake.bc.ca). A floating boardwalk winds its way through this 40-hectare (99-acre) wetland past resident swans; the adjacent Nature House supplies feeding grain on request.

PARAGLIDING

Vancouver Island Paragliding ($\textcircled{c}$ **250/514-8595;** www.viparagliding.com) offers tandem paraglide flights for C$175. The pilot steers; you hang on and enjoy the adrenaline rush. Flights last around 25 minutes. They also offer 1-day training courses that allow you to take off on your own.

SAILING

One of the most exciting ways to explore the Strait of Juan de Fuca is aboard the *Thane*, on a **3-hour sail tour** ★★ for C$60 per person. The vessel is moored in front of the Fairmont Empress. Daily summer sailings leave at 9am, 1pm, and 5pm. Guests are welcome to bring a picnic. Contact the **SV *Thane*** (© **877/788-4263** or 250/885-2311).

SKIING

Mount Washington Ski Resort, P.O. Box 3069, Courtenay, B.C. V9N 5N3 (© **888/ 231-1499** or 250/338-1380; 250/338-1515 for snow report; www.mtwashington.bc.ca), in the Comox Valley is British Columbia's third-largest ski area, a 5-hour drive from Victoria and open year-round (for hiking or skiing, depending on the season). A 480m (1,575-ft.) vertical drop and 50 groomed runs are serviced by four chairlifts and a beginners' tow. The terrain is popular among snowboarders and well suited to intermediate skiers. For cross-country skiers, 31km (19 miles) of track-set Nordic trails connect to Strathcona Provincial Park. Full-day rates are C$59 for adults, C$48 for seniors and students, C$31 for youths 6 to 12, and free for kids 5 and under. Equipment rentals are available. Located 100km (62 miles) north of Nanaimo; take Hwy. 19 to exit 130.

WATERSPORTS

The **Crystal Pool & Fitness Centre,** 2275 Quadra St. (© **250/361-0732**), is Victoria's main aquatic facility. The 50m (164-ft.) lap pool; children's pool; diving pool; sauna; whirlpool; and steam, weight, and aerobics rooms are open Monday through Thursday 5:30 to 11pm, Friday 5:30am to 10:30pm, Saturday 6am to 6pm, and Sunday 8:30am to 4pm. Drop-in admission is C$4.75 for adults, C$3.75 for seniors and students, C$2.50 for children 6 to 12, and free for children 5 and under. **Beaver Lake** in Elk and Beaver Lake Regional Park (see "Birding," above) has lifeguards on duty as well as picnicking facilities along the shore.

Surfing has recently taken off on the island. The best surf is along the west coast at **China, French,** and **Mystic beaches** ★. To get there, take Blanshard Street north from downtown, turn left onto Hwy. 1 (Trans-Canada Hwy.), then after about 10km (6¼ miles), take the turnoff onto Hwy. 14A (Sooke Rd.). Follow Hwy. 14A north along the coast. The beaches are well signposted.

Windsurfers skim along outside the Inner Harbour and on Elk Lake when the breezes are right. Though French Beach, off Sooke Road on the way to Sooke Harbour, has no specific facilities, it is a popular local windsurfing spot.

WHALE-WATCHING

The waters surrounding the southern tip of Vancouver Island teem with orcas (killer whales), harbor seals, sea lions, harbor and Dall porpoises, and bald eagles. All whale-watching companies offer basically the same tour; the main difference comes in the equipment they use: Some use a 12-person Zodiac, where the jolting ride is almost as exciting as seeing the whales, whereas others take a larger, more leisurely craft. Both offer excellent platforms for seeing whales. In high season (June–Labour Day), most companies offer several trips a day. Always ask if the outfitter is a "responsible whale-watcher"—that is, doesn't go too close to disturb or harass the whales.

Seafun Safaris Whale Watching, 950 Wharf St. (© **877/360-1233** or 250/360-1200; www.seafun.com), is just one of many outfits offering whale-watching tours in Zodiacs and covered boats. Adults and kids will learn a lot from the naturalist guides, who explain the behavior and nature of the orcas, gray whales, sea lions, porpoises, cormorants, eagles, and harbor seals encountered along the way. Fares for the Zodiac tour are C$109 for adults and C$79 for children.

Other reputable companies include **Prince of Whales,** 812 Wharf St. (© **888/383-4884** or 250/383-4884; www.princeofwhales.com), just below the Visitor Info Centre, and **Orca Spirit Adventures** (© **888/672-ORCA** [6722] or 250/383-8411; www.orcaspirit.com), which departs from the Coast Harbourside Hotel dock.

Victoria Strolls & Biking Tour

Victoria has always been a transient's town, from miners and mariners to loggers and lounge-lizards, from hard-core hippies to retired but involved investment counselors. On three occasions I've packed up and moved from Victoria myself.

—Folk Singer Valdy

Victoria's ambience is made for the wanderer, its pavements picture-perfect for perambulation—Victoria, in short, is a great place to walk, bike, in-line skate, skateboard, or scooter. The tours below work no matter what your favored form of transportation.

WALKING TOUR 1	THE INNER HARBOUR

START AND FINISH:	The Visitor Centre (812 Wharf St.) on the Inner Harbour.
TIME:	2 hours, not including shopping, museum, and pub breaks.
BEST TIME:	Late afternoon, when the golden summer sunlight shines on the Fairmont Empress.
WORST TIME:	Late in the evening, when the shops close and the streets empty.

Victoria was born on the Inner Harbour. When the Hudson's Bay Company's West Coast head of operations, James Douglas, happened across this sheltered inlet in 1843 while searching for a new corporate HQ, it was love at first sight. "The place appears a perfect Eden," he wrote to a friend. High praise indeed, although as Douglas was pretty deep into local real estate, his words should be taken with a wee bit of salt. His confidence in the location certainly paid off, however, for less than 20 years after Douglas set foot onshore, the native stands of Garry oak had been supplanted by small farms, the town was choked with miners and mariners, and the harbor was full of ships, many of which had circled the globe. This tour circumnavigates the Inner Harbour, showing some of its lesser-known nooks and crannies while providing an opportunity to enjoy the same view seen by many a Victorian sailor.

We begin our tour at the:

❶ Victoria Visitor Centre
At 812 Wharf St., this is without a doubt one of the finest-looking visitor centers in the world—a masterful Art Deco pavilion topped with a shining white obelisk rising high above the Inner Harbour. It would be a tribute to the taste and vision of city tourism officials, except that it started out life as a gas station.

From the Visitor Centre, thread your way south through the jugglers and musicians on the causeway until you're opposite 721 Government St., where stands:

❷ The Fairmont Empress
"There is a view, when the morning mists peel off the harbor, where the steamers tie up, of the Houses of Parliament on one hand, and a huge hotel on the other, which is an example of cunningly fitted-in

waterfronts and facades worth a very long journey." Thus spoke Rudyard Kipling during a visit to the city in 1908. If he'd come only 5 years earlier, he would've been looking at a nasty, garbage-choked swamp. The causeway was then a narrow bridge over the tidal inlet, and as Victorians made a habit of pitching their refuse over the rail, the bay was, not surprisingly, a stinking cesspit of slime. In 1900, the ever-shrewd Canadian Pacific Railway made an offer to the city—we'll build a causeway and fill in the stinky bay if you let us keep the land. The city jumped at the offer. Little was expected—the land was swamp after all. But taking their cue from the good folks in Amsterdam, the CPR drove long pilings down through the muck to provide a solid foundation. And on top of that, they built the Fairmont Empress. The architect was Francis Rattenbury, and his design was masterful, complementing his own Provincial Legislature Buildings to create the view that has defined the city ever since.

Around the south side of the Fairmont Empress is a formal rose garden—worth poking your nose in for a sniff. Cut through the garden, cross over Belleville Street, and continue another half-block east to the corner of Douglas Street, where you'll find:

❸ Thunderbird Park

The park is instantly recognizable by its forest of totem poles. Even if you've over-dosed on the ubiquitous 6-inch souvenir totem, take a second look at these. The original poles on this site had been collected in the early 1900s from various villages up and down the coast. Some decades later, when officials decided the severely weathered poles needed restoring, they discovered the art of native carving had eroded even more than their collection of poles. From all the thousands of carvers on the coast, only one man still carried on the craft. In 1952, Kwakiutl artist Mungo Martin set up a carving shed on the park grounds and began the work of restoration. Martin replaced or repaired all the existing poles

while teaching his son and step-grandson-in-law to carve. Seeing them at work renewed public interest in the form. Other young artists came to learn and train, which led to a revival of totem carving and native artistry among coastal natives.

All poles have a purpose; most tell a story. The stories associated with the poles in Thunderbird Park have unfortunately been lost, but many of the figures are easily recognized, including Thunderbird (look for the outstretched wings and curly horns on the head), Raven, Bear, and Killer Whale.

On the edge of the park is the shed where Martin carved many of the poles. Feel free to poke your head in to take a look and ask the carvers what they're up to. The artists generally welcome questions and enjoy sharing their stories.

Farther back in the park, at 610 Elliott St. Sq., stands the:

❹ Helmcken House

Dr. John Sebastian Helmcken, a surgeon with the Hudson's Bay Company, set up house here in 1852 when he married the daughter of Governor Sir James Douglas. Originally a three-room log house, the house was built by Helmcken and expanded as both the prosperity and size of the family grew. It's now the oldest house in B.C. to remain on its original site. Helmcken went on to become a statesman and helped negotiate the entry of British Columbia as a province into Canada. May through September, the house is open daily 10am to 5pm. Admission is C$5.

Walk west along Belleville past the modern-looking Carillon Tower (a gift from the Dutch people who settled in B.C.) and the not-to-be-missed Royal B.C. Museum (p. 243) and cross Government Street. You're now standing in front of 501 Belleville St. at the:

❺ Provincial Legislature Buildings (Parliament Buildings)

In 1892, a 25-year-old Yorkshireman arrived on the West Coast just as an architectural competition for a new Legislature

1 Victoria Tourist Info Centre
2 The Fairmont Empress
3 Thunderbird Park
4 Helmcken House
5 Provincial Legislature
  (Parliament Buildings)
6 Coast Hotel Docks
6a Fisherman's Wharf
7 West Bay
8 Songhees Point
9 Johnson Street Bridge
10 Bastion Square
11 Floatplane Docks

Building in Victoria was announced. Francis Mawson Rattenbury had no professional credentials but was blessed with both talent and ambition. He submitted a set of drawings and, to the surprise of all, beat out 65 other entries from around the continent. For more about Rattenbury, who was murdered in 1935, see "Francis Rattenbury: Famous Architect and Murder Victim," in chapter 2.

The Provincial Legislature Buildings are open for tours 9am to 5pm. In summer, the 40-minute tours start every 20 minutes (p. 242).

Across the street, the Greek-temple-style **Royal London Wax Museum** (p. 243) is another Rattenbury creation, built originally as the CPR's Steamship ticket office. From here, ocean liners once departed for San Francisco, Sydney, and China.

From the Legislature lawn, make your way past the horse-drawn calèches parked on Menzies Street, and walk west on Belleville Street for 2 blocks to Pendray Street. The road takes a sharp right, but follow the path leading down to a waterfront walkway as it curves around Laurel Point. This headland was long the site of a stinking, fuming paint factory, so residents were delighted when it finally shut down and the luxurious Inn at Laurel Point (p. 212) was erected in its place. Continuing around the pathway past the first few jetties takes you to the:

Here is one of several ports of call for the **Victoria Harbour Ferries** (p. 206; **℃ 250/708-0201**).

From here, the official Frommer's route is to take the ferry all the way across the harbor to West Bay (the next stop on this tour). If the weather's clear you'll enjoy views of the Olympic Mountains to the south and possibly spot a seal or bald eagle. You have several options here: You can take a short hop out to **Fisherman's Wharf** (6A on the map on p. 259), where fresh fish is sold when in season; go directly across to Spinnakers Brewpub on the far shore; take the ferry across to Songhees Point (stop 8); or go directly to Canoe (see "Take a Break," after stop 9). You can even give up on your feet entirely and take the full Harbour Ferries tour.

If you stick with the program, however, the next stop is:

7 **West Bay**

While a pleasant little residential neighborhood with a picturesque marina, West Bay isn't anything to write home about. What is worthwhile, however, is the waterfront walkway that winds its way from here back east toward the city. The trail twists and curves through several parks, and views south through the harbor look out to the Strait of Juan de Fuca and the Olympic Mountains beyond. After about 20 minutes of walking, it may be time to:

> **☕ TAKE A BREAK**
> Excellent beer brewed on the premises combined with an above-average patio make **Spinnakers Brewpub**, 308 Catherine St. (**℃ 250/386-BREW** [2739]), a dangerously time-consuming port of call. For those looking for more substantial fare, the pub grub's very good and the entrees are above average. The on-site bakery makes inspired beer bread, as well as a range of more delicate goods. Open daily 11am to 11pm. See p. 230.

From the pub, continue along the shoreline until you see the totem pole standing at:

8 **Songhees Point**

The point is named for the First Nations tribe that once lived on the site. The Songhees had originally set up their village close to Fort Victoria, near the current site of Bastion Square, but relations with the Hudson's Bay Company were always strained. In 1844, a dispute over a pair of company oxen slaughtered by the Songhees was settled only after Commander Roderick Finlayson blew up the chief's house. A few years later, after a fire started in the native village, spread, and nearly burned down the fort, Finlayson told the Songhees to relocate across the Inner Harbour. They refused at first, pointing out quite rightly that as it was their land, they could live wherever they liked. They assented to the move only after Finlayson agreed to help dismantle and transport the Songhees' longhouses.

The totem pole here is called the **Spirit of Lakwammen,** presented to the city to commemorate the 1994 Commonwealth Games.

Continue on the pathway around the corner. The patio of the Delta Victoria Ocean Pointe Resort (p. 211) provides a great view of the Fairmont Empress. A little farther on is the:

9 **Johnson Street Bridge**

The same guy who designed San Francisco's Golden Gate Bridge also designed Victoria's Johnson Street Bridge. Alas, while the soaring Golden Gate span is justly famous for its elegance, this misshapen lump of steel and concrete is something designer Joseph Strauss would likely wish forgotten.

Cross the bridge, walk past the Esquimalt and Nanaimo (E&N) Railway station, and turn left onto Store Street. Walk 1 block north to Swift Street, turn left, walk downhill to the end of the street, and:

TAKE A BREAK
While having a drink at **Canoe,** 450 Swift St. (⟨**℃**⟩ **250/361-1940**), it's hard to know whom to admire more: the 19th-century engineers who built everything with brick and beam and always twice as thick as it had to be; the restorers who took this old building (once the site of the City Light Company) and turned it into a sunlit cathedral of a room; the owner, who had the vision to pay the restorers; the chef, who made the delicious plate of appetizers now quickly disappearing from your table; or the brew master, whose copper cauldrons produce such a superior brew. Try the taster option—six small glasses of different brews for about the price of a pint—and toast them all. Canoe is open daily 11am to midnight or 1am. See p. 229.

Salutations complete, wander back up Swift Street, turn right, and continue south down Store Street for 2 blocks, where Store Street becomes Wharf Street. Walk another 3 blocks until you reach:

❿ Bastion Square

This pleasant public space stands on the site of the Hudson's Bay Company's original Fort Victoria. The fort was demolished in 1863 and the land sold off for development. When the B.C. government bought and renovated the Rithet Building on the southwest corner of the square, workers uncovered Fort Victoria's original water well, complete with mechanical pump. It's now in the building's lobby.

Continue south on Wharf Street another 2 blocks until you come to the pinkish Dominion Customs House. Built in 1876, it was one of the first tangible signs of British Columbia's new status as a Canadian province. The Second Empire style was meant to impart a touch of European civilization in the midst of this raw wilderness town. Take the walkway by the Customs house down to the waterline and walk out on the:

⓫ Floatplane Docks

Early in the morning these docks buzz with activity as floatplanes fly in and out on their way to and from Seattle, Vancouver, and points farther north. The docks are also the place to come to arrange diving and whale-watching tours.

Back up on Wharf Street, you're just a hop, skip, and a jump from the Visitor Centre tower, where the tour began.

WALKING TOUR 2   **THE OLD TOWN & CHINATOWN**

START AND FINISH:	The Fairmont Empress, 721 Government St.
TIME:	2 hours, not including shopping, sightseeing, and eating stops.
BEST TIME:	Any day before 6pm.
WORST TIME:	Any day after 6pm, when the shops close.

This tour also begins at one of Victoria's most impressive landmarks. In front of you is:

❶ The Fairmont Empress

At 721 Government St., this architectural delight was designed by Francis Rattenbury (see "Francis Rattenbury: Famous Architect and Murder Victim," chapter 2).

Walking north up Government Street, you'll find a number of historic buildings. British Columbia's oldest brick structure, at 901 Government St., is the:

❷ Windsor Hotel building

Built in 1858 as the Victoria Hotel, the building's actually a perfect metaphor for the city. The original structure was a robust yet stylish piece of frontier architecture, with heavy red bricks formed into graceful Romanesque arches. Then, in the 1930s, when the city began pushing the "little bit of England" shtick, the original brick was covered with stucco and fake Tudor half-timbering. Somewhere under the phony gentility, however, the robust frontier structure survives. (It's been through worse: In 1876, the hotel underwent major unexpected remodeling after the owner searched for a gas leak with a lit candle.)

On the next block, you'll find a brass sidewalk plaque at 1022 Government St., indicating the former site of:

❸ Fort Victoria

The fort was constructed in 1843 by the Hudson's Bay Company as the western headquarters of its fur-trading empire. Bound by Broughton and View streets, between Government and Wharf streets, the fort had two octagonal bastions on either side of its tall cedar picket walls. It was torn down during the 1860s gold boom to make room for more businesses. You can get an idea of its size and shape from the line of light-colored bricks—inscribed with the names of early settlers—in the sidewalk that delineates the boundaries of the original walls. The first school in British Columbia was built on this site in 1849.

Continue north 2 more blocks, just past View Street, where a little byway cuts off on the right, running 1 block to Broad Street. It's known as:

❹ Trounce Alley

This is where miners and mariners spent their extra cash on the ladies. The alley is still lit by gas lamps, hung with heraldic crests, and ablaze with flower baskets and potted shrubs. You can stroll through shops selling jewelry, fashions, and crafts, or stop for a bite to eat. Trounce Alley ends abruptly at Broad Street.

Turn left on Broad Street, walk north 1 block, turn left on Yates Street, and walk west 1 block until you come to the:

❺ Legacy Art Gallery and Cafe

At 630 Yates St., this ex-bank building is one of the city's finest examples of the Moderne style, but what makes it worth a visit is the gallery inside. When Victoria art collector and architectural preservationist Michael Williams died in 2000, he willed his collection of contemporary Canadian art to the University of Victoria, which shows it here, along with changing exhibitions. Williams was one of the leading figures in the fight to save Victoria's

Old Town. There's a gallery shop and a deli-style cafe as well. The gallery is open Wednesday to Sunday from 10am to 5pm.

From here, go 1 more block west on Yates. Between Government and Store streets, on the north side of the block, is a collection of mid-19th-century brick storefronts, including the former Majestic Theatre, at 564 Yates, dating from 1860. From Yates, turn left on Langley Street, and go 1 block south. Turn right on View Street and you're in:

❻ Bastion Square

This square was a bustling area with waterfront hotels, saloons, and warehouses during the late 19th century. Earlier, it had been the site of one of Fort Victoria's octagonal gun bastions. In 1963, the area was restored as a heritage square. This is a good place to:

☕ **TAKE A BREAK**
If you're in the mood for a big, healthy glass of organic juice, or some delicious vegetarian grub, stop in at **rebar**, 50 Bastion Sq. (✆ **250/361-9223**), downtown Victoria's best and funkiest spot for wholesome food and drinks. It's open Monday through Thursday 8:30am to 9pm, Friday and Saturday 8:30am to 10pm, and Sunday 8:30am to 3:30pm. See p. 235.

The provincial courthouse and hangman's square were once located on Bastion Square, but now you'll find the:

❼ Maritime Museum

At 28 Bastion Sq. you can get a glimpse into Victoria's naval and shipping history (p. 242). The museum is housed in Victoria's original courthouse and jail, which opened in 1889.

Turn north up Commercial Alley. Cross Yates Street, and a few steps farther west, turn north again up Waddington Alley. On the other side of Johnson Street is:

❽ Market Square

This restored historic site was once a two-story complex of shipping offices and supply stores. It now contains more than 40

1 The Fairmont Empress
2 Windsor Hotel building
3 Fort Victoria
4 Trounce Alley
5 Legacy Art Gallery and Cafe
6 Bastion Square
7 Maritime Museum
8 Market Square
9 Chinatown
10 Fan Tan Alley
11 Gate of Harmonious Interest
12 Chinese Settlement House
13 Chinese Imperial School
14 McPherson Playhouse
15 Congregation Emanu-El Synagogue
16 St. Andrew's Roman Catholic Cathedral
17 Greater Victoria Public Library

VICTORIA STROLLS & BIKING TOUR

17

THE OLD TOWN & CHINATOWN

shops that sell everything from sports equipment and crafts to books and toys. In the summer, musicians often perform and restaurants set up outdoor seating in the large open-air court.

More than a century ago, Victoria's business was transacted in this area of winding alleys and walkways. Warehouses, mariner's hotels, and shipping offices have been carefully restored into shops, restaurants, and galleries. You'll occasionally find historic plaques explaining the function of a building before it was renovated.

Go north 1 block on Store Street, and turn right (away from the harbor) onto Fisgard Street. You're now in North America's oldest:

9 Chinatown

Established in 1858 when the first Chinese arrived as gold seekers and railroad workers, this 6-block district (roughly between Store and Blanshard sts. and Herald St. and Pandora Ave.) fell into decline after World War I (as did many West Coast Asian communities when the U.S. and Canadian governments restricted Asian immigration). What remains is a fascinating peek into a well-hidden and exotic heritage.

On your right, halfway up the block, you'll find:

10 Fan Tan Alley

The world's narrowest street, it's no more than 1.2m (4 ft.) wide at either end, and expands to a little more than 1.8m (6 ft.)

in the center. Through the maze of doorways (which still have their old Chinese signage) are entries to small courtyards leading to even more doorways.

During the late 1800s, this was the main entrance to "Little Canton," where the scent of legally manufactured opium wafted from the courtyards. Opium dens, gambling parlors, and brothels sprang up between the factories and bachelor rooms where male immigrants shared cramped quarters to save money.

Today, you won't find any sin for sale here—just a few little shops dealing in crafts and souvenirs. You can enter the **Chinatown Trading Company,** 551 Fisgard St., from Fisgard Street or via a back door facing Fan Tan Alley. Hidden in its back room are a couple of minimuseums cleverly displaying artifacts from old Chinatown, including the original equipment from a 19th-century Chinese gambling house.

When you're finished exploring the alley, return to Fisgard Street and continue heading east. At the corner of Government and Fisgard streets is the:

⑪ Gate of Harmonious Interest

This lavishly detailed, dragon-headed red-and-gold archway was built in 1981 to commemorate the completion—after years of deterioration—of Chinatown's revitalization by the city and the Chinese Consolidated Benevolent Association. The gate is guarded by a pair of hand-carved stone lions imported from Suzhou, China.

A half-block up at 1715 Government St. is the former location of the:

⑫ Chinese Settlement House

Newly arrived Chinese families once lived upstairs in this balconied building and made use of social services here until they were able to secure work and living quarters. The original **Chinese Buddhist temple** has been moved from the storefront to the second floor, but it's still open to visitors. Although admission is free, hours vary. You will have to check with temple staff to see if you may enter.

A half-block up from the Gate of Harmonious Interest at 36 Fisgard St. is the:

⑬ Chinese Imperial School (Zhongua Xuetang)

This red-and-gold, pagoda-style building with a baked-tile roof and recessed balconies was built by the Chinese Benevolent Society. In 1907, the Victoria School Board banned non-Canadian Chinese children from attending public school, and in response, the society started its own community elementary school the following year. The school is open to the public during the week, and still provides children and adults with instruction in Chinese reading and writing on weekends.

Just east of the school at 3 Centennial Sq. is the:

⑭ McPherson Playhouse

Formerly a vaudeville theater, this was the first of the vast Pantages Theatres chain (Alex Pantages went into showbiz after striking it rich in the Klondike gold fields). The building was restored in the 1960s, and is now Victoria's main performing arts center (© **250/386-6121**). The center is usually open during the day, although no formal tours are given; if you ask nicely, you may be allowed to take a peek inside at the ornate interior. You could also try to get tickets to a show there. City Hall and the police department are located in the office plaza surrounding the playhouse.

When you get to the southeast corner of Centennial Square, walk east 1 more block on Pandora Avenue to Blanshard Street. At 1461 Blanshard St. (at Pandora Ave.), you'll find:

⑮ Congregation Emanu-El Synagogue

This is the oldest surviving Jewish temple on North America's west coast. Built in 1863, it has been proclaimed a national heritage site. The temple (which is not particularly impressive on the outside) is not open to the public.

Turn south on Blanshard Street, and walk 3 blocks to 740 View St., where you'll see the impressive:

⓰ St. Andrew's Roman Catholic Cathedral

Built during the 1890s, this is Victorian High Gothic at its best. The facade is 23m (76 ft.) across, the spire 53m (174 ft.) tall, and no frill, flounce, or architectural embellishment was left out of the design. Renovations in the 1980s incorporated the works of First Nations artists into the interior. Go inside and see the altar by Coast Salish carver Charles Elliot.

One block south at Fort Street is the beginning of Antique Row, which stretches 3 blocks east to Cook Street. Ignore that for the moment (or go explore and then come back), and continue 1 more block south on Blanshard. Walk across the plaza to 735 Broughton St., where you'll find the:

⓱ Greater Victoria Public Library 265

The attraction here is the huge skylit atrium, complete with George Norris's massive hanging artwork, *Dynamic Mobile Steel Sculpture.* Built in 1979, the library complex takes up most of the block. The library is open Monday through Saturday from 9am to 6pm (until 9pm Tues and Thurs; Sun 1–5pm Oct–Apr).

Duck out through the portal on Broughton Street, and walk west to Douglas Street; turn left and walk 1½ blocks south on Douglas until you see the entrance to the Victoria Convention Centre. Walk in and admire the indoor fountain and aviary. The Centre connects to the Fairmont Empress, which was our starting place.

BIKING TOUR	DALLAS ROAD

START AND FINISH:	Cycle B.C. Bike Rental, 707 Douglas St.
TIME:	2 hours, not including picnic stops, sightseeing, shopping, or food breaks.
BEST TIMES:	Clear, sunny days when the Olympic Mountains are revealed in all their glory.
WORST TIMES:	Gray, rainy days.

Victoria cries out to be biked. The hills are modest, the traffic light and very polite, and the views incredible. When touring around by bike, you rarely have time to stop and pull out a point-by-point guide, so the descriptions offered here are shorter than for walking tours. The route is designed to take you a bit beyond what would be possible on foot, without getting into an expedition-length tour.

This tour is about 15km (9⅓ miles) long and stays on bike paths through much of its length, although some of the streets in the second half of the tour are lightly trafficked. The ride from the Dallas Road shoreline to Craigdarroch Castle involves an elevation gain of about 150m (492 ft.).

Start at **Cycle B.C. Bike Rental,** 707 Douglas St. (© **250/380-2453;** www.cyclebc.ca). Follow Douglas Street down to **Thunderbird Park** and have a look at the totem poles. From there, continue east along Belleville Street past the **Legislature** and the **Coho ferry terminal;** then go round the corner onto Kingston Street, and left through the small park to **Fisherman's Wharf.** From here, continue south along **Dallas Road,** past the helijet pad and the car-ferry docks, and stop at the entrance to the breakwater at **Ogden**

Point. By this time, if the sky's clear, you should have a fabulous view of the Olympic Mountains. Park your bike and wander out along the breakwater, or stop in at the **Ogden Point Cafe,** 199 Dallas Rd., for the same view without the wind.

Continue east along the seaside bike path or on Dallas Road. Stop here and there as the mood strikes for some beach-combing. A little ways on, past Douglas Street, cross Dallas and cut north into **Beacon Hill Park** (p. 248). Stop at the petting zoo, look at the 38m (125-ft.)

totem pole, or just enjoy Victoria's favorite park. Exit the park by the northeast corner on Cook Street, and cycle a few blocks north into **Cook Street Village.** This is a good spot to stop for a coffee and dessert or to shop for picnic supplies at the local deli or supermarket. Head back south on Cook Street to Dallas Road; turn left and continue east a kilometer or so to **Clover Point,** a short peninsula sticking out into the Strait of Juan de Fuca. It makes a fine picnic spot. From here, head east to **Ross Bay Cemetery** (p. 245), Victoria's second oldest, where many local notables are buried, including former governor James Douglas and painter Emily Carr (see "Emily Carr: Visionary from Victoria," in chapter 2). From the north side of the cemetery, ride up the hill on **Stannard Street,** skirting the eastern edge of **Government House** (p. 248), the official residence of the lieutenant governor.

When you reach **Rockland Avenue,** turn right and ride a few hundred meters past the many fine homes of this elite enclave to the main entrance to Government House. Though the residence itself is closed to the public, the formal gardens are open and well worth a wander. Round back, the hillside of Garry oaks is one of the last places to see what the area's natural fauna looked like before European settlers arrived. The rose garden in front is sumptuous. Just west of the gate on Rockland Avenue, turn right onto **Joan Crescent** and ride up the small hill to opulent **Craigdarroch Castle** (p. 240), built by coal magnate Robert Dunsmuir for his wife, Joan. The castle is open for self-guided tours. From here, continue up Joan Crescent to Fort Street; turn right and go a very short way east to Yates Street; turn left and go 1 block to Fernwood Street; turn right and go 1 block north to **Pandora Street;** then turn left again and ride west down the hill. Watch for the **Christian Science church** at 1205 Pandora St. (where the street widens to include a boulevard in its center). Another 6 blocks west, and you're at **Pandora** and **Government streets,** with **Chinatown** (see stops 9–13 of "Walking Tour 2," above) to your right, **Market Square** (see stop 8 of "Walking Tour 2," above) to your left, and the Fairmont Empress and the bike-rental spot just a few blocks south.

18

Victoria Shopping

Victoria has dozens of specialty shops, and because the city is built on a pedestrian scale, you can easily wander from place to place seeking out whatever treasure you're after. Nearly all of the areas listed below are within a short walk of the Fairmont Empress (or in it); for those shops located more than 6 blocks from the hotel, bus information is provided. Stores in Victoria are generally open Monday through Saturday from 10am to 6pm; some, but not many, are open on Sundays during the summer.

1 THE SHOPPING SCENE

Explorers beware: The brick-paved **Government Street promenade,** from the Inner Harbour 5 blocks north to Yates Street, is a jungle of cheap souvenir shops. There are gems in here—Irish linen, fine bone china, quality Pacific Coast Native art, and thick Cowichan sweaters—but to find these riches, you'll have to pass T-shirt stores, knick-knack emporiums, and countless maple-syrup bottles.

Farther north, the **Old Town district** and **Market Square** feature a fascinating blend of heritage buildings and up-to-date shops. Victoria's **Chinatown** is tiny, and since most of the city's Chinese population has moved elsewhere, it lacks some of the authenticity and vitality of Chinatowns in Vancouver or San Francisco. The area has been charmingly preserved, however, and there are a number of gallery-quality art and ceramic shops, and quirky back alleys (including Canada's thinnest commercial street, Fan Tan Alley).

A small new **Design District,** lined with home furnishing stores, begins 1 block north of Chinatown on Herald Street and stretches west to Wharf Street and south along Wharf. On the eastern edge of downtown, **Antique Row** is known for its high-quality British collectibles. And if you're at all interested in the Pacific Coast Native art of the Pacific Northwest, Victoria is a good place to look for pieces to add to your collection.

2 SHOPPING A TO Z

ANTIQUES

Victoria has long had a deserved reputation for antiques—particularly those of British origin. Many of the best stores are on **Antique Row,** mentioned above. In addition to those listed below, check out **Romanoff & Company Antiques,** 837 Fort St. (*C* **250/ 480-1543**); and for furniture fans, **Charles Baird Antiques,** 1044A Fort St. (*C* **250/ 384-8809**).

David Robinson Antiques Here you'll find Oriental rugs, silver, oil paintings, brass, porcelain, and period furniture. Though it's not as large as Faith Grant's shop (see below), Robinson's pieces—especially his furniture—are particularly well chosen. 1023 Fort St. *C* **250/384-6425.** Bus: 10 to Blanshard or Cook St.

Faith Grant's Connoisseur Shop Ltd. (Finds)   The farthest from downtown, this shop is also the best. The 16 rooms of this 1862 heritage building contain everything from Georgian writing desks to English flatware, not to mention fine ceramics, prints, and paintings. Furniture is especially strong here. 1156 Fort St. ℂ 250/383-0121. www.faith grantantiques.com. Bus: 10 to Fort and Cook sts.

Vanity Fair Antiques & Collectibles (Value)   This large shop is fun to browse, with crystal, glassware, furniture, and lots more. If you're feeling flush, it's certainly possible to spend here, but many items can be easily snapped up without taking out a bank loan. 1044 Fort St. ℂ 250/380-7274. www.vanityfairantiques.com. Bus: 10 to Blanshard or Cook St.

ART

Fran Willis Gallery   Soaring white walls and huge arched windows make this one of Victoria's most beautiful gallery spaces. The collection is strong in contemporary oils, mixed media, and bronzes, almost all by B.C. and Alberta artists. 1619 Store St. ℂ 250/381-3422. www.franwillis.com. Bus: 5 to Douglas and Fisgard.

Open Space   When does self-confidence start edging into pretension? This artist-run gallery and self-declared flag-bearer of the avant-garde has trod on both sides of that line since 1972. Mostly, they get it right, so the gallery is usually worth a visit. Exhibits run the full gamut, from paintings and sculpture to literary and dance performances. 510 Fort St. ℂ 250/383-8833. www.openspace.ca.

Winchester Galleries   This slightly daring gallery features contemporary oil paintings. Unlike elsewhere in town, very few wildlife paintings ever make it onto the walls. 1010 Broad St. ℂ 250/386-2773. www.winchestergalleriesltd.com.

BOOKS

Avalon Metaphysical Centre   Avalon specializes in New Age books, crystals, rune stones, body oils, and videotapes of gurus who've already trodden the path to enlightenment. 62-560 Johnson St. (in Market Sq.). ℂ 250/380-1721.

Crown Publications Inc.   In addition to dry, but informative, government publications, this store stocks an excellent selection of books covering the history, nature, and culture of the Victoria area. Keeping up with the times, digital maps are available on CD-ROM. 563 Superior St. ℂ 250/387-6409. www.crownpub.bc.ca.

Munro's Books (Finds)   All bookstores should look so good: a mile-high ceiling in a 1909 heritage building, complete with heavy brass lamps and murals on the walls (never mind that the building was originally a bank). The store stocks more than 35,000 titles, including an excellent selection about Victoria and books by local authors. The staff is friendly and very good at unearthing obscure titles. The remainder tables have some incredible deals. 1108 Government St. ℂ 888/243-2464 or 250/382-2464. www.munrobooks. com.

Russell Books (Value)   This shop offers two floors of used, new, and remaindered books. 734 Fort St. ℂ 250/361-4447. www.russellbooks.com.

Western Canada Wilderness Committee (WCWC)   Committed to protecting Canada's endangered species and environment, the WCWC store raises funds for the cause. Choose from beautiful gift cards, posters, and souvenir T-shirts or mugs. 651 Johnson St. ℂ 250/388-9292. www.wildernesscommittee.org.

CHINA & LINENS

Irish Linen Stores Everything Irish since 1910: handkerchiefs, scarves, doilies, napkins, lace, and more. 1019 Government St. ☎ 250/383-6812. www.irishlinenvictoria.com.

Sydney Reynolds This building opened as a saloon in 1908, became a bank in 1909, was converted into a shop in 1929, and now houses a wide array of porcelains, including tea sets and Victorian dolls. 801 Government St. ☎ 250/383-3931.

CHINESE ARTS & CRAFTS

Chinatown Trading Company (Finds) This unobtrusive storefront on Fisgard opens onto a veritable bazaar—three connected shops stocked with Chinese goods either useful, endearingly corny, or both. Who wouldn't want kung fu shoes or a tin pecking chicken? Browse through bamboo flutes, origami kits, useful and inexpensive Chinese kitchenware, and a few small museum displays of artifacts from Chinatown's past. Look for the sneaky back entrance off Fan Tan Alley. 551 Fisgard St. ☎ 250/381-5503. Bus: 5 to Douglas and Fisgard sts.

CIGARS & TOBACCO

Old Morris Tobacconist Ltd. This small shop maintains a century-old tradition of custom-blending pipe tobacco. You'll also find an impressive selection of cigars, including Cubans. Cuban cigars can't be brought into the United States, but a few brands like Horvath Bances duck the blockade by importing the tobacco into Canada and rolling the cigars here. 1116 Government St. ☎ 250/382-4811. www.oldmorris.com.

DEPARTMENT STORE & SHOPPING MALL

The Bay Centre The Bay Centre is named after its new anchor store, Hudson's Bay Company. Canada's oldest department store sells everything from housewares to cosmetics and the classic (and expensive) Hudson's Bay woolen point blankets. The store also has a large china and crystal department. The rest of the complex houses a full shopping mall disguised as a block of heritage buildings. Between Government and Douglas sts., off Fort and View sts. The Bay: ☎ 250/385-1311. Mall: ☎ 250/389-2228. www.thebaycentre.ca.

FASHION
For Women

Breeze This high-energy store carries a number of trendy lines such as Mexx, Powerline, and Mac+Jac. Shoes by Nine West and Steve Madden, plus stylish accessories, complete the look. 1150 Government St. ☎ 250/383-8871.

Hughes Ltd. This local favorite features designer fashions and trendy casual wear. 564 Yates St. ☎ 250/381-4405. www.hughesclothing.com.

The Plum Clothing Co. This local chain features quality dressy casuals designed with the baby boomer in mind. 1298 Broad St. ☎ 250/381-5005.

For Women & Men

The Edinburgh Tartan Shop If there's even a drop of Celtic blood in ye, this shop can set ye up in a kilt made from your family tartan. It also stocks sweaters, blankets, tartan by the yard, and kilt pins. 921 Government St. ☎ 250/953-7790.

Still Life Originally known for its vintage clothes, Still Life has updated and moved to a contemporary style that includes fashions from Diesel, Workwear, and Toronto designer Damzels-in-this-Dress. 551 Johnson St. ☎ 250/386-5655.

W. & J. Wilson's Clothiers   Canada's oldest family-run clothing store, this shop has been owned/managed by the Wilsons since 1862. Look for sensible casuals or elegant cashmeres and leathers from British, Scottish, and other European designers. 1221 Government St. ℭ 250/383-7177.

For Men
British Importers   Victoria may be laid-back, but a man still needs a power suit, and this is the place to get it. Designer labels include Calvin Klein and Hugo Boss. Ties and leather jackets are also for sale. 1125 Government St. ℭ 250/386-1496.

FIRST NATIONS ARTS & CRAFTS
Natives from the nearby Cowichan band are famous for their warm, durable sweaters knit with bold motifs from hand-spun raw wool. In addition to these beautiful knits, craftspeople create soft leather moccasins, moose-hide boots, ceremonial masks, sculptures carved from argillite or soapstone, baskets, bearskin rugs, and jewelry. The **Quw'utsun' Cultural and Conference Centre** (p. 246) also has a large gift shop where you can watch artisans at work.

Alcheringa Gallery   What began as a shop handling imports from the Antipodes has evolved into one of Victoria's truly great stores for aboriginal art connoisseurs. All the coastal tribes are represented in Alcheringa's collection, along with pieces from Papua New Guinea. The presentation is museum quality, with prices to match. 665 Fort St. ℭ 250/383-8224. www.alcheringa-gallery.com.

Art of Man Gallery   Beautiful and expensive First Nations artwork is sold in this shop, located off the Tea Lobby in the Fairmont Empress hotel. You'll find high-quality works by some of the best-known artists in British Columbia. In the Fairmont Empress hotel, 721 Government St. ℭ 250/383-3800. www.artofmangallery.com.

Cowichan Trading Company   A downtown fixture for almost 50 years, Cowichan Trading follows the standard layout for its displays: junky T-shirts and gewgaws in front, Cowichan sweaters, masks, and fine silver jewelry farther in. 1328 Government St. ℭ 250/383-0321. www.cowichantrading.com.

Hill's Native Art   Hill's is the store for established artists from up and down the B.C. coast, which means the quality is high, and so are the prices (although you can find good-quality work here for under C$300). Of course, you don't stay in business for 50 years without pleasing your drop-in customers, so Hill's has its share of dream catchers and other knickknacks. 1008 Government St. ℭ 250/385-3911. www.hillsnativeart.com.

FOOD & WINE
English Sweet Shop   All those old-fashioned English sweets you love but can never find in North America (such as horehound drops and lemon sherbets) are sold in this 20-year-old candy shop. They also sell English marmalade, lemon curd, jam, chutneys, tea and biscuits—you get the picture. There's a smaller version, the **British Candy Shoppe,** 2 blocks away at 638 Yates St. (ℭ 250/382-2634). 738 Yates St. ℭ 800/848-1533 or 250/382-3325. www.englishsweets.com.

Murchie's   It's worth coming here just to suck up the coffee smell or sniff the many specialty teas, including the custom-made blend served at the Fairmont Empress' afternoon tea. 1110 Government St. ℭ 250/383-3112. www.murchies.com.

Rogers' Chocolates Rogers' bills itself "Quite possibly the best chocolates in the world," and with original Tiffany glass, old-fashioned counters, and free samples, this 100-year-old shrine could possibly live up to the claim. 913 Government St. (℃ **800/663-2220** or 250/881-8771. www.rogerschocolates.com.

Silk Road Aromatherapy and Tea Company (Value) Before setting up shop, the two Victoria women who run this store first trained to become tea masters in China and Taiwan. Their Victoria store on the edge of Chinatown sells a wide variety of teas, including premium loose blends and tea paraphernalia such as teapots, mugs, and kettles; they offer a full line of aromatherapy products as well. The latest addition is the spa, which offers a range of treatments at very reasonable prices; their 2-hour full facial and full-body massage at C$99 is a steal. 1624 Government St. (℃ **250/704-2688.** www.silkroadtea.com. Bus: 5 to Douglas and Fisgard sts.

The Wine Barrel This shop sells more than 300 B.C. VQA (Vintner Quality Alliance) wines and wine accessories. It's known for carrying the largest selection of B.C. ice wines (a type of wine where grapes have to be picked when the temperature has been below 0°C/32°F for a certain amount of time) in Victoria. 644 Broughton St. (℃ **250/388-0606.** www.thewinebarrel.com.

JEWELRY

Artina's High-quality, handcrafted Canadian jewelry is sold in this shop. 1002 Government St. (℃ **250/386-7000.** www.artinas.com.

Jade Victoria Here you'll find jewelry made from British Columbia jade, which is mined in northern Vancouver Island, then crafted in Victoria and China into necklaces, bracelets, and other items. 911 Government St. (℃ **250/384-5233.**

Le Soleil Jewellers In business since 1976, this store sells one-of-a-kind pieces created in on-site workshops using the finest of materials. 608 Courtney St. (℃ **250/388-5162.** www.lesoleiljewellers.com.

MacDonald Jewelry Ian MacDonald designs and makes all his own jewelry: diamonds cut in squares and triangles, and styles from the traditional to cutting edge. It's a great place to hunt for rings and pearls, as well as precious gems like sapphires, rubies, and emeralds. 618 View St. (℃ **250/382-4113.**

The Patch The Island's largest provider of body jewelry has studs, rings, and other bright baubles for your nose, navel, or nipple, much of it quite creative and reasonably priced. 719 Yates St. (℃ **250/384-7070.**

OUTDOOR CLOTHES & EQUIPMENT

Ocean River Sports This is the place to go to arrange a sea kayak tour—they'll be happy to rent (or sell) you a boat and all the gear. This is also a good spot for outdoor clothing and camping musts, such as solar-heated showers or espresso machines. 1824 Store St. (℃ **250/381-4233.** www.oceanriver.com.

Pacific Trekking An excellent source for rain and hiking gear, this store is also good for advice on local hiking trails. 1305 Government St. (℃ **250/388-7088.**

Walkers Shoes This store specializes in the finest European walking shoes for men and women. 1012 Broad St. (℃ **250/381-8608.**

Market Square Constructed from the original warehouses and shipping offices built in the 1800s, this pleasant and innovative heritage reconstruction features small shops and restaurants surrounding a central courtyard, often the site of live performances in summer. 560 Johnson St. ⓒ **250/386-2441.**

19

Victoria After Dark

*Victoria is God's waiting room. It's the only cemetery
in the entire world with street lighting.*

—a visitor from Gotham, as quoted in *Monday Magazine*

Ouch. That's harsh. More important, it's not exactly accurate. True, with retirees and civil servants making up a sizable segment of the population, Victoria is never going to set the world on fire. But the U. Vic. students, tourists, and a small but dedicated cadre of Victoria revelers form a critical mass large enough to keep a small but steady scene alive.

Monday Magazine, a weekly tabloid published on Thursdays, is the place to start. Its listings section provides comprehensive coverage of what's happening in town and is particularly good for the club scene. If you can't find *Monday* in cafes or record shops, visit it online at **www.mondaymag.com**.

For information on theater, concerts, and arts events, contact the **Tourism**

Victoria Visitor Centre, 812 Wharf St. (**(C) 800/663-3883** or 250/953-2033; www.tourismvictoria.com). You can also buy tickets for Victoria's venues from the Visitor Centre, but only in person.

Whatever you decide to do with your Victoria evenings, chances are that your destination will be close at hand: One of the great virtues of Victoria's size is that nearly all of its attractions—concert halls, pubs, dance clubs, and theaters—are no more than a 10-minute walk from the Fairmont Empress, right in the heart of the city, and easily reached by taking bus no. 5 to the Empress Hotel/Convention Centre. For those few nightlife spots a little farther out, bus information is provided throughout the chapter.

1 THE PERFORMING ARTS

The **Royal Theatre,** 805 Broughton St., and the **McPherson Playhouse,** 3 Centennial Sq., share a common box office (**(C) 888/717-6121** or 250/386-6121; www.rmts.bc.ca). The **Royal**—built in the early 1900s and renovated in the 1970s—hosts concerts by the Victoria Symphony and performances by the Pacific Opera Victoria, as well as touring dance and theater companies. The **McPherson**—built in 1914 as the first Pantages Vaudeville Theatre—is home to smaller stage plays and performances by the Victoria Operatic Society.

THEATER
Performing in an intimate playhouse that was once a church, the **Belfry Theatre Society** ★★, 1291 Gladstone Ave. (**(C) 250/385-6815;** www.belfry.bc.ca; bus no. 22 to Fernwood St.), is an acclaimed theatrical group that stages four productions (usually dramatic works by contemporary Canadian playwrights) October through April, and one show in August. Tickets are C$21 to C$36.

The **Intrepid Theatre Company,** 2-1609 Blanshard St. (℃ **250/383-2663;** www. intrepidtheatre.com), runs two yearly theater festivals. In spring it's the **Uno Festival of Solo Performance** ★★, a unique event of strictly one-person performances. Come summer, Intrepid puts on the **Victoria Fringe Festival** ★★. Even if you're not a theater fan—*especially* if you're not—don't miss the Fringe. More than 50 performers or small companies from around the world put on amazingly inventive plays. The festival runs from late August to early September, and performances are held at six downtown venues daily noon to midnight.

Theatre Inconnu, 1923 Fernwood Rd. (℃ **250/360-0234;** www.theatreinconnu. com), is Victoria's oldest alternative theater group, celebrating 20 years of performances. The actors are local and often semiprofessional, but quality is excellent and tickets are inexpensive. They stage a two-man adaptation of Charles Dickens's *A Christmas Carol* every year.

The **Langham Court Theatre,** 805 Langham Court (℃ **250/384-2142;** www.langham courttheatre.bc.ca), performs works produced by the Victoria Theatre Guild, a local amateur society dedicated to presenting a wide range of dramatic and comedic works. From downtown take bus no. 14 or 11 to Fort and Moss streets.

OPERA

The **Pacific Opera Victoria** ★★, 1815 Blanshard St. (℃ **250/385-0222;** www.pov. bc.ca), presents three productions annually from October to April. Performances are normally at the McPherson Playhouse and Royal Theatre. The repertoire covers the classical bases, from Mozart and Rossini to Verdi and even Wagner. Tickets cost C$30 to C$110.

The **Victoria Operatic Society,** 10-744 Fairview Rd. (℃ **250/381-1021;** www.vos. bc.ca), presents Broadway musicals and other popular fare at the McPherson Playhouse. Tickets cost C$18 to C$45.

ORCHESTRAL & CHORAL MUSIC

The well-respected **Victoria Symphony Orchestra** ★, 610-620 View St. (℃ **250/385-9771;** www.victoriasymphony.bc.ca), kicks off its season on the first Sunday of August with Symphony Splash, a free concert performed on a barge in the Inner Harbour. Regular performances begin in September and last through May. The Orchestra performs at the Royal Theatre or the University Farquhar Auditorium. Tickets are C$14 to C$60 for most concerts.

DANCE

Dance recitals and full-scale performances by local and international dance troupes such as DanceWorks and the Scottish Dance Society are scheduled throughout the year. Call the **Visitor Centre** at ℃ **250/953-2033** to find out who's performing when you're in town.

COMEDY & SPOKEN WORD

Mocambo, 1028 Blanshard St. (℃ **250/384-4468**), a coffeehouse near the public library, hosts a range of spoken-word events through the week (multimedia fusion demos, philosopher's cafes, argument for the joy of it, slam poetry), then lets loose on Saturdays with improv comedy. There is no cover.

MUSIC FESTIVALS

Folkfest ★   A free multicultural celebration of song, food, and crafts, Folkfest is the largest outdoor event on Vancouver Island. It takes place late June through early July on Ship Point (the parking space below Wharf St. on the edge of the Inner Harbour). ℂ **250/388-4728.** www.icafolkfest.com.

Summer in the Square   Every day at noon from early July to late August, this popular festival in downtown's Centennial Square offers free music. Each day features a different band and musical style: Monday features mostly jazz; Tuesdays offer a selection of Big Band golden oldies; Wednesday through Saturday is potluck (show up at noon and take your chances). The festival's showstoppers are the Concerts Under the Stars held each Sunday from 7 to 9:30pm; the series features some 15 local bands over the 6-week length of the festival. Centennial Sq. ℂ **250/361-0388.**

Victoria Jazz Society/JazzFest International ★   The Jazz Society is a good place to call any time of year to find out what's happening; it runs a hotline listing jazz events throughout the year. Its raison d'être, however, is **JazzFest International,** held from late June to early July. The more progressive of Victoria's two summer jazz fests, this one offers a range of styles from Cuban, salsa, and world beat to fusion and acid jazz. Many free concerts are given in the Market Square courtyard; others are held in live-music venues around the city. This organization also puts on the excellent **Blues Bash** on Labour Day weekend on an outdoor stage in Victoria's Inner Harbour. ℂ **888/671-2112** or **250/388-4423.** www.jazzvictoria.ca.

LIVE MUSIC

Swans Pub (see review under "Bars & Pubs," below) presents a live band every night.

Hermann's Jazz Club   This venue cultivates a community-center feel, which is definitely and defiantly *not* chic. Still, the reasonable cover charge gets you in for some good old-time jazz and Dixieland. Open Thursday through Saturday at 8pm, Sunday at 4:30pm. 753 View St. ℂ **250/388-9166.** www.hermannsjazz.com. Cover C$5–C$10.

Lucky Bar   This long, low, cavernous space has a pleasantly grungy feel to it. DJs spin house and trance on the weekends, with bands often showing up earlier in the week. 517 Yates St. ℂ **250/382-5825.** www.luckybar.ca. Cover C$5–C$20.

Steamers ★   One of the best places to catch live music on the cheap, Steamers features live music 7 nights a week. Once a strip bar, this long, narrow downtown spot got a new interior and was reborn as the city's premium blues bar. "Blues" here isn't taken too literally: Acts often stray into the realms of zydeco, Celtic, and world beat. Mondays present an open-stage acoustic jam (no cover). 570 Yates St. ℂ **250/381-4340.** No cover–C$5.

The Upstairs Lounge   Victoria's newest hot spot for live music sits overtop Darcy's Wharf Street Pub (see below) on the edge of Bastion Square. The Upstairs has space, good sightlines, and a crowd of attractive Victoria locals who come for touring bands and DJ'ed house and Top 40. 15 Bastion Sq. ℂ **250/385-5483.** Cover about C$6, bigger shows up to C$12.

Most places are open Monday through Saturday until 2am, and Sunday until midnight. Drinks run from C$4 to C$8.

The Red Jacket Opened in 2004, Red Jacket quickly became *the* hoppin' hot spot thanks to Caramel @ The Red Jacket, a Friday night bash featuring some of Victoria's finest urban DJ talent. 751 View St. 🕐 **250/384-2582.**

Sugar Groove the night away under an old-fashioned disco ball. Open Thursday through Saturday only; lineups start at 10pm so come early. DJs spin mostly hip-hop, house, and Top 40 tunes. 858 Yates St. 🕐 **250/920-9950.** www.sugarnightclub.ca. Cover Fri–Sat C$3–C$6.

---

3 LOUNGES, BARS & PUBS

LOUNGES

Bengal Lounge ★ The Bengal is one of the last outposts of the old empire—a Raffles or a Harry's Bar—except the martinis are ice-cold and jazz plays in the background (and on weekends, live in the foreground). The couches are huge and covered in leather thick enough to stop an elephant gun. The cocktail list is extensive. The combination has lately attracted the young and elegant lounge-lizard crowd. In the Fairmont Empress, 721 Government St. 🕐 **250/384-8111.**

Med Grill@Mosaic ★ Bistro by day, this cool, contemporary space turns into a martini spot at night (happy hour nightly 9–10pm), when DJs spin mellow sounds. Everything's reasonably priced and pretty. 1063 Fort St. 🕐 **250/381-3417.**

The Reef This Caribbean restaurant transforms into a funky reggae lounge when the sun has faded away. Features include great martinis and good tunes, and a DJ now and again. 533 Yates St. 🕐 **250/388-5375.** www.thereefrestaurant.com.

BARS & PUBS

Big Bad John's Victoria's first, favorite, and only hillbilly bar is a low, dark warren of a place, with thick gunk on the walls, inches of discarded peanut shells on the plank floor, and a crowd of drunk and happy rowdies. In the Strathcona Hotel, 919 Douglas St. 🕐 **250/383-7137.**

Canoe ★ If it's a nice night, head for this fabulous outdoor patio overlooking the Upper Harbour. The beer is brewed on the premises (try the taster option—six small glasses of different brews for more or less the price of a pint). The century-old brick-and-beam building is a joy to look at, and the food is fun and hearty. 450 Swift St. 🕐 **250/361-1940.** www.canoebrewpub.com.

Darcy's Wharf Street Pub Eating anywhere on Wharf Street would be a foolish newbie move, but drinking? That's another story. This large, bright, harborfront pub features a range of fine brews, pool tables, occasional live bands, and a lovely view of the sunset. The crowd is young and lively. 1127 Wharf St. 🕐 **250/380-1322.** www.darcyspub.ca.

Spinnakers Brewpub ★ One of the best brewpubs in town, Spinnakers did it first and did it well. Overlooking Victoria Harbour on the west side of the Songhees Point Development, Spinnakers' view of the harbor and Legislature is fabulous. On sunny days it's worth coming here for the view alone. At other times (all times in fact), the brewed-on-the-premises ales, lagers, and stouts are uniformly excellent and the pub grub is always good. An on-site bakery sells various beer breads. The weekends often feature a band. There are also dartboards and pool tables. 308 Catherine St. (✆ 250/386-2739. www.spinnakers.com. Bus: 24 to Songhees Rd.

The Sticky Wicket   This is yet another pub in the Strathcona Hotel (see Big Bad John's, above)—but the Wicket is a standout. The beautiful wood interior—including dividers, glass, and a long teak bar—spent many years in Dublin before being shipped here to Victoria, making it about as original an Irish bar as you're likely to find. Elevators can whip you from deepest Dublin up three floors to the mini-Malibu on the outdoor patio balcony, complete with beach volleyball. In the Strathcona Hotel, 919 Douglas St. (✆ 250/383-7137.

Swans Brewpub ★   Few drinking spots are more intriguing—or more enjoyable—than Swans. The intrigue comes from the founding owner's vast Pacific Northwest and First Nations art collection. The enjoyment comes from the room itself, on the ground floor of a beautifully converted 1913 feed warehouse across from the Johnson Street Bridge. The beer here is brewed on-site and delicious. There's live entertainment every night. In Swans Hotel, 506 Pandora Ave. (✆ 250/361-3310.

4 GAY & LESBIAN BARS

Victoria's entertainment options for the gay and lesbian community are few. A good resource for local contacts can be found online at **www.gayvictoria.ca**.

Hush   This straight-friendly space (crowd is about fifty-fifty) features top-end touring DJs spinning house, trance, and disco house. Open Wednesday to Sunday. 1325 Government St. (✆ 250/385-0566. Cover on weekends C$5.

Prism Lounge   Drag shows, karaoke, techno, Top 40—something different every night. 642 Johnson St. (entrance on Broad St.). (✆ 250/388-0505. www.prismlounge.com.

20

Pacific Rim National Park Reserve of Canada

The west coast of Vancouver Island is a magnificent area of old-growth forests, stunning fjords, rocky coastline, and long sandy beaches. And though **Pacific Rim National Park Reserve of Canada** ★★★ was established in 1971 as Canada's first marine park, it wasn't until 1991 that it really became significant in the consciousness of people outside the area. That was when thousands of environmentalists from across the province and around the world gathered to protest and blockade the clear-cutting of old-growth forests on Meares Island in Clayoquot Sound. It was the largest act of civil disobedience in Canada's history. When footage of the protests ran on the evening news, people who saw the unspoiled beauty of this coastal landscape for the first time were moved to come experience it firsthand. Tourism in the area has never looked back, and because of its importance as a pristine marine environment, Clayoquot Sound was designated a UNESCO Marine Biosphere Reserve in 2000. This designation doesn't add any legal protection (the paper companies are again eyeing the old-growth trees) but it does boost the park's environmental visibility.

The three main areas to visit are **Ucluelet, Tofino,** and the **Long Beach section** of Pacific Rim National Park. Tofino and Ucluelet are small towns on the northern and southern edges of a peninsula about halfway up the western shore of Vancouver Island, with the Long Beach section of the park between them. From Victoria, the trip by car—along a highway considered one of the top three scenic drives in Canada—takes about 4½ hours and includes such highlights as massive old-growth trees (Cathedral Grove), an enormous mountain lake (Kennedy Lake), snow-covered peaks, and brief stretches of oceanside highway.

The park receives about one million visitors a year, most of them June through August. In those high-season months, traffic between Ucluelet and Tofino becomes an all-day jam, beaches are crammed with vacationers, and every restaurant, hotel room, and B&B is full (in the summer it's essential to book a hotel before you go). Thick fog that doesn't burn off until midafternoon is typical in August. As locals will tell you, September and October are actually the best times to visit, and coming out for winter storm-watching is increasingly popular. This is a coastal rainforest area, so be prepared for rain no matter when you visit.

The town of **Ucluelet** (pronounced you-*clue*-let, meaning "safe harbor" in the local Nuu-chah-nulth dialect) sits on the southern end of the peninsula, on the edge of Barkley Sound. It's the first town you come to if you're driving across the island from Victoria. Back when fishing was the dominant local industry, Ucluelet was the primary town on the peninsula. When tourism began to take over, Tofino became more popular (it's better developed). Ucluelet has about 2,100 permanent year-round residents; in the summer, however, its population jumps tenfold. Like Tofino, it's a small coastal town with mostly new houses and businesses, so don't expect a quaint old fishing village.

At the far northern tip of the peninsula, about a 25-minute drive from Ucluelet, **Tofino** (pop. 1,800) sits on beautiful Clayoquot Sound, and is the center of the West Coast's growing eco-tourism business. Hikers and beach-combers come to Tofino simply for the scenery—few landscapes in the Pacific Northwest are more majestically diverse, with the Island Mountains rising to the east of island-studded Clayoquot (pronounced *clay*-oh-quot) Sound, and the thundering-surf beaches of the Pacific just to the west. The town, with its eco-tour and fishing outfitters, a growing number of restaurants, and new beach-front lodges, provides all the ingredients necessary for a memorable getaway.

Long Beach stretches between Tofino and Ucluelet. The beach is more than 30km (19 miles) long, broken here and there by rocky headlands and bordered by groves of cedar and Sitka spruce. The rocky coastline is popular with countless species of birds and marine life—bald eagles routinely nest in the vicinity, and between March and May as many as 20,000 Pacific gray whales pass by as they migrate to their summer feeding grounds in the Arctic Circle.

1 ESSENTIALS

GETTING THERE
To get to Vancouver Island, see "Getting to Victoria," p. 38.

BY BOAT   A 4½-hour ride aboard the Alberni Marine Transportation passenger ferry **MV *Lady Rose*** ★★ (© **250/723-8313;** www.ladyrosemarine.com) takes you from Port Alberni to Ucluelet, making brief stops along the way to deliver mail and packages to solitary cabin dwellers along the coast and to let off or pick up kayakers bound for the Broken Islands Group. This is a wonderful way to see portions of Vancouver Island aboard a heritage vessel; the round-trip takes 11 hours. The *Lady Rose* departs at 8am Monday, Wednesday, and Friday from June to mid-September (Tues, Thurs, and Sat the rest of the year) from Alberni Harbour Quay at 5425 Argyle St. in south Port Alberni. The round-trip fare to Ucluelet is C$72.

BY BUS   Greyhound Lines (© **800/661-8747;** www.greyhound.ca) operates regular daily bus service between Victoria, Nanaimo, Port Alberni, and Tofino/Ucluelet. The 6-hour trip, departing Victoria at 7:30am and arriving in Tofino at 2:30pm, costs from C$70 to C$135 round-trip, the lower fares for advance purchase tickets. During the summer months, **Tofino Bus** (© **866/986-3466** or 250/725-2871; www.tofinobus. com) provides the same route service, departing Victoria at 8:25am and arriving in Tofino at 2:30pm; the price is the same as Greyhound.

BY CAR   Once you are on Vancouver Island, the same scenic, easy-to-follow route takes you to Ucluelet, Long Beach, and Tofino. Considered one of the top scenic drives in Canada, the paved route, mostly two lanes, gets twisty toward the end, and takes about 4 to 4½ hours from Victoria. From Victoria, take Hwy. 1 north along the Saanich Peninsula to Nanaimo, where you take the Island Highway (Hwy. 19) north for 52km (32 miles). Just beyond the town of Parksville, turn west on Hwy. 4, which leads past **Cathedral Grove** ★★—worth a stop to see the old-growth inland forest—to the mid-island town of Port Alberni (about 38km/24 miles west). Hwy. 4 continues west, past giant Kennedy Lake, and reaches the Pacific Ocean just north of Ucluelet (103km/64 miles west of Port Alberni). Hwy. 4, also called Pacific Rim Highway, then turns north, passing through the Long Beach section of Pacific Rim National Park, to Tofino (34km/21 miles north of Ucluelet). If you arrive on Vancouver Island by ferry, rent a car from **Budget** (© **888/368-7368**), which offers customer pickup at all the ferry terminals in Victoria and Nanaimo.

BY PLANE   Tofino's airport is tiny (only small planes can land) and the airline companies serving it change frequently. **Orca Airways** (© **888/359-6722;** www.flyorcaair.com) is currently the only Canadian company providing daily service between Vancouver/Victoria and Tofino/Ucluelet. The flight takes 55 minutes from Vancouver.

VISITOR INFORMATION

The **Pacific Rim Visitor Centre** (© **250/726-4600;** www.pacificrimvisitor.ca), at the junction of Hwy. 4 and Ucluelet, serves as a general information gateway for Ucluelet, Tofino, Port Alberni, and Bamfield. Pick up information on area accommodations and attractions, and buy a **day-use park pass** (C$8 adults, C$7 seniors, C$4 youths 6–16, C$20 families/groups per day), which you'll need if you want to visit the beaches and park at any of Pacific Rim's official parking lots (passes can also be purchased with credit cards only from machines at the parking lots). The Visitor Centre is open daily 9am to 5pm (9am–7pm July–Aug; 10am–4pm Oct–Mar).

The **Ucluelet Visitor Info Centre** (© **250/726-4641;** www.uclueletinfo.com), in town at 100 Main St., is open daily June through September from 9am to 5pm. The **Tofino Visitor Info Centre** (© **250/725-3414;** www.tofino-bc.com), 380 Campbell St., outside Tofino, is open the same hours. For information on the park itself, stop in at the **Long Beach Unit of Pacific Rim National Park Reserve of Canada** (© **250/726-4701**), north of Ucluelet (take the Wickaninnish Interpretive Centre exit from Hwy. 4). This park office, with a spectacular location above Wickaninnish Beach, is home to the **Wickaninnish Interpretive Centre** and a scenically stunning restaurant (see listing for Wickaninnish Restaurant, p. 287). The center is open daily from mid-March through mid-October from 10am to 6pm.

SPECIAL EVENTS

About 20,000 whales migrate past this section of Vancouver Island annually. In March, the **Pacific Rim Whale Festival** (© **250/726-7798;** www.pacificrimwhalefestival.org) is held in Tofino and Ucluelet. The **Edge to Edge Marathon** in June is a distance run between Tofino and Ucluelet through Pacific Rim National Park; contact **Ucluelet Chamber of Commerce** for details (© **250/726-4641;** www.uclueletinfo.com).

---

2   UCLUELET ★

Ucluelet is 292km (181 miles) NE of Victoria

Ucluelet enjoys a beautiful location on a sheltered harbor. You can choose from a number of fine B&Bs and cabin accommodations, but Ucluelet has yet to develop the same range of restaurants and activities as Tofino. If you want to stay in a seaside resort or lodge, head for Tofino.

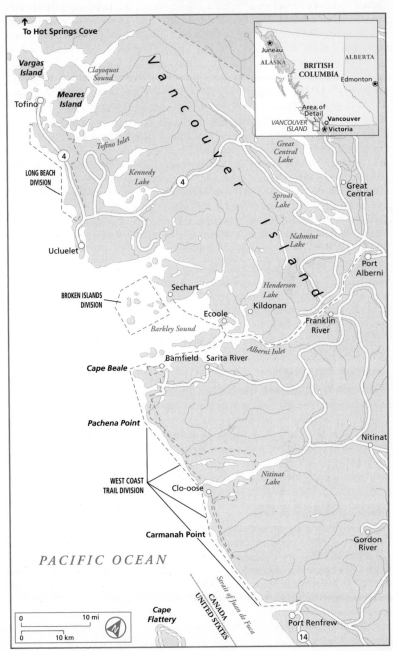

↑
To Hot Springs Cove

Vargas Island

Clayoquot Sound

Vancouver Island

Juneau

ALASKA

BRITISH COLUMBIA

ALBERTA

Edmonton

Area of Detail

VANCOUVER ISLAND

Vancouver

Victoria

Tofino

Meares Island

Tofino Inlet

4

LONG BEACH DIVISION

Kennedy Lake

4

Great Central Lake

Great Central

Ucluelet

Sproat Lake

Nahmint Lake

Port Alberni

BROKEN ISLANDS DIVISION

Sechart

Henderson Lake

Kildonan

Ecoole

Barkley Sound

Franklin River

Bamfield   Sarita River

Alberni Inlet

Cape Beale

Pachena Point

Nitinat

WEST COAST TRAIL DIVISION

Nitinat Lake

Clo-oose

Carmanah Point

Gordon River

PACIFIC OCEAN

Cape Flattery

Strait of Juan de Fuca

CANADA
UNITED STATES

Port Renfrew

14

0 — 10 mi

0 — 10 km

If you're backpacking and want budget accommodations or a place to pitch a tent, try **Ucluelet Oceanfront Hostel**, 2081 Peninsula Rd., Ucluelet, B.C. V0R 3A0 (✆ 888/434-6060 or 250/726-7416; www.cnnbackpackers.com). The hostel, on its own private beach, provides free linens, use of a kitchen, Internet, and kayak and bike rentals. Rates are C$65 for a private room, C$25 for a single dorm bed. Campers seeking a family-friendly campground close to the park can reserve a spot at **Ucluelet Campground** (✆ 250/726-4355; www.ucluraletcampground.com), located at the edge of the village. The 125 campsites range from no service to full service; prices range from C$20 to C$38.

Black Rock Oceanfront Resort ★★
Ucluelet's newest and most upscale hotel sits on a rocky promontory overlooking the Pacific and surrounded by the Wild Pacific Trail. Opened in March 2009, Black Rock is carefully designed to maximize its dramatic location. Studios, one- and two-bedroom suites feature floor-to-ceiling windows (the least expensive rooms have rainforest, not ocean, views), balconies, and a smart but unobtrusive air of luxury. Fetch, the hotel's fine-dining restaurant, sits on a surge channel with spectacular views. The center of town is a 15-minute stroll away.

596 Marine Dr., Ucluelet, B.C. V0R 3A0. ✆ **877/762-5011** or 250/726-4800. www.blackrockresort.com. 133 units. C$135–C$500 double. AE, MC, V. **Amenities:** Restaurant, bar; free airport transfers; good fitness center; spa. *In-room:* TV/DVD, movie library, kitchenette, minibar, free Wi-Fi.

Pacific Rim Motel (Kids)
If you're looking for a clean, simple, inexpensive motel room, this is a good place to know about. The motel overlooks the harbor and offers one- and two-bedroom units, some with kitchenettes, a couple with full kitchens. The rooms are plain, the property well maintained and well run, and you're close to the Wild Pacific Trail. They can help you arrange whale-watching or fishing tours.

1755 Peninsula Rd., Ucluelet, B.C. V0R 3A0. ✆ **800/810-0031.** www.pacificrimmotel.com. 55 units. C$85–C$150 double. MC, V.

WHERE TO DINE

Matterson Teahouse and Garden PACIFIC NORTHWEST
Located on Ucluelet's main street, this is a good spot for lunch; sandwiches, salads, and a great seafood chowder are served in the two front rooms of a small frame house. On a nice summer day, you have the option of sitting on the shady porch or the sunny back deck. The Teahouse also serves dinner, with seafood always on the menu along with other eclectic offerings.

1682 Peninsula Rd. ✆ **250/726-2200.** Reservations recommended for dinner in summer. Soup and sandwiches C$5–C$8; lunch and dinner C$17–C$25. MC, V. Daily 7:30am–8pm; winter Sat-Sun 9am–8pm.

WHAT TO SEE & DO

Fishing remains the big outdoor activity in Ucluelet, and salmon is still the most sought-after catch. Charter companies that can take you out include **Island West Resort** (✆ 250/726-7515; www.islandwestresort.com), **Castaway Charters** (✆ 250/726-2628; www.castawaycharter.com), and **Long Beach Charters** (✆ 877/726-2878 or 250/726-3474; www.longbeachcharters.com).

The recently completed **Wild Pacific Trail** ★★★ skirts the rugged coastline with fabulous views of the Pacific and the Broken Islands; bald eagles nest along parts of the trail. For an easy and wonderfully **scenic walk**, take the 2.7km (1.6-mile) stretch from Peninsula Road in Ucluelet to the lighthouse. On this 30- to 45-minute hike along a gravel-paved trail, the path winds as close as possible to the ocean's edge, passing surge mation on walks and access points.

For **kayaking,** contact **Majestic Ocean Kayaking** (📞 **800/889-7644;** www.ocean kayaking.com) about their half-day harbor trips, full-day paddles to Barkley Sound or the Broken Islands, and weeklong adventures in Clayoquot Sound.

Long Beach Nature Tours ★★ (📞 **250/726-7099;** www.oceansedge.bc.ca), run by retired Pacific Rim Park chief naturalist Bill McIntyre, does **guided beach, rainforest,** and **storm walks** that explain the ecology and wildlife of the area.

---

3 TOFINO ★★

Tofino is 316km (196 miles) NE of Victoria

The center of the environmental protest against industrial logging—and the center of the ecotourism business ever since—**Tofino** was, and to some extent remains, a schizophrenic kind of town. Until very recently, about half of the town was composed of ecotourism outfitters, nature lovers, and activists, while the other half was loggers and fishermen. Conflict was common in the early years, but gradually the two sides learned how to get along—more important than ever, now that a million visitors a year come to experience the area's natural wonders. Recently, the balance has definitely swung in favor of the eco-preservationists, who seek to manage growth and preserve the diverse habitats in a sustainable manner. But the town faces big pressures now that it's been "discovered" and has become such a popular destination.

WHERE TO STAY

Tofino sits at the tip of Long Beach peninsula. One paved road—Hwy. 4—runs along the spine of the peninsula from Ucluelet up through Pacific Rim National Park to Tofino. The big resort hotels are all located on their own private roads, each of which has a name and connects to Hwy. 4. Big signs on Hwy. 4 advise drivers of the location of these private access roads, which will help you find your way to your hotel.

Expensive

Long Beach Lodge Resort ★★   This luxurious beachfront resort perched on the edge of Cox Bay, 3.2km (2 miles) south of Tofino, was built to resemble a grand West Coast–style home. The central great room (with bar and restaurant) features a massive granite fireplace and stunning ocean views. The guest rooms are luxuriously comfortable, some with fireplaces, balconies, and soaker tubs; all have marvelous beds and fine linens. Two-bedroom cottages, located in the forest and without ocean views, feature a ground-floor master bedroom and bathroom with soaker tub and separate shower, a sitting area with gas fireplace, dining area, fully equipped kitchen, private hot tub, and a second bedroom and bathroom upstairs. The dining room serves fresh regional cuisine with a hint of Asian influence.

1441 Pacific Rim Hwy., P.O. Box 897, Tofino, B.C. V0R 2Z0. 📞 **877/844-7873** or 250/725-2442. Fax 250/725-2402. www.longbeachlodgeresort.com. 61 units. C$299–C$429 double; C$319–C$649 cabin. Rates include continental breakfast. AE, DC, MC, V. At the Pacific Rim Hwy. junction, turn right (north), and travel through Pacific Rim National Park; watch for lodge sign on the left after you exit the park. **Amenities:** Restaurant, lounge; access to beach. *In room:* TV, DVD/CD player, fireplace (in some rooms), fridge, hair dryer, high-speed Internet; Jacuzzi (in some rooms).

The Wickaninnish Inn ★★★ The Wickaninnish Inn is the most beautifully designed and built of all the Long Beach resorts, and the place to stay if you're looking for absolutely the best of everything. The service is exceptional, the detailing remarkable, and the setting spectacular. The inn sits on a rocky promontory, surrounded by an old-growth spruce and cedar rainforest and the sands of Chesterman Beach. From the two buildings, no matter which room you book, you'll wake to a magnificent view of the untamed Pacific. Don't be surprised if a bald eagle soars past your window. All rooms in the original lodge feature handcrafted furniture, richly printed textiles, and local artwork, as well as a fireplace, soaker tub, and private balcony. The Wick's new wing features deluxe rooms and suites with more space, more light, and a higher price. Ancient Cedars is the hotel's on-site Aveda spa. **The Pointe Restaurant** (p. 285) is the most accomplished restaurant in the area. A stay at The Wick is a relaxing, rejuvenating and memorable experience.

500 Osprey Lane (at Chesterman Beach), P.O. Box 250, Tofino, B.C. V0R 2Z0. ✆ **800/333-4604** or 250/725-3100. Fax 250/725-3110. www.wickinn.com. 75 units. C$280–C$680 double; C$400–C$1,500 suite. AE, DC, MC, V. Drive 5km (3 miles) south of Tofino toward Chesterman Beach to Osprey Lane. **Amenities:** Restaurant, bar; babysitting; access to beach; concierge; room service; small fitness center; spa; rooms for those w/limited mobility. *In room:* TV/DVD player, movie library, CD player, CD library, hair dryer, minibar, raingear, free Wi-Fi.

Moderate

Brimar Bed and Breakfast ★ The location, right on Chesterman Beach, is what makes this place special. From your room, you can step onto the sand and start exploring the wild Pacific. All three nonsmoking rooms have antique furnishings and lots of natural light. The upstairs Loft room features a queen-size bed, a bathroom with claw-foot tub and separate shower, and a bay window with a seat—and view of the ocean. The small Moonrise room has a queen-size sleigh bed and its own private bathroom across the hall. The larger, brighter Sunset room has a king-size bed and bathroom with shower. Breakfast and common areas look out over the ocean.

1375 Thornberg Crescent, Tofino, B.C. V0R 2Z0. ✆ **800/714-9373** or 250/725-3410. Fax 250/725-3410. www.brimarbb.com. 3 units. C$110–C$220 double. Rates include breakfast. AE, MC, V. Stay on Hwy. 4 going north through Pacific Rim National Park until you pass the turnoff for the Pacific Sands Resort; take the next left on Chesterman Beach Rd., and proceed to the fork in the road. Take Thornburg Crescent (the left fork), and follow it to the end. No pets. No children 11 or under. *In room:* TV, no phone.

The Inn at Tough City Right in town, overlooking Clayoquot Sound, this is Tofino's nicest and quirkiest small inn. Built in 1996 from salvaged and recycled material, it's filled with antiques, stained glass, and bric-a-brac. Several of the spacious rooms feature soaker tubs, fireplaces, or both. Rooms at the back enjoy views over the Sound and Tofino harbor. Three rooms on the main floor are wheelchair accessible. The excellent and reasonably priced sushi restaurant on the Inn's main floor is open for dinner only.

350 Main St., P.O. Box 8, Tofino, B.C. V0R 2Z0. ✆ **877/725-2021** or 250/725-2021. Fax 250/725-2088. www.toughcity.com. 8 units. C$99–C$229 double. MC, V. Drive into town and you'll see it on your right—it's impossible to miss. **Amenities:** Restaurant; 3 rooms for those w/limited mobility. *In room:* TV, Jacuzzi (in some).

Middle Beach Lodge ★★ (Kids) This appealing resort complex is on a headland overlooking the Pacific, and features Middle Beach Lodge at the Beach, for adult guests only, and Middle Beach Lodge at the Headlands, a lodge and cabins suitable for families. The centerpiece of the first and smaller of the lodges is a large but rustically cozy common room with big windows that look out over crashing waves. Accommodations here are simple lodge rooms (26 of them) with private bathrooms and balconies, and no phone or TV. The 38 rooms and suites in the second lodge have more of the standard amenities, and nearby are 19 cabins designed for one to six people, with decks, kitchenettes, and wood-burning fireplaces, some with soaker tubs or outside Jacuzzis. This is a very comfortable, unpretentious place with a good restaurant and wonderful views of the ocean and beaches.

P.O. Box 100, Tofino, B.C. V0R 2Z0. © **866/725-2900** or 250/725-2900. Fax 250/725-2901. www.middle beach.com. 64 units, 19 cabins. Lodge rooms C$110–C$360 double; C$200–C$450 cabin. Rates include continental breakfast. AE, MC, V. **Amenities:** Restaurant; exercise room. *In room:* TV/VCR (in Headlands rooms), kitchenette, no phone (in Beach rooms).

Inexpensive

Whalers on the Point Guesthouse (Kids)   Located at the foot of Main Street in "downtown" Tofino, right beside Clayoquot Sound, this 1990s building is part of the Hostelling International network of backpackers' hostels. It's clean and inexpensive, and everything in Tofino is within walking distance. As in other HI properties, you can rent a shared dorm room (four to six beds in a room), a private double room, or a larger family room. Rooms H to K, and N to Q are the best—all have views of Clayoquot Sound. There's an outdoor patio with a barbecue and a steam sauna.

81 West St., P.O. Box 296, Tofino, B.C. V0R 2Z0. © **250/725-3443.** Fax 250/725-3463. www.tofinohostel. com. 17 units. C$24–C$32 dorm room; C$50–C$100 double. Nonmembers pay slightly higher rates. AE, MC, V. At the foot of Main St. in downtown Tofino. **Amenities:** Kitchen; sauna. *In room:* No phone.

Campgrounds

The 94 campsites on the bluff at **Green Point** ★★ are maintained by Pacific Rim National Park. Reservations are required in high season as the grounds are full every day in July and August, and the average wait for a site is 1 to 2 days. To make a reservation, call © **877/RESERVE** [737-3783], or go online at **www.pccamping.ca**. The cost is C$24 per night. You're rewarded with a magnificent ocean view, pit toilets, fire pits, and pumped well water, but no showers or hookups. The campground is closed mid-October through mid-March.

   Bella Pacifica Resort & Campground, P.O. Box 413, Tofino, B.C. V0R 2Z0, 3km (1¾ miles) south of Tofino on the Pacific Rim Highway (© **250/725-3400;** www.bella pacifica.com), is privately owned. March through November, it has 165 campsites from which you can walk to Mackenzie Beach or take the resort's private nature trails to Templar Beach. Flush toilets, hot showers, water, laundry, ice, fire pits, firewood, and full and partial hookups are available. Rates are C$25 to C$48 per two-person campsite. Reserve at least a month in advance for a summer weekend.

WHERE TO DINE

Tofino is gaining a reputation for fine dining, with new restaurants opening every year, but it's also a laid-back place where you can grab a bite with the locals. For the best handmade chocolates and gelato on Vancouver Island, visit **Chocolate Tofino,** 1180 Pacific Rim Hwy. (© **250/725-2526;** www.chocolatetofino.com), about 3.3km (2 miles) south of town at the Live to Surf location next to Groovy Movies.

Expensive

The Pointe Restaurant ★★★ PACIFIC NORTHWEST   Tofino's finest restaurant is perched on the water's edge in the Wickaninnish Inn (see above) with a 280-degree view of the roaring Pacific. The Relais & Château kitchen team deliciously interprets

Pacific Northwest cuisine with an array of fresh and locally organic West Coast ingredients, including fish, shellfish, lamb, and rabbit; there's a daily vegetarian creation as well. To sample the best of everything, try the value-packed tasting menu. A recent one included pan-roasted scallops with lemon and celeriac panna cotta; pan-roasted sweetbreads with white asparagus and watercress puree; slow-roasted pork shoulder with bacon, apple, endive and walnuts; and ended with pineapple mousse. The wine list is international in scope but also features the best B.C. vintages. The breakfast omelet here is memorable.

In the Wickaninnish Inn (p. 284), 500 Osprey Lane (at Chesterman Beach). 𝒞 **250/725-3100.** Reservations required. Main courses C$30–C$46; C$80 tasting menu. AE, MC, V. Daily 8am–2:30pm, 2–5pm (snacks), and 5–9:30pm.

The Schooner ★★ SEAFOOD/PACIFIC NORTHWEST Established in 1949, The Schooner is the most venerable of Tofino restaurants and also one of the best for fresh seafood. The restaurant has two dining areas, one on the second floor with big windows looking out toward Clayoquot Sound. If you love fresh oysters, start with the "six pack," fresh shucked and served over ice with Tabasco and lemon. The classic signature dish here, served for more than 3 decades, is the Mates Plate, which includes fresh seafood from Clayoquot Sound (charbroiled salmon and halibut, grilled oysters, and garlic-sautéed prawns and scallops). Lamb, chicken, and pasta dishes are also available, but I'd stick with the seafood. A good wine list and wonderful desserts complement the menu.

331 Campbell St. 𝒞 **250/725-3444.** Reservations recommended for dinner. Main courses C$19–C$39. AE, MC, V. Mon–Sat 9–11:30am, noon–3pm, and 5–9pm; Sun 9am–12:30pm, 1–3pm, and 5–9pm.

Moderate

Shelter PACIFIC NORTHWEST Shelter is a three-in-one place: there's a casual pub area with a big-screen TV; an informal lounge area with tables and a big fireplace; and a romantic fine-dining restaurant on the second floor. The same lounge menu (halibut burger, pizza, teriyaki street bowl with fish, chicken, or tofu) is available in both areas on the main floor. If they're on the menu, try panko-crusted Fanny Bay beach oysters—a succulent treat. Then I'd recommend the pan-seared wild salmon; it was the best sockeye salmon I've ever had. Shelter is also famous for its marinated pork chop and yellow thai curry. This is a good place for a casual lunch, too.

601 Campbell St. 𝒞 **250/726-3353.** Reservations recommended in summer. Lounge meals C$9.50–C$14; restaurant main courses C$18–C$29. AE, MC, V. Daily 11:45am–midnight. On your left as you drive into town.

SOBO ★ (Kids) FUSION PACIFIC NORTHWEST SOBO started life as a humble food truck and became so popular that it expanded into a bright, glass-walled, sit-down restaurant in "downtown" Tofino. The truck is gone now, but you can still taste the famous fish tacos made with wild salmon and halibut topped with fresh-fruit salsa; you won't find a better lunch treat in Tofino. SOBO is short for "sophisticated bohemian," which is how chef Lisa Ahier describes her cooking: She's interested in street food and tastes from all over the world. The dinner menu includes seafood tapas, soups, salads, and complete meals with offerings such as Vancouver Island seafood stew, hand-cut pasta with duck ragout, and oven-smoked-chicken pizza. There's a kids' menu, too.

311 Neill St. 𝒞 **250/725-2341.** www.sobo.ca. Lunch and snacks C$5–C$21; main courses C$21–C$33. MC, V. Wed–Thurs 11:30am–5:30pm; Fri–Sun 11:30–9pm. Closed Jan and the last 2 weeks of Dec.

Wickaninnish Interpretive Centre, is notable for the incredible ocean views from its wall
of glass windows. It's a good lunch spot, with lots of fresh seafood on the menu, plus
soups, salads, sandwiches, and fresh daily specials. Main courses include roasted chicken,
baked salmon, and a fish trio (salmon, halibut, prawns). To reach the restaurant you have
to park in the nearby lot (the restaurant will give you a parking sticker) and follow a short
boardwalk.

In the Wickaninnish Interpretive Centre (p. 280). ℭ **250/726-7706.** Reservations recommended in summer. Main courses C$18–C$29. MC, V. Daily mid-Mar to Oct 11am–9pm (until 10pm in summer). North of
Ucluelet off Hwy. 4 (take Wickaninnish Centre exit).

Inexpensive
Common Loaf Bakeshop COFFEE/SANDWICHES/BAKED GOODS A cozy,
comfy gathering spot, this a good place to get a homemade breakfast sandwich or muffin
and a good cup of coffee. The Loaf does baked goods really well and has a modest lunch
and dinner menu of soup and sandwiches.

180 1st St. ℭ **250/725-3915.** Sandwiches C$7–C$12. MC, V. Daily 8am–9pm.

Tuff Beans COFFEE/LIGHT MEALS If you're looking for a good espresso or latte
or a light meal—or want to check your e-mail—it's hard to beat Tuff Beans, located at
the entrance to town. The cafe is a little short on style but it serves good pizzas, paninis,
salads, a curry bowl, and homemade soup. You can rent computers with Wi-Fi access for
a nominal fee.

151 Campbell St. ℭ **250/725-2739.** Pizzas and paninis C$13–C$15. MC, V. Daily 7am–9pm.

WHAT TO SEE & DO
For a good, overall introduction to the unique ecology of this area, stop by the 5-hectare
(12-acre) **Tofino Botanical Gardens** ★, 1084 Pacific Rim Hwy. (ℭ **250/725-1220;**
www.tofinobotanicalgardens.com), just south of town. The garden is laid out with paths
and boardwalks that wind through the forest and along the shoreline; guided walks,
special workshops, and naturalist programs are offered seasonally. The garden is open
daily from 9am to dusk; admission is C$10 for adults, free for children 12 and under.

Also in the gardens is the **Raincoast Education Society,** located in the Clayoquot
Field Station (ℭ **250/725-2560;** www.raincoasteducation.org). Open daily in summer,
this center features exhibits on local flora, fauna, and history, and often has guest speakers and nature walks; off-season hours vary, so call ahead. **Wickaninnish Interpretive
Centre,** described under "Visitor Information," earlier in this chapter, has exhibits on
coastal life and stunning views over Wickaninnish Beach.

BIRDING The Tofino/Ucluelet area is directly in the path of the Pacific Flyway, and
attracts tens of thousands of birds and wildfowl; it's also home to bald eagles. The area
celebrates its rich birdlife with the annual **Flying Geese & Shorebird Festival** every April
and May. During those months, large flocks of migrating birds fill the skies and estuaries
along Barkley Sound and Clayoquot Sound. Avid bird-lovers should contact **Just Birding** (ℭ **250/725-2520;** www.justbirding.com), run by keen birders who can show you
the best bird spots on shore (very early in the morning) or on the open ocean. **Bird &
Breakfast,** 1430 Pacific Rim Hwy., Tofino, B.C. V0R 2Z0 (ℭ **250/725-2520**), is a bed-
and-breakfast run in conjunction with Just Birding. Perfect for birders, it's located adjacent to the walking trail in the Tofino Mudflat Conservation Area, right in the middle of

the second-biggest shorebird pit stop this side of North America. April, May, and early June, sees literally thousands of shorebirds of all species fly by in their annual migration.

FIRST NATIONS TOURISM Clayoquot Sound is the traditional home of the Nuu-chah-nulth peoples, some of whom have recently gone into the cultural and ecotourism business. **Tla-ook Cultural Adventures** ★★★ (✆ 877/942-2663 or 250/725-2656; www.tlaook.com) runs three different tours: a 6-hour Cluptl-Chas **(canoeing and salmon barbecue)** Adventure (C$140), in which participants paddle ancient fishing grounds and clam beds, explore the rainforest, hear traditional stories, and feast on fresh local salmon; a 2½-hour **Inlet** (or **Sunset**) **Paddle** (C$44), in which participants paddle the local waters and learn about historical sites and local wildlife; and a 4-hour **Meares Island Tour** ★★★ (C$64), which explores the ancient rainforest on Meares Island and offers insight into the trees, plants, and animals that make it their home. All tours are led by First Nations guides and often use traditional Nuu-chah-nulth canoes. These are among the most informative and memorable ecotours on Vancouver Island.

FISHING Sport fishing for salmon, steelhead, rainbow trout, Dolly Varden char, halibut, cod, and snapper is excellent off the west coast of Vancouver Island. Long Beach is also great for bottom fishing. To fish here, you need a nonresident saltwater or freshwater license. Licenses (including the salmon surcharge) for nonresidents cost C$7.50 for 1 day, C$20 for 3 days, and C$33 for 5 days. Tackle shops sell licenses, have information on current restrictions, and often carry copies of *B.C. Tidal Waters Sport Fishing Guide* and *B.C. Sport Fishing Regulations Synopsis for Non-Tidal Waters.* Independent anglers should also pick up a copy of the *B.C. Fishing Directory and Atlas.*

Jay's Clayoquot Ventures, Box 652, 564 Campbell St., Tofino V0R 2Z0 (✆ 888/534-7432 or 250/725-2313; www.tofinofishing.com), offers half- and full-day fishing charters (saltwater and fresh) throughout the Clayoquot Sound area.

GOLF Year-round golf is available at **Long Beach Golf Course** (✆ 250/725-3332; www.longbeachgolfcourse.com), one of the most challenging—and scenic—9-hole champion courses in British Columbia; guest rate is C$24.

GUIDED NATURE HIKES Owned and operated by Bill McIntyre, former chief naturalist of Pacific Rim National Park, **Long Beach Nature Tours** ★★ (✆ 250/726-7099; www.oceansedge.bc.ca), offers guided beach walks, storm-watching, land-based whale-watching, and rainforest tours customized to suit your needs. **Raincoast Education Society,** Tofino Botanical Garden (✆ 250/725-2560; www.raincoasteducation.org), also offers seasonal guided rainforest and shore walks.

HIKING The 11km (6.75-mile) stretch of rocky headlands, sand, and surf along the **Long Beach Headlands Trail** ★★ is the most accessible section of the Pacific Rim National Park system, incorporating Long Beach, the West Coast Trail, and the Broken Islands Group. Take the Wickaninnish Interpretive Centre exit on Hwy. 4.

In and around **Long Beach,** numerous marked trails .8 to 3.3km-long (.5–2 miles) meander through the thick, temperate rainforest edging the shore. The 3.3km (2-mile) **Gold Mine Trail** near Florencia Bay still has a few artifacts from the days when a gold-mining operation flourished among the trees. The partially boardwalked **South Beach Trail** (less than 1.6km/1 mile) leads through the moss-draped rainforest onto small quiet coves and rocky tidal pools of Lismer Beach and South Beach.

For a truly memorable walk, take the 3.3m (2-mile) **Big Cedar Trail** ★★★ through the dense rainforest on Meares Island in Clayoquot Sound. The best and most memorable way to experience Meares Island is to canoe over and enjoy a guided walk with

---

(Moments) **Two Trips of a Lifetime**

These two trips are within striking distance of Vancouver or Victoria and can't be done anywhere else on earth.

Sailing the Great Bear Rainforest ★★★ About halfway up the west coast of British Columbia, the Great Bear Rainforest is an area accessible only by boat. The lush landscape, the largest expanse of intact temperate rainforest left on the planet, encompasses fjords, rivers, streams, and waterfalls; the forest is filled with old-growth hemlock and cedar forests, and shelters the rare white spirit bear, as well as grizzlies and wolves. In 2006 a landmark agreement between First Nations tribes, environmentalists, timber companies, and the Canadian government designated the Great Bear Rainforest a protected habitat, thus preserving its unique splendor for ages to come.

With 3 decades of sailing experience in the region, Tom Ellison and his wife, Jen, run **Ocean Light II Adventures** (⟨© **604/328-5339;** www.oceanlight2. bc.ca), the only company to offer trips to this magical part of the world on a 21m (69-ft.) sailboat. Skipper Tom Ellison is extremely knowledgeable and takes great delight in exploring the waters and coastline looking for whales, dolphins, and grizzlies. Prices for trips to the Great Bear Rainforest range from C$3,500 to C$3,600. All include excellent home-cooked meals and comfortable, but not luxurious, accommodations aboard the *Ocean Light II.*

Horse Trekking the Chilcotin Plateau ★★ The high plateau country of the B.C. interior has some of the most impressive scenery around. Soaring peaks rise above deep valleys, and mountain meadows are alive with flowers that bloom for just a few weeks in high summer. In British Columbia, one guide company is granted exclusive rights to run tours through particular sections of wilderness. The territories are typically 5,000 sq. km (1,931 sq. miles) of high-country wilderness, where you won't meet another horse team. One of the guide-outfitters closest to Vancouver is **Chilcotin Holidays Guest Ranch,** Gun Creek Road, Gold Bridge (⟨© **250/238-2274;** www.chilcotinholidays.com), in the Chilcotin Mountains north of Whistler. Their trips, running from 4 to 13 days and costing C$322 to C$3,450, inevitably involve encounters with wildflowers, bighorn sheep, grizzly bears, and wolves.

Tla-ook Cultural Adventures (see "First Nations Tourism," above). Built in 1993 to protect the old-growth temperate rainforest, the boardwalked trail is maintained by the Tla-o-qui-aht First Nations band, and has a long staircase leading up to the Hanging Garden Tree, the province's fourth-largest western red cedar.

HOT SPRINGS COVE ★★★ A natural, coastal hot springs about 67km (42 miles) north of Tofino, accessible only by water, makes a wonderful day trip from Tofino. Once there, you can soak in the small, steaming pools and douse yourself under a hot waterfall. A number of kayak outfitters and boat charters offer trips to the springs. I'd recommend **Jamie's Whaling Station,** 606 Campbell St. (⟨© **800/667-9913** or 250/725-3919; www. jamies.com), which runs daily trips in a 12-passenger boat. The 90-minute trip (each way) takes you past dozens of the quiet, green islands in Pacific Rim National Park; once you dock, there's a gorgeous and easy 30-minute hike along a boardwalk through old-growth forest to the hot springs. The cost is C$109 per person. Your experience of the hot springs might be ruined if you go during the day in summer, though, when up to 70 people can jam the place. To experience the full magic, go on the earliest boat or float-plane, or camp overnight (Jamie's will drop you off on their last trip and pick you up in the morning).

KAYAKING   Perhaps the quintessential Clayoquot experience, and certainly one of the most fun, is to slip into a kayak and paddle out into the calm waters of the sound. For beginners, half-day tours to Meares Island (usually with the chance to do a little hiking) are an especially good bet. For rentals, lessons, and tours, try **Tofino Sea Kayaking Company,** 320 Main St. (© **800/863-4664** or 250/725-4222; www.tofino-kayaking.com); **Pacific Kayak,** 606 Campbell St., at **Jamie's Whaling Station** (© **250/725-3232;** www.jamies.com); or **Remote Passages Marine Excursions,** 71 Wharf St. (© **800/666-9833** or 250/725-3330; www.remotepassages.com). Kayaking packages range from 4-hour paddles around Meares Island to weeklong paddling and camping expeditions. Instruction by experienced guides makes even your first kayaking experience a comfortable, safe, and enjoyable one. Single kayak rental averages around C$40 per day.

STORM-WATCHING   Watching winter storms from behind big glass windows has become very popular in Tofino. For a slight twist on this, try the outdoor storm-watching tours offered by **Long Beach Nature Tours** (© **250/726-7099;** www.oceansedge.bc.ca). Owner Bill McIntyre used to be chief naturalist of Pacific Rim National Park, and can explain how storms work and where to stand so you can get close without getting swept away.

SURFING   The wild Pacific coast is known as one of the best surfing destinations in Canada, and most surfers work in the tourism industry around Tofino, spending all their free time in the water. To try this exciting and exhilarating sport, call **Live to Surf,** 1180 Pacific Rim Hwy. (© **250/725-4464;** www.livetosurf.com). Lessons start at C$55 without gear. Live to Surf also rents boards at C$25 and wet suits (don't even think about going in without one) at C$20. Another option is **Pacific Surf School,** 430 Campbell St. (© **888/777-9961;** www.pacificsurfschool.com); or try the all-female surfing school, **Surf Sister** (© **877/724-7873;** www.surfsister.com).

WHALE-WATCHING & BEAR-WATCHING   A number of outfitters conduct tours through this region, which is inhabited by gray whales, bald eagles, black bears, porpoises, orcas, seals, and sea lions. One of the oldest, **Jamie's Whaling Station,** 606 Campbell St. (© **800/667-9913** or 250/725-3919; www.jamies.com), uses a glass-bottomed 20m (66-ft.) power cruiser as well as a fleet of Zodiacs for tours to watch the gray whales March through October. A combined Hot Springs Cove and whale-watching trip is offered year-round. Three-hour bear-watching trips are normally scheduled around low tides when the bruins forage for seafood on the mudflats. Fares (for this and other companies) generally start at around C$79 per person; customized trips can run as high as C$200 per person for a full day. For an interesting combination, try the Sea-to-Sky tour, a 5-hour trip with a boat ride, a hike through the rainforest to the hot springs, and a return to Tofino by floatplane, at the cost of C$165 for adults.

   Remote Passages Marine Excursions, 71 Wharf St. (© **800/666-9833** or 250/725-3330; www.remotepassages.com), runs 2½-hour-long whale-watching tours in Clayoquot Sound on Zodiac boats, daily March through November. Fares are C$84 for adults

whale-watching and hot springs trip at C$120 for adults and C$99 for children 12 and
under. Reservations are recommended.

INDOOR PURSUITS   Browse the excellent selection at **Wildside Booksellers,** 320
Main St. (© **250/725-4222**), in the same building as the Tofino Sea Kayaking Com-
pany. Or tour some of the 20 **galleries;** the Tourist Info Centre has a pamphlet with
a map and contact info for all of them. Standouts include **Sandstone Jewellery and
Gifts** ★, 346 Campbell St.(© **250/725-4482**), and the **Reflecting Spirit Gallery,** 441
Campbell St. at 3rd Street (© **250/725-2472**).

Fast Facts

1 FAST FACTS: SOUTHWESTERN BRITISH COLUMBIA

AREA CODES The telephone area code for all of Vancouver Island, including Victoria and most of British Columbia, is **250.** For Vancouver and the greater Vancouver area, including Squamish and Whistler, it's **604.**

AUTO CLUB Members of the **American Automobile Association (AAA)** can get emergency assistance from the **British Columbia Automobile Association** (BCAA; ✆ **604/293-2222)** by calling ✆ **800/222-4357** (or the number listed on the back of their AAA membership card).

CONSULATES In Vancouver, the **U.S. Consulate** is at 1075 W. Pender St. ((✆ **604/685-4311).** The **British Consulate** is at 800-1111 Melville St. (✆ **604/683-4421).** The **Australian Consulate** is at 2050-1075 W. Georgia St. (✆ **604/684-1177).** Check the Yellow Pages for other countries' consulates.

DRIVING RULES Canadian driving rules are similar to regulations in the U.S. Seat belts must be worn, children 5 and under must be in child restraints, and motorcyclists must wear helmets. It's legal to turn right on a red light after you've come to a full stop. Unlike in the U.S., daytime headlights are mandatory.

ELECTRICITY As in the U.S., electric current is 110 volts AC (60 cycles).

EMERGENCIES Dial ✆ **911** for fire, police, ambulance, and poison control. This is a free call.

GASOLINE (PETROL) Gas stations are basically the same as in the U.S., but gasoline is sold by the liter, not by the gallon. (3.8 liters equals 1 U.S. gallon). Gas prices in British Columbia fluctuate as they do everywhere else in the world; as of press time, 1 liter cost about C$1.10. Taxes are included in the printed price.

HOLIDAYS For a list of holidays in Canada, see "Vancouver & Victoria Calendar of Events," in chapter 3.

HOSPITALS For a list of doctors and hospitals in Vancouver, see "Fast Facts Vancouver," in chapter 5; for doctors and hospitals in Victoria, see "Fast Facts Victoria," in chapter 13.

INSURANCE For travel overseas, most U.S. health plans (including Medicare and Medicaid) do not provide coverage, and the ones that do often require you to pay for services upfront and reimburse you only after you return home.

If you require additional medical insurance, try **MEDEX Assistance** (✆ **800/527-0218;** www.medexassist.com) or **Travel Assistance International** (✆ **800/821-2828;** www.travelassistance.com; for general information on services, call the company's **Worldwide Assistance Services, Inc.,** at ✆ **800/777-8710).**

Travelers from the U.K. should carry their European Health Insurance Card (EHIC), which replaced the E111 form as proof of entitlement to free/reduced cost medical treatment abroad (📞 **0845/605-0707**; www.ehic.org.uk). Note, however, that the EHIC only covers "necessary medical treatment," and for repatriation costs, lost money, baggage, or cancellation, travel insurance from a reputable company should always be sought (www.travel insuranceweb.com).

Travel Insurance You can get insurance estimates from various providers through **InsureMyTrip.com**. Enter your trip cost and dates, your age, and other information, for prices from more than a dozen companies.

U.K. citizens and their families who make more than one trip abroad per year may find an annual travel insurance policy works out cheaper. Check **www.money supermarket.com**, which compares prices across a wide range of providers for single- and multi-trip policies.

Most big travel agents offer their own insurance and will probably try to sell you their package when you book a holiday. Think before you sign. **Britain's Consumers' Association** recommends that you insist on seeing the policy and reading the fine print before buying travel insurance. **The Association of British Insurers** (📞 **020/7600-3333**; www.abi.org.uk) gives advice by phone and publishes *Holiday Insurance*, a free guide to policy provisions and prices. You might also shop around for better deals: Try **Columbus Direct** (📞 **0870/033-9988**; www.columbus direct.net).

Trip Cancellation Insurance Trip-cancellation insurance will help retrieve your money if you have to back out of a trip or depart early, or if your travel supplier goes bankrupt. Trip cancellation traditionally covers such events as sickness, natural disasters, and State Department advisories. The latest news in trip-cancellation insurance is the availability of **expanded hurricane coverage** and the **"any-reason"** cancellation coverage—which costs more

but covers cancellations made for any reason. You won't get back 100% of your prepaid trip cost, but you'll be refunded a substantial portion. **TravelSafe** (📞 **800/523-8020**; www.travelsafe.com) offers both types of coverage. Expedia also offers any-reason cancellation coverage for its air-hotel packages. For details, contact one of the following recommended insurers: **Access America** (📞 **800/284-8300**; www. accessamerica.com); **Travel Guard International** (📞 **800/826-4919**; www. travelguard.com); **Travel Insured International** (📞 **800/243-3174**; www.travel insured.com); and **Travelex Insurance Services** (📞 **800/228-9792**; www. travelex-insurance.com).

Automobile Insurance Auto insurance is compulsory in British Columbia. Basic coverage consists of "no-fault" accident and C$200,000 third-party legal liability coverage. If you plan to drive in Canada, check with your insurance company to make sure that your policy meets this requirement. Always carry your insurance card, your vehicle registration, and your driver's license in case you get pulled over or have an accident. AAA also offers low-cost travel and auto insurance for its members. If you are a member and don't have adequate insurance, take advantage of this benefit.

Note: If you rent a car in British Columbia and plan to take it across the border into the U.S., let your rental company know in advance.

LIQUOR LAWS The legal drinking age in British Columbia is 19. Spirits are sold only in government liquor stores, but beer and wine can be purchased from specially licensed, privately owned stores and pubs. Most LCBC (Liquor Control of British Columbia) stores are open Monday through Saturday from 10am to 6pm, but some are open until 11pm.

MAIL At press time, letters and postcards up to 30 grams cost C98¢ to mail to the U.S. and C$1.65 for overseas airmail service; C54¢ within Canada. You can buy stamps and mail parcels at the main post office (for locations see "Post Office," in "Fast Facts Vancouver," p. 66, and "Fast Facts Victoria," p. 208) or at any of the postal outlets inside drugstores and convenience stores. Look for a POSTAL SERVICES sign. For more information visit www.canadapost.ca.

PASSPORTS See "Entry Requirements," in chapter 3.

SMOKING Smoking is prohibited in all public areas, including restaurants, bars, and clubs. Many hotels are now entirely smoke-free.

TAXES Hotel rooms are subject to a 10% tax. The **provincial sales tax (PST)** is 7% (excluding food, restaurant meals, and children's clothing). For specific questions, call the **B.C. Consumer Taxation Branch** (© **604/660-0858;** www.sbr.gov.bc.ca/ctb). Most goods and services are subject to a 6% **federal goods and services tax (GST)**. *Note:* The GST Visitors Rebate Program was eliminated in 2007, so it's no longer possible to get a rebate on goods and services purchased in Canada.

TIME ZONE Vancouver and Victoria are in the Pacific time zone, as are Seattle,

Portland, San Francisco, and Los Angeles. Daylight saving time applies the second Sunday in March to the first Sunday in November.

TIPPING Tipping etiquette is the same as in the United States: 15% to 20% in restaurants, C$1 per bag for bellboys and porters, and C$1 to C$4 per day for the hotel housekeeper. Taxi drivers get a sliding-scale tip—fares under C$4 deserve a C$1 tip; for fares over C$4, tip 15%.

VISITOR INFORMATION For tourist office locations in Vancouver, see "Visitor Information," in chapter 5; for Victoria, see chapter 13.

If you're planning to spend time outside Vancouver and Victoria, you may wish to contact the **Vancouver Coast and Mountains Tourism Region** (© **800/667-3306** or 604/739-9011; www.vcmbc.com). For travel information on Vancouver Island and the Gulf Islands, contact **Tourism Vancouver Island,** 501-65 Front St., Nanaimo, B.C. V9R 5H9 (© **250/754-3500;** www.vancouverisland.travel).

For information about travel and accommodations elsewhere in the province, contact **Tourism British Columbia,** 300-1803 Douglas St., Victoria, B.C. V8T 5C3 (© **800/hello-bC** [435-5622] or 250/356-6363; www.tourismbc.com).

2 AIRLINE, HOTEL & CAR RENTAL WEBSITES

MAJOR AIRLINES

Aeroméxico
www.aeromexico.com

Air France
www.airfrance.com

Air Jamaica
www.airjamaica.com

Air New Zealand
www.airnewzealand.com

Alaska Airlines/Horizon Air
www.alaskaair.com

American Airlines
www.aa.com

British Airways
www.british-airways.com

China Airlines
www.china-airlines.com

Continental Airlines
www.continental.com

Delta Air Lines
www.delta.com

Finnair
www.finnair.com

Frontier Airlines
www.frontierairlines.com

Hawaiian Airlines
www.hawaiianair.com

Japan Airlines
www.jal.co.jp

JetBlue Airways
www.jetblue.com

Korean Air
www.koreanair.com

Lan Airlines
www.lan.com

Lufthansa
www.lufthansa.com

Midwest Airlines
www.midwestairlines.com

North American Airlines
www.flynaa.com

Northwest Airlines
www.nwa.com

Olympic Airlines
www.olympicairlines.com

Qantas Airways
www.qantas.com

Pan Am Clipper Connection
www.flypanam.com

PenAir (The Spirit of Alaska)
www.penair.com

Philippine Airlines
www.philippineairlines.com

South African Airways
www.flysaa.com

Swiss International Air Lines
www.swiss.com

TACA
www.taca.com

Thai Airways International
www.thaiair.com

Turkish Airlines
www.turkishairlines.com

United Airlines
www.united.com

US Airways
www.usairways.com

Virgin America
www.virginamerica.com

Virgin Atlantic Airways
www.virgin-atlantic.com

BUDGET AIRLINES

Aegean Airlines
www.aegeanair.com

Aer Lingus
www.aerlingus.com

AirTran Airways
www.airtran.com

BMI Baby
www.bmibaby.com

easyJet
www.easyjet.com

InterJet
www.interjet.com.mx

Jetstar (Australia)
www.jetstar.com

Ryanair
www.ryanair.com

Southwest Airlines
www.southwest.com

Spirit Airlines
www.spiritair.com

Volaris
www.volaris.com.mx

WestJet
www.westjet.com

FAST FACTS

21

AIRLINE, HOTEL & CAR RENTAL WEBSITES

Best Western International
www.bestwestern.com

Clarion Hotels
www.choicehotels.com

Comfort Inn Hotels
www.comfortinn.com

Courtyard by Marriott
www.marriott.com/courtyard

Crowne Plaza Hotels
www.ichotelsgroup.com/crowneplaza

Days Inn
www.daysinn.com

Doubletree Hotels
http://doubletree1.hilton.com

Econo Lodges
www.choicehotels.com

Embassy Suites
http://embassysuites1.hilton.com

Fairfield Inn by Marriott
www.fairfieldinn.com

Four Seasons
www.fourseasons.com

Hampton Inn
http://hamptoninn1.hilton.com

Hilton Hotels
www.hilton.com

Holiday Inn
www.holidayinn.com

Howard Johnson
www.hojo.com

Hyatt
www.hyatt.com

InterContinental Hotels & Resorts
www.ichotelsgroup.com

La Quinta Inns and Suites
www.lq.com

Loews Hotels
www.loewshotels.com

Marriott
www.marriott.com

Motel 6
www.motel6.com

Omni Hotels
www.omnihotels.com

Quality
www.qualityinn. com

Radisson Hotels & Resorts
www.radisson.com

Ramada
www.ramada.com

Red Carpet Inns
www.bookroomsnow.com

Red Lion Hotels
www.redlion.rdln.com

Red Roof Inn
www.redroof.com

Renaissance Hotels & Resorts
www.renaissancehotels.com

Residence Inn by Marriott
www.marriott.com/residenceinn

Rodeway Inn Hotels
www.rodewayinn.com

Sheraton Hotels & Resorts
www.starwoodhotels.com/sheraton

Super8 Motels
www.super8.com

Travelodge
www.travelodge.com

Vagabond Inns
www.vagabondinn.com

Westin Hotels & Resorts
www.starwoodhotels.com/westin

Wyndham Hotels & Resorts
www.wyndham.com

CAR RENTAL AGENCIES

Advantage
www.advantage.com

Alamo
www.alamo.com

Auto Europe
www.autoeurope.com

Avis
www.avis.com

Budget
www.budget.com

Dollar
www.dollar.com

Enterprise
www.enterprise.com

Hertz
www.hertz.com

Kemwel (KHA)
www.kemwel.com

National
www.nationalcar.com

Payless
www.paylesscarrental.com

Rent-A-Wreck
www.rentawreck.com

Thrifty
www.thrifty.com

FAST FACTS

21

AIRLINE, HOTEL & CAR RENTAL WEBSITES

INDEX

See also Accommodations and Restaurant indexes, below.

ACCOMMODATIONS— VANCOUVER

ACCOMMODATIONS— VICTORIA

ACCOMMODATIONS— OTHER AREAS